Hunger Redraws the Map

The First World War resulted in major economic and agricultural strains to neutral and belligerent countries alike, including shifts in trading patterns, blockades, and extensive physical destruction on a unique scale.

The resulting hunger crises transformed relationships between the state, citizens, and civil society and had a profound and lasting impact on the twentieth century. As civilians across Europe and the Middle East struggled to survive, new emphasis was placed on the state's responsibility to provide food for its citizens, leading to emerging concerns about "nutritional sovereignty," the viability of new states, and a huge expansion of international humanitarianism. This innovative history utilizes both contemporary and modern maps to analyze food shortages and responses to them across Europe and the Ottoman Empire from 1914 to 1923. Through a comparative approach, the authors demonstrate the consequences of civilian hunger in its military, international, political, social, economic, and cultural dimensions.

Mary Elisabeth Cox is Assistant Professor of International Relations at the Central European University, Vienna and author of *Hunger in War and Peace: Women and Children in Germany, 1914–1924*.

Claire Morelon is Lecturer in Modern European History at the University of Manchester. She is the author of *Streetscapes of War and Revolution: Prague, 1914–1920*.

Studies in the Social and Cultural History of Modern Warfare

In recent years the field of modern history has been enriched by the exploration of two parallel histories. These are the social and cultural history of armed conflict, and the impact of military events on social and cultural history.

Studies in the Social and Cultural History of Modern Warfare presents the fruits of this growing area of research, reflecting both the colonization of military history by cultural historians and the reciprocal interest of military historians in social and cultural history, to the benefit of both. The series offers the latest scholarship in European and non-European events from the 1850s to the present day.

A full list of titles in the series can be found at:www.cambridge.org/modernwarfare

Hunger Redraws the Map

Food, State, and Society in the Era of the First World War

Edited by

Mary Elisabeth Cox
Central European University

Claire Morelon
University of Manchester

CAMBRIDGE
UNIVERSITY PRESS

CAMBRIDGE
UNIVERSITY PRESS

Shaftesbury Road, Cambridge CB2 8EA, United Kingdom

One Liberty Plaza, 20th Floor, New York, NY 10006, USA

477 Williamstown Road, Port Melbourne, VIC 3207, Australia

314–321, 3rd Floor, Plot 3, Splendor Forum, Jasola District Centre, New Delhi – 110025, India

103 Penang Road, #05–06/07, Visioncrest Commercial, Singapore 238467

Cambridge University Press is part of Cambridge University Press & Assessment, a department of the University of Cambridge.

We share the University's mission to contribute to society through the pursuit of education, learning and research at the highest international levels of excellence.

www.cambridge.org
Information on this title: www.cambridge.org/9781009441308

DOI: 10.1017/9781009441278

When citing this work, please include a reference to the DOI 10.1017/9781009441278

First published 2026

A catalogue record for this publication is available from the British Library

A Cataloging-in-Publication data record for this book is available from the Library of Congress

ISBN 978-1-009-44130-8 Hardback

Contents

Colour versions of a selection of the maps are available at www.cambridge.org/cox-morelon

Figures

Maps

Tables

Contributors

MUSTAFA AKSAKAL, Georgetown University

MARY ELISABETH COX, Central European University

SOPHIE DE SCHAEPDRIJVER, Penn State University

JOËL FLORIS, University of Zurich

FRANCESCO FRIZZERA, Italian War History Museum, Rovereto

MARK HARRISON, University of Oxford

ĒRIKS JĒKABSONS, University of Latvia and Maria Curie-Skłodowska University, Lublin

FRIEDERIKE KIND-KOVÁCS, Technical University of Dresden

SAMUËL KRUIZINGA, University of Amsterdam

CLAIRE MORELON, University of Manchester

MELANIE SCHULZE TANIELIAN, University of Michigan

NICHOLAS SIEKIERSKI, Polish Academy of Sciences

KASPAR STAUB, University of Zurich

HEW STRACHAN, University of Oxford and University of St Andrews

STEPHEN G. WHEATCROFT, University of Melbourne

Acknowledgments

This book is the result of a coordinated effort at collaborative writing that is still rare in edited volumes in history. Thanks to a generous Network Grant from the Leverhulme Trust, as well as additional funding from the Hoover Institution Library and Archives and the History Faculty at the University of Oxford, the members of this project were able to meet over a period of three years to explore the themes covered in this book. The participating scholars brought not only their expertise on a specific region or country (and the language skills that go with it) but also their different approaches and historical methodologies. Our work unites the perspective of economic historians, historians of medicine, cultural and social historians, political historians, and military historians, tackling the subject of hunger from various angles.

We decided early on to produce a book that focused on themes rather than to divide the chapters into individualized country-based case studies in order to better understand the multifaceted impact of hunger in the First World War era. Each chapter was written by one or two authors, but with input and material provided by other members of the project, so that everyone worked not only on their own chapter but also on the others. This collaborative way of writing history means that some countries and themes receive less attention in the book. However, this structure gives more weight to the major themes that emerged from our discussions.

Several institutions have provided crucial support to be able to carry out this project. We are grateful to the University of Oxford History Faculty for financial support from the John Fell Fund. We particularly wish to thank the Hoover Institution Library & Archives and the director of this institution, Eric Wakin. The Hoover Institution hosted one of our research workshops and its librarians and archivists provided invaluable help in sourcing material for this book.

We extend a special thanks to Jeanette Atkinson and Tiffany Shumaker for their administrative support. For help with the creation of our maps we wish to thank Tiffany Shumaker, Thomas Caton Harrison (British

Antarctic Survey), and Geodienst at the University of Groningen, especially its director Dr. Govert Schoof, and Johan Bergsma.

We also wish to thank scholars who contributed their time and ideas to this project. Bertrand Patenaude (Stanford University), Andy Newby (University of Jyväskylä), Adrian Gregory (University of Oxford), and John Horne (Trinity College, Dublin, emeritus) all contributed valuable insights and discussions at one or more of our meetings.

We owe special thanks to Jay Winter and Robert Gerwarth for accepting this book into their series and to Michael Watson, our editor at Cambridge University Press, for working with us on this volume. We also very much appreciated the feedback of the two anonymous reviewers that have helped us improve the manuscript.

Finally, we especially wish to thank the outstanding scholars whose essays appear in this book. They have embarked with us on this project and have devoted much of their time and energy to it. We value both the chapters they wrote and the contributions – of sources and ideas – that they shared with others.

Introduction

Hunger Redraws the Map

Mary Elisabeth Cox and Claire Morelon

> Paris is very self-important. It believes it is making a new Europe, that it is writing history with a large and firm hand, but history is being made elsewhere. It is being made in 1,000 hospitals, in innumerable homes all over Europe. The cry of the child for bread is hushed in a nameless grave, but surely his voice will waken again. It will resound down our century.[1]

With these words on the Paris Peace Treaties, Save the Children founders Dorothy and Eglantyne Jebb sought to mobilize British public opinion to help feed hungry European children. Their words on the imprint of hunger on Europe in 1919 invite us to shift our vantage point away from the rooms filled with diplomats and experts in the Paris suburbs towards the empty kitchens of ordinary citizens across the continent. In the wake of the conflict, the world was not only remade by maps, treaties, new borders, and violence, but also by the experiences of hunger that shaped the lives of millions of people. By positioning hunger as a central experience of the First World War, this book explores how it restructured societies and reshaped the continent.

While the significance of hunger in sparking the Russian Revolution has long been acknowledged, the broader global political consequences of hunger in the era of the First World War have only recently received more attention.[2] Food gained particular political significance during this period: lack of food spurred protests for social change across the globe, and strengthened or undermined the legitimacy of states, while

[1] Cited in Bruna Bianchi, 'That massacre of the innocents has haunted us for years': Women Witnesses of Hunger in Central Europe', in *Living War, Thinking Peace (1914–1924): Women's Experiences, Feminist Thought, and International Relations*, ed. by Bruna Bianchi and Geraldine Ludbrook (Newcastle: Cambridge Scholars, 2016), 76; on Save the Children, see Emily Baughan, *Saving the Children: Humanitarianism, Internationalism, and Empire* (Oakland, CA: University of California Press, 2021).

[2] On hunger riots in Russia, see Barbara Alpern Engel, 'Not by Bread Alone: Subsistence Riots in Russia during World War I.' *The Journal of Modern History*, 69:4 (1997), 696–721.

they, and non-state actors, used food to further political aims.[3] Scholars who approach hunger as a multifaceted problem that encompasses the cultural, social, and emotional dimensions of food are beginning to trace the long-term transformations brought on by wartime hunger. This book builds upon these new directions. Hunger in the First World War was a definitive and life-changing experience at the personal, local, state, and global level.

When placed in the long history of wartime famine, hunger in the First World War was nothing new. War has always reduced available food supplies: through aggressive military tactics with the use of sieges, blockades, the disruption of trade, scorched earth combat as well as through the destruction of arable land, the fielding of armies that consume civilian foodstuffs, and reduced agricultural manpower due to the needs of militaries.[4] Furthermore, whether from poor harvests or natural disasters, episodes of famines had been regular occurrences before the modern period. By the twentieth century, however, progress in transportation and agriculture meant that famine was more likely the result of human actions, such as war.[5] Furthermore, the First World War was not the most lethal episode of famine in the twentieth century compared with the USSR famines of the 1930s and the deaths by starvation during the Second World War.[6]

[3] On the multifaceted aspects of hunger in the twentieth century, see Alice Weinreb, *Modern Hungers: Food and Power in Twentieth Century Germany* (Oxford: Oxford University Press, 2016), 16; on new approaches to the economic consequences of war, see Tara Zahra et al., 'A World of Contradictions: Globalization and Deglobalization in Interwar Europe', *The American Historical Review*, 128:2 (2023), 703–881.

[4] On siege warfare in Early Modern Europe, see Anke Fischer-Kattner, Jamel Ostwald, eds., *The World of the Siege: Representations of Early-Modern Positional Warfare* (Leiden: Brill, 2019).

[5] See, Guido Alfani and Cormac Ó Gráda, eds. *Famine in European History* (Cambridge: Cambridge University Press, 2017); Declan Curran, Lubomyr Luciuk, and Andrew Newby, eds., *Famines in European Economic History: The Last Great European Famines Reconsidered* (London: Routledge, 2015).

[6] Economic historians have found that 'Anti-Ukrainian bias in Soviet policy explains up to 92% of famine mortality in Ukraine and 77% in Ukraine, Russia and Belarus'. Andrei Markevich, Natalya Naumenko, and Nancy Qian, 'The Causes of Ukrainian Famine Mortality, 1932–33', National Bureau of Economic Research, Working Paper 29089, July 2021, revised May 2023; on hunger during the Second World War, see Wendy Z. Goldman and Donald Filtzer, eds., *Hunger and War: Food Provisioning in the Soviet Union during World War II* (Bloomington, IN: Indiana University Press, 2015); Violetta Hionidou, *Famine and Death in Occupied Greece, 1941–1944* (Cambridge: Cambridge University Press, 2006), 219; Tatjana Tönsmeyer, Peter Haslinger, and Agnes Laba, eds., *Coping with Hunger and Shortage under German Occupation in World War II* (London: Palgrave, 2018); Alexis Peri, *The War Within: Diaries from the Siege of Leningrad* (Cambridge, MA: Harvard University Press, 2020).

Yet hunger in the First World War was also exceptional. It stands out from crises before and after because of the far-reaching consequences it had on transforming relationships between states, citizens, and civil societies. The historical significance of hunger in the First World War is visible in three major ways: first, through a new emphasis on the state's responsibility to provide food; second, in shaping emerging concerns about 'nutritional sovereignty'; and third, through the expansion of international humanitarianism. These changes were possible because of the interconnected nature of the world prior to 1914, especially with regard to the globalized food economy, and because of the unprecedented global scale of the War.

State Responsibility

The conflict was a turning point in public sentiment regarding food shortages. Hunger became something the state should solve. Rationing systems put in place by the various belligerent states in Europe were more developed and complex than anything that had existed previously (see Chapter 3 by Francesco Frizzera).[7] Expectations of state intervention in economic policy and welfare provision were transformed. Hunger and destitution during the First World War were important catalysts of the expansion of social safety nets and the development of the welfare state in subsequent years in Europe.[8] The War marked, in many countries, an important step in the transition from poor relief to state welfare. As conceptions of citizenship changed in wartime through massive participation in the war effort, welfare turned into an expected state provision – part of the political contract. As more and more people suffered from shortages, food became a political priority, and material security was increasingly conceived of as a state responsibility (see Chapter 9 by Melanie Schulze Tanielian and Mustafa Aksakal).[9] This expectation was new

[7] On rationing during the Franco-Prussian war, see Bertrand Taithe, *Defeated Flesh: Medicine, Welfare, and Warfare in the Making of Modern France* (Lanham, MD: Rowman & Littlefield, 1999), 106–21.

[8] On food policies in general, see John Burnett and Derek Oddy, eds., *The Origins and Development of Food Policies in Europe* (London: Leicester University Press, 1994); on the development of the welfare state, see Susan Pedersen, *Family, Dependence, and the Origins of the Welfare State: Britain and France, 1914–1945* (Cambridge: Cambridge University Press, 1993); Young-Sun Hong, *Welfare, Modernity, and the Weimar State, 1919–1933* (Princeton: Princeton University Press, 1998); Maria Sophia Quine, *Italy's Social Revolution: Charity and Welfare from Liberalism to Fascism* (Basingstoke: Palgrave, 2002).

[9] On the public–private mix in welfare, see Célia Keren, Fabio Giomi, and Morgane Labbé, eds., *Public and Private Welfare in Modern Europe: Productive Entanglements* (London: Routledge, 2022); on welfare as the basis for state legitimacy, see Claire Morelon, *Streetscapes of War and Revolution: Prague, 1914–1920* (Cambridge: Cambridge

to many municipal and state leaders. As the Mayor of Vienna, Richard Weiskirchner explained in 1916, 'In peacetime nobody demanded from me that I should get him potatoes. It didn't occur to anybody that I should provide flour or meat; it was never the legal duty of the municipality to do so … It is neither in a statute or found in law that it is the city's duty to take care of food.'[10]

These expectations formed during the War continued into the 1920s and beyond. Food was an important driver in the transformations of the state in the early twentieth century. Recent studies of totalitarian regimes show the central role that the control of food production played in fascist as well as communist ideology, and the First World War's massive experience of shortages is key to understanding this development.[11] With more attention focused on food supplies and distribution during wartime, governments carefully assessed their agricultural production capabilities and vulnerabilities in the aftermath of the Great War. Some continued food distribution practices that had begun during the War and increased their agricultural monitoring. The British government, for example, published a comprehensive study on food supplies and agricultural potential following the First World War, as well as a secret study of the impact of blockades on food supplies.[12] In Germany, agricultural surveys were created to better estimate how much food could be produced per farm.[13] State agricultural surveys had existed well before the War, but came with renewed interest and greater focus on national self-sufficiency afterwards.

Nutritional Sovereignty

The First World War hit an unprecedently globalized food economy. Prior to the War's outbreak, agricultural production and trade had become increasingly interdependent.[14] Food production was specialized.

University Press, 2024), 198–205; on citizenship rights and welfare in the post-war, see Dominique Kirchner Reill, Ivan Jeličić, and Francesca Rolandi, 'Redefining Citizenship after Empire: The Rights to Welfare, to Work, and to Remain in a Post-Habsburg World', *The Journal of Modern History*, 94:2 (2022), 326–62.

[10] Maureen Healy, *Vienna and the Fall of the Habsburg Empire: Total War and Everyday Life in World War I* (Cambridge: Cambridge University Press, 2004), 59.

[11] Tiago Saraiva, *Fascist Pigs: Technoscientific Organisms and the History of Fascism* (Cambridge, MA: MIT Press, 2016).

[12] See, for example, A. C. Bell, *A History of the Blockade of Germany and of the Countries Associated with Her in the Great War: Austria-Hungary, Bulgaria, and Turkey 1914–1919* (London: His Majesty's Stationery Office, 1937).

[13] Avner Offer, *The First World War: An Agrarian Interpretation* (Oxford: Oxford University Press, 1989).

[14] Hew Strachan, 'The First World War as a global war', *First World War Studies*, 1:1 (2010), 3–14.

Countries and entire regions increasingly relied on each other for their sustenance (see Chapter 1 by Samuël Kruizinga). European diets had benefited from these exchanges and, in many countries, people ate more calories than ever before as well as a more varied diet.[15] People in Europe and the Ottoman Empire had grown dependent on international markets for food, or on food produced within their own empires. Even domestic agricultural production, particularly in the case of Germany, was dependent on the importation of chemical fertilizers. When global and domestic trade slowed or broke down during the War, many states could not make up the losses. Furthermore, as blockades imposed on seaports in the Mediterranean and the North Sea tightened, food insecurity dramatically deepened for millions of people.

As Tara Zahra has argued, the widespread experience of hunger during and following the War tempered enthusiasm for the benefits of free trade and fostered calls for economic autonomy in the interwar years.[16] Concerns over states' capacity to feed their populations and to rely less on foreign imports obsessed politicians and citizens alike. The First World War fundamentally reshaped the basis of political sovereignty. For many, sovereignty meant, concretely, having enough food for basic survival. This notion of 'nutritional sovereignty', as Carolyn Taratko has called it, was especially essential for Central Europeans in both old states and in the new states that emerged following the War.[17] New definitions of state viability often considered the potential to be economically self-sufficient as one of the essential requirements. The viability of new states such as Austria and the Baltic countries was questioned based on their ability to feed their populations.[18] Adequate provisioning was also the basis for political stability and for neutralizing discontent. For experts and decision-makers, economic factors – informed by the experience of shortages and economic collapse – were essential in conceptions of what a state was and what it should be. On the ground, food also played a vital role in boosting – or undermining – the legitimacy of new states. In regions claimed by differing

[15] See in the case of Germany, Corinna Treitel, *Eating Nature in Modern Germany: Food, Agriculture, and Environment, c. 1870 to 2000* (Cambridge: Cambridge University Press, 2017), 4; on Britain: Chris Otter, *Diet for a Large Planet: Industrial Britain, Food Systems, and World Ecology* (Chicago, IL: University of Chicago Press, 2020).

[16] Tara Zahra, *Against the World: Anti-Globalism and Mass Politics between the World Wars* (New York, NY: W. W. Norton & Company, 2023).

[17] Carolyn Taratko, 'Autarky from the Ground Up: Settlement and Agricultural Independence in Weimar Germany', *American Historical Review*, 128:2 (2023), 842–61; on the redefinition of sovereignty, see Leonard Smith, *Sovereignty at the Paris Peace Conference of 1919* (Oxford: Oxford University Press, 2018).

[18] Klaus Richter, 'The Catastrophe of the Present and That of the Future: Expectations for European States from the Great War to the Great Depression', *Contemporary European History*, 33 (2024), 1002–30.

states, loyalties were often determined by food provisioning rather than by national sentiment. Economic arguments were decisive in the plebiscites that enshrined the principle of self-determination. Similarly, food allowances played an important role in the motivation of men joining the Hungarian Red Army.[19] Access to food was an essential factor in ordinary citizens' decisions to get involved in post-war transformations, be it political revolutions or the redrawing of borders.

International Humanitarianism

The hunger crises gave rise to new modes of national and international economic intervention. Hunger, particularly in Austria, played a central role in paving the way for supranational financial stabilization through the League of Nations.[20] In the immediate post-war era, the range, scope, and sheer size of humanitarian aid was unprecedented (see Chapter 13 by Ēriks Jēkabsons).[21] While this outpouring of care was far from commensurate with the previous national budgets for armaments, the involvement of so many different actors in terms of nationality, language, and religious background, as well as the amount of international aid being sent across borders was greater than it ever had been before. As part of

[19] See Brendan Krach, 'Plebiscites and Postwar Legitimacy', in Marcus M. Payk and Roberta Pergher, eds., *Beyond Versailles: Sovereignty, Legitimacy, and the Formation of New Polities after the Great War* (Bloomington, IN: Indiana University Press, 2019), 25; Jernej Kosi, '"Yugoslavia Has Nothing. Yugoslavia Has No Bread. But Hungary Gives Us Bread": Access to Food and (Dis)Loyalty in a "Redeemed" Yugoslav Borderland', *Austrian History Yearbook*, 55 (2024): 283–97. Tamás Révész, 'A National Army Under the Red Banner? The Mobilisation of the Hungarian Red Army in 1919', *Contemporary European History*, 31 (2022), 82.

[20] Patricia Clavin, 'The Austrian Hunger Crisis and the Genesis of International Organization after the First World War', *International Affairs*, 90:2 (2014), 265–78; see also, Peter Becker and Natasha Wheatley, eds., *Remaking Central Europe: The League of Nations and the Former Habsburg Lands* (Oxford: Oxford University Press, 2021).

[21] Bruno Cabanes, *The Great War and the Origins of Humanitarianism, 1918–1924* (Cambridge: Cambridge University Press, 2014); the literature on humanitarianism in the wake of the First World War is currently expanding: see, Paul Weindling, *International Health Organisations and Movements, 1918–1939* (Cambridge University Press, 1997); Julia Irwin, *Making the World Safe: The American Red Cross and a Nation's Humanitarian Awakening* (Oxford: Oxford University Press, 2013); Branden Little, 'An Explosion of New Endeavours. Global Humanitarian Responses to Industrialized Warfare in the First World War Era', *First World War Studies*, 5:1 (2014), 1–16; Elisabeth Piller and Neville Wylie, eds., *Humanitarianism and the Greater War, 1914–24* (Manchester: Manchester University Press, 2023); Jaclyn Granick, *International Jewish Humanitarianism in the Age of the Great War* (Cambridge: Cambridge University Press, 2021); Clotilde Druelle, *Feeding Occupied France during World War I: Herbert Hoover and the Blockade* (London: Palgrave Macmillan, 2019); on the link between humanitarianism and modern conceptions of hunger, see James Vernon, *Hunger: A Modern History* (Cambridge, MA: Harvard University Press, 2007).

this outpouring, the First World War saw the development of a rationalized scientific system of aid.[22] It was a central moment in the transition of food assistance from traditional local charity, such as soup kitchens, to highly organized international bureaucratic procedures.[23] Both state and international institutions attempted to introduce scientifically designed rations that took into account the specific needs of the different parts of the populations they served. Milk was set aside for children, and increased rations were provided for certain groups that were deemed to need them most. Everywhere, those responsible for providing aid sought to precisely assess who was in greatest need, so that they could be provided for first. A 1923 article called this kind of relief 'machine age humanitarianism'.[24]

In addition to feeding the most hungry, humanitarian projects also aimed to bring new forms of organization and governance to help foster political stability in the new post-war order.[25] Humanitarianism at this crucial juncture also replaced imperial projects that had been increasingly failing with new forms of international influence. Humanitarian aid deployed to Europe and the Middle East revealed the implicit imperial dimensions of who was deemed worthy of hunger relief, and who was not. The wave of empathy for European victims of famine and the argument that hunger relief was needed to save European or Christian civilization highlighted the contrast with pre-war famines in European colonies.[26] Humanitarian aid in the wake of the war was accompanied by a discourse of worthiness that underlined the necessity to rebuild healthy European nations.

The Experience of Hunger

By focusing on civilian hunger in the First World War period, this book shows not only major shifts towards state responsibility to provide a minimum level of provisioning, the idea of nutritional sovereignty, and the growth of humanitarian aid, but also the unique and collective responses people used to combat it. Induced hunger was considered to be of strategic importance, with some authorities at the time believing that it played

[22] See Cabanes, *The Great War and the Origins of Humanitarianism.*

[23] Tom Scott-Smith, *On an Empty Stomach: Two Hundred Years of Hunger Relief* (Ithaca, NY: Cornell University Press, 2020).

[24] Scott-Smith, *On an Empty Stomach*, 82.

[25] Doina Anca Cretu, *Foreign Aid and State Building in Interwar Romania: In Quest of an Ideal* (Stanford, CA: Stanford University Press, 2024); Nel de Mûelenaere, 'International development contested: the American Child Health Section in Belgium (1922–1924)', *European Review of History: Revue Européenne d'histoire*, 30:5 (2023), 747–69.

[26] On humanitarianism as a means for the reconstruction of European civilization, see Tomás Irish, *Feeding the Mind: Humanitarianism and the Reconstruction of European Intellectual Life, 1919–1933* (Cambridge: Cambridge University Press, 2024).

a key role in winning the war (see Chapter 2 by Hew Strachan).[27] Avner Offer's pathbreaking research thirty-five years ago underlined the impact of agrarian factors and the production and trade of grain on the course of the military conflict.[28] Yet the consequences of hunger reached even further. Issues of food production and consumption were not only objects of economic policy, but cultural and social practices as well. Even when severe nutritional deprivation could be avoided, significant changes in diet – usually because of losses of specific foodstuffs – transformed tastes, or even self-perceptions in terms of class and national identity. In the short term, hunger was not just a subject of supply levels, political discussions, or strategies of blockade. Ordinary people devoted much of their energy to finding food and developed their own strategies to circumvent deficient official provisioning systems (see Chapter 4 by Friederike Kind-Kovács). The striking experience of hunger also integrated more tangible aspects: sensations such as disgust at the tastes of available food, the drabness of ersatz products, and disappointment at empty market stalls (see Chapter 5 by Sophie De Schaepdrijver). Hunger gave rise to new representations (Chapter 6 by Nicholas Siekierski) and brought new feelings such as fear, anxiety, or the humiliation of relying on charity for sustenance (see Chapter 8 by Claire Morelon).

At its core, hunger is a physiological response by a person to not having enough food to eat. Fats, proteins, vitamins, carbohydrates, and sugars are the building blocks of human diets, and necessary for life. They support physical growth and development in children, maturation of the nervous system, cardiovascular health as one ages, and an overall feeling of wellness at all stages of life. In times of famine, when chronic hunger is not abated, a person will have less energy to engage in their normal activities. Responses to hunger may include self-imposed limitations on work, leisure, and housework. Indeed, all kinds of activities are reduced that use up precious energy. If additional forms of nutrition are not forthcoming, individuals suffering from such chronic energy deficiency (CED) will eventually be driven to give up all nonessential activities unrelated to obtaining food and shelter.[29] Hence, hunger was not only a physical experience but also a social one. It

[27] Ferdinand Foch believed that the blockade could explain 50 per cent of the outcome, and Lloyd George's sentiments were similar. See Isabel V. Hull, *A Scrap of Paper: Breaking and Making International Law during the Great War* (Ithaca, NY: Cornell University Press, 2014), 170.

[28] Avner Offer, *The First World War: An Agrarian Interpretation* (Oxford: Oxford University Press, 1989).

[29] Roderick Floud, Robert W. Fogel, Bernard Harris, and Sok Chul Hong, *The Changing Body: Health, Nutrition, and Human Development in the Western World since 1700* (Cambridge: Cambridge University Press, 2012).

became an all-encompassing feature of social life, even in cases where people were not threatened with terminal starvation. In the era of the First World War, hunger impacted national economies, transformed the cultural relationship to food, determined and was determined by social status, and influenced the perception of citizens towards their governments and each other.

A common perception among those suffering from hunger was that access to food was a zero-sum game: one experienced hunger because another person or entity deliberately harmed them, cheated, or took more than their share. This perception could also be found at a societal level and at an international level, as different groups and countries vied to convince aid agencies that they were more deserving.[30] Different responses depended in large part on the varied and changing circumstances that peoples, governments, and institutions found themselves in. Whether fault was attributed to foreign enemies or occupiers, to greedy farmers in the countryside or to wealthy city dwellers, to incompetent government leaders, or to racketeers in the shadows, people sought to make sense of the difficult and confusing conditions of food insecurity in which they found themselves. Casting blame was one part of trying to understand, and perhaps change, difficult and unwanted experiences (see Chapter 7 by Mary Elisabeth Cox).

Although estimates vary, a significant part of the civilian losses during the First World War can be attributed to starvation or nutritional deprivation. To this day, we only have a very imprecise picture of the number of civilian victims of hunger as it can be difficult to determine the exact breakdown of the causes of civilian deaths. The high number of refugees and changing state borders also complicate the assessment, which could be comprised between 2 and 5 million people in Europe and the Ottoman Empire.[31] Distinguishing the number of civilian deaths resulting from starvation from deaths due to disease during World War I and its aftermath can be difficult to parse.[32] Malnutrition weakens the immune system and makes people more vulnerable to disease, including diseases that they

[30] Michael McGuire, 'At (Red) Cross Purposes: American Red Cross Humanitarian "arrogance" and France's Great War Relief and Reconstruction, 1917–20', *European Review of History: Revue Européenne d'histoire*, 30:5 (2023), 705–26.

[31] See Antoine Prost, 'War Losses', in Ute Daniel et al., eds., *1914–1918-online. International Encyclopedia of the First World War* (Berlin: Freie Universität Berlin, 2014). On the origins and use of the German number of civilian victims: see Nicolas Patin, 'Histoire d'un chiffre. Réflexions autour des victimes allemandes du blocus de 1914–1918', *Les Cahiers Sirice*, 26 (2021), 95–107.

[32] See Joel Mokyr and Cormac Ó Gráda, 'What Do People Die of during Famines: The Great Irish Famine in Comparative Perspective', *European Review of Economic History*, 6:3 (2002), 339–63; Hionidou, *Famine and Death in Occupied Greece*.

might otherwise have been able to overcome. The longer morbidity period of individuals weakened by malnutrition also aids in the spread of disease. The rate of death by tuberculosis had gone down in many European cities before the First World War yet jumped in the wake of the War. The high mortality rate from the Spanish flu, which is generally excluded from war-induced losses, might have been facilitated by the diminished physical condition of populations (on disease and hunger, see Chapter 11 by Mark Harrison). Finally, even those who survived death from hunger continued to suffer from poor physical health, reduced life spans, anxieties, and inescapable memories of hunger and deprivation.

Probably the most frequently used contemporary definition of famine was built on the work of Stephen Devereux and Paul Howe, who have argued over the past several decades that famines need to be defined in terms of intensity and magnitude scales to provide better responses and accountability by the international community.[33] These ideas led to the Integrated Food Security Phase Classification (IPC). Level V, considered 'famine' is defined as '20% of households facing an extreme lack of food, at least 30% of children suffering from acute malnutrition, and two people for every 10,000 dying each day due to outright starvation or to the interaction of malnutrition and disease'.[34] (On the measurements of hunger during the First World War, see Chapter 10 by Joël Floris and Kaspar Staub.) Death statistics during the First World War, including those for civilians, are imperfect and vary in quality (see Chapter 12 by Stephen G. Wheatcroft). Given this, it did not make sense to restrict the use of the terms famine and hunger, although they have been successfully applied to food crises in the past, most notably the Dutch Hunger Winter of 1944–1945.[35] Authors throughout this book use the words hunger, starvation, and famine in non-restrictive ways as they appear in their contemporary sources.

The severity of food shortages varied within and across countries. This book does not focus only on famine and the most extreme, life-threatening cases of hunger, but also on more widespread struggles to keep minimum living standards and previous expectations surrounding food and mealtimes. The terms used in different societies at different stages of the conflict to describe the experience of hunger reflected these variations. They reveal how much these different groups suffered, as well as how they made sense of that suffering. Shortages of common

[33] Paul Howe and Stephen Devereux, 'Famine Intensity and Magnitude Scales: A Proposal for an Instrumental Definition of Famine', *Disasters*, 28:4 (2004), 353–72.

[34] IPC 'What Is Famine?' <www.ipcinfo.org/famine-facts/>

[35] Ingrid de Zwarte, *The Hunger Winter: Fighting Famine in the Occupied Netherlands, 1944–1945* (Cambridge: Cambridge University Press, 2020).

goods were first understood in continuity with pre-war times as crises of the cost of living. In France, where shortages remained relatively limited throughout the war, complaints against the *vie chère* (high prices) were nonetheless frequent, as were those against the *carovita* (high prices) in Italy. In Central Europe, the high prices (*Teuerung* in German, *drahota* in Czech, and *drożyzna* in Polish) were also blamed at first. From cost of living, terms were developed to describe experiences of hunger and suffering as a whole. In Germany, for example, the period of hunger from 1914–1919 was known as *die Hungerblockade* (the hunger blockade), emphasizing the external origin of the shortages and casting blame away from themselves or their government. In Austria, the experience became known as *die Hungerkatastrophe* or 'the hunger catastrophe'. This implies hunger to be a total disaster rather than imputing blame solely to foreign forces. In Mount Lebanon, then part of the Ottoman Empire, it was called, 'the Great Famine'. With a population of some 400,000 people, it is estimated that between 100,000 and 250,000 people died of starvation. This depth of severity meant that the war was primarily identified with the experience of hunger in popular memory.[36]

War and Redrawing the Map

By examining the impact of food shortages on wartime societies, this book contributes to a renewed historiography of the First World War. Scholarly focus has moved away from the muddy trenches of the Western Front to the global dimensions of the conflict and its impact on larger sections of civilian populations worldwide. Increased attention has been paid to the neglected belligerents, the colonial territories, and the neutrals. Territories, from Latin America to Japan, less exposed to direct fighting were nonetheless directly impacted by the economic, political, social, and cultural consequences of the First World War. Some polities were thoroughly transformed by the conflict, especially in Eastern Europe and the Middle East.[37] Analyzing the conflict through the lens of hunger automatically expands the focus to more than just the Western front. Famine and food crises also played a major role in regions even

[36] Melanie S. Tanielian, *The Charity of War: Famine, Humanitarian Aid, and World War I in the Middle East* (Stanford, CA: Stanford University Press, 2017), 7; see also, Tylor Brand, *Famine Worlds: Life at the Edge of Suffering in Lebanon's Great War* (Stanford, CA: Stanford University Press, 2023).

[37] See Olivier Compagnon and Pierre Purseigle, 'Geographies of Mobilization and Territories of Belligerence during the First World War', *Annales: Histoire, Sciences Sociales*, 71:1 (2016), 37–60.

further away from the European battlefields, including in colonies that were exploited by European powers wanting more raw material to fuel their war effort. The First World War may have been less of a turning point in the history of colonial territories, which repeatedly suffered famines as a matter of European policy.[38] Even when concentrating primarily on Europe and the Ottoman Empire, our study of hunger redraws the map, revealing a new geography of the conflict that highlights experiences on the Eastern side of the continent and in the Middle East. Our book confirms the status of Central Europe as 'ground zero' not only for the international order, but also in the economic reordering that took place after the war.[39] Once the focal point is moved eastwards, hunger is more clearly delineated as one of the most consequential factors in the conflict and its aftermath.

The study of food shortages and nutritional deprivation also implies a time frame that extends beyond 1918. Hunger did not end with the Western front armistice. The situation continued to be just as critical in the immediate post-war years. Historians have recently highlighted the complexity of the years following the armistice, which were characterized by state and non-state violence, uncertainty, political instability, and economic difficulties. For several years following official peace treaties and border agreements, border conflicts and ideological strife blurred the boundaries between peace and war in large parts of the European continent. Even in relatively spared Britain or France, the recovery from war cast a heavy shadow over the immediate post-war period.[40] This historiographical shift therefore involves a rethinking of the conflict's temporal limits, extending the direct impact of the First World War on civilians until at least the early 1920s. Our book ends in 1923 to reflect the continued impact of hunger on the continent in the years following 1918. Crop yields only slowly returned to pre-war levels, human bodies only recovered incrementally, and disrupted trade routes, enforced or otherwise, were only gradually reestablished.

[38] On famine in colonial contexts, see Steven Serels, 'Starving for Someone Else's Fight: The First World War and Food Insecurity in the African Red Sea Region', in *Environmental Histories of the First World War*, ed. by Richard P. Tucker et al. (Cambridge: Cambridge University Press, 2018), 208–30; Yan Slobodkin, *The Starving Empire: A History of Famine in France's Colonies* (Ithaca, NY: Cornell University Press, 2023).

[39] Natasha Wheatley, 'Central Europe as Ground Zero of the New International Order', *Slavic Review*, 78 (2019), 900–11.

[40] See, Robert Gerwarth, *The Vanquished: Why the First World War Failed to End, 1917–1923* (London: Allen Lane, 2016); Robert Gerwarth and John Horne, eds., *War in Peace: Paramilitary Violence in Europe after the Great War* (Oxford: Oxford University Press, 2012).

In some regions, active combat prevented major recovery entirely. New and old states only progressively lifted the various regulations of the food economy in the early 1920s.

Finally, more recent studies have explored another dimension of the conflict by examining the experience of different types of populations beyond the soldiers of conventional armies. Research on internees, refugees, and civilians has revealed the high impact of war on non-combatants and showed that the First World War was a major step in the 'civilianization of war'.[41] Hunger during the First World War disproportionately affected civilians. The deleterious effect of hunger was certainly not a civilian-only phenomenon – many soldiers ended up starving in the armies of the Central Powers – but the priority given in most belligerent countries to feeding armies left less available food for civilian populations. All the belligerent armies recognized the importance of food rations in maintaining soldiers' morale.[42] This book therefore focuses on civilian experience and only marginally deals with soldiers' hunger.[43]

Hunger during the war has largely been examined through local studies, dealing with a specific city or region.[44] As food distribution was

[41] See, Jay Winter, *The Day the Great War Ended, 24 July 1923: The Civilianization of War* (Oxford: Oxford University Press, 2022); Tammy M. Proctor, *Civilians in a World at War, 1914–1918* (New York, NY: New York University Press, 2010); Matthew Stibbe, *Civilian Internment during the First World War: A European and Global History, 1914–1920* (Cham: Palgrave Macmillan, 2019); Peter Gatrell and Lyubov Zhvanko, eds., *Europe on the Move: The Great War and Its Refugees* (Manchester: Manchester University Press, 2017); Alex Dowdall, *Communities Under Fire: Urban Life at the Western Front, 1914–1918* (Oxford: Oxford University Press, 2020); Sophie De Schaepdrijver, 'Populations under Occupation', in Jay Winter, ed., *The Cambridge History of the First World War* (Cambridge University Press, 2013), 476–504; Sophie De Schaepdrijver, *La Belgique et la Première Guerre Mondiale* (Brussels: Lang, 2004); Yigit Akin, *When the War Came Home: The Ottomans' Great War and the Devastation of an Empire* (Stanford, CA: Stanford University Press, 2018).

[42] Emmanuelle Cronier, 'Food and Nutrition', in Ute Daniel et al., eds., *1914–1918-online. International Encyclopedia of the First World War* (Berlin: Freie Universität Berlin, 2014).

[43] For more on this topic: on the British case, see Rachel Duffett, *The Stomach for Fighting: Food and the Soldiers of the Great War* (Manchester: Manchester University Press, 2012); soldiers' insufficient food supply was a greater issue in the East; on the Italian front, see Rok Stergar, 'L'expérience des soldats austro-hongrois sur le front austro-italien: le problème du ravitaillement en vivres', in Giovanni L. Fontana and Marco Mondini, eds., *Soldati e quotidianità della guerra* (Ospedaletto: Pacini editore, 2019), 13–30; Holger H. Herwig, *The First World War: Germany and Austria-Hungary 1914–1918* (London: Bloomsbury Academic, 2009), 280.

[44] For example, see Roger Chickering, *The Great War and Urban Life in Germany: Freiburg, 1914–1918* (Cambridge: Cambridge University Press, 2007); Belinda J. Davis, *Home Fires Burning: Food, Politics, and Everyday Life in World War I Berlin* (Chapel Hill, NC: University of North Carolina Press, 2000); Maureen Healy, *Vienna and the Fall of the Habsburg Empire: Total War and Everyday Life in World War I* (Cambridge: Cambridge University Press, 2004); Robert E. Blobaum, *A Minor Apocalypse: Warsaw during the First World War* (Ithaca: Cornell University Press, 2017).

often a local matter managed at the municipal level, such demarcations make sense.[45] There are far fewer studies which portray the food situation at the national, regional, or international level.[46] In many cases, the most detailed accounts are still the volumes that were part of the 'Economic and Social History of the World War' series published by the Carnegie Endowment for International Peace in the aftermath of the war. The country studies attempted to capture how much food different countries had been able to produce, import, and export during the conflict.[47] By contrast, experiences of hunger during the First World War have often been memorialized primarily as a national experience. National memories have been exploited for political goals or even to justify later wars. Memories of hunger experienced by Germans during the war were multifaced in the interwar period but were then weaponized by the Nazis: first to get votes,[48] as propaganda against the British,[49] and to undergird fascist predatory occupation policies[50] that resulted in the deaths of millions of people.

No comprehensive study provides an overall picture of the impact of hunger on the continent.[51] The pioneering volumes edited by Jay Winter and Jean-Louis Robert compared the three European capital

[45] On Belgium and Northern France, see Jan Naert, 'Ventre Affamé n'a Pas d'oreilles: Une Histoire Sociale de l'approvisionnement Par Les Autorités Locales Dans Les Territoires Occupés En Belgique et En France (1914–1918)', *Guerres mondiales et conflits contemporains*, 272:4 (2018), 35–50.

[46] Mary Elisabeth Cox, *Hunger in War and Peace: Women and Children 1914–1924* (New York, NY: Oxford University Press, 2019); Tanielian, *The Charity of War.*

[47] See, among others, Riccardo Bachi, *L'alimentazione e la politica annonaria in Italia* (Bari: Laterza, 1926); William H. Beveridge, *British Food Control* (London: Oxford University Press, 1928); Albert Henry, *Le Ravitaillement de La Belgique pendant l'occupation allemande* (Paris: Presses Universitaires de France, 1924); Hans Loewenfeld-Russ, *Die Regelung der Volksernährung im Kriege* (Vienna: Hölder Pichler Tempsky, 1926); Pierre Pinot, *Le Contrôle du ravitaillement de la population civile* (Paris: Presses Universitaires de France, 1925); August Skalweit, *Die deutsche Kriegsernährungswirtschaft* (Stuttgart: Deutsche Verlagsanstalt, 1927); P. B. Struce, *Food Supply in Russia during the World War* (New Haven, CT: Yale University Press, 1930).

[48] Gesine Gerhard, *Nazi Hunger Politics: A History of Food in the Third Reich.* (London: Rowman & Littlefield, 2015), 44–5.

[49] Werner Schaeffer, *Krieg Gegen Frauen und Kinder: Englands Hungerblockade gegen Deutschland 1914–1920* (Stuttgart: Berlin Deutsche Verlag, 1940); see also, Elisabeth Piller, 'German Child Distress, American Humanitarian Aid and Revisionist Politics, 1918–1924', *Journal of Contemporary History*, 51:3 (2016), 453–86; on national memorializations of hunger, see the 'Heritages of Hunger' project funded by the Dutch Research Council and led by Professor Marguérite Corporaal at Radboud University in Nijmegen, Netherlands.

[50] Lizzie Collingham, *The Taste of War: World War II and the Battle for Food* (London: Penguin Publishing Group, 2011), 25–38.

[51] Two edited collections provide some elements of comparison, see Ina Zweiniger-Bargielowska, Rachel Duffett, and Alain Drouard, eds., *Food and War in Twentieth Century Europe* (London: Routledge, 2011); Frank Trentmann and Flemming Just,

cities of London, Paris, and Berlin showing the centrality of hunger in the everyday lives of metropolitan inhabitants. Berliners clearly suffered from hunger more than their counterparts in Paris and London.[52] Our ambition is not to systematically compare levels of hunger over Europe and in the Ottoman Empire, but to give a better sense of how civilians throughout the continent experienced shortages as their living standards significantly fell during the war. The present chapters cover a variety of regions from Western to Eastern Europe and the Ottoman Empire. The debates on hunger and the First World War still revolve in large part around the blockade of Germany or the occupations in Belgium and Northern France.[53] The countries chosen for this book reflect the diversity of experiences on the continent, from occupied territories to neutral states, and home fronts in belligerent countries. We redrew the geography of hunger in the First World War to include lesser studied regions. The countries covered here range from Belgium, Switzerland, Hungary, Latvia, Austria, Czechoslovakia, Italy, Germany, Finland, the Netherlands, and Poland to parts of the Ottoman Empire.[54] While it was not possible to include the experiences of every belligerent into our study, this book is a major step towards establishing commonalities and differences in experience and response to nutritional deprivation.

******

This book focuses on themes rather than individualized country-based case studies in order to explore the interlinked nature of hunger in the First World War. It shows the multifaceted impact of hunger on societies. The themes presented in this book combine different approaches to the topic, including a top-down analysis of responses to hunger across the continent, and a comparison of the manner in

eds., *Food and Conflict in Europe in the Age of the Two World Wars* (New York, NY: Palgrave Macmillan, 2006).

52 Jay Winter and Jean-Louis Robert, eds., *Capital Cities at War: Paris, London, Berlin 1914–1919, vol. 1* (Cambridge: Cambridge University Press, 1997).

53 Paul Vincent, *The Politics of Hunger: The Allied Blockade of Germany 1915–1919* (Athens, OH: Ohio Press University, 1985); Cox, *Hunger in War and Peace*; on Belgium, see Luis Angel Bernardo y Garcia, *Le Ventre des Belges: Une histoire alimentaire des temps d'occupation et de sortie de guerre* (Brussels: Algemeen Rijksarchief, 2017). On France, see Druelle, *Feeding Occupied France during World War I.*

54 Some areas of Europe are not as systematically covered; first among them, France (occupied and non-occupied). See, Dowdall, *Communities under Fire*; Druelle, *Feeding Occupied France*; Stéphane Lembré, *La guerre des bouches. Ravitaillement et alimentation à Lille, 1914–1919* (Villeneuve-d'Ascq: Presses universitaires du Septentrion, 2016); Caroline Poulain, ed., *Manger et boire entre 1914 & 1918* (Dijon: Bibliothèque municipale de Dijon, 2015); on Romania, see David Hamlin, 'The fruits of occupation: food and Germany's occupation of Romania in the First World War', *First World War Studies*, 4:1 (2013), 81–95.

which ordinary people dealt with the shortages. A transnational history of hunger from 1914 to 1923 is necessary both to understand the lives of the millions of people it touched, and the emerging world that was created as a result of the hostilities. We acknowledge that a single book cannot offer a comprehensive survey of hunger and food-related issues across Europe and the Ottoman Empire, and this book does not claim to do so.

The first two chapters analyze the role of hunger within the international system and as part of the war campaigns. Chapter 1 offers an overview of the war's impact on the worldwide food distribution system, the disruption of trade routes and the decline in agricultural production. While this chapter considers the war as an external event with consequences on the dynamics of food supply, the following chapter (Chapter 2) examines the intentional restriction of food as a means of warfare. It focuses on the weaponization of hunger during the conflict. From there, the book moves to the top-down management by states of food scarcity in wartime in Chapter 3. The First World War marked a moment of systematic deployment of state intervention in the food economy that would have far-reaching consequences for the role of state as welfare provider in the rest of the twentieth century. This chapter constitutes a comparison, unique in the literature, of the various modes of food controls used during the war.

Official state policies only accounted for part of the modes of obtaining food. Many people increasingly relied on self-provisioning strategies, which enabled them to cope with the shortages of food and complement the state-mandated rations. This unofficial world of alternative strategies constitutes the theme of Chapter 4. This is followed by two chapters that explore the issue of hunger from the perspective of lived experience, trying to get as close as possible to the perceptions and feelings of ordinary Europeans. Chapter 5 reveals the profound transformations of tastes and smells, the substitute goods, the changes in diet and in modes of eating. It shows how a cultural history of food and hunger can give more depth to our understanding of the war experience on the continent. Chapter 6 examines the increased number of artistic and cultural productions representing the challenges of hunger, which reflect the large place that the phenomenon took in the lives of ordinary citizens. From cultural issues, we move on to social issues in the next two chapters (Chapters 7 and 8), which explore the social consequences of hunger in societies. The certainties of pre-war social hierarchies were turned upside down by the experience of hunger while communities broke apart in the increased competition for food. The strong demand for social justice, equal food allocation and just reward for sacrifice that emerged from these fragmented societies led to more articulated political projects, which are the subject of Chapter 9.

The last part of the book takes us further into the search for remedies to the challenges posed by hunger during the war itself and in its immediate aftermath. Chapters 10 and 11 examine contemporary understandings of the issue of hunger informed by the history of science including systems of measurement and the relationship between malnutrition and hunger-related diseases. Chapter 12 is entirely devoted to a quantitative overview of famine conditions, offering a comparison between wartime famines and the Russian famine of the early 1920s. Finally, the book ends with a discussion of humanitarian aid in Chapter 13.

These different themes not only draw a varied picture of hunger in the era of the First World War from the perspective of different subdisciplines of history, they also show a logical trajectory of the causes, consequences, and solutions to the crisis triggered by hunger. This book highlights the links between social transformations brought on by hunger and the political transformations such as the collapse of the four main Empires on the continent (Habsburg, Romanov, Hohenzollern, Ottoman). The loss of legitimacy of each of these regimes cannot be understood without considering the major hunger crisis that their societies went through. Neither can the difficult stabilization processes the new states went through as they faced the same issues. The First World War was a moment when food was uniquely linked to the notion of political sovereignty. In this crucial period around 1919, hunger was at the center of citizens' relationship to their state, governmental economic policies, conceptions of international order, and humanitarian endeavors to bring political stability. In that sense, hunger profoundly redrew the map of Europe.

1 War of Want

The Impact of the First World War on the Global Food Economy

Samuël Kruizinga

Introduction: Food and War

Food's centrality to the conduct of warfare was not a feature that was unique to the Great War.[1] However, the armies of 1914–1918 were not only much larger than those engaged in previous conflicts, they waged a war in which new weapons systems combined with the frequency and duration of battles to produce physical and mental strains simply not comparable to any conflict that had come before. Moreover, many of the soldiers and the hundreds of millions of civilians on whose (enthusiastic, tacit, or enforced) continued support the engines of modern warfare had depended, in the decades before the war, became accustomed to a much more varied diet. That diet, in turn, consisted of foodstuffs produced by a global market, which was severely disrupted by the equally global scale of the war.[2]

This chapter analyses the First World War's impact on global patterns of food production, distribution, and consumption. It will do so by briefly charting the development of the first global and modern agricultural market (1750–1913) and then detailing the impact of the war on three of its key elements: productivity, trade, and transport. This chapter's level of analysis is global and structural;[3] it serves both as an introduction to the reader on the impact of the First World War on food, and vice versa, and provides essential contexts for the chapters that follow.

[1] For example, see Graham Oliver, *War, Food, and Politics in Early Hellenistic Athens* (Oxford: Oxford University Press, 2007), 114–15, 265.

[2] Peter Lummel, 'Food Provisioning in the German Army of the First World War', in Rachel Duffett and Alain Drouard, eds., *Food and War in Twentieth Century Europe* (Farnham: Ashgate, 2011), 16, 19.

[3] Most economic histories of the war, on which this chapter is largely based, focus primarily on Europe and the USA, and in some cases on the Ottoman Empire and Japan, and it is unavoidable that this geographic bias has been, in part, replicated in this chapter. See Jamie Martin, 'Globalizing the History of the First World War: Economic Approaches', *The Historical Journal* 65 (2022), 838–55.

Towards a Global Food Economy, 1750–1913

Food production is a unique economic sector. Unlike most other economic goods, demand for basic foodstuffs is not elastic: cereal grains such as wheat or rice provide fuels so vital to human survival as to make them irreplaceable. What is more, humans must intake a certain number of calories in order to function. Food production is also heavily dependent on the environment. Plants require nutrients, chiefly nitrogen, phosphorus, and potassium found in the soil, but also sunlight and water; yields will fall when any of these are not available in adequate quantities, or if temperatures rise or fall below certain levels. Agriculture, moreover, has a seasonal pattern, since plants grow according to a biologically determined life cycle.[4] Everything and everyone that consumes plants also becomes beholden to that seasonality, as most foods cannot be stockpiled for very long. For most of humanity's existence, food's indispensability combined with the fickleness of its production induced checks on the growth of the population.[5]

There are only a limited number of ways to increase food production substantially for an extended period. One is to increase *inputs*, such as labour, land, and livestock; more livestock produces more meat and milk, more land increases yearly yields, and more labour allows for more intensive cultivation. This produces so-called extensive growth. Alternatively, one can improve production through intensive growth, by increasing productivity through fertilization, mechanization, or irrigation. Throughout much of the nineteenth century, agricultural production increases were mostly of the extensive variety. Technological progress that is indispensable to intensive growth remained limited to improvements made to existing tools and by introducing new plant varieties and cultivation practices. Crucially, outside Europe (and China), the total stock of land that was made available for agriculture was still growing, mainly due to the (forced) expropriation of vast swathes of land from their native inhabitants. Developments in transport technology (especially due to the introduction of more fuel-efficient compound steam engines in trains

[4] Giovanni Federico, *Feeding the World: An Economic History of Agriculture 1800–2000* (Princeton, NJ: Princeton University Press, 2009), 7–11.

[5] Avner Offer, *The First World War: An Agrarian Interpretation* (Oxford: Clarendon Press, 1991), 23–4; Jörg Friedrichs, 'Escapology, or How to Escape Malthusian Traps', in Fredrik Albritton Jonsson et al., eds., *Scarcity in the Modern World: History, Politics, Society and Sustainability, 1800–2075* (London: Bloomsbury Academic, 2019), 115–18, 122–3; Richard Wilk, 'Rethinking the Relationships between Scarcity, Poverty and Hunger: An Anthropological Perspective', in Fredrik Albritton Jonsson et al., eds., *Scarcity in the Modern World: History, Politics, Society and Sustainability, 1800–2075* (London: Bloomsbury Academic, 2019), 51–2.

and ocean-going ships) significantly lowered transport costs, enabling a rapid integration process of agricultural markets.[6]

In 1873, wheat prices in London still exceeded those in the American interiors by a factor of ten, but by 1880 transit costs had lowered to such a degree that European land found itself in direct competition with the vast and fertile land endowments of the New World. For the first time in global history, long-distance trade began to have economy-wide effects on the allocation of resources, and hence on factor prices and distribution of income.[7] In some countries, most notably in the United Kingdom, the 'grain invasion' caused the domestic agricultural sector to shrink.[8] And other invasions were to follow: sugar, oilseeds, fruits, and vegetables were increasingly transported from the Americas, Asia, and Africa to be sold in Europe. During the last decades of the century the invention of mechanically refrigerated transport systems in ships and boxcars allowed perishables such as meat to join them.[9]

The spread of modern communications technology allowed for the further incorporation of the expanding European empires in Africa and Asia in the developing global agricultural markets, albeit in a deeply unequal relationship of dependence on Europe. The 1841 cross-Channel and the 1866 permanent transatlantic telegraph cable enabled the mobilization of European capital to build railroads in Asia, abattoirs in South America, and port facilities in Africa. Colonial trading firms established inland trade stations or plantations, from where African cocoa and groundnuts, Indian rice, and Indonesian coffee were transported by rail or ship to specially built entrepôt ports, to be transhipped to European harbours.[10] These developments, suggests economic historian Giovanni Federico, caused the trade/gross output ratio of global agricultural production to grow from about 5 per cent in 1870 to 15 per cent in 1913, meaning that

[6] Lizzy Collingham, *The Taste of War: World War Two and the Battle for Food* (New York: Penguin Books, 2011), 19; Michael Tracy, *Government and Agriculture in Western Europe 1888–1988*, 3rd ed. (New York, NY: New York University Press, 1989), 17; Per Högselius, Arne Kaijser, and Erik van der Vleuten, *Europe's Infrastructure Transition: Economy, War, Nature* (Houndmills: Palgrave Macmillan, 2016), 24–8, 188.

[7] Ronald Findlay and Kevin H. O'Rourke, *Power and Plenty: Trade, War, and the World Economy in the Second Millennium* (Princeton: Princeton University Press, 2007), 378–85.

[8] Stephan Broadberry and Peter Howlett, 'The United Kingdom during World War I: Business as Usual?', in Stephan Broadberry and Mark Harrison, eds., *The Economics of World War I* (Cambridge: Cambridge University Press, 2005), 211.

[9] James Vernon, *Hunger: A Modern History* (Cambridge, MA: Harvard University Press, 2007), 5.

[10] Högselius, Kaijser, and van der Vleuten, *Europe's Infrastructure Transition*, 117–20; Alice Weinreb, *Modern Hungers: Food and Power in Twentieth-Century Germany* (Oxford: Oxford University Press, 2017), 13–14.

in the last year before the First World War, 15 per cent of all agricultural production entered the global marketplace, where it accounted for 50 per cent of its total volume.[11] Given the expansion of both domestic consumption due to rapid population growth and productivity due to technological innovations, these numbers stand out even more.

The continued integration of global agricultural markets had a double impact on European agrarian production. It enabled cheap imports of fertilizers and feeding stuffs, improving yields and increasing the slaughter weight of livestock, but also exposed European farmers to global competition.[12] This, in combination with European population growth that made land scarce, created incentives to increase the productivity of existing plots. Farmers started to focus on intensive growth by increasing rotations and using chemical fertilizers to increase the supply of nitrogen in the soil. Additionally, they began to purchase feed stuffs (maize and oilseed cakes) on global markets to save on land previously used for producing livestock feed.[13] But farmers also began to demand some measure of protection from extra-European competition, calls that were augmented by a strong current of cultural nationalism and the notion that farming communities represented a purer form of society than those found in rapidly expanding industrial cities. Only those countries whose agricultural sector had already shrunk as a result of increased food imports and emigration (Britain) or had transformed their agricultural sectors to be highly export-dependent rather than self-sufficient (the Netherlands, Denmark) remained wedded to free trade.[14]

However, the extent of the impact of this protectionist surge in most of Europe should not be overstated. The degree of protection was real enough, ranging from duties of 15 per cent in the Ottoman Empire to an average of between 20 and 30 per cent in continental Europe.[15] But they only affected wheat; other products remained free from protection. Moreover, continuing strong population and economic growth meant that the dependence on extra-European sources of agricultural

[11] Federico, *Feeding the World*, 23, 28; Offer, *The First World War*, 157.

[12] Broadberry and Howlett, 'United Kingdom during World War I', 211.

[13] Jan Luiten van Zanden, 'The First Green Revolution: The Growth of Production and Productivity in European Agriculture, 1870–1914', *The Economic History Review* 44:2 (1991), 216, 232–4.

[14] Luiten van Zanden, 'The First Green Revolution', 227–8; Frank Trentmann, 'Coping with Shortage: The Problem of Food Security and Global Visions of Coordination, c. 1890s–1950', in Frank Trentmann and Flemming Just, eds., *Food and Conflict in Europe in the Age of the Two World Wars* (Houndmills: Palgrave Macmillan, 2006), 15.

[15] Tracy, *Government and Agriculture*, 22–3; Şevket Pamuk, 'The Ottoman Economy in World War I', in Stephan Broadberry and Mark Harrison, eds., *The Economics of World War I* (Cambridge: Cambridge University Press, 2005), 14–15.

supply only increased; in general, tariff increases did little to change the overall course of global agricultural integration.[16] Germany provides an excellent example. In 1913, it imported about 25 per cent of its food, particularly eggs, dairy products, vegetable oils, fish, and meat, as well as wheat. Moreover, domestic German agriculture was dependent on imports as well; to sustain high yields, German farmers imported Chilean nitrates and fed their draught animals barley and clover from Russia and their livestock maize from Argentina and oil cakes from the United States.[17]

Germany's pre-war imports also shed light on the changing expectations of the average European as to what to find on their dinner table. As in other industrialized or industrializing countries, the German urban workforce had developed a taste for meat. German meat consumption had nearly doubled from 36 to 52 kg yearly between 1897 and 1912; their intake was surpassed only by the British, who in 1913 consumed a yearly average of 60 kg.[18] Potatoes and bread were and remained a staple of working-class diets, but animal proteins and fats (meat, but also butter and margarine) played increasingly large roles. Moreover, foodstuffs that were previously considered luxuries, such as coffee, tea, fresh and tinned milk, granular sugar, fine wheaten flour, and chocolate were now increasingly available for the working classes to buy as, especially during the last quarter of the nineteenth century, the price of food declined relative to incomes.[19]

[16] Federico, *Feeding the World*, 190; Offer, *The First World War*, 85, 95–6.

[17] Robert Chickering, *Imperial Germany and the Great War, 1914–1918*, 2nd ed. (Cambridge: Cambridge University Press, 2004), 41; Friedrich Aereboe, *Der Einfluss des Krieges auf die landwirtschaftliche Produktion in Deutschland* (Stuttgart: Deutsche Verlags-Anstalt, 1927), 23; Gerd Hardach, *Der Erste Weltkrieg: 1914–1918* (Munich: Deutscher Taschenbuch Verlag, 1973), 121; Ute Daniel, *Arbeiterfrauen in Der Kriegsgesellschaft. Beruf, Familie Und Politik Im Ersten Weltkrieg* (Göttingen: Vandenhoeck & Ruprecht, 1989), 183–4; August Skalweit, *Die deutsche Kriegsernährungswirtschaft* (Stuttgart: Deutsche Verlags Anstalt, 1927), 11–12, 15–16; Anne Roerkohl, *Hungerblockade und Heimatfront: die kommunale Lebensmittelversorgung in Westfalen während des Ersten Weltkrieges* (Stuttgart: Steiner, 1991), 18. Britain, too, heavily depended on imports; in the years before the war, 78.7 per cent of consumed wheat and flour and 56.2 per cent of total cereals and pulses originated from outside the country. See Mary Elisabeth Cox, 'Food', in *The British Home Front and the First World War*, ed. Hew Strachan (Cambridge: Cambridge University Press, 2023), 475.

[18] Belinda Joy Davis, *Home Fires Burning: Food, Politics, and Everyday Life in World War I Berlin* (Chapel Hill, NC: University of North Carolina Press, 2000), 62; Högselius, Kaijser, and van der Vleuten, *Europe's Infrastructure Transition*, 120. The European average was 50 kg yearly in 1914; in Asia, especially in Japan, animal protein consumption was on the rise as well. Collingham, *The Taste of War*, 18, 51–2.

[19] Collingham, *The Taste of War*, 19; Offer, *The First World War*, 39–40; Rachel Duffett, 'British Army Provisioning on the Western Front, 1914–1918', in Rachel Duffett and Alain Drouard, eds., *Food and War in Twentieth Century Europe* (Farnham: Ashgate, 2011), 28.

For military reasons, as well as to improve industrial productivity, governments and industrialists alike had begun to awaken to the relationship between food, health, and productivity. Aided by new sciences related to demography, statistics, and nutrition, notions of 'hunger' slowly began to transform. Where the teachings of Thomas Malthus and Adam Smith suggested that the market must be free to generate plenty or want, and thus to regulate demography, during the nineteenth century the question of the prevention of starvation slowly became one of human responsibility and culpability rather than of impersonal forces.[20] The Great Famine of 1845–1849, for example, was initially portrayed as the fault of the Irish themselves: with their wasteful and primitive ways, they had brought their misfortune upon themselves. But soon photos of the famine's victims joined those of the hungry and starving in Europe's slums; these *reportages* turned their subjects from fools into victims denied their basic human and citizen rights by an uncaring government. By the outbreak of the First World War, writes James Vernon, 'the effectiveness of government had come to be measured by the absence, not the presence, of hunger and famine'.[21] So, in 1913, for many of those in the Western world food had transformed into something that was essentially inexhaustible. The global marketplace and increasing productivity were, naturally, subject to market forces, but those affected prices and not the availability of food. This does not mean that everyone enjoyed the same level of access to the global agricultural market, but it does mean that when food shortages occurred, they were considered deplorable and, crucially, avoidable.[22]

War, Labour, and Productivity

In Summer 1914, as Germany invaded Belgium and France, Austria-Hungary shelled Belgrade, and Russia attacked Germany in East Prussia, millions of people, most of them drawn from Europe's predominantly agrarian society, were conscripted or volunteered: Russia mobilized 4 million men in July, Germany 3.8 million, the Ottoman

[20] See, e.g., Raymond Pearl, *The Nation's Food: A Statistical Study of a Physiological and Social Problem* (Philadelphia, PA: W. B. Saunders Company, 1920), 17.

[21] Vernon, *Hunger*, 5, 20–2, 41–2, 273–4; Weinreb, *Modern Hungers*, 3, 6, 9. Imperial-colonial relationships, however, made sure that not everybody's hunger was treated as equally serious and not everyone's suffering deserved the same response. Declan Curran, Lubomy Luciuk, and Andrew G. Newby, 'Famines in European Economic History: Introduction', in Declan Curran, Lubomy Luciuk, and Andrew G. Newby, eds., *Famines in European Economic History: The Last Great European Famines Reconsidered* (London: Routledge, 2015), 11–13.

[22] See, e.g., Pearl, *The Nation's Food*, 17.

Empire 2.85 million, and France 2.9 million, while in Britain 300,000 men volunteered for service in early August.[23] Before the Armistice of 11 November 1918, many millions more, from all over the globe, would join them, either as part of the armed forces of the warring empires or to work in special Labour Battalions behind the front.[24] All in all, about 50 per cent of the pre-war labour force of Europe was called up.[25] The European agricultural sector faced an immediate shortage of labour, which grew worse as the war progressed. In Italy, of the 4.8 million men aged over eighteen years employed in agriculture, 2.6 million were called to arms; in Russia, about 12 of the nearly 16 million males called into the army between 1914 and 1919 were peasants; France mobilized about 4 million peasants during the war, representing about 43 per cent of the pre-war agricultural workforce; Germany mobilized about 3.3 million farmers, or an astonishing 60 per cent of all those who worked the fields before July 1914.[26] At least 10 million civilians were displaced by the violence, adding to the labour shortage.[27] And as the armies of the Great War expended never-before-seen amounts of ammunition, armaments industries had to quickly ramp up production, creating new employment opportunities for farm workers, especially since the strategic value of their labour translated into attractive wages.[28] The war also

[23] Matteo Ermacora, 'Rural Society', in Ute Daniel et al., eds., *1914–1918-online. International Encyclopedia of the First World War* (Berlin: Freie Universität Berlin, 2015); Benjamin Ziemann, 'Agrarian Society', in Jay Winter, ed., *The Cambridge History of the First World War, Vol. II: The State* (Cambridge: Cambridge University Press, 2014), 396. On mobilization more generally, see Adrian Gregory, *The Last Great War: British Society and the First World War* (Cambridge: Cambridge University Press, 2008), 9–39; Jean Jacques Becker, *1914. Comment les Français sont entrés dans la guerre: contribution à l'étude de l'opinion publique printemps-été 1914* (Paris: Presses de la Fondation nationale des sciences politiques, 1977), 277–309; Jeffrey Verhey, *The Spirit of 1914: Militarism, Myth and Mobilization in Germany* (Cambridge: Cambridge University Press, 2006), 11–13.

[24] Barry Supple, 'War Economies', in Jay Winter, ed., *The Cambridge History of the First World War, Vol. II: The State* (Cambridge: Cambridge University Press, 2014), 302–3; Richard Fogarty, 'The French Empire', in Robert Gerwarth and Erez Manela, eds., *Empires at War: 1911–1923* (Oxford: Oxford University Press, 2014), 118.

[25] Federico, *Feeding the World*, 191.

[26] Benjamin Ziemann and Alex Skinner, *War Experiences in Rural Germany, 1914–1923* (Oxford: Berg, 2007), 45–52; Peter Gatrell, 'Poor Russia, Poor Show: Mobilising a Backward Economy for War, 1914–1917', in Stephan Broadberry and Mark Harrison, eds., *The Economics of World War I* (Cambridge: Cambridge University Press, 2005), 251; Davis, *Home Fires Burning*, 23; Pierre-Cyrille Hautcoeur, 'Was the Great War a Watershed? The Economics of World War I in France', in Stephan Broadberry and Mark Harrison, eds., *The Economics of World War I* (Cambridge: Cambridge University Press, 2005), 174.

[27] Peter Gatrell, 'World Wars and Population Displacement in Europe in the Twentieth Century', *Contemporary European History* 16:4 (2007), 418–24.

[28] Ziemann and Skinner, *War Experiences in Rural Germany, 1914–1923*, 403.

closed most international borders, curbing transnational flows of seasonal labour.[29] It additionally took both fishermen and their equipment, as many smaller boats were drafted into Navy service.[30]

Making good this shortage of labour proved to be an impossible task. Especially for smallholdings, now deprived of their one full-time worker, the effects were disastrous.[31] The farming communities' women, now soldiers' wives, mothers and daughters, had no choice but to take up additional duties; however, they could not possibly replace the labour lost.[32] Therefore, government-sponsored schemes quickly emerged to send schoolchildren, the urban poor, refugees, and prisoners of war to the fields. But most of them lacked the training or the physical energy to be effective workers.[33] Attempts to draw in new seasonal labourers from allied or neutral countries mostly failed, as they had plenty of employment opportunities closer to home. In some cases, such as in France, the army agreed from 1915 onwards to send some of the soldiers home in time for seed-time and the harvest, but never in numbers sufficient to make up the deficit.[34] Replacing manual with machine labour also did not offer a solution: not only could most farmers not afford to mechanize, but machine shops were inundated with war-related orders and lacked raw materials for civilian construction and maintenance.[35] Of the European belligerents, only Britain was able to keep up with agricultural labour demand, but it had the smallest agricultural workforce to begin with.[36]

In addition to labour shortages, European agricultural productivity suffered from a reduction in cultivated land. The Russian invasion of Galicia and the Bukovina and its eventual defeat by Austro-Hungarian and German forces caused widespread destruction to a part of the Dual Monarchy that before the war had produced about a third of its

[29] Collingham, *The Taste of War*, 72–3; Gatrell, 'Poor Russia, Poor Show', 257; Pamuk, 'Ottoman Economy', 120.

[30] Rob Robinson, 'Fishing', in Hew Strachan, ed., *The British Home Front and the First World War* (Cambridge: Cambridge University Press, 2023), 186–7, 190.

[31] Hautcoeur, 'Was the Great War a Watershed?', 173–4.

[32] Susan R. Grayzel, 'Men and Women at Home', in Jay Winter, ed., *The Cambridge History of the First World War, Vol. III: Civil Society* (Cambridge: Cambridge University Press, 2014), 110; Werner Plumpe, 'Die Logik Des Modernen Krieges Und Die Unternehmen: Überlegungen Zum Ersten Weltkrieg', *Jahrbuch Für Wirtschaftsgeschichte* 56:2 (2015), 341.

[33] Federico, *Feeding the World*, 191; Offer, *The First World War*, 62; Michel Augé-Laribé, *L'agriculture pendant la guerre* (Paris: Les Presses universitaires de France, 1925), 67–84.

[34] Hautcoeur, 'Was the Great War a Watershed?', 174; Frank M. Surface, *The Grain Trade during the World War: Being a History of the Food Administration Grain Corporation and the United States Grain Corporation* (New York: The MacMillan Company, 1928), 1–3.

[35] Collingham, *The Taste of War*, 72–3.

[36] Ziemann, 'Agrarian Society', 391–2.

cereal harvest.[37] Similarly, the Central Powers' invasion and subsequent occupation of Northern France (1914), Poland (1915), Serbia (1915), Montenegro (1916), Rumania (1916), and Northern Italy (1917), as well as parts of Russia (1915–1918), destroyed crops, farms, and food-processing plants.[38] Scorched-earth tactics by retreating forces ensured the damage, while not permanent, was often long-lasting.[39] Agricultural lands near the fronts not conquered or destroyed were subject to army requisitioning, to be used for training grounds, air fields, supply bases, and the construction of defences.[40] The use of mines and submarines, finally, made many of the European salt-water fishing grounds inaccessible.[41]

To combat the scarcity of arable land and fishing grounds, efforts to expand cultivation were undertaken by city dwellers and even by armies. The British Expeditionary Force on the Western Front, for example, instituted the creation of vegetable gardens in rest areas behind the trenches, where vegetables, potatoes, and even some grains were cultivated.[42] More dramatically, the Central Powers attempted to take advantage of land gained by invasion. However, successfully exploiting these territories proved to be near-impossible.[43] Not only did retreating armies destroy production capacity and infrastructure, but significant parts of the population fled before the invading forces, further depriving the conquered territories of labour.[44] Additionally, integrating conquered territories in the Central Powers' economies was difficult. The agricultural regions of Northern France, for example, depended on French credit facilities that were now inaccessible and lacked sufficient infrastructural

[37] Max-Stephan Schulze, 'Austria-Hungary's Economy in World War I', in Stephan Broadberry and Mark Harrison, eds., *The Economics of World War I* (Cambridge: Cambridge University Press, 2005), 92–3; Hans Loewenfeld-Russ, *Die Regelung Der Volksernährung Im Kriege* (Vienna: Hölder Pichler Tempsky, 1926), 46–58.

[38] Katherine Blunt and Florence Powdermaker, 'Part I: Food and the War', in *Food and the War: A Textbook for College Classes* (Boston, MA: Houghton Mifflin Company, 1918), 166–7; Frank M. Surface and Raymond L. Bland, *American Food in the World War and Reconstruction Period: Operations of the Organizations under the Direction of Herbert Hoover 1914 to 1924* (Stanford, CA: Stanford University Press, 1931), 23.

[39] Tait Keller, 'Destruction of the Ecosystem', in Ute Daniel et al., eds., *1914–1918-online. International Encyclopedia of the First World War* (Berlin: Freie Universität Berlin, 2014), DOI: 10.15463/ie1418.10371.

[40] Collingham, *The Taste of War*, 73.

[41] Blunt and Powdermaker, 'Part I: Food and the War', 72–5; Collingham, *The Taste of War*, 96, 229.

[42] *Statistics of the Military Effort of the British Empire during the Great War 1914–1920* (London: His Majesty's Stationery Office, 1922), 582.

[43] Sophie de Schaepdrijver, 'Military Occupation, Political Imaginations, and the First World War', *First World War Studies* 4:1 (2013), 2–3.

[44] Frank Pentland Chambers, *The War behind the War 1914–1918: A History of the Political and Civilian Fronts* (London: Faber & Faber, 1939), 143, 460–1; Grayzel, 'Men and Women', 100–3.

links to Germany.[45] Ukraine, separated from Russia following the March 1918 Brest-Litovsk Treaty, proved, from the Central Powers' military and political leadership's point of view, to be especially disappointing. It was to supply the populations of Germany, Austria-Hungary, Bulgaria, and the Ottoman Empire with a staggering million tons of grain per year. On paper, this seemed perfectly doable: pre-war, Ukraine had accounted for about a fifth of the total world export of grain. However, the country quickly became embroiled in a revolution followed by a civil war. Even after the German Army had propped up a new government, getting local farmers to sell their produce for now nearly worthless Ukrainian roubles was a hard task. Moreover, rolling stock to transport the goods that were for sale westwards was simply unavailable, while infighting amongst factions of German and Austrian officials only added to the confusion. Before the November 1918 Armistice annulled the Brest-Litovsk treaty, the fabled Ukrainian 'bread basket' supplied only 113,400 tons of grain, wheat, bread, and feed to the Central Powers.[46]

Another crucial factor in the decline of European productivity was a lack of fertilizers. Artificial fertilizers, widely in use, were made predominantly from nitrogen and phosphorus. Here, too, army demands clashed with those of farmers; nitrogen and phosphorus were also key ingredients in the manufacture of explosives, which the armies needed in previously unheard-of quantities.[47] Natural potash deposits were too limited to satiate both farmers and the army. In Germany, scientists had experimented with a process of creating nitrogen quite literally out of thin air since 1909,[48] and the first chemical plant using this

[45] Hautcoeur, 'Was the Great War a Watershed?', 173; Leonard V. Smith, Stéphane Audoin-Rouzeau, and Annette Becker, *France and the Great War, 1914–1918* (Cambridge: Cambridge University Press, 2003), 43–6.

[46] Wolfram Dornik and Peter Lieb, 'Die Wirtschaftliche Ausnutzung', in Wolfram Dornik, et al., eds., *Die Ukraine Zwischen Selbstbestimmung Und Fremdherrschaft 1917–1922* (Graz: Leykam, 2011), 281–323; Adam Tooze, *The Deluge: The Great War and the Remaking of the Global Order, 1916–1931* (London: Allan Lane, 2014), 150–3; Weinreb, *Modern Hungers*, 25. Data from Loewenfeld-Russ, *Die Regelung Der Volksernährung Im Kriege*, 428. The German experience in Romania was not much better: see David D. Hamlin, *Germany's Empire in the East: Germans and Romania in an Era of Globalization and Total War* (Cambridge: Cambridge University Press, 2017), 211–15. The Central Powers' hoped-for agricultural exploitation fared little better: see David D. Hamlin, *Germany's Empire in the East: Germans and Romania in an Era of Globalization and Total War* (Cambridge: Cambridge University Press, 2017), 211–15.

[47] Chambers, *War behind the War*, 151–2; Dieter Ziegler, 'Die Kriegswirtschaft Im Ersten Weltkrieg – Trends Der Forschung', *Jahrbuch Für Wirtschaftsgeschichte* 56:2 (2015), 313–15.

[48] More accurately: from atmospheric nitrogen. See Christine Strotmann, 'Nitrogenous Fertilisers in Germany: Paths of Distribution from Chile Saltpetre to Haber-Bosch-Ammonia and Cyanamide (ca 1914–1930)', *Jahrbuch Für Wirtschaftsgeschichte* 62:1 (2021), 159–89.

Haber–Bosch process started operations in 1913. Others were built during the war but demand vastly outstripped supply.[49]

Often the factors that negatively impacted European and Middle Eastern agricultural productivity reinforced each other. Labour scarcity and the lack of financial incentives (due to political pressures or inflation), for example, could lead farmers to convert wheat- or rye-growing areas to pastures, which were less labour-intensive, or even to abandon them completely, which in turn led to a further decline in production. Similarly, the lack of draught animals in and of itself depressed production but also caused a dearth of naturally available manure, which further depressed farm yields.[50]

In addition, natural shocks also reinforced the negative effects of the war on agricultural production. During 1915, swarms of desert locusts (*Schistocerra gregaria*) devastated crops, fields, and fruit and olive trees in Ottoman Palestine, Lebanon, and Syria.[51] Moreover, an unusually strong influx of cold marine air from the North Atlantic caused average temperatures to cool and precipitation to increase over Europe and parts of the Middle East during the First World War period. Winters were unusually long, cold, and wet, further impacting crop yields. The highest increase in marine air proxies occurred in the summer–autumn of 1915 and the winter of 1915–1916, resulting in heavy rains from the spring of 1915 to December 1916, with only a short interruption in July–August and December 1915. Starting in January 1916, precipitation in Europe increased steadily throughout the year, with a peak in December 1916. After a brief respite, rain and cold returned again in the summer and autumn of 1917, followed by another influx of torrential rains accompanied by decreasing temperatures in the autumns of 1917 and 1918. On and around the Western Front, it rained for 648 of the 1,563 days of the war, or once every three days.[52] World Bank climate data suggests that precipitation in Germany in June 1916 was 16 per cent higher than in the average for 1909–1913, while temperatures in April 1917 were more than

[49] Davis, *Home Fires Burning*, 22; Federico, *Feeding the World*, 83; Weinreb, *Modern Hungers*, 17–18; Högselius, Kaijser, and van der Vleuten, *Europe's Infrastructure Transition*, 146.

[50] Ermacora, 'Rural Society'.

[51] Zachary J. Foster, 'The 1915 Locust Attack in Syria and Palestine and Its Role in the Famine during the First World War', *Middle Eastern Studies* 51:3 (2015), 370–94; Melanie Tanielian, *The Charity of War: Famine, Humanitarian Aid, and World War I in the Middle East* (Stanford, CA: Stanford University Press, 2017), 51–2, 69–70.

[52] Alexander F. More et al., 'The Impact of a Six-Year Climate Anomaly on the "Spanish Flu" Pandemic and WWI', *GeoHealth* 4:9 (2020), https://doi.org/10.1029/2020GH000277; Edwige Savouret et al., 'Au temps météorologique de la Grande Guerre. Approche séquentielle des périodes contraignantes dans les tranchées sur le front de la Marne et de la Meuse, 1914–1918', *Climatologie* 8 (2011), 59–77.

three degrees lower compared to the pre-war average.[53] Weather data outside Europe is much less conclusive, but anecdotal evidence suggests that the Middle East, too, experienced an exceptionally cold and wet winter in 1914–1915 and 1915–1916, followed by a heatwave in the summers of 1915 and 1917.[54] In peaceful times, agriculture would have adapted to these climatic events, but the First World War limited its ability to do so.[55]

We can see some of the effects of the war and the climatic conditions on agricultural production in Europe in Table 1.1. By 1917, the League of Nations calculated in 1943 based on the best available

Table 1.1 *Wheat, rye, and potato crops in 1917 compared to pre-war averages*

	Wheat			Rye			Potatoes		
	Land under cultivation (%)	Yield (%)	Yield/ ha (%)	Land under cultivation (%)	Yield (%)	Yield/ ha (%)	Land under cultivation (%)	Yield (%)	Yield/ ha (%)
France	79.2	55.3	69.8	83.6	64.2	76.8	93.6	82.3	88.0
Britain	101.5	98.6	97.1	66.8	?	?	106.9	100.1	93.6
Italy	90.1	76.4	84.8	92.1	83.7	90.8	103.3	79.1	76.6
Finland	65.7	61.8	94.0	100.7	114.5	113.7	117.6	108.2	92.0
Germany	110.5	116.7	106.0	134.0	133.8	99.7	93.6	85.8	91.7
Hungary	?	?	102.6	?	?	100.6	?	?	102.4
Cisleithania	70.4	44.1	31.3	77.3	45.8	29.5	70.2	45.0	34.2
Switzerland	93.1	189.4	203.5	76.3	86.7	113.7	125.1	155.4	124.2
Spain	100.3	113.7	113.4	102.7	92.2	89.8	107.1	104.5	97.5
Sweden	92.3	73.9	80.1	93.9	61.3	65.3	97.3	99.3	102.0
Netherlands	77.3	70.8	91.6	95.2	96.1	100.9	94.6	83.8	88.6
Belgium	?	47.2	?	?	27.5	?	?	?	?

'Land under cultivation' denotes the total area harvested, '?' indicates that information is not available, *'Yield' the total yield thereof, and 'Yield/ha' the average yield per hectare. For all figures the average of 1909–1913 = 100.*[56]

[53] Davis, *Home Fires Burning*, 22–5; Christian Pfister, 'Auf Der Kippe: Regen, Kälte Und Schwindende Importe Stürzten Die Schweiz 1916–1918 in Einen Nahrungsengpass', in Christian Pfister, Daniel Krämer, and Daniel Mark Segesser, eds., *Woche für woche neue preisaufschläge. Nahrungsmittel-, energie- und Ressourcenkonflikte in der Schweiz des Ersten Weltkrieges* (Basel: Schwabe Verlag, 2016), 67–76. World Bank climate data can be found at http://sdwebx.worldbank.org/climateportal/index.cfm?page=climate_data.

[54] Tanielian, *The Charity of War*, 53.

[55] Geoffrey Parker, *Global Crisis: War, Climate Change & Catastrophe in the Seventeenth Century* (New Haven, CT: Yale University Press, 2013), 20–3.

[56] International Institute of Agriculture, *Annuaire international de statistique agricole 1909 à 1921* (Rome: Institut international d'agriculture, 1922), 22–81.

statistical material at the time, that European production of cereals (wheat, rye, maize, barley and oats) and potatoes dropped by about 30 per cent compared to the 1909–1913 pre-war average. The decline in crops in Western Europe was more pronounced than it was in the East.[57] Of particular interest are the results for France, which suffered the loss of some 2.5 million hectares of farmland after the German invasion, the 'Austrian' half of the Dual Monarchy, and Belgium, where yields more than halved.[58] Some countries actually managed to expand the crop area and/or increase the average yield per hectare, but these could not compensate for the loss of pre-war imports or for increased consumption.

Naturally, given the enormous varieties in agricultural systems of production, and states', communities', and individuals' resilience to (temporal) changes in them, we can only speak of the effects of the war on agricultural productivity in very general terms. Some early estimates on the effects of the First World War on agricultural production can be found in Table 1.2, although data for the war years itself are missing. Nevertheless, available sources suggest that between 1914 and 1918, global agricultural production declined by about 8–10 per cent, with the bulk of the decline situated in Europe.[59] The table will hide large regional and product discrepancies, however. Comparing official records on wheat yields of the last pre-war years with those of 1917, for example, shows France's production dropping 41 per cent, Italy's 30 per cent, the Ottoman Empire 24 per cent and Russia 13 per cent.[60]

The negative impact of the war on productivity did not end with the signing of the Armistice on 11 November 1918, even when one discounts the continuing violence that plagued much of Europe and Asia until the early 1920s. The war had killed millions of farm workers and cattle: in Serbia, ravaged by invasions and occupations, one-fourth of the country's cattle, one-third of its horses, and half its pigs, sheep, and goats were either killed or confiscated by the occupiers, while Bulgaria lost a third of its cattle and agricultural machinery. Farms and farm tools also suffered

[57] *Agricultural Production in Continental Europe during the 1914–18 War and the Reconstruction Period* (League of Nations, 1943), 11–12.

[58] Arable land in France under German occupation from Augé-Laribé, *L'agriculture pendant la guerre*, 93–105.

[59] Federico, *Feeding the World*, 190–1.

[60] Data on Russia: Peter Gatrell, *Russia's First World War: A Social and Economic History* (Harlow: Longman, 2005), 159. Data on the Ottoman Empire: Vedat Eldem, *Harp ve Mütareke Yıllarında Osmanlı İmparatorluğu'nun Ekonomisi* (Ankara: Türk Tarih Kurumu Basımevi, 1994), 30–3. Data on Italy and France: Chris Wrigley, 'The War and the International Economy', in Chris Wrigley, ed., *The First World War and the International Economy* (Cheltenham: Edward Elgar, 2000), 7.

Table 1.2 *Indices of global agricultural production, 1911–1922 (1913 = 100)*

	1911 (%)	1912 (%)	1913 (%)	1920 (%)	1921 (%)	1922 (%)
Gross value added agriculture, total	94.1	98.1	100	85.3	88.7	93.0
Europe	89.9	95.7	100	75.5	75.3	81.4
Northwestern Europe	95.5	97.8	100	80.4	82.3	86.4
Southern Europe	97.0	92.8	100	97.9	96.1	101.8
Eastern Europe	79.9	94.4	100	59.3	57.1	66.0
Asia	103.6	103.2	100	98.9	108.2	111.9
South America	69.8	101.9	100	111.3	111.6	112.7
Canada, Australia and the USA	95.3	99.1	100	94.3	100.3	101.4
Gross output agriculture, total	94.4	98.6	100	87.8	92.1	96.9
Livestock	94.9	96.7	100	88.2	93.9	98.0
Crops	95.9	99.0	100	88.6	92.9	97.7

Agricultural production is measured by 'gross output', which is defined as the total market value of all agricultural products, minus reuses thereof within the agricultural sector itself (as seed or feed, but not as farmers' consumption). Value added is the gross output minus the costs of inputs purchased from outside the sector. The first measures the capability of agriculture to provide food, clothing, and heating, while value added measures its capability to create income. Furthermore, the ratio of value added to gross output is a simple proxy for the relative importance of industrial inputs (fertilizers, fuel, industrial feeding stuffs) used in agriculture.[61]

destruction or damage.[62] Moreover, in Central and Eastern Europe, the war accelerated demands for land reform, which usually resulted in larger plots of land being subdivided into smallholdings. Land was redistributed to fulfil political promises in return for continued support for the war effort, to colonize ethnically mixed territories, especially prevalent in new states such as Yugoslavia, or to effectuate radical agricultural reforms.[63] And in the former Ottoman Empire, new borders were drawn with an eye

[61] Giovanni Federico, 'The Growth of World Agricultural Production 1800–1938', *Research in Economic History* 22 (2004), 127–8. An up-to-date data set can be found at www.rug.nl/ggdc/historicaldevelopment/na/ [last accessed 10 March 2022].

[62] Andrej Mitrović, *Serbia's Great War, 1914–1918* (West Lafayette, IN: Purdue University Press, 2007), 193–244; Ian Innerhofer, 'Post-War Economies (South East Europe)', in Ute Daniel et al., eds., *1914–1918-online. International Encyclopedia of the First World War* (Berlin: Freie Universität Berlin, 2017).

[63] Gert Von Pistohlkors, 'Tiefgreifende agrarische umwälzungen und Umstrukturierungen in den neu gegründeten baltischen Staaten Estland, Lettland und Litauen 191/1920/1922: Motivationen Und Ergebnisse Bis 1940', in Karl-Peter Krauss, ed., *Agrarreformen und Ethnodemographische Veränderungen. Südosteuropa Vom Ausgehenden 18. Jahrhundert Bis in Die Gegenwart* (Stuttgart: Franz Steiner Verlag, 2009), 181–9; Dietmar Müller, 'Landreformen, Property Rights und Ethnische Minderheiten. Ideen- und Institutionsgeschichte Nachholender Modernisierung und Staatsbildung in

more to imperial strategic interests than to the nutritional needs of their inhabitants.[64] It took until 1925 for European agricultural production to once again reach pre-war levels, further underscoring both the (political) importance and the vulnerability of food production. The governments of the 1920s therefore funded massive agricultural reconstruction and improvement programmes, which would only intensify after the 1929 financial crisis.[65]

Agricultural Trade Flows and Transport

The complicated flows of people, trade, and finances that emerged during the nineteenth century to bind the European agricultural markets to those of other continents developed in large part in response to rising European demands, and the possibilities this offered to agricultural businesses to produce for a global market rather than local or national markets. The First World War, however, disrupted or redirected many of these flows. Most dramatically, the war divided a formerly highly interconnected world into distinct regions divided by front lines.[66] The consequences of the sudden fracture of the pre-war agricultural globalization process were all the more serious as they affected not only the availability of agricultural products or supplies, but also impacted trade balances and therefore states' abilities to purchase other agricultural supplies or control their currency rates.

First of all, upon entering the war, belligerents and neutrals alike enacted laws which forbade the export of an ever-growing list of items deemed of strategic value, while the two belligerent blocs made trading with their enemies illegal.[67] Russia, for example, which before the war exported about one-sixth of its total agricultural production, now

Rumäninen und Jugoslawien 1918–1948', in Karl-Peter Krauss, ed., *Agrarreformen Und Ethnodemographische Veränderungen. Südosteuropa Vom Ausgehenden 18. Jahrhundert Bis in Die Gegenwart* (Stuttgart: Franz Steiner Verlag, 2009), 213–20.

[64] Leonard V. Smith, 'Empires at the Paris Peace Conference', in Robert Gerwarth and Erez Manela, eds., *Empires at War: 1911–1923* (Oxford: Oxford University Press, 2014), 270–1.

[65] Charles Hilliard Feinstein, Peter Temin, and Gianni Toniolo, *The World Economy between the World Wars* (Oxford: Oxford University Press, 2008), 91–2; League of the Nations, *Agricultural Production in Continental Europe during the 1914–18 War and the Reconstruction Period* (Geneva: League of the Nations, 1943), 33.

[66] Weinreb, *Modern Hungers*, 13; Hautcoeur, 'Was the Great War a Watershed?', 181; Antje Hagen, 'Anglo-German Economic Relations before, during and after the War', in Hartmut Berghoff and Robert von Friedeburg, eds., *Change and Inertia, Britain under the Impact of the Great War* (Bodenheim: Philo), 67–9, 72–3.

[67] Ernst Grünfeld, *Die deutsche Aussenhandelskontrolle (Die Politik der Sperren) vom Kriegsausbruch bis zum Inkrafttreten des Friedensvertrages* (Bonn: Schroeder, 1922), 2.

blocked all trade with its enemies, who in turn halted most economic contact with the European Allies. Its traditional trade routes – the land frontier with Germany and Austria-Hungary, the Black Sea, and the Baltic – closed and with alternative outlets for grain unavailable, Russia had nowhere to export its agricultural surpluses.[68] The Allies' doomed Gallipoli campaign, therefore, was designed in part to force the Ottoman Straits connecting the Black Sea to the Aegean and Mediterranean seas, re-opening a vital supply route. As a consequence of its failure, the value of the Russian rouble on foreign exchanges plummeted.[69] Germany, Austria-Hungary, and the other Central Powers, meanwhile, faced not only the loss of Allied agricultural markets but also the impossibility of finding alternatives for them, at least outside of Europe. The North Sea and Mediterranean were blockaded by Allied fleets, cutting off Germany and its allies from direct trade with Asia, Africa and, crucially, the Americas. The only foreign markets open to Central Powers' merchants were those contiguous to Germany and Austria-Hungary: Norway, Sweden, Denmark, the Netherlands, and Switzerland. However, their agricultural production could never replace what was lost due to Allied maritime interference, and had to be bought at a steep price.[70] Moreover, Allied economic measures made sure that agricultural surpluses from these countries tapered off from 1916 onwards, while a combination of preclusive purchasing, bullying, and control of merchant shipping (some 55 per cent of which was owned or controlled by British interests) combined to monopolize large amounts of extra-European sources of supply for the exclusive use of the Allies, limiting merchants' ability to supply Germany and Austria via neutral ports. Taken together, these measures had a dramatic impact on the Central Powers' ability to procure foodstuffs, feed, and fertilizers from outside of Europe.[71]

The Allied blockade in effect grounded the German, Austrian, and Ottoman ocean-going merchant fleets. This produced a global effect, since before 1914 commercial shipping companies had operated a dense network of trans-oceanic lines, bringing cargo to a wide variety of

[68] League of the Nations, *Agricultural Production in Continental Europe*, 11, 15.

[69] Gatrell, 'Poor Russia, Poor Show', 248, 257–8.

[70] Samuël Kruizinga, 'Neutrality', in Jay Winter, ed., *The Cambridge History of the First World War, Vol. II: The State* (Cambridge: Cambridge University Press, 2014), 559–60; Hew Strachan, *Financing the First World War* (Oxford: Oxford University Press, 2004), 161–6.

[71] Charles Ernest Fayle, *The War and the Shipping Industry* (London: Humphrey Milford, 1927), 2–3, 17; Nicholas Lambert, *Planning Armageddon: British Economic Warfare and the First World War* (Cambridge, MA: Harvard University Press, 2012), 238–40; Kruizinga, 'Neutrality', 565–8.

Table 1.3 *Gross tonnage of ocean-going steamers of 100 tons and upwards (measured in 1000 tons)*

	1912	1913	1914	1915	1916	1917	1918	1919	1920
British Empire	19,323	19,934	20,540	20,819	20,385	18,577	17,498	18,326	19,872
Allies	2,783	3,076	3,337	3,443	3,553	3,406	2,974	3,424	4,985
USA	1,861	2,007	2,147	2,604	3,068	4,273	6,299	9,923	12,346
Neutrals	9,217	10,045	10,853	11,105	11,260	10,735	10,262	10,880	13,564
Central Powers	5,359	5,870	6,232	—	—	—	—	122	410
World	*38,543*	*40,933*	*40,512*	*37,972*	*38,266*	*36,991*	*37,032*	*42,514*	*51,177*

Tonnage is measured in gross register tons (GRT), a measure for total internal volume of the ship, which is a good proxy for the vessel's total carrying capacity. One GRT equals 100 cubic feet (or 2.832 m^3*).*[72]

destinations irrespective of nationality.[73] The global tonnage available for agricultural shipments was further diminished by the demands of the Allied military; not only were ships sequestered for troops transport or patrol duty, shipyards switched to the production of warships and suffered from a lack of raw materials, and the shipping sector suffered the same labour shortages as other parts of the war economy.[74] Finally, contact mines and submarines destroyed thousands of tons of merchant ships, even those flying a neutral flag.[75] What remained of the world's tonnage (see Table 1.3) often had to travel longer distances, decreasing their yearly carrying capacity. For example, with Russia out of reach, British ships in the grain trade were instead directed to undertake significantly longer voyages to North America, India, Australia, and Argentina. Convoying, whereby groups of merchant ships sailed under naval escort to guard them against commerce raiders, further limited the available tonnage per year, as the speed of the convoy was restricted to that of its slowest ships. Longer travel was also more expensive due to higher fuel demands, and costs increased further as both wages and

[72] Jan Tore Klovland, 'Navigating through Torpedo Attacks and Enemy Raiders: Merchant Shipping and Freight Rates during World War I', *Norwegian School of Economics Discussion Paper* 4:17 (2017).

[73] See e.g. Samuël Kruizinga, 'Sailing in Uncharted Waters: Dutch Steamship Companies and the First World War', *International Journal of Maritime History* 27:2 (2015), 228–9, 232.

[74] Jon T. Sumida, 'Forging the Trident. British Naval Industrial Logistics, 1914–1918', in John A. Lynn, ed., *Feeding Mars: Logistics in Western Warfare from the Middle Ages to the Present* (Boulder, CO: Westview Press), 223–31, 248 (esp. table 10.8).

[75] Henri Cangardel, *La Marine Marchande Française et La Guerre* (Paris: Les Presses Universitaires de France; New Haven, CT: Yale University Press, 1927), 24–6, 83–6.

insurance premiums were raised in response to the dangers of sailing in wartime. These increases, in turn, also affected wholesale food prices, as the costs of importing grains but also natural fertilizers and feeding stuffs increased.[76]

The combination of increased demand from the European Allies and neutrals and a limited supply of shipping space had enormous consequences for extra-European production. North America, which, prior to the outbreak of war was the world's second-largest grain-producing area after Russia, saw an enormous increase in demand in grain, wheat, livestock, and dairy products. High prices, guaranteed by the US and Canadian governments, stimulated North American farmers to significantly extend their production by increasing the land under cultivation. Between 1913 and 1919 the acres of wheat harvested in the United States alone increased from 50 million to 75.7 million, while in Canada crop acreage increased from 35 million to 53 million.[77] Those that could pay the inflated prices – chiefly the Allies in Europe – were therefore in a position to dominate the markets, to the detriment of other consumers. Foodstuffs and routes that were deemed less essential, more often than not those that served European imperial possessions, were simply sacrificed to the interests of the metropoles.[78]

Other imbalances, too, reflected or increased existing socio-economic divides. In the USA as well as in Argentina, meat packers profited handsomely from an immense increase in the prices their products fetched, while smallholders failed to profit.[79] The high prices agricultural products fetched on the world markets induced North and South American farmers to expand the land under cultivation, hastening the process of expropriating indigenous peoples.[80] And in those areas of Asia and Africa under European or Japanese control, the exploitative properties of imperialism came to the fore as the needs of the metropole were deemed as far outweighing those of the colonies, dominions, or protectorates

[76] Broadberry and Howlett, 'United Kingdom during World War I', 214; Wrigley, 'The War and the International Economy', 7–8; Arthur Salter, *Allied Shipping Control: An Experiment in International Administration* (Oxford: Clarendon Press, 1921), 3, 69, 80, 102, 105.

[77] Data on US crops from Ermacora, 'Rural Society'; Keller, 'Destruction'. For Canada, see Wrigley, 'The War and the International Economy', 8. Exports from Findlay and O'Rourke, *Power and Plenty*, 436–7. Weather conditions from Thomas Hudson Middleton, *Food Production in War* (Oxford: Clarendon Press, 1923), 4–5.

[78] Fogarty, 'The French Empire', 113–14; Collingham, *The Taste of War*, 68; Wrigley, 'The War and the International Economy', 5.

[79] Richard Perren, 'Farmers and Consumers under Strain. Allied Meat Supplies in the First World War', *Agricultural History Review* 52:2 (2005), 218–20, 224–5.

[80] See David Wood, 'American Indian Farmland and the Great War', *Agricultural History* 55:3 (1981), 249–65.

Table 1.4 *Estimates of the total value of world exports in millions of 1913 US dollars*

	1911	1912	1913	1914	1915	1916	1917	1918	1919	1920	1921	1922
Africa	844	899	863	718	619	756	854	711	805	731	848	988
North and South America	3,879	4,354	4,495	4,438	5,096	6,433	6,794	5,963	6,830	6,991	5,279	5,258
Asia	2,004	2,176	2,349	2,215	2,210	2,373	2,960	3,369	2,605	2,491	2,251	2,482
Europe	9,438	9,935	10,473	7,968	5,016	5,340	3,982	3,255	4,264	6,010	5,263	7,277
Oceania	471	469	500	466	458	412	331	343	459	529	585	591

Source: Giovanni Federico and Antonio Tena-Junguito, 'World Trade, 1800–1938: A New Data-Set', *European Historical Economics Society Working Papers* 0093 (2016), https://doi.org/10.13140/RG.2.1.4013.1602.

under their control (see Table 1.4). In British India, for example, the wheat purchase was brought under control of imperial bureaucrats, who then shipped massive amounts of foodstuffs and animals to its armies in Mesopotamia and Europe. Although some plantations profited and basic food-processing plants were established, the redirection of a significant portion of the domestic wheat output for export created or exacerbated gross internal imbalances within India; price rises and decreased supply heightened the susceptibility to the epidemics that ravaged the subcontinent in 1918, resulting in tens of millions of deaths.[81] In Africa, finally, mass starvation in present-day Tanzania and Malawi could be attributed to the forced confiscation of all food resources to feed Allied and Central Powers soldiers.[82]

As the belligerents redirected seaborne agricultural transports towards their armies and industries, they not only faced higher transport and insurance prices and slower turnarounds, but also the added difficulty of shipping food from ports to consumers. Motorized road traffic still being in its infancy, trains were the key linchpin of land-based transport

[81] Budheswar Pati, *India and the First World War* (New Delhi: Atlantic Publishers and Distributors, 1996), 78, 81–4, 87. For the French Empire, see Jacques Frémeaux, *Les Colonies Dans La Grande Guerre. Combats et Épreuves Des Peuples d'Outre-Mer* (Saint Cloud: 14–18 éd., 2006), 91–3. For the Japanese Empire, see Frank Jacob, *East Asia and the First World War* (Munich: De Gruyter Oldenbourg, 2022), 125–6. And for the Italian Empire, see Massimo Zaccaria, '"Not a Hectare of Land Shall Remain Uncultivated This Year!" Food Provisions for Italy and the Role of the Colonies, 1917–1918', *Afriche e Orienti* 21:3 (2019), 25–41.

[82] Maartje Abbenhuis and Ismee Tames, *Global War, Global Catastrophe: Neutrals, Belligerents and the Transformations of the First World War*, New Approaches to International History (London: Bloomsbury Academic, 2022), 1, 99.

systems, even more so in Germany, Austria, and the Ottoman Empire, where coastal trade was made impossible by Allied interdiction.[83] If rail networks towards the battle lines even existed pre-war, they were not built for wartime purposes but to ply trade routes that mostly or completely disappeared once the war broke out. Building new tracks and infrastructure was costly and time-intensive.[84] Even when this could be done, shortages of manpower and the progressive deterioration of equipment due to overuse combined to make the task of keeping trains rolling to or near the front line even more Herculean, and the need to redirect trains away from civilian service ever greater. While trains connecting Ottoman Beirut with Damascus had run twice daily before the war, the redirection of rolling stock away from civilian routes reduced the service to once a week; food surpluses in Syria therefore failed to reach starving Lebanon.[85] Finally, train-based transport systems were incredibly vulnerable to strikes, riots, human error, or mechanical failings, and to extreme weather conditions.[86] During the harsh winter of 1916–1917 the German transport system nearly crashed; rivers were frozen over and trains not only moved slowly but also required extra coal to do so, which, ironically, made it much harder to transport coal from the mines to where it was needed. Only the diversion of some 40,000 extra men from the front to the coal mines prevented a shutdown.[87] In the Ottoman Empire, which had become dependent on coal imports from Britain before the war, trains had to run on firewood, which was not only less efficient but also caused widespread deforestation.[88]

Interruptions of ship, rail, truck, or pack animal connections could temporarily disable or even sever vital links in the food distribution system. A lack of shipping space in Asia meant that during the second

[83] Gerald D. Feldman, *The Great Disorder: Politics, Economics, and Society in the German Inflation, 1914–1924* (New York, NY: Oxford University Press, 1993), 254–5; Pamuk, 'Ottoman Economy', 115–16.

[84] Ziemann, 'Agrarian Society', 388–9; Gatrell, *Russia's First World War*, 56, 156.

[85] Tanielian, *The Charity of War*, 61–5.

[86] See for examples related to Germany and Italy Francesco Galassi and Mark Harrison, 'Italy at War, 1915–1918', in Stephan Broadberry and Mark Harrison, eds., *The Economics of World War I* (Cambridge: Cambridge University Press, 2005), 292–3; Tooze, *The Deluge*, 94; Gerald D Feldman, *Army, Industry and Labor in Germany 1914–1918* (Princeton, NJ: Princeton University Press, 1966), 257–62.

[87] Feldman, *Army, Industry and Labor*, 254–63; Chickering, *Imperial Germany*, 78–81; C. Paul Vincent, *The Politics of Hunger: The Allied Blockade of Germany, 1915–1919* (Athens, OH: Ohio University Press, 1985), 175.

[88] Jeffrey D. Reger, '"Lamps Never Before Dim Are Being Extinguished from Lack of Olive Oil": Deforestation and Famine in Palestine at War and in Peace Under the Late Ottoman Empire and Early British Empire, 1910–1920', in Selena Daly, Martina Salvante, and Vanda Wilcox, eds., *Landscapes of the First World War* (Cham: Palgrave Macmillan, 2018), 39–40, 44–5, 51.

half of the war a food crisis could develop in India while warehouses in Australia were overflowing with wheat.[89] Transport issues also combined with institutional barriers: various overlapping authorities, both civil and military, were in competition with each other for food supplies and transport facilities, exacerbating local shortages and causing potentially devastating delays. In Austria-Hungary, customs barriers between the two constituent parts of the dual monarchy combined with serious shortages of rolling stock and coal to hamper efforts at effective countrywide food distribution, and even its ability to feed its soldiers at the various fronts towards the end of the war; these, in turn, were chiefly blamed on Hungarian 'egoism' in refusing to release its grain stocks for use in the 'Austrian' half of the Empire.[90] These examples highlight not only the interplay of the various factors impacting food supply, but also how declining productivity and transport capacities could serve to undermine inter-allied, inter-imperial or even inter-state solidarities crucial in wartime.

The effects of the trade dislocations of the First World War did not fundamentally alter the globalizing tendencies of the world economy, but nevertheless lasted until deep in the twentieth century. The post-war settlement drew new borders which cut across formerly interdependent territories, and new tariff barriers were erected by governments of both existing and new states to protect their own agricultural markets, production centres, and industries, and in the political uncertainties of the 1920s and the 1930s, to economically justify their own existence.[91] In most of Central and Eastern Europe, it took time to redirect agricultural trade flows and create the new administrative and infrastructural preconditions for renewed production growth. Meanwhile, it took time for international trade flows to adjust to post-war political conditions. Having lost access to the Russian market, exporters in the Baltic states found new buyers in Britain, Sweden and, increasingly, in Germany.[92] The

[89] Mancur Olson, *The Economics of the Wartime Shortage. A History of British Food Supplies in the Napoleonic War and in World Wars I and II* (Durham, NC: Duke University Press, 1963), 88–9; Surface, *Grain Trade*, 289–93.

[90] See Holger H. Herwig, *The First World War: Germany and Austria-Hungary, 1914–1918* (London: Arnold, 1997), 238; Manfried Rauchensteiner, *Der Tod des Doppeladlers. Österreich-Ungarn und der Erste Weltkrieg* (Graz: Styria, 1993), 212–14. For transportation difficulties in the Austro-Hungarian Empire, see Robert J. Wegs, 'Transportation: The Achilles Heel of the Habsburg War Effort', in Robert A. Kann, Béla Király, and Paula S. Fichtner, eds., *The Habsburg Empire in World War I* (New York, NY: Columbia University Press, 1977), 121–34.

[91] Jan Kofman, *Economic Nationalism and Development: Central and Eastern Europe between the Two World Wars* (Boulder, CO: Westview Press, 1997), 54–9, 110–12, 205–7; Feinstein, Temin, and Toniolo, *The World Economy*, 30–5.

[92] Kofman, *Economic Nationalism*, 88–9.

First World War also proved the final campaign in the extra-European 'grain invasion'. During the war, wheat production in the Americas and Australia had expanded dramatically as it fed the European allies and neutrals. The recovering European economies formed the perfect outlet for the wheat surplus: in 1924, Canada produced 15.2 million tons of wheat, the USA 8.8 million tons, Argentina 7.6 million tons and Australia 4.8 million tons; of these roughly 40 million tons total, 19 were exported, mostly to Europe. Other agricultural goods, such as meat and sugar, which had seen their production massively expanded during wartime, also continued to expand even when European production was slowly restored to pre-war levels after 1918.[93]

The Militarization of Food

Adequately supplying the massive armies of the First World War with men and materiel proved an enormous organizational and technical challenge. Often, as we had seen, the requirements of these armies clashed with civilian demands, with the latter nearly always losing out. It is telling, in this regard, that even the armies of the Central Powers that ended up losing the war were largely able to supply their soldiers with adequate weaponry and munitions right up until the last months before the Armistice.[94]

The scale of the challenges faced by both the Central Powers and the Allies in first bringing millions of troops to the battlefields and then supplying them, was staggering. On the mostly-static Western Front, both belligerent armies constructed enormous storage facilities at the end of the remaining transport links, such as the Channel ports or railheads deep in occupied France. From these stores, goods were transported by new railway links to forward posts nearer to the front and then transhipped via light rail systems ('field railways') to the trenches. The last part of the journey was, naturally, the most perilous: it was only undertaken by

93 Findlay and O'Rourke, *Power and Plenty*, 447–71; Feinstein, Temin, and Toniolo, *The World Economy*, 64–9. See for an analysis of the economic effects of the disintegration of empires e.g. István Deák, 'The Habsburg Empire', in Karen Barkey and Mark von Hagen, eds., *After Empire. Multiethnic Societies and Nation-Building. The Soviet Union and the Russian, Ottoman, and Habsburg Empires* (Boulder, CO: West View Press, 1997), 129–41.

94 Ian Brown, 'Logistics', in Jay Winter, ed., *The Cambridge History of the First World War, Vol. II: The State* (Cambridge: Cambridge University Press, 2014), 224; William H. McNeill, *The Pursuit of Power. Technology, Armed Force, and Society Since A.D. 1000* (Oxford: Basil Blackwell, 1983), 340; Gustav Gratz and Richard Schüller, *Der wirtschaftliche Zusammenbruch Österreich-Ungarns die Tragödie der Erschöpfung* (Vienna: Hölder-Pichler-Tempsky, 1930), 106.

carts to keep noise to a minimum, and usually at night.[95] At the more fluid Eastern, Mesopotamian, Galician, and African fronts, rail transport presented unique difficulties.[96] By mid-August 1915, for example, following the Austro-German Gorlice-Tarnów Offensive which pushed the Russians out of much of present-day Poland, German field railways stopped 125 km short of the front lines.[97] Where trains were unavailable, trucks, human carriers and, critically, draught animals had to take up the burdens of carrying food to the front.[98]

When it came down to food priorities, humans usually did not rank first. Soldiers can fight when hungry, but guns need to be fed continuously to be of use. Artillery and howitzers expended staggering amounts of munition during the First World War. But feed for draught animals, too, had to be given priority over human foodstuffs. On 31 August 1917, the British Army alone employed 591,324 horses and 213,321 mules on the various fronts, who all needed to be fed.[99] Nevertheless, army leaders were very cognisant of the importance of trying to feed their soldiers better than the average civilian to ensure continued performance under extreme duress but also to instil loyalty and attract recruits.[100] Given the enormous number of men at the fronts and the higher caloric requirements of military men on active duty, significant amounts of foodstuffs were diverted from civilian markets to the army.[101] During the first two years of the war, the German army alone shipped almost 1.2 billion kg of flour, 1 million heads of cattle, 1 million pigs and more than half a million sheep as well as 275 million kg of canned meat to its forces in

95 Duffett, 'British Army Provisioning', 32; Lummel, 'Food Provisioning', 18.

96 For a telling example, see the Cameroon campaign detailed in: Isidore Pascal Ndjock Nyobe, 'Rain and Bad Weather During War: The Role of Climate and Environment During the Great War in Cameroon (1914–1916)', in Selena Daly, Martina Salvante, and Vanda Wilcox, eds., *Landscapes of the First World War* (Cham: Palgrave Macmillan, 2018), 64–5.

97 Brown, 'Logistics', 233.

98 Vejas Gabriel Liulevicius, *Kriegsland Im Osten. Eroberung, Kolonisierung Und Militärherrschaft Im Ersten Weltkrieg* (Hamburg: Hamburger Edition, 2002), 117–18; Rudolf Kučera, 'Entbehrungen Und Nationalismus. Die Erfahrung Tschechischer Soldaten Der Österreichisch-Ungarischen Armee 1914–1918', in Bernhard Bachinger and Wolfram Dornik, eds., *Jenseits Des Schützengrabens. Der Erste Weltkrieg Im Osten: Erfahrung-Wahrnemung-Kontext* (Innsbruck: StudienVerlag, 2013), 126–7.

99 *Statistics of the Military Effort of the British Empire during the Great War 1914–1920*, 400.

100 Duffett, 'British Army Provisioning', 28–9.

101 Collingham, *The Taste of War*, 9. According to modern nutritional scientists, a moderately active young man needs somewhere in the region of 2,800 to 3,000 calories a day. A soldier in training requires about 3,500, whereas a soldier in active condition in cold weather needs to consume about 4,250 calories daily. See Fritz Hartmann, *Die Heeresverpflegung in Volkswirtschaftliche Abteilung des Kriegsernährungsamts. Beiträge zür Kriegswirtschaft* (Berlin: Verlag der Beiträge zur Kriegswirtschaft, 1917), 4, 29; Lummel, 'Food Provisioning', 18.

the field. They also received luxury items that were nearly impossible to procure on the German civilian markets: 62.5 million kg of coffee, 15 million kg of cocoa and tea, 2.7 million hectolitres of beer and an astonishing 8.5 million cigars and cigarettes.[102] In the spring of 1917, General Hindenburg estimated that the German army consumed about 70 per cent of the total German food supply.[103] The British Army faced an even greater task, since it supplied not only its own Expeditionary Force but also parts of the armed forces of its allies as well as various labour battalions drafted from its Empire and beyond, although these often received less than white soldiers.[104] From 9 August 1914 until 10 November 1918, the British Army shipped a grand total of 25,497,151 tons across the English Channel, including 3,240,948 tons of food. British ships carried 45 per cent of imports to both France and Italy in 1917 to 1918.[105] But it was not just armed forces that required enormous quantities of food; key war industries massively expanded their operations, and their workers needed to be adequately fed to make sure supply kept up with demand.[106]

The vastly increased military production also had unexpected side-effects on civilian food availability. The belligerent armies virtually monopolized the production of canned goods in order to produce long-lasting army rations, meaning that non-military consumers lacked means to supplement their diets with canned fruit or vegetables; also, the need to replace canned goods with fresh produce placed additional strains on infrastructure and on cooling and storage facilities.[107]

Conclusion

The First World War catastrophically impacted a global economy of specialized agriculture that had been created during the nineteenth and early twentieth centuries. That network consisted of links, both visible and invisible, which combined to create, mostly to the benefit of the

[102] Hartmann, *Die Heeresverplfegung*, 2, 29.

[103] Daniel, *Arbeiterfrauen*, 201.

[104] Anna Maguire, '"A Pageant of Empire?" Untangling Colonial Encounters in Military Camps', in Santanu Das, Anna Maguire, and Daniel Steinbach, eds., *Colonial Encounters in a Time of Global Conflict, 1914–1918* (London: Routledge, 2021), 37–41; Kyle J. Anderson, *The Egyptian Labor Corps: Race, Space, and Place in the First World War, The Egyptian Labor Corps* (University of Texas Press, 2022), 109–13, https://doi.org/10.7560/777361; Guoqi Xu, *Strangers on the Western Front: Chinese Workers in the Great War* (Cambridge, MA: Harvard University Press, 2011), 107, 119–20, 122, 134.

[105] *Statistics of the Military Effort of the British Empire during the Great War 1914–1920*, 485.

[106] Collingham, *The Taste of War*, 9.

[107] Hudson Middleton, *Food Production*, 150–2.

European consumer a complicated global chain of production and distribution. As a result, the average European's daily bread, butter, potatoes, and meat was produced either abroad or grown using imported feed and fodder. The expanding population of Europe, even the working classes, profited from these networks – even though many in the areas of Africa and Asia under European formal or informal control did not – and had become accustomed to cheaper and more plentiful food. Moreover, governments increasingly saw ensuring food supply as an urgent matter of state policy, and a key component in creating a socially and physically healthy 'body politic'.

The outbreak of the First World War seriously, but temporarily, disrupted many of the links connecting Europe to overseas sources of supply, and the battle lines drawn across the globe caused enormous damage to established pre-war patterns of trade. Efforts to compensate for the loss of these trade links, or to forge new ones, were made more difficult by rampant wartime inflation and trade imbalances, resulting in (local) scarcities and price rises. In South Africa, far away from the fronts, consumer prices rose by over 15 per cent over the war, and in the Gold Coast the costs of living rose by 50 per cent. Brazil, Iraq, and Trinidad, as well as many other places saw food riots, labour actions, mass strikes, and revolutionary violence near or after the Armistice, primarily motivated by high food prices and the failure of wages to keep pace.[108]

Transport capabilities, too, often failed to meet the increased demands: there were simply too few ships and trains available, and those that were moved more slowly than they would in peacetime. The war also impacted food production in various ways: the farm boys that volunteered or were drafted were taken out of food production roles and changed into privileged food consumers, as well as destroyers of food production.[109] Agricultural production was further affected by a lack of machinery, fertilizers, fodder, and feed. Farmers, meanwhile, reacted to the dearth of agricultural supplies, the changing and expanding demands of consumers, and state pressures, resulting in changing patterns of production and trade. In extreme cases, they deemed it more profitable to seize trading surpluses and increase their own consumption rather than submit to terms of trade they considered unfair.

The catastrophe that befell global agriculture was not a natural one, but was man-made. Its impact was shaped and directed by a variety of agents, both within and outside government, and experienced in various

[108] Martin, 'Globalizing', 846–7, 855.
[109] Brown, 'Logistics', 218–39, 224.

ways by different societal strata, as their actions were mediated by racial and socio-economic identities and power differentials. Their efforts to mitigate or accommodate to the changing global structures of agricultural production, distribution, and consumption produced seismic shifts in global understandings of the relationship between food, war, and everyday lives. But they also tried to shift the effects or the blame of hunger to others, in attempts to profit, to vilify, or to destroy, with equally far-reaching effects. And they replicated, and enhanced, the pre-war systemic global inequalities, making them more visible and infusing them with 'the grief and anger that the violence of the war had unleashed on the world'.[110] This was done in a variety of ways, first and foremost by governments and armies using sieges and blockades to starve their enemies into submission. This will be the subject of Chapter 2.

[110] Abbenhuis and Tames, *Global War, Global Catastrophe*, 173. Cf. Martin, 'Globalizing', 855.

2 Siege and Blockade

Starvation as a Weapon of War

Hew Strachan

Starvation as a Weapon of War before 1914: Its Legal and Practical Status

All the original belligerents in the First World War, except Serbia and Austria-Hungary, had fought colonial wars in the couple of decades preceding its outbreak. In doing so they regularly used starvation as a weapon of war. They sought to bring their opponents to battle by destroying their means of subsistence and their homes, in ways which ignored any clear distinction between combatant and non-combatant. 'Only the most cowardly of savages and irregulars', Charles Callwell wrote in the standard British textbook of the day, 'will allow their cattle to be carried off or their homes to be destroyed without making some show of resistance'.[1]

Their doctrines, however, distinguished between 'savage war', waged outside Europe, and 'civilised warfare', a phrase used to denote the war on which they imagined they were embarking in 1914. Here the laws of war had gained traction. Between the treaty of Paris in 1856 and the Hague Conventions of 1899 and 1907, the great powers sought to define the rights of combatants and non-combatants. Despite this sustained effort to contain conflict, starvation retained its potential as a weapon of war.[2] In positional war the law effectively endorsed its employment, and in manoeuvre warfare it remained ambiguous and so implicitly permissive, not least thanks to changes in the character of war itself.

Sieges were the classic form of positional warfare. 'Investment, bombardment, assault, and regular siege are severally and jointly legitimate means of warfare', the British army's guidance on the laws of war on land published in 1912 stated, citing the 1899 Hague conference. The only

[1] Charles E. Callwell, *Small Wars: Their Principles and Practice*, 3rd ed. (London: His Majesty's Stationery Office, 1909), 145–6.

[2] Isabel V. Hull, *A Scrap of Paper: Breaking and Making International Law during the Great War* (Ithaca, NY: Cornell University Press, 2014), 164–6.

restriction was that 'their application ... is strictly limited to defended localities'. The scope for flexibility was wide: although fortified places were *prima facie* deemed to be defended, and so open to attack, defended localities did not have to be fortified, and so the absence of fortifications was not in itself a reason for deeming a town free from assault.[3]

A central ambition of international law, beginning with the St Petersburg declaration of 1868, had been to protect non-combatants from the terrors of war, and the Hague provisions reflected that. Defended cities which were besieged and then stormed had, from antiquity to the Napoleonic wars, been subject to looting, destruction, rape and indiscriminate killing. That was now outlawed. However, the very business of saying what was illegal implicitly rendered legal the other consequences of a siege, of which the most immediate was hunger. An effective siege cut a town off from all outside sources of supply, but as a result those conducting it could not easily discriminate between combatants and non-combatants. Moreover, the very fact that the garrison had to share its supplies with the civilian population would increase the pressures on the defenders, so much so that the town's investors were permitted to force back into a city those non-combatants trying to leave. 'The famine has become more atrocious', the author of a journal kept during the siege of the Ottoman city of Adrianople during the 1st Balkan War wrote on 31 January 1913. By the time the siege ended, on 26 March, mortality was running at fifty to sixty a day, 'the result not of any epidemic, but of pneumonia affections and physiological starvation. Many have eaten unwholesome or poisonous bodies.'[4]

Revolution and civil war were another effect of hunger, and they in turn could divide a nation from within and so cause its defeat. 'Every great State', Ivan Bloch told the British journalist, W. T. Stead, in 1899, 'would in time of war be in the position of a besieged city, and the factor which always decides sieges is the factor which will decide the modern war. Your soldiers may fight as they please; the ultimate decision is in the hands of *famine*.'[5] He stressed the effects of hunger on future war because he believed that the war would be long. Since countries would struggle to import, they would have to rely on their own resources but their capacity

[3] J. E. Edmonds and L. Oppenheim, *Land Warfare: an Exposition of the Laws and Usages of War on Land for the Guidance of Officers of His Majesty's Army* (London: His Majesty's Stationery Office, 1912), paragraphs 117–20.

[4] Carnegie Endowment for International Peace: Division of Intercourse and Education. Publication no. 4, *Report of the International Commission to Inquire into the Causes and Conduct of the Balkan Wars* (Washington, DC: Carnegie Endowment, 1914), 110–11, 405.

[5] I. S. Bloch, *Modern Weapons and Modern War, Being an Abridgement of 'The War of the Future in Its Technical, Economic and Political Relations'* (London: Grant Richards), xlix. Italics in the original.

to do so would be massively diminished. The creation of mass armies would result in their own supply problems, and conscription would suck labour out of the agricultural workforce. States would struggle to satisfy 'the vital needs of populations' and some would confront 'the danger of revolutionary movements, not only political but also socialistic'.[6]

Land Warfare in the First World War

In the event, the First World War was not as marked by sieges as the precedents of the previous century had suggested. In 1914 itself, those that occurred in the west, at Liège and Namur for example, were brief, or revolved round towns like Verdun which were not fully invested. Belgrade, despite its position on Serbia's frontier with Austria-Hungary, was taken without a fight. The most protracted sieges of the war's first year were those of the German colony in China at Tsingtao, captured in six weeks by the Japanese (with some British support), and at Przemyśl in Galicia. The latter, designed as a jumping-off point for the Austro-Hungarian armies facing Russia, was left isolated as they fell back in September 1914. The city was besieged from 21 September, but relieved on 9 October. Its food stocks were in large part eaten by those who came to its rescue, a move which also swelled its garrison from 85,000 to 130,000. Ten days later, the Russians closed in once more, and the Austrians readied themselves for a renewal of the siege, but the railway lines they now needed to bring supplies forward had been destroyed in the earlier fighting. One calculation is that only six days' rations arrived for a siege that resumed for five more months, until 22 March 1915.[7] Mortality rates from starvation and disease peaked at 300 a day.[8]

The opening months of the war on all fronts were characterised not by sieges, but by manoeuvre. Towns and cities had been fortified precisely to provide bulwarks against advancing armies. The Austro-Hungarian defence of Przemyśl sucked in the advancing Russians and so protected the Habsburg Empire from further invasion, but elsewhere defended

6 Bloch, *Modern Weapons*, 294–5; Jean de Bloch, *La guerre, traduction de l'ouvrage russe La Guerre Future aux points de vue technique, économique et politique*, 6 vols (Paris: Guillaumin, 1898–1900), vol. 3, 289, 386; 4, 243–67, 353–514.

7 Manfred Rauchensteiner, *Der Erste Weltkrieg und das Ende der Habsburgermonarchie 1914–1918* (Wien: Böhlau, 2013), 250–1, 257, 306–18; Alexander Watson, *Ring of Steel: Germany and Austria-Hungary at War 1914–1918* (London: Allen Lane, 2014), 186–8; Graydon A. Tunstall, *Written in Blood: The Battles for Fortress PrzemyślPrzemyśl in WW1* (Bloomington, IN: Indiana University Press, 2016), 16–17, 102.

8 Helena Jablońska z Seifertów, *Dziennik z Oblężonego Przemyśla (1914–1915)*, ed Stanisław Stępień (Przemyśl: Południowo-Wschodni Instytut Naukowy w Przemyślu, 2017), 295–6, 392; reference provided and trans. by Nicholas Siekerski.

towns performed less well than expected, and generals thereafter favoured field fortifications and extended trench lines instead. Civilians were still affected but in different ways. Vitally, these linear positions were open to the rear and so could be more readily supplied. Indeed, the spread of static war from siege to field meant that light railways could be constructed and motorised transport extended, so facilitating the distribution of food. Sieges became the exception, not the rule. In January 1916, when the Russians advanced from the Caucasus into eastern Anatolia, the fortified town of Erzurum was the principal obstacle in their path: it was taken, not by siege, but with an assault which penetrated between the outer forts over five days in February.[9] This Ottoman defeat was offset by victory in Mesopotamia at the end of April, when the Turks forced the surrender of the British and Indian force holding Kut al-Amara. Kut was a regular siege, lasting five months and brought to a successful conclusion specifically by starvation, but it pointed back in time, not forward.[10]

The declining significance of siege warfare, traditionally defined, in the First World War did not in itself eliminate the use of hunger in the war's land campaigns. Napoleon had sought to minimise the place of sieges in warfare and to accelerate the movement of his armies by feeding off the land. In 1913 the historical section of the German general staff told those responsible for the supply of the army that their role was simply auxiliary, and that accordingly their logistical concerns should not shape the conduct of operations. Self-evidently, this was an impossible requirement to impose on the armies of industrialised powers in 1914. Those of France, Germany and Russia mustered nearly 3 million men after mobilisation. The arrival of a single corps of perhaps 30,000 men was equivalent to erecting a new town overnight, with direct consequences for the supply of the non-combatants living in the area. 'As the greatest efforts of army supply then extend to the exploitation of the stocks of the area of operations', the historical section advised in 1913, 'so must it also become a priority to ensure that the food, which has not been consumed, does not on any account fall into the hands of the enemy.' Chillingly, it went on: 'Concern for the local inhabitants cannot hinder these measures.'[11]

In the following year the supply arrangements of the German armies advancing into France and Flanders collapsed the moment they passed

[9] W. E. D. Allen and Paul Muratoff, *Caucasian Battlefields: A History of the Wars on the Turco-Caucasian Border 1828–1921* (Cambridge: Cambridge University Press, 1953), 344–63.

[10] Nikolas Gardner, 'Sepoys and the Siege of Kut-al-Amara, December 1915–April 1916', *War in History* 11 (2004), 307–26.

[11] Großen Generalstabe, Kriegsgeschichtliche Abteilung I, *Studien zur Kriegsgeschichte und Taktik: VI: Heeresverpflegung* (Berlin: Mittler, 1913), 279, 309–10.

beyond their railheads. When the battle of the Marne opened on 6 September 1914, the key railheads for the three German armies on the right wing were between 136 and 168 km to their rear. Soldiers plundered, looted and requisitioned, and did so at the expense of the civilian population.[12] It was a pattern repeated across other theatres of war for the next four years. In 1918 in East Africa, Ludwig Deppe, a German medical officer, wrote in his diary: 'Behind us we leave destroyed fields, ransacked magazines and, for the immediate future, starvation. We are no longer the agents of culture; our track is marked by death, plundering and evacuated villages, just like the progress of our own and enemy armies in the Thirty Years War.'[13]

Military necessity became the escape clause for many, and probably most, breaches of international law in the First World War. In 1912, Paul Schneider, in another pre-war German text on army supply, mirrored these arguments when he advised that, 'The resources of the theatre of war must be as fully exploited as possible. If anything else is done, it is not the enemy that shoulders the burden, but your own side.' Schneider acknowledged that the Hague conventions forbade looting, but by ensuring that food was taken in an organised fashion, and not plundered, armies blurred the boundary between what was permissible and what not: 'Requisition', Schneider wrote, 'extends to everything of which the army has need, and makes no distinction between public and private property.'[14]

The German army was not alone in the First World War in using the argument of military necessity to prioritise its own need for food over that of the local non-combatant population; it just did so more often because it invaded more territory between 1914 and 1916 than did any other country. By the autumn of 1914 Germany occupied most of Belgium and north-eastern France, and a year later it had added the Baltic states and much of Poland. Belgium imported four-fifths of the food it needed before the war, and so was directly hit by the allied economic blockade. The Hague conventions did not formally require an army to supply the civilians in areas under its occupation, and the chief of staff of the quartermaster of the German armies in the west in December 1914 specifically rejected that they had any such obligation. Because they argued that they had to feed their own soldiers first, the Germans could use the idea that military necessity constituted its own law of war. Believing

[12] Martin van Creveld, *Supplying War: Logistics from Wallenstein to Patton* (Cambridge: Cambridge University Press, 1977), 109–41; Larry H. Addington, *The Blitzkrieg Era and the German General Staff* (New Brunswick: Rutgers University Press, 1971), 15–21.

[13] Ludwig Deppe, *Mit Lettow-Vorbeck durch Afrika* (Berlin: August Scherl, 1919), 393.

[14] Paul Schneider, *Die Verpflegung des Feldheeres* (Berlin: Mittler, 1912), 48, 53.

themselves to be under no obligation to satisfy the requirements of the civilian population, they were able to see whatever they did give as evidence of generosity.[15] In the east they regarded the land they conquered as empty and neglected, populated by inhabitants who lacked even a basic knowledge of agricultural science. They improved farming methods, but for their own benefit and not that of the local population, in order to legitimise and make permanent its possession.[16]

Germany's ally, Austria-Hungary, experienced the pros and cons of these arguments about 'hunger war' in rapid succession in 1914. The war emergency law of 26 September 1912 gave the army almost unfettered rights to requisition. On mobilisation, it became effectively a 'third state' alongside each of Austria and Hungary, but unlike them had powers that spanned both. It also 'concerned itself with the army only, not with the affairs of the civilian population'.[17] Despite this authority, unmatched in any other belligerent, supply collapsed when the army invaded Serbia in August. At the beginning of September, as it retreated from Galicia in the face of the advancing Russian armies, the 3rd Army burned the hard-won supplies of one of its own corps for fear they would fall into the hands of the enemy.[18] The competition for food, with the enemy as well as with the indigenous population, implicitly intensified by the army's approach to supply, interacted with these cultural and social fears to produce atrocity and devastation. Arable production in Galicia, the nearest Austria (as opposed to Hungary) had to a bread basket of its own, was hit hard by the fighting, the number of horses and cows in the region falling by 40 per cent and of pigs by 70 per cent.[19] When, in the spring of 1915, the Central Powers turned about, cleared Galicia and pushed into Poland, their supply problems were compounded not just by the self-inflicted wounds of the previous eight months, but also by Russia's deliberate use of scorched earth methods. At the beginning of August, the Russian army decided on a full-scale retreat. It destroyed what it could not take, its chief of the general staff determined to leave the invaders nothing but a wilderness. Over 3 million refugees, deprived

[15] Hull, *A Scrap of Paper*, 116–24; Philippe Nivet, *La France occupée 1914–1918* (Paris: Armand Colin, 2014), 85–93, 150–77.

[16] Vejas Gabriel Liulevicius, *War Land on the Eastern Front: Culture, National Identity, and German Occupation in World War I* (Cambridge: Cambridge University Press, 2000), 64–75.

[17] Victor Heller, 'Government price fixing and rationing in Austria during the war of 1914–18', report for the National Bureau of Economic Research, January 1941, 3–4; I am grateful to Francesco Frizzani Frizzera for this reference.

[18] John R. Schindler, *Fall of the Double Eagle: The Battle for Galicia and the Demise of Austria-Hungary* (Sterling, VA: Potomac Books, 2015), 132–3, 220.

[19] Watson, *Ring of Steel*, 199.

of subsistence, clogged the roads going eastwards: 'We were forced to burn our homes and crops, we weren't allowed to take our cattle with us'.[20] When in February 1917 the German supreme command decided to abandon the Somme battlefield and withdraw to the *Siegfriedstellung* (or Hindenburg line as the British called it), they were directly influenced by the problems that the Russians had created in 1915.[21] The British official history quoted a German order to the effect that 'the enemy must find a land sucked completely dry'.[22]

Starvation and War at Sea: Pre-1914 Thinking

In the literature on the First World War, the employment of hunger as a method of war focuses disproportionately on the British blockade at sea and its effect on Germany. However, the full impact of the blockade on Germany was delayed until late 1916, and by then vast swathes of Europe, Central Asia, the Middle East and Africa were already reeling from over two years of war. Also by then, other influences, addressed in Chapters 1 and 3, some the product of human design and others not, had set the conditions which the blockade could exploit. Among the first were governmental priorities in how to manage food collection and distribution, and whether to do so by fixing the prices paid to the producer or by rationing at the point of sale. Among the second were the weather conditions experienced across Europe in 1916, which resulted in poor harvests everywhere, or the plagues of locusts in Palestine and Syria which caused famine in 1917. Both man and nature had the capacity to determine how the blockade would bite.

Before the war peasant societies had tended to assume that they would prove more resilient if confronted with protracted conflict. In February 1914 the Carnegie Endowment for International Peace's report on the Balkan Wars of 1912–13 found that the war had minimal impact on Serbia and Bulgaria because the loss of labour on the land generated by the mobilisation of men for military service had been offset by the efforts of women and children.[23] By 1918–19, with

[20] Peter Gatrell, *A Whole Empire Walking: Refugees in Russia during World War I* (Bloomington, IN: Indiana University Press, 1999), 15–16; Reichsarchiv, *Der Weltkrieg. Die Operationen des Jahres 1915*, Band 8 (Berlin: Mittler, 1932), 453. See also Chapter 1 of the present work.

[21] Oberkommando des Heeres, *Der Weltkrieg, Die Kriegführung im Frühjahr 1917*, Band 12 (Berlin: Mittler, 1939), 121.

[22] James E. Edmonds (ed), *History of the Great War Based on Official Documents: MilitaryOoperations: France and Belgium, 1917*, 3 vols (London: Macmillan, 1940–1948), vol. I, 118.

[23] Carnegie Endowment for International Peace, *Report into the Balkan Wars*, 246–7, 250–1.

revolutions in Russia, and with Bulgaria and then the Ottoman Empire leading the way in the succession of armistices negotiated by the Central Powers, this argument would look much less convincing. Russia had believed it was better equipped for a long war precisely because it was agriculturally self-sufficient. However, in 1914 mobilisation took 2.1 million horses from the land with no compensating gain in modern technologies: increased food production could not be achieved by more intensified farming but only by bringing more land under cultivation, and that itself was dependent on the labour lost to the army.[24] The length of the war exposed the weaknesses of self-sufficient agricultural economies.

The Carnegie enquiry had also found that the Balkan Wars had a greater adverse effect on industrial production than they did on agriculture.[25] No industrialised state was more aware of its vulnerability than Britain. Its worries were not generated by the possible absence of men on active service, the problem that had beset the Balkan states, but by its adoption of the principles of free trade, and its corollary, its reliance on imported grain. In 1903 the government responded by appointing a Royal Commission on Food Supply and Raw Materials in Time of War. Its report, published in 1905, was reassuring: the navy could cope, merchant ships would continue to sail if war insurance were introduced, and the working classes were likely to be more resilient than alarmists suggested. In reality, as the First World War was to prove, Britain's position was even more positive. Even at the height of the German submarine campaign, in 1917–18, Britain was never in danger of starvation.[26] Instead of a threat, the Royal Commission scented an opportunity. German workers spent proportionately more on food than did British workers, and by 1906 Germany was importing 20 per cent of its annual consumption of grain. In the run-up to the outbreak of the First World War, it increased its production of rye and oats, but did so at the expense of barley. Imports of the latter, used for animal fodder, grew from 650,000 tonnes in 1889 to 2.6 million tonnes in 1909. As a result, although Germany was apparently self-sufficient in meat, its cattle-farming depended on imported fodder, and by 1913 Germany also imported about 60 per cent of its fats. In the

[24] Alexandre Sumpf, *La grande guerre oubliée: Russie, 1914–1918* (Paris: Perrin, 2014), 128–32; generally, see Peter Gatrell, *Russia's First World War: A Social and Economic History* (Harlow: Pearson Longman, 2005), 154–75, 269–70.

[25] Carnegie Endowment for International Peace, *Report into the Balkan Wars*, 250.

[26] P. E. Dewey, *British Agriculture in the First World War* (London: Routledge, 1989), 201–10; J. M. Winter, *The Great War and the British People* (Basingstoke: Macmillan, 1986), 215–29, 239, 244.

last year before the war, the value of German food imports exceeded exports by £100 million.[27] The Trade Division of the Admiralty's Naval Intelligence Department concluded that Germany looked just as vulnerable as Britain to economic war, and planned accordingly in the decade before 1914.[28]

The pre-war thinking of both sides therefore incorporated the possibility of a British-led war on trade. In Germany, the propaganda promoting fleet construction emanating from Alfred von Tirpitz, the head of the Reichsmarinesamt (Imperial Naval Office), emphasised Germany's dependence on overseas trade to justify the costs of naval building. The plans of the chief of the general staff, Alfred von Schlieffen, for a speedy land campaign on two fronts reflected his fear of German vulnerability if the war became protracted, and the danger of working class discontent which supply problems would generate.[29] In Britain the principal naval theorist of the day, Julian Corbett, noted that Britain's geographical position lay athwart Germany's exits from the North Sea, to the south by way of the Channel and to the north between Orkney and Norway. He argued that a navy did not necessarily have to bring its enemy to battle, provided it could exercise sufficient control of the sea to protect its trade. Such thinking was not purely defensive, since protection of one's own commerce implied the disruption of the enemy's. Corbett believed that naval war had to make itself felt through its impacts on finance and on the economy, which would in turn have political effects in modern democracies.

Corbett disseminated his ideas through his links with the First Sea Lord, Sir John Fisher, and with successive Directors of Naval Intelligence.[30] One of them was Edmond Slade, who wrote a memorandum on Germany's growing vulnerability to blockade in 1906 and in 1908 argued that the role of the battle fleet was to protect the blockading cruisers from enemy battleships, so that the cruisers could fight the war against enemy trade.[31] However, the arguments in favour of blockade as a war plan confronted three sets of challenges.

[27] Lothar Burchardt, *Friedenswirtschaft und Kriegsvorsorge. Deutschlands wirtschaftliche Rüstungsbestrebungen vor 1914* (Boppard am Rhein: Boldt, 1968), 96–106; Louis Guichard, *The Naval Blockade 1914–1918*, trans. and ed. Christopher Turner (London: Philip Allan, 1930), 11.

[28] Avner Offer, *The First World War: An Agrarian Interpretation* (Oxford: Oxford University Press, 1989), 218–32.

[29] Burchardt, *Friedenswirtschaft und Kriegvorsorge*, 20–9.

[30] Julian Corbett, *Some Principles of Maritime Strategy* (London: Longmans, Green, 1911; 2nd ed., Eric Grove, ed., Annapolis, MD: Naval Institute Press, 1988).

[31] Stephen Cobb, *Preparing for Blockade 1885–1914: Naval Contingency for Economic Warfare* (London: Routledge, 2013), 95–108.

The first was commercial. The use of maritime blockade in earlier wars had not targeted food supply, given the relative agricultural self-sufficiency of most states, so much as the revenues derived from other forms of trade and their use to fund the procurement of war-related goods.[32] By December 1904, however, international trade had become much more sophisticated. Sir George Sydenham Clarke, the Secretary of Britain's Committee of Imperial Defence, pointed out that indirect trade with the enemy via adjacent neutral powers would be almost impossible to track, and that in any case an effort to prevent it could prove counter-productive, alienating non-aligned powers and cutting off Britain's own imports. If Britain wanted to wage economic war on Germany, it would somehow have to control the trade with the adjacent states, the Netherlands, Denmark, Norway and Sweden.[33] Schlieffen's successor as the chief of the Prussian general staff, Helmuth von Moltke the younger, recognised this very point, adjusting German war planning in 1911 so that the army's invasion of France did not infringe Dutch neutrality.

Secondly, the technological transformation of naval war, manifested by steam power and armour plate, and which enabled ships to stay on station, both buttressed the case for blockade and challenged it. Mines, coastal batteries, torpedo boats and submarines all strengthened the defence of states whose coasts and harbours were blockaded. Navies which came too close to the shore were liable to lose ships in a steady process of attrition, an opportunity which the German navy proposed to exploit in the event of war. From 1908 onwards, the Royal Navy reviewed various options for mounting a distant, as opposed to a close, blockade in recognition of this reality, and by 1913–14 the Admiralty had finally settled on a distant blockade, so using Britain's land mass as part of the blockade and keeping the navy's ships closer to their bases. It rendered the North Sea a maritime no man's land and required flotillas to protect Britain's east coast from German raids.

The problem with this solution was the third challenge confronted by blockade: a distant blockade could be contrary to international law. In 1856 the declaration of Paris on maritime law stipulated that a blockade had to be effective and to do that it had to prevent access to the coast, which implied it would be close. In 1911 the Admiralty was advised

[32] Andrew D. Lambert, 'The Crimean War Blockade, 1854–56', in Bruce Elleman and S. C. M. Paine, eds., *Naval Blockades and Seapower: Strategies and Counter-strategies, 1805–2005* (London: Routledge, 2006), 54.

[33] A. C. Bell, *A History of the Blockade of Germany and of the Countries Associated with Her in the Great War, Austria-Hungary, Bulgaria, and Turkey 1914–1918* (London: His Majesty's Stationery Office, 1937; made publicly available in 1961), 9.

that a distant blockade could be legal, even at a distance of 800 nautical miles, if the navy could intercept all ships in the North Sea.[34] The declaration of Paris had also abolished privateering and shored up neutral rights. It prohibited the seizure of enemy or neutral property, except contraband, from neutral ships (the principle of 'free ships, free goods') or of neutral property from enemy ships.[35] Although it eroded Britain's maritime rights as a belligerent, it served British interests in two ways. It minimised the risks of offending neutrals (and particularly the USA) if Britain were a belligerent, and it strengthened Britain's economic opportunities in war if it itself were neutral.

Between the Crimean War and the First World War Britain fought only one international war, that with the Boer republics in 1899–1902. In all the other inter-state wars fought over almost six decades it was able to use the size of its merchant fleet to profit as a cross-trader. During the American Civil War, it did so by breaking the Union blockade of the Confederacy. The Union challenged neutral rights by asserting the doctrine of continuous voyage, that contraband whose ultimate destination was the Confederacy, even if its intermediate destination was a neutral port, could be seized. Increasingly, what was contraband and what not, an issue not addressed at Paris in 1856, would define how a blockade could be conducted. The Hague Convention of 1907 proposed the formation of an international prize court in order to rule on these issues.

So far Britain had, by virtue of its maritime supremacy, been able to make much of the running, and in particular had used its own prize courts to establish norms. Worried that its power to set the rules would be undermined by the proposed prize court, it convened its own meeting in London in 1908–9 to discuss the laws of war at sea. It sought clarity on three issues. First, what law would the international prize court apply? Second was the definition of contraband. The declaration of London distinguished between free goods, absolute contraband, most obviously munitions of war, and conditional contraband. The latter included food if it was likely to be destined for belligerent consumption, but the burden of proof lay with the blockading power, not the shipper. Third was the principle of continuous voyage. The declaration of London restricted its application to absolute contraband. With many convinced that a blockade would struggle to be effective, and others worried that Britain's pursuit of belligerent rights might upset neutrals, both the Foreign Office

[34] Nicholas A. Lambert, *Planning Armageddon: British Economic Warfare and the First World War* (Cambridge, MA: Harvard University Press, 2012), 135; Hull, *A Scrap of Paper*, 291.

[35] Adam Roberts and Richard Guelff, *Documents on the Laws of War* (Oxford: Oxford University Press, 2000), 47–52.

and Admiralty were ready to compromise. Those who were not fell back on military necessity: the imperatives of war would make the law.

The declaration of London enhanced the position of neutrals by establishing a strict and tight definition of absolute contraband and by permitting neutrals to trade a broad range of conditional contraband, at least indirectly, with the enemy. This made sense for Britain if it was not a belligerent and even, some argued, if it were. The declaration retained the principle of blockade and enhanced both its legitimacy and its enforceability by its greater clarity on contraband. The formal British position since 1856 had been that rules would help the power that had the strength to enforce them. Others were less convinced. 'Undiminished belligerent rights and the widest possible freedom for neutrals are opposite principles', T. G. Bowles told the House of Commons when it debated the declaration in 1911. Sir Edward Grey, the Foreign Secretary, responded that, 'We shall never bring a Continental enemy to his knees by dealing with contraband alone. There is the question of where he gets his supplies. … He can get them overland.'[36] The Commons passed the declaration, but the House of Lords did not. So, despite having convened the London conference, Britain did not ratify its outcome, and as a result nor did anyone else before 1914 except the USA. Nonetheless the Admiralty assumed that the declaration would apply in the event of war.

When the July crisis broke in 1914, Britain's entente partners sought its participation in the war precisely because of its navy and its capacity to wage economic warfare. As late as 30 July, the British ambassador in Paris, Lord Bertie, told Grey that a British decision to support France would 'almost certainly' prevent war, as Germany 'would not run the risk of having her sea-borne trade destroyed and of being starved out by the British fleet'.[37] When on 3 August 1914 Grey explained to the House of Commons why Britain had issued an ultimatum to Germany, he stressed that the war which Britain would be entering was one that it would wage overwhelmingly by sea, and to that extent it would be as affected as it would be as a maritime trading power that opted for neutrality.

The Blockade of Germany

On 20 August 1914, just over two weeks after its entry to the war and in response to a request from the USA for clarification on the issue, Britain

36 Eric W. Osborne, *Britain's Economic Blockade of Germany 1914–1919* (London: Frank Cass, 2004), 35–9.

37 Stefan Schmidt, *Frankreichs Außenpolitik in der Julikrise 1914. Ein Beitrag zur Geschichte des Ausbruchs des Ersten Weltkrieges* (Munich: De Gruyter, 2009), 132, 166.

published an order in council stating that it would adhere to the principles of the declaration of London, while reserving the right to modify its rules. The effect was to reverse its previous position, which had been to insist on clear rules and to demand that the declaration be adopted as a whole. Specifically, Britain reasserted the doctrine of continuous voyage: it would seize conditional contraband carried by neutrals irrespective of the port at which it was discharged on the presumption (unless proved to the contrary) that its ultimate consignee was the enemy. The USA objected to this infringement of neutral rights, but the British responded – both in a further order in council on 29 October 1914 and on 7 January 1915 – that it was up to the owner of the cargo to prove its final recipient. It referred Washington to the Union's espousal of continuous voyage in the Civil War. 'A similar presumption', the order in council of 20 August stated, 'arises if the goods are consigned to a fortified place belonging to the enemy'.[38] The idea that the blockade was simply a naval form of siege war, albeit fought at sea rather than on land, was there from the outset, and would intensify as the blockade tightened.

The trouble was that the blockade lacked the geographical and operational precision of a siege: a maritime blockade was conducted in an almost entirely unregulated environment, despite the fact that the declaration of Paris had started to impose rules on war at sea, and one which lay outside the territorial control of states. The sea was an international means of passage used by neutrals, who averred their right to do so freely just as belligerents asserted theirs to use it to wage war. A further difficulty in 1914 was that neither side had a clear view of what it thought economic war was or what its purpose might be. Was it to stop the flow of contraband or to close off all commerce? Was its purpose to starve the people so that they would be ready to mandate their government to negotiate, or to overthrow it if it did not? Or was its purpose more specific, to undermine the fighting power of the enemy's armed forces? What was the relationship between an attack on these assets and their defence, given that the sea was not nationally or territorially bound?

Because these questions were left unresolved, Britain entered the First World War without a clear plan for economic warfare, and what little it had done addressed the defence of its own trade rather than the attack of Germany's. The War Book, prepared for use in the event of mobilisation on behalf of the Committee of Imperial Defence by its secretary, Maurice Hankey, set up a scheme of maritime insurance to keep its merchant ships sailing despite the dangers of attack. Initially, German surface raiders caused chaos on the principal sea lanes, but by the end

[38] Guichard, *The Naval Blockade*, 23–4.

of 1914 they had been cleared from the world's oceans by the cruisers of the Royal Navy. The Germans turned instead to submarines early in 1915, so that in fact the respite was short. But submarines did not have the range or speed of cruisers, and were disadvantaged by the laws of cruiser warfare, which required them to surface and identify the nationality of the ship and the nature of its cargo before capturing or sinking it. Moreover, Germany had not prepared for U-boat warfare. It would take another two years before they could mount an effective *guerre de course* and, even then, they had too few submarines to match the geographical scale of the undertaking.

Britain's plans for the offensive use of economic warfare had been set back after the retirement of Fisher as First Sea Lord in 1909. When on 23 August 1911 during the second Moroccan crisis the Committee of Imperial Defence reviewed its options in the event of war with Germany, it was alarmed by the incoherence of naval planning.[39] Neither blockade nor economic warfare more generally was among them, despite the fact that the committee's secretary was Charles Ottley, who as Director of Naval Intelligence in 1905–7 had worked closely with Corbett and recognised Germany's vulnerability to blockade. By 1914 the blockade meant at least three different things. For some, the aim was to cause panic on financial markets so great that the wheels of international commerce would seize and revolution would follow.[40] For others, the target of economic war was not the stock exchange and international credit, but commodities like food and raw materials.[41] Those who thought about economic war in these terms, as Ottley and Hankey did, reckoned its effects would take years, not months. Theirs was a plan for a long war, not a quick one. After Fisher was recalled as First Sea Lord in August 1914, he too was wont to associate talk of a long war with pressures on German food supplies. The third group, made up mostly of naval officers, saw economic war as a means solely to force Germany fleet out of harbour in a bid to break 'the siege', and so to bring on a decisive battle. These divergent objectives were not incompatible but they were not clearly articulated. When taken in combination they ensured that blockade was not a precise instrument, and that those who were charged with its implementation could harbour differences in conception that were not immediately self-evident.

[39] Keith Wilson, 'Hankey's Appendix: Some Admiralty Manoeuvres during and after the Agadir Crisis', *War in History* 1 (1994), 81–97.

[40] This is the principal, if tendentious, argument of Lambert, *Planning Armageddon*; see also Marion Siney, *The Allied Blockade of Germany, 1914–1916* (Ann Arbor, MI: University of Michigan Press, 1957).

[41] Schmidt, *Frankreichs Außenpolitik in der Julikrise 1914*, 100, 166–7.

It was Germany rather than Britain that first came to characterise the blockade as 'a starvation war'. A study by a group of German experts, edited by Paul Eltzbacher and published in December 1914, appeared in English in 1915. It spoke of 'a scheme from which our opponents hoped great things even before the war, and which is now, after a succession of defeats, doubly important to them. It is the famous starvation scheme'. The book's evidence for the plan's pre-war origins was slender, but it gave an authority to the notion that hunger was being mobilised as a weapon of war which the blockade never lost. The irony was that the German experts believed it would not work because Germany could just about feed itself, even in a long war, provided that state regulation replaced the free market: 'No German woman or child can be starved', the British editor quoted the Germans as saying, 'unless by the direct action of the German Government'.[42] For the British this was a self-fulfilling argument: the greater the evidence of governmental control of Germany's food supply, the more Britain was able to justify the blockade as fulfilling a military purpose.[43] The further irony was that by 1915 many in Britain agreed, or at least accepted, that the blockade was not working.

Not least because Britain had no coherent war plan, it took time just to put the blockade in place. The simplest and most immediate action was naval. The Dover Patrol closed the Channel. To the north, the 10th Cruiser Squadron patrolled the inhospitable waters between Orkney and Norway. Initially, however, it did so with only eight obsolete and slow cruisers. The Admiralty had planned to deploy armed merchant cruisers but at the war's outbreak they were neither prepared nor armed, and not until early December were 23 vessels on station. On 5 November Britain used Germany's indiscriminate mining of the North Sea as an excuse to declare it a war zone, with the aim of getting neutral vessels to enter from the south where it was easier to inspect their cargos.[44]

The navy soon gave vent to its frustrations. Of 341 vessels sent in to Lerwick and Kirkwall for examination of their cargos by the 10th Cruiser Squadron between 1 January and 31 March 1915, only 16 were detained. The commander-in-chief of the Grand Fleet, Sir John Jellicoe, was convinced that many were carrying goods destined for the enemy, and the evidence supported him: US exports to Germany doubled in value between January 1913 and February 1915.[45] Imports to

[42] Paul Eltzbacher, *Germany's Food. Can It Last? Germany's Food and England's Plan to Starve Her Out. A Study by German Experts*, ed. by S. Russell Wells (London: University of London Press, 1915), ix, 1–3.

[43] Hull, *A Scrap of Paper*, 171.

[44] Cobb, *Preparing for Blockade*, 243–51.

[45] Osborne, *Britain's Economic Blockade*, 59–60, 73–4, 85.

the Scandinavian neutrals soared, those of Sweden rising by value from £47 million in 1913 to £62 million in 1915, of Norway from £3 million to £48 million, and of Denmark from £38 million to £64 million.[46] Food prices were of course rising, but the increase in tonnages was real, and much of it was destined for onward transhipment to Germany, which still controlled the Baltic. Denmark's exports to Germany rose in value from 174 million kroner in 1913 to 691 million in 1916, and from 30 per cent of its exports to nearly 60 per cent; and Norway's did so from 67 million kroner to 292 million, or from 17 per cent of its exports to almost 30 per cent. Although Holland's trade with Germany declined, it did so from a much higher base point. Holland's total imports in 1915 were still equal in value to those of the three Scandinavian countries combined, and its exports to Germany were in similar proportions. Of 1.63 billion gold marks spent on agricultural imports by the Zentral-Einkauf Gesellschaft, Germany's centralised import agency, between January and November 1915, 50 per cent by weight and 42 per cent by value entered the country from the Netherlands.[47] In other words, the principal challenge which the blockade faced lay in the application of the principle of continuous voyage. Germany could continue to import via its neighbours, just as those who were sceptical of the blockade's effectiveness had anticipated, and up until 1916 it was coping well enough, in terms of both food and industrial raw materials.

From the Entente's perspective, if the blockade were to become a 'siege', it needed to tighten the principle of continuous voyage. Part of the solution was better intelligence – on the firms that were acting for the Germans and the routes they used. Simple inspection of ships, their cargos and their accompanying manifests were insufficient. A database of commercial information had to be created from scratch, and that took time. But once it was in place, the allies could establish 'black lists' of those firms known to be trading with the enemy, and could license those businesses they knew to be in good standing by issuing letters of assurance or 'navicerts'. The navicert was a form of 'commercial passport', issued before the goods were shipped to ensure their undisturbed passage. If the naval patrols were the sticks of economic warfare, navicerts were the carrots to reward those shipowners who obeyed the rules.[48]

[46] Guichard, *The Naval Blockade*, 58.

[47] Marc Frey, 'Deutsche Finanzinteressen an den Vereinigten Staaten und den Niederlanden im Ersten Weltkrieg', *Militärgeschichtliche Mitteilungen*, 53 (1994), Heft 2, 327–53.

[48] Bell, *A History of the Blockade of Germany*, 456–8; Greg Kennedy, 'Intelligence and the Blockade 1914–1917: A Study in Administration, Friction and Command', *Intelligence and National Security*, 22 (2007), 699–721.

Part of this was diplomacy, designed to get the neutral powers to work with the blockade rather than against it. Here the British had limited leverage with the Scandinavian powers, not just because the Germans controlled the Baltic but also because Sweden in particular lay on the supply route to Russia, which it was in the Entente's interests to keep open. Entente powers were greater in relation to Holland, given its dependence on the North Sea, but initially the approach was wrong. The British Foreign Office assumed that it should broker a deal with the Dutch government, but Holland feared that an official agreement would weaken its claim to neutrality and could invite a German invasion. The impasse was unlocked in November 1914 by the creation of the Netherlands Overseas Trust, a non-governmental body made up of businessmen whose commercial interests made it sensible to work with the blockade rather than against it.[49]

The process of stopping ships, searching them and adjudicating on their cargos cost shipping companies time and money; it also disrupted the sailing patterns of those offering regular liner services. On 4 February 1915 Germany announced that its submarines would sink all vessels, including neutrals', in the North Sea. On 1 March Britain responded with an order in council which disregarded the treaty of Paris and presented its actions as reprisals for German illegality. Britain argued that the law of war at sea had to adapt to changing conditions. It used Germany's refusal to distinguish neutral from belligerent, or to sort out contraband from 'free goods', to justify reprisals against all German trade. So far the navy's efforts had been directed to stopping German imports; now it also sought to blockade its exports, not only hitting Germany's trade balance but also the viability of Rotterdam as a port. Although Britain continued to maintain that it was observing the declaration of London, it announced that it would requisition exports from, and imports to, Germany; that it would stop vessels bound for a neutral port if they were carrying goods intended for Germany or goods owned by Germans; and that vessels which proceeded to an enemy port after clearing a neutral one would be condemned if subsequently captured. The effect was to give the Netherlands Overseas Trust teeth, and to encourage other states to imitate its structure.[50]

[49] Samuël Kruizinga, 'NOT Neutrality. The Dutch Government, the Netherlands Oversea Trust Company, and the Entente Blockade of Germany, 1914–1918', in Johan den Hertog and Samuël Kruizinga, eds., *Caught in the Middle: Neutrals, Neutrality, and the First World War* (Amsterdam: Amsterdam University Press, 2011), 85–104; Samuël Kruizinga, 'Neutrality', in Jay Winter, ed., *The Cambridge History of the First World War*, 3 vols (Cambridge: Cambridge University Press, 2014), vol. 2, 542–75.

[50] Bell, *A History of the Blockade of Germany*, 233–4, 249–62.

In practice the application of the model was – at least until 1917 – variable. The most successful was that with the Swiss, the Société Suisse de Surveillance Économique or SSS, created in May 1915. The control of Switzerland's trade, being landlocked, was largely left to France.[51] The French government was in many respects more determined in its pursuit of economic warfare than was the British, partly because it was less fearful than Britain that ruthlessness in regard to neutrals would damage its own capacity to import. It proposed to ration the imports of Germany's border neutrals in line with their pre-war norms. Britain accepted this approach in 1916. The French also persuaded their allies to use their purchasing power to enter into preclusive arrangements to buy commodities, particularly Danish bacon and Dutch dairy produce, from Germany's border neutrals. Less controversial within Britain was the suggestion (adopted in October 1915) that it use its control of coal bunkers in ports around the world to restrict the sale of fuel only to those ships that obeyed British rules.

The USA was the neutral to which Britain paid most attention. As Grey put it, British policy was to get the maximum of blockade with the minimum of disruption to Anglo-American relations. Britain seemed to be in a strong position. Entente orders, underpinned by the convertibility of the pound sterling, by the City of London's global dominance of financial services and by the fact that over 47 per cent of the world's tonnage was British[52] pulled the USA out of recession in 1914. Americans made money out of the war. However, they knew that as neutrals they could make even more if they – like the British in the Civil War – could trade with both sides, not just one.

In February 1915 the German resumption of a *guerre de course*, using submarines rather than surface ships, had the potential to strengthen the Entente case, particularly when – as in the case of the *Lusitania* in May 1915 – U-boats sank ships with US citizens on board. By a mixture of patient diplomacy and purchasing power the British got what they wanted, while the Germans increasingly felt that America's neutrality was not preventing it becoming a *de facto* belligerent, at least in economic terms. Between 1915 and 1917 the Germans oscillated between respect for the laws of cruiser warfare, which robbed their U-boats of much of their effectiveness, and short-lived rejections of such restrictions.

[51] Marjorie Millbank Farrar, *Conflict and Compromise: The Strategy, Politics and Diplomacy of the French Blockade, 1914–1918* (The Hague: Martinus Nijhoff, 1974).

[52] C. E. Fayle, *History of the Great War Based on Official Documents: Seaborne Trade*, 3 vols (London: John Murray, 1920–4), vol. I, p. 18.

The Foreign Office's need to pander to American opinion was driven as much by British self-interest as by regard for neutral rights. However, the Royal Navy continued to feel that its efforts in the dangerous waters north and east of the British Isles were being undermined by an overly fastidious approach to prize law, respect for private property and excessive deference to states that were making good money from the war. British firms themselves were facilitating trade with the enemy, albeit indirectly and possibly unwittingly, either by consigning goods to agents in neutral countries without knowing their eventual destination or by financing the trade of Germany's border neutrals in the USA. Britain's role as the arsenal and financier of an alliance made it as dependent as Germany on imports and even on a balance of trade. The navy failed to recognise that, while its priorities were not those of the Foreign Office or of the Board of Trade, all three were making different contributions to a common goal. It also had to recognise the roles of their allies, and especially France, which effectively took over the running of the blockade on land, while Britain was responsible for its implementation on the sea.[53]

Developing the administrative structure to reconcile these agencies and their different priorities took time. On 15 August 1914 Britain formed an inter-departmental Contraband Committee, under the chairmanship of Sir Eyre Crowe of the Foreign Office, but it did not acquire executive powers until November 1914. In February 1915, a War Trade Department was formed by the Committee of Imperial Defence in a bid to centralise control further, particularly in the issue of export licences and in the pooling of intelligence. In February 1916, the government responded to parliamentary and press attacks on the blockade's implementation by creating a Ministry of Blockade. This brought the Contraband Committee and the War Trade Department under one head. The former commander of the 10th Cruiser Squadron, Admiral Dudley de Chair, was brought in as its naval adviser and Lord Robert Cecil, a junior Foreign Office minister, became its head. Much of the external criticism focused on what was seen as excessive regard for neutral rights, and in July 1916 Cecil at last announced that Britain would abandon the declaration of London.

France was in favour of keeping the declaration of London on two grounds. First, the clarity it provided on contraband was better than the ambiguity that had prevailed before 1909. Second, as the allies had not been able to mount an effective and close blockade, its provisions

[53] Greg Kennedy, 'Strategy and Power: The Royal Navy, the Foreign Office and the Blockade, 1914–1917', *Journal of Defence Studies*, 8 (2008), 190–206.

were not even formally applicable. France argued that what the allies were doing was better described as economic war because there was no blockade in the technical sense.[54]

Despite this difference, France's declarations on the blockade kept step with those of Britain's orders in council, but its efforts to achieve unity of effort in the opening two years of the war proved even less successful. Each of the finance, navy and war ministries guarded their independent responsibilities. A joint committee, *Comité R* (for restriction), involving not just these three departments but also those for justice, public works, commerce, agriculture and colonies, was set up in March 1915, with the task of overseeing policy. However, the committee on specific regulations remained separate. A year later, Denys Cochin became the president of *Comité R*, and made it function, even if its role was still advisory rather than executive. He did not become the effective minister of blockade until December 1916, and France did not create a fully-fledged ministry until Clemenceau became premier in November 1917.[55]

From 1915, despite their own lack of unity, the French began putting pressure on Britain not only to be tougher in its enforcement of the blockade but also to support the creation of a mechanism for allied coordination. In June 1916 the minister for commerce, Etienne Clémentel, convened a meeting in Paris principally directed towards the formation of a post-war economic order designed to give France and Britain a head-start over Germany. However, Britain's commitment to free trade prevented it from using protection to ensure a long-term economic advantage over Germany. Instead, the allies used the blockade as a short-term substitute. The war provided an opportunity to squeeze German goods out of overseas markets and created the openings into which Britain and France might insert themselves.[56] However, beyond French agreement to join Britain in abandoning the declaration of London, progress in the administration of the blockade during the war itself was limited until the USA entered the war.

Germany's pursuit of its own economic war prompted it finally to embrace unrestricted U-boat warfare on 1 February 1917. The consequence was a self-inflicted wound. Neutral ships stopped sailing for fear

[54] Yves-Henri Nouailhat, *France et Etats-Unis août 1914-avril 1917* (Paris: Publications de la Sorbonne, 1979), 304–5.

[55] Jean-Baptiste Duroselle, *La France et les Français 1914–1920* (Paris: Perrin, 1972), 257–8.

[56] Georges-Henri Soutou, *L'Or et le sang: les buts de guerre économiques de la première guerre mondiale* (Paris: Fayard, 1989), 233–71; Pierre Renouvin, 'Les buts de guerre du gouvernement français 1914–1918', *Revue historique*, 235 (1966), 8–9; V. H. Rothwell, *British War Aims and Peace Diplomacy 1914–1918* (Oxford: Oxford University Press, 1971), 272–7.

of being sunk, and thus reduced Germany's flow of imports. When neutrals resumed sailings, even those that had been less well disposed to the allies – like Sweden – changed their positions, favouring the Entente, not least because they were now more dependent on it than they had been before. The USA's decision to enter the war in April removed the biggest restraint on the allies' conduct of economic warfare. It was just in time, as the revolutions in Russia, and the decision of the Bolsheviks in December 1917 to pursue peace regardless of the territorial penalties, opened the granaries of Ukraine, western Russia and (from May 1918) Romania to the Central Powers.

France wanted the USA to embrace the blockade and to do so on its, not Britain's, terms. Initially America seemed reluctant to bend to either will. It had spent too much of the war calling for freedom of the seas (a demand that Wilson incorporated in his Fourteen Points in January 1918) and defending the rights of neutrals to be ready rapidly to abandon those principles. Congress passed a law controlling exports in June 1917, and by August Woodrow Wilson succumbed to British pressure to list those items that could not be exported without a licence. In practice the embargo was effectively total, embracing not just products whose military applications were direct, but also grain and foodstuffs. Specifically, it prohibited the export of food to the border neutrals until December 1917, so that the Americans would have time to examine the situation. The Americans banked on the border neutrals being able to feed themselves without imports between the gathering of that year's harvest and Christmas.[57] They were wrong, principally for the reasons explained in Chapter 1.[58]

The positions of the border neutrals became so dire that they were barely able to trade at all, particularly in the cases of Norway and the Netherlands, the two states most directly exposed to allied maritime controls. Norway's total trade in 1916 was valued at 988 million kroner and 29.6 per cent of that represented exports to Germany; by 1918 it was valued at 755 million, of which only 11.3 per cent was exported to Germany. Holland's trade, which had been valued at 3,113 million

[57] Guichard, *The Naval Blockade*, 103–34.

[58] Christian Pfister, 'Auf der Kippe: Regen, Kälte und schwindende Importe stürzten die Schweiz 1916–1918 in einen Nahrungsengpass', in Daniel Krämer, Christian Pfister and Daniel Marc Segesser, eds., *"Woche für Woche neue Preisaufschläge": Nahrungsmittel-, Energie- ind Ressourcenkonflikte in der Schweiz des Ersten Weltkrieges* (Basel: Schwabe, 2016), 76; Maartje M. Abbenhuis, *The Art of Staying Neutral: The Netherlands in the First World War, 1914–1918* (Amsterdam: Amsterdam University Press, 2006), 187–94, 219–22; Steven Koblik, 'Sweden 1917: Between Reform and Revolution', in Hans A. Schmitt, ed., *Neutral Europe between War and Revolution, 1917–23* (Charlottesville, VA: University Press of Virginia, 1988), 111–32.

guilders in 1912, and of which fully 50 per cent went to Germany, slumped to 386 million guilders in 1918, and only 40 per cent was exported to Germany. Sweden lost its leverage over the allies with the Bolshevik revolution, and its exports to Germany dropped from 36.9 per cent of its trade in 1915 to 21.7 per cent in 1918.[59]

Despite (and in part because of) this intensification of the blockade, its control was slipping away from Britain. By the end of 1917 London feared that the tightness of the American embargo would lead to the loss by Britain of neutral markets. In October 1917 Wilson established the War Trade Board, which regulated the overseas trade of American companies, created a blacklist of German-owned firms, especially in Latin America, and monitored the activities of businesses in neutral countries. In 1914 the United States had organised relief for the civilian population of occupied Belgium; in 1917 its policies hit neutral non-combatants. Unlike Britain in 1914, the USA in 1917 had no reason for caution in how it handled the issue of neutrality. It dealt with the countries bordering Germany as states, not, as Britain had done, through trading companies as intermediaries. In effect the allies were blockading states that were not belligerents as well as those that were. If Germany had reacted by widening the war to Holland, Denmark or Switzerland, on the grounds that America's embargo meant that they were no longer neutrals, it would only have hastened its own defeat through military over-extension. Now more than ever, the economic power of a belligerent made neutrality relative, not absolute.

After the USA's entry to the war, its economic dominance also enabled it to force the allies into greater cooperation. They set up cartels to purchase and so control world supplies of commodities, including grain and meat. In November 1917 an Allied Maritime Transport Council united responsibility for food and transport, and established a permanent secretariat to manage both. By providing ships to the allies, the neutrals could barter for food. So great was the purchasing power of these bodies and so pervasive their effective monopolisation of global markets that non-aligned states had little option but to cooperate. The Allied Blockade Committee first met in December 1917, in the Foreign Office in London, with Cecil in the chair, and became effective in March 1918. British mechanisms were replaced with allied ones, including Joint Allied Trade Committees in neutral states, even if they still operated through British legations, and British committees, like the Contraband Committee, became allied committees. The Foreign Office grew as

[59] Lance E. Davis and Stanley E. Engerman, *Naval Blockades in Peace and War: An Economic History since 1750* (Cambridge: Cambridge University Press, 2006), 208.

frustrated with the Americans as it had been with the Royal Navy, and with as little justification. Sir Eyre Crowe wrote in October 1917, that 'it becomes more and more evident that the United States do not want to co-operate with us; they only want to see our cards'. By November he was arguing that Britain would have to decide on its course of action in relation to all neutrals 'for ourselves, apart from anything the United States may do'.[60]

For the French too, frustration mounted. While happy with the tightening of the blockade and ready to accept draconian policies in regard to the neutrals as the British were not, they realised that their hopes for some form of short-term protectionism, provided by an extension of the blockade beyond the restoration of peace, would not get American support.

The Mediterranean: The Blockade of Austria-Hungary, Bulgaria and the Ottoman Empire

All three powers – Britain, France and the USA – enjoyed at least one feature in common: an almost obsessive fixation with Germany to the exclusion of its allies. Both during the war and in the histories written thereafter, they focused on the blockade against Germany and the handling of its border neutrals. In the American case, this neglect of the economic war waged against Germany's allies is understandable: it did not declare war on Austria-Hungary until December 1917, and it never did so against Bulgaria and the Ottoman Empire. In the case of Britain and France, as well as Italy after its entry in 1915, this oversight is extraordinary. After all it was effectively maritime and economic power which prised Italy and Greece away from the Central Powers. The threat of blockade gave the Entente leverage over Italy, given its long coastline, a vulnerability which Bulgaria lacked.

Greece resisted this pressure and paid a price. In late 1915 an Anglo-French naval squadron was based at Milo, athwart the approaches to Salamis and Piraeus. Aboard HMS *Hibernia*, Rear-Admiral Sydney Fremantle demanded more forceful action: 'we are not sufficiently in evidence', he wrote in December 1915, 'to produce the full effect we ought to on the Greek *people*'.[61] Having landed in Salonika (formally part of Greece since 1913) in October 1915, the allies provided a haven

[60] Bell, *A History of the Blockade of Germany*, 666–7.

[61] Fremantle to Vice-Admiral Arthur Limpus, 7 December 1915, in Paul Halpern, ed., *The Royal Navy in the Mediterranean 1915–1918* (Aldershot: Navy Records Society, 1987), 48; emphasis in original.

for the pro-Entente Eleutherios Venizelos and his followers, who set up a provisional government and so divided the country. The armies on the Macedonian front requisitioned supplies in Thessaly, and the British and French deepened the political split by their pressure on the royalist government in Athens. The British established oversight of Greek imports and exports during the summer of 1916 and a system of certification was introduced to ease relations with Greek shipowners.[62] In September 1916 British and French ships appeared off Salamis, demanding control of Greek ports and telegraphs and the surrender of interned Austro-Hungarian and German ships. In October they seized the Greek fleet and in December the French put troops ashore in Athens. That winter Greece was blockaded and food shortages generated what was described as famine in Thessaly and the Peloponnese. The situation was only resolved in June 1917 when King Constantine was forced to abdicate in favour of his son. Venizelos formed a government, and Greece entered the war on the allied side.

In other words, 'siege' warfare at sea was far easier to impose in the eastern Mediterranean than it was in the Atlantic approaches. Effectively freed from the constraint of American objections, the Entente was much less circumspect in its handling of neutrals than in the North Sea. In 1916 Britain and France proposed that the Mediterranean be declared a war zone, but Italy objected, principally because of its dependence on neutral tonnage to maintain its trade and its fear that freight rates would soar.[63] Neutral opinion in the Mediterranean – in 1916 essentially that of Spain and Greece – was a secondary factor, and by the end of the war not a single neutral power both had access to the Mediterranean and a common frontier with the Central Powers. The sea was itself closed at Gibraltar and at the Suez Canal, both held by the British. As the Italians pointed out, a supercargo at each could control neutral traffic at the points of entry.

The Turks twice attacked the canal from the Sinai desert but failed. They could at least dispute control of the Black Sea at the war's outset, but they lost it by the end of 1915 as the Russians brought new warships into service.[64] The poverty of Turkey's inland transport network,

[62] Compton Mackenzie, *Greek Memories* (London: Chatto and Windus, 1939), 223–4; for what follows I have drawn on a paper given by Vlasis Vlasidis on feeding the armies in Macedonia, presented at the conference on 'The Macedonian Front 1915–1918: Politics, Society and Culture in Time of War', at the Aristotle University, Thessaloniki, 10–13 May 2018.

[63] Paul G. Halpern, *The Naval War in the Mediterranean 1914–1918* (London: Allen and Unwin, 1987), 235, 242.

[64] See George Nekrasov, *North of Gallipoli: The Black Sea Fleet at War, 1914–1917* (Boulder, CO: East European Monographs, 1992).

and particularly the incomplete state of its railways, made it far more dependent on coastal trade for domestic commerce than was the case for its allies with their internal waterways and railway links. Here was an agricultural economy robbed of labour and draught animals by mobilisation, and so increasingly unable to generate a marketable surplus or to move its produce to its four fronts – the Dardanelles, the Caucasus, Mesopotamia and Syria – located at four different points of the compass, or to its principal city, Istanbul. The allied invasion of Gallipoli in 1915 may have failed but it cut any maritime links between the capital and the Levant by way of the eastern Mediterranean. Palestine was afflicted by drought for the three years preceding the war, and then in the summer of 1915 locusts attacked the harvest. By the end of 1915 famine prevailed. It is estimated that up to half a million people, or an eighth of the population of Ottoman Syria, died of hunger by the end of 1918. Reports of men committing suicide because they could not provide for their families and of mothers eating their own dead children spread across Lebanon. In Istanbul a telegraph operator with a large family complained that, 'We are literally starving ... I have had to sell everything we had merely to keep my family and myself alive.'[65] The government tried to contain prices in order to ensure that food was affordable, but peasants responded by withholding their produce from the market. The government's response – to put the army in charge of grain distribution – showed how directly the use of hunger as a weapon could diminish military effectiveness on the battlefield.[66]

The Ottoman people blamed the famine on the government and the government blamed the allied blockade. Fearing an amphibious invasion in March 1915, Cemal Pasha, the military governor of Syria, ordered the movement of supplies to the interior and the destruction of the grain stocks that remained in storage on the coast. His measures prompted a mass migration into the interior, but not on a sufficient scale to avoid appalling conditions in Beirut.[67] Refugees compounded the problems. Again, the government was complicit: the policies of the Young Turks drove the Armenians out of eastern Anatolia into the Levant. In 1916 Enver Pasha, the minister of war, used the argument of military necessity to plead for humanitarian assistance from the Vatican, saying that

[65] Leila Tarazi Fawaz, *A Land of Aching Hearts: The Middle East in the Great War* (Cambridge, MA: Harvard University Press, 2014), 89–110, 114–15; Irfan Orga, *Portrait of a Turkish Family* (first published 1950; London: Eland, 2011), 155, 166, 170.

[66] Yiğit Akin, *When the War Came Home: The Ottomans' Great War and the Devastation of an Empire* (Stanford, CA: Stanford University Press, 2018), 129–30, 135–6.

[67] Fawaz, *A Land of Aching Hearts*, 89, 101–6.

the army's supply needs had to be prioritised over that of the Ottoman empire's own civilian population.[68]

Italy's entry to the war effectively ended any worries about the implementation of blockade against Austria-Hungary from the south. Although the French navy, which exercised primary responsibility for the Mediterranean at the war's outset, could not mount a close blockade of the Habsburg Empire's principal commercial port, Trieste, it was able to bottle up the Adriatic at the straits of Otranto, so also closing off the naval bases at Pola and Cattaro. Bulgaria entered the war on the side of the Central Powers not least because it was less susceptible to maritime pressure from the Entente, but its limited access to the Aegean and to the Black Sea meant it could not escape the constraints to which its allies in the region were also subject, especially after the Entente occupation of Salonika in autumn 1915. The Central Powers were therefore 'besieged' even more effectively from the south than from the west.

By 1917 their hopes for escape from the stranglehold of the blockade lay with exaggerated anticipations of what could be reaped from Russia's collapse. By 1918 all four of the Central Powers looked to the Black Sea as a route by which to bring in grain from Ukraine and to open routes to the oilfields of Baku. As they scrabbled over the spoils, they fell out with each other. From the start of the war Austria-Hungary had, like Germany, portrayed the Entente's strategy as one of starvation. If that had been the case, it should not have been worried, because before the war the Habsburg Empire was effectively self-sufficient in food. At its outset the allied blockade caused shortages of cotton and war metals, not of food. When shortages nonetheless took hold, the blockade did indeed prevent imports from filling the gap, but the Austrians correctly realised that the immediate culprit was not so much Britain as their fellow subjects, the Hungarians, who hoarded grain at their expense.[69] The government's response was not to make a long-term plan, but 'to behave like a man who, in the face of a sudden flood mounting on all sides, struggles for his life by jumping from one spot of dry ground to another'.[70]

In spring 1918 Austria hoped that its problems would be eased by imports from Romania and Russia, given that both were now defeated, but the best deal they could negotiate with the Germans in the division

[68] Eugene Rogan, *The Fall of the Ottomans: The Great War in the Middle East* (New York, NY: Basic Books, 2015), 290–1.

[69] Maureen Healy, *Vienna and the Fall of the Habsburg Empire: Total War and Everyday Life in World War I* (Cambridge: Cambridge University Press, 2004), 36–7, 47–53.

[70] Heller, 'Government Price Fixing and Rationing in Austria', 4, 24.

of the spoils left them dissatisfied.[71] The Bulgarians were even more disgruntled by German behaviour. By 1918 their hopes of agricultural self-sufficiency fed by the Balkan Wars had been undermined through the loss of manpower and of draught animals sent to the front. To their rear the Germans were taking food for their own troops and for dispatch back to Germany. The Bulgarians hoped that, under the terms of the treaty of Bucharest imposed on Romania in May 1918, they would get compensation in the form of the grain-rich Dobrudja, but they did not: it was put under joint Austro-Bulgarian-German administration. 'The officers and men lost faith in the loyalty of our allies, the Germans', one Bulgarian officer later wrote.[72] At the end of September 1918 his army was the first to surrender. As the alliance of the Central Powers fragmented, the effect of food shortages was a vital component in the breakdown of mutual trust.

Conclusion

By 1918 the success of the blockade was measured by the revolutions in the Hohenzollern and Habsburg empires. During the war the allied powers had increasingly taken signs of domestic dissent and evidence of food shortages as inducements to go further. On 2 February 1915, when the United States requested that Britain ease the pressures on civilian food consumption in Germany, Hankey told the prime minister that its proposal showed that the blockade was working and should therefore be intensified (as it was in March).[73] He believed that the Germans could be starved into surrender.

They were not.[74] In 1937 the British official historian cast doubt – moral as well as strategic – on the value of 'hunger' war. Bell's view was that the operations of the Germans in the field had not been affected by the blockade.[75] He was right: those who were weak and vulnerable, too old or too young for military service, suffered precisely because they were of no military or economic value.[76] In other words the blockade,

[71] Ottokar Landwehr, *Hunger. Die Erschöpfungsjahre der Mittelmächte 1917–18* (Vienna: Amalthea, 1931), 159–63.

[72] Lieutenant-Colonel Nédelf, *Les operations en Macédoine. L'épopée de Doïran 1915–1918*, trans. by Commandant Goetzmann (Sofia: Imprimerie Armeyski Voeno-Isdatelski Fond, 1927), 212, 78–9.

[73] Stephen Roskill, *Hankey: Man of Secrets*, 3 vols (London: Collins, 1970–4), 1, 157–8, 180, 184.

[74] A point argued in full in Offer, *The First World War*.

[75] Bell, *A History of the Blockade of Germany*, 673.

[76] Anne Roerkohl, *Hungerblockade und Heimatfront. Die kommunale Lebensmittelversorgung in Westfalen während des Ersten Weltkrieges* (Stuttgart: Franz Steiner, 1991), 147, 297.

because it focused on food supplies, failed to respect the principle of non-combatant immunity, towards which so much of the effort of international law had been bent before 1914. However, that argument itself confuses a central controversy surrounding the blockade: whether food was conditional or absolute contraband, with the issue of where the blockade had greatest effect. Self-evidently the legal and ethical defence for economic war was most robust in relation to absolute contraband, munitions of war and the materials for their manufacture. The Central Powers did not seek terms in autumn 1918 because they had exhausted their stocks of bullets and shells, and for that reason we can too easily neglect the effects that the blockade had on their supply, not least in their prioritisation in terms of production with reciprocal and indirectly deleterious effects elsewhere. The blockade was not in the first instance a war on food, although as the war progressed that increasingly became its principal target. As a result, it has been made to carry responsibility for food shortages to which other factors contributed.[77]

The First World War required the mobilisation of all the resources of the nation, in a phenomenon which later generations would call 'total war'. As a result, distinctions between munitions and food, and between combatant and non-combatant, were in a very real sense artificial. Citizen armies by 1918 were aware that those at home were going hungry. Their motivation was diminished if the families to which they hoped to return on the war's conclusion were in danger of starvation or of disease brought on by malnutrition. To weigh the economic war against military operations in determining the overall outcome is therefore to create a false antithesis: they were not choices but two aspects of a many-sided war which interacted with each other.[78] Even the allied generalissimo and victor on the western front in 1918, Ferdinand Foch, is said to have credited the blockade with half the responsibility for the outcome of the war.[79]

An armistice is a temporary pause in the fighting, which might or might not lead to a peace settlement. That signed with Germany on 11 November 1918 was binding for 36 days in the first instance, although provision was made for its renewal. All five agreements reached with the Central Powers between 29 September 1918 and 13 November

[77] Alexander B. Downes, *Targeting Civilians in War* (Ithaca, NY: Cornell University Press, 2008); Paul C. Vincent, *The Politics of Hunger: The Allied Blockade of Germany 1915–1919* (Athens, OH: Ohio University Press, 1985).

[78] Basil Liddell Hart, *A History of the World War, 1914–1918* (London: Faber, 1934), 587–8, made the case for the blockade; Paul Kennedy, *The Rise and Fall of British Naval Mastery* (London: Macmillan, 1983) attacked it.

[79] Hull, *A Scrap of Paper*, 170.

1918 were overwhelmingly military arrangements, designed to strip the enemy of the capacity to resume fighting and to give the allies the maximum strategic freedom of movement in the war's aftermath. Neither the Bulgarian nor Ottoman terms made any reference to the blockade. According to the British official historian, economic warfare in the Mediterranean had been established by 'regular blockades of the enemy countries' and the fact that they were not mentioned meant that they simply continued. Economic warfare in the North Sea, by contrast, had been waged only by agreements with the border neutrals, and so blockade was specifically mentioned in the armistice agreements with Austria-Hungary and Germany, with the merchant ships of both remaining liable to capture.[80]

In the eyes of the vanquished, therefore, hostilities had only ceased in respect of their armed forces; their societies, and especially their non-combatants, remained under attack. Indeed, the blockade could now be waged with a ferocity that was unprecedented, as both the Baltic and the northern Adriatic were stripped of their defences, and the capacity to import overland was shattered by the surrender of railway rolling stock. In early 1919 the hunger it caused fractured the carapace of allied unity. The Americans wanted to lift the blockade; their European partners did not, albeit each for differing reasons. When the armistice terms of 11 November were renewed on 16 January 1919, the Germans had not delivered their allocated quota of railway rolling stock and they were ordered instead to provide agricultural machinery. Now there could be no doubt: hunger was being used as a weapon.

The period 1918–19 was when the starvation aspects of the blockade became firmly etched in the public consciousness of Germany and Austria, and so shaped their post-war memories. We shall never know how many people in the First World War died as a result of starvation and, even if we did, we would still not be able to calculate whether their deaths were attributable to the deliberate action of the enemy, as opposed to the random workings of nature or the poor administration of governments. Not even the Germans, who had the greatest motivation to calculate their losses, could agree on a figure. On 18 December 1918 they put excess civilian mortality due to the blockade at 762,796. In 1920 Arthur Dix calculated that live births had fallen by 4 million over the course of the war, a quarter of which the government health office attributed to the blockade. Dix combined the increase in death rates and the fall in the birth rate to produce a loss of nearly six million 'due to undernourishment'. These figures have come down over the years,

[80] Bell, *A History of the Blockade of Germany*, 709.

with Jay Winter suggesting 300,000 in 1988.[81] For the other blockaded powers we do not even have estimates.

Roughly 9 million soldiers and sailors died in the war, some of them no doubt as a result of starvation, but they were the unlucky ones: normally states gave their soldiers priority in the allocation of food. Civilians were not so privileged. We do not know how many non-combatants died as a result of the war, not least because there are no established criteria for determining which causes should be treated as war-related, beyond the obvious one of direct enemy action. As a result, we have no quantitative basis for assessing the effectiveness of hunger as a weapon of war between 1914 and 1918, let alone up until 1923, when the last peace treaty was signed. In its absence, we fall back on more subjective, and hence more open-ended, arguments to explain the role of hunger in the outcome of the war.

[81] Hull, *A Scrap of Paper*, 169; Arthur Dix, *Wirtschaftskrieg und Kriegswirtschaft. Zur Geschichte des deutschen Zusammenbruchs* (Berlin: Mittler, 1920), 294.

3 The Politics of Food
State Reactions

Francesco Frizzera

Introduction

In 1914, Europe's politicians could rely on a long tradition of practicing food rationing and imposing price ceilings in the event of war. This practice was deep rooted in both medieval and modern history.[1] Even at the time of the Franco-Prussian war (1870–71), it had been necessary to set up a system of rationing during the Siege of Paris, which lasted four months, thereby creating a precedent that was close in time and relevant in terms of the size of the population to be fed.[2] Nevertheless, European military planners failed to recognize the importance of this historical precedent. For economic theorists and decision makers, 'rationing continued to be viewed as an emergency measure for provisioning urban areas coping with local shortages in essential goods'.[3]

The outbreak of the war destroyed the fragile equilibrium regulating the complex network of trade in foodstuffs that guaranteed Europe subsistence, setting new challenges for European politicians and state officials. The First World War, with its static and impermeable fronts and limits to naval and transoceanic trade, reversed the assumptions underlying the state non-intervention model, which was widespread among the ruling classes of the European continent. The war prompted all European countries to address the problem of sourcing and rationing foodstuffs. The usual import channels were lacking. Domestic agriculture, already scarcely sufficient, saw its performance gradually decline, given the inability to maintain intensive cultivation systems (lack of fertilizers, intensive work force and machinery). Enemy occupation deprived

[1] G. Alfani and M. Rizzo, 'Politiche annonarie, provvedimenti demografici e capitale umano nelle città assediate dell'Europa moderna', in G. Alfani and M. Rizzo, eds., *Nella morsa della guerra. Assedi, occupazioni militari e saccheggi in età preindustriale* (Milan: Franco Angeli, 2013), 15–46.

[2] M. Howard, *The Franco-Prussian War: The German Invasion of France, 1870–1871* (London: Routledge, 1990), 220–4.

[3] D. Southerton, *Encyclopedia of Consumer Culture* (London: SAGE Publications, 2011), vol. I, 1198.

countries of their most fertile – or most agriculturally productive – regions (northern departments in France; Galicia in Austria; East Prussia in Germany; Ukraine in Russia). And, last but not least, the authorities responsible for managing food supplies had not considered prior to the war the eventuality of having to reorganize their food procurement systems.[4] State officials in most cases envisioned a short war,[5] and moreover it was believed that a slight contraction in consumption (which had grown significantly since the 1870s) would not starve the population.[6]

The outbreak of the war interrupted transnational trade patterns and affected long-term economic practices. The decision makers had to identify new solutions to counteract food shortages and these solutions in many cases envisaged direct involvement of the State.[7] There was only marginal pre-existing know-how on which these measures could be based. Despite a gradual tendency towards state intervention in the economy at the end of the nineteenth century,[8] before the First World War liberal economists considered the idea of establishing state monopolies or regulated economic systems unrealistic (and unrealizable) hypotheses, almost as if they were a legacy of a primitive economic conception.[9]

In order to address the new food crisis brought about by the war, decision makers across Europe faced many new challenges, which were based on needs and not according to an organic plan.[10] The solutions, at least in theory, could vary from country to country, according to the extent to which there was dependence on foreign trade, the ability of the various agricultural economies to cope with shortages of certain products and their political economies. Since the quantity of food

[4] G. Hardach, *The First World War, 1914–1918* (Berkeley: University of California Press, 1981), 111; A. Skalweit, *Die deutsche Kriegsernährungswirtschaft* (Stuttgart: Deutsche Verlags Anstalt, 1927), 146.

[5] J. Leonhard, *Die Büchse der Pandora: Geschichte des Ersten Weltkrieges* (Munich: C.H. Beck, 2014), 255.

[6] A. Offer, *The First World War: An Agrarian Interpretation* (Oxford: Clarendon Press, 1991), 25; A. Seidl, *Deutsche Agrargeschichte* (Frankfurt am Main: DLG-Verlag, 2013), 215–17; P. Eltzbacher, *Die deutsche Volksernährung und der englische Aushungerungsplan: Eine Denkschrift* (Berlin: Springer-Verlag, 1914), 62.

[7] I. T. Berend, *An Economic History of Twentieth-Century Europe: Economic Regimes from Laissez-Faire to Globalization* (Cambridge: Cambridge University Press, 2016), 11–12. K. Burk, ed., *War and the State: The Transformation of British Government, 1914–1919* (London: Routledge, 2014).

[8] T. Davis and E. Spilman, 'Proto-Economic Nationalism in the Early Nineteenth Century', in H. Schulz and E. Kubo, eds., *History and Culture of Economic Nationalism in East-Central Europe* (Berlin: Berliner Wissenschafts-Verlag, 2006), 89–108; Berend, *An Economic History*, 46–7.

[9] Berend, *An Economic History*, 55–8.

[10] Skalweit, *Kriegsernährungswirtschaft*, 146.

available was less than the requirement, new purchasing systems were needed to snatch up the few remaining goods; hence, it first of all had to be decided whether to leave the food supply to the free market in line with prevailing economic thought, or introduce controlled economies. Furthermore, the scarcity of food resulted in widening the gap between supply and demand, which inevitably triggered spiralling inflation. As a result, authorities across Europe had to decide whether containing inflation was a priority or, on the contrary, whether to relieve food shortages by organizing rationing and controlling food distribution. These were two sides of the same coin, but the solutions adopted to limit one problem tended to exacerbate the other. Finally, in the attempt to tackle the food shortages, they had to decide whether to focus first on the control and expansion of imports or on encouraging self-sufficiency. When the decision was made to support domestic production, this presented two different solutions: to encourage greater production or enforce more diverse production. In many cases, countries responded to losses in food supply by requisitioning foodstuffs in lands under their occupation as a rough and ready mean to overcome food shortages.

By devising innovative solutions to these questions, the decision makers established new models – though not always coherent – for state intervention in the economy. This chapter will analyse the ways in which state authorities in Europe, regardless of whether their countries were belligerent or neutral, created long-term expertise and radical solutions to the absence of food. This development follows similar patterns across Europe, partly due to reactions to analogous problems, partly due to the path dependancy resulting from the first measures taken in many countries. In a broad sense, it was the result of the expansion of the sphere of competence of public authorities. The purpose of this chapter is to show how a transfer of experience, which often went beyond the war's boundaries, existed in Europe. One of the key aspects of this chapter concerns therefore the analysis of the methods and timing through which rationing and state intervention were devised and implemented in individual countries, with the aim of proposing a comparative analysis on a transnational scale.

These measures to control food markets and distribution were believed to be temporary and were the result of economic distortions brought about by the conflict. When the First World War ended, however, the distortions did not disappear: indeed, some were definitely aggravated through direct intervention by the State. Moreover, the world market itself underwent decisive changes and the centres of gravity of production and credit shifted. It follows that armistice and the end of the War did not coincide with the end of controlled economies. This chapter concludes with analyses of the gradual back-flow of measures to control the production, distribution and purchase of foodstuffs, demonstrating how slow and reluctant state authorities were to abandon these instruments of control.

Creating a Controlled Economy

Pressured by the need to guarantee sufficient food supplies for their populations within a context of shortages, many European governments decided as a first step to gradually incorporate control of imports and exports. There were many reasons for this choice. First, it was the only area in which decision makers could rely on previous experience. Prior to then, during and in the aftermath of the Great European Depression in the late nineteenth century (1873–96), many states on the continent had resorted to restrictions on exports or the creation of trade barriers.[11] In 1879 Germany had applied moderate tariffs on both agricultural and industrial products, introducing from 1902 onwards a new high level of protection; Italy, Switzerland and France respectively had introduced effective protection in 1887, 1884 (and then 1906) and 1892 (which then increased in 1910). The same had happened in Russia.[12] The only exceptions were Britain, Holland and Denmark, which had continued to operate free market economies.[13] As a result, it was generally accepted that the State could broaden its competences in this area.

Furthermore, it was believed that if the State could prove itself capable of importing all the necessary food, it would be possible to leave the distribution mechanisms unchanged. In this way, state intervention would be limited and in line with traditional notions of the limits of government competences in the economic field. Finally, the application of export restrictions and lower duties on imports could be brought into force immediately. The idea – though not even considered initially – of focusing internal production on the foodstuffs in short supply instead required long timescales, skills and had a high political cost. As the general opinion was that it was going to be a short war, authorities opted to rely on previous long-term practices.

[11] N. P. Petersson, 'Das Kaiserreich in Prozessen ökonomischer Globalisierung', in S. Conrad and J. Osterhammel, eds., *Das Kaiserreich transnational. Deutschland in der Welt 1871–1914* (Göttingen: Vandenhoeck & Ruprecht, 2004), 49–67; R. Boch, *Staat und Wirtschaft im 19. Jahrhundert* (Munich: Oldenbourg, 2004), 39; C. Torp, *Die Herausforderung der Globalisierung: Wirtschaft und Politik in Deutschland 1860–1914* (Göttingen: Vandenhoeck & Ruprecht, 2005).

[12] Berend, *An Economic History*, 46–7.

[13] M. Graff, A. G. Kenwood and A. L. Lougheed, *Growth of the International Economy, 1820–2015* (London: Routledge, 2014), 83–5.

Control of Imports

The differences between individual countries' decisions to resort to direct control of food imports lay simply in timing. Those countries who found themselves in difficulty because they were highly dependent on foreign trade acted very quickly. Those that had stocks decided only later to block exports or organize a government-controlled import system. Almost all the European states, however, followed a similar pattern: by mid 1915 nearly all belligerent and neutral countries had applied stringent rules to foreign trade, which provided for direct state intervention. Even the few states that attempted to remain neutral and to assert their right to trade with the belligerent countries, like Sweden, had to forcibly adapt to the new situation. In this case, the Allies stopped a large percentage of Sweden's trade. This, however, not only affected Sweden's exports to Germany, but also from 1916 caused a severe shortage of food in Sweden.[14]

In Germany, the state began to regulate foreign trade early on. The importation of goods in short supply was promoted whilst other goods were banned from being exported. In order to control international trade towards Germany, the *Reichseinkaufsgesellschaft* (Federal Purchasing Company) was founded on 3 August 1914.[15] In December 1914 it was renamed *Zentraleinkaufsgesellschaft* (ZEG, Central Purchasing Company) with the aim of centralizing foreign trade into one organization. The ZEG was financed by the German *Reich*, individual German states and some large companies, like the the Hamburg Amerika Linie:[16] the goal was to achieve low-cost cumulative purchases in neutral countries and limit the competition of individual buyers.[17] Even in the limited field of action left to German foreign trade because of the Allied blockade (see Chapter 2), the ZEG achieved significant results: in 1916 it imported 1,684,000 tons of food, which fell to 412,000 in 1918.[18]

[14] M. Cox, *Hunger in War and Peace* (New York, NY: Oxford University Press, 2019); S. Koblik, *Sweden. The Neutral Victor. Sweden and the Western Powers 1917–1918. A Study of Anglo-American-Swedish Relations* (Stockholm: Läromedelsförlagen, 1972), 15–64.

[15] O. Barber, *Einrichtung Und Aufgaben Der Zentral-Einkaufsgesellschaft* (Berlin: Stellvertretendes Generalkommando VI. Armeekorps, 1917).

[16] Skalweit, *Kriegsernährungswirtschaft*, 22.

[17] G. Corni and F. Frizzera, 'Die Diskussion um die „Zwangswirtschaft“ während des Ersten Weltkrieges und in der Nachkriegszeit', *Journal for Agricultural History and Sociology – Zeitschrift für Agrargeschichte und Agrarsoziologie* 66:1 (2018), 23–5; G. Corni and F. Frizzera, 'Erster Teil: Vom Ersten Weltkrieg bis zum Ende der Weimarer Republik', in H. Möller et al., eds., *Agrarpolitik im 20. Jahrhundert: Das Bundesministerium für Ernährung und Landwirtschaft und seine Vorgänger* (Berlin: De Gruyter Oldenbourg, 2020), 13–19.

[18] Skalweit, *Kriegsernährungswirtschaft*, 24–5; S. Kruizinga, *Overlegeconomie in oorlogstijd. De Nederlandsche Overzee Trustmaatschappij en de Eerste Wereldoorlog* (Zutphen: Walburg Pers, 2012), 113–21.

This development, whereby the State acted as the controller of imports, was not specific to Germany, which was quickly forced to ration the supply of foodstuffs from abroad due to the Blockade. The same strategy was adopted by all states for products that were in short supply. Even Italy, which was still a neutral country, followed the same pattern. In August 1914 the exportation of grain was banned and import duties were lowered. The closure of the Dardanelles made it impossible to import 14 million tons of wheat from Russia and Romania, which had secured Italy's food balance before the war. In January 1915, the *Ufficio Temporaneo Approvvigionamento Grano* (UTAG, Temporary Grain Supply Office) was created, through which the State managed the purchase, transportation and centralized distribution of foodstuffs from abroad. Finally, after Italy entered the war, the Italian government agreed with France and Britain (January 1916) to create a single inter-allied body, the Joint Committee, to carry out this task on a transnational scale.[19]

The same development was evident in occupied countries such as Belgium that had been net importers of wheat prior to the war. The *Comité National de Secours et d'Alimentation* (CNSA) was created in Belgium in September 1914 as a network through which aid brought in by the international Commission for Relief in Belgium (CRB) could be distributed within the national territory since Belgium relied on supplies of imports for almost three-quarters of all food consumed.[20]

This trend to control foreign trade from the very beginning of the conflict also characterized states that were known for their a priori support of a laissez faire dogma or those that possessed a food surplus. From August 1914 onwards Britain created independent state purchasing committees, the best known of which was the *Commission Internationale de Ravitaillement* (International Commission for the Purchase of Food Supplies).[21] This was the result of an agreement with the French government, and its object was to coordinate the purchase of food supplies and military and naval equipment of the two governments, thereby preventing damaging competition in the same markets and a consequential

[19] M. C. Dentoni, *Annona e consenso in Italia, 1914–1919* (Milan: Franco Angeli, 1995), 12–25.

[20] H. Pirenne, *La Belgique et la Guerre Mondiale* (Paris: Presses Universitaires de France, 1928), 134–47; O. von der Lancken, M. Amara and H. Roland, *Gouverner en Belgique occupée: Oscar von der Lancken-Wakenitz, rapports d'activité 1915–1918* (Brussels: Peter Lang, 2004), 32–3; S. De Schaepdrijver, *La Belgique et la Première Guerre mondiale* (Brussels: Peter Lang, 2004).

[21] M. Barnett, *British Food Policy during the First World War* (London: Routledge, 2014), 23–5; A. Salter, *Allied Shipping Control: An Experiment in International Administration* (Oxford: Clarendon Press, 1921); E. Clémentel et al., *La France et la politique économique interalliée* (Paris: Les Presses universitaires de France, 1928), 60.

inflation of prices. This was followed in November by the creation of the Royal Commission on Sugar Supplies, in March 1915 by a Ban of Export and in October 1916 by the Royal Commission on Wheat Supplies.[22] Therefore,

> although 'Business As Usual' remained the ideal, the Liberal government had diverged significantly from peacetime modes of official practice by the spring of 1915. They had taken a big step on the road to control of the food supply by becoming partially or totally responsible for the acquisition of three important imported foodstuffs – wheat, meat and sugar. This has provided a nucleus of administration that was to feed the future control mechanism.[23]

The same pattern could also be identified in other countries, both belligerent and neutral: in September 1914 the Swiss government established the Federal Cereal Supply Office.[24] In Austria-Hungary, which on paper was self-sufficient, a ban on exports and the suspension of protectionist duties were imposed by August 1914, followed in October 1915 by the creation of a central office for the importation of foodstuffs and in December 1915 by a bilateral agreement with Romania.[25] Also the Netherlands, which like Britain had a long tradition of free trade, on 26 August 1914 established the State Bureau for the Distribution of Grain and Flour, which would supply the Dutch populace with bread partially made from subsidized imported grain from US and British markets.[26] Finally, Russia, a traditional grain exporter, also ordered an embargo on the exportation of food from the Western Provinces in November 1914, and in November 1915 it created a Special Council for Food Supply.[27]

These actions represented perhaps a first step in the ability of states to intervene in their economies. The measures succeeded in alleviating shortages, but not in solving the problem. The foodstuffs purchased abroad during the war cost far more than those produced on

[22] Hardach, *First World War*, 123–4; Barnett, *British Food Policy*, 41.

[23] Barnett, *British Food Policy*, 44.

[24] A. Bellwald-Roten and M. Jorio, 'Wirtschaftliche Landesversorgung', *Historisches Lexikon Schweiz*, online ed., 2015 [www.hls-dhs-dss.ch/textes/d/D42887.php, accessed 26 April 2023].

[25] H. Loewenfeld-Russ, *Die Regelung Der Volksernährung Im Kriege* (Vienna: Hölder Pichler Tempsky, 1926), 48–55.

[26] Nota betreffende de werkzaamheden van het Rijksbureau voor de Distributie van Graan en Meel, loopende tot 1 Juli 1918 (Den Haag: Departement van landbouw, nijverheid en handel, 1918), 4–7. M. Frey, 'Bullying the Neutrals: The Case of the Netherland', in S. Förster and R. Chickering, eds., *Great War, Total War: Combat and Mobilisation on the Western Front, 1914–1918* (Cambridge: Cambridge University Press, 2000), 230–1.

[27] P. Gatrell, *Russia's First World War: A Social and Economic History* (London: Pearson, 2005), 154–69.

the domestic market: insurance costs, which sky-rocked with the added risks of death by submarine attack, increased transport fees in a world of limited oceanic tonnage and high demand caused these goods to command very high prices if resold on the domestic market. Moreover, these purchases were not always sufficient to meet requirements. Germany imported 9,017,919 tons of foodstuffs in 1913,[28] whilst in the year in which ZEG's operations reached their highest level (1916) it imported 1,684,000 tons.[29] Britain also recorded negative performances: in 1913 it imported 6,135,000 tons of wheat and flour while in 1918 it imported 4,632,000 tons; data for dairy products and sugar were even worse.[30] An obvious gap was therefore created between supply and demand, which led to distortions of the market.

Centralization of the Market

The gap between supply and demand led governments to further extend their field of action, resulting in more incisive and long-term outcomes. In fact, many governments decided to impose a total monopoly on purchases from abroad and on the resale of those goods on the internal market to prevent price differences between domestic and imported products of the same category. This enabled them to implicitly influence price dynamics, with the aim of avoiding inflation. The differences between individual policies lay in the incisiveness and timing of these measures, but the sequence of actions carried out was similar everywhere.

In this case once again Germany provides the best example of overall development.[31] The ZEG quickly became a monopolistic body for the importation and marketing of foreign goods, which were sent to the individual *Kommunalverbände* (associations of municipalities) according to their requirements. The management of purchases and wholesale trade was organized as follows: a *Kriegsstelle* (Central Coordination Office) was created for each category of goods. The Empire was divided into about 1,100 *Kommunalverbände* and those producing an agricultural surplus had to notify the competent *Kriegsstelle*, which organized the redistribution of the surplus produce to the non-self-sufficient *Kommunalverbände*. If agricultural produce available on the domestic market was not sufficient to cover needs, the shipment of foodstuffs to the *Kommunalverbände* was supplemented with food purchases from

[28] Eltzbacher, *Deutsche Volksernährung*, 35.
[29] Skalweit, *Kriegsernährungswirtschaft*, 25.
[30] W. B. Henry, *British Food Control* (London: Milford, 1928), 135.
[31] Corni and Frizzera, 'Erster Teil', 16–23.

abroad (which was the ZEG's duty). In this way, the *Kriegsstellen* eliminated the entire market and distribution mechanism at the import and wholesale level.[32]

Italy followed the same path, though for different reasons. Here an attempt was made initially to leave the importation and marketing of wheat in the hands of private entrepreneurs. Despite numerous transport and credit facilities created by government decree, the new trusts of companies were unable to take on this task. The government was forced to create UTAG (the equivalent of the ZEG), taking over responsibility for imports; finally, UTAG distributed the purchased grain to the association of municipalities. The freedom to trade continued at the retail distribution level.[33]

Even in Britain, bastion of classic-liberal economic thought, the pattern was not dissimilar. Any differences lay in the desire to keep the supply chain and retail trade alive, as happened in many neutral countries such as the Netherlands. Here too the large purchases of food imported from abroad (which accounted for the majority of the total) were managed by the army or the government. This tendency is evident in the case of sugar, the first commodity to be monopolized in Britain during the war. The British government assumed that 'State control of food does not need to produce a problem of distribution'. In this case, 'if the State is prepared to meet all the demands ... it has nothing to decide what agents will be and what commission they will receive'. This line of action proved to be adequate for wheat, since it was possible until 1916 'to meet its demands for human consumption in the form of bread or flour'. However, its limits became apparent in the case of sugar: here soon 'demand began to outrun supplies'.[34] Beveridge explains clearly how the Sugar Commission acted in this regard:

> Having no other principle on which to act, and feeling a natural desire to disturb the existing channels of trade as little as possible, the Commission resorted inevitably to the principle of the 'datum period'; that is to say, in 1916 and thereafter, it limited the issue of sugar to each wholesaler to a percentage of the amount handled by that wholesaler in 1915, and met increasing stringency of supplies by decreasing this percentage. It required the first-hand wholesalers to pass on the supplies – to smaller wholesalers or retailers or manufacturers – on the same principle.[35]

[32] K. P. Müller, *Politik Und Gesellschaft Im Krieg. Der Legitimitaetsverlust Des Badischen Staates 1914–1918* (Stuttgart: Kohlhammer, 1988), 316–81; Skalweit, *Kriegsernährungswirtschaft*, 146–79.

[33] Dentoni, *Annona*, 19.

[34] William H. Beverdige, *British Food Control* (London: Oxford University Press, 1928), 183.

[35] Beveridge, *British Food Control*, 184.

Beveridge points out that this 'rough and ready' system adopted for sugar was then expanded to other commodities: 'almost all important foods, except bread-stuffs, passed through this stage'.[36] Intervention here was less pervasive than in other states, because it did not affect the retail market for some time. However, even here the state broadened its competences in the areas where there was a shortage (sugar, for instance), following the same pattern already seen in Germany and Italy.

By creating state bodies that took over the distribution of foodstuffs, the second step towards controlling the food economy was accomplished: these bodies were then able to extend their competences in the collection and distribution of internal production. This pattern was not, however, a prerogative of Germany, Italy or Britain. Even in neutral or occupied countries the development was similar, both in terms of timing and the types of offices created.

Price Ceilings

It was possible to limit state intervention to a monopoly over imports and wholesale distribution, at least until food could be distributed in sufficient quantities to meet demand. This mechanism, however, is no longer sufficient to maintain equilibrium when a shortage is recorded, because such a situation will trigger inflation. As a consequence, several governments decided to impose price ceilings; that is, a government-imposed price control to protect consumers from conditions that could make commodities prohibitively expensive. This was the first step towards a wartime 'moral economy':[37] all citizens had to contribute equally to the war effort and share the same food-related privations.

By setting maximum prices, we notice the tendency of authorities to proceed step by step, being afraid of intruding with force into the mechanisms regulating the market. This action, based on attempts that proved at times to be clumsy, shows clearly how from this moment onwards decision makers found themselves on completely unexplored territory, unable to rely on previous experience. The inconsistency of these policies led to distortion of the market of worrying proportions: in many cases the measures taken to address regional shortages tended to exacerbate the general food crisis rather than solve it, causing path dependency.

Again, the German case stands as an example, both of the gradual introduction of price controls and of the limits of this policy, which

[36] Beveridge, *British Food Control*, 184.

[37] D. R. Stabile and A. F. Kozak, *Markets, Planning and the Moral Economy: Business Cycles in the Progressive Era and New Deal* (Cheltenham: Edward Elgar Publishing, 2012), 74–5.

consequently led to a controlled economy. According to Jens Flemming, the government wanted to 'keep the food that was vital to the broader strata of the population as cheap as possible under given conditions and without affecting production'.[38] In order to achieve this goal, a law was passed on 4 August 1914 which allowed for the introduction of price regulation measures. The law was to be applied by the individual federal states. As a result, 'there were significant regional distortions, with the effect that goods migrated to markets that promised maximum profit'.[39] The system was revised several times and extended to other products in the following months, before it was finally coupled to central price ranges specified by the government.[40] However, as a result of this measure, peasants were reluctant to market products with a limited profit margin, forcing the government to ration some food, starting with bread, grain and flour.[41] In fact, in November 1914 the government set federal maximum prices for grain to be applied to purchases from producers.[42] These consequently directed production towards more profitable commodities, causing additional shortages.

In fact, setting maximum prices at the local level would only have provided a rough-and-ready solution, without any prospect of long-term success. In Germany it was often recorded that 'the goods pass through several hands, often 6–7, before they reach the consumer'.[43] This happened despite the publication of regulations prohibiting price increases (23 June 1915).[44] The attempts of local authorities to limit the number of authorized dealers,[45] the measures to promote control of trade by the local police[46] and the imposition of measures which prescribed that wholesalers had to sell goods only to selected sellers ended in a fiasco.[47] The goods moved in accordance with market laws to where prices were highest.[48]

38 J. Flemming, *Landwirtschaftliche Interessen Und Demokratie. Ländliche Gesellschaft, Agrarverbände Und Staat 1890–1925* (Bonn: Verlag Neue Gesellschaft, 1978), 98.

39 Flemming, *Landwirtschaftliche Interessen*, 98.

40 Deutsches RGBl, 1914, p. 528, 19 December 1914.

41 Flemming, *Landwirtschaftliche Interessen*, 98–9.

42 Loewenfeld-Russ, *Die Regelung*, 49; Hardach, *First World War*, 115.

43 Der Oberbürgermeister von Elberfeld an die Reichsprüfungsstelle für Lebensmittel, 28/12/1915, BA/R3601/404.

44 Preisprüfungsstelle für Lebensmittelpreise Berlin an den Oberbürgermeister von Elberfeld, 7/01/1916, BA/R3601/404.

45 Entwurf einer Vorschrift über den Verkehr mit Gegenständen des notwendigen Lebensbedarfes, 1/04/1916, BA/R3601/404.

46 Nachrichtendienst für Ernährungsfragen Nr. 161, 27/05/1916, BA/R3601/404.

47 Städtische Preisprüfungsstelle Frankfurt am Main an die Reichsprüfungsstelle für Lebensmittelpreise Berlin, 16/05/1916, BA/R3601/404.

48 Öffentliches Untersuchungsamt der Stadt Freiburg im Breisgau an die Schriftleitung der Reichsprüfungsstelle für Lebensmittelpreise Berlin, 26/06/1916, BA/R3601/404.

Figure 3.1 Food caricature, 1916.
Source: Postcard from the European collection: www.europeana.eu/fr/item/2020601/https___1914_1918_europeana_eu_contributions_118, Europeana 1914–1918

To avoid these distortions, in May 1916 it was decided to set maximum prices for all consumer foodstuffs at the federal level.

This tendency to extend control towards ever larger sections of the market (from the producer to the wholesaler, right through to the consumer), to control more and more products (usually starting with wheat or sugar) and to move from local regulations to federal or central values occurred across Europe. The learning curve was the same, as were the mistakes made and the situations experienced. In Russia in January 1915 the government set maximum prices to be paid to producers for grain. In November 1915 this control was extended to other goods. In June 1916 selling prices were imposed for mills. From November 1916 onwards a forced economy was established, with consequent control over the entire production and distribution cycle.[49] In Italy, from August 1914 onwards the municipalities were obliged to set maximum retail prices. In March 1916, price ceilings were established throughout the country for wheat, maize, flour, pasta and sugar. In August 1916, a forced economy system was established, with set prices also for producers and wholesalers.[50]

[49] Gatrell, *Russia*, 154–69.
[50] Dentoni, *Annona*, 22–33.

In Belgium, given the particular situation with regard to shortages since the German occupation, as early as September 1914 maximum prices were set for six food products;[51] in December 1915 these provisions were extended to pork and in January 1916 to potatoes.[52] In another occupied area, Ober Ost, maximum prices for cereals and legumes were fixed in July 1915; in April 1916 for meat and grain; in July 1916 for potatoes; in December 1916 the occupying authorities finally set the maximum sales and requisition prices for 21 food products.[53]

Maximum retail price fixing characterized other states, with different timescales depending on the severity of shortages: in September 1917 they were introduced in Britain (where the introduction of price ceilings had, however, been discussed in Parliament as early as November 1914);[54] in Austria in November 1914 maximum prices were set at the local level and in November 1916 these were fixed by the central authority;[55] in the Netherlands the government mandated in August 1916 that it could set maximum prices for all foodstuffs and introduced stiff penalties for those who sold goods above the maximum price. Price ceilings for certain goods had already been introduced much earlier.[56]

Rationing and Food Regimes

Price ceilings did in some cases inhibit price increases, but they did not prevent the disappearance of goods from the market. On the contrary, to the chagrin of leaders and frustration of civilians, price ceilings often encouraged products to become unavailable as production prices made it uneconomical to trade them: in many cases the prices set by governments between 1915 and 1916 did not take into account the rising production costs.[57] This is explained clearly in the introduction to a collective study published in Germany in 1914 entitled *Die deutsche*

51 A. Vrints, 'Food and Nutrition (Belgium)', *International Encyclopedia of the First World War (WW1)* [https://encyclopedia.1914-1918-online.net/article/food_and_nutrition_belgium [accessed 26 April 2023].

52 J. Pirenne and M. E. A. Vauthier, *La législation et l'administration allemandes en Belgique* (Paris: Les Presses Universitaires de France; New-Haven: Yale University Press, 1925), 34–7.

53 *Die amtlichen Befehle, Verordnungen u. Bekanntmachungen für Libau, erlassen in d. Zeit vom 7. Mai 1915 bis 3. März 1918* (Libau: Gottl. D. Meyer, 1918). Verordnungen 68, 271, 309, 348, 436.

54 Barnett, *British Food Policy*, 37; Hardach, *First World War*, 129.

55 Loewenfeld-Russ, *Die Regelung*, 49–56.

56 W. Klinkert, S. Kruizinga and P. Moeyes, *Nederland neutraal: de Eerste Wereldoorlog 1914–1918* (Amsterdam: Boom, 2014), 242–7.

57 Corni and Frizzera, 'Erster Teil', 18–28; E. F. Heckscher et al., *Sweden, Norway, Denmark and Iceland in the World War* (New Haven, CT: Yale University Press, 1930), 16.

Volksernährung und der englische Aushungerungsplan. The book written by German experts from the food and agricultural sector asserts that it was the duty of governments to reverse the balance of power between production and consumption: whilst in a free market scenario it was necessary to encourage production, so that this could also be sold on foreign markets, now efforts had to be centred upon controlling consumption and the rational use of the goods available.[58] Thus, for some selected products food regimes were established. These included the control of production, the requisition of the harvest and the management of distribution at prices fixed by the authorities, in quantities determined from above to guarantee a minimum required amount for all.

In this situation, the actions of the governments concentrated mainly on identifying substitute goods or encouraging the use of canned vegetables, rather than increasing internal production. For instance, states like Austria-Hungary aimed to regulate the trade with such 'preserved vegetables', requiring all producers not only 'to report their entire product to the Fruit and Vegetable Bureau in Vienna or to the agency designated' but also to 'offer these preserved vegetables for sale to this Bureau or to its designated agency'. Exceptions were only made for those who produced not more than '10 q of canned vegetables or vegetables in brine, or not more than 20 q of cucumber pickles, or sauer kraut, or of pickled beets'.[59] (See Chapter 4 for further insights on coping with food shortage.)

The ability of governments to curb inflation and to organize impartial distribution served to establish a 'moral economy', which was to become a tangible symbol of the union sacrée.[60] Many considered a strong internal front to be essential to a final victory.[61] Consequently, both in neutral as well as belligerent countries, yet at different paces and with different outcomes, rationing was introduced as a 'burden-sharing scheme' in this 'highly controlled economy'[62] as a means of

[58] Eltzbacher, *Deutsche Volksernährung*, 7.

[59] HILA, USFAR, Alphabetical File, Box 95, Folder 9, Austria-Hungary, Food Ministry, Fruits and Vegetables, Hungary-Food Administration, Reg-Vegetables, Information Bureau Library, 15 December 1917.

[60] J. J. Becker, 'Union Sacrée et idéologie bourgeoise', *Revue Historique*, 264:1 (1980), 65–74; J. J. Becker, *1914, comment les Francais sont entrés dans la guerre. Contribution à l'étude de l'opinion publique printemps-été 1914* (Paris: Presses de la Fondation nationale des sciences politiques, 1977); S. Bründel, *Volksgemeinschaft oder Volksstaat. Die 'Ideen von 1914' und die Neuordnung Deutschlands im Ersten Weltkrieg* (Berlin: Akademie Verlag, 2003).

[61] A. Bauerkämper and E. Julien, eds., *Durchhalten!: Krieg und Gesellschaft im Vergleich 1914–1918* (Göttingen: Vandenhoeck & Ruprecht, 2010).

[62] K. Allen, 'Sharing Scarcity: Bread Rationing and the First World War in Berlin, 1914–1923', *Journal of Social History*, 32:2 (1998), 372.

ensuring fair distribution of the available foodstuffs.[63] Many governments resorted first to admonishing consumers to reduce their consumption. Then, when this action proved insufficient, the authorities organized the imposition of formal controls, usually consisting of the planned and restrictive allocation of scarce resources and consumer goods, which were distributed on the basis of quantities established from above.

Also in this field, the differences between states lay in timing, and not in the solution they ultimately adopted. While Germany started to ration its bread in the summer of 1915, Britain did not introduce an organized rationing system until spring 1918.[64] In France rationing of local grain[65] was introduced in October 1915 and general rationing in June 1918.[66] In Italy there was an attempt to counteract the grain shortage by baking an increasing proportion of bran at first, following the German and Austrian example. In March 1915 an 80 per cent whipped breading was imposed; in September 1917 general rationing was finally introduced.[67] In Russia there was a step-by-step process: initially (October 1915) the consumption of meat was rationed; then sugar (June 1916); in February 1917 the rationing of bread was introduced[68] and in March 1918 a complete rationing system controlled from above was created.[69] In Britain, the rationing of sugar to be distributed to wholesalers was regulated from November 1914; at the beginning of 1916 the same system was also introduced for other products; in February 1917, given the continuous increase in queues at shops and rising disparities, an attempt was made to introduce voluntary rationing of consumption;[70] in July 1917, given the decline in food intake, rationing was extended to the retail level; finally, between February and June 1918, ration cards were introduced for several products.[71]

Neutral Switzerland also followed the same pattern: from November 1915 attempts were made to guarantee access to basic foods for all through the establishment of soup kitchens in large cities; from March

[63] K. Hunt, 'Gender and Everyday Life', in Tammy M. Proctor and Susan R. Grayzel, eds., *Gender and the Great War* (Oxford: Oxford University Press, 2017), 156.
[64] T. M. Proctor, *Civilians in a World at War. 1914–1918* (New York and London: New York University Press, 2010), 84.
[65] Dentoni, *Annona*, 20.
[66] Hardach, *First World War*, 132.
[67] Dentoni, *Annona*, 41–3.
[68] Gatrell, *Russia*, 154–69.
[69] Peeling Siobhan, 'War Communism', *International Encyclopedia of the First World War (WW1)*, [https://encyclopedia.1914-1918-online.net/article/war_communism, accessed 26 April 2023].
[70] Hardach, *First World War*, 123–8.
[71] Hardach, *First World War*, 130; Beveridge, *British Food Control*, 183–218.

1917, rationing for rice and sugar was introduced at the cantonal level, followed in July 1917 by the introduction of ration cards for corn and pasta. In October the government introduced the rationing of bread and cereals at the federal level,[72] followed in March 1918 by the distribution of ration cards for fats. The case of Austria is very similar to that of Italy. In 1914, attempts were made to compensate for the lack of certain products through the use of substitutes or whipped breading.[73] In February 1915 flour was rationed, in April bread. In 1916 the government rationed sugar and in July 1916 meat.[74] Between November 1916 and March 1917, general rationing at the central level was finally introduced.[75] In the occupied areas of Eastern Europe, the occupying authorities replicated the control system already adopted in their hinterland. In Ober-Ost the rationing of bread, grain, potatoes and the introduction in April 1916 of a *Brotkarte* and *Zuckerkarte* was followed in August 1916 by the distribution of a *Milchkarte* and in October 1916 by the creation of a general rationing system based on the German example.[76] Even countries that had tried to maintain the free trade and free distribution practices had to surrender: Sweden started rationing in the Spring of 1917 after food riots broke out across the country in April of that year.[77]

Although the system appeared egalitarian on paper, it was, however, fraught with operational problems.[78] In Germany the shortage of coal frequently caused a breakdown in the system for transporting and distributing potatoes to urban and industrial areas: in some weeks up to 70 per cent of deliveries by train were cancelled.[79] The food situation in Bohemia revealed furthermore how inefficient the official supply and rationing system was. In fact, ration cards were often equally useless, as the necessary foodstuffs were often simply not available.[80] Those who did not have access to the black market and based their diet exclusively

72 J. Ruchti, *Geschichte der Schweiz während des Weltkrieges 1914–1919: politisch, wirtschaftlich und kulturell* (Bern: Haupt, 1930), vol. II, 242.

73 Loewenfeld-Russ, *Die Regelung*, 48.

74 Anfange der Rationierung in Oesterreich, Kriegsernährungsamt, 01/10/1916, BA/R3601/486.

75 Loewenfeld-Russ, *Die Regelung*, tab. 147.

76 *Die amtlichen Befehle*, Verordnungen 68, 76, 82, 371 and 418.

77 M. Richardson, *The Hunger War: Food, Rations & Rationing 1914–1918* (Barnsley: Pen and Sword, 2015), 256.

78 T. Bonzon and B. Davis, 'Feeding the Cities', in J. Winter and J. L. Robert, eds., *Capital Cities at War. Paris, London, Berlin 1914–1919* (Cambridge: Cambridge University Press: 2009), 320.

79 Wochenbericht des KEA vom 28. Oktober bis 3. November 1917, BA/R3601/16.

80 ÖStA, AdR, Volksernährungsamt, AR, K151, no. 96062, Stimmungsbericht from the Military Commander in Prague, 30 June 1918.

on food distributed by the authorities risked starvation: 65 per cent of Italian-speaking psychiatric patients housed in Austrio-Hungarian asylums died because of hunger or malnutrition-related diseases during the war, relying solely on official rations.[81]

The apparent fairness guaranteed by the ration cards left some problems unresolved even in the States of the Entente. From the spring 1917 it is frequently reported in London that the women waiting at the food shops in the working-class districts crowded into long queues. It was not uncommon that many of these – in some cases thousands – were sent away unsupplied, due to the lack of rations, although they did have the coupon.[82] In Italy, the transport crisis of late 1917 and errors in the distribution caused the collapse of the supply system in mountain areas and in the southern regions of the country at the beginning of 1918. Rationing cards became almost useless in these regions, as there was no surplus of food to be distributed for almost two months.[83]

Lastly, the management of the rationing cards was incredibly complicated in the eyes of the citizens. In Budapest, for instance, the authorities issued two different types of rationing cards in October 1916. As reported by the *New York Times*, the first 'one for general victualing, a general kind of a ticket without which single tickets for bread, meat, maize, potatoes, etc. are useless'. Only residents of Budapst and Transylvanian refugees got these general tickets from the municipal authorities. Then, the authorities issued a 'second ticket, ... to holders of the general tickets', that 'entitles every inhabitant to buy half a pound of beans per month'. To sum up, there were 18 tickets in use, whose management 'involves the loss of half a day's work' every week.[84]

From the point of view of state organization, the creation of complex rationing systems implicitly required the creation of a central control authority. A dedicated food administrator, often referred to as a food dictator, was required on an on-going basis in several countries during the First World War.[85] In Germany the government instituted in May 1916 the *Kriegsernährungsamt* (KEA, War Food Office) whose task was to control and manage centrally price ceilings, import, rationing and distribution of foodstuff. In August 1916, a Ministry of

[81] A. Grillini, *La guerra in testa. Esperienze e traumi di civili, profughi e soldati nel manicomio di Pergine Valsugana (1909–1924)* (Bologna: Il Mulino, 2018), 85.

[82] Bonzon and Davies, *Feeding the Cities*, 330.

[83] U. Ricci, *La politica annonaria dell'Italia durante la Guerra* (Bari: Laterza, 1939).

[84] 'Famine in Hungary while women riot', Special Cable to the *New York Times*, 16 October 1916, 2.

[85] R. J. Hammond, *Food*, Vol. 1*: The Growth of Policy* (London: HMSO, 1951), 237; Hardach, *First World War*, 118.

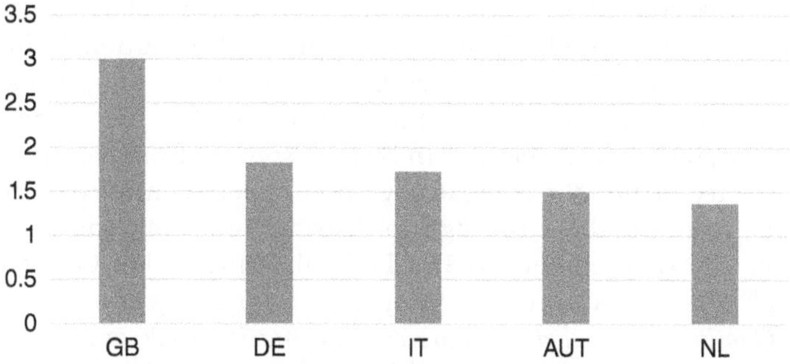

Figure 3.2 Weekly bread/flour consumption (1918) per head in kg.

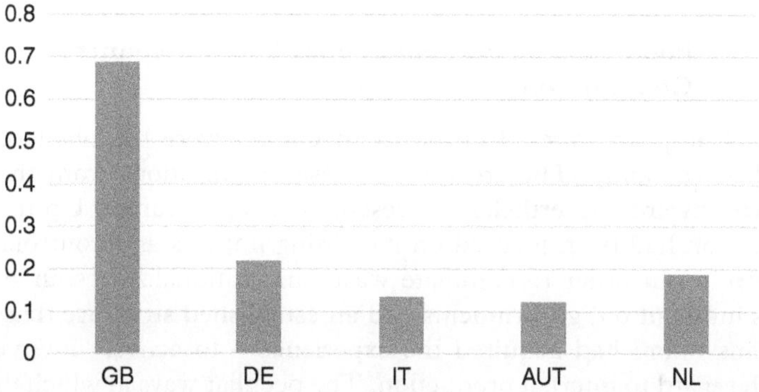

Figure 3.3 Weekly meat consumption (1918) per head in kg.

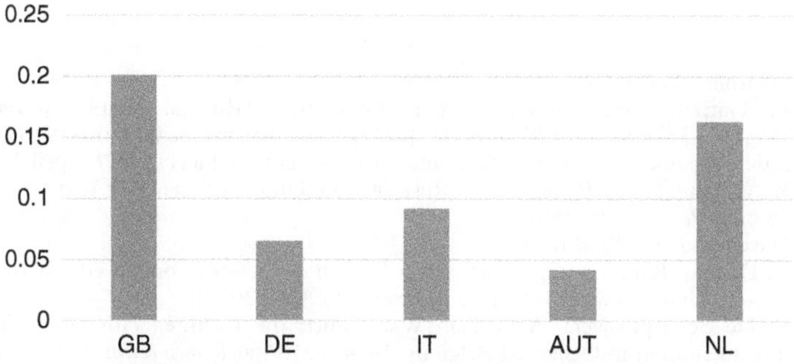

Figure 3.4 Weekly fat consumption (1918) per head in kg.
Source: Beverdige, *Food* Control, 317; Löwenfeld-Russ, *Regelung der Volksernährung*, 335; Bachi, *L'alimentazione*, 294, Skalweit, *Die deutsche Kriegsernährungswirtschaft*, 247–9. Period: November 1918

Food was created in Italy, with the task of controlling all the main food consumer goods, from production to distribution.[86] In Russia, from November 1915, a Special Council for Food Supply was operational,[87] subsequently replaced in May 1918, after the change of government, by a food dictator.[88] In Britain, starting from December 1916, a Ministry of Food was created with complete control over imported goods, from purchase through to distribution.[89] In Switzerland, even if very late (September 1918) a Federal Alimentation Office was created,[90] which was to remain in operation for many years. In Belgium, the *Comité National de Secours et Alimentation* took over these duties de facto from 7 August 1914.[91] In Austria, from November 1916 the *Amt fuer Volksernähurung* was in operation[92] and worked alongside the Hungarian *Országos Közélelmezési Hivatal.*[93]

Food Control across Europe: A Cross-country Comparison

The European states' Central Food Offices were the pivot of a controlled economy. The creation of these organizations from the end of 1916 onwards nevertheless represented an opportunity. Up until 1916 attention had been focused on increasing imports and controlling consumption in order to eliminate waste and rationalize resources. From this moment on, governments had an established structure that had the means – and had acquired the experience – to actively intervene also with regard to internal production. The peculiar ways in which the single state models addressed the food crisis can be seen in their interventions to enhance domestic production and in the development of inter-allied cooperation rather than in their restrictive policies.

[86] Dentoni, *Annona*, 33.

[87] P. Gatrell, 'Organization of War Economies (Russian Empire)', *International Encyclopedia of the First World War (WW1)* https://encyclopedia.1914-1918-online.net/article/organization_of_war_economies_russian_empire [accessed 26 April 2023].

[88] B. M. Patenaude, 'Peasants into Russian. The Utopian Essence of War Communism', *Russian Review*, 54:4 (1995) 554.

[89] Hardach, *First World War*, 125.

[90] B. Degen, 'Rationierung', *Historisches Lexicon der Schweiz*, online ed., 2010 www.hls-dhs-dss.ch/textes/d/D13782.php [accessed 26 April 2023].

[91] S. De Schaepdrijver, 'A Civilian War Effort: the Comité National de Secours et d'Alimentation in Occupied Belgium, 1914–1918', in *Remembering Herbert Hoover and the Commission for Relief in Belgium* (Brussels: Fondation Universitaire, 2007), 24–37.

[92] Loewenfeld-Russ, *Die Regelung*, 56.

[93] E. Langthaler, 'Food and Nutrition (Austria-Hungary)', *International Encyclopedia of the First World War (WW1)*, https://encyclopedia.1914-1918-online.net/article/food_and_nutrition_austria-hungary [accessed 26 April 2023].

Steering Domestic Agricultural Production

The tendency to set up 'moral economies', which aimed to keep prices low and divide resources equally clashed with the need to increase domestic production. The effort to reduce retail prices and limit inflation, in fact, discouraged the production of certain goods. The prices paid to farmers for agricultural produce were lower than production costs and therefore farmers specialized in the production of other more profitable crops or restricted the introduction of the produce onto the market, waiting for prices to be set higher. This challenge – to maintain low prices but increase and intelligently steer domestic production – saw the differences between the various centralized control systems come into play.

In general terms, the tendency to keep retail prices low was regarded by rulers as an unavoidable necessity in order to avoid strikes and production stoppages (see Chapter 9). The price ceilings succeeded in many cases in artificially slowing down the upward pressure on the prices of goods that were in short supply. This happened for instance in Britain and Germany, where the imposition of price ceilings on food products allowed to contain inflation.[94] This would suggest that the centralized control system functioned systematically both in Britain and in Germany; it did nevertheless conceal major internal disparities, which emerge if domestic agricultural production is analysed. The British and German cases are in this regard good examples to explain how different state policies aimed at greater agricultural production worked.

In Germany, despite the mobilization of huge numbers of experts and the creation of control systems early on,[95] attention towards domestic production came late.[96] In fact it was not until the '*Verordnung über die Preise für landwirtschaftliche Erzeugnisse aus der Ernte 1917*' (Decree on the prices of agricultural production for the year 1917) was issued that any overall consideration was given to issues concerning domestic production:[97] only from this point onwards was a conscious effort made to guarantee farmers fair prices for the goods they sold and for seeds, labour and fertilizers.[98] This belated consideration for the needs of farmers had undermined many of the government's efforts to guarantee

94 Beveridge, *British Food Control*, 324. Adam Tooze, *The Deluge. The Great War and the Remaking of the Global Order, 1916–1931* (London: Allan Lane, 2014), 213–14.

95 Eltzbacher, *Die deutsche Volksernährung*; Flemming, *Landwirtschaftliche Interessen*, 98.

96 A. Weinreb, *Modern Hungers. Food and Power in Twentieth-Century Germany* (Oxford: Oxford University Press, 2017), 21.

97 Corni and Frizzera, 'Die Diskussion', 30–1.

98 W. Wygodzinski, *Produktionszwang Und Produktionsförderung in Der Landwirtschaft*, Volkswirtschaftlichen Abteilung des Kriegsernaehrungsamts, ed. (Berlin: Volkswirtschaftlichen Abteilung des Kriegsernaehrungsamts, 1917), 38.

that food distribution remained close to the high pre-war standards: the decrees on maximum prices and bans on using cereals as animal fodder proved in fact to be ineffective as long as the profitability of farms could not be guaranteed.[99] As a result, yields per hectare and the total surface area farmed in Germany fell drastically between 1914 and 1916.[100]

The most notable case brought about by attempts to centrally steer and manage domestic agricultural production without providing appropriate financial incentives for farmers was the so-called *Schweinemord.* This occurred in early 1915 when farmers started shifting production towards goods that were not subject to price ceilings. Rather than placing low priced cereals and potatoes on the market, they used these instead to feed their cattle so they could then produce more profitable dairy products. The government therefore ordered the slaughtering of around 5 million pigs to bring the ratio between fodder and livestock back to a sustainable level. The rationale for this measure was apparently accurate: feeding livestock destined for the food market required many more calories than the equivalent cultivation of vegetable foodstuffs. Therefore, it was inefficient in conditions of food shortage. As assessed by the experts, the logic of scientific use of every available calorie should favour a diet with a lower intake of dairy products. As a result, however, the market was inundated with meat-based products and meat prices dropped significantly, only then to rise steeply once again in the autumn of 1915 when maximum prices then needed to be introduced for pork.[101] The consequences were threefold: the number of pigs in Germany fell from 25.3 million in 1914 to 17 million in 1916, which led to shortages in the meat industry; the problem of the scarcity of animal feed was not resolved; farmers did not shift production towards the goods that were in short supply. The absence of a centrally coordinated policy up to 1916 allowed farmers to find profitable prices for goods that were not yet subject to controls[102] on other regional markets.

In this sense, the federal structure of the German government, just like the dual structure of Austria-Hungary,[103] restricted the possibility

[99] H. Steeg, 'De Extensivierung Der Rheinischen Landbaus Unter Der Wirkung Der Hoechstpreise Und Der Zwangswirtschaft' (unpublished PhD thesis, Cologne University, 1923); W. Baumann, 'Das Sinken Der Grundrente Landwirtschaftliche Grossbetriebe Durch Den Weltkrieg' (unpublished PhD thesis, Frankfurt University, 1921).

[100] Corni and Frizzera, 'Die Diskussion', 32.

[101] R. Chickering, *Imperial Germany and the Great War, 1914–1918*, 2nd ed. (Cambridge: Cambridge University Press, 2004), 57.

[102] Corni and Frizzera, 'Die Diskussion', 26–30.

[103] C. Horel, 'Il Compromesso austro-ungherese alla prova della Grande guerra', in P. Pombeni, ed., *La Grande guerra e la dissoluzione di un Impero multinazionale* (Trento: FBK Press, 2017), 211.

of agreeing on rigorous solutions. Frictions between local and central governments made these policies uneffective. Moreover, these actions were underminded by the disregard for farmers' interests. An analysis conducted by US experts on European agricultural production during wartime highlights the limits of these policies, which were intended to force farmers to produce more.[104] In particular, referring to the systems in use in Germany and Austria-Hungary, it states that 'federal control with far-reaching jurisdiction and responsibility must be the starting point of any successful national effort'. However, before arriving at this observation, the experts reported that 'It was not until after two years of muddling along and irreparable harm had been done, that a federal control under Batocki [KEA, Germany] was inaugurated'.[105] In this field, the food policies of Germany and Austria-Hungary, however invasive and defined they were in detail, differed substantially from those developed in Britain.

In Britain, where access to foreign resources continued, the greatest effort was put into regulating imports and distribution. If decision makers here decided to establish food regimes, these were based for the greatest part on imported goods, which were easier to collect, control and manage centrally. Therefore, there was more time available to think about self-sufficiency and plan it on the basis of economic conditions. On the other end, unbroken import channels made it easier to focus on domestic production. Also in Britain, just as in Germany, up until 1916 there was uncertainty about the measures to be implemented to guarantee adequate domestic production: 'under the first coalition government, in June 1915, three Committees – for England and Wales, Scotland and Ireland – had been appointed to consider the steps necessary to increase food production, and had provided a remarkable diversity of advice'. The England Committee intended to guarantee a fixed sales price for grain for 4 years; 'the Scottish Committee reported unanimously against it; the Irish Committee reported in favour of a guarantee for one year'. The government, for its part, came out against paying farmers a minimum price.[106] As in Germany, decision makers followed at first fluctuating policies, with the difference that in Britain imports could make up for shortfalls in domestic agriculture.

In the British case, Food Controllers did not realise until 1917 that price fixing was an 'essential factor governing the production of grain at

[104] R. S. MacElwee, 'Bread Bullets Concerning Agricultural Mobilisation in the United States', in Walter B. Pitkin, ed., *Columbia War Papers*, vol. 11 (New York, NY: Division of Intelligence and Publicity of Columbia University, 1917), 15.

[105] MacElwee, 'Bread Bullets', 4–5.

[106] Beveridge, *British Food Control*, 104–38.

home', and ordered that minimum prices be set on 16 April of the same year. The crucial element of the British pricing system was that the Food Controllers 'never fixed a price for home-grown grain until, after consulting the agricultural departments and listening first hand to what the producers had to say, they were satisfied, not simply that the price would allow a fair profit, but that it would be substantially accepted by producers as something worth working for'.[107] As a result of these measures and other government financial incentives, production was directed towards goods that were in short supply, namely cereals.[108] Guaranteed selling prices and planning by local committees, which ensured additional labour, horses and machinery, enabled the 'production of grain and potatoes [to be raised] ... some 40 per cent above the average for the years 1904–13' by the end of 1918.[109] This policy, though costly, enabled the British people to successfully cope with the gradual decline in imported goods: even if net imports of principal foodstuffs had dropped from 10.5 million tons in 1913 to 6.4 million in 1918,[110] the weekly consumption of bread and flour in Britain had actually increased, from 6.12 lb (1913) to 6.57 lb (1918) per person.[111] In return, however, to enable farmers to amortize the costs of installations for the new crops, minimum prices had to remain fixed long-term. This was to prevent the entire agricultural sector from collapsing. Therefore, once hostilities had ceased, the British government found itself compelled to guarantee farmers 'minimum prices for five years', starting from 1917,[112] with the need consequently to keep a number of control mechanisms running.

In short, the differences in the two cases did not concern so much the timing as the learning curve: in neither Britain nor Germany was there any noticeable sign of attention towards issues regarding increasing domestic production until 1916. The differences lay in the ability to access foreign imports during the period required for crop conversion and the method chosen: Germany tried to compel farmers to produce more; in Britain farmers were urged to produce different crops. According to Martin Schumacher, in Germany the *Kriegsernährungsamt* remained for a long time 'a sword without sharpness'[113] that only

107 Beveridge, *British Food Control*, 106–7.

108 E. M. H. Lloyd, *Experiments in State Control at the War Office and the Ministry of Food* (Oxford: Clarendon Press, 1924); Hardach, *First World War*, 126.

109 Hardach, *First World War*, 127.

110 Beveridge, *British Food Control*, 354.

111 Beveridge, *British Food Control*, 316.

112 MacElwee, 'Bread Bullets', 18.

113 M. Schumacher, *Land Und Politik. Eine Untersuchung Über Politische Parteien Und Agrarische Interessen, 1914–1923* (Düsseldorf: Droste Verlag, 1978), 60.

slowly managed to impose its agricultural policy decisions upon reticent local authorities.[114] Moreover, despite the introduction of complex mechanisms to control prices paid to producers,[115] in Germany's case there was no public acknowledgement of the need to agree with farmers on increasing production until 1920, rather than relying on obligation as the sole means. Only on 14 May 1920 did the new Federal Minister for Nutrition and Agriculture, Andreas Hermes, state that 'through sympathetic cooperation with agriculture and the cooperative organizations ... we will be able to produce far more potatoes than by continuing with the previous forms of coercive economy'.[116] By then the war had been over for a year and a half. In Britain, on the other hand, the guaranteed minimum price instrument was accompanied for several years by a bold compulsory crop conversion policy, directed from above and put into practice by local committees after consulting with farmers from 1917 onwards.

The two cases of Germany and Britain highlight the decision-maker's sphere of action. All the policies adopted in the other countries move within these two poles. The differences underlying policies undertaken by belligerent and neutral countries to strengthen domestic production are surprising, and do not take into account military alliances and borders. In Switzerland, although the centralized control of the food economy was established very late, the State was able to intelligently stimulate the domestic production of goods, which were previously imported. The results were so significant that the government decided to maintain some control mechanisms running for many years after the conflict, since it was possible to create a form of pre-litteram *Marktordnung* in some sectors, such as the dairy industry.[117] In Italy, despite the country being an ally of the Entente, attempts to stimulate greater domestic production only through coercion and by rejecting favourable price policies for the peasants proved to be a fiasco, comparable to that which characterized Germany.[118]

114 Corni and Frizzera, *Erster Teil*, 27–49.

115 Die Getreidepreise im Weltkriege. Denkschrift zur Frage der Gestaltung der Getreidepreise aus der Ernte 1918. Bearbeitet im Kriegsernaehrungsamt. 1918, BA/R3601/483, 170.

116 Auszug aus dem Protokoll der Sitzung des Reichsministeriums. 14/05/1920, BA/R43-I/2535, fol. 32.

117 M. Cottier, *Liberalismus oder Staatsintervention: die Geschichte der Versorgungspolitik im Schweizer Bundesstaat* (Zürich: Verlag Neue Zürcher Zeitung, 2014), 67–70.

118 R. Bachi and G. Zingali, *L'alimentazione e la politica annonaria in Italia: con una appendice su 'Il rifornimento dei viveri dell'esercito italiano' di Gaetano Zingali* (Rome: G. Laterza, 1926), 432; Dentoni, *Annona*, 76.

Inter-allied Cooperation

The second element of cross-country comparison, which highlights major differences between operational choices, is inter-allied cooperation. In the first case (Central Powers), collaboration in the field of food supply was minimal. In the second case (Entente), cooperation was good, also because there was a foreign producer who had a vested interest in selling its surplus (USA) and one of the partners (Britain) also had an interest in developing the economic activities of its dominions.

The lack of collaboration among the Central Powers is not surprising if we consider that the Austrian government did not even agree with Hungary, nor did it obtain foodstuffs produced in the Hungarian portion of the Empire, which was a traditional exporter of grain, maize and flour before the outbreak of the war.[119] Some sources report that 'aid from Hungary was only granted to Austria reluctantly and only against exchanges; thus in the case of the purchase of frozen [foods] .... Austria was to deliver a corresponding quantity of shoes and clothing to Hungary, whose demands caused great indignation in Vienna'.[120] The administrative facility charged with handling exchanges of foodstuffs between the two parts of the Empire was inadequate: according to Langthaler, 'the Joint Food Committee (*Gemeinsamer Ernährungsauschuss*) formed in early 1917 ... was largely a toothless institution lacking power over the national food administration in the two halves of the Empire'.[121] Given this, one can only imagine what collaboration with Germany was like since Austria did not have any desirable trading goods. Connections with Bulgaria and the Ottoman Empire were for a long time also completely lacking, at least until Serbia was defeated, and then only minimal: just one railway line connected the Central Powers and the capacity of this line was insufficient to allow for trading on a large scale.[122]

In essence, cooperation in terms of food trading between Germany, Austria-Hungary and the Ottoman Empire proved to be a failure. The same scarce cooperation also emerged in the dynamics involved in occupying and plundering the territories being conquered, where disputes – especially between Austria-Hungary, Germany and Bulgaria – exceeded

[119] M. S. Schulze, 'Austria-Hungary's Economy in World War I', in S. R. Broadberry and M. Harrison, eds., *The Economics of World War I* (Cambridge: Cambridge University Press: 2005), 94; Richardson, *The Hunger War*, 213–20.

[120] HILA, USFAR, Alphabetical File, Austria Hungary, Box 95, Folder 7, Economic Situation: Austria-Hungary during the first half of 1918, 'Meat. Hungary', 15.

[121] Langthaler, 'Food and Nutrition (Austria-Hungary)'.

[122] A. Mitrović, *Serbia's Great War, 1914–1918* (West Lafayette, IN: Purdue University Press, 2007), 221; A. J. May, 'The Novibazar Railway Project', *The Journal of Modern History*, 10:4 (1938), 496–527.

agreements. The most obvious case was exploitation of Romania's occupied areas.[123] In particular, according to Gustavo Corni, 'the Romanian occupation policy was marked by a reciprocal diffidence: the Austrians feared German military and economic superiority. German authorities, in turn, suspected that their Ally's claims concealed a desire to take control of the occupied territory after the war.' The attempt to find an agreement, by exchanging the respective spheres of influence in Romania and Poland, was discussed unsuccessfully at the Kreuznach conference in April 1917.[124] The bones of contention were specifically food, petroleum and the control of large companies.

Figure 3.5 Austro-Hungarian soldiers distribute food to the civilian population after the occupation of Veneto.
Source: Museo Storico Italiano della Guerra (MSIG), Archivio fotografico (AF), 59/69

[123] L. Mayerhofer, 'Making Friends and Foes: Occupiers and Occupied In First World War Romania, 1916–1918', in H. Jones, J. O'Brien and C. Schmidt-Supprian, eds., *Untold War. New Perspectives in First World War Studies* (Leiden: Brill, 2008), 119–50.

[124] G. Corni, 'Occupation during the War', in U. Daniel, Peter Gatrell, Oliver Janz, et al., eds., *1914–1918-online. International Encyclopedia of the First World War* (Berlin: Freie Universität Berlin, 2015).

Collaboration between the Allied countries instead represented an example of successful conciliation of individual interests. Margaret Barnett maintains that 'both the British and the French conceded after the war that the inter-allied system had worked well'. In particular, 'the waste and expense stemming from competition among the Allies for the same goods and services had been virtually eliminated, and it was agreed that stock levels had been higher than they would have been if the inter-allied organization had not existed'.[125] On the other hand, the creation of this system had a great impact on the food control mechanisms of European countries: in practice, 'because of the United States' economic power and role as major supplier, the American authorities … had the predominant voice in the decision-making process'.[126] As a matter of fact, the requirements of individual states were discussed and examined during joint meetings and the demands of individual countries aimed to maintain 'a proper balance between the needs of the Allied countries … in regard to their food supply as a whole'.[127] Put simply, the Entente's cooperation system worked, while that of the Central Powers proved to be substantially deficient.

Transnational Learning and Neutral Countries

The development of food supply systems seemed at first to resist external influences or, at most, to be conditioned by relations between the Allies. On the other hand, when a state intervened resolutely to economically control foodstuffs, other states felt justified to do the same. In some cases, these policies were adopted by reaction, others by emulation. The decisive role in this context was played by neutral countries, which became the channels through which information extended beyond the frontlines.

The first two examples concern Romania and Italy during the period they were neutral. The extremely high demand for agricultural produce in Austria-Hungary indirectly also caused prices to rise on the Romanian domestic market, since envoys from the Habsburg *Kriegsstellen* purchased goods at high prices in neutral countries that were in short supply on the domestic market. This forced the Romanian government first to tax the exportation of some agricultural produce

[125] Barnett, *British Food Policy*, 164.
[126] Barnett, *British Food Policy*, 163.
[127] United States Army, Center of Military History, in Eric B. Setzekorn ed., *The U.S. Army in World War I: Complete History of the U.S. Army in the Great War, Including the Mobilization, The Main Battles & All Official Documents of the U.S. Government during the War* (Washington, DC: Madison & Adams Press, 2018), 481.

(24 February 1915), then to temporarily suspend exports (21 June 1915, cereals and meat).[128] In the meantime, the Central Powers took steps to overcome these hurdles: in Germany the ZEG was established to administer foreign imports as a monopoly; Austria followed suit and created the *Kriegsgetreideverkehrsanstalt*. These institutions jeopardized Romanian domestic supplies through their ability to purchase substantial quantities at reduced prices: the government in Bucharest was therefore compelled to extend its control over the entire system from exports to production right through to domestic consumption. Between November 1915 and April 1916 therefore Romania also introduced a controlled economy system, as a reaction to intrusion by buyers from the Central Powers.[129]

Even in the case of minor pressures, disruptions in the movement of food due to the war caused similar reactions in other neutral countries, which responded to shortages by following the example of those that had already adopted similar measures. In Italy, Vincenzo Giuffrida, who was appointed in December 1914 to coordinate policy for procuring goods and creator of UTAG, soon found himself forced to 'reappraise the entire chain of state intervention, from setting minimum prices to the monopoly, right through to rationing'.[130] The examples he refers to in a publication after the war concern measures already implemented in Switzerland, France, Britain and Germany,[131] from which he, by his own admission, gained extensive insight.

A similar pattern was recorded in Switzerland.[132] Here too *Importstellen* were created early on for specific categories of products, though private initiative was permitted until early 1915. France, however, began as early as December 1914 to put pressure on Switzerland to establish a single centralized organization for imports. Consequently, in January 1915 a federal monopoly for the importation of cereals was created, in October 1915 one for the importation of rice and in February 1916 one for sugar, which were then followed by other products. The *Lebensmittelbureau für Zivilversorgung* (Bureau for Civilian Food

128 G. Ionesco-Sisesti, *L'Agriculture de la Roumanie Pendant La Guerre* (Paris: Les Presses Universitaires de France, 1929), 22.

129 Ionesco-Sisesti, *L'Agriculture*, 28–36.

130 Dentoni, *Annona*, 20.

131 V. Giuffrida and G. Pietra, *Provital: approvvigionamenti alimentari d'Italia durante la grande guerra 1914–1918* (Padua: Cedam, 1936), 77–9.

132 J. Käppeli and M. Riesen, *Die Lebensmittelversorgung der Schweiz unter dem Einfluss des Weltkrieges von 1914 bis 1922* (Bern: Verbandsdruckerei A. & G., 1925); D. Krämer, C. Pfister and D. M. Segesser, eds., *'Woche für Woche neue Preisaufschläge': Nahrungsmittel-, Energie- und Ressourcenkonflikte in der Schweiz des Ersten Weltkrieges* (Basel: Schwabe Verlag Basel, 2016), 173–257.

Supply) was then appointed to distribute these goods internally. Finally, Switzerland created the SSS (*Societè Suisse de Sorveillance Economique*) along the lines of the Netherlands Oversea Trust Company: in some neutral states, trade with the Entente was therefore controlled by a single company. It is evident that there was a transfer of measures adopted, including the introduction of maximum prices, rationing and control over domestic production.[133]

The situation in the Netherlands, generally speaking, followed a similar pattern. Here too, in line with Britain, efforts were made to intervene in the least intrusive way possible in the distribution chain. For imported foodstuffs, primarily grains, the Dutch government sought to offset price hikes by both subsidizing imports – by paying part of the transit costs – and dividing the imported foodstuffs amongst established distributors, which preserved the pre-war supply chain, whilst preventing 'unnatural' competition and, therefore, unemployment.[134] However, as in Romania, the government was forced to react to the presence of German buyers on Holland's territory: Dutch agricultural business deliberately underestimated domestic demand so that it could export as much as possible to Germany, where prices were much higher. When the Dutch government closed the borders in order to re-balance domestic supplies, agricultural businesses simply stopped selling in order to force the government to reconsider its decision. To break this deadlock, from 11 September 1915 onwards, the Minister for Agriculture, Folkert Posthuma, attempted to rectify the situation by increasing governmental oversight.[135]

The introduction of a more coherent compulsory economic mechanism shows how significant the experience of bordering countries – Germany especially – was for Holland's decision makers. The Dutch government decided to replace the food distribution system with a much more invasive food rationing system, in which the government would set maximum prices and amounts for certain foods in order to share the burdens of an expected shortfall in both imported and homegrown foodstuffs. On 27 December 1916 the Minister for Agriculture informed city councils that from 5 February onwards bread, flour, meal and grain would be rationed.[136] The German derivation of these measures was evident as far as domestic production was concerned. In addition to rationing food, the Dutch government attempted to

[133] Cottier, *Liberalismus oder Staatsintervention*, 49–69.
[134] Nota betreffende, 4–7.
[135] Kruizinga, *Overlegeconomie*, 126–9.
[136] Minutes Second Chamber Dutch Estate General, Session 1916–1917, 20 December 1916, 942.

stimulate domestic food production: in an effort to free up acreage for the production of basic foodstuffs and lessen dependency on imported animal feed, Posthuma ordered the wholesale slaughter of a significant number of the country's pigs in the summer of 1917, creating – as the German *Schweinemord* had – a temporary glut of meat on the market. The effects were short-lived and meat was officially rationed on 25 March 1918.[137]

In Sweden, the government put off measurements for as long as possible, despite pressure from both Germany and Britain. They assumed that their right as a neutral country to export and import goods was protected by international law, and overlooked pressure and blockades from Britain until 1917, when the government in Sweden had to resign. The government consequently resorted to the imposition of price caps. Those, nevertheless, were consistently set too low, and instead of selling their meat, farmers withheld their goods or were tempted to sell them illegally. The overall development then followed that of the other states: during the summer and the autumn of 1917 sugar and bread were rationed, followed by meat, eggs, milk and butter. Food shortage became an everyday experience for Swedish people, who had to change their diet: an animal-based nutrition was replaced by a food regime based on potato flakes, mushrooms and carrots.[138]

Other cases of transnational learning existing in the food supply system can be seen in two examples. In 1917 the German *Kriegsernährungsamt* appointed a specific committee to study the economy established in Belgium's occupied territories, to evaluate whether any of its aspects – it seemed to be performing better than the German economy – could be applied to the context of the *Reich*.[139] The idea of introducing improvements based on the experience of the *Generalgouvernement Belgien* was discarded,[140] but the analysis was detailed and there was widespread interest in the application of these measures. A similar work was carried out as early as 1916 to assess the merits and flaws of the Austrian system.[141] Moreover, as early as 1915 Germany successfully put pressure

[137] F. E. Posthuma, 'Food Supply and Agriculture', in H. B. Greven, ed., *The Netherlands and the World War. Studies in the War History of a Neutral* (New Haven, CT: Yale University Press, 1928), vol. II, 210–13.

[138] Heckscher, *Sweden*, 13–19; S. Qvarnström, 'Sweden', in U. Daniel, Peter Gatrell, Oliver Janz, et al., eds., *1914–1918-online. International Encyclopedia of the First World War* (Berlin: Freie Universität Berlin, 2015), https://encyclopedia.1914-1918-online.net/article/sweden, [accessed 26 April 2023].

[139] Die Verwaltungschef für Flandern und Wallonien, Brussel 2.3.1918, an Staatssekretaär des Reichsamts, Berlin, 01/03/1918, BA/R3601/486.

[140] Reichstelle für Speisefette an KEA, 06/08/1918, BA/R3601/486.

[141] Anfänge der Rationierung in Österreich, 17/10/1916, BA/R3601/486.

on Austria to build a number of *Kriegszentralen* to administer food stocks centrally.[142] This system was based on the experience of the German *Kriegsgetreidegesellschaft*.

The Struggle for Food at the End of the War

The end of the war did not mean the end of the forced economy. The scarcity of food in fact was a feature of many European economies for years after the conflict. Furthermore, the global economic context had radically changed. As a result, state policy governing the control of imports and production, setting sales prices, rationing and combating the black market were only slowly dismantled; in some cases, as in Soviet Russia and Hungary, these institutions actually reached their peak after 1918, once the war was over.

The Economic Blockade and New State Borders

Firstly, the economic blockade of the Central Powers was only lifted after the signing of the peace treaties, so Germany, German-Austria and Hungary had very little opportunity to buy agricultural produce abroad even after the end of hostilities.[143] Moreover, when the naval blockade was removed, a slump in international trade was recorded.[144] The difficulties in importing foodstuff through traditional trade channels were only partially relieved by humanitarian aid sent to Europe through the American Relief Administration (ARA).

In a situation of low domestic agricultural yields Europe-wide, this situation forced governments and especially the new governments of Germany and German-Austria to keep the forced economy firmly in place. In order to stop revolutionary uprisings[145] and limit as far as possible the internal war being waged between producers (who were concealing stocks or selling them on the black market) and consumers (who

[142] Wolfram Dornik, 'Verwaltung des Mangels: die österreichisch-(ungarisch)en Kriegszentralen 1914–1918', in Gerald Schöpfer and Barbara Stelzl-Marx, eds., *Wirtschaft. Macht. Geschichte: Brüche und Kontinuitäten im 20. Jahrhundert* (Graz: Leykam, 2012), 268.

[143] N. P. Howard, 'The Social and Political Consequences of the Allied Food Blockade of Germany, 1918–19', *German History*, 11:2 (1993), 182–4.

[144] Berend, *An Economic History*, 60–1.

[145] U. Kluge, *Die deutsche Revolution: 1918/1919; Staat, Politik und Gesellschaft zwischen Weltkrieg und Kapp-Putsch* (Berlin: Suhrkamp, 1997); H. A. Winkler, *La Repubblica di Weimar: 1918–1933: storia della prima democrazia tedesca* (Rome: Donzelli Editore, 1998); G. Hirschfeld, G. Krumeich and I. Renz, *1918: Die Deutschen zwischen Weltkrieg und Revolution* (Berlin: Ch. Links Verlag, 2018).

were demanding draconian requisitioning policies),[146] it became even more imperative to rely on rationing as a fair means of distribution. This was emphasized by the fact that control of German agricultural policy had ended up in the hands of representatives of the SPD,[147] who were keen to protect consumers rather than producers.[148] In Austria the political situation was similar.[149]

The continuing shortage of foodstuffs on the domestic market restricted the actions of decision makers, who remained inevitably entrenched in the wartime economy: on 10 March 1919, with the Allied blockade still in force and no imports allowed into the country, the Federal Minister of Nutrition and Agriculture was forced to admit before the German Constituent Assembly that he was unable to abandon the forced economy as far as food was concerned, although the farmers' associations demanded that this policy, whose limitations were by now obvious, be abolished.[150] The agreement signed in Brussels on 14 March 1919 with the Allies, which allowed Germany to import 270,000 tons/month of foodstuffs,[151] may have partially alleviated immediate nutritional needs. Yet it did not solve the food shortage issue at its root: there was widespread lack of credit in Germany and, moreover, that was not enough to cover the enormous German food deficit. The Blockade on Germany was finally lifted in July 1919.[152] Despite numerous attempts by Federal Minister for Alimentation, Robert Schmidt, to liberalize the movement of marginal products (measures that were quickly rescinded due to the complete disappearance of these products from the market, as in the case of oats),[153] people had to wait until the summer of 1920[154] to see the first decisive provisions made for the

146 U. Kluge, *Agrarwirtschaft und ländliche Gesellschaft im 20. Jahrhundert* (Munich: Oldenbourg, 2005), 18; R. G. Moeller, *Peasants and Lords in Modern Germany: Recent Studies in Agricultural History* (Winchester, MA: Allen & Unwin, 1986), 97; R. G. Moeller, 'Winners as Losers in the German Inflation: Peasant Protest over Controlled Economy, 1920–1923', in G. D. Feldman et al., eds., *Die Deutsche Inflation. Eine Zwischenbilanz* (Berlin: De Gruyter, 1982), 257–88.

147 Corni and Frizzera, 'Die Diskussion', 36–7.

148 Flemming, *Landwirtschaftliche Interesse*, 164.

149 H. Loewenfeld-Russ, *Im Kampf gegen den Hunger: aus den Erinnerungen des Staatssekretärs für Volksernährung, 1918–1920* (Munich: Oldenbourg, 1986), 220.

150 *Verhandlungen des Reichstages*, Bd. 326, 1919/20, Berlin, 1920, 627, Nationalversammlung. – 24. Sitzung. Montag den 10. März 1919.

151 *Akten der Reichskanzlei, Weimarer Republik*, Bd. 1: *Das Kabinett Scheidemann, 13. Februar bis 20. Juni 1919* (Boppard: H. Boldt, 1971), 50: Doc. 14b, Kabinettsitzung vom. 15. März 1919, Lebensmittelabkommen in Brüssel.

152 Howard, 'The Social and Political Consequences', 194.

153 Der Reichswirtschaftsminister an dem Reichspräsident, 24/09/19, BA/R 43-I/1255, foll. 200–3.

154 Auszug aus dem Protokoll der Sitzung des Reichsministeriums, 14/05/1920, BA/R43-I/2535, fol. 32.

withdrawal of meat and potatoes from the forced economy in Germany, which was implemented by the new Minister, Andreas Hermes.[155]

The situation in German-Austria was similar, if not worse. After the borders had been redrawn, there were 1.3 million self-supplying civilians in Austria, counterbalanced by 5.7 million people who relied on state distribution.[156] Accounting for the reduction in yields of Austrian farmland and the need to import grain from Hungary, which were a feature of regional trade relations prior to the conflict, in 1919 the Austrian *Staatsamt fuer Volksernährung* was able to distribute just 103 grams of bread per person per day. In fact, in order to reach the pre-war consumption of 386 g/day, 73 per cent of the bread grain had to be imported, in an international context that had been completely transformed by the Austro-Hungarian's Empire collapse.[157]

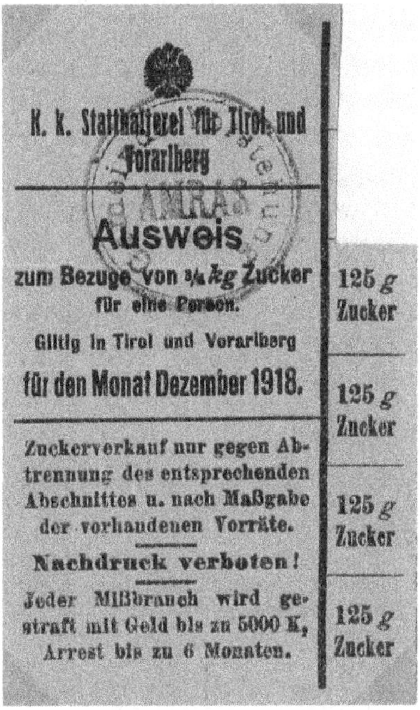
K. k. Statthalterei für Tirol und Vorarlberg

AMRAS

Ausweis

zum Bezuge von ¾ kg Zucker für eine Person.

Giltig in Tirol und Vorarlberg

für den Monat Dezember 1918.

Zuckerverkauf nur gegen Abtrennung des entsprechenden Abschnittes u. nach Maßgabe der vorhandenen Vorräte.

Nachdruck verboten!

Jeder Mißbrauch wird gestraft mit Geld bis zu 5000 K, Arrest bis zu 6 Monaten.

125 g Zucker

125 g Zucker

125 g Zucker

125 g Zucker

Figure 3.6 Ration card, Tyrol (Republic of Austria), December 1918. Source: Museo Storico Italiano della Guerra (MSIG), Archivio fotografico (AF), 114/127

155 Schumacher, *Land*, 182.

156 H. Loewenfeld-Russ, *Ernährungswirtschaftliche Gegenwartsprobleme in Österreich: Vortrag geh. in d. Vollversammlung d. N.-ö. Gewerbevereines am 28. Nov. 1919* (Vienna: Manz, 1919), 6.

157 Loewenfeld-Russ, *Ernährungswirtschaftliche Gegenwartsprobleme*, 7–8.

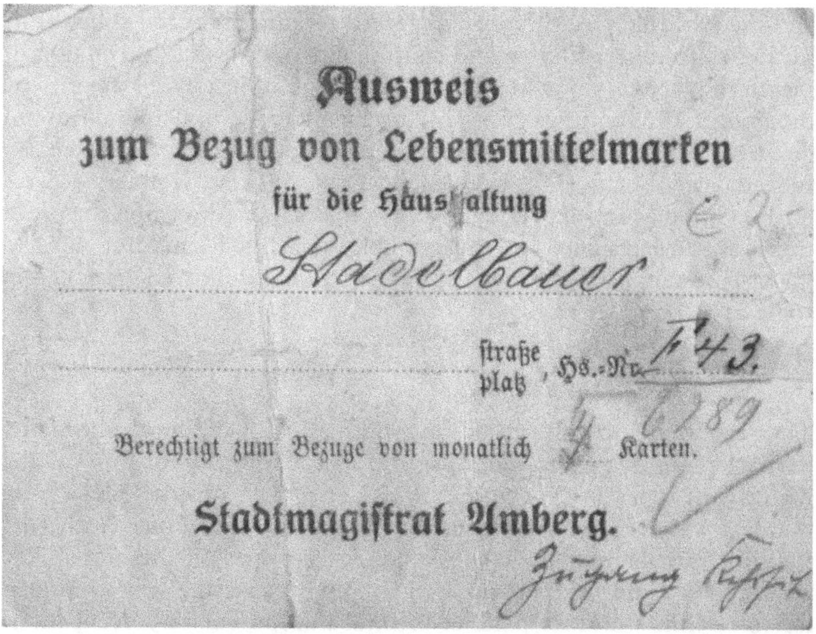

Ausweis
zum Bezug von Lebensmittelmarken
für die Haushaltung
Stadelbauer
straße
platz , Hs.-Nr.
Berechtigt zum Bezuge von monatlich 4 Karten.
Stadtmagistrat Amberg.

Figure 3.7 Card for food coupons, Hans Stadlbauer, 1919.
Source: Europeana. www.europeana.eu/fr/item/2020601/https___1914_1918_europeana_eu_contributions_3088

The limited international movement of foodstuffs was a result of the radical change that the European trading structure had undergone after the war. The great empires of Eastern Europe had disappeared from the map of Europe. The new borders redesigned by the peace treaties did not take into account pre-existing economic areas but were based on national and/or political considerations. This created major economic obstacles for Eastern European countries, not least with regard to food supply: 'Once the borders were redrawn, thirty-eight independent economic units replaced the pre-war twenty-six, and twenty-seven currencies were in use instead of the pre-war fourteen. The frontiers, i.e. tariff borders, increased by 2,000 kilometers.'[158] Cities of enormous size, like Vienna, were isolated from the hinterland that guaranteed their sustenance and economic role. Before the war 850,000 litres of milk a day were consumed in Vienna; of these, 200,000 came from Bohemia, Moravia and Silesia (now in Czechoslovakia), while 100,000 came from Hungary. These distribution channels were cut off when hostilities ended

[158] Berend, *An Economic History*, 54.

and the Austrian government was forced to administer the shortfall by further restricting rationing and controlling imports and distribution. It therefore managed to guarantee a daily ration of just 1,271 calories by the end of 1919 and was not able to abandon the principle of rationing, because the conditions that had created it had not ceased to exist. Indeed, according to Hans Loewenfeld-Russ, Austrian Secretary of State for Food, total control over imports was maintained even after the peace treaties had been signed and the naval blockade lifted 'since not only had the circumstances brought about by the war not improved, they had in some cases even deteriorated'.[159]

Regional Wars beyond 1918

The second element to prompt a continuation of the forced economy in many states was even more practical. In many parts of Europe, the war did not end in November 1918. The most obvious cases were the civil war in Russia between Bolsheviks and the White Army, the Polish-Ukrainian war and the Greco-Turkish war. In these areas the war economy did not end in 1918 simply because the war continued for some time. In other parts of Central Europe, military occupations (the Rhineland, for instance) prevented normal economic recovery; in other contexts, political power was contended by stakeholders with conflicting aspirations, some of whom had set their sights on revolutionary solutions (Hungary, Slovakia). This of course led to states needing to continuously intervene to tackle the food crisis. In these situations, state control was at its most pervasive after November 1918.

In Hungary when the war ended, the 'social democratic workers' movement ... temporarily acquired control over the entire public supply in the country'. Mór Erdélyi, 'the head of the General Consumer Cooperative, became the commissary for public supply' and the centralized control and distribution system in this stage became omnipresent: during the four and a half months of the 'dictatorship of the proletariat', there existed, de facto, a 'dictatorship of urban food consumers over rural food producers, or the dictatorship of worker consumers over other urban consumers'.[160]

The most evident case of this development is provided by Bolshevik Russia where, in particular in the so-called war communism period,[161]

[159] Loewenfeld-Russ, *Ernährungswirtschaftliche Gegenwartsprobleme*, 10–26.

[160] Zsombor Bódy, 'The Food as Political Issue during and after WWI in Hungary', in *State and Food Supply during the Wars of the 20th Century* (Journée d'étude, Sciences Po, Paris, 25 November 2016).

[161] Silvana Malle, *The Economic Organization of War Communism 1918–1921* (Cambridge: Cambridge University Press, 2002).

governmentalization and requisitioning measures reached their peak, inevitably involving also the food production, processing and distribution chain. This stage (mid 1918 to 1920) saw a further 'enforcement of compulsory food requisitioning from farmers as the main means to supply food to the urban areas'.[162] As early as May 1918 the creation of a 'food dictatorship, the subsequent formation of poor peasants' and local food committees, and a more aggressive promotion of collective forms of agriculture' had been announced. The food dictatorship 'reasserted the principles of the state grain monopoly and fixed grain prices, both of which had been introduced by the Provisional Government', with the substantial difference being that peasants were ordered to hand over all grain surpluses to the state and the government was authorized to use armed force to collect cereals.[163] Initially this method was applied only to grain and fodder, but then was widely extended to other agricultural products and raw materials as well. Only in 1919 was the concept of monopoly gradually replaced by that of '*razverstka*', a policy and campaign of confiscation of grain from peasants at nominal fixed prices according to specified quotas. It was therefore necessary to await the New Economic Policy in April 1921 to see the official end to compulsory requisitioning, this being replaced by a tax in kind, named '*prodnalog*', which corresponded to part of the harvest.[164] Indeed, this did not immediately solve the food crisis and worse aspects of the famine followed the harvest of 1921.

Finally, one of the most evident features that shows the long duration of government intervention in the agricultural and food supply field beyond the end of the war is given by land reforms. The state – and particularly the new states of Central and Eastern Europe – continued the practice of intervening in the economic life of farmers and consumers, transforming the secular structure of agricultural property. However, 'post-war agrarian reforms carried out in all South East European countries had all the characteristics of land redistribution but did not have any plans to enhance the economic efficiency of the agricultural sector'. Nevertheless, land redistribution rates reached 40 per cent of

162 Antony Heywood, 'Post-War Economies (Russian Empire)', in U. Daniel, Peter Gatrell, Oliver Janz, et al., eds., *1914–1918-online. International Encyclopedia of the First World War* (Berlin: Freie Universität Berlin, 2015), https://encyclopedia.1914-1918-online.net/article/post-war_economies_russian_empire [accessed 26 April 2023].

163 Patenaude, 'Paesants into Russian', 554.

164 P. Kenez, *A History of the Soviet Union from the Beginning to the End* (Cambridge: Cambridge University Press, 2006), 47–8; V. P. Tīmoshenko, *Agricultural Russia and the Wheat Problem* (Stanford, CA: Pub. jointly by the Food Research Institute and the Committee on Russian Research of the Hoover War Library, 1932), 86; L. Lih, 'Bolshevik Razverstka and War Communism', *Slavic Review*, 45:4 (1986), 673–88.

total agricultural area of Greece, 20 per cent in Romania, 17 per cent in Yugoslavia and 6 per cent in Bulgaria.[165] This practice also characterized Eastern Europe, where land reforms also served for nationalist purposes, 'because landlords belonging to new national minorities … were disproportionately affected'.[166] In this region the territory affected by reforms and distributed to small or medium-sized owners reaches 42 per cent of Latvian, 25 per cent of Estonian, 17 per cent of Lithuanian, 14 per cent of Czechoslovak, 10 per cent of Hungarian and 6 per cent of Polish agricultural area.[167]

The Slow Return to the Free Market

The economic situation of countries emerging from the war in a new international context prevented a rapid return to a free market. The reasons were partly associated with the difficulties in accessing credit, in a situation in which currencies were drastically depreciating, as in Germany[168] and Austria.[169] This led to difficulties in financing the importation of the enormous quantities of foodstuffs that could not be produced internally. The forced economy therefore persisted for some time and was only dismantled very slowly.

In Germany, the end of total requisitioning of the cereal harvest did not come until April 1921 and was replaced by the obligation to deliver a considerable share of the harvest at a fixed price set by the State.[170] Only in October 1920 did meat and potato rationing come to an end,[171] though the subsidized distribution of imported meat and potatoes continued.[172] The legal end to compulsory consignment of part of the cereal

[165] I. Innerhofer, 'Post-War Economies (South East Europe)', in U. Daniel, Peter Gatrell, Oliver Janz, et al., eds., *1914–1918-online. International Encyclopedia of the First World War* (Berlin: Freie Universität Berlin, 2015), https://encyclopedia.1914-1918-online.net/article/post-war_economies_south_east_europe [accessed 26 April 2023].

[166] I. Livezeanu, T. Ort and A. Drace-Francis, 'The Cultures of East Central Europe: Imperial, National, Revolutionary', in I. Livezeanu and A. von Klimo, eds., *The Routledge History of East Central Europe since 1700* (Abingdon: Routledge, 2017), 345.

[167] League of the Nations, *Agricultural Production in Continental Europe during the 1914–18 War and the Reconstruction Period* (Geneva: League of the Nations, 1943), 48.

[168] Statistischen Reichsamt, *Deutschlands Wirtschaftslage Unter Den Nachwirkungen Des Weltkrieges. Unter Verwendung von Amtlichen Material Zusammengestellt Im Statistischen Reichsamt* (Berlin: Zentralverlag, 1923), 12–24; C. L. Holtfrerich, *The German Inflation 1914–1923: Causes and Effects in International Perspective* (New York: Walter de Gruyter, 2013), 197.

[169] Loewenfeld-Russ, *Im Kampf*, 236–49.

[170] Schumacher, *Land*, 162.

[171] Corni and Frizzera, 'Die Diskussion', 39.

[172] Schumacher, *Land*, 154–68.

harvest did not come until July 1923, and only came into effect in the first half of 1924,[173] followed by the end of bread rationing.[174]

The situation was comparable in the European Balkans and the Habsburg Empire successor states: Romania, which in 1914 had been the world's fourth largest exporter of wheat, 'had to import grain and other foodstuffs in order to meet the urgent needs of the population'.[175] It was necessary to wait as long as February 1924 for permission to export grain to be reintroduced and December 1924 for the export of oilseed crops to be liberalized. In the meantime the requisitioning of harvests was maintained until April 1921, accompanied by production bonuses and the distribution of seeds.[176] In Yugoslavia and in particular in Croatia, Slovenia, Bosnia and Dalmatia, the Habsburg *Kriegszentralen* were reopened and requisitioning as well as rationing of grain and livestock were implemented: the new government thus extended the forced economy and rationing until 1921.[177] In Czechoslovakia the situation was by no means any better and state control over foodstuffs not only continued for another three years after the end of hostilities (rationing and price ceilings until 1921, foreign exchange control until 1922),[178] but this also had to be supported, as in Germany, Austria, France and Hungary, by substantial consignments of food coordinated by the ARA which supplied millions of tons of foodstuffs to these areas.[179]

In other cases, the end of inter-allied cooperation rendered the organizing, financing and collective purchasing of foodstuffs from overseas more complex: in August 1919 the Wheat Executive (composed of a representative of, respectively, the French, British and Italian governments) was abolished[180] and the work of the Commission for Relief

[173] Schumacher, *Land*, 182.

[174] S. Hadry, 'Ernährungskrise, Revolution Und Der Bauernbund – Zur Geschichte Des Ersten Bayerischen Staatsministeriums Für Landwirtschaft (1919–1932)', *Archivalische Zeitschrift*, 92:1 (2011), 232; B. Ziemann, *War Experiences in Rural Germany: 1914–1923* (Oxford: Berg, 2011), 348.

[175] Innerhofer, 'Post-War Economies (South East Europe)'.

[176] Ionesco-Sisesti, *L'Agriculture*, 112–14.

[177] Innerhofer, 'Post-War Economies (South East Europe)'; J. R. Lampe and M. R. Jackson, eds., *Balkan Economic History, 1550–1950: From Imperial Borderlands to Developing Nations* (Bloomington, IN: Indiana University Press, 1982), 348–49.

[178] J. Krejcí and P. Machonin, *Czechoslovakia, 1918–92: A Laboratory for Social Change* (Basingstoke: Macmillan, 1998), 59.

[179] B. Berglund R., '"We Stand on the Threshold of a New Age": Alice Masarykova, the Czechoslovak Red Cross, and the Building of a New Europe', in M. Stibbe and I. Sharp, eds., *Aftermaths of War: Women's Movements and Female Activists, 1918–1923* (Leiden: Brill, 2011), 364.

[180] Dentoni, *Annona*, 25.

in Belgium (CRB) came to an end,[181] which resulted in France, Italy, Belgium and Britain having to organize their own purchases from abroad. Italy attempted prematurely (March 1919) to return to a free market since the cost of importing cereals risked exhausting the government's finances. However, the Italian government was forced a few months later to reintroduce all the restrictive regulations that had been enacted during wartime: the shortage of food and extremely high prices caused the outbreak of numerous popular protests.[182] People had to wait until 1921, in other words until after the 'Biennio Rosso' – a two-year period of intense social conflict and popular protests – for price ceilings to be revoked for bread, for domestic trade and the distribution of cereals to be freed and to see the end of rationing.[183]

In France, the state policy with regard to the control over the harvest and distribution of foodstuffs developed along the same lines. Also, in this case exit from the controlled economy was gradual and fraught with difficulty. Limits on production and the sale of condensed milk (January 1919), butter and cheese (March 1919) were slowly abolished, but the end of inter-allied cooperation prompted the government to issue lists of goods that were banned from being exported (July 1919). Meanwhile recourse to requisitioning was gradually restricted: in May 1919 the requisitioning of maize and oats ceased and in August 1919, after the harvest, regulation of other cereals (except for grain) also came to a halt. As in Italy, however, the government was then forced to partially backtrack, reintroducing set prices for producers for cereals and bread flour (February 1920), reappointing the commissions that set maximum prices for grain, sugar and rye (July 1920) and continuing to control exports. The exportation of potatoes was only liberalized in February 1921, followed a month later by the end of maximum sales price setting and, in May 1921, by the free movement of cereals on national territory and by the end of sugar rationing, the last vestige of the controlled economy.[184]

This development reflected precisely what was happening in Belgium: here too, after the operations of the CRB ceased, the government shouldered the responsibility for supervizing and administrating the purchase

[181] B. Little, 'Commission for Relief in Belgium (CRB)', in U. Daniel, Peter Gatrell, Oliver Janz, et al., eds., *1914–1918-online. International Encyclopedia of the First World War* (Berlin: Freie Universität Berlin, 2015), https://encyclopedia.1914-1918-online.net/article/commission_for_relief_in_belgium_crb [accessed 26 April 2023].

[182] Dentoni, *Annona*, 165–71; Bachi and Zingali, *L'alimentazione*, 175.

[183] Bachi and Zingali, *L'alimentazione*, 185–90.

[184] M. Augé-Laribé, *L'agriculture pendant la guerre* (Paris: Les Presses Universitaires de France; New Haven, CT: Yale University Press, 1925), 291–7.

of foodstuffs abroad, creating the *Ministère du Ravitaillement* (Ministry of Food Supply), which remained in existence until December 1921. As in France, the rationing system was only gradually dispensed with and the last step in its dismantling was ending sugar rationing, which occurred in July 1921.[185]

In Britain, the need to maintain minimum guaranteed prices for farmers who had converted their crops and the simultaneous end to inter-allied cooperation led to the same outcomes. When inter-allied import agreements ended, it was forbidden for private citizens to import meat and only in August 1921 did the Food Commission stop trading flour. In the retail sector there were the same fluctuations experienced in France, Germany and Italy: in May 1919 the end of setting of maximum prices for milk was decreed, but in December of the same year the price caps were reintroduced. The same happened with bread: first the order was given to end maximum retail prices for bread in April 1920, then these were reintroduced in August; finally, in October 1920, bread and flour prices were liberalized. With regard to requisitioning (December 1918) the gathering up of pigs was halted immediately, but meat continued to be stockpiled and in April 1921 the government was still distributing 100 per cent of bread grain to the mills. The same applied to general rationing, which was maintained until May 1920 and only came to an end in November 1921 when sugar rationing ceased.[186]

Conclusion

The First World War forced countries throughout Europe to intervene radically in their food supply chains, thereby extending the State's perview and its authority. Measures to control prices, rationing, centralized distribution, requisitioning and steering agricultural production became routine for both consumers and producers. Countries equipped themselves with gargantuan bureaucratic machinery for this purpose.

The prevalent aspects of this interference in the laws of the free market and conditioning the day-to-day lives of the civilian population can be summarized in three main elements. Firstly, this intervention by the state was to a large extent improvized: a large number of the measures taken during the first two years of war proved to be partial; some even caused an aggravation of the food shortages rather than easing them. A learning curve can thus be denoted over the course of the war, which

185 A. R. Fleissig and G. A. Whitney, 'Belgium Relief Fund, Post War Food Shortages and the "True" Cost of Living', *Explorations in Economic History*, 58 (2015), 98–101.
186 Beveridge, *British Food Control*, 295–301.

led to increasingly more complex and centralized provisions being issued, to the point where in many cases, by the end of the conflict, we can even speak of a centrally planned food economy. This development also highlights path dependency: once the decision makers had undertaken the road to centralized control, it became increasingly difficult to renounce restrictive measures in administering food shortages.

The second important element is the omnipresence of these measures. The control systems were not caused *ipso facto* by the Allied naval blockade but were a constant of Europe at war. All the belligerant countries and even neutral states in Continental Europe had to face the challenges posed by food shortages because of violence to man and land, foreign occupation and devastating blockades. Perhaps most interesting is the close resemblance of the measures taken, albeit in countries with highly diverse agricultural economies, and conditions of war that could not have been more different – belligerents and neutrals alike. The timing and the radicality of the measures varied in relation to the severity of shortages and to the organization of power relations within states. What did not change were the responses and solutions adopted across the whole of Europe. Hence there was a widespread transfer of competences.

Lastly, these controlled economic measures, which were the result of the emergencies brought about by the war, did not disappear when the war ended. For a long time afterwards, countries were to continue to affect the daily lives of their citizens where food was concerned. For a period that in some cases lasted as long as ten years, ordinary people were forced to live with shortages, rationing and maximum prices. When peace was restored, the administrative structures created during wartime to manage the food emergency took far longer to dismantle than the time required to demobilize the armed forces.

4 Individual Strategies of Survival

Friederike Kind-Kovács

Introduction

In the past decade, a collective and partly illegal social movement has spread throughout urban spaces in Europe and beyond known as 'guerrilla gardening'. It embraces all kinds of initiatives to collectively grow food in neglected areas or vacant spaces as a means of contributing to urban food security.[1] While in our day this social movement reflects an attempt to collectively resist food globalization and unite communities, there have been times in history when initiatives to use neglected or public urban spaces for food production were a reaction to a scarcity or even entire lack of certain foodstuffs. During the First World War, home-based agriculture became one of the most widely used individual strategies of survival. People planted and harvested food wherever they could. Yet, this was just one of the various means civilians employed to fight hunger in war and post-war Europe. The progressive shortages of certain commodities and increasing food insecurity made hungry people around the continent improvise and search for alternative modes to gain access to basic and otherwise unavailable foodstuffs.

This chapter focuses on how ordinary civilians responded to the shortcomings of official food provisioning systems using a variety of individual survival strategies. Transnational comparisons show the diverse modes and means employed throughout Europe by civilians to survive the scarcity of food during the Great War and its aftermath. In all European countries that suffered from hunger, governments tried to equally distribute the available food and introduced rationing systems but the reality of the limited supply available through official channels meant that populations needed to access additional food resources. People across the continent employed a diversity of strategies to respond to the lack of food. Some of them corresponded to pre-war methods of competent

[1] Stephan Barthel, 'Resilience', in *A Companion to Urban Anthropology*, edited by Donald M. Nonini (Oxford: Wiley Blackwell, 2014), 432.

housekeeping: people tried to use food more efficiently, or to produce it themselves. They also circumvented official distribution means by relying on the alternative economies of the grey and black markets, crossing into illegality. They sometimes resorted to even more illegal activities such as fraud and theft. It was often women who utilized such strategies to meet the daily challenge of feeding their families in times of food scarcity.[2] As many men were at the front, women turned into 'soldiers in the food wars', and in their new role they often stole or smuggled food to provide for their families.[3] These strategies were not isolated from each other and could be used together or in succession as the war unfolded. Women and families of course took actions in different forms throughout the continent, depending on the severity of the food scarcity, but the strategies they used also shared many similar features and delineated new modes of social interactions, and new relationships to the licit and the illicit in wartime.

The Need for Alternative Food Strategies

In times of war and conflict food – the most essential necessity of daily life – becomes the centre of attention and thus reflects 'micro- and macrohistorical processes, as individuals, families, cities and states struggle for provisions'.[4] During the First World War food was not only required for soldiers at the front but for the civilian populations as well.[5] The scarcity of food made it impossible for many governments to meet both the nutritional needs of its army and its civilians.[6] When governments had to choose between feeding their soldiers or civilians, they tended to prioritize feeding their soldiers.[7] Civilians understood this inequality as illustrated by the people they targeted when they begged. In Warsaw, for example, by March 1916 'the stretched hands of beggars to those in military uniform' and 'professional beggars' who used their children to occupy the main squares and spots were becoming an everyday sight.[8]

[2] Karen Hunt, 'Gender and Everyday Life', in *Gender and the Great War*, edited by Tammy M. Proctor and Susan R. Grayzel (Oxford: Oxford University Press, 2017), 154.

[3] Tammy M. Proctor, *Civilians in a World at War: 1914–1918* (New York, NY: New York University Press, 2010), 95.

[4] Melanie Schulze Tanielian, 'Feeding the City: The Beirut Municipality and the Politics of Food during World War I', *International Journal of Middle East Studies* 46:4 (2014), 740.

[5] Hunt, 'Gender and Everyday Life', 150.

[6] Proctor, *Civilians in a World at War*, 5.

[7] Ute Daniel, *Arbeiterfrauen in der Kriegsgesellschaft: Beruf, Familie und Politik im Ersten Weltkrieg* (Göttingen: Vandenhoeck & Ruprecht, 1989), 201.

[8] Robert Blobaum, *A Minor Apocalypse: Warsaw during the First World War* (Ithaca, NY: Cornell University Press, 2017), 87.

If begging was not successful, 'desperation' over the lack of sufficient nutrition 'led people to look for it even in dumps and waste bins'.[9]

Although the prioritization of militaries over civilians was widespread, it was rarely done without consideration of civilians on the Homefront. Indeed, as Chapter 3 in this volume shows, most European governments introduced rationing systems in an effort to help secure the survival of their civilian populations. However, given the scarcity of food, state rationing systems and price controls were rarely able, on their own, to consistently provide civilian populations with the sufficient food supplies they needed. Rationing tickets did not necessarily translate into the availability of the rationed good. A diary of a teacher from Trentino in Southern Tyrol from 27 April 1917 recalls '[p]eople have been hungry since the flour of the ration card has not been distributed as prescribed!'.[10] Even people who were not exclusively dependent on state provisions and who had the means to purchase additional foodstuffs could often not do so, as the desired foodstuffs were simply not available. It was not only in Tyrol where ration cards did not always translate to actual food. This was a common experience. To cite an example from Bohemia from June 1918, a military commander reported the story of a mother of six who was 'in the highest despair, because she has been unable for fourteen days to get bread and flour from her bread and flour cards'. This was 'not an isolated case'.[11]

The food situation for people housed in government institutions throughout Europe demonstrates how insufficient official supply systems were even when the rationed goods were available and delivered.[12] As the ability to obtain additional food became vital, people who could not leave the institution's premises were unable to secure additional calories. As one report from Bohemia explained, inmates of psychiatric asylums were 'the only people in the [Austro-Hungarian] monarchy who actually had to live on the rations which the state had established, and who could

9 Agnieszka Drozdowska, *Kobiety w czasie Pierwszej wojny światowej [Women during the First World War]* (Białystok: Książnica Podlaska im. Łukasza Górnickiego, 2018), 114 and Povilas Dogelis, *Mano gyvenimo prisiminimai [Memories of my Life]* (Kaunas: „Šešupės" spaustuvė Marijampolėje 1936), 206, both cited in Andrea Griffante, 'Food and Nutrition (East Central Europe)', in *1914–1918-online. International Encyclopedia of the First World War*, edited by Ute Daniel et al., (Berlin: Freie Universität Berlin, 2022), https://encyclopedia.1914-1918-online.net/article/food_and_nutrition_east_central_europe/?version=1.0.

10 FMST, ASP, Daniele Speranza, Diario, c. 76. Fondazione Museo storico del Trentino, Archivio della Scrittura Popolare.

11 ÖStA, AdR, Volksernährungsamt, AR, K151, no. 96062, Mood Report from the Military Commander in Prague, 30 June 1918.

12 On Germany, see Mary Elisabeth Cox *Hunger in War and Peace: Women and Children in Germany, 1914–1924* (New York, NY: Oxford University Press, 2019), 89.

not procure for themselves anything more'.[13] Certainly in Vienna, the Steinhof asylum recorded an excess mortality of 4,000 inmates for the period 1914–1923.[14] In Germany, people in government institutions lost weight and had higher mortality rates than the rest of the civilian population.[15] From 1914 to 1918, 4,434 additional patients died in Belgian psychiatric asylums as a result of the wartime context.[16] Inmates in Riga prisons experienced similar outcomes as it was difficult for inmates to live on the state rations alone. In 1919, the diet in Latvian prisons consisted of only 1,500 calories per day.[17] These examples of food dependency show that the rationing systems alone rarely met the minimum nutritional standard and requirements.

Ordinary people, whose daily movements were not restricted because of institutions or asylums, were able to seek alternative ways to obtain necessary commodities as state rations were not sufficient. They primarily did so in the common framework of neighbourhoods and communities. These networks were often independent from official state provisions and outside formal markets.[18] To obtain sufficient food alongside often unreliable daily food rations, individuals and communities turned to bartering, home-based agricultural production, trips to the countryside, black and grey market participation and crime and theft. These alternative ways to obtain food were not exclusively hunger-driven survival strategies. They were also useful means to combat rising prices, to add more sought-after foodstuffs often unavailable through the market, and for some, even a way to earn extra income.

It should be noted that the various strategies people used to source additional foodstuffs reveal a situation of relative choice for individuals. In extreme cases of famine, hungry civilians simply ate whatever they could find, especially in times of desperation and panic. For example, by late 1915, especially in Beirut and Mount Lebanon, which had become

[13] NA, MZd/R, ka 5, no. 2374, Report from the Bohemian Governor's Office to the Austrian Ministry of Health, 29 August 1918.

[14] Peter Schwarz, '"Die Opfer sagen, es war die Hölle": Vom Tremolieren, Faradisieren, Hungern und Sterben: Krieg und Psychiatrie in Wien', in *Im Epizentrum des Zusammenbruchs: Wien im Ersten Weltrieg*, edited by Alfred Pfoser and Andreas Weigl (Wien: Metroverlag, 2013), 330–4.

[15] Max Rubmann, *Hunger! Wirkungen moderner Kriegsmethoden* (Berlin: Verlag von Georg Reimer, 1919), 60.

[16] Benoît Majérus and Anne Roekens, 'Deadly Vulnerabilities. The Provisioning of Psychiatric Asylums in Occupied Belgium (1914–1918)', *Journal of Belgian History* 47:4 (2017), 18–48.

[17] 'Mūsu cietumnieku pārtika', *Policijas Vēstnesis* 65 (1923), 2.

[18] Jay Winter, 'The Practices of Metropolitan Life in Wartime', in *Capital Cities at War: Paris, London, Berlin 1914–1919*, edited by Jay Winter and Jean-Louis Robert (Cambridge: Cambridge University Press, 1997), 4.

the epicentre of the Ottoman hunger crisis, this meant consuming items that were normally not considered food, and that were dangerous to human health. In an account by Najwa al-Qattan, Antun Yamin recalled the hunger years and the transgressions it wrought. Under the header 'Stories That Would Shake Rocks', he described what he had seen: near a school, namely 'two children, picked sesame seeds from piles of excrement'. In another story, 'a young man died after gorging himself on lemon peels'. He also recalled a situation when a group of 'forty people ate the carcass from head to hoof' of a diseased horse that had been left behind by German soldiers.[19] This proclivity occurred elsewhere as well, when the choice was either to eat something previously unimaginable, or to not eat. Once the Italian town of Udine, for example, had been occupied by German troops in 1917, the people in the cities were doomed to eat 'bad bread and rotten vegetables'.[20] Hungry people across Europe and the Ottoman Empire were willing to eat poor-quality, sometimes rancid food.

In such an atmosphere, it is perhaps not surprising that rumors of cannibalism circulated. Najwa al-Qattan elaborates on two, though unverified, moments when a man had eaten 'three human corpses' and when a woman by the name of Helena had consumed 'the corpse of her nephew'.[21] Rumors of cannibalism also surfaced in other regions affected by extreme food scarcity. During the famine in the Volga region, various cases of cannibalism and corpse-eating were reported by two Russian physicists who produced studies on the subject. One of the doctors recalled in his study a moment of corpse-eating at a cemetery 'where twelve people had dug up the corpse of a man who had died of an infectious disease and were eating the flesh "quite raw on the spot"'.[22] Cases of cannibalism were also reported by a Russian university professor who worked for the American Relief Administration (ARA): '[f]amilies were killing and devouring fathers, grandfathers and children'.[23] In a context of millions of hungry people, such accounts, whether true or not, remain limited. If practiced at all, only a very few individuals resorted to cannibalism in countries like the Soviet Union and the Ottoman Empire that

[19] Najwa al-Qattan, 'When Mothers ate Their Children: Wartime Memory and the Language of Food in Syria and Lebanon', *International Journal of Middle East Studies* 46 (2014), 720.

[20] Allison Scardino Belzer, *Women and the Great War: Feminity under Fire in Italy* (New York, NY: Palgrave Macmillan, 2010), 132.

[21] Najwa al-Qattan, 'When Mothers Ate their Children', 720.

[22] Cited in: Bertrand M. Patenaude, *The Big Show in Bololand: The American Relief Expedition to Soviet Russia in the Famine of 1921* (Stanford, CA: Stanford University Press, 2002), 265.

[23] Patenaude, *The Big Show*, 265.

suffered from mass starvation. The vast majority of people, even in these starving Empires, did not succumb to this practice. But rumors of such practices perhaps made it easier for desperate people to justify their own actions of eating other, less edible things, such as vegetable peels, grass and the carcasses of dead animals described earlier.

Beyond people's very basic needs, 'the notion of well-being in wartime' had a subjective dimension.[24] It differed from individual to individual, from community to community and from country to country. Yet, most people shared a common desire to maintain some part of their pre-war eating habits. People found it difficult to give up on certain dishes and ways of eating. The 'unquestionable lack of consideration of people's dietary habits and eating habits' in a German report from August 1917 was considered to have a 'depressing impact on the whole [German] population'.[25] While in the first years of the war it might have been easier to 'accept sacrifice for the greater good',[26] sacrifice in the later years of the war became less and less bearable.

To better understand the necessity to rely on alternative modes of provisioning, it is important to underline how difficult obtaining food had become for many urban dwellers across wartime Europe. Day after day, people queued for many hours, which was exhausting and frustrating to many, particularly if the long wait did not result in the anticipated foodstuffs. In Germany, the term 'promenade' was frequently used for this practice of going out and waiting in long lines hoping to obtain food. In post-war Budapest, in January 1920, 'long queues of women and children ... [began] to form about midnight before the bakers' shops, waiting for them to open in the morning'.[27] Sometimes, children would also go unsupervised to queue for food. Yet, because of a the lack of adequate clothing, as a report from 2 January 1920 states, children in Budapest had to take turns so that they would not freeze: 'three children take turns too at going out at midnight to stand before the shop in order to get some bread when the shop opens'.[28] A Hungarian relief worker recalled in 1920 the 'wasted

[24] Winter, 'The Practices of Metropolitan Life in Wartime', 11.

[25] Auszug aus dem Monatsbericht des K.W. Kriegsministeriums an Herrn Geheimrat Stadthagen, August 1917, Nr. A II 10152, Bundesarchiv Berlin/R3601/405.

[26] Winter, 'The Practices of Metropolitan Life in Wartime', 13.

[27] Archives d'État de Genève (The State Archives of Geneva), Archives de l'Union internationale de secours aux enfants (Archive of the Save the Children International Union), Archives privées 92.21.3, Secours à la Hongrie, Correspondence et rapport de Mme J.E. Vajkai, Julia Eva Vajkai, 'Supplementary report on the conditions of children in Hungary', 20 January 1920, 1–6, 1.

[28] Archives d'État de Genève, Archives de l'Union internationale de secours aux enfants, Archives privées 92.21.3, Secours à la Hongrie, Correspondence et rapport de Mme J.E. Vajkai, Julia Vajkai, 'The Need of Hungary.' Extract from the Report of Miss. R. Vajkai, Secretary of the Delegation of the International Red Cross

face' of a 10-year-old girl 'who had been on duty that night and had stood in the queue from 1 o'clock till 9', but who could not obtain any foodstuffs when her turn came.[29] When people were unable to wait for hours in those lines, either because of work obligations, age or illness, this most basic strategy to secure one's own survival could not be employed.

If certain products were simply unavailable, even after hours of waiting outside in the cold or even at night, some civilians chose to respond with violence and rioting.[30] The lack of certain food products and the massive amount of time which was needed, and often wasted, to secure one's everyday food resulted in emotional outbursts, including complaints, anger and even riots to those believed to be responsible. Moreover, queuing had at times a damaging effect on social relations, as it ignited 'rudeness, envy and violence'.[31] Major social struggles arose when some individuals who had queued for hours left empty-handed. In those cases, the lack of available commodities forced many to look for alternative strategies to obtain food.

Practices of Self-Provisioning

Because civilians could not always depend on rationed foods for their sustenance, they incorporated patterns of food self-provisioning. This included gathering and hoarding food, as well as cooking and preserving food in new ways. Housekeeping itself developed into a subsistence economy, which relied on the home production of foodstuffs, enabling people to cope with the shortage of food and complement the official food rations.[32] People often went directly to the countryside to collect and obtain foodstuffs. Many people attempted to obtain food in the countryside or to purchase it from black market retailers. Such journeys could last days or even weeks. For example, a report from 8 September 1918 from the Bohemian governor describes a 'real migration movement starting in June-July' of that year. Northern Bohemians, the report continues, traveled through the countryside sometimes even to Bavaria or Southern Bohemia to get food in exchange for their last piece of laundry. The inspector observed some of these exhausted women, children and elderly

in Budapest, concerning her visit in the suburb of Budapest called 'Angyalföld', Budapest, 2 January 1920.

29 Archives d'État de Genève Julia Vajkai, 'The Need of Hungary.' Extract from the Report of Miss. R. Vajkai, Secretary of the Delegation of the International Red Cross in Budapest, concerning her visit in the suburb of Budapest called 'Angyalf.ld', Budapest, 2 January 1920.

30 Maureen Healy, *Vienna and the Fall of the Habsburg Empire: World War and the Everyday Life in World War I* (Cambridge: Cambridge University Press, 2004), 35.

31 Healy, *Vienna and the Fall*, 77.

32 Daniel, *Arbeiterfrauen in der Kriegsgesellschaft*, 216.

Figure 4.1 The Food Hunt, board game, 1918.
Source: Spielzeugmuseum Stadt Nürnberg, Gertrud Caspari, 'Die Lebensmitteljagd'

men at the train stations in Neudek, Carlsbad and Plan, many of whom had been travelling for weeks.[33] The complexity of the 'hunt' for foodstuff was satirized in a contemporary German board game, where players had to go through different steps to find food (Figure 4.1).

Civilians also hoarded foodstuffs, some starting as early as in the first month of the war in 1914, before any food rationing was introduced. People were fixated on hoarding non-perishable foods as a form of insurance against the unknowns that the war, and later the official rationing, might bring. While the working classes were less in a position to hoard food, the German-American journalist Wolf von Schierbrand noted in

33 Report from the Bohemian governor to the Ministry of Alimentation, ÖStA, AdR, Volksernährungsamt, AR, K113, no. 135989, 8 September 1918.

1917 of Austria-Hungary that the well-to-do classes were the main problem. They started to hide 'immense stores of eatables not easily perishable such as smoked meats, bacon, ham, sausage, also flour, macaroni, rice, peas, beans, lentils, sugar, coffee, tea, cocoa, condensed milk, cheese, butter, lard, canned goods'. Because of people's immense obsession with hoarding food – as a 'private piling-up of eatables' – many food articles in Austria and Hungary completely 'disappeared from the open market, such as macaroni and noodles, rice, peas, beans, lentils, sardines and other fish preserves',[34] many of the exact items hoarded by the well-to-do.

In Hungary not only the landowners, but also the famers who profited from the war 'hid fat, flour and grain in underground pits or in holes beneath the dung heap and even raised poultry and pigs in them', which would later end up on the black market.[35] The farmers may also have been hiding foodstuffs from the military, who might requisition it. This occurred throughout southern Germany, when farmers would hide foodstuffs while working in the fields from fear of military – or hungry urban civilians on 'visits' to the countryside – might steal it.[36] Hence, individual survival strategies mirrored existing social and economic differences. Hoarding also became a strategy to prevent the access of the invading or occupying armies to the foodstuffs in occupied or seized territories. In occupied territories such as Belgium, hatred of enemy occupiers provided further fuel to resentment about food controls.[37]

In cellars and pantries, one could still find stockpiles of hoarded and canned foods, which became signs of the accumulated wealth of the better-off classes and prosperous famers. These stocks were also the subject of 'food fantasies' for hungry civilians,[38] but everyone who could tried to hoard as much non-perishable food as possible, as these private stocks enabled individuals to bridge days and weeks of food shortage. Hence, to shopkeepers and individuals, the proper storing and conservation of foodstuffs became even more essential to guarantee the even and daily distribution and consumption of food. The issue of how to best store food not only motivated individuals to prepare their own preserves and pickled food, it even engaged nutrition scientists to publish books on topics such as 'Our Foodstuffs: Their Character, Transformation and

[34] Wolf von Schierbrand, 'The Food Situation in Austria-Hungary', *The North American Review* 205:734 (1917), 51.

[35] Ignác Romsics, 'The Peasantry and the Age of Revolutions: Hungary, 1918–1919', *Acta Historica Academiae Scientiarum Hungaricae* 35:1/4 (1989), 120.

[36] Benjamin Ziemann, *War Experiences in Rural Germany: 1914–1923* (Oxford: Berg, 2007), 172.

[37] Proctor, *Civilians in a World at War*, 89.

[38] Healy, *Vienna and the Fall of the Habsburg Empire*, 69.

Conservation',[39] which appeared in Germany in 1917. Its author, Dr J. Roland, wished to provide not only doctors and pharmacists, but also teachers, farmers, shopkeepers and anyone interested in food preservation with instructions on how to best handle certain foodstuffs. While the storage of wheat and sugar, as the publication argues, did not pose much of a challenge, fresh vegetables, fresh fruits, dairy products and meat were difficult to store for prolonged periods.[40] While rejecting chemical preservation, he encouraged his readers to rely on natural food preservation through fungal cultures and bacteria, light, heat and cold.[41] Roland also proposed ways to prevent the 'unwanted and harmful decomposition' of foodstuffs and appealed to his readers to turn 'waste products, that had previously only been used as fertilizers and cattle feed', by means of suitable processing, into 'valuable foodstuffs and luxury items'. He wished to remind his readers of the fate of beer yeast, of which only a tiny part was being used as a leavening agent in bakeries, while the main part ended up in the gutter.[42] People bottled and canned available fruits and vegetables as a means of preserving food for later, which reduced the available stocks of fruits on the market. A report from Hungary in 1918 noted that the 'provision market had very little fruit on sale'.[43]

Shopping and cooking also turned into an 'exhausting struggle', as certain fundamental ingredients were often unobtainable, and housewives had to become creative in preparing their families' everyday meals.[44] Historian Heather Perry has described German housewives as 'kitchen soldiers', whose everyday efforts to obtain food could 'help or hinder the nation at war'.[45] Wartime cookbooks appeared that instructed housewives how to best handle the food crisis in the kitchen and prepare some dishes even without certain unavailable ingredients. Often published early in the conflict, they provided instructions on nutrition and practical recipes. For example, a cookbook published in 1914 in Bohemia introduced ordinary people to the principles of 'good cooking' by outlining the scientific foundation of modern nutrition and providing

[39] Dr J. Roland, *Unsere Lebensmittel: Ihr Wesen, Ihre Veränderung und ihre Konservierung* (Dresden: Verlag von Theodor Steinkopf, 1917).

[40] Roland, *Unsere Lebensmittel*, IV.

[41] Roland, *Unsere Lebensmittel*, 175 onwards.

[42] Roland, *Unsere Lebensmittel*, VII.

[43] HILA, USFAR, Alphabetical File, Reel 118, Box 95, Folder 6, Austria-Hungary Agriculture, Market Prices-Hungary, 10 August 1918.

[44] Karen Hunt, 'Gender and Everyday Life', in *Gender and the Great War*, edited by Tammy M. Proctor and Susan R. Gryzel (Oxford: Oxford University Press, 2017), 149–68, 150.

[45] Heather R. Perry, 'Onward Kitchen Soldiers! Gender, Food and Health in Germany's Long Great War', in *Food, Culture and Identity in Germany's Century of War*, edited by Healther Merle Benbow and Heather R. Perry (Cham: Palgrave Macmillan, 2019), 34.

a collection of cooking recipes.[46] Such cookbooks represented a manual of how to overcome daily obstacles in the food crisis. They helped women to cook nutritious dishes in the absence of essential ingredients. In the Netherlands, special cooking classes geared towards providing healthy and affordable meals became very popular.[47] Even in the United States, where the majority of people were not hungry, recipes were published by the state for simplified meals that did not use normal staples such as sugar or eggs, so that these basics might be saved to be shipped to Europe.[48]

Ruralization of Urban Space

In many countries that suffered from food scarcity, it was also common for people living in urban areas to bring agricultural practices into their cities. While growing food was much easier in the countryside and in villages, urban areas also began to grow vegetables. Cities and towns went through a process of 're-ruralization',[49] which meant that people in urban areas adopted features of a more rural lifestyle. This involved learning or relearning traditional farming techniques and applying them to the smaller spaces available to them. People across Europe reverted to home-based agricultural practices and started to grow vegetables in gardens or apartments or reared farm animals in homes. In German Westphalia, the improvisational transformation of the city dwellers into urban farmers and the widespread appearance of 'window-sill gardens' [*Fensterbrettplantagen*] may not have been of major economic significance, but 'for the individual urban consumer their own piece of land and cattle was of vital importance'.[50] When, for instance, the food situation in Riga became so bad in March 1919 that institutions could not even distribute food cards to children and ill people or deliver milk, articles appeared in the press urging people to grow vegetables wherever they could, including

46 Rudolf Kučera, *Rationed Life: Science, Everyday life, and Working-Class Politics in the Bohemian Lands, 1914–1918* (New York, NY: Berghahn, 2016), 32.

47 L. Bückmann, 'Distributiejaren', in *25 jaar geschiedenis van Nederland 1898–1923: gedenkboek, uitgegeven ter gelegenheid van het zilveren regeeringsfeest van Hare Majesteit Koningin Wilhelmina der Nederlanden*, edited by W. G. de Bas et al. (Amsterdam: Fongers & Co, 1923), 580; M. W. F. Treub, *Herinneringen en Overpeinzingen* (Haarlem: H.D. Tjeenk Willink & Zoon, 1931), 320.

48 Helen Zoe Veit, *Modern Food, Moral Food: Self-Control, Science, and the Rise of Modern American Eating in the Early Twentieth Century* (Chapel Hill, NC: University of North Carolina Press, 2013), 5.

49 Roger Chickering, *The Great War and Urban Life in Germany: Freiburg, 1914–1918* (Cambridge: Cambridge University Press, 2007), 181.

50 Anne Roehrkohl, *Hungerblockade und Heimatfront. Die kommunale Lebensmittelversorgung in Westfalen im Ersten Weltkrieg* (Stuttgart: Franz Steiner Verlag, 1991), 37.

in cities and towns.[51] The need for self-help to secure one's survival resulted in the widespread acceptance of small-scale animal husbandry in flats, houses and urban gardens. This occurred even among the better-off classes; a source from German Lüdenscheid points out that '[g]oats, cows and pigs have moved into the most noble households'.[52]

In wartime Prague, many published books and pamphlets explained in detail how to rear and cook small poultry or rabbits in an urban setting, or how to dry vegetables. It was suggested that rabbits could be kept on an inner balcony after receiving the neighbours' permission, and that the rabbits could then be fed and maintained through all kinds of waste. Titles of some of these Czech books, such as *Practical tables for the cultivator of vegetables and grains, small and big*; *The home grocer: a short introduction to the cultivation, care, harvesting of all types of vegetables and roots in the home garden: for the usage of the broadest classes*; and *Cheap providers of meat, fat, butter, milk, cheese and eggs: practical advice for breeders of rabbits, guinea pigs, goats and poultry*, show how important instructions became for those who relied on urban self-provisioning and farming.[53] Pop-science books and instructions were very widespread in wartime Europe as experts and would-be experts sought to provide practical knowledge and strategies to others on how to adapt to the scarcity of food. These publications represent one of the strategies people turned to whether by following the instructions, or by creating, sharing or distributing them. The practice of animal-rearing also gave rise to parodies. One Czech caricature (Figure 4.2) shows two men chatting while a woman feeds a group of small rabbits in an apartment's kitchen: 'So you are raising rabbits at home? – Yes, but my wife got so used to them, that she said she would jump off the balcony if I killed them'.[54]

Even in neutral Switzerland, individuals profited from the governmental strategy to teach people how to breed rabbits and then process their meat and fur. Apart from securing a significant additional income, every now and then breeding rabbits also enriched the dinner tables of poor families with a roast rabbit [*Hasenbraten*].[55] Apart from rabbits, goats

[51] 'Sīkie darbi' *Zu Priekšu* 66 (23 March 1919), 3.

[52] Cited in Roehrkohl, *Hungerblockade und Heimatfront*, 43.

[53] Claire Morelon, 'A Threat to National Unity?: The Urban-rural Antagonism in Prague during the First World War in a Comparative Perspective', in *Frontwechsel. Österreich-Ungarns 'Grosser Krieg' im Vergleich*, edited by Wolfram Dornik, Julia Walleczek-Fritz, Stefan Wedrac (Vienna: Böhlau, 2014), 332.

[54] *Humoristické listy*, 20 April 1917, 241.

[55] Adrian Knoepfli, 'Mit Kaninchenzucht gegen den Hunger. Winterthur im Ersten Weltkrieg', in *Kriegs- und Krisenzeit. Zürich während des Ersten Weltkriegs*, edited by Erika Hebeisen, Peter Niederhäuser and Regula Schmid (Zürich: Chronos, 2014), 41.

Figure 4.2 Czech caricature on raising rabbits in apartments.
Source: *Humoristické listy*, 60, no. 17 (1917), 241. Czech Digital Bibliography research infrastructure by the Institute for Czech Literature of the Czech Academy of Sciences, P.R.I., https://clb.ucl.cas.cz/ (ORJ Code: 90243)

were also frequently used as animals to breed in urban areas. Breeding small animals was considered a powerful means to counter hunger for the poorer classes. In contrast to rabbits and chicken, breeding pigs in German cities was difficult because of the space required and the unpleasant stench. For this reason, city dwellers who could afford it bought pigs and sent them 'in pension' to farmers in the countryside. These so-called 'pension pigs' [*Pensionsschweine*] would be fattened in the countryside and would then be slaughtered and consumed by the city dweller. The 'pension pig' came to symbolize the social inequalities of war-time food consumption, as only wealthier individuals could afford buying a pig to be fattened up in the countryside and later slaughtered for their convenience.[56]

[56] Roehrkohl, *Hungerblockade und Heimatfront*, 41–3.

People and communities also started to plant vegetables in public parks to help provide for the city population. Municipalities sometimes organized the plots. In the Prague suburb of Karlín, for example, lettuces, kohlrabi, celery and other vegetables were grown in public parks for local consumption.[57] Often, even without official permission, people in Austria-Hungary started to use public parks and appropriated uncultivated land to grow vegetables and feed livestock.[58] In Westphalia, the municipal authorities explicitly called upon individual city dwellers, especially families of draftees and those whom the war had impoverished, to take up small garden plots in industrial areas to circumvent the difficult supply situation.[59] In Stuttgart, schoolyards that had previously been used for play were converted into large city gardens that the schoolchildren helped tend. The vegetables grown were later consumed by the schoolchildren themselves.[60] In Paris, too, the fortifications around the city were used for cultivation (a novelty commented upon by contemporaries) and private vegetable gardens developed to reach 3,000 in the inner city and 2,500 in the nearby municipalities by 1917.[61]

In German-occupied Belgium, urban gardening also became ubiquitous. The *Ligue du Coin de Terre* (the 'Plot-of-Land League') had 180,000 members by 1918; and, beyond these, many other households supplemented their food supply by cultivating small plots of 'leftover' land in cities; for instance, near railway embankments or around industrial plants. The Plot-of-Land League had been created in 1896 by a Catholic government intent on keeping workers away from the temptations of modern life. During the war, urban gardening in Belgium acquired more of an urgent edge. Municipalities allied themselves with the *Ligue*, as did the National Committee for Relief and Provisioning. Unexpected parts of city land were put to the plough and allotted to needy families. In the Schaerbeek district of Brussels, for instance, the stately Boulevard Lambermont became half 'ruralized': the lanes reserved for cyclists and horseback riders – now unused because of the occupation regime's

[57] Claire Morelon, *Streetscapes of War and Revolution: Prague 1914–1920* (Cambridge: Cambridge University Press, 2024), 191.

[58] Ernst Langthaler, 'Food and Nutrition (Austria-Hungary)', in *1914–1918-online. International Encyclopedia of the First World War*, edited by Ute Daniel et al., (Berlin: Freie Universität Berlin, 2016), https://encyclopedia.1914-1918-online.net/article/food_and_nutrition_austria-hungary.

[59] Roehrkohl, *Hungerblockade und Heimatfront*, 45 and 48.

[60] Keith Allen, 'Sharing Scarcity: Bread Rationing and the First World War in Berlin, 1914–1923', *Journal of Social History* 32:2 (1998), 377.

[61] Emmanuelle Cronier, 'The Street', in *Capital Cities at War: Paris, London, Berlin, 1914–1919*, edited by Jay Winter and Jean-Louis Robert (Cambridge: Cambridge University Press, 2007), 65.

restrictions and requisitioning – were broken up to make way for potatoes and cabbages.[62] Even so, the 'moral' benefits of urban gardening continued to be extolled: the Schaerbeek municipality praised its effects on the self-esteem of men who worked in them that had been thrown out of work because of the war.[63]

In the Netherlands, families turned their gardens into vegetable plots and learned to cook with little or no fat on fires made from *brikken* (bricks of pulped combustible materials) instead of wood or coal.[64] Some Dutch city councils allocated small plots of land for the purpose of growing vegetables.[65] Farmers likewise looked for alternative sources of fertilizers, including a special 'sea manure' made from seaweed, while the population was urged to adopt vegetarianism and to eat nuts, because they grew in abundance in city parks every autumn.[66] From 1917 onwards, city councils in the Netherlands began to create special communal plots in city gardens, and the Utrecht City Council even bought its own pigs for breeding and slaughter purposes. Everywhere, strips of undeveloped land were sown for communal use, especially after the bad weather of Winter and Spring 1917 partially ruined that year's crops.[67] All over Europe, cities and towns saw the development of garden plots in spaces previously used for other purposes as every inch of land could become valuable in times of scarcity.

Smuggling and Trading Food

Faced with growing shortages, augmenting their own production was only one of the strategies used by populations. Traveling further distances

[62] Louis Gille, Alphone Ooms and Louis Delandsheere, *Cinquante mois d'occupation allemande* (Brussels: Dewit, 1919), 358–9.

[63] Florence Loriaux, '1914–1918: le chômeur entre suspicion et héroïsme', in *Le chômeur suspect: histoire d'une stigmatization*, edited by Florence Loriaux (Brussels: Centre d'Animation et de Recherche en Histoire Ouvrière et Populaire (CARHOP) / Centre de Recherche et d'Information Socio-Politiques (CRISP), 2015), 75–94, 78.

[64] Robert van Kamp, *De kolenvoorziening van Nederland gedurende de Eerste Wereldoorlog* (Amsterdam: Het Parool, 1968), 32.

[65] Jan Verseput, 'Gevolgen van de gesloten wapenstilstands- en vredesverdragen, welke een einde aan de eerste wereldoorlog maakten, voor Rotterdam', *Rotterdams Jaarboekje* 8 (1960), 228.

[66] Cornelis Broekema, 'Landbouw' in *Nederland in den oorlogstijd. De geschiedenis van Nederland en van Nederlandsch-Indië tijdens den oorlog van 1914 tot 1919, voor zoover zij met dien oorlog verband houdt*, edited by Hajo Brugmans (Amsterdam: Elsevier, 1920), 279–323, 316–17.

[67] Bob Benschop, *Kanongebulder in de verte. Hellevoetsluis en omgeving tijdens de mobilisatie 1914–1918* (Zaltbommel: Aprilis, 2008), 116–17; Annie van der Velden, 'Gemeentevis en regeringsvarkens. Voedselvoorziening in Utrecht 1914–1918', *Oud-Utrecht* 81: 6 (2008), 162–6.

in search of food also became more frequent. Due to the variations in food supply in the various European countries, smuggling and trading food between city and countryside, between different regions and across imperial or national borders increased. For instance, within the Austro-Hungarian empire there were wide differences in the food situation from one region to another. The situation in Vienna appears to have been far worse than in Budapest. Contemporary sources recount numerous occasions when Austrian travelers attempted to smuggle food products out of Hungary. Such illegal traffic was severely punished. On 29 September 1918, at the train station in the Hungarian border town Szombathely, the local police conducted a raid before the departure of a train to Vienna. A Hungarian newspaper stated that '[t]hey caught 10 Viennese travelers who wanted to smuggle out smaller or larger amounts of food', which is why a 'legal procedure against them ha[d] been started'.[68] The state authorities tried to contain illegal domestic trade through a strict 'surveillance of train stations, trains and other transport means',[69] instructing the police to regularly raid trains and food warehouses. A report from September 1918 from the train station in Szombathely in Hungary describes how the 'police conducted a raid before the departure of the train to Vienna. They caught ten Viennese travelers who wanted to smuggle out smaller or larger amounts of food.'[70]

The Austrian authorities tried manifold policies to stop the 'flow of human traffic between city and countryside' and across borders.[71] The attitude of the Austrian authorities towards this type of self-provisioning of the population (backpack traffic or *Rucksackverkehr*) was inconsistent and changed during the course of the war.[72] There were complaints among the public that people who simply tried to buy food were arrested at train stations by the police or gendarmerie. For example, the German radical association in Bohemian Leitmeriz/Litoměřice sent a formal complaint in November 1917 about the lack of food in the city and asked for more tolerance regarding self-provisioning, denouncing the 'razzia' at train stations at the end of October.[73] A proposal to fully ban backpacks on trains was discussed, in the hope to discourage

68 'Razzia a vonaton', *8 Órai Ujság* 4:228 (29 September 1918), 5.

69 Hans Loewenfeld-Russ, *Die Regelung der Volksernährung im Kriege* (New Haven, CT: Yale University Press, 1926), 359.

70 'Razzia a vonaton', 5.

71 Healy, *Vienna and the Fall of the Habsburg Empire*, 55.

72 The *Rucksackverkehr* was more tolerated during the last year of the war, see Loewenfeld-Russ, *Die Regelung der Volksernährung im Kriege*, 175.

73 ÖStA, AdR, Volksernährungsamt, AR, K147, no. 117227/17 in 748/18, Beschwerden über die Ernährungsverhältnisse in Leitmeritz, Complaint from Josef Schuh (German radical association), 24 November 1917.

people from plundering fields and carrying home their stolen goods, but it was not implemented as it was considered to exclusively punish the poorest classes.[74]

In Russia in 1917, so-called 'bagmen' (*meshochniki*) became a new phenomenon and a frequent sight.[75] Similar to their German and Austro-Hungarian counterparts, they went with large bags to the countryside to find food supplies.[76] Apparently there existed two different types of bagmen: those who searched for and carried food for themselves and then those who traded food as currency. Both types of food traders were united in their reliance on mobility as a means to enable access to foodstuffs.[77] Yet, 'bagging' – as this illegal food trading practice was called – went so far as to paralyse railway traffic in Russia, as bagmen highjacked trains, blocked train stations and brought chaos to the whole railway system. According to Orlando Figes, 'millions of townspeople, from all classes relied on this petty trade ... to feed themselves', trading bags of clothes and other material goods for foodstuffs.[78]

In Hamburg in 1918, authorities decided to restrict railway traffic between the city and the surrounding villages. Trains from the villages to the city would only run once a day in one direction, so that the hoarders would have to stay overnight in the city and could only return the next day, which would make these trips an expensive and time-consuming undertaking. The State Secretary of the War Food Office [*Kriegsernährungsamt*], Wilhelm von Waldow, was hoping to prevent the extensive illicit food traffic between the villages and the starving city of Hamburg, which he held responsible for the 'imminent collapse of the German food economy and of the entire state and economic order'.[79] Yet, a report from 19 December 1917 shows that the state secretary had also become aware of the municipal authorities' involvement in the massive illicit trade in livestock and fertilizers. Instead of securing their equal distribution, the communal authorities traded goods for their private

[74] Healy, *Vienna and the Fall of the Habsburg Empire*, 55.

[75] Iaroslav Golubinov, 'Food and Nutrition (Russian Empire)', in *1914–1918-online. International Encyclopedia of the First World War*, edited by Ute Daniel et al., (Berlin: Freie Universität Berlin, 2018), https://encyclopedia.1914-1918-online.net/article/food_and_nutrition_russian_empire/2018-08-13?version=1.0.

[76] See Mauricio Borrero, *Hungry Moscow: Scarcity and Urban Society in the Russian Civil War, 1917–1921* (New York, NY: Peter Lang, 2006).

[77] Arup Banerji, *Merchants and Markets in Revolutionary Russia, 1917–30* (London: Palgrave Macmillan, 1997), 27, 143.

[78] Orlando Figes, *A People's Tragedy: The Russian Revolution* (London: The Bodley Head, 2017), 611.

[79] Der Staatssekretär des KEA, Bekämpfung Schleichversorgung durch Hamsterfahrten, November 11 1918, Bundesarchiv Berlin/R3601/432.

consumption.[80] This participated in the undermining of the official control organs' credibility among the civilian population.

Populations strongly resented the harsh control of illicit trading on railway lines. In September 1918, checks onboard the railway line Berlin-Königsberg were met with 'vigorous outbursts of anger' as well as verbal insults to officials.[81] A civilian, Wilhelm Neuhaus, complained on 28 September 1918 to the German authorities about the introduction of severe controls of illicit trading and kindly requested to further permit the 'poor people in the countryside to use illicit trade for their supply'.[82] A military major even complained about excessive controls giving the example of an inspector who had confiscated eight eggs from a woman, who had collected them from her own chickens in order to bring them to her husband in a military hospital. The major not only considered this type of control too harsh but also doubted that the inspector actually delivered the confiscated goods to the appropriate authority and instead used them for himself.[83] Smuggling and trading food was not limited to the poorer classes; state employees and policemen were also reported to participate in this type of informal trade.

Railway structures were overwhelmed by this influx of passengers and goods and asked the authorities to intervene. The management of the railway administration in German Elberfeld, for example, organized in October 1918 several extra trains to ease the individual delivery of potatoes, butter, eggs and grain in large quantities to neighbouring cities. The passenger cars were on 24 October overfilled to such an extent with bags of individually obtained foodstuffs, that the 'passengers were virtually sandwiched' and that they even used the windows for getting on the trains and leaving them. The police considered the control of smaller train stations an impossible endeavor. Like the Austrian authorities who considered banning large backpacks, the German railway administration had tried to forbid any individual transport of foodstuffs in large bags. However, this regulation could not be implemented. They hoped that a state authority would regulate and thereby prevent any illicit trade because only then could the farmers actually deliver their goods to the food authorities.[84]

80 Preuss. Staatskomm. für Volksernährung an die Herren Regierungspräsidenten, 19 December 1917, Bundesarchiv Berlin/R3601/407.

81 'Niederschrift über Beschwerde des Major Hahnemann'. Berlin, 11 September 1918, Bundesarchiv Berlin/R3601/431/ Bekämpfung Schleichhandels/1918–1919.

82 Der Staatssekretär des KEA an Bezirksamtmann Metz, 28 September 1918, Bundesarchiv Berlin/R3601/431.

83 'Niederschrift über Beschwerde des Major Hahnemann'. Berlin, 11 September 1918, Bundesarchiv Berlin/R3601/431/Bekaempfung Schleichhandels/1918–1919.

84 Abschrift aus dem Montatsbericht des Reg. Präs. Cöln, Weitere Wünsche und Anregungen, 24 October 1918, Bundesarchiv Berlin/R3601/432.

This type of traffic did not only take place on a domestic scale but also beyond national borders. A report on smuggling between Northwest Bohemia and Germany recounts how 300 working-class and middle-class persons crossed the ridge of the mountain between four and five o'clock in the morning to go into Saxony with rucksacks and hand carts to buy swedes, parsnips and potatoes. The district officer in Olbernhau authorized them to cross the border at certain times of the week to obtain these products. The report quotes some of these Bohemian 'pilgrims' who acknowledged that they had to temporarily rely on bread from the 'foreign and better supplied Saxony'. A local Saxon official expressed his compassion for those 'poor devils', who were far more exposed to the 'hyenas of the hinterland' than in Germany and offered them help.[85]

Dutch border communities also swelled their income by smuggling foodstuffs across the border. The number of convicted smugglers, for example, rose from just 29 during 1914 to a massive 10,960 in 1916 – and we can only assume, given the long land border the Netherlands shared with both Germany and Belgium, that an even greater number managed to escape detection.[86] In the landlocked province of Drenthe, bordering Germany, the total number of criminal convictions rose by a massive 400 per cent during the First World War. Roughly two-thirds of these convictions were the result of offences related to the distribution and rationing statutes and laws promulgated by local councils and the central government, such as ignoring mandated maximum prices and smuggling foodstuffs into Germany.[87]

From Bartering to Black Marketeering

In those direct exchanges between consumer and producer, money was sometimes not the main currency used to obtain food. Bartering had several causes, such as the simple lack of money, the changing value of certain foodstuffs, and the inflation-related distrust towards money in general. In Trentino in Southern Tyrol, the diary of Don Degara, a priest from Breguzzo, describes (probably in January 1918), how people 'hid in the ditch and in the bed wheat, beans, often potatoes', whereas they cared little about hiding their money, as money was

[85] ÖStA, AdR, Volksernährungsamt, AR, K148, no. 54687, Situationsbericht, Ernährungsinspektor Brüx, 8 April 1918.

[86] Warner Rudolph Emmen Riedel, 'De smokkelarij. Een terugblik', *Vragen des Tijds* 2 (1919), 209.

[87] Albert Eggens, *Van daad tot vonnis. Door Drenten gepleegde criminaliteit voor en tijdens de Eerste Wereldoorlog* (PhD thesis, University of Groningen, 2005), 157.

neither lacking nor could one buy with it anything to satisfy one's hunger. The priest explained that '[t]he only way to get the flour, sugar, meat, coffee was the change with other goods'.[88] Unlike money, material wealth, in the form of furniture, jewellery and clothing, could be converted into food.

Because of the different and changing availability of certain foodstuffs in some cities and areas, people relied on their social and familial ties to exchange and obtain food products. For instance, in Swiss Lausanne, some foodstuffs were easier to obtain than in the municipality of Swiss Dürnten. Hence, Anna, a daughter, sent 'chocolate, rice, macaroni, flour and cones' from Lausanne to Dürnten, in return for which the mother sent apples and vegetables.[89] Such behaviour was considered to strengthen family relations, as the material exchanges were based on 'reliability and sustainability'.[90] As food had turned into the new luxury good, people in cities like Vienna were forced to sell their 'real' valuables such as 'porcelain, housewares, pianos, fine clothing' in exchange for everyday consumables.[91] Relying on informal channels, the hungry population traded clothes for potatoes or furniture for meat. On 3 October 1918, women from the Anatolian town of Yozgat complained to the state that while their children were 'sacrificing their lives for the nation, performing their military service and even dying as martyrs', they themselves remained without breadwinners and had no source of income, which is why they sold their household items to meet their everyday needs.[92] In Riga, at the end of 1918, when there was almost nothing left to eat, people walked all day long in search of food. The only way to find a little saccharin was to barter it from 'speculators' by giving them 'a pair of boots' or three kg of salt.[93]

By 1918, barter had become so widespread in Bohemia as a means to exchange material goods that some districts attempted to ban it altogether. In Komotau/Chomutov, the district officer reported that artisans sold nails, chains, ploughshares, clothes or tobacco for food and

[88] FMST, ASP, Silvio Degara, Cronaca di Breguzzo. Memorie della terribile guerra scoppiata all'1° agosto 1914–3 novembre 1918 in quanto riguarda il paese di Breguzzo, cc. 15–16.

[89] Heidi Witzig, 'Alltagsleben und Alltagserleben während des Ersten Weltkriegs. Frauen und Männer der Mittel- und Oberschicht im Zürcher Oberland', in *Kriegs- und Krisenzeit: Zürich während des Ersten Weltkriegs*, edited by Erika Hebeisen, Peter Niederhäuser and Regula Schmid (Zurich: Chronos Verlag, 2014), 81.

[90] Witzig, 'Alltagsleben und Alltagserleben', 85.

[91] Healy, *Vienna and the Fall of the Habsburg Empire*, 53.

[92] Quoted in Yiğit Akin, 'War, women, and the State. The Politics of Sacrifice in the Ottoman Empire during the First World War', *Journal of Women's History* 26:3 (2014), 25.

[93] -ņš, 'Mēs atminamies…' *Darba Dzīve* 45 (4 November 1939), 1, 3.

that some of them only accepted to perform repair works or ironwork against food. He asked for an immediate cessation of these practices.[94] At a consumers' council meeting in Prague in March 1918, almost all speakers commented that banning black market trading would be difficult because most municipalities, industries and other institutions relied on the black market for 75 per cent of their supply and received only 25 per cent through state provisioning.[95]

The porous border between bartering and black market trading meant that more and more citizens were willing to break the law to obtain food. The unavailability of most basic foodstuffs gave ground to a 'moral trauma', as usually law-abiding civilians started to mistrust the state and circumvent official regulations, paving the way towards illegality and criminality.[96] The inability of European governments to 'provide citizens with an acceptable quantity of foodstuffs at reasonable prices fuelled the growth of black [and grey] markets'.[97] While grey markets 'occurred in a pre-existed network' of individuals and happened everywhere, black markets were situated 'in public places' and involved anonymous trade between buyer and seller.[98] Black and grey marketing in goods and foods helped civilians to survive, especially 'in regions where rationing and price-control policies were ineffective or where transport systems broke down'.[99] When getting involved in black and grey market activities, people faced various challenges. Individuals who wished to make the highest profit would most likely try to sell or trade their goods on a black market. While anonymity between buyer and seller was more likely in a black market, the risks of being detected by the authorities were much greater as black markets tended to have fixed locations. On the other hand, participation in a grey market sacrificed anonymity, but allowed exchanges to occur in non-centralized locations. Differential risks and flow of economic information, particularly the market prices of goods, could be asymmetric depending on which market an individual chose to participate in.[100]

As the lack of foodstuffs affected all social strata – though to differing degrees – the black and grey markets were widely used at various times

94 *Deutsche Zeitung Bohemia*, 6 September 1918 (evg ed.), 4.

95 ÖStA, AdR, Volksernährungsamt, AR, K151, no. 37819, Situationsbericht, Ernährungsinspektor Prag, 16 March 1918.

96 Proctor, *Civilians in a World at War*, 94.

97 Allen, 'Sharing Scarcity', 371.

98 Vincent Bignon, *Black Markets and Grey Networks for Illegal Exchanges in post WW2 Germany* (Geneva: Graduate Institute for International and Development Studies, 2007), 16–18.

99 Proctor, *Civilians in a World at War*, 94.

100 Bignon, *Black Markets and Grey Networks*, 3.

by those who could afford them. Even in the neutral Netherlands, many people turned to the black market to supplement their staple diet of *noodbrood*, a little milk, and *eenheidsworst*.[101] While they helped people to improve their daily food, the emergence of this type of parallel economy also affected and even impaired the official food supply. Hans Loewenfeld-Russ, the Austrian State Secretary for Public Nutrition considered the proliferating and intensifying 'Schleichhandel', illicit trading, the main cause of the failing official food supply system.[102] It has been shown in other contexts that while black markets help to supplement the food rations of their customers during wars and in times of political and economic crisis, they always also undermine the official rationing system by pulling available foodstuffs out of the official food market.[103]

The food distribution system turned into a real quandary: the less the state was able to meet the needs of the populations, the more products would end up on the black, grey or dark grey markets. These markets coexisted with the normal market, and competed and represented a diverse parallel economy.[104] Indeed, the more food would circulate in these different types of markets, the less the state could requisition and distribute.[105] Even if the black market, as Jay Winter pointed out, 'may deliver the goods to those who know how to work it', it still 'diminished the standard of living of the many by more than the items it purloins and distributes at exorbitant prices'.[106] There are low estimates that 20 to 40 per cent of total economic production was rerouted from official channels to the black and grey markets, in particular in those countries, such as occupied Belgium or Germany, where food continued to be much dearer – both quality and quantity-wise – than for instance in the Netherlands.[107] A report of the German War Ministry from 3 August 1918 complained there was 'almost no [food] item which

[101] Marius Jacoubus van der Flier, 'War finances in the Netherlands up to 1918', in *The Netherlands and the World War. Studies in the War History of a Neutral*, edited by H. B. Greven, vol. 1 (Oxford: The Clarendon Press, 1923), 108.

[102] Loewenfeld-Russ, *Die Regelung der Volksernährung im Kriege*, 358.

[103] For a similar analysis on WWII Soviet Union, see Wendy Z. Goldman, 'Not by Bread Alone: Food, Workers, and the State', in *Hunger and War: Food Provisioning in the Soviet Union during World War II*, edited by Wendy Z. Goldman and Donald Filtzer (Bloomington, IN: Indiana University Press, 2015), 84.

[104] Bignon, *Black Markets and Grey Networks*, 2 and 16–18.

[105] Daniel, *Arbeiterfrauen in der Kriegsgesellschaft*, 168.

[106] Winter, 'The Practices of Metropolitan Life in Wartime', 12.

[107] Hein Klemann, 'Ontwikkeling door isolement. De Nederlandse economie 1914–1918', in *Wankel evenwicht. Neutraal Nederland en de Eerste Wereldoorlog*, edited by Martin Kraaijestein and Paul Schulten (Soesterberg: Aspekt, 2007) 271–309, 279–80.

remained untouched from black marketing'.[108] It went on to describe the many 'secret slaughters and the flourishing illicit trade with meat', due to which two restaurants in Allenstein (Olsztyn) had to be closed. Similarly, in Austria, many farmers, mills or bakers, particularly around larger consumption centres, succumbed to the temptation of illicit trading.[109] Farmers in various countries started to hoard their foodstuffs for their own consumption or to trade it to the destitute urban population for excessive prices.

In cities, specific locations turned into hubs for the illegal purchase and sale of food. In 1918, a Czech publication contained the 'confessions' of a repenting profiteer who explained how easy it was to make a profit during the war by selling food. Operating around the Bohemian Reichenberg/Liberec region, he went to the countryside to get provisions and sold it back at the train stations or in cafés. He described cafés as places where it was especially easy to meet someone willing to sell some black-market goods, with waiters transmitting information to customers about the potential traffics.[110] In Budapest, a flea market at Teleki square had turned into 'a hot bed of the black market' during the last years of the war. The police tried to discontinue it, but it could 'hardly eliminate the black market's professional structures'.[111]

Illicit trade and black marketeering caused severe problems: unreasonable prices of the products, extensive travels between the countryside and the cities, the loss of wages for those days when people were trading food, the overburdening of the railway connections, thefts, premature harvesting of certain vegetables, a decline of the state economy and an imbalance in the distribution of vital goods.[112] Only those who had something worth bartering could obtain additional calories. Additionally, only those who felt comfortable skirting the law did participate. Some Catholic farmers in Germany chose not to participate in black marketeering or hoarding because they felt that doing so would be 'an offence against fundamental moral principles to which commodity prices must

108 Kriegsministerium, Kriegsamt. Zusammenstellung der Monats-Berichte der Sellv. Generalkommandos vom 3.8.2018, Berlin. Akten betreffend: Berichte der stellvertretenden Generalkommandos über die Lebensmittelversorgung. BA/R3101/3409.

109 Loewenfeld-Russ, *Die Regelung der Volksernährung im Kriege*, 359.

110 Kamil Gollin, *Ket'asová zpověd': autentické líčení života, zákulisí a tajů řetězového obchodu po dobu pěti měsíců ve válce od 1. srpna 1917 až do ledna 1918* (Prague: A. Svěcený, 1918).

111 'Rendőrileg beszüntették', *8 Órai Ujság* 4, no. 37 (12 February1918), 3.

112 Kriegsministerium, Kriegsamt. Zusammenstellung der Monats-Berichte der Sellv. Generalkommandos vom 3.8.2018, Berlin. Akten betreffend: Berichte der stellvertretenden Generalkommandos über die Lebensmittelversorgung, 11. BA/R3101/3409.

not exceed purchasing costs'.[113] Yet, at the same time, some authorities viewed illicit trade as a lesser evil, as it was a means of 'self-help' which enabled people to secure for themselves at least some kind of access to certain foodstuffs. A German military report even argued that it thereby helped to prevent social unrest and revolts.[114]

Black marketing also affected the general mood, especially when authorities were accused of colluding or taking part in it. A monthly report about the over-all food supply in Germany speaks of the unhappiness which the illicit trade caused among the civilian population, as some communal authorities seemed to have been involved in and benefited from these activities. An example from Hamburg illustrates the degree of official protection afforded to some illegal sellers. Mr Prahl, the director of the wholesale cooperative in Hamburg, reported a discussion he had witnessed in a shop in the Wandsbek neighbourhood. A woman, Mrs Hampel, was offering rice and flour to the shop's owner for an exorbitant price. While the shop owner dismissed her, Prahl followed her and offered to buy large quantities of rice and flour from her. They agreed to first meet in a café where Mrs Hampel would provide samples of her foodstuffs. After that, they went first to a cellar, where a man, named Rosenbaum, sold 500 kg of sausage to Mr Prahl for an exorbitant price, and then to a storage place in the harbour where Mr Prahl bought large quantities of beans and peas. A criminal officer, who had been called to the scene and had been following the suspicious traders, then arrested Mr Rosenbaum, Mr Prahl and Mrs Hampel. Rosenbaum had previously told Mr Prahl, when he asked how the foodstuffs could be transported, that they could offer him not only a military car but also a sergeant and a police officer to protect it, if needed. The discovery of this illicit trade did not even prevent its continuance: just a week later, the aforementioned Mrs Hampel went from shop to shop in Wandsbek as before and proposed the very same products for the very same prices.[115] The 'odd impression of the silent tolerance' of the 'silent illicit trade' on the part of the police and the state authorities did not help to halt this second, alternative economy.[116]

113 Benjamin Ziemann, *War Experiences in Rural Germany: 1914–1923* (Oxford: Berg, 2007), 177.

114 Kriegsministerium, Kriegsamt. Zusammenstellung der Monats-Berichte der Sellv. Generalkommandos vom 3.8.2018, Berlin. Akten betreffend: Berichte der stellvertretenden Generalkommandos über die Lebensmittelversorgung, 11. BA/R3101/3409.

115 Preuss Staatskommission für Volksernährung an KEA. Monatsbericht über die Volksernährung für die Zeit vom 21.1–20.2.1919, 13 May 1918, A II 2778. BA/R3601/430.

116 Auszug aus dem Monatsbericht des K. W. Kriegsministeriums an Herrn Geheimrat Stadthagen, August 1917, Nr. A II 10152, Bundesarchiv Berlin/R3601/405.

Breaking the Law: Fraud, Theft and Plundering

During periods of famine and hunger the general crime rate tends to increase dramatically.[117] Swindling and theft on an individual or collective scale become more commonplace strategies to obtain increasingly unavailable food. As early as September 1914, reports spoke of food-related fraud. In September 1914 civilian men in Warsaw dressed in military uniforms went to visit the relatives of soldiers and pretended to deliver news of their 'comrades'. They then claimed that they had to quickly join their comrades at the front and, as the relatives gave them food parcels for their loved ones, they either kept them or sold them.[118] Forging food coupons and ration cards represented one of the earliest illegal modes to obtain additional rations. In Warsaw in January of 1916, a dozen people were arrested and charged for the possession of counterfeit bread tickets. Some women were even arrested for registering 'dead souls' for bread and flour rations which they then used for resale or for their own consumption.[119] In Austrian Braunau am Inn, in June 1917, refugees from South Tyrol were known to buy bread cards from adults and children at the distribution place, even if it was illegal to purchase such tickets for money and then exchange them for bread.[120] A report from the food inspector in Prague in March 1918 also mentioned 'numerous cases of deception or forgery with bread tickets'.[121] In some cases, not only the bread tickets, but also the food itself was fake. In marketplaces in Riga, in January and February 1919, Latvian authorities caught various farmers who had tried to sell milk which had been mixed with water for the price of real milk; they then imposed 'severe fines and arrest terms on tens of peasants'.[122]

The theft of food also developed quickly during the conflict. During the extreme conditions of the siege of Galician Przemyśl by the Russian army, between September 1914 and March 1915, civilians stole food where it was still available. The Polish woman, Helene von Seifert Jabłońska, whose diary has survived, recalls that by December 1914 people in Przemyśl started to plunder private food stores: 'Every

[117] Guido Alfani, Cormac Ó Gráda, ed., *Famine in European History* (Cambridge: Cambridge University Press, 2017), 42.
[118] Blobaum, *A Minor Apocalypse*, 81.
[119] Blobaum, *A Minor Apocalypse*, 87.
[120] K. K. Bezirkshauptmannschaft Braunau am Inn. 25 Juni 1917. Beschwerde gegen die Flüchtlinge. ÖStA/ADR/BKA/KFL/77/Zl. 24131.
[121] ÖStA, AdR, Volksernährungsamt, AR, K151, no. 37210, Bericht über die Reise des General-Ernährungsinspektors nach Prag, 25 March 1918.
[122] 'Sodīti piena viltotāji' *Latvijas Sargs* (20 February 1919 and 26 March 1919), 3.

day, cellars, attics, pantries are broken into somewhere'.[123] In occupied Belgium, theft was particularly focused on the newly 'ruralized' parts of the city. The attacks by marauders on the little plots of 'ruralized' land were very upsetting, which forced tenants to stand guard in the same way as farmers in the countryside. For instance, 400 workers' families from Brussels had been allotted parcels of land on the vast site of the 1910 World's Fair; from mid-1917, men from this collective took turns, day and night, to watch out for pilferers.[124] In Vienna, theft rose rapidly as well, sometimes taking place collectively on the streets: in March 1917, for example, thirty women and children stole a bread wagon, while shouting 'We want bread! We are hungry!', after they had been denied potatoes at the marketplace.[125] When bread disappeared in 1919 from stores in Riga, hungry crowds robbed the city's bakeries. For instance, they broke into the bakery on Cēsu Street, because 'of the smell of bread coming from its windows', as they later stated. But in reality, there had been no bread in the bakery at that moment, so the smell had been nothing but an illusion.[126] In Berlin, bread rationing offices were regularly burglarized.[127] Such acts of violence mirror, at times, the irrational character of some individual and collective attempts to secure food. Stealing in Riga took many forms, from more modest individual actions to large-scale robberies. The clerk of a workshop's office, Mr Aleksandres Krastiņš, who had received a large supply of herring meant for the workshop's workers, simply fled with all the supply instead of distributing it.[128] In the same year, the private apartment of Mrs Augusta Walden was robbed by groups of soldiers who were searching for 'butter, meat, different flour, grease'.[129]

Theft of food supplies could take place on an individual level, in an organized collective way, or even be a matter of international dispute. As the conflicts over borders and territories in the former Habsburg empire continued beyond 1918, the agrarian products in newly seized territories turned into an especially thorny issue between the neighbouring

[123] Jabłońska, Helena z Seifertów, *Dziennik z Oblężonego Przemyśla* (1914–1915), edited by Stanisław Stępień (Przemyśl: Południowo-Wschodni Instytut Naukowy w Przemyślu, 2017), 293.
[124] Gille, Ooms and Delandsheere, *Cinquante mois d'occupation allemande*, 358–359.
[125] Healy, *Vienna and the Fall of the Habsburg Empire*, 40.
[126] 'Maizes smaka' *Uz Priekšu* 6 (10 January 1919), 3.
[127] Allen, 'Scarcity', 371.
[128] 'Kantorists un reņģes', *Uz Priekšu* 7 (11 January 1919), 3.
[129] 'Iebrucēji', *Uz Priekšu* 48 (2 March 1919), 3.

states. Hungarian sources from 16 November 1918 speak of the plundering of Hungarian food trains and food stores in the territories occupied by Czechoslovakia, Serbia and Romania. 'In the afternoon hours' of 15 November 1918, as a source outlines, in the Hungarian town of Szabadka (Subotica), which had been occupied, 'Serbian soldiers started to plunder a [Hungarian] train filled with food and a storage filled with military tools'. The officers then were reported to have 'distributed the food and the collected objects among the [Serbian] population' in Szabadka.[130] This resulted in anger towards the invading army that distributed food that was meant for Hungary's civilian population. Similarly, the Czechs in Pozsony (Bratislava) were reported not only to have collected money 'but also food, in numbers of train coaches, in the northern parts of Hungary (Felvidék) and shipped away entire trains of food that had been bitterly collected for the population of the Hungarian territories into Czechoslovakia'.[131] Detailed descriptions of the plundering of food stores in Budapest by Romanians during their occupation of Budapest in the summer of 1919 also featured particularly prominently in contemporary Hungarian media.[132] In other Hungarian towns and villages, the Romanians were also reported to have brought damage to the local Hungarian population, mostly through the theft of 'livestock, coaches, food, cloths, underwear, jewelries and cash', but without causing any physical harm.[133]

Even American food relief delivered to Eastern Europe after the end of the war was not exempt from theft. The day the first ARA cargo ship arrived into Petrograd, on 1 September 1921, stevedores secretly filled their 'pockets, hats, trousers, legs and even the seats of their trousers' with milk, flour, sugar and other urgently needed commodities.[134] Similarly, in June 1919 in Latvian Liepāja (Libau), much of the relief food, once unloaded, was stolen by the labourers.[135] In June 1922, when the stevedores in Riga were searched by local police guards, the group was gathered together, and once forced to move away, the floor of the ARA warehouse was left 'literally covered with small sacks of sugar [and] flour'.[136] Even the Latvian soldiers who were assigned to guard

[130] 'Czehek, szerbek, románok Magyarországon', *Friss Ujság* 23:269 (16 November 1918), 2.
[131] 'Czehek, szerbek, románok Magyarországon', 2.
[132] 'Halas a román megszállás allat', *Kiskun-Halas Helyi Értesítője* 19:22 (26 November 1919): 3.
[133] 'A vörös rémuralom utolsó napja Szabolcsban', *Nyírvidék* XI:120 (29 May 1919): 1–3, 2.
[134] Patenaude, *The Big Show in Bololand*, 614.
[135] From the telegram of M. Svenson (ARA officer) to Herbert Hoover, 26 June 1919, HILA, ARA, EU, box 336, folder 3.
[136] Baltic Port Operations, June 1922, HILA, ARA, EU, box 463, folder 12.

the ARA warehouses were reported to have been involved in stealing '26 cases of bacon and 17 cases of milk'.[137]

Most European governments implemented measures to prosecute and punish the offenders of food-related crimes. In the Netherlands in January 1917, war-related crimes were considered such a threat to public order that the government made any breach of the 1916 Distribution Law and other foodstuff-related laws punishable by a heavy prison sentence. In March 1917, prisons were already overflowing.[138] The government then turned to religion to provide a deterrent to crime. Acting on its advice, Dutch Protestant, Catholic and Jewish priests, pastors and rabbis denied religious services, such as Holy Communion, to offenders.[139] In Riga, in June 1919, a determined effort was made to stop stevedores from stealing relief food. As 'this evil' was apparently '[s]o great' and 'so prevalent' among the workmen, the grain corporation agent even went to the point of 'using soldier guards from the Latvian Army' to 'search the workmen at the end of the morning as well as at the end of the day's work'.[140] The head of ARA Child Relief Mission in Latvia, Thomas Orbison, announced in December 1919 a reward of 500 Latvian rubles for receiving reliable information about thieves who had stolen five sacks of flour, two sacks of sugar and three sacks of rice from one of the children's kitchens in Riga.[141] Despite the manifold attempts to stop the ongoing illicit trade, people kept obtaining much of their nutrition through illegal channels.

Conclusion

This chapter discussed various ways in which ordinary people responded to hunger that was induced or magnified as a part of the conflicts during and following the First World War. They modified their cooking practices, preserved foodstuffs, created new spaces in their apartments, homes, balconies and parks for food production, they hoarded, bartered, stole and risked capture in efforts to secure enough food.

[137] Letter By George F. Felker to the Minister of Supplies. Riga, 25 July 1919, HILA, ARA, EU, box 336, folder 4.

[138] Albert Eggens, *Van daad tot vonnis. Door Drenten gepleegde criminaliteit voor en tijdens de Eerste Wereldoorlog* (Assen: Van Gorcum, 2005), 157.

[139] P. H. Ritter Jr., *De donkere poort. Een boek, behelzende tal van Persoonlijke Herinneringen van vooraanstaande Mannen, Stemmingsbeelden, Indrukken, Beschouwingen, Belangrijke en Onbelangrijke Gebeurtenissen, Verhalen en Anecdoten over Nederland in de jaren 1914–1918* II (The Hague: s-Gravenhage Daamen, 1931), 196.

[140] 'Report of Port activities', ARA, Riga, 1 August 1919, HILA, ARA, EU, box 336, folder 7.

[141] '500 rubljej nagradi' *Segodnia* 79 (19 December 1919), 3.

Ordinary civilians ate things they normally would not have eaten, sometimes things that had little nutritive value or that were even unsafe. Such strategies were used by individuals to try and secure adequate food supplies for themselves, and for their families. One can only imagine the fear and anxiety they must have felt in the uncertainty of their ability, after attempting any of the methods discussed here, to obtain basic food items. In many instances, despite their best efforts and the manifold strategies they used, people were not successful in curbing the hunger they felt. There was simply not enough food to be had. It is little wonder then that food obsessions, discussed elsewhere in this book, took root. This chapter detailed some of the methods used to obtain food, but it does not and cannot measure the success, or not, of the people who employed them. If just one of the individual and collective survival strategies outlined here had worked perfectly, then millions of people would not have died of hunger, succumbed to disease, experienced lassitude because of insufficient nutrition, and children and infants would not have had their growth rates reduced. Unfortunately, the employed survival strategies were not enough for many to prevent this kind of suffering in war and post-war Europe.

5 Food as Experience

Sophie De Schaepdrijver

Introduction

In old age, the playwright Suzanne Lilar (b. 1901), looking back on her lower-middle-class childhood in German-occupied Ghent (Belgium), remembered how, twice a week, her father would reverentially unwrap the family's allotted loaf of bread, a staple once so taken for granted. "Humble food," Lilar recalled, "had become a sacred matter again."[1] So it had been for Otto Rees (b. 1910) from a Freiburg working-class family, who recalled eighty years on how he and the other neighborhood children would rush to the baker's after school, clutching their precious bread coupons in white-knuckled little hands.[2] Across First World War Europe, the vast majority of civilians experienced food in ways that differed significantly from pre-war times. They came by their food differently; they ate different things, in altered quantities and qualities; they ate in changed environments. And they found themselves thinking about food obsessively. In July 1916, a sixteen-year-old forester's daughter from the Harz mountains in Saxony wrote that her war diary was "becoming really quite humdrum, I go on about food all the time!"[3] Albeit with stark, indeed tragic variations, changes in food experience held across regions and even across much of the social spectrum; they obtained for civilians living under military occupation as well as for those on home fronts; for the "settled" as for refugees; for urban populations but also for rural ones; for "free" civilians and for internees; for citizens of belligerent as well as neutral states; for those bereft of food relief but also for those who had access to it. This chapter takes a closer look at these changes in the experience of food.

1 Suzanne Lilar, *Une enfance gantoise* (Paris: Grasset, 1976), 100.

2 Otto Rees, 1994, quoted in Nina Régis, "1917, année de rupture: le rôle du pain de guerre (*Kriegsbrot*) en Allemagne," *Revue d'Allemagne et des pays de langue allemande* 49:2 (2017), 417.

3 July 7, 1916 diary entry by Agnes Kiendl née Zenker (1900–1991), Gerold Kiendl ed., www.zenker.se/History/nessi_tagebuch.shtml [retrieved May 1, 2019].

To begin with the most obvious: The war changed diets. People did not just eat less; they ate different food. Because of war shortages and also the way authorities had to – or chose to – allocate resources, "war diets" differed considerably from pre-war ones for all but the very affluent and very well-connected. Some of these changes would not last, even if they did linger for a long time after the Armistice; others by contrast took hold.

Wartime European populations did not just eat different things; they also ate in different ways. As more and more civilians depended on food relief, they had to eat in common at soup kitchens and canteens; as to the food they ate at home, they had to restrict their choices to the rations doled out in relief warehouses – imperfectly and intermittently complemented by what they could grow themselves (if they had access to land), or obtain on various black markets (if they had funds, connections, and means of transportation). This regimentation of food clashed with established mores. Impoverished members of the middle class felt it a great humiliation to have to queue, which deepened social tension, especially in the hardest-hit regions (in Berlin, queueing could last all night with no guarantee of any food to be had); and "shoppers" balked at having no choice but to consume fodder crops like rutabagas. The war brought hunger but also disgust: at the musty-smelling, quick-to-spoil "war bread," the slimy or moldy sausages, the dubious substitute goods, the smell of unwashed bodies, the sight of greasy pots in soup kitchens, fellow eaters' noisy chewing – a quotidian attack on all five senses at a time when the idea of *enjoying* one's daily meals had come within reach of an ever larger percentage of citizens. In view of this disheartening regression, what drove some contemporaries to profiteering (or at least to types of behaviour lambasted as profiteering) was not just the promise of plenty, but also of cleanliness, privacy, and enjoyment; a respite from the sights, smells, and taste of wartime food and its enforced public consumption.

Changes in Diet

As other chapters in this volume demonstrate, the food supply and the quality of food diminished across belligerent Europe and the Ottoman Empire, including in neutral countries such as the Netherlands and Switzerland. Of course, as these chapters also show, this general recession covers a wide variety of changes: regional, across classes, between civilians and the military, between those with connections and those without. In September 1917 Germany, to give only one example, Victor Klemperer observed the great difference between districts: "in Driburg

[*Bad Driburg near Paderborn, where he went on holiday in September 1917, SDS*], things were almost as they were in peacetime, whereas famine reigned at a few hundred kilometres' distance."[4]

The shrinking supply of food translated into changes in diet. In the United Kingdom, statistics recorded how calorie intake might remain constant while the provenance of those calories changed. The Working Class Cost of Living Committee observed that in June 1918, working-class Britons could afford the same amount of calories as in June 1914, and the unskilled were even somewhat better off than before the war. But recent research shows that the continuity in calorie intake hides worrisome changes in the weekly "food basket." By June 1918, British working-class families ate (even) more bread than they had on the eve of war. They also ate twice as much processed meat (sausages, bacon, tinned meat), but only one-third of the 1914 amount of fruits and vegetables, if that. These changes do not reflect direct war shortages so much as choices made by those in charge. The British food control authorities did not see fruit and vegetables as key foodstuffs, so did not regulate them; as production therefore fell and prices rose, fruit and vegetables became too expensive for many working-class families. In 1918, British workers also consumed more condensed milk, vastly more margarine than they did in 1914, and less butter and cheese. As a result of these changes in diet, workers' energy levels might be maintained, but their intake of vitamins A, B12, D, riboflavin, and C were reduced. The drop in vitamin A was significant enough to suggest a deficiency.[5] To conclude, even in the United Kingdom, where food imports had not dropped too much and where the food policy was alert and nimble, the working-class diet regressed. Elsewhere, it regressed more dramatically. In German-occupied Belgium, even though the international Commission for Relief in Belgium (hereafter CRB) imported 5,174,431 tons of food from 1914 to 1918,[6] food insecurity was rampant. By the winter of 1916–1917, working-class families ate as wretchedly as they had in 1860 (when they had been on the eve of a generations-long improvement in their standard of living). Once again, their diet consisted largely of starch – specifically, mold-prone bread made out of potato flour; potatoes with

[4] Victor Klemperer, *Curriculum Vitae: Erinnerungen 1881–1918*, edited by Walter Nowojski (Berlin: Aufbau-Verlag, 1996), Vol. 2, 565. Klemperer, the later chronicler of life as a Jewish intellectual in Nazi Germany, was at the time working as a book censor for the German-occupied Baltic, stationed first in Kaunas (Lithuania), then at the main office in Leipzig.

[5] Ian Gazeley and Andrew Newell, "The First World War and Working-Class Food Consumption in Britain," *European Review of Economic History* 17 (2013), 71–94.

[6] George I. Gay, *Public Relations of the Commission for the Relief in Belgium: Documents* (Stanford, CA: Stanford University Press, 1929), Vol. 2, 474.

onion sauce when they could get them – on occasion supplemented with some inferior-quality processed bacon (or, as aid recipients called it, "American lard") from the CRB stores. Dairy and meat were out of reach. By April 1917, working-class Belgians were reduced to some 350 grams of food per person per day, most of it bread, plus half a liter of generally thin and protein-poor relief-issue soup.[7] Many among the middle classes were barely better off. That same month of April 1917, the Brussels journalist Charles Tytgat described how his household too had to make do with the food relief stores' 350 grams per person per day: 300 grams of bread, the rest made up of dried beans, lard, and noodles with no meat or cheese. This insubstantial fare sapped away at people's bodily resistance: "the old die in great numbers, as do children."[8] (To compare: in 1913, in bread alone, the average male's daily intake was 670 grams.[9] For the institutionalized, the drop in quantity came earlier: By the start of 1915 already, the boys at the main orphanage of German-occupied Ghent (Belgium) received 250 grams of bread a day, whereas, before the war, the older teenage boys received 800.[10])

Not only did people have less to eat, they also had to go without familiar fare. Some contemporaries were at pains to argue that such changes were for the better. In 1917, the German-American author Wolf von Schierbrand painted the appalling food situation in Vienna as a bracing return to health: "the Austrian people, in their vast majority, are now subsisting on about half the amount of food that they consumed before the war. They must also go without many accustomed articles of diet. With robust, healthy adults, this Spartan fare may often be beneficial, especially in the case of the Viennese, who are naturally

[7] This regression would last a while beyond the war: In 1919, Belgian miners' families still had to spend 85 percent of their income on food. Peter Scholliers and Frank Daelemans, "Standards of Living and Standards of Health in Wartime Belgium," in *The Upheaval of War: Family, Work and Welfare in Europe, 1914–1918*, edited by Robert Wall and Jay Winter (Cambridge: Cambridge University Press, 1988), 139–58.

[8] Charles Tytgat, *Bruxelles sous la botte allemande* (Brussels: Charles Bulens, 1919), 285–90 (April 17, 1917). The mortality rate among the elderly did go up. In 1918, it had increased by a factor of 2.23 compared to the average over 1911–1913: Benoît Majerus, "War Losses (Belgium)" in *1914–1918-online. International Encyclopedia of the First World War*, edited by Ute Daniel et al. (Berlin: Freie Universität, January 2016), https://encyclopedia.1914-1918-online.net/article/war_losses_belgium.

[9] Giselle Nath, *Voedselschaarste en voedselbedeling, tactieken en strategieën. Twee episodes uit de Belgische bezetting tijdens de Eerste Wereldoorlog*. Master's thesis, University of Ghent, 2011, 45.

[10] January 1, 1915 entry in the diary of the Ghent novelist Virginie Loveling: *In oorlogsnood. Oorlogsdagboek 1914–1918*, edited by Bert Van Raemdonck (Ghent: KANTL/UGent, 2005), http://lib.ugent.be/fulltxt/RUG01/000/924/065/BIB-G-025872_2005_0001_AC.pdf.

rather prone to overfeeding."[11] Likewise, the Heidelberg history professor Karl Hampe lauded culinary austerity, for, he told himself in his diary, people too used to sophisticated eating were bound to appreciate it less.[12] But those busy fighting hunger were less complacent. As Herbert Hoover, head of the CRB and, after the war, of the American Relief Administration, perceptively noted, unfamiliar foods compounded the effect of insufficient nutrition:

> However carefully national food supply may be adjusted, from the point of view of ... nutrition ..., yet no mere sufficiency of the needed calories and balanced protein, fats and carbohydrate content in the ration will necessarily make it a satisfactory one. People of different kinds, with different traditions and habits of food use, must have, in some measure at least, the particular kinds of food they are used to. They eat more effectively, one may say, the kinds of food they like than the kinds they do not like. Taste and appetite must be consulted and satisfied in some degree.[13]

Hoover was right: People experienced the imposition of unfamiliar and unloved foods on top of an insufficient diet as particularly vexing. In the Netherlands, during 1915–1916, middle-class diarists when discussing food focused on its mounting price; but by 1917–1918 it wasn't just the price of food that had changed, it was food itself. Diarists complained about the lack of familiar fare, the ever-declining rations, the unfamiliar taste of rationed goods, the inability to cook as one was used to because of a lack of familiar ingredients and a dearth of fuel.[14] They also complained about the circumstances in which one had to eat: under wartime conditions, even eating at home had become *unheimlich.* "I keep my coat on all day indoors," wrote a woman in The Hague. "The oilcloth on the table is so cold to the touch. This afternoon we went out into the street to get warm."[15] In occupied Belgium,

[11] Wolf von Schierbrand, "The Food Situation in Austria-Hungary," *The North American Review* 205:734 (1917), 46–52, 51.

[12] Karl Hampe war diary, quoted in Régis, "1917, année de rupture," 414.

[13] Herbert Hoover, "Preface," in Vernon Kellogg and Alonzo Taylor, *The Food Problem* (New York, NY: Macmillan, 1917), vi.

[14] For example, C. J. F. M. Wentholt, ed., *Den Haag '14–'18: fragmenten uit een dagboek* (The Hague: Haags Gemeentemuseum, 1986), diary entry Miep de Zaaijer February 7, 1917, 18; J. P. de Valk and M. van Faassen, *Dagboeken en aantekeningen van Willem Hendrik de Beaufort 1874–1918* (The Hague: Huygens Instituut voor Nederlandse Geschiedenis, 1993), diary entry June 19, 1916, 807; "Sien Metz over het aardappeloproer in de Jordaan," in *Getuigen van een Generatie. Waarden, idealen en het leven van alledag in de jaren na de Eerste Wereldoorlog in Nederland*, edited by Marijke Verduyn and Sietske van Weerden (Zoetermeer: Meinema, 1992), 32–6.

[15] Diary entry Miep de Zaaijer, April 13, 1918, in *Den Haag '14–'18: fragmenten uit een dagboek*, edited by C. J. F. M. Wentholt (The Hague: Haags Gemeentemuseum, 1986), 18.

loving descriptions of (rare) decent meals cropped up in diaries: The middle-aged novelist Georges Eekhoud from Easter 1916 got into the habit of recording good meals in all their details, which he had never once done up until then. Likewise, in occupied Poland, a priest, Father Rokoszny, described a dinner organized on Easter Monday 1916 in terms befitting what was clearly a rare occasion: "Yesterday evening I was at the gathering of Dr. Szczepaniak – the war was unknown: dinner with wine, porter, plum brandy, hot sirloin and compotes, cold appetizers, as if there was no war!"[16] In Victor Klemperer's memoir, the most sensuous recollection of the First World War years is that of a dinner spent at the lavishly appointed house of a friendly war profiteer in Leipzig: "You can't imagine," Klemperer's young host told him, "what lovely peacetime things [*was für gute Friedensdinge*] we will eat and drink and smoke." He was as good as his word: "There was rhine wine and burgundy and *Sekt* and cherry brandy and mocha coffee from hand-painted, thickly gilded little cups, there was roast goose, and there were pastries, baked with no *Ersatz* at all and with a great deal of eggs and sugar."[17] These fond descriptions of the by now all-too-rare experience of eating one's fill both in terms of quantity and, importantly, in terms of quality, all of it enhanced by elegant surroundings and sumptuous wines, were, for those who wrote them down, a means to remind themselves that another life was still possible – a life away from the ever more drab and depressing daily food routine.

In what follows, this section will take a closer look at changes in the consumption of particular foodstuffs.

"Bread First"

In the early twentieth century, Europeans consumed much more bread than they would a century later. (The drop in bread consumption seems particularly pronounced in France, where it stood at 600 grams per person per day in 1900, dropped to 425 grams on the eve of the Second World War, and sank to an estimated 90 grams in 2020.)[18]

[16] J. Rokoszny, *Diariusz Wielkiej Wojny 1915–1916*, Vol. 2, W. Caban and M. Przeniosło, eds. (Kielce: Wydawn. Wyższej Skoly Pedag. im. Jana Kochanowskiego, 1998), 24 IV 1916, 163, quoted in Katarzyna Sierakowska, *Śmierć, wygnanie, głód w dokumentach osobistych. Ziemie polskie w latach Wielkiej Wojny 1914–1918* [Death, Exile, Hunger in Personal Accounts. Polish Lands during the Great War, 1914–1918] (Warsaw: Instytut Historii PAN, 2015), 197.

[17] Victor Klemperer, *Curriculum Vitae: Erinnerungen 1881–1918*, Walter Nowojski, ed. (Berlin: Aufbau-Verlag, 1996), Vol. 2, 591.

[18] Steven L. Kaplan, *Pour le pain* (Paris: Fayard, 2020), 24. Another statistic quotes the figures of 900 grams in 1900 and 150 grams in 2013: "L'évolution de notre

Unsurprisingly, therefore, many if not all wartime official food offices and non-governmental relief efforts pursued a fierce "bread first" policy.[19] Berlin had a Bread Supply Office before the end of 1914.[20] In the United Kingdom, the Corn Production Act of 1917 returned grassland to grain production.[21] And, as a third example, by the winter of 1917–1918 the search for grain dominated not just Austria-Hungary's interior policy, but also its foreign affairs policy.[22] The provision of food was held to stand or fall with the provision of bread. As two CRB agents stated in 1917,

> Bread has not infrequently been referred to as the stuff of life. But it really is. We of the Relief Commission found it so in feeding Belgium. The loudest call of the people, their principal anxiety, and our first care, all converged on wheat. The German experience, as well as the Belgian one, has shown that a dietetic regimen for a semi-starving people is strong or weak, appeasing or dangerous, in proportion to the bread it contains. If the bread ration is normal, or sufficient, much repression or substitution can be used in the case of the other foods. Thus, considered either from the standpoint of physiology or psychology, seeing to the bread supply is the matter of first importance in the case of peoples living on short rations and getting occasional glimpses into the abyss of starvation.[23]

consommation de pain," *Ouest-France*, September 29, 2013, www.ouest-france.fr/normandie/falaise-14700/levolution-de-notre-consommation-de-pain-1151361. In Germany, the consumption of bread cereals fell from 133 kg per person per year in 1910 to 66 kg in 1970: Hans-Jürgen Teuteberg, "Die Rolle von Brot und Kartoffeln in der historischen Entwicklung der Nahrungsgewohnheiten," *Ernährungs-Umschau*, 26:5 (1979), 146–54, 151. With thanks to Nina Régis.

19 In Russia, by contrast, the tsarist state and provisional government were unable to mobilize grain on a national scale, though city governments were more proactive. Lars Lih, *Bread and Authority in Russia, 1914–1921* (Berkeley, CA: University of California Press, 1990) (with thanks to Bertrand Patenaude); Iaroslav Golubinov, "Food and Nutrition (Russian Empire)," in *1914–1918-online. International Encyclopedia of the First World War*, edited by Ute Daniel et al. (Berlin: Freie Universität, August 2018), https://encyclopedia.1914-1918-online.net/article/food_and_nutrition_russian_empire.

20 Keith Allen, "Sharing Scarcity: Bread Rationing and the First World War in Berlin, 1914–1923," *Journal of Social History* 32:2 (1998), 371–93, 375.

21 Theo Balderston, "Industrial Mobilization and War Economies," in *A Companion to World War I*, edited by John Horne (London: Wiley-Blackwell, 2010), 217–33, 227.

22 Clifford F. Wargelin, "A High Price for Bread: The First Treaty of Brest-Litovsk and the Break-up of Austria-Hungary, 1917–1918," *The International History Review* 19:4 (1997), 757–88. See also David Hamlin, "The Fruits of Occupation: Food and Germany's Occupation of Romania in the First World War," *First World War Studies* 4:1 (2013), 81–95, 83.

23 Kellogg and Taylor, *The Food Problem*, 5. In June 1917, a CRB memorandum pointed out that "Bread occupies in the physiology and psychology of the diet the position of keystone of the arch. If the bread intake be normal, the consumer will tolerate many other alterations in the diet." HILA, Graham Lusk Papers, Box 1, Folder 1, "Memorandum," June 11, 1917.

Yet the "war bread" provided through "bread first" arrangements often had very little in common with people's familiar loaves.[24] A leitmotiv in wartime diaries and other personal accounts is the abysmal quality of war bread; all the more disheartening as bread was a staple and a comfort food. "War bread" dough was watered down, and/or mixed with inferior ingredients, like potato flour, or, as shortages increased and even potatoes were hard to come by, flour made out of peas or beans, and ultimately adulterated with wood dust, straw, talcum powder, or other inedible ingredients.[25] In the Ottoman Empire, hard-up civilians stretched flour with ground legumes, chickpeas, and lentils; and with potatoes, though they seem to have done so with (even) more reluctance than elsewhere, disgusted as they were with the resulting bread: "white talc that was like a white glue," wrote one inhabitant of Lebanon.[26]

Still, chickpeas and lentils did have nutritional value; more in general, we should note, as an aside, that a few "war breads" were coarse but not inferior. The return, in some regions, of the dense, dark "poverty breads" of the early modern era, made of whole wheat or rye or other cereals, was a nutritional gain, and some contemporaries knew this: early twentieth-century research on vitamin deficiency had demonstrated the inferiority of the white bread which consumers across Europe had come to like. (If with regional differences: in Central and Eastern Europe's "rye belt," naturally more suited to growing rye than wheat, "black" bread remained much more common.[27] Still, by the early twentieth century, much German-grown rye was used for fodder, and Germany imported 3 million tons of wheat a year.[28])

But "poverty bread" could also mean a return to organic but non-cereal ingredients: In northern Germany, for instance, by August 1918, bread was reported to contain "46% wheat, 46% reindeer moss, and 8% nitrate of soda to offset the moss."[29] And most "war breads" were actively unwholesome because of cereal problems, which were greatest among the Central Powers. In the Bohemian lands, from 1915 wheat

[24] As strikingly demonstrated for Germany in Nina Régis, *Le pain de guerre allemand: une histoire culturelle de l'arrière (1914–1919)* (PhD dissertation, Université de Toulouse-Jean Jaurès, November 2022). I thank Dr. Régis for her permission to refer to this work.

[25] Arnulf Scriba, "Ersatzprodukte," Deutsches Historisches Museum, Berlin, 2014, www.dhm.de/lemo/kapitel/erster-weltkrieg/alltagsleben/ersatzprodukte.html.

[26] Quoted in Melanie Schulze-Tanielian, "Food and Nutrition (Ottoman Empire/Middle East)," in *1914–1918-online. International Encyclopedia of the First World War*, edited by Ute Daniel et al. (Berlin: Freie Universität, October 2014), https://encyclopedia.1914-1918-online.net/article/food_and_nutrition_ottoman_empiremiddle_east.

[27] On "poverty breads," the "rye belt," and on German bread culture, William Rubel, *Bread: A Global History* (London: Reaktion, 2011), 45; 91–3.

[28] Allen, "Sharing Scarcity," 375.

[29] HILA, USFAR, Office of Foreign Information, Report of September 28, 1918.

flour had to be mixed not just with flour from other cereals like barley, oats, or corn, but also with non-cereal substitutes like malt products, potato starch, and sugars.[30] People in the Baltic region, too, experienced a dearth of flour. For instance, in December 1916, the municipal authorities in the city of Riga attempted to centralize the flour supply and sell it to bakeries who had to then sell bread for a fixed, low price. However, the system failed because many bakers used the worst kind of flour (and, one presumes, a great many non-cereal fillings) for civilians, and sold the better-quality loaves to the Russian army.[31] In Vienna, by July 1918, wheat and rye made up no more than 10 percent of the content of loaves.[32] In Germany, from the start of the war, "war bread" contained potato flour;[33] bread was rationed from June 1915 (from February 1915 in Berlin);[34] and the quest for substitute ingredients was continuous. In May 1916, for instance, the *Münchner Neueste Nachrichten* reported that bread could be baked with whey instead of water; this made bread more nutritious and used the whey that would otherwise go to waste since there were no pigs to feed. But even this deliberately optimistic report had to admit one drawback: this bread quickly turned sour, so could not be transported outside of the cheese-making districts themselves.[35] In September 1916, German legislation ratified the plunge in standards with a decree that loosened the rules on what bakers could put in bread; it would remain in effect until well after the war.[36]

Meanwhile, in occupied lands, desperate women prostituted themselves to the occupying troops for bread: "a tryst for a loaf of bread," wrote the observer of sexual mores Magnus Hirschfeld, "that is the unvarnished truth." And he cited a motto ascribed to Flemish women: "for hours we will bang / for a *Kommissbrot* [a German army-issued loaf, SDS] and a franc."[37] Still, in Belgium and northern France, the

[30] Martin Franc, "Bread from Wood: Natural Food Substitutes in the Czech Lands during the First World War," in *Food and War in Twentieth Century Europe*, edited by Iva Zweiniger-Bargielowska, Rachel Duffett, and Alain Drouart (Farnham: Ashgate, 2011), 73–83.

[31] *Jaunākās Ziņas*, 1916, December 18, 19, 24.

[32] HILA, USFAR, Office of Foreign Information, Alphabetical File, Box 95, Folder 8, Austria-Hungary, Food Ministry, Dairy Products, "Special Report on Bread Situation – Austria-Hungary," July 6, 1918.

[33] Scriba, "Ersatzprodukte."

[34] Roger Chickering, "Imperial Germany's Peculiar War, 1914–1918," *Journal of Modern History* 88:8 (2016), 856–94.

[35] HILA, USFAR, Clippings, *Münchner Neueste Nachrichten*, May 31, 1916, translated clipping in file.

[36] Régis, *Le pain de guerre*, 388–9, 558.

[37] Magnus Hirschfeld, *Sittengeschichte des Ersten Weltkriegs*, 2nd ed. (Hanau: Müller & Kiepenhauder, n.d.), 268 [original edition, *Sittengeschichte des Weltkrieges*, 1929, 2 vols].

occupying forces could not seize the local wheat harvest because of international agreements. But they were able to do so in occupied Poland, where all harvested grains were sent to Germany; some were returned to Poland as flour, mixed with additives. This measure, together with bread rationing, profoundly impoverished the diet. In Warsaw, one hunger riot in May 1917 saw angry people banging on the doors of sweetshops catering to German officers; the teacher and social activist Władysława Głodowska-Sampolska later recalled that "people demanded increased food rations, above all bread. The bread at that time was very bad; people became sick from eating it. It contained a bare amount of flour and a multitude of other ingredients such as potato peels, field peas, and milled chestnuts. This bread fell apart a day after baking and had a terrible stench."[38] In that same Spring of 1917, in German-occupied Courland (current-day Latvia), the occupation authorities began to mix bread flour with straw.[39] A summer 1917 decree by the occupation authorities ordered bakers to use at least 50 percent of non-cereal ingredients.[40]

The change in the supply and the composition of bread, the ultimate staple and the ultimate comfort food, may, then, have been the most keenly felt and remembered "food experience" of the entire war.

Dairy

Meanwhile, other pre-war staple foods, such as dairy, became rare. Dairy's importance was well known. A 1917 CRB report highlighted how

> [m]ilk, including of course butter and cheese, supplies the essential growth vitamin for children, balanced protein for children and adults … A certain amount of milk is required in the preparation of our food and if absent this would so disorganize the condition of our food and alter its qualities from the psychological point of view as to exert a disastrous influence upon national alimentation.[41]

Authorities therefore made stringent choices regarding the allocation of dairy. The German Milk Office, created in 1916, collaborated with municipal authorities to apportion the available milk by preference to pregnant women, small children, and the sick. But the policy, as Belinda

[38] Robert Blobaum, *A Minor Apocalypse: Warsaw during the First World War* (Ithaca, NY: Cornell University Press, 2017), 89–90.

[39] April 1917. Arnolds Aizsilnieks, *Latvijas saimnieciskā vēsture 1914–1945* (Stockholm: Daugava, 1968), 75.

[40] Klāvs Zariņš, *Policies of the German Military Administration in the occupied Courland Governorate (May 1915-March 1918)* (PhD dissertation, University of Latvia, January 2023), 145. I thank Dr. Zariņš for his permission to refer to this work.

[41] Cited in Kellogg and Taylor, *The Food Problem*, 145–6.

Davis has shown in the case of Berlin, was not strictly enforced in the face of angry queuing crowds who resented others' "privileges," and, what with the War Food Office's tendency to favour the war effort over demographic concerns, extra rations of foodstuffs went to heavy laborers and munitions workers rather than to women and children.[42] In occupied Belgium, by contrast, the combined efforts of the CRB and the *Comité National* (hereafter CN), the vast voluntary organization tasked with charting need and allocating supplies, kept up the provision of extra rations for pregnant and lactating women, and for babies and small children; this plethora of preventative health efforts even diminished infant mortality compared to the pre-war years, especially in 1915 and 1916.[43] Meanwhile, there was less dairy available to the general population, and its quality diminished. In Germany, there were Ersatz products for dairy as there were for thousands of articles. In immediate post-war Riga, which had been occupied by German troops in 1917–1918, British sailors marveled at the dairy Ersatz products they saw in shops, claiming (not altogether correctly) that the Entente had known no such products at all, and buying Ersatz butter and cheese in shops as a curiosity "to show them in their homeland," as the local press reported.[44]

Meat

In the years prior to the war, per capita intake of meat had risen; modestly enough for the mass of the population, but sufficient to bolster a sense of progress. Meat was prestigious, which is why bourgeois dishes – *filet de boeuf à la truffe*, *poularde à la royale*, and so on – were entirely centered around imposing pieces of roast beef, mutton, or stuffed poultry, in contrast to the stews of traditional farming and working-class families: the *pots-au-feu*, *Eintöpfe*, *dalmatinska pašticadas*, and so on, where meat was a mere component (and sometimes even a minor one). The war caused meat intake to drop across the continent. Even in relatively well-fed France, families were urged to observe meatless days. The Catholic journal *La Croix* helpfully printed sample menus – taking care to differentiate between "families of modest means" (who were curtly presented

[42] Belinda J. Davis, *Home Fires Burning: Food, Politics, and Everyday Life in World War I Berlin* (Chapel Hill, NC: University of North Carolina Press, 2000), 151–8.

[43] Albert Henry, *Le ravitaillement de la Belgique pendant l'occupation allemande* (Paris: Presses Universitaires de France, 1924), 198; Godelieve Masuy-Stroobant, "Les enfants et la guerre," and Catherine Jacques and Valérie Piette, "Une grande bataille: sauver l'enfance," both in *Une guerre totale? La Belgique dans la Première Guerre mondiale* (Brussels: Rijksarchief, 2005), edited by Serge Jaumain et al., 157–70, 171–82.

[44] "Angļu jūrnieki," *Jaunākās Ziņas*, 1918, December 31.

with a list of ingredients for a lentil-and-rice soup), "bourgeois families of middling condition" (who by contrast received a great deal of attention, with a week-long day-by-day enumeration of lunches and dinners: "boiled chestnuts," potatoes fried in *végétaline* [a kind of margarine], cheese macaroni, dried fruit, and so on), and, thirdly, "families of means," who were invited to sample permutations of meatless fare that required more expensive ingredients, a cook's attention, and a fully equipped and well fuelled kitchen: the chestnuts now came in a pâté, the potatoes were new, the macaroni was adorned with mushrooms, the dried fruit comprised dates, and so on.[45] Elsewhere in the world-at-war, "meatless days" were less of a choice. They were introduced, by necessity, in Austria-Hungary. From May 1915, the Viennese had to observe two meatless days per week: an empty measure for most working-class families, who by then were unable to afford meat.[46] Even in Budapest, where the food situation was better than in Vienna, the daily *Pesti Napló* ran an article in late September 1916 entitled "How do we live without meat? A Wednesday Walk in Budapest." It painted a picture of closed butcher shops and slaughterhouses, and lively traffic at fishmongers; there was also a brisk trade in live poultry, since the ban had been unclear on that score. Eggs, by contrast, were unobtainable, partly as an unintended consequence of official policies.[47] In spite of the paper's fairly cheerful tone, the meat problem in Budapest would deepen: by the early summer of 1918 a report noted that "Matters have reached such a climax in Budapest that large sections of population can get no meat at all."[48] Meatless days were also introduced in several Russian cities and provinces, as well as in Petrograd and in the province of Livland, from July 1917. It was forbidden to sell and eat meat in public eating places from Tuesdays through Fridays. As a result, other sources of animal protein, particularly fish, became much more expensive.[49]

In April 1918, the Dutch government introduced the so-called *eenheidsworst* ("regulation sausage"), sold at fixed prices and rations (100 grams per person per week) (Figure 5.1). Butchers were banned from

45 "Menus sans viande établis d'après les règles de l'alimentation rationnelle," *La Croix*, May 19, 1917, 4.

46 Reinhard Sieder, "Behind the Lines: Working-class Family Life in Wartime Vienna," in *The Upheaval of War: Family, Work, and Welfare in Europe, 1914–1918*, edited by Richard Wall and Jay Winter (Cambridge: Cambridge University Press, 1988), 112.

47 "Hogyan élünk hus nélkül?" [How do we live without meat?], *Pesti Napló*, 67:270, September 28, 1916, 10.

48 HILA, USFAR, Office of Foreign Information, Alphabetical File, Austria Hungary, Box 95, Folder 11, Food Ministry, Livestock and Meat. "Meat Situation-Hungary," June 8, 1918.

49 *Jaunākās Ziņas*, July 25, August 6, 1917.

Figure 5.1 Sale of “regulation sausages” in Haarlem during the First World War, 1918.
Source: North Holland Archives, 1100 – Beeldcollectie van de gemeente Haarlem, no. 32910

selling both cheap and expensive cuts; they had to mince all available meats together and add sugar and spices to make the mix palatable. A similar meat item had been introduced in Germany in 1916 under the name *Einheitswurst*. In the Netherlands, its introduction led to an explosion of mockery (cartoons, satirical songs, skits), and the term stuck: to this day, *eenheidsworst* refers to any standardized and unattractive item.

Sugar

The wartime fate of sugar is paradoxical. Supplies diminished due to the vast slump in beet sugar production.[50] But this only increased the call for sugar, which contemporaries saw as a provider of energy and not as "empty calories" (a notion that did not yet exist).[51] This conflation of energy with nutrition informed the provisioning of mass armies, all the more so as sugar provided an easily packaged, compact, non-perishable boost. On home fronts, authorities touted sugar as a substitute foodstuff in spite of its diminishing supply: German posters exhorted housewives to cook with sugar, claiming that it was "plentiful" and had "great nutritional value."[52] Housewives rallied by and by: in the summer of 1916, German women took to the streets to protest having to substitute nutritious bread spreads with sugary ones ("Away with jam!"), but they accepted it one year later.[53] (In addition, German and Austrian consumers seem to have used saccharin: in April 1916, at any rate, the German authorities in Courland reported a dearth of saccharin because it was exported to the German home front.[54] Consumers deplored the change: One March 1918 reader's letter from the *Neue Freie Presse* in Vienna thought "war tea with saccharin, the lethe of today" a poor substitute for pre-war treats.[55]) In the United Kingdom, which by 1914 already had the highest per-capita consumption of sugar in the world and where "it was commonly believed by the

[50] On the slump in production, Thierry Bonzon and Belinda Davis, "Feeding the Cities," in *Capital Cities at War: Paris, London, Berlin 1914–1919*, edited by Jean-Louis Robert and Jay Winter (Cambridge: Cambridge University Press, 1997), Vol. I, 305–41, 310; see also Marie-Thérèse François, "La production et la consommation du sucre dans le monde," *Revue de botanique appliquée et d'agriculture coloniale* 17:191 (1937), 496–513.

[51] As one official noted in the case of Belgium: Henry, *Le ravitaillement de la Belgique*, 137.

[52] Roger Chickering, *The Great War and Urban Life in Germany: Freiburg, 1914–1918* (Cambridge: Cambridge University Press, 2007), 264.

[53] Davis, *Home Fires Burning*, 190.

[54] Aizsilnieks, *Latvijas saimnieciskā vēsture*, 75.

[55] Quoted in Edgar Haider, *Wien 1918: Agonie der Kaiserstadt* (Vienna: Böhlau, 2018), 196.

working classes that children would die unless they ate a pound of sugar a week" – a belief widely shared in the middle and upper classes – the Royal Commission on Food Supplies went out of its way from August 1914 to keep sugar imports flowing, and, in 1918, berated the government's "stupidity" in concentrating on cereal imports when it could have focused all its energy on sugar.[56] Sugar beets became more desirable than they had ever been. One Czech woman recalled after the war how her household produced their own sugar from sugar beets they stole in the carts on their way to the factory. "With this we bake gingerbread adding some rye flour. We spread it on the children's bread. Our sugar is actually some kind of dark brown sweet thick fluid."[57] Meanwhile, in Syria, grape molasses substituted for sugar.[58] The prioritizing of sugar was no less intense among the besieged and occupied. In encircled and starving Przemyśl, to quote a rather arresting set of data, the *Festungskommando* opened a warehouse for civilians in January 1915. This warehouse distributed an average of 13 kg of foodstuffs per month for two people. This encompassed "thick and dark" barley-rye flour, 1/4 kg of onions, a maximum of 2 kg of processed meat (of different quality depending on the customers' social status), and, startlingly, "3/4 kg of sugar."[59] Inhabitants of eastern Anatolia, after the war, praised their former Russian occupiers by pointing out that local work crews building roads for the Russian forces received "tea with plenty of sugar."[60]

As a result of this heightened demand, after the war, sugar consumption would rise; in Germany and France, it almost reached the level of the United States (the world's second-largest consumer after the United Kingdom), and would remain high.[61] In Belgium, the Flemish novelist Stijn Streuvels noted how eating sweets had become commonplace in the countryside, whereas, before the war, "grown men looked down on sweets as children's stuff."[62]

[56] L. Margaret Barnett, *British Food Policy during the First World War* (Boston: Allen & Unwin, 1985), 30–1.

[57] Alois Žipek, ed., *Domov za války: svědectví účastníků* (Praha: Pokrok, 1929), vol. IV, 218.

[58] Schulze-Tanielian, "Food and Nutrition (Ottoman Empire/Middle East)."

[59] January 23, 1915 entry from the diary of Helena Jabłońska: Jabłońska, Helena z Seifertów, *Dziennik z Oblężonego Przemyśla* (1914–1915), edited by Stanisław Stępień (Przemyśl: Południowo-Wschodni Instytut Naukowy, 2017), 325.

[60] Quoted in Halit D. Akarca, "The Imperial Transformation of a Russian-Occupied Ottoman City during the First World War," *War & Society*, 41 no. 1 (2022), 21–35, 22.

[61] François, "La production et la consommation du sucre," 499.

[62] An observation from 1923, quoted in Jakob P. Kruijt, *België: boeren en arbeiders sedert den Wereldoorlog* (Groningen-Batavia: Noordhoff, 1932), 66.

Changes in Food Practices

Communal Eating

In reaction to the overwhelming unfamiliarity and unattractiveness of wartime food regimes, wartime societies fiercely clung to their cultures of conviviality centered around food and drink. Even if the food and drink itself were in short supply. The two hundred or so Berlin cafés raised the alarm in late 1915: because of the dwindling supply of coffee beans and the official ban on serving an unadulterated brew (see below), clients stayed away. Yet the overhead stayed the same, for, as café owners explained, an establishment's standards had to be kept up regardless of the number of patrons: "just like in peacetime, one has to provide live music in the afternoons, newspapers, and attentive service – which is particularly hard, since skilful waiters have become rare. Customers should feel the restrictions as little as possible."[63] Likewise, in The Hague, the swank tea-rooms with their string orchestras kept up the show, though the fare had changed. Instead of proper tea, they served a concoction named "thea." One diarist recorded that "when we asked what that was, they told us they themselves had no idea, but that it smelled of mulled wine and tasted of saffron. We decided not to risk it."[64] In Brussels, society ladies visiting each other for tea brought their own sandwiches (in stylish little boxes called *tartinières*, which were all the rage), and the typical hostess gift was a satchel of potatoes, exquisitely presented, of course.[65] In Budapest, in September 1916, a newspaper reported on the cityscape on the first meatless day:

> We started our walk at the most famous cook-shop [kifőzés], at Aunti Mari. … Today this was the menu: mushroom soup, deep-fried carp with potatoes and cabbage, pastry filled with nuts, poppy-seeds or cottage cheese or marmalade. This menu costs two crowns and twenty filler and one needs to admit that the portions are satisfactory. … At the "Aunt Mari" at Ó-street … there were the following choices: war stew, minced lung, Transylvanian gulyás with beef heart, fried veal liver, sour lung with dumplings. The war stew was prepared like the normal stew, just instead of the beef or veal meat they use kidney, heart and liver.[66]

63 HILA, USFAR, Clippings, "Die Kaffeehaüser ohne Kaffee," undated clipping (late 1915?), unidentified German newspaper.

64 Diary of Miep de Zaaier, March 10, 1918 in Wentholt ed., *Den Haag '14–'18*, 18.

65 Potatoes: C. Sorgeloos and G. Veirman, "La guerre du silence ou le journal de la Comtesse d'Oultremont," *Revue belge d'Histoire militaire* 29 (1991), 123–44 and 209–28, specifically 142–3. On the *tartinières*: *Belgian Bulletin*, October 17, 1918, 1.

66 "Hogyan élünk hus nélkül?" ["How do we live without meat? A Wednesday Walk in Budapest"], *Pesti Napló*, 67:270, September 28, 1916, 10.

This description conveys a fierce desire not to give in to scarcity: restaurants served familiar if downsized fare such as the traditional gulyás, except made with inferior types of meat. These were actual restaurants, and they served an actual menu, with choices, which mitigated customers' sense of having to eat "war dishes." An article from February 1916 describes the creation of another type of public feeding space: the student canteen. Students were particularly suffering from famine, as many Hungarian students had come as refugees to Budapest, because their universities had been closed in Transylvania. "[T]he capital's student canteen opened its doors … [T]he pure white table is being laid – day after day – for two hundred university students, with healthy and good foods—for free or for very little money."[67]

Similar locales abounded in occupied Belgium, where, for a small fee, hard-up middle-class people could take meals in so-called *restaurants économiques* (budget restaurants). By war's end, almost all of Belgium's middle-class families ate in these places: the monthly budget for their operation rose by a factor of a staggering twenty-nine between June 1917 and December 1918. All was done to maintain a modicum of distinction: some of the restaurants were located in tony pre-war locales; "customers" sat at proper restaurant tables, with table linen (like the "pure white table" of the Budapest student canteen),[68] waited on by white-aproned *garçons*.

Meanwhile, still in Belgium, communal eating increased across the board. Concerns for children's growth overrode prejudices of social status, so that, at war's end, almost all of the schoolchildren in Brussels ate the lunch offered by the CN (the so-called *couque scolaire*, a small loaf with lard, and a cup of cocoa).[69] The vast majority of working-class Belgians, by war's end, ate in soup kitchens; endless queuing upended family life,[70] as it did in German-occupied Liepāja in today's Latvia. The artist Aleksandrs Janševskis, a boy during the war, later recalled how "the town council [issued] soup and bread for the needy once a day. … It was

[67] "Diakmenza" ["Student canteen"], *Fővárosi Közlöny*, 27:8, February 11, 1916, 1.

[68] The *restaurants économiques* distinguished themselves from soup kitchens by the use of table linen, although they could not keep this up: by April 1918, even ordinary restaurants and cafés were forbidden to use table linen so as to preserve laundry soap for essential uses (Georges Eekhoud, *Journal*, manuscript, Archives et Musée de la Littérature, Brussels, entry from April 24, 1918).

[69] Peter Scholliers, "La faim à Bruxelles en '14-'18. Soupe populaire et restaurants économiques," in *Bruxelles en '14-'18: la guerre au quotidien*, edited by Serge Jaumain and Valérie Piette (Brussels: La Fonderie, 2005): 34–40, 36.

[70] After the war, a priest in the Brussels district of Molenbeek wrote that children misbehaved because their parents were away queuing all day. State Archives, Belgium, Archepiscopal Archive First World War Reports, Commune of Sint-Jans-Molenbeek, parish of Sint-Jan-Baptist, report by the parish priest, n.d. [1919], folio 3.

necessary to go early in the morning because there were long queues. Almost half a day passed until one reached the pot."[71]

In Budapest, the Relief Committee devised a specific arrangement: a Central Kitchen where "lunch for 10.000 to 15.000 people could be cooked. ... This central kitchen would also distribute food dishes to the poor and to the poor part of the middle class. ... On the space outside the kitchen they would build a kiosk [sütőde] and a sausage factory [hurkagyarat]."[72] The kitchen opened in the fall of 1916; it prepared and delivered food to the soup kitchens as well as to the families that could not attend them.[73] To serve these latter families, Budapest's Relief Committee also provided mobile kitchens, a kind of Meals-on-Wheels: these "for little money bring tasty warm foods home to families with many children where the father was drafted, the mother needs to do war work ... and can therefore not cook, and who ... do not have the time or the money to travel to faraway soup kitchens." The report went on to say that when these kitchens were launched, "masses of people" thronged them; they clearly filled a need.[74]

At Home

Although more people ate ready-made meals at or from soup kitchens, mobile kitchens, central canteens, budget restaurants, and so on, cooking still went on in families, though with vast changes, few of them for the better. "Making do" was a bitter skill to have to learn. As the CRB wrote in 1917, with regard to Germany:

> It is impossible to prepare foods without milk or butter or other fat, and have them meet the normal taste of the Germans. When the German housewife no longer had milk for use in the kitchen and was denied the use of cooking fats, she stood helpless before the task of preparation of food; and throughout the last two years the German people have subsisted upon food that to their tastes was unnatural and definitely unsatisfying.[75]

Civil society did what it could: municipal authorities, relief agencies, companies, friendly societies, and other collectives disseminated tips and recipes. In Austria-Hungary, by 1915, cookbooks explained to housewives how to use wartime ingredients. In Vienna, recipes were even printed on tram tickets to reach a broader audience.[76] One War Relief

71 Quoted in Zariņš, *Policies of the German Military Administration*, 156.
72 "A középponti konyha," *Budapesti Hírlap* 34:284, November 12, 1914, 14.
73 "A középosztály ételei," *Budapesti Hírlap* 36:20, July 23, 1916, 4–5, 5.
74 "Mozgókonyhák a főváros utcáin," *Fővárosi Közlöny* 27:25, May 19, 1916, 4.
75 Kellogg and Taylor, *The Food Problem*, 79.
76 Reported in *Prager Tagblatt*, February 10, 1915, 5.

Agency cookbook explained how to cook one's way around scarcity, since, as a Czech newspaper reported, "many foodstuffs, which cooks and housewives used until recently, are either completely unavailable, or [only available] in reduced quantity."[77] This book also offered seventy-five recipes for communal eating to cook in large portions in hospitals or relief locales.[78] Another cookbook published in the same year gave instructions about substitution flours and how to prepare desserts (*Mehlspeisen*) without flour (*Mehl*).[79] Enterprising women attempted to market their skill in war cookery: in April 1916, a woman from a village outside Budapest advertised how, "for 1 Krone and 20 Filler I send food replacement recipes (40 items). Mrs. Zsigmond, from Pilisszántó, Pestmegye."[80] But discouragement rose as the food crisis became more serious in 1917 and 1918. One Czech housewife described her morning routine from 1917 on: "I wake up ... to a painful day. I cook breakfast. For me, my mother, and my sister a caraway soup without caraway, for my small daughter a sweet decoction of linden flowers and an egg. ... Even just looking at the caraway soup without caraway, we feel sick, to say nothing of eating it."[81]

The lack of fuel for cooking was another hardship. In 1915, the board of directors of Budapest's central gas company – which presumably liked to see households continue to cook at home, using gas – organized a public talk on "The Preparation of War Foods" (March 1915). The company offered a cooking course "in which we not only showed the handling of gas cookers ... but we also taught the participants the preparation of cheap war foods." But as scarcity deepened, lack of fuel might have interfered with the cooking of even substitute meals. One diary from The Hague described how by way of fuel many people used "balled-up paper, steeped in salt water, wrung, then placed on the fire half humid." The diarist (stoically?) added: "It seems to suit some people all right."[82] An example among many of how cultural efforts – from diary writing over the decoration of communal kitchens to the painstaking preparation of paltry meals – endeavored to recreate a sense of normalcy amidst the deeply disorienting experience of wartime food; an effort that was, in many cases, doomed to fail, as food quality plummeted.

[77] *Národní Listy*, March 2, 1915, 4.

[78] Gisela Urban, *Österreichisches Kriegs-Kochbuch vom k.k. Ministerium des Innern überprüft und genehmigt* (Wien: Stefan, 1915).

[79] Anna Larisch, *150 Kochrezepte für die Kriegszeit* (Brünn: k. k. Hofbuchhandlung Carl Miniker, 1915), 42.

[80] Advertisement in *Tolnai Világlapja* 15, April 13, 1916, 35.

[81] Žipek ed., *Domov*, vol. IV, 216.

[82] Diary of Miep de Zaaier, February 28, 1917, in Wentholt ed., *Den Haag '14–'18*, 18.

Food Quality, Substitution Goods, and Sensory Experience (Taste, Touch, Smell)

Substitution and Falsification

As indicated above, statistics on calories hide the fact that the quality of food had changed. Substitution and falsification were the order of the day. Many foodstuffs – butter, milk, sausages – contained far more water than they had before the war. Others came on the market spoiled: rotten fish was sold in the working-class districts of Petrograd. From 1915, "war sausages" in Austria contained barely any proper meat: instead, they consisted of one-third potatoes (until even potatoes became rare, after which they may have been replaced by turnips), one-third offal, and one-third thickened blood from slaughterhouse animals (also used as an ingredient in bread and "chocolate" and as a substitute for eggs).[83] These substitutes were perfectly legal; and the Austrian government did what it could to make citizens accept them, up to and including organizing an exhibition on food substitutes in the Prater Park in Vienna in 1918.[84]

But next to these legal practices, out-and-out falsification was rampant. In Germany, coloured curd cheese was sold illegally as "butter" and milk was likewise adulterated. In August 1918, the *Berliner Tageblatt* cried foul: butter contained over 50 percent water; flour dust made its way into bread, ashes in pepper, and bark in cocoa (if indeed there was any cocoa left in the cocoa); and sausages were made of slaughterhouse waste, of which there was a brisk trade: sinews and tendons, hitherto dog food, were "now sold at astonishing prices."[85] In occupied Belgium, wartime cartoons showed greedy farmers diluting their milk with water, and memoirists would long remember how farmers sold large lumps of butter which on unwrapping were found to contain turnips thinly spread with the precious stuff.[86] In urban Russia, by war's end, the substance sold as "butter" was a foul mix containing industrial food waste.[87]

[83] Judith Fritz, "Vom Strecken, Wässern und Dünnen," https://ww1.habsburger.net/de/kapitel/vom-strecken-waessern-und-duennen; Lena Hallwirth, *Die Versorgung der Zivilbevölkerung mit Lebensmitteln und Ersatzlebensmitteln während des Ersten Weltkriegs*, Social Ecology Working Paper 171, Alpen-Adria Universität, Klagenfurt (2016), www.aau.at/wp-content/uploads/2017/04/WP171_Web.pdf, 122.

[84] Hubert Weitensfelder, "Die Ersatzmittel-Ausstellung im Prater 1918," https://ww1.habsburger.net/de/kapitel/die-ersatzmittel-ausstellung-im-prater-1918.

[85] HILA, USFAR, Clippings, translated clipping, August 20, 1918.

[86] In occupied Liège. Georges Rem [pseud. of Georges Rémy], *Le roman de ma maison* (Ans: Printex, 1975), 155.

[87] Golubinov, "Food and Nutrition."

Disgust

The abysmal quality of wartime food naturally disgusted contemporaries. In the Bohemian lands, bread contained 60 percent of wheat substitutes by 1916. A woman writing to her husband in a POW camp complained about the quality of this war bread: "One gets used to everything with time, only we cannot get used to this damned corn. It stays in the stomach for three days."[88] Likewise, in Germany, in September 1917, a German medical weekly noted the repugnant, even stomach-turning taste and smell of wartime bread.[89] In Italy, from January 1917, bread could only be sold stale to limit consumption; coupled with the inferior quality of the large lumpy loaves (it was forbidden to sell loaves of under 700 grams), this made for a dismal sensory experience.[90] In Vienna, a 1918 report stated that the bread had never been so poor in quality. "It is a solid yellow mass, without any holes, and it goes mouldy only a few days after it is baked." Containing only 10 percent of wheat and rye, it resembled, the report went on to say, "the flat cakes of prehistoric man. Similar flat, dried cakes are still made in the remote dales of South Tyrol and Sweden." Though heavy, it did not keep: "Bakers have to clear out their stock daily, and sell the week's loaf to single purchasers in four lots."[91] This report mixes revulsion over the bread's inferior quality – seventy years on, in the 1980s, inhabitants of Vienna would still shudder at the memory of the war bread they had as children during the First World War[92] – with distaste for its "primitive" aspect ("the remote dales of South Tyrol and Sweden"). Recipients of food aid in regions hardest hit by scarcity had to suffer particularly ghastly food: in occupied Liepāja (today's Latvia), for instance, the soup kitchen offerings featured "white beetroot soup, blood soup, frog soup. The latter was unusually glum, it seemed disgusting to take in the mouth."[93]

Explaining (away) Hardship

Some contemporaries, as we have seen, were at pains to present war food as spare and healthy. Officially sanctioned publications – but also

[88] ÖStA, KA, FA, AOK, Evb/NA, K3746, no. 4240, undated letter in a censorship report from September 1, 1916.

[89] The *Deutsche Medizinische Wochenschrift*, quoted in Régis, "1917, année de rupture," 420.

[90] Marie Concetta Dentoni, *Annona e consenso in Italia 1914–1918* (Milan: Franco Angeli, 1995), 36–9.

[91] HILA, USFAR, Office of Foreign Information, Alphabetical File, Box 95, Folder 8, Austria-Hungary, Food Ministry, Dairy Products, "Special Report on Bread Situation – Austria-Hungary," July 6, 1918.

[92] Reinhard Sieder, "Behind the lines," 110.

[93] Aleksandrs Janševskis, quoted in Zariņš, *Policies of the German Military Administration*, 156.

lifestyle movements like the German *Lebensreformbewegung*[94] – attempted to persuade the public that "war bread" meant a return to spartan, sturdy national habits. One Finnish periodical praised the virtues of bread made with lichen (moss).[95] Lichen, a traditional emergency food across Scandinavia, including Finland, was presently revived. To this day, the National Museum collection in Helsinki exhibits a lichen loaf from 1918. The illustrated weekly *Suomen Kuvalehti* ran cheerful pictures of women preparing birch bark for emergency bread, and printed recipes that mixed edibles – spinach, onions and potatoes – with emergency ingredients like leaves, giving the dishes French names to make them more palatable to middle-class sensibilities.[96] Examples abound of efforts made by authorities (local and supra-local) as well as by "self-mobilizing" civil society to present substitution goods as an improvement. The meatless menus presented in the French daily *La Croix* (see above) were put together by Jules Lefèvre, a lifelong champion of vegetarianism (he himself preferred the term "vegetalianism"), who saw the war as an opportunity to present his fellow French citizens with the fare that his family had thrived on for decades – or so he claimed.[97] The same Finnish periodical that hailed lichen bread illustrated a didactic piece on budget-friendly cooking with an attractive picture of a housewife cooking soup from foraged herbs: "Lovely! Let's slurp it down."[98] Meanwhile, in German-occupied Courland, in 1916, the occupation authorities ordered civilians to collect crows' eggs, and prodded local peasants to shoot crows, arguing that their flesh was perfectly edible and in fact very healthy.[99] In Bohemia, newspaper articles would frame war foods, such as nettle soup, as a return to sturdy tradition.[100] Likewise, the Prague daily *Národní listy* cozily described linden tea as an old custom, reactivated in wartime: "tea can be well replaced by the favorite drink of those times when our grandfather married grandmother; still in

94 The *Lebensreformbewegung*, which had championed black bread before the war, tried to persuade consumers that by reverting to rye they were not being shortchanged. Nutritionists concurred; see, for instance, Volkmar Klopfer (a food chemist from Dresden), *Die Verbesserung des Brotes durch Aufschliessung der Kleie und Vervollkommung des Backverfahrens* (Dresden: Globus, 1918). More in general: Rudolf Otto Neumann, *Die im Kriege 1914–1918 verwendeten und zur Verwendung empfohlenen Brote, Brotersatz- und Brotstrechmittel unter Zugrundelegung eigener experimenteller Untersuchungen* (Berlin: Springer, 1920).

95 *Helsingin Sanomat*, August 12, 1917.

96 *Suomen Kuvalehti* July 13, 1918 and September 28, 1918.

97 "Menus sans viande établis d'après les règles de l'alimentation rationnelle," *La Croix*, May 19, 1917, 4.

98 *Helsingin Sanomat*, August 12, 1917.

99 Aizsilnieks, *Latvijas saimniecības vēsture* 1914–1945, 62.

100 *Národní Listy*, May 15, 1916, 3.

the memory of older readers."[101] So, while some commentators – such as the 1918 Viennese report that compared war bread to the loaves produced in "remote dales" – were appalled at the return to primitive conditions, another discourse presented war austerity as a return to ancestral, hence (it was implied) healthy and indeed regenerative ways of living.

Stubborn Nostalgia for the Familiar

Nostalgia usually served to highlight not the return to traditional foodstuffs but the unavailability of familiar treats: the *gute Friedensdinge* of Klemperer's host. On April 11, 1916, a journalist in Brünn/Brno marked the one-year anniversary of the bread coupon by recalling freely available bread in bakeries and restaurants and stating that if pre-war-quality bread and rolls were to return after the war, people would never again take them for granted.[102] A Czech memoirist records how, during the war, having been deprived of potatoes for half a year, he was presented with some: "I felt close to heaven when in the autumn of I don't remember which war year, my colleague procured me with them as a great delicacy."[103] Over ten years on, he could not remember the exact date, but the sensation lingered.

So did the disagreeable taste of wartime substitutes. In Bohemia, beer and coffee, two commodities at the heart of conviviality in pre-war times, suffered much wartime adulteration. Home beer brewing in both Bohemia and Moravia occurred "on a large scale," to the dismay of the health authorities who called for stricter regulation.[104] A Czech memoir recalled that "there was no beer, people made it at home, to this day the memory of it makes one's stomach turn."[105] Coffee was home-made from crushed rosehip beans.[106] Even barley coffee was hard to get; and one report observed frequent complaints about the poor quality of wartime coffee.[107] A Prague bookbinder recalled his distaste: "In the coffeehouse, they gave us some dark brown liquid which they nicknamed "black coffee" and sweetened with a little saccharine."[108]

101 *Národní Listy*, June 28, 1916 (evening edition), 2.

102 *Tagesbote aus Mähren und Schlesien*, April 11, 1916, 5.

103 Rudolf Pánek, *Od černého orla k bílému lvu: 1918–1928* [From the black eagle to the white lion] (Prague: Alois Lapáček, 1928), Vol. II, 46.

104 ÖStA, AdR, Bundesministerium für soziale Verwaltung, Volksgesundheit, K1593, no. 4132, Report from June 16, 1917.

105 Vladimír Vondráček, *Lékař vzpomíná 1895–1920* [A Physician Remembers] (Prague: Avicenum, 1978), 287.

106 *Duch české ženy za války* [The Spirit of the Czech Woman during the War] (Prague: Ženský obzor, 1928), 26.

107 ÖStA, AdR, Volksernährungsamt, AR, K151, no. 37210, Bericht über die Reise des General-Ernährungsinspektors nach Prag, March 25, 1918.

108 Josef Vieulzoeuf, *Memoáry pražského knihaře* [Memoirs of a Prague Bookbinder] (Prague: Svaz pomocnictva knihařského, 1929), 149.

Indeed, continental Europe's favourite pick-me-up, coffee, was a transoceanic import and so supplies suffered heavily from the war situation. Up until and including the spring of 1915, Germany got by, partly because of the vast stores of coffee found in the warehouses of Antwerp when the German military seized that city in October 1914. But eventually, German consumers felt the pinch: by the end of 1915, Berlin cafés were officially forbidden from serving unadulterated bean coffee; they had to mix the brew with chicory, malt, barley, or any other substitute, and even the small amount of actual beans that made the concoction palatable was running out.[109] In occupied Belgium, even among the still relatively affluent, bean coffee had become a rare treat, enjoyed only on special occasions such as Christmas Eve, and sipped with the awe hitherto reserved for champagne.[110] People made do with a substitute that went by the name of *torréaline*, made from roasted rye. Post-war ads would play on customers' well-remembered distaste for the stuff: "How about a nice cup of *torréaline*? No thanks! No more of *that* for me! Three cheers for proper coffee."[111]

Substitution goods, then, in spite of official efforts to render them acceptable, evoked keen revulsion, so much so that they could lead to violent clashes. In both the neutral Netherlands and occupied Belgium, consumers bitterly resented the dearth of potatoes because they knew that they were available; both countries produced much more than their needs. In many a Belgian and Dutch diary, potatoes became a leitmotiv, as they were in conversations in the street.[112] Imported rice was widely rejected as a substitute: rice was unfamiliar, considered fodder at best. In February 1916, in the working-class district of Molenbeek (Brussels), angry women attacked the city hall; in July 1917, Amsterdam housewives, rejecting the city council's offer of rice, plundered potato stores.[113]

[109] HILA, USFAR, Clippings, "Die Kaffeehaüser ohne Kaffee," undated clipping (late 1915?), unidentified German newspaper. This article refers extensively to *bean* coffee being imported, which may or may not qualify Belinda Davis's observation that "as Germany had no imperial markets in bean coffee, most of the population had never drunk anything but domestic coffee, made from inexpensive chicory and sugar beets" (Davis, *Home Fires*, 190).

[110] A news item transmitted to the Belgian army on the Yser front, quoted in François Bertrand, *La presse francophone de tranchée au front belge 1914–1918* (Brussels: Musée royal de l'armée, 1971), 39.

[111] Quoted in Sophie De Schaepdrijver, *Gabrielle Petit: the Death and Life of a Female Spy in the First World War* (London: Bloomsbury Academic, 2015), 139.

[112] E.g., Brussels: Louis Gille, Alphone Ooms and Louis Delandsheere, *Cinquante mois d'occupation allemande* (Brussels: Dewit, 1919), Vol. II, 317 (September 28, 1916).

[113] Molenbeek: Brand Whitlock, *Belgium: A Personal Narrative* (New York, NY: Appleton, 1919), Vol. II, 203; Amsterdam: Paul Moeyes, Samuël Kruizinga, and Wim Klinkert, *Nederland neutraal. De Eerste Wereldoorlog 1914–1918* (Amsterdam: Boom, 2014), 262–5.

Even where revulsion did not lead to clashes, plummeting food quality tended to sap the legitimacy of warring states. As the historian Nina Régis argues, in Germany the "impossible year" 1917 (to quote the title of Jean-Jacques Becker's book) was a turning point not just politically but also in terms of nutrition. Or, to be more precise, both were intimately linked: "the exacerbated vulnerability (*la grande précarisation*) of daily life in 1917 silenced much patriotic discourse."[114] In short, when it came to food quality, making do with worse – and/or making others accept making do with worse – became a war effort in its own right; an increasingly heavy-going one.

Conclusion

The war impacted Europeans' food experience in many ways: a diminishing supply, diminishing quality, or a return to coarser (and often, if not always, nutritionally inferior) fare; unfamiliar composition, unfamiliar and very often off-putting tastes, textures, smells. This combined with unfamiliar modes of procuring food – queueing, coupon-clutching, scavenging, hoarding, smuggling – and ways of consuming it in unfamiliar settings: canteens; soup kitchens; or one's own kitchen become cold and squalid and unrecognizable. These changes in food experience were undergone, not chosen, which rendered them all the more bewildering and disheartening. It testifies to the force of civil society that myriad efforts, by local governments, organizations of all stripes, and individual citizens, aimed not just at food relief but at framing the unfamiliar food experience as familiar, cosy, possibly even healthy. How successful were these efforts? In other words, did they manage to legitimize this particular war effort (imposed even on citizens in neutral countries)? Did they succeed in defining food hardship as a worthy, justified collective effort; an active choice, instead of unjustifiable victimization passively undergone? The answer to this question depends in part, and most obviously, on states', civil societies', and relief organizations' material resources and on the sheer level of hardship experienced by different belligerent societies, or groups inside societies. But it may also depend on the intricacies of the food experience itself: lichen bread and moldy loaves, "white tables" and queues and *restaurants économiques*, *Ersatz*, adulterations, "vegetalian" dinners, sugary spreads: the history of these quotidian but essential experiences unites food and legitimacy, corporeality and the political.

[114] Régis, "1917, année de rupture," 414.

6 Hunger Envisioned

Nicholas Siekierski

In a letter to his wife in December 1915, Polish historian Wacław Borowy wrote of "feeling the claws of war" while looking at a long, snaking line of desperate people in Warsaw waiting for food.[1] He envisioned hunger and scarcity as the wounds inflicted by a vicious creature preying on the civilian population. Many Europeans of that time would feel hunger dig deep into their skin as the conflict dragged on. At the furthest extreme, some faced starvation. While starvation of the type that devastated entire regions of Soviet Russia in the early 1920s did not occur on the same scale in Europe during the First World War era, the term was still used to elicit support for humanitarian programs.

The turmoil of war brought the issue of food to the forefront of people's minds. In Eastern and Central Europe in particular, the instability of food supplies, marked by shortages, was not a linear process of degeneration that took years of war to worsen. Many people felt the consequences of scarcity within months or even weeks of the war's beginning. As soon as the privation began, a variety of ways to represent that hunger emerged in different mediums. People envisioned hunger through descriptive language using metaphors as Wacław Borowy did, they represented hunger as death itself in cartoons, and they placed newspaper advertisements seeking the barter of goods for food, which implicitly told readers that hunger was encroaching on their everyday reality. Individuals and institutions tried to comprehend and express the causes of hunger, how it could be assuaged, who or what was responsible for it, and what its continuation portended for the future.

The threat of hunger upended the lives of millions, forcing many of them to sell once-valuable items for a fraction of their pre-war worth to purchase food. Hunger not only posed a threat to individuals but to

[1] Quoted in Katarzyna Sierakowska, *Śmierć Wygnanie Głód w dokumentach osobistych: Ziemie polskie w latach Wielkiej Wojny 1914–1918* [Death, Exile, Hunger in Personal Documents: Polish Lands in the Years of the Great War, 1914–1918] (Warsaw: Tadeusz Manteuffel Institute of History, Polish Academy of Sciences, 2015), 198.

governments as well, which tried to convince civilian populations to re-imagine such basic foodstuffs as bread or meat by suggesting previously unthinkable substitutes. Censorship aimed at preventing the news of hunger and poverty from undermining regimes both domestically and in the eyes of enemies. Humor spread in the form of cartoons in magazines, newspapers, and even postcards, offering both levity to the readers and commentary on the changing social situation. For some, hunger presented an opportunity to make money that bore great risks, later immortalized in song and passed down through the generations. For those that were in a position to do something about it, such as Herbert Hoover and the relief organizations that sprang into action during the First World War and its aftermath, hunger took on biblical proportions. Attempts of varying efficacy were made to convey the gravity of the situation to faraway viewers with photographs and the fledgling medium of film. The phenomenon of hunger served as a prism that refracted many images. This chapter evokes in turn several such depictions across Europe, to provide examples of the ways Europeans represented, envisioned, and related to hunger.

Hunger as Change

Above all, the prospect of hunger represented a change in the status quo. The value of money relative to food became deflated, the quantity and variety of foodstuffs available in peacetime dwindled, the type of meals that people had eaten previously became smaller and less varied. Expensive furniture, equipment, and artwork became superfluous unless it could be sold for cash or bartered for food. Even fashionable clothing could become a hindrance if its owner was forced to take up manual labor to survive as the demand for intellectual work dried up. These outward changes in dress and standards were physically visible, even without figurative representation. The specter of hunger, foreshadowing starvation, disease, and death, was the motivating force behind these dramatic lifestyle changes.

One gauge of hunger as a change agent can be found in newspaper advertisements, which serve as proxies for the devolving economic situation across social classes. In Poland, the increase in advertisements of goods for sale was commonplace as the war lengthened, though as early as 1916, even non-essential goods were increasing in price in proportion to growing food prices. As noted by Klemens Bąkowski, a lawyer in Kraków, "Like poison, high prices are even entering into people's smallest arteries. Everyone is spending more on indispensable needs so they want more for whatever they sell, therefore even the price of old junk is going up, fiddles, paintings, prints, pieces of metal and wood."[2] This "poison" was produced by the scarcity of food that led to hunger. As poison spreads through the veins of a victim, hunger spreads through communities that cannot afford or even access food.

Because of the low food supplies in Latvia, public service announcements were the closest thing to food-related advertising. In 1916, the German administrators of the occupied Courland proposed that local peasants could shoot crows because they were edible and their meat was very healthy, and to collect their eggs as well.[3] In March 1918, the German language newspaper, *Rigasche Zeitung*, published an article on crows being eaten in Germany as a delicacy and proposed the organizing of crow hunting in Riga.[4] Despite appeals to German culinary sophistication, this unconventional food choice did not take root among local populations beyond the immediate needs of the moment. Crows are scavengers that will even eat human meat and have been seen as a bad omen throughout history.

The idea of eating crow meat presented a desperate vision of the gravity of the food situation where the scavengers themselves were all that was left to eat. The attempt of the occupying authorities to have their subjects re-envision what constituted appropriate sustenance failed and may have backfired, reminding Latvians that Germans bore much responsibility for their lack of food. Not until mid-July 1919 did some bakeries begin to advertise their bread in Riga newspapers, as foodstuffs had been in very short supply until then. The main point of these advertisements was to state that "our bread is not mixed with oat flour."[5] It is unlikely that such advertising had been used before the war as the food supplies were better. It does indicate, however, that Latvians (largely out of necessity) did accept adulterated bread during the war and afterwards, when there was a period of readjustment to what "normal" bread consisted of and tasted like.

By 1918 in Bohemia, some advertisements for the bartering of food in exchange for raw materials or consumer goods reflected the severity of the provisioning situation. One ad offered food in exchange for all types of quality leather while another offered drying equipment for vegetables to store home-grown or collected food in urban apartments.[6] In another case, men's shoes, a sofa, a night stand, a desk, a gas meter,

[2] Quoted in Sierakowska, *Śmierć Wygnanie Głód*, 211.

[3] Aizsilnieks Arnolds, *Latvijas saimniecības vēsture 1914–1945* (Stockholm: Daugava, 1969), 62.

[4] *Līdums*, March 27, 1918.

[5] *Latvijas Sargs*, July 17, 1919.

[6] *Národní Listy*, May 18, 1918, 6.

and petroleum lamps were offered in exchange for food.[7] In the imaginations of the sellers, a pair of good shoes might have come to represent hope for feeding their family for a while longer. The mental arithmetic of the value of things underwent a sea change as economic pressures forced reflection on the utility of possessions in the new, unstable reality. Advertisements for seasonings that were "copious and aromatic"[8] or "containing appropriate levels of protein,"[9] were presented as supplements to the thin soups being consumed. While these were probably meager substitutes for soups made in times of plenty, the experience of making do with less surely affected the perception of what was nutritious once the conflict ended.

After the war, there were complaints about false advertising that exploited the desperate situation of the suffering people of Bohemia: "A caste of middlemen, food 'commissaries' proliferates who do not report any business or pay taxes – men and women – but advertise and offer everything possible."[10] This demonstrates the role that advertising played in enabling an alternative market for scarce foodstuffs.

Hunger as Threat

As shortages and high prices transformed hunger from a distant possibility to an everyday reality, it became an immediate threat to the well-being of individuals and families, but also a dangerous social force that could undermine the authority of governments and the war effort. In Austria-Hungary, a strict censorship regime monitored both private correspondence and newspapers, essentially forbidding the description of food shortages on the home front, in part for fear of damaging soldiers' morale.[11] This mechanism sought to prevent information about the problem of shortages and concomitant hunger from spreading and reflecting back negatively on the government. Nonetheless, some women defied the censorship to covertly communicate their anxieties to their men at the front or in captivity. One police report in Prague warned that secret messages about the desperate situation could be sent in hollowed-out nuts.[12] The danger posed by hunger loomed larger than any penalties the authorities could impose, especially when families with many

[7] *Národní Politika*, August 4, 1918, 9.
[8] *Prager Tagblatt*, February 20, 1918, 8.
[9] *Prager Tagblatt*, June 26, 1918, 10.
[10] F. P. Vožický, *Kronika světové války 1914–1919* (Na Král Vinohradech: F. P. Vožický, 1919–21), 370.
[11] Maureen Healy, *Vienna and the Fall of the Habsburg Empire: Total War and Everyday Life in World War I* (Cambridge: Cambridge University Press, 2004), 131.
[12] CNA, PP HSt, ka 28, sig. H 1/11, no 4777, October 10, 1916.

mouths to feed were involved. The heavy-handed attempts to censor such messages could have the opposite effect by suggesting to common citizens that hunger was a problem that the authorities created and were now trying to cover up.

As the war dragged on, it became impossible to stifle increasing complaints about the contracting food supply. A censor's report in June 1917 on correspondence from Bohemia refers to "the countless descriptions of downright hunger, [or] dreadful misery, which particularly in children cannot be looked at anymore."[13] A censored letter from a woman in a small village in Moravia to her husband in Russia is typical:

> We are threatened with death by starvation and are ready for everything. Before I should hear the children cry of hunger, I would rather throw them in the river and then throw myself in, that would be a quicker death. The agrarians become millionaires and we have become beggars. That's holy justice! Lightning should strike such a justice and make an end to it ... When the misters from the censorship read this letter, they will say, that I don't have all my senses, but I have all of them and even an extra one, despair.[14]

Agonizing outbursts like this never made it to the addressee, however, and the tragic plea of a wife to her husband was muzzled by the censors who aimed to silence negative assessments of the food supply and civilian hunger. Occasional reports of suicides or suicide attempts in the Polish press usually give desperation over food as the reason, but there is no evidence that suicides actually increased, and at least in Warsaw, their incidence dropped during the war.[15]

A question worth exploring is how closely expressions of angst over the food situation were correlated to the supplies available and whether the relative plenty of peacetime exacerbated the perception of the serious but not yet critical supply of food. In any case, the spread of communications relating to hunger, and other wartime complaints among the populace, were seen as serious enough a threat to the Austrian regime to merit being monitored by the complex censorship machinery.[16]

[13] ÖStA, AVA, MdI, Präs, 22, 1917, K2070, no. 14234.

[14] Letter originally in Czech from Pribislawitz (Přibyslavice), March 5, 1917, ÖStA, KA, FA, AOK, GZNB, K3751, no. 4618.

[15] Sierakowska, 208.

[16] Paweł Brudek, Jan Molenda, and Jerzy Z. Pająk, "The Great War in Polish Correspondence Intercepted by Austro-Hungarian Censorship: Materials of Polish Censorship Groups from 1914–1918" in *Metamorfozy Społeczne* [Social Metamorphoses] 21: *The First World War on Polish Lands; Expectations, Experiences, Consequences*, edited by Włodzimierz Mędrzecki (Warsaw: Tadeusz Manteuffel Institute of History, Polish Academy of Sciences, 2018), 199–224; Péter Hanák, "Vox populi: Intercepted Letters of the First World War," in *The Garden and the Workshop: Essays on the Cultural History of Vienna and Budapest* (Princeton: Princeton University Press, 1998), 179–212.

Austro-Hungarian press censorship was used to remove entire columns of newspaper articles relating to the food and economic situation to prevent foreign enemies from gaining an advantage. An unintended result was that the domestic population was left in the dark about actual conditions at home and could not make informed decisions about their own provisioning situation. According to Hans Löwenfeld-Russ, who worked in the office for food provisioning, "The infamous white spaces created more damage in the scared imagination of public opinion than the calm discussion of the economic situation could have done."[17] An article from 1918 titled "In the Kingdom of Hunger,"[18] describing the hunger crisis in the Ore Mountains of North Bohemia, is an extreme example of the "white spaces" left after censorship redaction, where more than two and a half of the article's four columns are blank. These spaces, empty like their pantries at home, were filled in by the reader's imaginations and speculation, which may have had an even more damaging effect than had the situation been discussed openly or simply censored in its entirety.

The censorship was inconsistent, however, especially towards the end of the war, when articles describing the food crisis or criticizing censorship itself escaped scrutiny. One newspaper in Bohemia published information on hunger oedemas, and complained that a reference to this issue in the published version of a speech by the mayor of Reichenberg/Liberec had been removed. They commented: "Does the censorship believe that the hunger oedema will disappear if it is forbidden to talk and write about it in Prague?"[19] In certain ways, what was left unsaid or unwritten spoke louder than any representations of the desperate food situation could have.

In Warsaw, the German regime's "preventive censorship" prevented mention of the June 1916 or May 1917 food riots in the official press. What information that can be found is in unpublished lists of looted grocery stores and in the underground press.[20] News of these events got out by word of mouth among family, friends, and neighbors and stood in stark contrast to the deafening silence of the official media.

The threat generated by hunger was even felt by individual government officials. Folkert Posthuma, the Dutch Minister of Agriculture during the First World War and the author of deeply unpopular

[17] Hans Loewenfeld-Russ, *Die Regelung der Volksernährung im Kriege* (Vienna: Hölder Pichler Tempsky, 1926), 108.
[18] *Prager Tagblatt*, March 29, 1918, 2.
[19] *Deutsche Zeitung Bohemia*, August 3, 1918, 3.
[20] Robert Blobaum, *A Minor Apocalypse: Warsaw during the First World War* (Ithaca, NY: Cornell University Press, 2017), 15.

decisions with relation to food distribution, surely experienced no small level of fear. He was the target of angry correspondence, "Now it's the milk distribution! Are you crazy?" and even death threats, "Minister Posthuma! If you have not improved food distribution before 7 February, you are a dead man. Beware!"[21] some of which took particularly creative forms, a testament to the way he embodied the causes of food shortages for some. He even received an invitation to his own funeral and a miniature gravestone with his name carved into it.[22] In Berlin, the Director of the War Food Ministry (*Kriegsernährungsamt*), Adolf Tortilowicz Batocki, was rumored to have lost 15 kg during his tenure.[23] Apparently, the food meant to be delivered to his residence in Berlin was looted along the way.

The threat posed by social unrest generated by hunger was utilized as a weapon directed against political and national enemies. Hunger was heavily factored into propaganda. For example, during the Latvian War of Independence (1918–1920) practically all political parties in Latvia used hunger in their messaging. Hunger was used to show the "cruelty" of both the Bolsheviks and the Germans. In January 1919, when most of Latvia, including Riga, were under Bolshevik control, *Latvijas Sargs* the pro-government newspaper in Libau wrote:

> Somebody coming from the Bolshevik side of the frontline brought to the editorial office a piece of bread – what is given by Bolshevik authorities to the people. It is impossible to describe this piece of bread. It looks like a lump of straw, inside of it we can see thickened pieces of dough, completely unpeeled oats and glume. Much worse than so called "oil cakes" given before the war to cows. How humans can eat such 'bread' is impossible to imagine. We asked the people who had been in Russia about this and they confirmed it – this really is Bolshevik bread. It would be good for every worker to come to the editorial office to look at this bread so as to realize the truth about the "Bolshevik paradise," it is impossible to work and later renew one's strength with such bread.[24]

Unlike the unpleasant but palatable bread mixed with oat flour, "Bolshevik bread" was wholly unsuitable for consumption. The bread served as a symbol of the corruption of the entire Bolshevik regime and was held up as a warning and a foretaste of what the 'main course' of this political and economic system would mean for Latvians. In this case hunger was envisioned not simply as a consequence of unavoidable

[21] Dutch National Archives, 2.21.026.07/9.

[22] Dutch National Archives, 2.21.026.07/9.

[23] "Aus Batockis Amtszeit," *Berliner Zeitung am Mittag*, August 8, 1917; M. E. Cox, *Hunger in War and Peace: Women and Children in Germany, 1914–1924* (New York, NY: Oxford University Press, 2019), 238.

[24] "Lielinieku maize," *Latvijas Sargs*, January 25, 1919.

wartime disruptions, but a product of Bolshevik policy. To buttress this argument, fragments from intercepted private letters of Red Army soldiers were published in the Latvian government press in the winter and spring of 1919 when the Bolsheviks controlled most of the country. The main reason the soldiers gave for enlisting was hunger and the access to food the army provided. In an excerpt from a letter written in Riga on 11 February 1919:

> The situation with food is very bad. Already for three weeks we have not seen a piece of bread ... We are living only on some sour cabbage and some beets but even beets are impossible to get now. The beets cost about 90–100 rubles per lb. We could die from hunger. Because of this I had to enter into the Army and this was the only way, there are no work places in Riga now ... Now I have the salary of 250 roubles a month, 2 lb. of bread and soup, although this soup is very bad.[25]

Whether the bread provided to new recruits in this case was the same "Bolshevik bread" described above, remains unclear. Claims about food and hunger were an important feature of political discourse during those years, as a way to recruit for a cause or undermine the opposition.

Hunger as Tragic Comedy

Despite the privations of the war, humor was expressed in various ways as both a direct confrontation with reality and a type of escape from it. Theories of dark humor, such as those posited by Carl Jung and Sigmund Freud,[26] though interesting, seem insufficient in explaining the phenomenon. More recent research suggesting that "in the face of stressful imagery, comedy is a more effective coping strategy than solemnity" is a more credible explanation for humor being a long-standing and perhaps even reflexive survival mechanism to relieve stress in psychologically and physically threatening situations.[27] Pierre Purseigle argues that humor (specifically humorous cartoons) "held a mirror to English and French societies and can also inform us about how these societies experienced the First World War."[28] Cartoons as well as different types

[25] "Sarkanā gvarda vēstule," *Latvijas Sargs*, April 3, 1919.

[26] "To be able to laugh at evil and error means that we have surmounted them. Comedy may be a philosophic as well as psychological compensation." (quoted in "The Meanings of Comedy" edited by Wylie Sypher in *Comedy: An Essay on Comedy* (Doubleday: 1956), 246).

[27] Andrea Samson and James Gross, "Humour as Emotion Regulation: The Differential Consequences of Negative Versus Positive Humour," *Cognition & Emotion*, 26 (2012), 375–84.

[28] Pierre Purseigle, "Mirroring Societies at War: Pictorial Humour in the British and French Popular Press during the First World War," *Journal of European Studies*, xxxi (2001), 290.

of humor (jokes, songs, etc.) also served as a reflection of the culture of the societies of Central and Eastern Europe and how they responded to the threat posed by hunger.

Food-related jokes frequently appeared as the provisioning situation became the prime concern of people in Bohemia. Cartoons and jokes on this theme abound in 1917 and 1918 in the Czech satirical weekly *Humoristické listy* (Humorous Papers). In one cartoon (Figure 6.1) the central panel shows a woman visiting a fortune teller who tells her: "card reading is quite simple nowadays." The surrounding images each show different scenes revolving around food: a woman in front of a shop with

Figure 6.1 Card reading is quite simple nowadays.
Source: *Humoristické listy*, 61:24 (1918), 251. Czech Digital Bibliography research infrastructure by the Institute for Czech Literature of the Czech Academy of Sciences, P.R.I. – https://clb.ucl.cas.cz/ (ORJ Code: 90243)

a sign "No bread": "What awaits you?," a worrying woman thinking "I wish the war was over!": "What is in your heart?," a woman in front of a shop with a sign announcing increased prices, "What did you find out?"[29] A joke from the same newspaper several months later highlighted the difficulty of laughing in dire circumstances, "And this man is really a good comedian? Does he have humor? – I would think so! Yesterday, he even brought a bread line to laughter."[30] The levity displayed here could have reflected a sense of solidarity felt by the Czechs who found themselves in similarly difficult circumstances. Even if hunger could not be satisfied, at least it could be mocked and ridiculed.

In post-war Vienna, posters appeared asking readers whether they had friends or relatives in the United States (increasingly envisioned as a land of plenty). If so, they were directed to contact them to request food packages, which would be delivered through the American Relief Administration (ARA), which became a very popular idea and hope. A satirical play called "The Prodigal Son" published in the *Arbeiter Zeitung* was written as a series of telegrams from 1914 and 1920. The protagonist was portrayed as a morally dissolute and wicked son who stole money and left Vienna in disgrace, moving to New York. He was disowned by his family and "cursed" via telegram. Yet, once the opportunity to receive food from the United States arose in 1920, all was forgiven, and communication was re-established. His aunt wrote to him saying: "Darling, at last I have learned your address. [I] Had a burning desire to see you all these years. Haven't you also heard of the 'Dollar parcels' (big parcels)? Kisses."[31] In the same way that massive ships were presented as the saving grace of famine-stricken Russians on ARA posters (see Figure 6.2), these food remittance packages could make a world of difference for an individual family.

ARA personnel came to be portrayed as saviors of sorts both in Russia and East-Central Europe. Figure 6.2 depicts a gigantic steamship with US flags arriving at a shore filled with emaciated Russian peasants, some kneeling and with arms raised. Figure 6.3 depicts a US-flag-draped woman (personifying the US) ladling food into the bowls of hungry Russian children.

A song, "Have you an uncle in America?" written by Rudolph Enrich was supposedly sung throughout Vienna in "leading vaudeville houses." The song was translated and published in *The New York Times*:

[29] *Humoristické listy*, June 7, 1918, 251.
[30] *Humoristické listy*, August 9, 1918, 323.
[31] "Misery Tales from Europe: Vienna Keeps Laughing Habit Despite Sufferings – Hoover Relief Machine Still Busy." *The New York Times*, October 17, 1920, 123.

Figure 6.2 America to the starving people of Russia.
Source: HILA, Poster collection, RU/SU 1213

Figure 6.3 Gift of the American nation.
Source: HILA, Poster collection, RU/SU 502B

What is it that alarms
Our native Vienna so suddenly?
What is the one thing in the world
Inspiring us still with interest?
What is this very last of hopes
Before our dreadful death?
A poster is, from the New World,
Telling of food to get.

Have you an uncle in America?
Have you an aunt in America?
Have you a relative
Or a friend
In Chicago
Or any other place?

Have you an uncle in America?
Have you an aunt in America?
Have you a relative
In America?
Then all right you are.[32]

On the German home front, postcards served as pictures blending both humor and social commentary. On one a woman enjoys several pieces of cake, cream, and coffee, while the caption reads "Es war einmal" (depending on the translation) "Once upon a time" or "It used to be" (see Figure 6.4).

While such delicacies may still have been available to the wealthy, they were out of reach for the general population. Flour used in the baking of cookies and cakes was regulated, among other things. A second postcard shows an empty bowl in front of two sad puppies and a dog wiping away a tear looking up at a mirage of a meat bone, the caption also reads, "It used to be" or "Once upon a time!" Food, of the plentiful, delicious, fattening type, was envisioned as a thing of the past, while hunger was the new reality.

On another postcard titled "Ein schöner Traum!" "A Beautiful Dream!" (Figure 6.5) a plump woman sleeps on a chair with a smile on her face, surrounded by hanging meats, butter, sugar, eggs, flour, and potatoes. But not only luxury foods like cake, meat, sugar, and eggs were depicted on postcards.

Another postcard (Figure 6.6) pictures two young boys eating fruit looking longingly at a butcher's stand filled with veal, mutton, and pork products, the title reads "iss mehr Gemuse und Obst" or "eat more vegetables and fruit."

[32] "Misery Tales from Europe."

Figure 6.4 It used to be.
Source: Private collection of Mary Elisabeth Cox

Figure 6.5 A beautiful dream (1916).
Source: Private collection of Mary Elisabeth Cox

Figure 6.6 Eat more vegetables and fruit.
Source: Private collection of Mary Elisabeth Cox

Two postcards picture maids wearing aprons covered in pockets for bread, meat, butter, milk, fat, pasta, potatoes, soap, and petroleum ration cards (Figure 6.7). One of the postcards pictures a plump, grinning woman against the backdrop of a food line and a policeman looking to maintain order. Next to her are the words "fill your bags with all the beautiful cards; (without cards, believe me, you can wait a long time). Everyone eats themselves fat and full – who still speaks of poverty? Whoever has enough cards has everything today!" The postcard to the right shows a similar theme and states simply "Das Dienstmädchen mit der Kriegs-Schüerze" or "The maid with the war apron."[33] Ration cards were no guarantee of securing food, however, as supply and distribution problems were a persistent and increasingly painful issue as time went on. Citizens began to see the ration cards as an increasingly meaningless proxy for the food that they did not have, while privileged bureaucrats had easier access to supplies.

[33] Das Dienstmädchen mit der Kriegs-Schüerze [Postcard] (1914–1918, estimate), MEC.

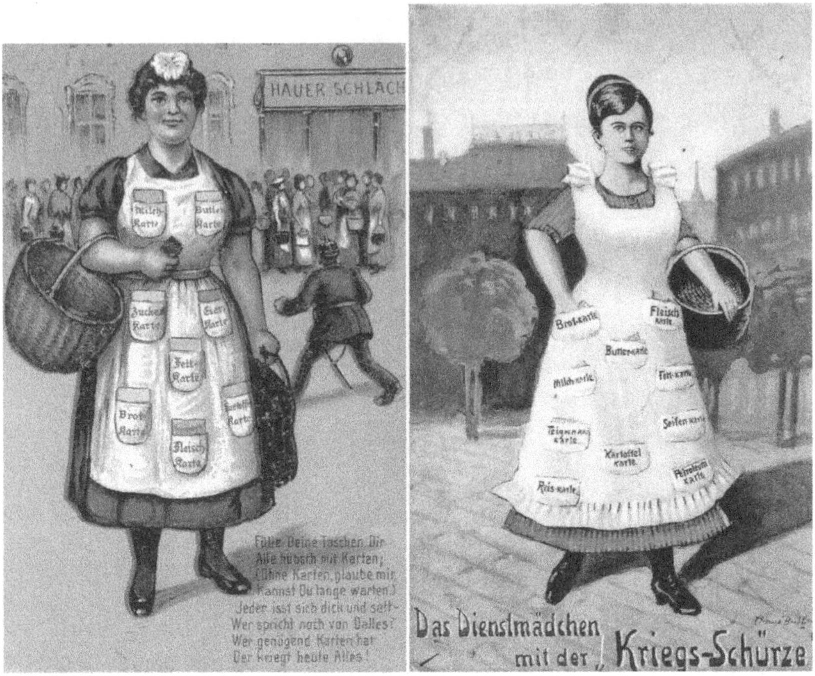

Figure 6.7 War aprons.
Source: Private collection of Mary Elisabeth Cox

Gallows humor was also common and several cartoons from the Swiss satirical magazine *Nebelspalter* reflect this dark theme. One, by artist Karl Czerpien (Figure 6.8), is titled "Europe's Congratulators for 1917" and features a shocked doorman under a sign that reads "Madame Europe" extending his hand to stop a line of mostly terrifying figures.[34] The first (from left to right) is the only well-fed and muscular of the bunch, dressed as a Roman soldier, labeled "war"; the second, "death," a skeleton, bears a bouquet of skulls and crosses; the third, an emaciated figure, "hunger," holds a bouquet of ration cards; the fourth, a near-skeleton with a bloated stomach, "pestilence," has a bouquet consisting of a viper poised to strike and appears to hold a thurible of burning incense; and the last, "poverty," is a gaunt figure, hat in hand, his torso an open, empty wallet.

[34] Karl Czerpien, "Europas Gratulanten für 1917," *Nebelspalter: das Humor-und Satire-Magazin*, 43:1 (1917), [13].

Figure 6.8 Europe's Congratulators for 1917.
Source: *Nebelspalter: das Humor-und Satire-Magazin*, 43:1 (1917), [13]

This cartoon commented on the effects of the war, including hunger, outside of the borders of the country in which it was published. The fact that Switzerland maintained armed neutrality during the First World War, and did not suffer its consequences to the same extent as its neighbors did, created a buffer in which gallows humor of this type appears detached from any profound suffering by the Swiss people, though relative to the pre-war situation it may have been perceived as such. The second cartoon, Figure 6.9, is titled "America and the Neutrals"[35] showing a group of five surprised children, labeled as "Switzerland," "Norway," "Holland," "Denmark," and "Sweden," cowering before Uncle Sam who holds a bundle of branches in his right hand as if to beat them and a bag labeled "rationing" in his left, while straddling bags labeled "grain," "sugar," and "flour." The caption at the bottom reads: "You shall learn to love me, once the hunger is big enough." While the United States was seen as a savior for millions after the war, here it was presented as the cause of their plight. Though the blockade and Anglo-American pressure on neutrals did contribute

[35] "Amerika und die Neutralen," *Nebelspalter: das Humor-und Satire-Magazin*, 43:48 (1917), [4].

Figure 6.9 America and the neutrals.
Source: *Nebelspalter: das Humor-und Satire-Magazin*, 43:48 (1917), [4]

to the difficult provisioning situation, cartoons like these were also an attempt to deflect blame for hunger and scarcity away from the local authorities onto a distant interloper.

Hunger as Opportunity

Hunger could lead to unforeseen consequences that went beyond the immediate situation of the needy. Smugglers at the borders between neutral countries and the Central Powers met the demands unsatisfied by the legal economy but often risked their lives to do it. Despite the risks involved, smugglers envisioned hunger as a great opportunity, or at least a means of making ends meet. These new realities, such as the evolution of smuggling and its hazards, found a reflection in contemporary culture.

An example of the tragic side of smuggling was captured in the Dutch poem "De Grenssoldaat" (The Border Guard):[36]

[36] Rob Kammelar, Jacques Sicking, and Menno Wielinga, eds., *Het monster van de oorlog. Nederlandse liedjes en gedichten over de Eerste Wereldoorlog* (Amsterdam: Nijgh & Van Ditmar, 2004), 236–7.

He was a soldier guarding a border crossing rife with smugglers.
But he would not forsake his duties and vowed to shoot all the smugglers and thieves.
In the border village he had found his sweetheart, they loved each other with all their hearts.
Even though her dad was a smuggler, he saw not him but only her.

One day, when they were making love she said: 'my dearest, promise me
If you catch my father in the act, think of me and spare his life.'
He said: 'Dearest, my duty comes even before love though it pains me
I would never violate my soldiers' oath even when it means losing you.'

'But tell your father to be careful and keep his smuggling out of my sight.
So my watchful eye will not surprise him when he flouts the export prohibitions.
I just hope that you will never be tempted to follow in his footsteps
As it is dangerous and wicked, please promise me!'

Through salty tears, she did not reply he kissed and caressed her.
'I know that you will never lower yourself to his standards. Will you, my dear? I know you won't.'
Later, at night, he stood guard once more. For hours he guarded the border
Thinking of his beloved whilst his eyes pierced the darkness.

Suddenly he heard the rushing of leaves, where before it had been silent.
There, at the edge of the border, two shadows in the dark.
'Stop! Who goes there?' he yelled, not once, but thrice. A shot rang out, a scream was heard, a shadow went down.
The second shadow fled the scene and stillness descended once more.

In the darkness he knelt alongside the body, hit by waves of agony and pain.
His beloved lay on the forest floor, a bullet had struck her heart.
Grimly, he decided his fate and a second shot rang across the darkness.
He had been loyal to his oath; the soldier met his end.

Despite the potential of fines, prison sentences, and even death, the smuggling of goods across the Rhine at the border between Austria and Switzerland during the First World War was particularly alluring. There were even violent clashes between smugglers and soldiers in 1918, resulting from increased traffic due to a shortage of cotton articles in Austria-Hungary, which prompted Rhine Valley inhabitants, who blackened their faces as camouflage, to smuggle fabrics and yarn spools across the river. Coffee and saccharin were also in great demand in Vorarlberg. One inhabitant of Widnau, on the Swiss side, became so rich that he donated a statue of the Virgin Mary for the church, which was nicknamed "Mary of the Yarn." In 1919, a man from Lustenau, on the Austrian side, was asked to which state he preferred to belong in the future: Switzerland, Austria, or Germany. He answered: "I don't care, as long as it's at a border."[37]

The lyrics of this song variant probably originate from an inhabitant of Lustenau on the Austrian side of the border. The creator of the melody is unknown.

> I am a poor smuggler, I always earn my money in danger, but when the border guard rests on the shore, the smuggling goes well as before.
>
> Then we sleep until four in the morning, then there is a quiet knock at the door: 'Stand up my smuggler, so young and beautiful, now we want to go smuggling again!'
> Then we go out to the Rhine, and cast out our sacks, and there come Austrians tall and short, every one of them, every one wanting a small sack.
>
> And if we are caught then once, then we come before the jury, six thousand francs we must pay, then we are allowed to continue immediately again.
>
> And when the month of May is over, I'll give up smuggling, then I'll lead my love to the altar, long live, long live the smuggling couple!
>
> And once I have died, put a tombstone, on which the words are written, Only now, only now will I let the smuggling go.[38]

Hunger as Apocalypse and Salvation

One of the darker visions of what hunger represented was taken from the Book of Revelation in the New Testament, and depicts the Four Horsemen of the Apocalypse (Pestilence, War, Famine, Death). This grim image surfaced in various contemporary sources around the globe. Herbert Hoover, United States Food Administrator from 1917 and then Director of the American Relief Administration (ARA) from 1919 frequently referred to it in the first volume of his memoirs. Indeed, the section that deals with the War (300+ pages)

[37] See exhibition catalogue: Heidi Witzig, Wolfgang Steiger, Jolanda Spirig, and Marcel Zünd, *Grenzland – Jacob Rohner und die Stickereizeit im Rheintal* (Altstätten: Muesum Prestegg, 2017), 10.

[38] See exhibition catalogue: Heidi Witzig, Wolfgang Steiger, Jolanda Spirig, and Marcel Zünd, *Grenzland – Jacob Rohner und die Stickereizeit im Rheintal* (Altstätten: Muesum Prestegg, 2017), 10.

is titled "Four Horsemen in World War I."[39] In lengthy discourse on the Horsemen in a later footnote, he offers one of numerous, deeper reflections, on Revelations 6:8:

> "And I looked, and behold a pale horse; and his name that sat on him was Death, and Hell followed with him. And power was given … to kill with sword, and with hunger, and with death." The rider's equipment certainly embraced FAMINE. However, as Hell followed with him, he was at least an intimation of further aftermaths and wrath to come.[40]

In South America, a book was published in 1916 called *Los cuatro jinetes del Apocalipsis* (*The Four Horsemen of the Apocalypse*) that depicted the horrors of the War, with a subsequent film produced in 1921 starring Rudolph Valentino.[41] A poster of the Four Horsemen of the Apocalypse was also used by the US National Council for Prevention of War, among other representations.[42]

Despite the foreboding picture displayed by so many, Hoover simultaneously presented hopeful visions for the relief of the misery induced by these specters of doom. Hoover had been raised as a Quaker, and though he was not active in religious services as an adult, this formative experience undoubtedly influenced his actions, which carried the undertones of a salvific mission, focused as a crusade against hunger. In his view, though the situation was dire, the United States, as a land that had exited the war relatively unscathed and in possession of a food surplus, had a duty to aid people everywhere. No individual was in a better position to initiate such a necessarily enormous machinery of relief, which had already been tested in practice on a much smaller scale through the Commission for Relief in Belgium (CRB), which he had co-founded. Alongside his ARA, a series of other organizations would answer the calls of the hungry and at the same time utilize new ways of recording images and disseminating information to those on

[39] Herbert Hoover, *The Memoirs of Herbert Hoover: Years of Adventure, 1874–1920* (New York, NY: Macmillan, 1951), 149.

[40] Herbert Hoover, *The Memoirs of Herbert Hoover: Years of Adventure, 1874–1920* (New York, NY: Macmillan, 1951), 325.

[41] Ibáñez, Vicente Blasco, *Los cuatro jinetes del Apocalipsis*, 1916; Ibáñez's *The Four Horsemen of the Apocalypse*, was published in 1918 in English, becoming a best-seller in the United States.

[42] "Cost of last war, 9,998,771 – killed, 20, 297, 551 – wounded, 337,946,179,657 – dollars. Never again! 'Our hundred millions [sic] want less of armament and none of war' – President Harding," Digtial Poster Collection, US 5551, Hoover Institution Library & Archives, https://digitalcollections.hoover.org/objects/39075/span-classqueryhlcostspan-of-span-classqueryhll?ctx=b15edfae0e98214101dec0feb1b17a3fc0a7040c&idx=1.

the home front, who were in a position to offer financial support for continued operations.[43]

Although film was in its infancy as a mass medium during the First World War, it played a role in the dissemination of information, especially after the conflict ended and humanitarian organizations were seeking donations for their work in Europe. Of note is a series of four short films produced by the Quaker Friends in the early 1920 to aid civilians affected by the war.[44] The films are an early example of marketing by a humanitarian organization using this medium, as the American Friends Service Committee (AFSC) compass-style logo is prominently visible on buildings and even pots in some scenes. While these films were meant to showcase the organization's work, they also portrayed poverty and associated hunger. The four silent films in the series titled *New Worlds for Old* feature Austria, France, Poland, and Russia.

The film on Austria opens on images of rooftops of beautiful buildings in the city center of Vienna and then transitions to a shack, likely on the outskirts of town, where a goat eats from a table outdoors. A shortage of housing after the war forced families and individuals into spartan living conditions until large housing projects in the 1920s alleviated the situation. Intertitles throughout the films highlight the work of the AFSC to provide milk and housing, augmenting the powerful visuals.

The film on France (which also includes footage from Vienna) begins with the title of the series "New Worlds for Old" and text noting its approval by the Ohio Department of Education Division of Film Censorship and Pennsylvania State Board of Censors. This detail suggests that the film was also shown for educational purposes and may have been a component of broader propaganda to highlight the involvement of the United States in relief for Europe. The focus of the French portion of the film is children at a hospital, while the additional footage from Vienna shows houses being built, farming and milking of cows, welfare centers, and children in hospitals. Apparently well-off Viennese women in furs and fine hats also lined up to receive aid, demonstrating that the ghost of hunger and poverty could haunt people of all classes. The film ends with footage of a grateful recipient and a request for further aid (Figure 6.10).

[43] See Chapter 13 of this book.

[44] *New Worlds for Old—Austria* [Film] (1919–1924, estimate); *New Worlds for Old—France* [Film] (1922–1924, estimate); *New Worlds for Old—Poland* [Film] (1919–1924, estimate); *New Worlds for Old—Russia* [Film] (1919–1924, estimate). American Friends Service Committee Archives.

Figure 6.10 A still from *New Worlds for Old.*
Source: American Friends Service Committee Archives

The Poland film begins with the barren landscape rolling by from a moving train before text explains the peasant exodus and the "no man's land" created by the war, showing people wandering around military dugouts. They had returned from Russia where they had been evacuated in 1915, only to discover that their homes had been destroyed. The dugouts often consisted of trenches or similar earthworks covered with lumber or branches as a roof, and in the case of the film, snow. Despite the grim conditions, children are shown at one point smiling and laughing outside one of the dugouts. The happiest moments come at the end of the film with peasants dancing and celebrating the completion of a new house, which we can assume was built with relief funds.

The first forty seconds of the film on Russia consist of text explaining the situation in the country, and Quaker relief efforts, before moving to a view of Buzuluk, a city of densely packed, single-story wooden shacks and buildings. The sullen-looking city becomes lively as the next scene shows close-up activity of residents and animals. A woman uses a large mortar and pestle to grind up grass that is said to be used as bread filler, first mixed with flour. Two small children look on, making the image all the more moving, which would not have had the same effect as a still image, especially as they are surrounded by snow. Children are shown eating food at an outdoor kitchen and the film ends with a plea to continue sending aid so the 250,000 inhabitants of Buzuluk do not starve. Fuyuki Kurasawa explains the utility of such images in promoting relief work:

> This mechanism of collapse of ethical, sociocultural, and geographical distance through iconicity is precisely that upon which humanitarianism relies, for once iconic images of distant suffering circulate widely and ordinary citizens are exposed to them, publics lose their innocence. They can no longer claim ignorance by denying knowledge of an unfolding humanitarian crisis, becoming culpable of crass indifference if they decide not to act.[45]

The imagery of the film on Buzuluk is quite tame in comparison with shocking images of an emaciated girl taken in Buguruslan (north of Buzuluk) in the fall of 1921 and featured in an AFSC bulletin and European and US newspapers,[46] or that of piled bodies taken in the Buzuluk cemetery in December 1921, which also circulated in print media.[47] Posters meant for domestic consumption in the Soviet Union, such as "Remember the Starving" (Figure 6.11), depicting a finger raised above a loaf of bread, cup, and bowl, pointing at a nearly amorphous mass of struggling people, were less intended to shock than to guilt viewers into conserving food.

While photography had gained acceptance in the press over the course of the war, film, especially its use as an intercontinental informational medium for fundraising purposes, was perceived as new. For the International Commission of the Red Cross, "Filmmaking, in contrast, represented a complete innovation for the organization. While photos provided evidence and information about the activities of the ICRC, movies were intended to show the reality on the ground in a more truthful and emotional way than photos and text alone could."[48] It is debatable, however, whether films were truly "more truthful" in their presentation of the actual situation in a given place, or if their

45 Fuyuki Kurasawa, "The Making of Humanitarian Visual Icons: On the 1921–1924 Russian Famine as Foundational Event," in *Iconic Power: Materiality and Meaning in Social Life*, edited by Jeffrey Alexander, Dominik Bartmański, and Bernhard Giesen (New York, NY: Palgrave Macmillan, 2012), 69.

46 Kurasawa, "The Making of Humanitarian Visual Icons," 72.

47 Kurasawa, "The Making of Humanitarian Visual Icons," 73.

48 Francesca Piana, "Photography, Cinema, and the Quest for Influence: The International Committee of the Red Cross in the Wake of the First World War," in *Humanitarian Photography: A History*, edited by Heide Fehrenbach and Davide Rodogno (New York, NY: Cambridge University Press, 2015), 141.

Figure 6.11 Remember the starving.
Source: HILA, Poster collection, RU/SU 539R

immediacy in presenting an ostensible window into a distant world was not also used to manipulate the intended audience.

The latter appears to be the case, though for a good cause, in a film sequence created by the American Relief Administration in Russia in the village of Vasil'evka on 11 April 1922 during the arrival of a shipment of corn.[49] The description of the event as related through the telegraphic diary of Father Edmund A. Walsh, a Jesuit priest and head of the National Catholic Welfare Council, who accompanied the ARA men at that time, is not matched in its intensity by the film record of the scene. It was shown in the short documentary film *America's Gift to Famine Stricken Russia* from 1923, preceded by the intertitle: "Entire remaining population of the village found on their knees in thanks as first food

[49] Bertrand M. Patenaude, *The Big Show in Bololand: The American Relief Expedition to Soviet Russia in the Famine of 1921* (Stanford, CA: Stanford University Press, 2002), 504–7.

is brought by the ARA."[50] In the words of Walsh: "We arrived about noon. Village waiting—all on knees— 'You are our Saviours—We perish if you did not come.' Kissed our feet—hands—and touched foreheads to ground before us."[51] What is seen in the film, however, captured by Floyd Traynham, "the ARA motion picture man," appears to be a reenactment by the villagers that doesn't convey the same emotional impact that the apparently genuine immediate reaction did (one of likely hundreds of similar events of poor Russians expressing their gratitude). While we can imagine an ebullient group of people surrounding their "saviours" based on the earlier description, in the film we see a stiff group apparently prepositioned for a wide-angle camera shot.

In the same vein, the recorded evidence does not show what was described in a press release written by Harry Gilchriese of the ARA communications department, which describes a much larger group of enraptured peasants:

> Traynham's celluloid sucked the emotional content out of an episode that appears to have genuinely moved its US eyewitnesses. Gilchriese's melodramatic copy, with its Second Coming atmospherics, doubtless served the purposes of his publicity chiefs in New York. But for the ring of authenticity and a sense of immediacy to the event neither the film nor the press release can compare with the pencil jottings in Walsh's little journal.[52]

The author concedes that the film technology of the time would not have allowed for the event to be recorded as it unfolded so it remains for the viewer to decide whether such an obvious recreation still retained an air of authenticity.

Another factor to consider is that the sight of a film camera, certainly a foreign object in the Russian countryside of that time, would have altered the behavior of the villagers (not unlike the knowledge of being filmed changes individual behavior to this day). Whether the peasants acted out of modesty, not knowing how to act in the novel situation of being filmed (almost certainly for the first time), or simply the subduing of initial emotions by the time the recording began, this example reminds us that war films were a way to inform others of how hunger and deprivation could be visualized.

Jason Francisco has described photographs taken in wartime as "repositories of information and vaults of testimony, aesthetic productions

[50] *America's Gift to Famine Stricken Russia* (American Relief Administration, 1923) [Film] www.pbs.org/video/american-experience-americas-gift-to-famine-stricken-russia/ (the scene described is from 02:50 to 03:08).

[51] Patenaude, *The Big Show in Bololand*, 506.

[52] Patenaude, *The Big Show in Bololand*, 507.

that alternately magnify and diffuse acts of war, dramatize and deflect them."[53] Applying this same description to film helps us to appreciate the immense difficulty of conveying the "reality on the ground" to various audiences, including in the distant future, whose own experiences and values shape the perception of the images they see. A documentary photographer who worked for the American Red Cross during and after the First World War, Lewis W. Hine, believed: "On another level, a photograph can record reality and at the same time the photographer's comment on that reality. I wanted to show the things that had to be corrected. I wanted to show the things that had to be appreciated."[54]

Hunger Knows No Armistice

This broad survey of examples provides a sampling of the myriad ways in which hunger was envisioned, especially during years when the representation of hunger became pervasive in society and took on a heightened significance. Reflecting on how hunger and food shortages were perceived and represented gives a deeper glimpse into the psyche and circumstances shaped by scarcity, which on the one hand were dependent on local factors, but also reveal some universal features such as the desire to cast blame, to satisfy commonly understood "basic needs," to improve one's situation relative to others and to relieve stress with humor and restore some semblance of normalcy in an uncertain situation.

The changes wrought by hunger motivated individuals to reshape their lives to feed themselves and their loved ones. Even when they were successful, they almost always subsisted on a much lower level of sustenance than before the war, and advertisements for goods for sale or barter may in fact represent the better-off who still had something to exchange. Hunger threatened both the pauper and the prince alike; the former with physical suffering and the latter with political catastrophe. Certainly, in the case of the German and Austro-Hungarian empires, systematically censoring hunger-related news to prevent political fallout appears to have been as important as alleviating hunger itself. Humor, especially in the form of cartoons and caricatures, provided catharsis for those enveloped in one of the greatest traumas in Western history. The most enterprising individuals even found opportunity in the maelstrom and left songs of their exploits.

53 Jason Francisco, "War Photography in the Twentieth Century: A Short Critical History" (2005), http://jasonfrancisco.net/war-photography.

54 Barbara London, et al. *Photography*, 8th edition (Upper Saddle River, NJ: Prentice Hall, 2005), 379.

The "claws of war" dug deep and hunger was one of the most painful wounds that it left behind. It is no wonder that periods of hunger, and in the most extreme cases, famine and starvation,[55] left a permanent mark on those that lived through it. Like in Herbert Hoover's apocalyptic vision (which also offered the hope for salvation through humanitarian works), these fortunate ones saw the pale horse in one form or another, but survived the devastation left in its wake. More than 100 years after the First World War ended, the echoes of that international trauma are still cause for reflection and study, with the rich visual history of the period leaving the strongest reminders of its legacy.

[55] As Vernon Kellogg noted, after having returned to Warsaw following a survey of food conditions in various regions of Poland for the ARA, "here [in the cities] is hunger, there [in Poland's eastern and southern borderlands] starvation." "Letter of Colonel Grove to Dr. Kellogg Urging Immediate Supplies for Poland and Describing Political Conditions," January 29, 1919, *Documents of the American Relief Administration European Operations, 1918–1922*, Hoover Institution Library & Archives Reading Room, 121.

7 Hunger in Urban and Rural Areas, and Children on the Move

Mary Elisabeth Cox

When people in cities were unable to purchase food, it was easier for their governments to blame a foreign enemy rather than to admit internal distribution or production issues. Naturally, then, governments were happy to blame their enemies. For example, officials in Vienna suggested that the dwindling food supplies available in the city were caused by the Allied Blockade.[1] This particular attempt to blame hunger solely on a blockade is fascinating because, unlike most other places in Europe, the Austrian Hungarian Empire had been self-sufficient in food production before the war,[2] meaning there wasn't that much external food for the Allies to block. While the blockade did prevent some foodstuffs and fuel from entering the Austro-Hungarian Empire, and hurt the economy (money and fuel were necessary to move food along), there were other culprits that probably had a larger impact on food supplies in Vienna. The Russian occupation of agricultural Galicia containing "one-third of all Austrian farmland" early in the war took a decisive blow on food supplies.[3] So too did the production loss of roughly half of all cereals in Austria and Hungary.[4] Furthermore, the Hungarian half of the Dual Monarchy, which had previously served as the breadbasket for Austria, practically stopped their food shipments.[5] But casting blame on external enemies rather than their own military weakness, or, as is the focus of this chapter, on local farmers, was easier politically.

I argue in this chapter that while there were indeed hunger differences in some rural and urban places, we should exercise caution in attributing

[1] Maureen Healy, *Vienna and the Fall of the Habsburg Empire: Total War and Everyday Life in World War I* (New York, NY: Cambridge University Press, 2004), 37; Alexander Watson, *Ring of Steel, Germany and Austria-Hungary at War, 1914–1918* (London: Penguin, 2015), 244.

[2] Healy, *Vienna and the Fall of the Habsburg Empire*, 37.

[3] Pieter M. Judson, *The Habsburg Empire: A New History* (Cambridge, MA: Belknap Press: An Imprint of Harvard University Press, 2018), 398.

[4] Holger Herwig, *The First World War: German and Austria-Hungary 1914–1918*, 2nd ed. (London: Bloomsbury), 271.

[5] Judson, *The Habsburg Empire*, 399; Watson, *Ring of Steel*, 244.

the destitution of urban dwellers to the greed of rural farmers without careful scrutiny. Perceptions of dissimilar hunger levels between civilians in urban and rural areas did not always match reality. Human psychology may help explain why the urban/rural debate was so common. I begin with a discussion of the psychology of hunger based on the research of Ancel Keys. Next, I examine reasons for hunger in urban and rural areas. I then assess prejudices between rural and urban communities. Finally, I analyze hungry people on the move in urban and rural areas, with a focus on children in Central Europe.

The Psychology of Hunger

When a person is severely hungry, their psychology and their physiology are both affected. Indeed, "fear and desperation" may fill a person's thoughts as much as "hunger and food deprivation."[6] One experiment conducted on human starvation involved a group of thirty-two young men, all conscientious objectors, who volunteered to undergo a period of starvation and recovery in lieu of military service during the Second World War. This study, conducted from 1944–1945, sought to increase understanding of starvation through systematic observations by scientists with the aim of informing US efforts to assist starving Europeans ravaged by the war. Led by Dr. Ancel Keys at the University of Minnesota, this unique study sought to explore all conceivable aspects of starvation, especially biological responses induced by the breakdown of proteins, and how starvation impacted different organs in the body. The study also sought to clarify earlier ideas related to starvation that had been observed during previous periods of hunger and famine, including the effects of extreme hunger on physical strength, cognitive ability, libido, personality, and human psychology.

The study found that a starving person may become obsessed not only with food, but with their own changing body and bodily functions.[7] Under the strains of intense hunger, mood changes occur. Conscientious objectors who volunteered for the study were more subject to sadness, depression, and anger than a similar-aged control group. One generally amiable participant who had grown up abroad with missionary parents and "didn't have much experience with profanity" could not refrain from swearing at another volunteer when

[6] Ancel Keys, *The Biology of Human Starvation Vol. II* (University of Minnesota Press, 1950), 776. See also, Josef Stavěl, *Zum Aufbau der Psychodiagnostik* (Prague: nákladem vlastním, 1936), 140.

[7] Keys, *The Biology of Human Starvation*, 880–904.

they began reciting passages of Shakespeare referring to hunger during mealtime. The missionary's son wrote about the incident in his journal, expressing intense guilt.[8]

In other participants, deep neuroses arose. One man in the study cut off his middle fingers with an axe, maiming himself for life, in a moment of desperation.[9] Another man broke down after being unable to perform a menial test on a treadmill and sobbed uncontrollably.[10] While the exact psychological responses among the subjects differed as their personal hunger increased – the use of profanity, maiming oneself, sobbing uncontrollably, etc. – no one responded well.

The study found a fascinating and consistent discovery: participants remorselessly compared the amount of food they received to the amount of food other volunteers in the study received. Some of their comparisons were based on the structure of the experiment, as men were fed different amounts of calories from each other at different times, though they were not informed about who received more or less. Naturally the volunteers wondered how they were doing compared to their peers. Nevertheless, what was not anticipated prior to the study was that after a period of caloric reduction and weight loss, each participant in the study was convinced that *they* were receiving the fewest calories, even when they were not. In some instances, the differences in study diets ranged between 200 to 1,200 calories, with resultant physical differences. Independent of the calories received, all participants in the study were hungry, and this inequality – as they perceived it – with themselves the *worst* off, left them deeply unhappy. This was not simply a complaint, but a sincere belief that others in the study received more food than they did. This comparison and belief that everyone else received more food was universal among the participants, regardless of how many calories they received or the exercises they could complete.

This unique study conducted towards the end of the Second World War is still useful for scholars attempting to understand hunger and starvation, and can be applied to eras previous to when the study was made. In the context of this chapter, the importance of hungry people comparing their own plight to that of others, with the deeply held belief that others were receiving more calories, finds historical application to civilian experiences during the First World War. Indeed, such

8 Todd Tucker, *The Great Starvation Experiment: The Heroic Men Who Starved So That Millions Could Live* (New York: Free Press, 2006), 138–40.
9 Keys, *Biology of Human Starvation*, 896.
10 Tucker, *Great Starvation Experiment*, 157–8.

a construct may help explain some of the acrimony between civilians in urban and rural areas and, more generally, the “othering” that frequently occurred between people competing for the same food. City dwellers believed, and argued, that farmers received a larger share of available foodstuffs than they did. However, relying alone on perceptions of inequalities, no matter how sincere, may be insufficient when trying to tease out differences in hunger for urban and rural dwellers. Key’s study demonstrates that a universal reaction of people experiencing severe nutritional deprivation means that they *always* assume others have more food than they do. One of the key psychological results confirmed in the 1944/45 starvation study is that starving people hold distorted views of their own consumption levels relative to others. They may therefore not be in the best position to compare their own experience to that of others.

The idea that urban dwellers were hungrier than people living in rural areas rests on the belief that those physically closest to agricultural production had an intrinsically greater access to food than people who lived further away. The argument is logical. Rural workers closest to the food source would keep what they wanted for themselves, giving only secondary concern for their countrymen in the cities. If we accept that the human psychology of chronic hunger triggers comparison and the belief that others are better off, then this brings into question differences in urban/rural consumption. People in cities may have believed they were hungrier than people in the countryside when they were not.

Other than the idea that physical proximity to sources of food production gave people in rural areas an advantage, what else might explain food shortages in cities? There are many possibilities described throughout this book, but a few include militaries’ willingness to requisition foodstuffs from their own as well as foreign populations, worsened infrastructure and reductions in agricultural yields, the capacity and willingness of governments to intervene to prevent or reduce shortages, the movement and displacement of millions of people, and differences in land ownership and wealth. This short list also helps explain food shortages in rural communities.

Hunger Explanations: Requisitioning

Farmers were often subject to requisitioning by governments and militaries (their own and foreign). In Germany, for example, the *Kriegsernährungsamt* (War Food Office) which started operations in May 1916, had a difficult time enforcing any of its orders and requisitioning food, but the German military, which had its own leadership and enforcement, was different. The two organizations did not work in conjunction with each other, and the military had the right to go into the German countryside to requisition food from rural citizens to feed their soldiers.[11] Farmers had little choice. If they were caught hiding food (for themselves or to sell to others), their lands and farms were searched, and the food was taken. This reduced not only the overall amount of food allocated between rural and urban civilians, but requisitioning also reduced the amount of food agricultural workers themselves could eat. Farmers in Germany may have been closest to food production because they lived and worked on the land, but they could not always control what happened to the food after it had been produced.

Enemy troops also requisitioned food from local populations. German and Austrian troops, for example, regularly requisitioned foodstuffs in areas under their occupation. In parts of what is now known as Poland, foodstuffs were heavily requisitioned. Even worse, the Russian army scorched the earth as part of their retreat. "This was a terrible hardship for the population … four thousand villages were burned and two million people were made homeless."[12] These actions devastated rural populations in the Polish Lands. Yet there was also hunger in cities such as Warsaw with "widespread smuggling and thriving black markets."[13] Destroyed villages and fields and requisitioned food lowered available calories to both city dwellers and rural civilians.

Requisitioning occurred outside of Europe as well. Military and government leaders in the Ottoman Empire actively requisitioned food. Laws allowed, in practice, all goods from civilians to be requisitioned that could be used for the war effort. In addition to food and animals, "silk women's garments, stockings and petticoats, corsets, children's shoes and clothes, caviar, champagne, tableware, babies' slippers, and face powder" were requisitioned with the argument that they could be sold to support military operations.[14] Thus, requisitioning by the military hit both merchants and rural peasants. Furthermore, laws were

[11] Friedrich Aereboe, *Der Einfluss des Krieges auf die Landwirtschaftliche Produktion in Deutschland* (Stuttgart: Deutsche Verlags-Anstalt, 1927), 42; Benjamin Ziemann, *War Experiences in Rural Germany: 1914–1923 (The Legacy of the Great War)*, trans. Alex Skinner, 2nd ed. (Oxford: Berg, 2007), 167; Herwig, *The First World War*, 280–2.

[12] George I. Gay, *Public Relations of the Commission for Relief in Belgium: Documents* Vol. II (Stanford, CA: Stanford University Press, 1929).

[13] Robert E. Blobaum, *A Minor Apocalypse* (New York, NY: Cornell University Press, 2017), 22.

[14] Yiğit Akın, *When the War Came Home: The Ottomans' Great War and the Devastation of an Empire* (Stanford, CA: Stanford University Press), 115.

passed that all men and women who were not in military service could be required to work on land where there was insufficient labor. Farmers were required to harvest a certain area of land according to the number of oxen they owned, and in extreme circumstances, such as in Anatolia, "battalions of women were organized by the army and were sent to the fields to help with the cotton harvest."[15]

Overall Reduction in Agricultural Yields and Loss of Infrastructure

While women and children often assisted in agricultural work well before the outbreak of hostilities, particularly in subsistence farming, men played a large and central role in planting, harvesting, and husbandry. As young men were conscripted into their respective militaries, nations at war lost a fundamental part of their agricultural labor supply. While responses to this loss of men differed, in most cases women and children were expected to shoulder the extra burden, often with the assistance of prisoners. Soldiers with agricultural experience were frequently sent home seasonally to help harvest crops. Yet even in instances when men returned for longer visits in order to farm, women and children were often not able to make up the difference:

> Even though women assumed a greater burden in agriculture [in the Ottoman Empire], the acreage under cultivation and levels of output declined dramatically.[16]

In Germany, it is estimated that women supplied the labor needs of up to 80 percent of all small farms during the war.[17] Much of Europe also faced poor weather,[18] impacting not only the spread of disease but often reducing yields. An overall reduction in agricultural production across the continent during the war is illustrated in the maps created for this book.[19] While estimates of food production are included in Samuel Kruizinga's excellent chapter (Chapter 1), the overall reduction, and a breakdown in trade, is mentioned here to re-emphasize that this period was one of overall scarcity.

15 Sevket Pamut, "The Ottoman Economy in World War I," in *The Economics of World War I*, edited by Stephen Broadberry and Mark Harrison (Cambridge University Press, 2005), 122.

16 Pamut, "The Ottoman Economy in World War I," 120.

17 Herwig, *The First World War*, 293.

18 Alexander F. More et al., "The Impact of a Six-Year Climate Anomaly on the 'Spanish Flu' Pandemic and WWI," *Geohealth*, 4:9 (2021), e2020GH000277.

19 See Chapter 14, "Hunger Draws the Map."

Government Interventions

Governments intervened in a variety of ways, especially through forms of rationing and price controls.[20] Even in neutral countries, traditionally seen as experiencing less food insecurity during the war, governments intervened in multiple ways to try and ensure that there was sufficient food for their populations. New legislation was often created, and existing programs were increased and strengthened. Zurich, for example, had a progressive feeding program that provided meals to needy school children well before the onslaught of hostilities. In 1910, 3,000 school children in Zurich received a charitable meal provided by the city. By the 1918/1919 school year, over 78,000 children in Zurich took part in the program, an increase of twenty-six fold.[21] This suggests that charitable school meals were needed in cities, even in neutral Switzerland. It also points to the capacity that some cities had to provide additional meals to vulnerable members of their population. Living in a city could give a needy child access to additional meals if the city that they lived in could provide them.

Hunger and Extortion

A Pole wrote in his memoir of foraging as a nine-year-old in 1914 in the forest with his mother "When my mother did not go for firewood, she took me with her to the forest for *bedłki* [mushrooms] and berries, because we were faced with hunger more and more, forcing us to eat everything worse than potatoes, because they had become a delicacy."[22] Perhaps more common than foraging in forests were trips to the countryside. Civilians in the cities would visit friends or family in the countryside (even when they had none), to buy, barter, or steal food. One report from Prague in 1918 detailed how inhabitants of the city would visit the countryside: "At the station daily you could see cans of milk or empty milk cans. Empty, they were traveling to the countryside and they came back full. They had a little lock so that someone unauthorized could not open them."[23]

[20] Please see Francesco Frizerra's wonderful chapter on this subject (Chapter 3). To avoid repetition, I include an example not found in his chapter.

[21] Statististche Amt der Stadt Zürich, *Die Aufwendungen der Stadt Zürich für Armensfürsorge und Sozialpolitik, 1893 bis 1951* (Zürich: s.n., 1953), 105–6.

[22] Pamiętnik nr 8, in: Pamiętniki chłopów, ed. L. Krzywicki, Warszawa 1935, p. 81, in Katarzyna Sierakowska, *Śmierć Wygnanie Głód w dokumentach osobistych: Ziemie polskie w latach Wielkiej Wojny 1914–1918* [*Death Exile Hunger in Personal Documents: Polish Lands in the Years of the Great War 1914–1918*] (Warsaw: Institute of History, Polish Academy of Sciences, 2015), 190.

[23] Claire Morelon, "A Threat to National Unity? The Urban-Rural Antagonism in Prague during the First World War in a Comparative Perspective," in *Österreich-Ungarns*

In Prague, they called this practice "rucksack traffic" (*Rucksackverkehr/ bat'ohové zásobování*).[24] The Germans and Austrians had their own word for the actions of a city dweller who visited agricultural areas in search for food: "hamstering" (*hamstern*) which involved trips to the countryside to relatives (real or made-up) to obtain food, filling their mouths, bellies, and baskets with as much as they could, like hamsters. Indeed, in Germany, "the entire population" took visits to the countryside "to illegally buy food, exchange it or, doubly illegally, to steal it."[25]

Stealing continued as long as there was hunger. In Latvia in 1919:

> The last weeks the countryside was visited by potato thieves; during the day they come to peasants' homes asking for food as beggars (in reality looking where potatoes are stored) but during the night they break into cellars and steal potatoes. Stealing has become an everyday phenomenon ... footprints of thieves lead to the city.[26]

Occasionally the harm done to agrarian workers in the name of obtaining food was worse than "hamstering" or thievery or even state-sponsored requisitioning. As tensions rose, violence was not uncommon. Such was the case in Hungary:

> There is probably sufficient food in the country as a whole, but the peasants are unwilling to give it up, both because of their opposition to the system of government and because the Bolshevist money with which they are paid is virtually worthless, and there are no goods which the peasant desires on which to spend it. A large part of the food supply of Budapest at present is extorted from the peasants by sheer violence. The result is that even for the favored adherents of the government, life in Budapest is one of very great hardship. Everyone gets a fair quantity of poor bread.[27]

Note the words "there is probably sufficient food in the country as a whole," pointing to problems with distribution. Furthermore "everyone gets a fair quantity of food," if true, suggests that though people may have been hungry and dissatisfied with the food available, they were still surviving. Whatever their levels of deprivation, some in Budapest apparently responded with "sheer violence." This passage does not detail what kind of violence, but we know that occasionally farmers were killed while being robbed for their food. In Latvia, violence occurred on a mass scale in the

"Großer Krieg" im Vergleich, edited by Wolfram Dornik, Julia Walleczek-Fritz, and Stefan Wedrac (Vienna: Böhlau Verlag, 2014), 330.

[24] Morelon, "A Threat to National Unity?," 329.

[25] Ute Daniel, *The War from Within: German Women in the First World War* (Oxford: Berg Publishers, 1997), 172.

[26] Kartupeļu zādzības. In: *Latvijas Sargs*. 1919. Febr. 7.

[27] Emery Pottle and E. Dana Durand, "Conditions in Hungary," *American Relief Administration Bulletin*, 19 (1919), 30. Hoover Institution Library and Archives.

autumn of 1917 when the "Republic of Latvian Executive Committee" was founded with Bolsheviks in power. Almost immediately, robbing and physical violence towards peasants became standard practice through special army units and local "landless peasant committees."[28]

City people did not focus their aggression solely on peasants in the countryside. They also participated in acts of vandalism, theft, and protest in their own communities. Women and children in working-class neighborhoods in Berlin, after waiting in long lines to obtain food, fought and created public scenes when supplies ran out.[29] As hunger increased in Warsaw in the summer of 1916, a mass of people attacked a bread wagon in broad daylight, stealing some 1,200 lbs of bread. Later that summer nearly a third of all public stores in the city were ransacked.[30]

Rural Civilians Also Suffered

Even when rural civilians did not experience violence for their food, the physical effects of nutritional deprivation were recognizable. Stark images of starvation and want in villages challenged simple portrayals of rural society, yet even in these instances some still chose to blame villagers for their problems. An example of this can be found in Hungary:

> Due to malnutrition child mortality in the cities is especially high; this phenomenon, however, also occurs in many villages during the war throughout the country. The reason for this is not only the large degree of ignorance of the common people regarding health knowledge but above all the shameful practice that the rural population takes the great part of the foodstuffs (milk products, eggs, chicken) from their own families and brings it to the city to sell it for exorbitant prices. It is therefore natural that the children, weakened in this way, are more receptive to every epidemic, to which their organisms have less resistance.[31]

Not only were farmers accused of ignoring the needs of their children for personal gain, which is something that does not typically match what is known of families in nutritionally deprived circumstances, but equally insulting, the author suggested that children were dying and

[28] Straubergs Kārlis. "Kā Rīga tika ieņemta," in *Lāčplēsis*, 4 (1934). See also Ē. Jēkabsons, "*Latvijos ginkluotųjų pajėgų partizanų daliniai 1919 metais | From Guerrillas to Soldiers: The Activities of Guerrilla Units of the Latvian Army in 1919*," *Acta Historica Universitatis Klaipedensis* 28 (2014), 57–71.

[29] Belinda J. Davis, *Home Fires Burning: Food, Politics, and Everyday Life in World War I Berlin* (Chapel Hill: University of North Carolina Press, 2000), 51.

[30] Blobaum, *A Minor Apocalypse*, 88.

[31] László Zombory, *Gyermekvédelem a Háború Alatt* (Budapest: Stephaneum, 1916), 5.

malnourished in rural areas because they were stupid. These arguments can be handily refuted. Studies on the division of foodstuffs within families in times of need suggest that parents sacrifice and go without food for their children.[32] The second argument, that rural civilians in Hungary were starving because of their "large degree of ignorance," reeks of arrogance, coming off like an exaggerated form of the idiom that "poor people are poor because they are lazy." Where was the recognition that civilians in the countryside were hungry for the same reason that those in the cities were; simply because they did not have enough to eat? And finally, if agricultural workers were indeed taking "the great part of the foodstuffs (milk products, eggs, chicken) from their own families" to sell in the city, wouldn't that have reduced urban hunger levels? The farmers in this instance were damned when they fed their children, and damned and blamed when they could not.

Not surprisingly, rural peasants responded with frustration, and sometimes despair for their physical deprivation and for the judgments they received. They resented being called stupid for their suffering. One German woman expressed her feelings:

> They've left us with too few seeds per daily task [*Tagwerk*]. We in agriculture have to slave away and worry ourselves sick in order to feed all. Yet you're still now and later the stupid peasant.[33]

Perceptions and Prejudice

Despite a number of reasonable explanations for reduced food availability on the market other than farmers' avarice, these were not always on the minds of urban dwellers or members of the press. While local governments may have played off of the local/urban divide, national governments tried to unify rural and urban peasants. Farmers and munitions workers were both needed and working to support the nation and the war effort, as illustrated in this German poster, *Arbeit in Stadt und Land!* "Work in town and country!" (Figure 7.1). The image is divided into two, with a sketch of a muscular agricultural worker in the left panel leaning against a sickle in a field of wheat. In the right panel, a beefy

[32] S. Horrell and D. Oxley, "Crust or Crumb?: Intrahousehold Resource Allocation and Male Breadwinning in Late Victorian Britain," *Economic History Review* 52:3 (1991), 494–522; Gavin Wright and Howard Kunreuther, "Cotton, Corn and Risk in the Nineteenth Century," *The Journal of Economic History* 35:03 (1975), 526–51; Gary Becker, *A Treatise on the Family* (Cambridge, MA: Harvard University Press, 1991), 78–9; Mary E. Cox, *Hunger in War and Peace: Women and Children in Germany, 1914–1924* (New York, NY: Oxford University Press, 2019), 85–134.

[33] Ziemann, *War Experiences in Rural Germany*, 174.

Figure 7.1 *Arbeit in Stadt und Land!* (Work in town and country!). Source: Anker, Hans, "Arbeit in Stadt und Land!" Published by Meisenbach Riffarth & Co, 1918. [Poster] Herbert Hoover Library and Archives Poster Collection

munitions worker grasps an artillery shell in a factory. Both men are unshaven and strong, bearded, and both take up the same amount of space on the poster. The image itself emphasizes their equal importance to the war effort. Text confirms what the image shows:

> Arbeit in Stadt und Land!
> Der eine sät die Saaten
> und bindet Garben, schwer,
> der andre dreht Granaten
> und waffnet unser Heer.
> So geht's durch harte Zeiten
> zum Friedenserntefest,
> wenn keiner von den beiden
> die Hand vom Werke lässt.
>
> (Work in town and country!
> One sows the seeds
> and binds sheaves, heavy,
> the other spins shells
> and arms our army.
> So it goes through hard times
> to the harvest of peace,
> when neither of them
> leaves his hand from the work.)

In contrast to this image of national unity between urban and rural workers supporting the war effort in Germany, there was an exhibition sponsored by the Brussels City Museum in 1917 called "Concerning the Spoilage and Adulteration of Foodstuffs" (*Betreffende de Bederving en de Vervalsching der Eetwaren*) (Figure 7.2). Apparently, this was a local effort by officials in Brussels, not something from the Belgian government at large. Only the exhibition poster itself appears to have survived, and in it the Brussels City Museum spared no punches. Standing in front of a field with cows is a smiling man with rosy cheeks and a double chin. With his right hand he gently adds a small jug of milk to a large canister of water. His left hand turns the wheel of a tap shooting more water into the canister. Adding to the dishonesty of the scene is the label on the water-filled canister which reads "pure milk." Next to the man a pale woman holds her arm out in angry despair while a child clings to her. The Brussels City Museum was apparently doing its part to explain how food in the city of Brussels had been adulterated, and who – the double-chinned, rosy-cheeked man in the countryside – was to blame. If the graphics themselves were not clear enough, text on the poster states:

> De Vervalser is een Misdadiger Hij Benadeelt Gezondheid en Openbaar belang.
>
> (The counterfeiter is a criminal who harms health and the public interest.)

Figure 7.2 *Betreffende de Bederving en de Vervalsching der Eetwaren* (Concerning the Spoilage and Adulteration of Foodstuffs).[34]

[34] "Museum Betreffende de Bederving en de Vervalsching der Eetwaren." [Poster], 1917. Archives of the City of Brussels.

The theme of people in rural areas taking advantage of the food supply to the detriment of city dwellers was more common in the popular press than it was as exhibitions in city museums. Brussels seems to have been an exception. In Hungary it was the press that most notably blamed rural areas for hunger in cities:

> fortunes [are] being made by peasants in consequence of their ability to obtain higher prices in the rural districts than are paid in Budapest .... 'Their women wear silk stockings and pay as much as £ 2 or £ 3 for a pair of silk slippers. In the village of Abony 6,000 inhabitants put £ 100,000 in the savings bank during the last two years over and above their normal savings of pre-war years ... and they are said to have left half a million pounds hidden in their straw stacks and cupboards.[35]

A telling phrase here is "and they are said to have." The *New York Times* was reporting the rumors from a correspondent for a different newspaper (*The Morning Post*) and writing about *perceptions* of people in Budapest who found prices sky rocketing. The explanation they were told for the high prices in Budapest was that peasants in rural places such as Abony, a village about 85 km southeast of Budapest, were charging astronomical prices and using their new-found funds to purchase expensive silk stockings, discharge their debts, and store "half a million pounds hidden in their straw stacks and cupboards." Was the village of Abony truly a unique case of a luxurious rural fiefdom funded through high sales costs of their agricultural wares?

Even if all the ladies in rural Abony wore silk stockings and silk slippers, the proportion of actual foodstuffs agricultural workers could have kept for themselves at the expense of civilians in the cities was less than it had been before the fighting. While comparatively speaking there may have been more food in Hungary per person during the war than in Austria, there was still less overall because of the agricultural goods used to support the military and lower overall harvests compared to 1913.[36] In a world of shortages, the psychology of starvation – starving people believe that others receive more calories than they do – may at least partially explain some of the acrimony, alongside preexisting urban/rural biases. Even if agricultural yields had been perfectly and evenly distributed by a government amongst people in the countryside and people living in urban areas, as hunger crept in as

35 "Third Search for Food Ordered in Hungary. Peasants Growing Rich—Government Takes 50% as Exchange on Money Sent from America." *The New York Times*, February 2, 1917, 6.

36 Watson, *Ring of Steel*, 343–4; Judson, *The Habsburg Empire*, 399.

less food was available, both sides would have felt someone else was getting more than their share.

People on the Move: Long-term Stays

For people whose food supplies had been stolen, requisitioned, or were simply inadequate, often the only recourse they had was to leave their homes. Fourteen to fifteen million people were displaced in the era of the First World War.[37] Expulsions, violence and fear of violence, and hunger, led to and were a result of this displacement. Many people whose homes and fields had been destroyed poured into cities. Ethnic and religious minorities were driven from their homelands. These movements compounded issues of urban food supply. Agricultural workers as refugees were no longer harvesting and working the land. One of the earliest mass movements of agricultural workers during the First World War came with the Battle of Galicia, August 23 to September 11, 1914. Agrarian, poor, and subject to early violence, Galicia had over a million people leave, who not only could no longer feed themselves, but who were also no longer producing the wheat that had fed many in the same cities to which they fled, including Vienna and Prague.[38]

Refugees who ended up in cities faced entrenched biases, even among aid givers. One common view of international charities was to not assume responsibilities for poor people that were previously provided for by other institutions.[39] Even groups that shared the same religious background – for example, local leaders of the American Jewish Joint Distribution Committee (JDC) in Vienna – held this sentiment. Records from their meetings state the need to focus their aid not on the generally poor, but only on those who were poor because of the war:

> The JDC cannot take over the charity work for the poor that always, as in Vienna like every other large city, can be found. Our committee was founded to support those wounded by the War, and not for those that are due to difficult sociological and economic conditions.[40]

Of course, if a person in Vienna was in need of charity before the war, that need likely increased during and following the war.

[37] Peter Gatrell "Introduction," in *Europe on the Move: Refugees in the Era of the Great War*, edited by Peter Gatrell and Liubov Zhvanko (Manchester University Press, 2019), 3.

[38] David Rechter, *The Jews of Vienna and the First World War* (Oxford: The Littman Library of Jewish Civilization, 2008), 67–72.

[39] For example, the American Relief Administration saw itself as operating in the short term to help with emergencies.

[40] The National Library of Israel (NLI). Special Collections. V 770 / 1 Joint Distribution Committee Vienna Collection. Protokolle der Vollversammlung 1919/20. "Protokoll der Vollversammlung von 7. April, 1920," 3.

While people in cities may have been making short-term visits to the countryside for food, displaced peoples moving into cities frequently stayed much longer. "Temporary" displacement often stretched into months and years, and was often permanent. Unlike urbanites who visited the countryside for food and then returned home to their cities, returning home was extremely difficult for displaced persons. These movements blur conceptions of a strictly urban/rural divide during the First World War. Indeed, some of the same people in cities who complained about farmers keeping too much food may have recently been farmers themselves, or the children or grandchildren of transplants who had moved to urban areas in the decades leading up to the war.

Children on the Move

If the boundaries between civilians in the countryside and those in urban areas were not absolute, the countryside and the city still played a role in both urban and rural imaginations and expectations. People in cities believed there was food in the countryside, and used this belief not only to lay blame, but also to cast hope. Similarly, displaced peoples hoped that they would find food and safety upon their arrival to urban areas.

Lines dividing rural and urban populations are further blurred when one considers the vast undertaking of sending predominantly urban children to rural areas for better food and fresh air. While some children were sent relatively short distances to the local countryside, many were sent abroad. Whether with host parents or at a hotel or children's vacation camp, the aim was to help children receive better food than they could receive if they had stayed home with their families. Such visits could also serve political objectives. Visits tended to last several weeks or months, and once a child's health had improved, they would be sent home. Children from across Europe and the Ottoman Empire were on the move, bringing their languages, cultures, and experiences with them, mollifying the image of foreigner and enemy, and providing a meeting point for urban and rural.

We don't yet know exactly how many children participated, but the numbers we do have are considerable. Over 61,000 Hungarian children were sent to the Netherlands, Belgium, Switzerland, England, and Sweden between 1920 and 1930, in that order (see Table 7.1).

Furthermore, anywhere from 40,000 to 67,000[41] children from Germany arrived in Switzerland alone by 1921. From 1919 to 1921, some 200,000 Austrian children, primarily from Vienna and other cities, travelled to

[41] Cox, *Hunger in War and Peace*, 289.

Table 7.1 *Hungarian children sent abroad, 1920–1930*[42]

Netherlands	28,564
Belgium	21,542
Switzerland	10,608
England	603
Sweden	131

foreign countries for two months or more.[43] With a child population of 600,000 in the entire country, the Austrian numbers, which may be the highest, attest to the transformational experience on the First Austrian Republic: up to one-third of Austrian children may have left their homes for stints in countries with better food.[44] Most Austrian children were sent to hosts in Switzerland, the Netherlands, Germany, and Denmark, in that order (see Table 7.2), although would-be host parents offered to care for Austrian children as far away as Egypt, Iceland, and Transvaal.[45]

While the practice of sending urban children to the local countryside or abroad was especially prominent in Central Europe, children from other parts of Europe were also sent internationally for short stays during and following the war, including children from Poland, France, and Belgium.[46] Even urban children in the Balkans were sent abroad for help, though in much smaller numbers.[47] Research by Vera Hajtó and Friederike Kind-Kovács has added greatly to our understanding of these experiences for Hungarian children, and the posthumously published book by Isabella Matauschek on Austrian children sent to Denmark and the Netherlands, especially the interviews she conducted with former child participants, is especially noteworthy.[48]

42 Table 7.1 was created from data in Vera Hajtó, "The 'Wanted' Children. Experiences of Hungarian Children Living with Belgian Host Families during the Interwar Period," *History of the Family*, 14 (2009), 204.

43 Friedrich Reischl, "Die Ausländische Kinderhilfe in Wien," in *Volksgesundheit im Krieg I*, edited by Clemens Pirquet (Vienna: Carnegie Stiftung für Internationalen Frieden, Hölder Pichler Tempsky A. G. Yale University Press,1926), 365.

44 Some children took repeated trips, which would lower this ratio. Unfortunately, we don't know how many children took repeated visits. Reischl, "Die Ausländische Kinderhilfe in Wien," 368.

45 Reischl, "Die Ausländische Kinderhilfe in Wien," 365.

46 Oscar Bosshardt, *Die Schweizer Hilfsaktion für die hungernde Stadt Wien* (Bern: Francke, 1921), 158.

47 Ognjen Kovačević, "Putujuća škola: Izveštaj profesora Miloša S. Moskovljevića o srpskim đacima u Rusiji za vreme Prvog svetskog rata," *Istorijske sveske*, 11 (2014), 25–8. (Cyrillic).

48 Isabella Matauschek, *Lokales Leid – Globale Herausforderung: Die Verschickung österreichischer Kinder nach Dänemark und in die Niederlande im Anschluss an den Ersten Weltkrieg*. (Vienna, Böhlau Verlag, 2018).

Table 7.2 *Foreign food and board spots for Austrian children*

	Year			Total by country
	1919	1920	1921	
Switzerland	20,450	34,106	4,411	58,967
Holland	9,150	28,230	15,281	52,661
Germany	700	16,827	3,635	21,162
Denmark	1,050	12,670	4,713	18,433
Czechoslovakia		11,602	8,664	20,266
Sweden	1,400	7,556	1,492	10,448
Italy	2,700	5,568	226	8,494
Norway		2,884	761	3,645
Yugoslavia		1,501	3	1,504
England		1,040	22	1,062
Romania		988	2,759	3,747
Luxemberg		350	326	676
Belgium		220	121	341
Spain		98	223	321
France		50	68	118
Poland		30		30
Totals	35,450	123,690	42,705	201,845

Source: Adapted from table "Ausländische Kostplätze für österreichische Kinder" in Reischl, "Die Ausländische Kinderhilfe in Wien," 365.

The short-term movement of children sent by their caregivers to places with better food supplies, both abroad and within their own municipalities, occurred during the war itself.[49] As mentioned, these movements could be grounded in both charitable and political motivations. In the Bohemian Lands, the charity of the Czech nationalist Agrarian Party, Czech Heart (České srdce) set up feeding centers in urban areas, and organized programs for urban children to spend periods of time in the Czech countryside. This not only benefited children, but was part of the party's efforts to increase Czech solidarity and shake off blame placed on agriculture for hunger in the cities.[50] During the war, 71,851 Austrian children were sent to Hungary,[51] and groups of needy Hungarian children were sent to holiday camps on the coastlines of the Adriatic.[52]

[49] Cox, *Hunger in War and Peace*, 288.

[50] Morelon, "Urban-rural antagonism in Prague," 330; Judson, *The Habsburg Empire*, 403.

[51] Reischl, "Die Ausländische Kinderhilfe in Wien," 369.

[52] Friederike Kind-Kovács, "The 'Other' Child Transports: World War I and the Temporary Displacement of Needy Children from Central Europe," *Journal of the History of Irregular Childhood*, 15 (2013), 75–109.

These holiday camps were meant not only to help children, but were also supported by Karl I to try to create unity within the weakened Empire.[53] While smaller in scope compared to post-war movements, this wartime practice helps explain how numbers increased after the war. Simply put: many routes, organizations, and groups directing children already existed and became better established over time. Furthermore, as the political situation improved, it was safer for children to travel and to be away from their parents. Yet the comparatively small number of children who were sent abroad or to more local countrysides during the First World War are only one part of the explanation for the mass movement of children following the war. "Mass movement" is truly the appropriate term here when taking into account that over 200,000 Austrian children went abroad from 1919 to 1921.

There was already a precedent of children moving and living away from their parents for short periods, especially in the former Habsburg lands. Many German-speaking children were sent to live with Czech-speaking families, and vice versa, so that they could become bilingual. These exchanges included not only the middle classes, but also the children of peasants and farmers. Parents believed it would benefit their children if they learned an additional language.[54] The motivation behind these movements was different than the motivation to move hundreds of thousands of hungry children following the First World War. Yet this later movement of children, including people from different social classes and especially from the former Austrian-Hungarian Empire, was possible not only because of the acute need and willing charities and hosts, but also because temporarily moving children to places for their own improvement was not entirely new.

Children's stays with host parents and at summer camps also found a precedent in refugee camps. Wartime refugee camps in Austria-Hungary, which included many children, were a way to nourish bodies and minds of future citizens in times of need from the nethermost parts of the Empire. They were also an attempt to cement the state's legitimacy through its largess and power,[55] and to reduce the strain of landless refugees in the cities. For some, these "temporary" camps became long-term. While the stays of most children in foreign lands after 1918 were temporary, they can, like refugee camps during the war, fit within

[53] Friederike Kind-Kovács, *Budapest's Children: Humanitarian Relief in the Aftermath of the Great War* (Bloomington, IN: Indiana University Press, 2022), 248.

[54] Tara Zahra, *Kidnapped Souls: National Indifference and the Battle for Children in the Bohemian Lands, 1900–1948* (Ithaca: Cornell University Press, 2011), 2.

[55] Doina Anca Cretu, "Child Assistance and the Making of Modern Refugee Camps in Austria-Hungary during the First World War," *Central European History*, 55 (2022), 513.

the argument that mass migration in the twentieth century was seen as "a solution to demographic and social 'problems'."[56]

Just as Karl I had supported children's camps during the war to create unity and build legitimacy, others shared similar sentiments when offering aid to foreign children. In the aftermath of the war, some saw feeding children as a tool for building world peace. Early members of Save the Children, such as Emily Hobson, viewed feeding children, particularly German children, as "an inaugural act of political protest" against reparations and the continuance of the British blockade into the armistice period.[57]

Tables 7.1 and 7.2 show that countries that had been neutral during the war tended to host the most Austrian and Hungarian children. Yet Table 7.1 and Table 7.2 also show that countries hosted the children of those that had been their enemies during the war, not just their allies. With the movement of so many children, there were many different networks, including professional societies and religious institutions, that facilitated these exchanges, both formally and informally. The 20,000 Hungarian children who were sent to Belgium following the war, for example, were financially and practically supported by the British Save the Children Fund and the International Committee of the Red Cross and organized in Hungary by the National Child Protection League.[58] In Vienna too, a host of different groups and individuals supported the exchanges, both large and small. Hans Steiner, a twelve-year-old from Vienna, was sent to Faaborg, Denmark, to live with the married couple Ragnhild and Rasmussen Christiansen in 1920. Hans's father was a medical doctor, just like Rassa Christiansen, and it was probably this professional link that connected them.[59] Hans was mostly likely one of the 12,670 Austrian children that were hosted in Denmark in 1920 (see Table 7.2). The Methodist Episcopal Church supported sick German children in their stays in Davos and Locarno.[60] Forged with the experience of helping Belgian refugees during the war, people in the Netherlands hosted German and Austrian children from

[56] Tara Zahra, *The Great Departure: Mass Migration from Eastern Europe and the Making of the Free World* (New York: W. W. Norton & Company, 2016), 18.

[57] Tatjana Eichert and Rebecca Gill, "Children and the 'Hunger Politics' of 1919–20: Food Aid to German Children and the Founding of the International Save the Children Movement," in *Humanitarianism and the Greater War, 1914–24*, edited by Elisabeth Piller and Neville Wylie (Manchester University Press, 2023), 211–12.

[58] Kind-Kovács, "The 'Other' Child Transports."

[59] Based on oral interview with Ruth Steiner (daughter of Hans Steiner), September 21, 2021, Vienna [SFA]; see also Reischl "Die Ausländische Kinderhilfe in Wien," 366–7.

[60] *Schweizer Zentralkomitee für notleidende Auslandskinder*, Rapport no. 2, 1930. [Archives d'Etat de Genève, Box: Archives privées 92.10.2(1).]

1918 onwards, and in 1919 started hosting Hungarian children as well. During the summer of 1919, the Swedish Red Cross transported 125 undernourished children from Latvia to Stockholm and cared for them there for five to six months. It is recorded that the Latvian children returned in considerably better health and brought home substantial donations of clothes.[61] Germany hosted some 21,162 malnourished Austrian children,[62] even as thousands of German children were being sent abroad for help.[63] This mutual giving occurred while many children in Germany and Austria were themselves receiving foreign food aid after the war, and being transported to foreign countries for their own help. Finally, these large exchanges do not include the many daily child-feeding programs operating across Europe and the Ottoman Empire, which fed many more children.[64]

Despite the excitement, and the nutritional benefit, these visits could still be stressful. Children missed their homes and faced new experiences. In Latvia in 1922, the American Relief Administration (ARA) organized summer camps in the countryside and by the seaside for the most deprived children. In one camp a little girl was distressed by the new foods she was presented with:

> Children were not used to good quality food (vegetables, desserts, porridge, tomatoes etc.) and at the beginning they ate only potatoes, bread and sour cabbage. One small girl sat with a semolina pudding from cowberries before her and cried. When asked why she was crying, the girl answered: 'How can I eat such food, I have never seen such a red soup!'[65]

With hundreds of thousands of children living away from their parents, we know that there were also, tragically, instances of abuse.[66] And for a variety of reasons, some children who went on these supposedly short-term excursions never returned to their homelands.[67] Vera Hajtó estimates that of the 20,000 Hungarian children who visited Belgium in the First World War era, 4 percent became permanent residents.[68]

With so many children abroad, especially from cities like Vienna, people were interested in understanding the experiences of these children and their caretakers. Many of the records that remain were collected

[61] "Lai par cilvēku runā viņa darbs," *Zeltene*, no. 16 (August 15, 1932), 4–5.
[62] See Table 7.2.
[63] Cox, *Hunger in War and Peace*, 287–93.
[64] See Chapter 13, "Healing Hunger: Post-war Humanitarian Action" by Ēriks Jēkabsons.
[65] E. Klaustiņa, "Amerikāņu palīdzības darbs 1921. gadā." *Latvju Sieviete* 6 (1952), 18.
[66] Vera Hajtó, *Milk Sauce and Paprika: Migration, Childhood and Memories of the Interwar Belgian-Hungarian Child Relief* (Leuven University Press, 2017), 15, 112.
[67] Kind-Kovács, *Budapest's Children*, 248; Hajtó, *Milk Sauce and Paprika*, 112.
[68] Hajtó, *Milk Sauce and Paprika*, 112.

by the local aid organizations involved.[69] One such book is a collection of letters from Norwegian host parents to the parents of the Viennese children they hosted, as well as photographs of Viennese children in Norway sledding, skiing, and sitting in paddle boats.[70] Letters from these Norwegian host parents often contained requests that the children they were caring for stay longer. One letter, for example, from the Norwegian town of Lilleöen, addressed to "Gretel's loving parents and brother" and signed by Chr. and Margit Ch, begins with "Your Grete is so lively, enjoyable, and well-raised." It explains that they were told that all of the children were to return to Vienna on May 19. However, they hoped Grete could stay for the entire summer as "the summers here in Norway are so beautiful."[71]

Even a short children's fiction book about the experience of two Viennese siblings, Herta and her little brother Lixl, who lived with farmers in Switzerland, was published in 1925. Their location in the Swiss Alps is an important part of the storyline, where the children would "breath fresh strong mountain air, receive good milk and strong country bread as well as eggs and meat."[72] One book published in 1921 uses materials produced by Viennese children themselves such as letters, essays, and artwork.[73] The documents included were not random; schoolteachers, parents, and aid givers shared the children's material with the book's editors, but they do have a wide geographic spread, including sources credited to Viennese children who stayed in Switzerland, Sweden, the Netherlands, Denmark, Norway, England, France, Italy, Germany, Hungary, Bohemia and Moravia. The majority of these expressions are, not-surprisingly, positive. An 11-year-old girl named Kathe described with delight how she and the other children were met at the train station in Italy with oranges

[69] Examples from Vienna include: *Wiener Kinder in Norwegen 1. Was die norwegischen Pflegeeltern schreiben: eine Sammlung von Briefen mit zahlreichen Illustrationen* (self-published by the Norwegischen Hilfsaktion in Kristiania [Oslo], 1925); Oscar Bosshardt, *Die Schweizer Hilfsaktion für die Hungernde Stadt Wien* (Bern: Franke, 1921). (Bosshardt was the main secretary for *Die Schweizer Hilfsaktion für Wien.*); US American Relief Administration, *A Review of the Work of the American Relief Administration in Austria* (Vienna: s.n., 1921); US American Relief Administration, *Three Years Work of the American Relief Administration in Austria* (Vienna: s.n., 1922); Deutschösterreichischen Jugendhilfswerk in Wien, *Wiens Kinder und Amerika. Die amerikanische Kinderhilfsaktion 1919*. Friedrich Reischl (ed.), (Vienna: Gerlach & Wiedling, 1920).

[70] *Wiener Kinder in Norwegen.*

[71] *Wiener Kinder in Norwegen*, 22.

[72] Margit Ernst, *Wiener Kinder in der Schweiz* (Vienna: Seram Velag, 1925), 5.

[73] Anna Nussbaum and Else Feldmann (ed.), *Das Reisebuch des Wiener Kindes: Eine Sammlung von Briefen, Aufsätzen und Zeichnungen der Wiener Schulkinder im Ausland* (Vienna: Gloriette-Verlag, 1921).

Figure 7.3 Children's vacation home in Gmünd, Lower Austria.
Source: American Relief Administration, European Children's Fund Collection, Archives Center, National Museum of American History, Smithsonian Institution

and chocolate.[74] Hermine Pollak (age unknown) painted a beautiful scene of a windmill next to a river, small house, and boat. In the hilly green background is a church.[75] Ten-year-old Mariechen in England explained to her mother that she did not need to be blamed for letting her travel away. Rather, "you must be jolly and happy because maybe I would not have ever grown so much."[76]

Despite these positive letters and art, expressions of children's distress were also included in the book. Marie, aged eleven, who was staying at a children's camp in a rural coastline in Kent, England, asked her parents, "why don't you write to me? I walk to the post office every day and there is never any mail for me."[77] Twelve-year-old Herta was more forthright. She described her new home in Switzerland as "heavenly" but she closed her letter with: "it is beautiful here but it is more beautiful at home. Home is just home. Today I cried many tears for you."[78] Perhaps it was these expressions of homesickness that prompted vice president of the International Red Cross, Frédéric Ferrière, who wrote the book's preface, to express his hope that in the future Austrian children would stay closer to home in the "beautiful, healing, Austrian countryside."[79] Ferrière's suggestion may also have been practical. It would have been less expensive for an international organization like the Red Cross to support children close to their own homes or in a nearby countryside, than to send them to distant lands.

Anthropometric Measurements of Urban and Rural Children

Sometimes, in efforts to understand the health of children sent to the countryside, anthropometric data were collected. US aid workers in Hungary assessed their efforts of feeding 29,000 children between the ages of three and fourteen years old after five weeks of summer feeding in the countryside in 1921.[80] At the girls camp, the "really sick children" gained an average of 2.4 kg, and those "in better health [gained] an average of 4 kg each."[81]

[74] *Das Reisebuch*, 68.
[75] *Das Reisebuch*, 30.
[76] *Das Reisebuch*, 52.
[77] *Das Reisebuch*, 53.
[78] *Das Reisebuch*, 2.
[79] *Das Reisebuch*, ii.
[80] Russell W. Bell, "Summer Camps in Hungary," *American Relief Administration Bulletin* 2:17:1 (October 1921), 26–7, HILA.
[81] Russell W. Bell, "Experiences and Results of the 1921 Summer Camp Action in Hungary," *American Relief Administration Bulletin*, 2:20 (January 1922), 32, HILA.

Weights and heights of school children in urban and rural locations were also measured by local medical practitioners, both during and after the war. In instances where urban and rural indicators are included, it is possible to examine the question of rural/urban hunger. For example, an old medical publication on the heights and weights of school children in Strasbourg published in 1919 contains anthropometric data collected in 1914 and 1918 from schoolboys living in Strasbourg and the surrounding countryside. Uniquely, not only were the boys and their schools divided into whether or not they were rural or urban, but also by religion and wealth, with a total of six different identifiable socio-economic groups. Modern analyses show that boys from all backgrounds experienced nutritional deprivation between 1914 and 1918, and that these differences were highly related to socio-economic background. Indeed, once socio-economic background is controlled for, the differences between boys from rural areas outside of Strasbourg and those from the city disappear. So too do differences in religion. What mattered, at least in Strasbourg, was the wealth of the boys' families: wealthier children were heavier and taller than those that were less wealthy. Once wealth was accounted for, no other variable in the study had statistical significance.[82]

Anthropometric indicators of urban and rural children were also published in the Austrian Republic.[83] An initial study of the health of Austrian school children conducted from November 1920 to January 1921 with a sample size of 418,412 school children across cities and towns in Salzburg, Carinthia, Vorarlberg, Styria, Vienna, Upper Austria, and Lower Austria (Burgenland was not part of Austria then), stated that the nutritional status of school children was "bad everywhere, with only minor differences."[84] Any urban/rural disparities were not extreme. Still, within these "minor differences," Upper and Lower Austria had the least deprived children due to their "extensive fertile areas."

One way to think about urban/rural differences in a state is to look at differences between a city or cities and rural areas across the state as a whole. Vienna was the largest city in the First Austrian Republic. As the capital of the former Empire, it was "a head without a body" and approximately 2 million people lived there. Using surveys of

82 Cox, *Hunger in War and Peace*, 135–69.

83 In addition to "Ernährungszustand der Kinder," less aggregated statistics from the same studies used in the Carnegie edition were published in the appendix of Friedrich Reischl, ed., *Mitteilungen der American Relief Administration Band I* (Vienna: Unknown Publisher, 1921).

84 Clemens Pirquet, "Ernährungszustand der Kinder in Österreich während des Krieges und Nachkriegszeit," in *Volksgesundheit im Krieg I*, edited by Clemens Pirquet (Vienna: Carnegie Stiftung für Internationalen Frieden, Hölder Pichler Tempsky A. G. Yale University Press, 1926), 291.

anthropometric data from school children collected in the spring of 1920, Viennese children had a low nutritional status compared to other parts of Austria, such as Salzburg. As University of Vienna Medical Professor Clemens von Pirquet cautioned, these low numbers in Vienna hid variation across the city.[85] Some children, especially those in poorer districts of the city, were worse off than the statistics showed, and others were much better. However, according to Pirquet, Viennese children recovered very quickly relative to other parts of Austria. Viennese children as a whole had the fastest rate of recovery, and the fifth best nutritional status in Austria. This is also shown in the second large-scale anthropometric survey of Austrian school children, with a sample size of 379,864, taken in the spring of 1922.[86] Pirquet stated that the Amerikanische Kinder Hilfsaktion in Vienna and children vacation camps explained the faster rate of recovery of Viennese children relative to other parts of Austria.[87]

Another way to measure urban/rural differences in a state is to consider rural and urban areas that are geographically very close to each other. This has the advantage of minimizing possible genetic discrepancies. Dr. Kleinsasser did a large study of all school children in Tirol from mid-November 1919 to the end of December 1919,[88] separating children in "Stadt" (Innsbruck and its suburbs) and "Land" (twenty-six larger towns).

As Figures 7.4[89] and 7.5 show, the rural/urban differences in average height by age for boys and girls measured in Tirol was negligible. That said, at most ages, boys and girls living in urban areas in Tirol were slightly taller than children in more rural areas. When using a different anthropometric indicator that combined height and weight, the Pelidisi Index, children in the countryside had a slight advantage.[90]

The supposed urban/rural differences in Tirol were minimal. Given the geographical closeness of rural children to food sources, this does not fit the traditional paradigm. One possibility for practically no difference could be that in Tirol, the distances from city to farm were in fact not very large. The advantage a rural child might have had of being "closer" to the foodstuffs would have been dampened. Another

[85] Pirquet, "Ernährungszustand der Kinder," 296.
[86] Pirquet, "Ernährungszustand der Kinder," 298–9.
[87] Pirquet, "Ernährungszustand der Kinder," 296.
[88] Pirquet, "Ernährungszustand der Kinder," 300; Ernst Mayerhofer, "Medizinische Studie über die Amerikanische Kinderhilfsaktion in Österreich," in *Mitteilungen der American Relief Administration Band. I* edited by Friedrich Reischl (Mitteilungen des Generalkommissariates der A.K.H.A, August 1920), 16.
[89] Graph created from data in Table XVI in the appendix in *Mitteilungen*.
[90] Pirquet, "Ernährungszustand der Kinder," 300.

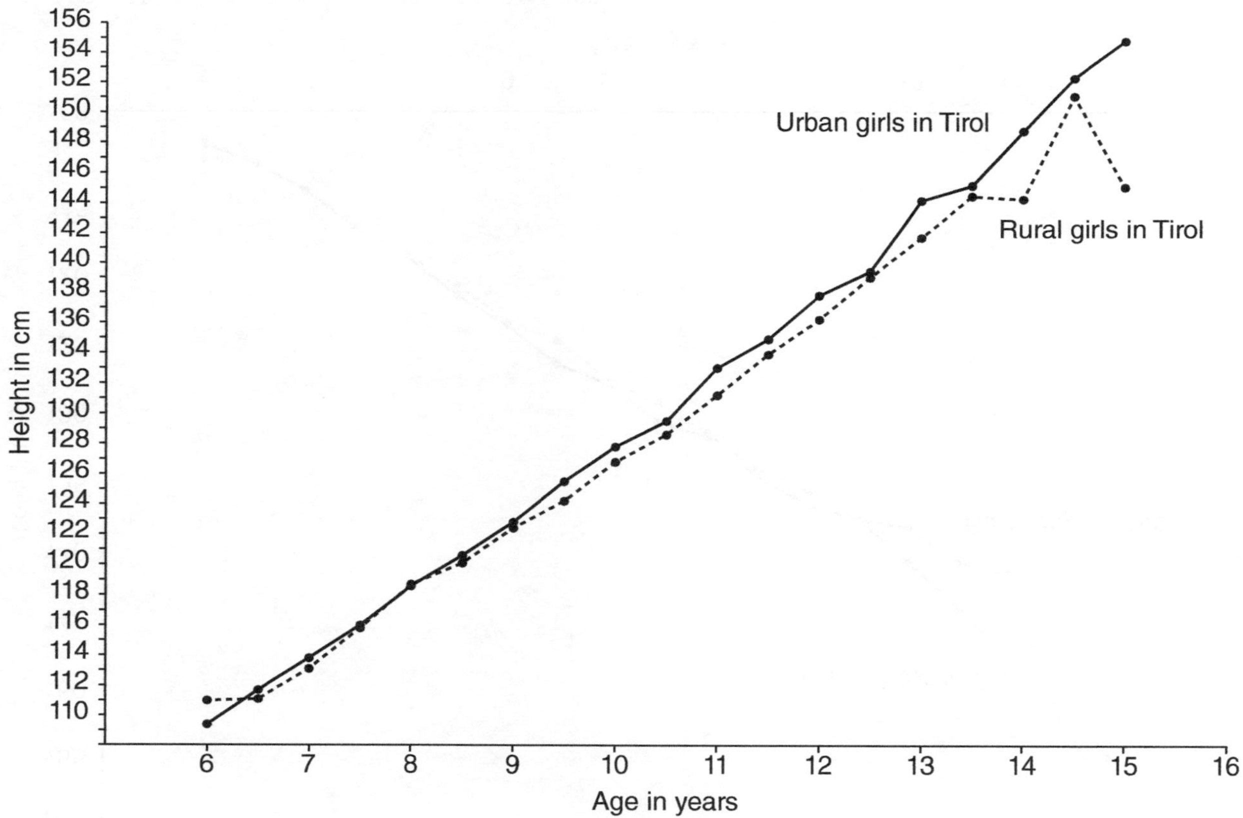

Figure 7.4 Heights of girls by age living in Tirol in 1920, in cm.

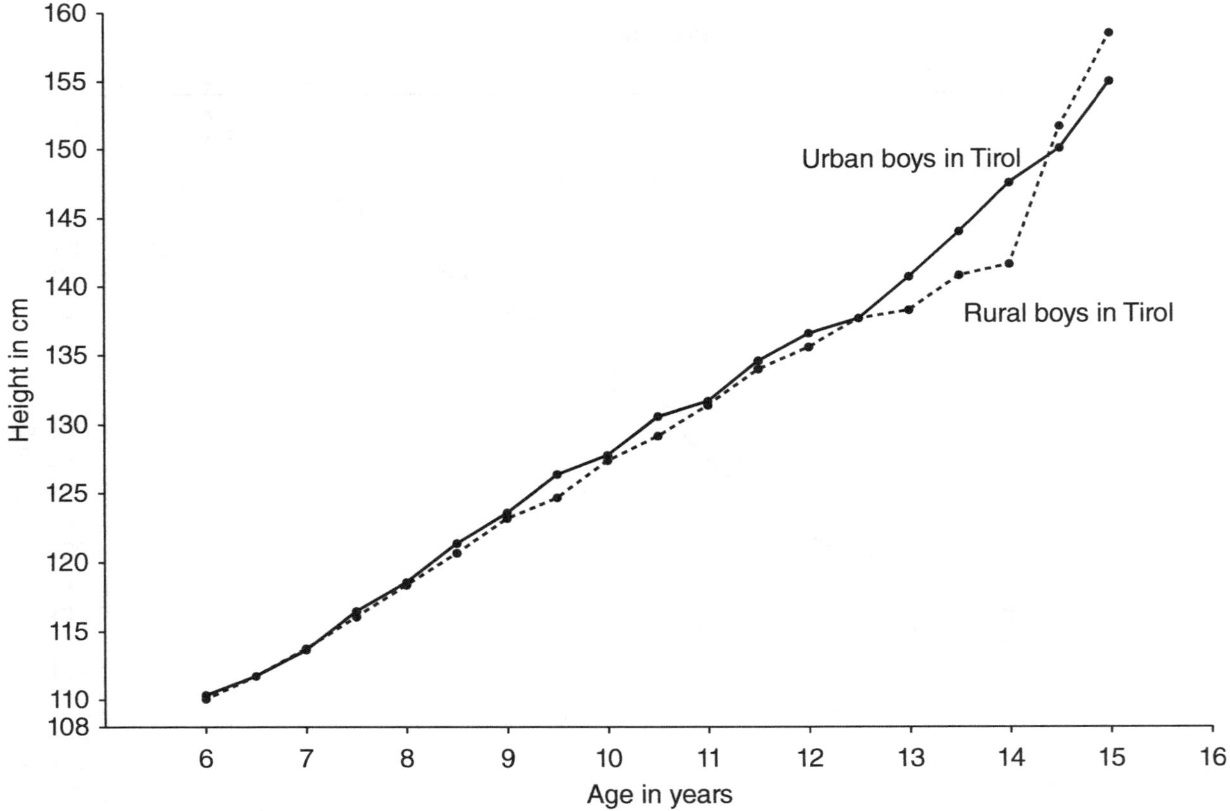

Figure 7.5 Heights of boys by age living in Tirol in 1920, in cm.

possibility likely lies in socioeconomic differences, which would also help explain variation in cities like Vienna.[91] Alongside the Strasbourg example from Germany, both of these findings – that children in Vienna were some of the most nutritionally deprived following the war, and yet had the *fastest* rate of recovery, and the finding that children living in cities and rural communities in Tirol had about the same anthropometric measurements – brings into question the simple rural/urban narrative that people in cities were hungry while those in rural communities were not, at least in Central Europe.

Post-war Recovery for Children was More Rapid in Urban Areas

Interpreting the results from Austria in relation to the urban/rural question we find two things. First, living in the capital city with the best infrastructure and connections to the rest of the empire does not appear to have given civilians living in Vienna a particular advantage over other civilians, at least those living in the Austrian half of the Empire, during the war. Second, living in Vienna *did* give civilians – children at least – an advantage once hostilities stopped.[92] Routes that had brought food into Vienna before the onslaught of hostilities slowed during the war. However, following the war, those same routes brought children out of Vienna to places where they could get more food, and moved essential foodstuffs into the city.

From May 1919 to September 1, 1921, some 30,237 *tons* of food from the American Relief Administration (ARA) designated for children in all of Austria arrived into Vienna.[93] Perhaps only living in a major port town such as Hamburg could get a child physically closer to more food supplies than having a Central Warehouse located in their city. ARA ships full of food and other supplies followed steamer routes into major harbors before being divided for further destinations, some of which went to Vienna. Stored in large warehouses in the Hofburg Palace and elsewhere in the city, Vienna became the major hub for food for the rest of Austria (see Map 14.9). In Map 7.1, "Plan of Feeding for Austria," "foodstuff stores" are represented in Vienna, Innsbruck, Graz, Linz, Salzburg, Klagenfurt, and Bregenz. From these foodstuff stores, food

[91] See Chapter 8, "Food Hierarchies: Class, Status, and Social Divisions" by Claire Morelon for more on socioeconomic differences.

[92] Pirquet suggested that children in Vienna may have had higher nutritional status than children in other parts of the country on the second measurement because the proportion of school children fed in Vienna was so high.

[93] *A Review of the Work of the American Relief Administration*, 25.

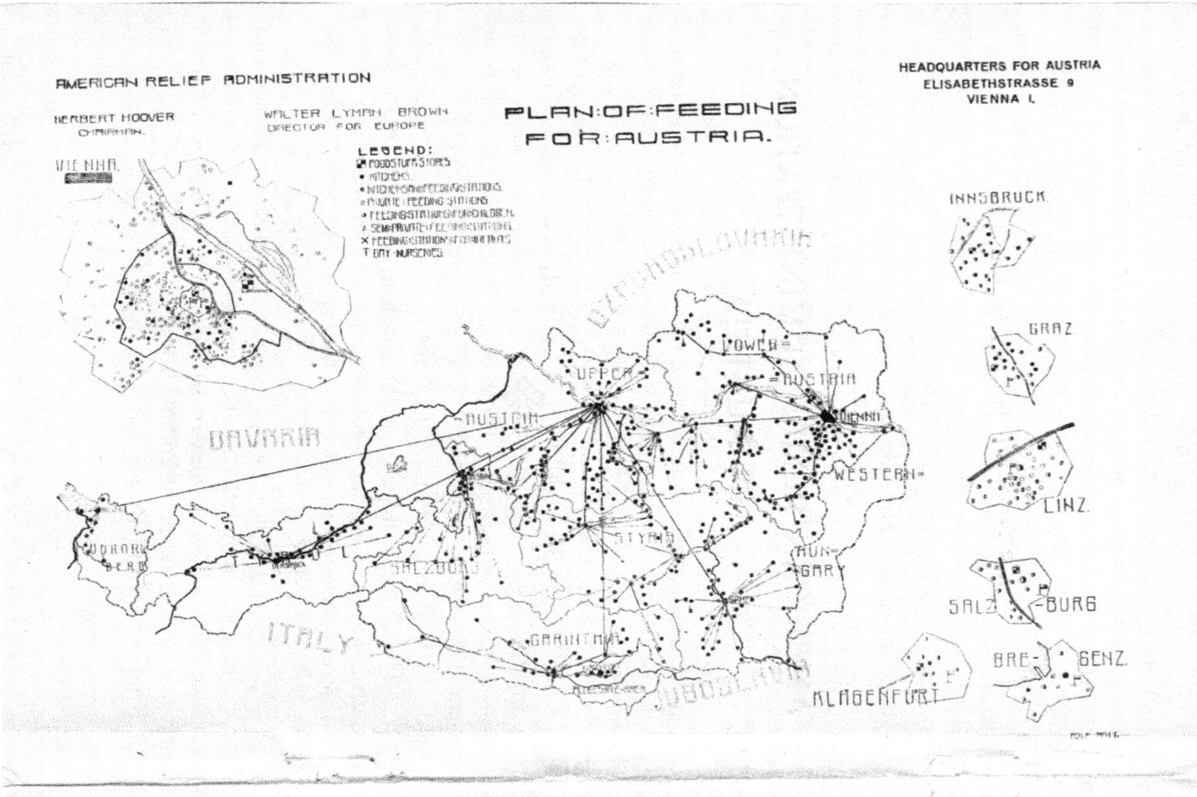

Map. 7.1 Plan of feeding for Austria.
Source: Herbert Hoover Presidential Library, US National Archives

was then delivered to kitchens and feeding stations across cities and to smaller locations across the Republic of Austria.

On the one hand these findings – that being closer to foodstuffs increased the likelihood of higher consumption – support the basic idea that proximity to food sources matter. On the other hand, it demonstrates that proximity was not simply determined by rurality. When the argument that people in the countryside generally had more food to eat during the war because they were physically closer to the food supply is considered, then so too should closeness to warehouses of food after the war. In both situations, closeness to foodstuffs only had value when a person had access to them. Furthermore, these findings show that the rural/urban divide was not consistent over time: all things equal it would have been worse for a child to live in urban Vienna during the war and better for a child to live in Vienna in 1921.

Perceptions are Not Always Wrong

While the examples and analyses of child feeding programs following the First World War in parts of the world I have used here – particularly in Germany, Austria, and Hungary – may question perceptions about urban/rural dichotomies in the nutritional status of civilians, questions about urban and rural differences in terms of hunger levels in the era of the First World War are important for other parts of the world as well. The famine in Russia and Ukraine in the early 1920s may have killed 5 million people, and "the rural population suffered the most."[94] This can be observed when looking at a map of net crop food grains per capita in 1921 in the Volga-Ural regions in the south (see Map 14.12). Yet this perception of rural suffering is widened when the famine dates are extended to include 1918–1920, following Stephen Wheatcroft's work. While not as severe as the later famine, "the northern urban famine of 1918–1920" more greatly impacted the urban north, and the "southern rural famine of 1921–1922" more greatly impacted the rural south.[95] The perception that people in rural communities suffered more than people in cities during the Russian Famine of 1921–1922 (as it is commonly called) needs no correction. Nevertheless, by including the 1918–1920

[94] Omelian Rudnytskyi, Stanislav Kulchytskyi, Oleksandr Gladun, and Natalia Kulyk, "The 1921–1923 Famine and the Holodomor of 1932–1933 in Ukraine: Common and Distinctive Features," *Nationalities Papers*, 48:3 (2020), 549–68, 564.

[95] Stephen Wheatcroft, "Eastern Europe (Russia and the USSR)," in *Famine in European History*, edited by Guido Alfani and Cormac Ó Gráda (Cambridge University Press, 2017).

famine in the urban north in his analysis, Wheatcroft is able to show how this earlier famine negatively influenced the 1921–1922 famine in the rural south.

In Mount Lebanon approximately one third of the total population died in the famine known as "the Great Catastrophe." Indeed, per capita, Lebanon had more casualties than any other bounded territory.[96] Although highly agricultural, people did not produce their own foodstuffs for consumption but instead grew mulberry leaves for silk production. They were primarily dependent on regional trade for their food supplies, importing up to 93 percent of all of their grains.[97] Many things contributed to the famine, and the Allied Blockade of the Mediterranean surely played a decisive and deadly role. So too did a lack of serious action from Ottoman, French, and British governments to intercede for the civilian population. That the people most influenced by this blockade were living under colonization in racist societies as well as being civilians, at least partly explains both the actions of those who ran and instigated the blockade, as well as the comparatively little scholarship that has been produced on this subject.[98]

When the silk economy fell apart with the outbreak of war, people in Lebanon were no longer able to receive money from their exports to purchase food, or to receive remittances from abroad.[99] Food stopped arriving in Lebanon. In these desperate circumstances, wealth mattered for gaining access to food more than any urban/rural divide. According to Graham Auman Pitts, while mostly ignored in the literature, "the poorest rung of the rural *and* urban working class suffered first and foremost."[100] (emphasis added). While society was dependent on agricultural trade, and the capitalism that came along with it, poor people in cities *and* in rural communities suffered and died. Here too, a wider perspective on hunger experiences in urban and rural areas, as Pitts'

[96] Graham Auman Pitts, "'Make Them Hated in All of the Arab Countries': France, Famine, and the Creation of Lebanon," in *Environmental Histories of the First World War*, edited by Richard P. Tucker, Tait Keller, J. R. McNeill, and Martin Schmid (Cambridge University Press, 2017), 175.

[97] Pitts, "Make Them Hated," 177.

[98] Heather Jones, "A Forgotten Front? The Mediterranean Blockade in the First World War," *The International History Review*, 7 May (2024).

[99] Remittances were the greatest source of income in Mount Lebanon prior to First World War. Just as people's ability to sell and trade their goods stopped, remittances were also choked off. Normal channels ended in January 1915. The US State Department facilitated transfers through its consulate in Beirut, but this ended when the US entered the war in 1917. Graham Auman Pitts, "The Ecology of Migration: Remittances in World War I Mount Lebanon," *The Arab Studies Journal*, 26:2 (2018), 102–4.

[100] Graham Auman Pitts, "Was Capitalism the Crisis? Mount Lebanon's World War I Famine," *Arcadia*, 3 (2021), Arcadia Collection: Terms of Disaster.

research suggests, is needed. Socio-economic background must be taken into account when assessing rural and urban differences.

Given the psychology of hunger, and the societal falling apart that can accompany it,[101] we should perhaps read expressions of blame from one group against another – city dwellers blaming rural farmers, farmers blaming city dwellers – with more caution. There was less food available in rural and urban areas because of agricultural slumps, requisitioning, blockades, and the violence of war. Even assumptions about the benefits of living close to infrastructure and trade routes do not always hold sway. Routes were stopped by blockades. Coal was being used by militaries who prioritized the needs of their troops over transporting food to civilians. Hence, living in a city close to a major road or trade route did not always translate into having enough food to eat. Once movement was again possible because blockades had been lifted, or coal and food became more available, then being on that route mattered, as demonstrated by my analyses of children in Austria. Children in Vienna during the war may have had some of the lowest health indicators, but following the war they improved the fastest. While this recovery was certainly multicausal, it surely helped that the Austrian hub for children to be sent to places where they could get better food was Vienna, and that Vienna itself served as a central location for international aid groups and their warehouses of food.

When relying on generalizations about different hunger levels between urban and rural civilians, or between any groups competing for the same foodstuffs, the psychology of hunger as well as existing biases must be taken into account. When one group blames their hunger on another group, their assessment may be correct, they may be demonstrating their own biases, or, in more severe cases, they may simply be demonstrating psychological symptoms typical of those who are experiencing starvation. In this chapter I have tried to add nuance to the urban/rural debate by analyzing biases against "stupid" peasants in places like Hungary. I have shown that, at least sometimes, urban/rural geography within a state is less important for gaining access to food than wealth is; certainly in Strasbourg, where rural and urban differences disappear once socio-economic background is taken into account, as well as in Lebanon, though not in the Russian Famine of 1921–1922, where the differential impact on rural and urban communities is decisively demarcated

[101] Healy, *Vienna and the Fall of the Habsburg Empire*, 300–3. For an example of society that coalesced to feed vulnerable citizens rather than fell apart during WWII, see Ingrid de Zwarte, *The Hunger Winter: Fighting Famine in the Occupied Netherlands, 1944–1945* (Cambridge University Press, 2020).

by geography. I have also underscored the importance of timing when assessing urban and rural differences. Finally, because of the mass movement of urban children into rural areas both locally and abroad, there were opportunities for some of the urban and rural biases, as well as national and international enmity, to be softened, though the extent to which this actually happened requires further research.

Taken together my findings suggest that a civilian's ability to obtain food depended on access, and that physical location in a rural or urban area was not a guarantee of access. Wealth and social connections, which were not particular to one specific geography, were vital. The determination by many to maintain and demonstrate social hierarchies through language and dress, even as the toils of war became ever more evident, may have served the elite, or would-be elite, as a tool to obtain food. Social hierarchies and socio-economic differences are the discussion of the next chapter.

8 Food Hierarchies
Class, Status, and Social Divisions

Claire Morelon

Food shortages did not only affect different countries in Europe with more or less severity, they also did not impact everyone equally within European societies. The First World War accentuated the existent disparities of wealth. The lack of available food reinforced previous differences between rich and poor in most countries but access to food also determined new social hierarchies. As seen in the previous chapter, class was often the biggest factor in determining the level of deprivation. Furthermore, the ability to secure food supply in wartime Europe could depend on some other factors: degree of personal connection to rural producers, merchants, or government distribution officers; physical fitness to stand in line or travel to the countryside; willingness to engage in illegal trading. A censorship report on letters sent from the home front in Austria-Hungary noted the anger generated by this asymmetry in suffering: 'The circles to which the war has brought economic downfall or stagnation look with envy and hatred to those whom the events have brought well-being and riches. As well as the opposition between rich and poor, other oppositions have been amplified.'[1] The meaning of social class itself was thus in flux and threatened through wartime shortages: social positions that seemed secured before the war could be turned upside down by the new food hierarchy. As most people saw a decline in their standard of living during this period, it is important to distinguish between the reality of impoverishment and the often imagined riches accumulated by other sections of society. Various narratives about profiteers and nouveaux riches often reflected more the fears and social insecurities of the times than a stable sociological category. Other prejudices and cleavages between national or religious communities could also be mobilized to explain unequal food consumption.

This chapter examines this reconfiguration of the hierarchies within European societies along perceptions and reality of food access. The

[1] ÖStA, KA, FA, AOK, GZNB, K3751, no. 4647, Censorship report May 1917.

rising costs of living everywhere meant that a higher proportion of household income had to be devoted to food. Employees on fixed incomes were particularly hit by the changing economic conditions. The level of wages did not keep up with the increased prices of food products. Within families even, the food was not shared equitably, with women often sacrificing their own portion to feed their husband or their children. Worsened material conditions sharpened old social divisions and created new ones. In many countries, it was easier for the rich to still obtain food despite rationing, which fed resentment against the comparatively better-off. The term 'profiteer' and its equivalent in other languages came to define the perceived enemy, who lived in opulence during times of scarcity and took advantage of the reduced circumstances of others. For middle-class people whose identity was linked to their class status, the struggles they experienced to obtain basic consumption goods were experienced as *déclassement*. Hunger both weakened and strengthened different communities: outsiders were increasingly considered as additional mouths to feed. In Central and Eastern Europe, the discourse against profiteers often targeted Jews and turned into virulent antisemitism. The growing numbers of refugees in many cities of the hinterland all over the continent also generated competition for dwindling food supplies with local populations trying to preserve rations and entitlements. Hunger thus transformed the self-perceptions of many Europeans and their positions within established social hierarchies.

Rising Cost of Living

As we have seen in previous chapters, the hunger crisis during the First World War developed progressively. It first manifested itself as a cost-of-living crisis, which more immediately affected the poorer sections of the population. European and Ottoman societies before the war were still characterized by strong disparities in wealth and income. Social structures varied enormously across the continent, but, despite overall improvement of living standards, food remained a primary item of expenditure for many. In France, Great Britain, and Germany, food purchases still accounted for a little under half of household budgets. In the German Empire, for example, in 1907 42.8 per cent of the budget was devoted to food among the general population and 60 per cent among workers.[2] An increase in prices still had the potential to endanger the ability to purchase sufficient food.

[2] Christophe Charle, *La Crise des sociétés impériales: Allemagne, France, Grande-Bretagne (1900–1940). Essai d'histoire sociale comparée* (Paris: Seuil, 2001), 45.

The very beginning of the war in July 1914 already created a slight movement of panic and hoarding, which led to short-term increases in food prices in several belligerent countries. In Riga, as early as 6 August (old Russian calendar, corresponding to 24 July) 1914, several food shops were demolished because of an increase in prices, as authorities assured the population that there was no reason for rising prices when the supplies of food were still sufficient.[3] In Prague, the high demand for flour, bread, and other food items in the first days after the mobilization created an immediate small penury. On 29 July, 100 kg of flour already cost 7 crowns more than a few days earlier (it went from 43 crowns to 50 crowns).[4] Great Britain also experienced a sudden rise in food prices after the outbreak of the war that was not caused by any scarcity.[5]

These first price increases receded in the following months, but the strains war put on global economies and state finances soon generated more lasting price changes. The First World War generated a global inflationary crisis on an unprecedented scale. All belligerent countries were affected to a greater or smaller extent. The experience of rising cost of living was shared across the globe, from Argentina to Japan.[6] Prices in basic commodities rose everywhere in Europe during the First World War. For consumers, it was a radically new experience as prices had been highly stable before 1910. Many countries during and immediately after the conflict started to compile for the first time index price numbers to measure the increase of the cost of living and compare them with the evolution of wages. These were used to settle labour disputes as the prices rose quicker than they had in previous decades and salaries did not always reflect the increase. The last two years of the war and the first post-war years were marked by numerous strikes all across Europe where workers asked for higher wages to be able to continue to purchase basic goods.

The International Labour Office (ILO) in the early 1920s compiled international comparisons of these index numbers. A true comparison of these different proportional values is very uneasy as different countries included different goods in their measurement and calculated them based on the prices observed in a greater or smaller number of towns. They sometimes only reflect the prices of certain goods in the capital city. They also registered official prices, which becomes particularly

[3] *Jaunākās Ziņas*, 25 July 1914.

[4] Alois Žipek, ed., *Domov za války: svědectví účastníků* (Prague: Pokrok, 1929), vol. I, 309.

[5] *The Lancet*, 22 August 1914, 511.

[6] Jamie Martin, 'Strained Interdependence: Inflation and Uprisings in Colonial Economies in the First World War', *American Historical Review* 128:2 (2023), 767–82.

problematic in economies that relied heavily on black market circuits where goods were unavailable for the official prices and could only be purchased at a much higher price (which was the case in the former Central Powers, for example). Despite these limitations, these numbers still provide an imperfect picture of the magnitude of the changes in food prices on the continent. Every major belligerent as well as neutrals experienced a rise in prices to various degrees. In many cases, prices continued to go up after 1918 although spikes occurred at different times for each individual case.

Looking at the rise in prices between 1914 and 1921 can give a relative sense of the various levels of fluctuation (see Map 8.1). During this period, food prices doubled in Great Britain, the Netherlands, or Switzerland, for example, while they tripled or almost quadrupled in France. In Belgium and Italy, prices were four or five times higher (depending on the estimate) than they had been six years before. Countries in Central and Eastern Europe, however, were hit on a different scale as can be seen in the case of Germany (12 times higher), Finland (12 times higher), Czechoslovakia (16 times higher), Austria (Vienna) (100 times higher), and Poland (Warsaw) (200 times higher). These numbers are partially explained by post-war hyperinflation and currency changes, especially in Austria or Poland, but the price increases in wartime were already substantial: in Vienna prices were 17 times higher in 1918 compared to 1914.[7] Wartime inflation explains the high increase in Czechoslovakia despite its relatively successful post-war economic stabilization. Other regions in the East not represented in the ILO survey indicate a similar upward spiral of prices aggravated by post-war instability. In Riga, prices in 1919 were 20 to 30 times higher than what they had been in peacetime.[8] In Hungary, according to the ARA, prices for basic food and clothing items in June 1920 were about 130 times higher than in 1914.[9] The methods of collection of these prices do not permit to establish a systematic ranking of countries, as each country devised their own model of measurement, but these numbers point to a more dramatic rise in prices in the East of the continent.

Nowhere, however, did increases in wages keep up with the increase in prices of foodstuffs, which implied falling standards of living all over the

[7] *International Labour Review*, IV:2 (1921), 88. On the different compiling methods, see *Methods of Compiling Cost of Living Index Numbers: Report Prepared for the Second International Conference of Labour Statisticians* (Geneva: International Labour Office, 1925). On the ILO, see Bruno Cabanes, *The Great War and the Origins of Humanitarianism, 1918–1924* (Cambridge: Cambridge University Press, 2014).

[8] *Latvijas Sargs*, 29 January 1919.

[9] American Relief Administration European Children's Fund, *Final Report of the Work in Hungary* (Budapest: The American Relief Administration, 1920), 5.

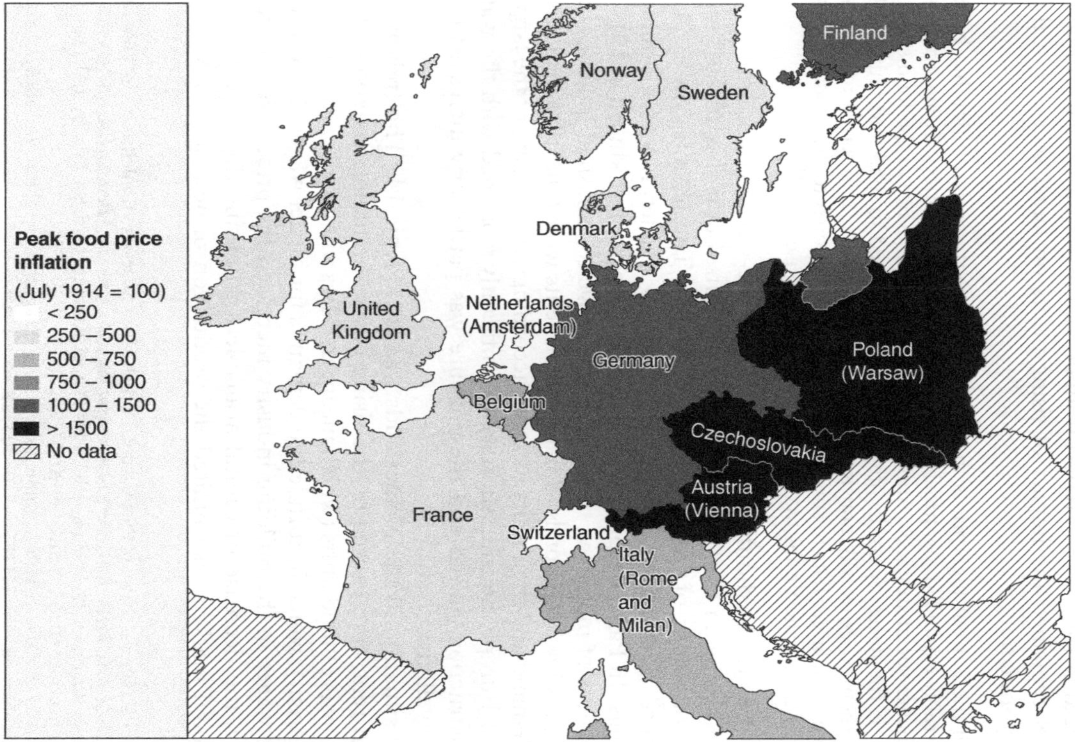

Map 8.1 Variations in index prices for food products in Europe, 1914–1921.
Credit: Geodienst

continent. Workers and employees had to spend a much higher part of their income to secure food, which had consequences on other essential costs such as housing or clothing. Even in neutral Switzerland the share of a worker's household budget devoted to food went from 44.1 to 47.7 per cent after the war.[10] A report from the municipal physician in Prague in 1918 explained the impact of rising prices on larger sections of the urban population:

> through the current high prices the concept of poverty or destitution has been considerably expanded, comprising through the increased prices always broader and broader social strata. ... Another important consequence of the food shortages ... is the necessity to devote all the money earned to food and reduce all other expenses, especially housing expenses. As a result, an internal move has occurred from larger flats to smaller ones, from smaller ones to the smallest ones and from the smallest ones to cellars, former warehouses, etc.[11]

Thus, the increased difficulty to get food at pre-war prices did not only mean a change in diets and consumption habits, but it also affected the living conditions of many urban populations. The tenants who could not afford their rent anymore had to move to smaller, less comfortable dwellings. In Paris, despite the moratorium on rents introduced in 1914, many wives of mobilized men needed to move to furnished lodgings or rent rooms in cheap hotels. Smaller apartments were thus in particularly high demand and their rents went up accordingly.[12] In many of the large cities of Europe, housing shortages significantly worsened with the war as construction slowed and the pressure was particularly increased on small dwellings.

The situation in the Netherlands was fairly typical.[13] The (relative) rises in rent were caused by the rising costs of building materials, the rising costs of foodstuffs (which meant that less money was available for paying rent), which in turn led to demands for higher wages. However, higher wages in the building industry increased the prices even more. Finally, the decrease of capital available for housing due to shortage on capital markets also limited the production of new houses, which

[10] Daniel Krämer, Chrisian Pfister, and Daniel Marc Segesser, 'Einleitung', in *"Woche für Woche neue Preisaufschläge": Nahrungsmittel-, Energie-, und Ressourcenkonflikte in der Schweiz des Ersten Weltkrieges*, edited by Daniel Krämer, Chrisian Pfister, and Daniel Marc Segesser (Basel: Schwabe, 2016), 25.

[11] Report from the health commission to the Prague City Council, ÖStA, AdR, Volkernährungsamt, K112, no. 103303, 28 May 1918.

[12] Susanne Magri, 'Les propriétaires, les locataires, la loi. Jalons pour une analyse sociologique des rapports de location, Paris 1850–1920', *Revue française de sociologie*, 37–3 (1996), 413.

[13] On Germany, see C. Edmunc Clingan, 'More Construction, More Crisis: The Housing Problem of Weimar Germany', *Journal of Urban History*, 26:5 (2000), 630–44.

declined from about 20,000 in 1913 to about 2,500 in 1918.[14] The Dutch government during the second half of the war enacted several laws (as did other wartime governments in France and Britain) to create price ceilings for rents and later make it illegal to evict tenants in rent-controlled housing. But this does not seem to have stopped rent hikes: rents in Amsterdam increased on average 12.9 per cent from March 1909 until October 1919 (corrected for inflation), with the lowest rents seeing the largest increases. Houses with a yearly rent up to Fl. 52 (lowest bracket) saw increases of about 31.8 per cent.[15] The increase in food prices (as the central expense in household budgets) formed part of a broader decline in living standards, as highlighted in the German caricatures in Figure 8.1. The first one shows the reduced amount of food obtained through 60 per cent of an average income from 1913 to 1923 and the other the prohibitive increases in living expenses (food, fuel, housing, clothing).

The surprise and anguish that the rising prices caused to European populations in their daily lives during the war is manifest in the frequent mentions of prices in diaries or letters sent from the home front. The diary of Edvard Beneš's wife for the year 1917 almost exclusively contains records of prices she paid for food in the countryside, sometimes comparing them with the current prices in Prague.[16] Diary entries or letters sometimes display a mix of disbelief and anger at the unprecedented cost of certain food items. In his diary, journalist Paul Max describes his reaction to some food prices in Brussels in 1917: 'A lassitude, a form of disillusioned philosophy takes you over as, walking by a pastry shop window, you see small biscuits for 0.50 francs, pralines for 2.50 francs per 100 grams, large cakes (large is a figure of speech) for 8, 9, 10 francs.'[17] Prices also reveal to soldiers how desperate the situation at home had become. A wife from Bohemia writing to her husband, for example, comments on the high prices at the black market: 'We don't do anything else but go to villages and there to ask people

[14] Joost van Genabeek and Louise Rietbergen, *De S.D.A.P. en de volkshuisvesting. Inhoud en resultaten van het sociaaldemocratische volkshuisvestingsbeleid in Nederland* (1894–1940) (Utrecht: s.l., 1991), 47–54; Martin Kraaijestein, 'Lokale noden en lokaal beleid', in *Leven naast de catastrofe. Nederland tijdens de Eerste Wereldoorlog*, edited by Hans Binnenveld, Martin Kraaijestein, Marja Roholl, and Paul Schulten (Hilversum: Uitgeverij Verloren, 2001), 63–77, here 68–9.

[15] van Genabeek and Rietbergen, *De S.D.A.P. en de volkshuisvesting*, 65–7.

[16] Dagmar Hájková and Eva Kalivodová (eds.), *Deníky Edvarda a Hany Benešových z období první světové války (1915–1918)* (Prague: Masarykův archiv, 2013), 202–4.

[17] Paul Max, *Journal de guerre de Paul Max. Notes d'un Bruxellois pendant l'occupation (1914–1918)*, edited by Benoît Majerus and Sven Soupart (Brussels: Archives de la Ville de Bruxelles, 2006), 110.

Figure 8.1 German cartoons on the rise of living expenses.
Source: Cadbury Research Library: Special collections, University of Birmingham, Eglantyne Jebb Papers: Germany, Box SCF A404

for an enormous amount of money to give us milk (1 liter for 1 crown) or butter.'[18] A priest also detailed the rise in prices of different foodstuffs in the parish chronicle.[19] In Dalmatia, where the shortages were particularly severe, a woman illustrated the unavailability of foodstuffs through their prices: 'Here there is no other food than herbs. Here a quart [65 kg] of corn costs 100 crowns.'[20] All these recordings of prices in ego documents, letters or chronicles underline the astonishment at the rapid increases. Comparisons with other locations also show the bewilderment at such huge variations and the uncertainty generated by the wartime conditions. A refugee in Innsbruck notes that eggs cost 90 heller [1 heller = 1/100 crown] there while 'in Germany the meat costs 16 crowns and the eggs 45 heller each'.[21] Rapid price increases made daily survival more difficult but also participated in the disorientating changes brought on by wartime. It was not just the price increases per se, but helplessness in the face of price variations one could not predict or even understand. In Paris, the changes of prices in real time were experienced as illogical and led to the feeling of being robbed among the public.[22]

In countries subject to post-war hyperinflation, the subjective sense of time was accelerated as money needed to be spent quickly.[23] Everywhere, the inflationary crisis reinforced the impression of uncertainty of those years and heightened anxieties about the future.

Unequal Access to Food

The price increase for common goods made access to food increasingly a matter of social class. As Herbert Hoover noted: 'famine does not occur according to popular ideas. In a country on a food supply below normal necessity all the people do not suffer in the same measure, nor die at the same time. The rich continue to live, despite any rigour in division; the

[18] ÖStA, KA, FA, AOK, GZNB, K3797, no 2352, Letter from Franziska P., Schlan, 25 August 1917.

[19] Státní Okresní Archiv Plzeň Sever, Farní Archiv, Vysoká Libyně, Kronika fary.

[20] ÖStA, KA, FA, AOK, GZNB, K3749, no. 4574, Letter from Milica M. to Italy without a date, Knin (Dalmatia) [report on March 1917].

[21] Diary written by Francesco Segato in Diego Leoni, Camillo Zadra (ed.), *La città di legno: Profughi trentini in Austria (1915–1918)* (Trento: TEMI, 1981), 145.

[22] Anaïs Albert, *La Vie à crédit. La consommation des classes populaires à Paris (années 1880–1920)* (Paris: Éditions de la Sorbonne, 2021), 125.

[23] Nathan Marcus, *Austrian Reconstruction and the Collapse of Global Finance, 1921–1931* (Cambridge, MA: Harvard University Press, 2018), 56–7; on German inflation, see Gerald D. Feldman, *The Great Disorder: Politics, Economics, and Society in the German Inflation, 1914–1924* (Oxford: Oxford University Press, 1997).

poor get weak, and weaker, and die—of something else than famine.'[24] Inequalities in food supply stoked existing social divisions. Richer sections of the population were better able to pay for food even at exorbitant prices, which emphasized the notion that wartime sacrifice was not shared equally. A mother writing to her son from Kolín in Bohemia expressed this resentment: 'The big merchants are becoming millionaires but we the poor people don't know what will become of us. The rich don't even know that there is a war on, they live in abundance.'[25] In the occupied industrial regions of Northern France, pre-war antagonism between workers and their bosses was further aggravated by the perception that the middle classes were still able to feed themselves properly and get provisions through gold while workers spent their whole income on food.[26] The notion that the war levelled class differences in terms of access to food could have a basis of truth in some societies. In Belgium or Switzerland, children from poorer backgrounds sometimes fared better than before the war because of the extent of aid.[27] In Britain as well, according to some measures, working-class diets improved during the war.[28] However, in societies where shortages were more substantial and with a thriving black market, access to basic items was determined by money.

As the war went on and food became scarcer, tensions grew: anyone else seemed relatively privileged for increasingly hungry citizens. It was not only the rich who were the target of envy. Other social groups were seen as better provided for; peasants and rural populations possessed the advantage of being closer to production in the minds of urban-dwellers (see Chapter 7). In Belgium, Baron von Falkenhausen, the Governor-General of Belgium noted that by the summer of 1917 tensions were high between classes and between city-dwellers and farmers.[29] Inflation

[24] Herbert Hoover, 'Preface', in *The Food Problem*, edited by Vernon Kellogg and Alonzo Taylor (New York, NY: Macmillan, 1917), v–ix, vii.

[25] NA, PP 1916–1920, ka 3076, no. 29091, report from 16 October 1916.

[26] James Connolly, *The Experience of Occupation in the Nord 1914–1918: Living with the Enemy in First World War France* (Manchester: Manchester University Press, 2018), 128.

[27] On Zürich, see Ismael Albertin, 'Die Massnahmen des Zürcher Stadtrats zur Verbesserung der Lebensmittelversorgung 1914–1921', in *'Woche für Woche neue Preisaufschläge': Nahrungsmittel-, Energie-, und Ressourcenkonflikte in der Schweiz des Ersten Weltkrieges* edited by Daniel Krämer, Chrisian Pfister, and Daniel Marc Segesser (Basel: Schwabe, 2016), 229; on Belgium, see Henri Pirenne, *La Belgique et la guerre mondiale* (Paris: Presses Universitaires de France, 1928), 163.

[28] See Jay M. Winter, *The Great War and the British People* (London, Macmillan, 1985); Ian Gazeley and Andrew Newell, 'The First World War in Working-Class Food Consumption in Britain', *European Review of Economic History*, 17 (2013), 71–91.

[29] J. Wullus-Rudiger, *Flamenpolitik: suprême Espoir allemande de domination en Belgique* (Brussels: Rossel, 1922), 12. See also Michaël Amara and Hubert Roland, eds., *Gouverner en Belgique occupée: Oskar von der Lancken-Wakenitz – rapports d'activité 1915–1918* (Brussels: Peter Lang, 2004).

also disproportionately affected people on fixed salaries that were not sufficiently adjusted to the change in prices compared to those reliant on other sources of income. Workers in many countries were often represented as comparatively more protected, especially those working for war industries. Middle-class clerks in Germany denounced the better wages of workers.[30] However, as Antoine Prost has shown, real wages for workers did not rise significantly during this period except in a few sectors in France and Britain and they fell in Germany, Italy, and Russia.[31] The loss in purchasing power for workers as well was more marked in Central and Eastern Europe. For workers in Austria-Hungary, the war experience defined new hierarchies based on the type of access to food (some factories were able to directly provide for their workers). The general declining living standards also affected workers in their pride as family providers.[32]

Unequal distribution of food was not only geographical or social: even within the family unit, once food had been acquired, it was not distributed equally among its members. Reinhard Sieder's study of working-class life in Vienna shows that, in continuity with pre-war practices, fathers as heads of households had priority over their children and wife, as his labour provided the most important source of family income. The older son then often took the place of the father as men left for the front and received a larger portion of the food the family could obtain.[33] The Austrian system of food rationing delivered tickets per household and this also meant that servants could be unfavourably treated by their employers in terms of food distribution within the household.[34] Women whose task it often was to find and purchase food for the household would sometimes reduce their own food intake to give more to their children. In Belgium, The *Comité National de Secours et d'Alimentation* took particular care of pregnant and breastfeeding women: they received extra meals, which they had to take in the official setting of the *cantines maternelles* ('mothers' canteens') to ensure they would not share with the

30 Jon Lawrence, 'Material pressures on the middle classes', in *Capital Cities at War: Paris, London, Berlin 1914–1919*, edited by Jean-Louis Robert and Jay Winter (Cambridge: Cambridge University Press, 1997), 254.

31 Antoine Prost, 'Workers', in *The Cambridge History of the First World War*, edited by Jay Winter (Cambridge: Cambridge University Press, 2014), vol. III, 343.

32 Rudolf Kučera, *Rationed Life: Science, Everyday Life, and Working-Class Politics in the Bohemian Lands, 1914–1918* (New York: Berghahn, 2016).

33 Reinhard Sieder, 'Behind the lines: working-class family life in wartime Vienna', in *The Upheaval of War: Family, Work, and Welfare in Europe, 1914–1918*, edited by Richard Wall and Jay Winter (Cambridge: Cambridge University Press, 1988), 114.

34 Maureen Healy, *Vienna and the Fall of the Habsburg Empire: Total War and Everyday Life in World War I* (Cambridge: Cambridge University Press, 2004), 70.

rest of the household. However, hunger could also break down parental links. The American Relief Administration in Czechoslovakia advised to make sure that the food would get delivered to the children themselves and not their parents, questioning parental care for food provision: 'The [parents] have often been accused of being the worst enemies of their children (with respect to food) and in one town (Asch) we were told that there was no maternal love.'[35]

Food shortages were not equally distributed throughout societies. They tended to magnify pre-existing divisions according to class (and gender) lines. Discourses emphasized the levelling of differences or the improved status of workers, but these remained exceptions on a continental scale. The difficulty to obtain food and to maintain living standards also impacted subjective perceptions of social status. It was not only the number of calories and the level of wages that mattered for many, but also the humiliation of downward social mobility.

Erosion of Status through Hunger

Across Europe, many accounts of wartime hardship often disproportionately focus on the downward social trajectory of the middle class. The category of the middle class encompassed different social categories depending on the country but, generally, educated employees on fixed incomes had indeed been particularly affected by rising prices: professors, army officers, artists, and governmental officials were all part of the 'nouveaux pauvres'.[36] This social category also attracted more sympathy from the journalists or the aid workers who wrote about the food crisis in wartime and post-war cities.

War disrupted the social hierarchies that had shaped pre-war societies until then. Inflation had devalued employees' wages and rentiers' incomes, which left many petit bourgeois households in reduced circumstances. To be sure, working-class households were even more constrained to abandon the consumption patterns to which they had grown accustomed.[37] Yet, the image of middle-class hardship symbolized the upturned social order. *The New York Times* reported about former Russian princesses and industrialists who sought work as typists

[35] HILA, ARA, EOR, Box 345, Folder 2, Czechoslovakia Child Relief Historical Record, report from Karlsbad, 24 May 1919.
[36] See, for example, a description for Hungary: American Relief Administration European Children's Fund, *Final Report of the Work in Hungary* (Budapest: The American Relief Administration, 1920).
[37] For a case study on Paris, see Albert, *La Vie à crédit*. 118–19.

or translators in Riga after having fled the Bolshevik Revolution.[38] The widow of an imperial tax officer in Prague complained of the demeaning aspect of having to stand in line 'in the crowd'. She considered it was more difficult for her than for working-class women to get coal as they 'were used to carrying burdens'.[39] A journalist in Warsaw made a similar argument about the hardships of unemployment for white-collar professionals who were 'physically more delicate' than workers and could thus not as easily find work.[40] The hardships suffered by these 'nouveaux pauvres' were not necessarily greater than those of the poorest sections of the population but the common perception was that their previous social standing gave an additional dimension to their suffering.

Clothing served as an indicator of the upturned social hierarchies in wartime. While the nouveaux riches ostentatiously wore expensive clothes which did not 'correspond' to their pre-war status, the impoverished middle classes' elegant garments sometimes seemed incongruous in their new situation. Writer Władysław Glinka who lived on an estate outside Warsaw described the new urban field workers they had recruited:

> While on holiday in Warsaw, my daughter got 40 men and women to agree to work for ten rubles per month and food (bread, flour, grits, pork fat, milk, salt, soap). Among them were typesetters, mechanics, painters, florists, seamstresses, lace makers, etc. None of them had ever held a hoe in their hands before, and they were dressed very lightly, in straw hats, dinner jackets, batiste blouses and lacquered slippers ...![41]

Eager people from various social backgrounds also came forward for organized public works. 'Alongside thick workers' jackets and women in headscarves, here and there are glimpses of a more elegantly cut, though now grayed overcoat, or hat, testifying to "better times" of not long ago.'[42] Similarly, the vision of better clothed people of all ages and genders felling their own wood and carrying it back to the city struck Lord Beveridge as a

[38] 'Princesses Work as Riga Typists', *New York Times*, 31 May 1921, 8.

[39] Claire Morelon, *Streetscapes of War and Revolution: Prague, 1914–1920* (Cambridge: Cambridge University Press, 2024), 179.

[40] Robert Blobaum, *A Minor Apocalypse: Warsaw during the First World War* (Ithaca, NY: Cornel University Press, 2017), 68.

[41] W. Glinka, 'Pamiętnik z wielkiej wojny. Narew – Berezyna, Warszawa 1927', in *Śmierć Wygnanie Głód w dokumentach osobistych: Ziemie polskie w latach Wielkiej Wojny 1914–1918* [Death Exile Hunger in personal documents: Polish lands in the years of the Great War 1914–1918], edited by Katarzyna Sierakowska (Warsaw: Institute of History, Polish Academy of Sciences, 2015), 221.

[42] *Tygodnik Ilustrowany*, 1 I 1916, nr. 1, pg. 6 quoted in Glinka 'Pamiętnik z wielkiej wojny', 221.

symbol of the 'breakdown of civilization' in post-war Vienna.[43] However, the constant rise in the price of clothing threatened even this visible remnant of social status. As a Viennese newspaper complained in 1918: 'until now it was at least possible to maintain a barrier in the external appearance through clothing to separate the middle classes from the army of the dispossessed'.[44] Another complained that women in middle-class professions (clerks, teachers) needed to look presentable and wear a hat, for example, while 'the proletarian woman can spend all that she earns for food'.[45] The outward signs of respectability was more difficult to uphold as every bit of money needed to be spent on food.

As William Rosenberg has recently argued for Russia, the experience of loss became a defining feature of this period as the scarcity of essential goods worsened.[46] Social descent was portrayed by the painter Ivan Vladimirov who, for example, showed the former elite living in large apartments gathering in a single room where the parquet floor had been ripped to be used for fuel.[47] In Vienna, the middle classes progressively sold their belongings to pay for food. As visitors to the city noticed, auction houses and shops were overflowing with Biedermeier furniture, Persian rugs, antiques and glass objects which could be purchased at a cheap price by foreigners or the nouveaux riches. As aid worker Ruth Fry remarked of their previous owners: 'Their houses remained, to haunt them like ghosts of former happiness, and to provide, one by one, treasured possessions which could be sold to obtain a little food.'[48] A newspaper reported the high number of objects on offer at the Dorotheum auction house in December 1920, lamenting the 'pauperization of the middle classes': 'Many families for which the privations have become unbearable sell their last heirlooms.'[49]

Popular figures of social downfall also underlined the inversion of values brought on by the war. In Hugo Bettauer's 'novel from our days' *The Joyless Street*, describing conditions in post-war Vienna, the bourgeois daughter of a former court councilor who left his family destitute after

[43] William Henry Beveridge, *Peace in Austria: A Study of Social and Industrial Conditions with a Programme for Reconstruction Based on a Personal Visit to Austria* (London: Fight the Famine Council, 1920), 14–16.

[44] *Wiener Neueste Nachrichten*, 19 August 1918, 4.

[45] *Die Frau*, 14 June 1919, 4.

[46] William G. Rosenberg, *States of Anxiety: Scarcity and Loss in Revolutionary Russia* (Oxford: Oxford University Press, 2023).

[47] Ivan Vladimirov, 'Miserable Life of Russian Nobles and Persons of High Rank during the Revolution', 1919, Ivan Alekseevich Vladimirov Paintings, HILA.

[48] A. Ruth Fry, *A Quaker Adventure: The Story of Nine Years' Relief and Reconstruction* (London: Nisbet, 1926), 225.

[49] *Neues Wiener Journal*, 7 December 1920, 2.

committing suicide is reduced to contemplate prostitution to survive.[50] Wartime inflation had sparked concerns all over Habsburg Austria that food shortages had driven women from 'better' social classes to prostitution. Some voices even expressed sympathy for the wives of state employees resorting to it to feed their families.[51] Indeed, in contrast with the pre-war period, a third of arrested clandestine prostitutes in Vienna in 1921 belonged to the middle classes, including female civil servants and officers' wives.[52] The middle classes also feared that class status could not be preserved in the next generation and that children could not afford to study as they had to start working as teenagers for their upkeep.[53] The image of middle-class despair at dire prospects leading to suicide became commonplace in post-war Germany even though there is no evidence that a higher proportion of middle-class persons committed suicide.[54]

Authorities in charge of food distribution often displayed particular sympathy for the humiliating aspect of shortages for the middle classes and found ways to mitigate the plight of those who had to rely on relief measures. In Belgium, the *Comité National de Secours et d'Alimentation* (National Committee of Aid and Food Supply) prided itself on being attuned to social sensitivities as its director Francqui wrote to Hoover.[55] Officers' wives, for instance, received help in cash, not kind. US minister to Brussels Whitlock reported the words of one *Comité* official: 'We can't say, … Madame, if you need a *chemise* you need only to come and ask us.'[56] The *Assistance discrète* (Discreet Help) in Belgium, an organization created at the initiative of members of the Brussels bourgeoisie, offered meals while sparing the shame of members of the middle class who were too proud to ask for charity or be seen to queue and needing assistance. As befitted its title, the *Assistance* distributed aid discreetly. One chronicle explained how respectable housewives

> who are in want but dare not present themselves at the soup kitchens because of their social rank, make their way in all discretion to the Collège Saint-Michel; upon entering, they hand in their empty shopping-bag, and at the end of a

[50] Hugo Bettauer, *Die Freudlose Gassse: ein Wiener Roman aus unseren Tagen* (Vienna: R. Löwit, 1925).

[51] Nancy Wingfield, *The World of Prostitution in Late Imperial Austria* (Oxford: Oxford University Press, 2017), 236.

[52] *Öffentliche Sicherheit: Polizei-Rundschau*, 1:1 (1921), 8.

[53] *Die Frau*, 25 December 1919, 2.

[54] Christian Goeschel, *Suicide in Nazi Germany* (Oxford: Oxford University Press, 2009), 19.

[55] Liane Ranieri, *Emile Francqui ou l'intelligence créatrice: 1863–1935* (Paris: Duculot, 1985), 164 (a letter of 5 November 1916).

[56] Brand Whitlock, *Belgium: A Personal Narrative* (New York, NY: D. Appleton and Company, 1919), vol. 1, 575.

corridor they pick it up again, filled with bread, vegetables, and bones. It is all done in silence, almost mysteriously. In this way, ladies who remain unseen … offer relief to mothers who would be mortified at being recognized – and who, in this way, acquire all they need to make a nourishing soup in the privacy of their own home.[57]

This issue was also prevalent in other European countries where attempts to spare the pride of the 'bashful poor' were common.[58] The middle classes who ran many of the aid programmes, both local and foreign, also felt a stronger empathy for people from a similar social background.

As war kitchens to feed hungry urban populations multiplied in the Central Powers and beyond, the demeaning aspect of their association with pre-war soup kitchens complicated their operation. In Zagreb, separate spaces were used for paupers and middle classes to avoid mixing, but many middle-class members still hid their faces in photographs, highlighting the shame associated with charity.[59] In Berlin, purpose-built public kitchens failed to attract as many clients as they hoped in 1916 because they were conceived as a mass dining arrangement for all classes and thus still felt like poor relief. Members of the lower middle class would not frequent them, which in return tarnished their image among working-class men and women.[60] In Freiburg, attempts to open three 'middle-class kitchens' more closely resembling restaurants in 1917 failed to make the prospect of communal eating more attractive for the target audience.[61] The opposite effect was true in Prague where the municipal council created public kitchens for the middle classes where meals had to be pre-paid (to avoid the formation of queues) and where the personnel was supposed to treat everyone politely. Despite being more expensive than regular public kitchens, these establishments were in the end frequented by a much broader section of the population, especially among the working classes.[62] Markers of class (white tablecloths, flower arrangements, table service) were a way to preserve pre-war social status (see Figure 8.2). The failure to target middle-class customers for

[57] Louis Gille et al., *Cinquante mois d'occupation allemande* (Brussels: Dewit, 1919), Vol. II, 312 (24 September 1916).

[58] *Die Frau*, 14 June 1919, 4.

[59] Stefano Petrungaro, 'Soup Kitchens and Yugoslav Poor Relief between the Two World Wars', *European Review of History: Revue Européenne d'histoire* 26:1 (2019), 150.

[60] Belinda Davis, *Home Fires Burning: Food, Politics, and Everday Life in World War I Berlin* (Chapel Hill, NC: University of North Carolina Press, 2000), 141.

[61] Roger Chickering, *The Great War and Urban Life in Germany: Freiburg, 1914–1918* (Cambridge: Cambridge University Press, 2007), 458.

[62] Kučera, *Rationed Life*, 40–3; for a comparison of the failure in Berlin and success in Vienna, see Jenny Sprenger-Seyffarth, *Kriegsküchen in Wien und Berlin: Öffentliche Massenverpflegung und private Familienmahlzeit im und nach dem Ersten Weltkrieg* (Berlin: Transcript, 2023).

Figure 8.2 Communal lunch in a German middle-class kitchen, 1916.
Source: *Sueddeutsche Zeitung* Photo / Alamy

war kitchens in Berlin had by association discredited them in the eyes of the working classes while the opposite was true in Prague, showing the importance of perceptions of social standing even in a context of food scarcity.

The special relief provided to the middle classes also stemmed from a belief of the importance of this class within the nation's whole in the context of post-war reconstruction. The sympathy felt for the impoverished middle classes did not only reflect the social class of relief workers or municipal authorities but in some cases concerns for the nation's future and culture. British humanitarian organization Save the Children founder Eglantyne Jebb found it was a priority to help the 'right sort' of children who were more deserving because the war had put them in a new position of poverty and they were more likely to help themselves in the long run.[63] As Tomás Irish has shown, help for intellectuals in the post-war was also a means to recast bourgeois Europe and avert the danger of Bolshevism.[64] The notion that elites formed an essential component of national communities shaped responses to the food crisis. The American Relief Administration saw measures targeted at the middle classes as part of national rebuilding. State collapse had made them particularly vulnerable. A statistical bureau in Austria recorded 140,000 needy members of the middle classes.[65] Hungary concentrated a particularly high number of newly impoverished members of the middle class, increased by the former civil servants who had fled the newly lost provinces. Due to their loss of citizenship in the ceded territories, they had to depart to the remaining Hungarian territory, where very few positions were available for additional state officials. The ARA in Hungary explained their action for the needy middle classes as targeting 'useful members of society':

> The Hungarian middle-class is having great difficulty in eking out an existence. … People are obliged to sell their jewels, pianos, furniture and often their linen and clothing to buy the most necessary food-stuffs. … First of all we helped parents having many children, also sick people, pregnant women and nursing mothers, widows and orphans, of the intellectual middle-class. Second, we gave our food packages to those needy middle-class people who are worthy, useful members of society. We requested the association of judges, attorneys, lawyers, clergymen, doctors, professors, teachers, engineers, journalists, writers, artists and actors to sends us the lists of their members, that we might be able to investigate the

[63] Emily Baughan, *Saving the Children: Humanitarianism, Internationalism, and Empire* (Oakland, California: University of California Press, 2022), 27.

[64] Tomás Irish, *Feeding the Mind: Humanitarianism and the Reconstruction of European Intellectual Life, 1919–1933* (Cambridge: Cambridge University Press, 2023).

[65] Irish, *Feeding the Mind*, 63.

urgent cases and help them. Experience taught us that the families of professors, teachers, writers, artists and pensioned people, were the most needy.[66]

The ARA also helped in creating a Professors' table in Vienna in 1920 funded by American donations to provide lunch for newly poor professors of the University of Vienna. This initiative both recognized that the crisis in Vienna had 'weighted particularly heavily on certain sections of the intelligence class' and acknowledged 'the high worth of Austria's cultural mission' and the 'significance of the intelligentsia for its reconstruction'.[67] In homage to better days past, the food was served in dishes adorned with an imperial eagle.

The loss of status through lack of food reinforced envy towards those who could still afford a regular diet, but even more so against the perceived 'winners' of wartime scarcity. The feeling that war, instead of rewarding patriotic sacrifice, had encouraged profiteering behaviours shaped the wartime and post-war moral economy in many European societies.

Reality and Perception of Profiteering

The idea that a class of people was able to avoid the general hardship of war was at the heart of complaints against 'profiteers' all over Europe. Those who could still afford luxuries were seen as not participating in the common sacrifice. In societies where food shortages were substantial, any lavish consumption was suspicious. The image of the rich easily morphed into that of the 'profiteer' who took advantage of the wartime prices to make their own fortune. The term itself gained a renewed importance in public discourse during the war years. Jean-Louis Robert has shown that the representation of the profiteer in English, French, and German caricatures stood in opposition to the patriotic sacrifice of the soldier. The 'profiteer' highlighted the moral norms of in acceptable behaviour in wartime: it could range from the grocer who refused to sell their goods to the industrialists who made large profits.[68]

In the French-speaking context, the term 'accapareur' with its origins in the French revolution also surfaced, focusing more on the food trade. In German, the term *Wucherer* (usurer) gained new traction through its

[66] Jrs. J. N. Laurvik, 'American Aid for the Hungarian Intellectual Middle-Class', 7 April 1921, *Bulletin of the American Relief Administration Budapest* 2:14 (1 June 1921), 21.

[67] *Mitteilungen der American Relief Administration*, no. 46–50 (May 1921), 236.

[68] Jean-Louis Robert, 'The image of the profiteer', in *Capital Cities at War. Paris, London, Berlin 1914–1919*, edited by Jean-Louis Robert and Jay Winter (Cambridge: Cambridge University Press, 1997), 104–32.

pervasive use during the war: overcharging was now perceived as a crime against the social community and not just against the individual.[69] In the eyes of the public, the food prices were distorted by the existence of many middlemen (*Kettenhändler* in German, *ket'asy* in Czech) who made a profit by reselling goods at a higher price. Even in neutral Denmark and Sweden, profiteers were nicknamed 'goulash barons' (due to the poor-quality food with which they made a fortune by selling it to the Central Powers) and also became the subject of contemporary satire in the press and in cabarets.[70] In the Netherlands, the term *Oorlogswinstmaker* (war profiteer) became so normalized that people began to use the abbreviation OW-er (OW was also a phonetic way of spelling 'oh wee', which roughly translates to 'oh woe is me').[71] The public image all across the continent corresponded to a social reality. Some industrialists made large wartime profits through war contracts, for example.[72] However, the profiteer also became a scapegoat figure to blame for the poor food supply conditions.

Less than a defined social category, the profiteer embodied negative wartime values of selfishness and immorality. In Belgium, in the collective imagination, 'profiteers' were everywhere. (And it was true that, especially in the larger cities, businesses catering to the 'war rich' thrived: night-bars, music-halls, restaurants, and even Belgium's first couture house, *Maison Norine*.) The clandestine press lambasted those they called 'shameless moneygrubbers' and 'despicable blood-suckers'.[73] A satirical piece in a Vienna newspaper posing for a special issue as an 'organ for the interests of the profiteers' called for their union: 'An invisible chain links the smuggler who sneaks on vertiginous mountain peaks and the trafficker who moves through city streets, the Jew in caftan from the dirty

[69] Martin Geyer, *Verkehrte Welt. Revolution, Inflation und Moderne, München 1914–1924* (Göttingen: Vandenhoeck & Ruprecht, 1998), 188.

[70] Bjarne Sondergar Bendtsen, 'Neutral Merchant Seamen at War: the Experience of Scandinavian Seamen during the First World War', in *Scandinavia in the First World War: Studies in the war experience in the Northern Neutrals*, edited by Claes Ahlund (Lund: Nordic University Press, 2012), 347.

[71] Paul Moeyes, Samuël Kruizinga, and Wim Klinkert, *Nederland Neutraal. De Eerste Wereldoorlog 1914–1918* (Amsterdam: Boom, 2014), 433.

[72] Máté Rigó, *Capitalism in Chaos: How the Business Elites of Europe Prospered in the Era of the Great War* (Ithaca, NY: Cornell University Press, 2022), 191–202.

[73] Hubert Bertrand, *La presse francophone de tranchée au front belge, 1914–1918* (Brussels: Musée royal de l'armée, 1971), 51, 67; Julienne Moulinasse, *Enghien: histoire, monuments, souvenirs* (Brussels; Van Buggenhoudt, 1931); Petrus Van Nuffel, *De Duitschers in Aalst* (Aalst: Vooruitgang, 1921), 107, 211–12; Peter Scholliers, 'België dreunt in zijn voegen. Sociale en politieke troebelen, 1914–1921', in *Mensen in Oorlogstijd*, edited by F. Vanhemelryck, J.-P. Peeters, and G. Janssens (Brussel: UFSAL, 1988), 161; different articles in the clandestine press (*La Libre Belgique*, *De Vlaamsche Wachter*, etc).

East and the smoking-gentleman in irreproachable white waistcoat.'[74] The variety of profiles reflected the different nature of what was perceived as undue profit in wartime and the range of social types accused of 'profiteering'.

In popular representations, the emphasis was always on the external signs of wealth that separated the profiteers from the masses who could not afford such luxuries. The ostentatiousness also revealed the quick social ascent and the ignorance of the bourgeois codes. In all the belligerent countries, caricatures shared similar features. French representations of profiteers underlined the vulgarity of newly acquired wealth, emphasizing their taste for new clothes and the manner in which their wives exhibited jewellery.[75] In Munich, 'profiteers' were represented with ostentatious style and cigars, a love of fast cars and nightclubs.[76] In pre-revolutionary Russia, popular theatre in large industrial cities mocked the lifestyle of 'profiteers' who were sometimes sitting in the audience.[77] Ottoman portrayals of profiteers included descriptions of plentiful meals with extravagant dishes and a taste for entertainment places, which reflected their moral degeneration. The immorality of the source of profiteers' wealth was linked to their immoral ways of spending it.[78] Clothes again often acted as a marker. As headteacher Lillian Bader recalls of her Vienna youth:

> The profiteers were very much in evidence after World War One. They speculated in every conceivable commodity from dried beans to legal tender. They usually were extremely young … The latest style for gentlemen at the time happened to be a very unusual one: bright yellow overcoats, worn with a belt, rather feminine. As the black marketeers were the only ones able to afford new clothes, one could spot them as easily as if they had worn a uniform.[79]

Profiteers were often accused of buying luxury items without understanding their value. Within the art market, the nouveaux riches were perceived as newcomers who had no real appreciation for art and only used it for speculation.[80] Criticizing the bad taste and poor manners of

[74] *Die Muskete*, 4 December 1919, 2.

[75] François Bouloc, *Les profiteurs de guerre, 1914–1918* (Bruxelles: Complexe, 2008), 102–4.

[76] Geyer, *Verkehrte Welt*, 244.

[77] Hubertus Jahn, *Patriotic Culture in Russia during World War I* (Ithaca, NY: Cornell University Press, 1995), 92.

[78] Çiğdem Oğuz, *Moral Crisis in the Ottoman Empire: Society, Politics, and Gender during WWI* (London: I.B. Tauris, 2021), 105–6.

[79] Leo Baeck Institute, ME 784, Lillian Bader, 'One life is not enough: Autobiographical vignettes' (1956), 103.

[80] Maddalena Alvi, 'The Land of Cockaigne: The German Art Market and the First World War', *German History* 38:4 (2020), 594–615; see also Morelon, *Streetscapes of War and Revolution*, 277.

the profiteers was sometimes a way for the 'nouveaux pauvres' to maintain disappearing class hierarchies.

Night bars in the major cities became one of the symbols of the moral deregulation of the period where fortunes were spent for pleasure while soldiers were fighting and women were struggling to feed their families. For this reason, they had been closed in Vienna during the war especially as the encounters between people leaving these establishments at dawn and people already queuing in front of bakeries before they opened had caused altercations.[81] Jean-Louis Robert's opposition of the profiteer with the soldier giving his life for the fatherland mostly holds true for France and Britain.[82] In the Central Powers and for occupied populations, the 'profiteer' also increasingly jarred with civilian suffering as the sacrifices of front and home front became more equalized. An article in the Austrian press underlined the indecency of lavish parties with wonderful clothes, and French champagne 'as if many thousands were not bleeding for us at the front, as if many hundred thousands of poor and poorest people in Vienna alone were not fighting freezing and hungry with bitter misery'.[83] Newspapers helped propagate the moral discourse against any form of luxury consumption in wartime, targeting coffee houses and night clubs more particularly. The Hungarian conservative daily *Budapesti Hírlap* published such a complaint: 'In respect to the milk question, Dr. Sándor Petö complains and criticizes that the coffee houses and the confectioners still receive milk. In Budapest even every night club was still open which did not suit the current times.'[84] This requirement for a restriction on personal enjoyment because of widespread hardship was a direct consequence of the wartime moral economy but it did not necessarily disappear with the end of hostilities as shortages persisted. In April 1920, the regional administration in Bohemia forbade the sale of milk in Prague cafés after repeated complaints from the public that they served in their coffees milk that could be used for children.[85]

Certain foodstuffs became symbols of excessive consumption in wartime. In France, a tax on luxury goods introduced in 1917 targeted some food items such as truffles. Even bread, as the most basic and common food, could show the new nuances of wartime class and

[81] *Neues Wiener Tagblatt*, 18 May 1919, 11.

[82] Robert, 'The Image of the Profiteer', 127–8.

[83] *(Österreichische) Volks-Zeitung*, 1 March 1917, 5.

[84] 'Országos kenyérjegy-rendszer [the state system of bread tickets]', *Budapesti Hirlap*, 35:349, 15 December 1915, 11.

[85] *Aprovisace obce pražské za války a po válce 1914–1922* (Prague: Aprovisační ústav hlavního města Prahy, 1923), 259.

moral hierarchies. The more expensive types of bread, which already indicated class distinctions in the pre-war era, now represented an immoral indulgence. The wartime ban on 'pains de fantaisie' in Paris exemplified both the necessary wartime seriousness, but debates around the ban also showed the disapproval of bourgeois purchasing habits.[86] Pastry shops were closed because this type of lavish consumption became unacceptable in the wartime moral economy.[87] Pastry shops were also a symbol of wartime profiteering in Prague where authorities attempted to regulate their use of eggs.[88] In a context of more drastic shortage, the presence of white bread became sign of black marketeering. A report from the Austrian military complaining about the poor supply for the army noted that in Lemberg 'there is no food scarcity especially for the better situated classes. ... Bread is available in all coffee houses and restaurants without bread coupons. The quality of the bread is very good, without mixing of maize flour.'[89]

In regions particularly affected by scarcity, food (and other goods of primary necessity) became an important yardstick to measure commitment to the community. Paul Max in his Brussels diary comments on coal merchants: 'Ah! The accapareurs, here are good patriots whose name it would be useful to know!'[90] Authorities in Vienna attempted to mitigate public anger towards profiteers by doing just that. In 1917, pillory lists were published to shame publicly those who had been arrested for black market activities. The reaction of the public, however, was mostly characterized by disappointment: many of the contraventions to the price regulations amounted to relatively minor profits (selling at a higher price, lowering the quality of food) but none of the imagined fabulously rich profiteers appeared on the list.[91] Many European states had to find mechanisms to punish economic wrongdoing to channel resentment against food profiteers.[92] Grievances towards profiteers could only partially be appeased through justice. They also stemmed from the

[86] Tyler Stovall, *Paris and the Spirit of 1919: Consumer Struggles, Transnationalism, and Revolution* (Cambridge: Cambridge University Press, 2012), 53.

[87] Erik Langlinay, 'Consommation et ravitaillement en France durant la Première Guerre mondiale (1914–1920)', in *Au nom du consommateur: Consommation et politique en Europe et aux États-Unis au XXe siècle*, edited by Alain Chatriot (Paris: La Découverte, 2005), 40.

[88] Morelon, *Streetscapes of War and Revolution*, 184.

[89] Report from AOK Chef des Gen Stabes. 'Schleichhandel in Lemberg', ÖStA, AdR, Volksernährungsamt, AR, K148, no. 19164, 9 February 1918.

[90] Paul Max, *Journal de guerre*, 102.

[91] Healy, *Vienna and the Fall of the Habsburg Empire*, 66–7.

[92] On Belgium in the post-war, see Martin Schoups, 'Prosecuting Food Profiteers after the Armistice: a Transitional-Justice Perspective, 1919–1923', in *Doing Justice in Wartime: Multiple Interplays between Justice and Populations during the Two World Wars*, edited by Melanie Bost and Anton Vrints (Cham: Springer, 2021), 45–68.

illusion that while one is suffering, someone else was necessarily much better off. However, as Martin Geyer pointed out in the case of Munich, while the profiteer became a 'type' ripe for contemporary caricature, the that was reproached to them (engaging in black market activities) was shared by much larger sections of the population who relied on alternative modes of provisioning.[93]

The profiteer and the impoverished member of the intelligentsia were two faces of the same coin of social deregulation in the wake of the war. Satire written or drawn by the new poor on the new rich, mocking their lack of education and their vulgarity could be a form of consolation. The purchase of pianos by those who had no knowledge of music was a recurring motif, which symbolized social and personal upheaval from England where rumours of munition workers buying pianos were widespread[94] to Austria where peasants were shown having obtained them through bartering.[95]

Falling Apart

Hunger reinforced preexisting divisions in European societies as individuals were pitted against each other in their search for food. In addition to social class, national and religious differences also fuel
led resentment among consumers. In the Habsburg Empire, with its variety of languages groups, narratives of victimization quickly became nationalized. Maureen Healy has documented this 'falling apart' of an urban community around food issues in the case of Vienna but this process was not limited to the capital city of the monarchy.[96] As the Hungarian half of the Empire stopped exporting food to the Austrian half, civilians in the latter blamed their neighbours for their own food shortages. A report from the censor on letters from the Austrian half in June 1918 comments: 'While some painfully experience the growth of class and race hatreds, others indulge in embittered statements about the crass selfishness displayed in the most provocative way by certain sections of society or nationalities. Sharp accusations are currently raised against the Hungarian sister state, which, itself rolling in well-being and opulence, has shamefully abandoned the population of the other half.'[97] Other national hatreds within the Austrian half focused

[93] Geyer, *Verkehrte Welt*, 247.
[94] Adrian Gregory, *The Last Great War: British Society and the First World War* (Cambridge: Cambridge University Press, 2008), 193.
[95] *Kirekiki*, 1 September 1918, 4.
[96] Healy, *Vienna and the Fall of the Habsburg Empire.*
[97] Censorship report, ÖStA, KA, FA, AOK, GZNB, K3759, no. 5723, 7 June 1918.

on the allocation of food among the different regions. In Bohemia, industrial German-speaking regions in the North and the West accused Czech peasants from the interior of starving them. Czechs themselves claimed that the reason for their hunger was that food from Bohemia was sent to Germany and Vienna. Conversely, access to food also determined national loyalties in the wake of imperial collapse. People often considered the likelihood to receive food as they claimed belonging to one nationality or another, for example in post-war Fiume where the number of Italians grew in the census.[98]

Austria-Hungary and its successor states might seem like an exceptional case with its diversity of nationalities, but the war provoked major displacement everywhere, which increasingly put new populations into contact with each other. The army invasions on the different fronts generated an influx of refugees throughout the conflict and its aftermath in different parts of the continent (estimates indicate that between 14 and 15 million people were displaced during this period in Europe).[99] The armistice did not mean the end of population movements: border changes and revolution created new flows of refugees in the former multi-ethnic Empires. In a context of food shortages, refugees were considered as an extra burden for local populations and cultural differences magnified tensions. Belgian refugees in the Netherlands in 1917 were, for example, accused of contributing to the food crisis.[100] There were increasing demands to send the foreigners home as they were taking 'Dutch' food.

Whether or not they benefitted from state support, refugees were often particularly hit by food scarcity in regions where they were not able to draw on the same networks of support as local inhabitants. Substantial food shortages in Russia caused tensions between locals and refugees around rationing. Merchants and peasants refused to sell food products to refugees while supply commissions sometimes felt that the refugees were not entitled to be integrated to the food distribution.[101] In Ottoman Beirut, the influx of 40,000 Armenian refugees put further strain on the system of supply.[102] In the Austro-Hungarian Empire, refugees from the

[98] Dominique Reill, *The Fiume Crisis: Life in the Wake of the Habsburg Empire* (Cambridge, MA: Harvard University Press, 2020), 148.

[99] Peter Gatrell, 'Introduction', in *Europe on the Move: Refugees in the era of the Great War*, edited by Peter Gatrell and Liubov Zhvanko (Manchester: Manchester University Press, 2017), 3.

[100] Michaël Amara, 'Belgian Refugees during the First World War (France, Britain, Netherlands)', in *Europe on the Move*, 209.

[101] Peter Gatrell, *A Whole Empire Walking: Refugees in Russia during World War I* (Bloomington, IN: Indiana University Press, 1999), 192.

[102] Melanie Tanelian, 'Politics of Wartime Relief in Ottoman Beirut (1914–1918)', *First World War Studies* 5:1 (2014), 70.

Eastern regions were not only accused of adding to the number of mouths to feed in wartime but also of food hoarding and profiteering, thereby contributing to the increase in prices. The accusation of black-market trading was one of the most frequent complaints about Jewish refugees in Vienna.[103] Italian-speaking refugees from Trentino were also perceived as competitors in the food market for populations in the interior of the monarchy, which even led to violence in 1918 when they ceased to be part of the same state.[104] Anti-refugee rhetoric in the Austro-Hungarian Empire often assumed anti-Semitic overtones as around half of the refugees who had fled from Galicia and Bucovina were of Jewish faith. Hostility was not reserved to Jewish refugees. Other groups of refugees were also resented by locals as illegitimate users of common resources but the hatred of Jewish newcomers was conflated with pre-existing anti-Jewish prejudices. The overlap between different forms of exclusion from the community strengthened claims to food entitlement for the insiders.

All over Central and Eastern Europe, antisemitic discourse grew as a result of the world war. In the immediate aftermath of the war, many of these countries attempted to limit the number of Jewish residents in their cities and to send the refugees back to a home where state boundaries had changed. In Germany, according to Martin Geyer, the 'almost archaic' association between usury and Jewishness shaped an anti-Semitic discourse blaming the Jews for profiteering and economic difficulties.[105] In Hungary after the war, the right-wing discourse crystallized around a pure Christian Hungary pitted against an 'other' Hungary undermining it.[106] Hungary's Jews were blamed for the raging famine: 'Christian Hungary is starving, while the Jews are collecting every money.'[107] Even within the bourgeoisie, Christian members tended to increasingly blame Jewish traders for the economic difficulties.[108] In Prague at the end of the war, the Municipal Council accused Jewish refugees of profiteering and taking advantage of state subsidies. They recommended suspending state aid and the distribution of rationing tickets to refugees.[109]

Further East, in Lemberg/Lwów/L'viv, the Polish and Ukrainian parts of the population suspected that the Jewish population was better

[103] David Rechter, 'Galicia in Vienna: Jewish Refugees in the First World War', *Austrian History Yearbook* 28 (1997), 113–30.

[104] Marco Mondini and Francesco Frizzera, 'Beyond the Borders: Displaced Persons in the Italian Linguistic Space during the First World War' in *Europe on the Move*, 188.

[105] Geyer, *Verkehrte Welt*, 280.

[106] Paul Hanebrink, *In Defense of Christian Hungary: Religion, Nationalism, and Antisemitism, 1890–1944* (Ithaca, NY: Cornell University Press, 2006), 54.

[107] 'Egy a sok közül' [One among the many], *Egyenlőség*, 2 September 1922, 5.

[108] Rigó, *Capitalism in Chaos*, 110.

[109] Morelon, *Streetscapes of War and Revolution*, 152.

fed and had a privileged access to food provisioning. This anti-Semitic discourse was linked with accusations of having avoided military service and controlling Austrian food supply agencies. The rumours questioned the equality of wartime sacrifices performed by the Jews in the city, casting them as outsiders taking advantage of the misery. The violent pogrom taking place in the city at the end of 1918 was nominally triggered by charges of disloyalty towards the Poles but was actually based on this earlier resentment.[110] The overrepresentation of Jews in the retail trade in Warsaw generated a conflation of economic grievances with racial hatred, making Jewish merchants responsible for the rise in prices.[111] Although Riga did not see any serious anti-Jewish violence, accusations of driving up prices and better provision also surfaced there. Newspaper articles relayed these rumours: 'Jewish traders are buying harvest in the countryside from the farmers and paying much more than the costs in the cities and towns at the moment'[112]; 'There is no more sugar available at the stores in Riga though one week ago Jewish traders were visible on the streets with sugar loads from Ukraine.'[113] As the American Relief Administration gave food to separate Jewish kitchens in Latvia in 1919–1922, there were rumours that the Jewish minority received more food than the rest of the population.

Food shortages were thus at the heart of an increasingly strong anti-semitism, which did not originate in the war but gained particular currency in the region through the wartime conditions. Building on previous prejudice, the Jewish population became an easy target for people looking for someone to blame for their hardship. Differences in food supplies did not only pit classes against each other but furthered other divides within local communities. Recriminations against social, national, ethnic, or religious groups often overlapped as this discourse mainly attempted to find a culprit for the general misery.

Conclusion

Class is a category defined by lived experience: the struggles and reconfigurations of class participate in the making of the different classes in society.[114] In wartime Europe differences in access to food highlighted

110 Christoph Mick, *Kriegserfahrungen in einer multiethnischen Stadt: Lemberg 1914–1947* (Wiesbaden: Harrassowitz, 2010), 182; 232–3.

111 Blobaum, *A Minor Apocalypse*, 145–7.

112 'Žīdu tirgotāji', *Jaunākās Ziņas*, 22 November 1918.

113 'Cukurs', *Jaunākās Ziņas*, 26 November 1918.

114 Selina Todd, 'Class, Experience and Britain's Twentieth Century', *Social History* 39:4 (2014), 489–508.

class distinctions and constitute a good vantage point to examine the changing perceptions of social hierarchies. The 'rich' became conflated with those who did not suffer equally from shortages and this category became both narrower (as standards of living were falling everywhere) and larger (as it could encompass anybody who was still able to maintain some form of pre-war consumption). The transformations to the pre-war social order that shortages implied did not necessarily mean that middle class or bourgeois households were disproportionately affected by the food crisis. Their plight was considered of particular interest to contemporary (often middle class) observers but there is plenty of evidence of working-class hardship. It would, however, be a mistake to underestimate the profound emotional toll of these years: the sense of loss and disorientation that scarcity provoked and the moral language used to denounce it. Insecurities around food consumption reveal the great uncertainty that characterized wartime societies. Social status was in flux as basic needs were not as easily met. The collectives formed by those who complained or who felt unfairly treated were not stable either. Overlapping class, gender, or national identities could shape alternative exclusions from the main community of sufferers. This process occurred to various degrees throughout the continent and did not end with the armistice in 1918. The wave of social conflict in the immediate post-war years, which has often been interpreted in light of the Bolshevik revolution, reflected the new reconfigurations of class in wartime and food featured as a central issue.

9 Hungry for Change

Civilian Challenges to the State and Demands for Food

Melanie Schulze Tanielian and Mustafa Aksakal

A young Ottoman conscript from Jerusalem, Ihsan Turjman, had been assigned to desk duty in the city of his birth, not too far from his parental home. His ability to read and write may have spared him from combat, but it could not protect him from hunger. Sitting with his pens and papers, Turjman recorded in his diary on 20 October 1915 the first news of lives lost to starvation in Palestine. This tragedy had been avoidable, he noted. Authorities had failed to keep markets functioning. By 17 December 1915, he remarked bitterly: "If the government had any dignity, it would have saved wheat" to feed the poor and the most vulnerable. "I haven't seen darker days in my life. Flour and bread have basically disappeared since last Saturday. Many people have not eaten bread for days now." Ihsan Turjman believed hunger would drive the people of Jerusalem to rebellion: "If these conditions persist, the people will rebel and bring down this government—and then it will be too late for the leaders to atone for their sins. We have so far tolerated living without rice, sugar, and kerosene. But how can we live without bread?"[1] This was a question that many of his Ottoman compatriots would ask as the war emptied markets, store shelves, and kitchens alike.

When it comes to addressing food and hunger as redrawing the map of World War I, the Ottoman empire cannot be ignored: hunger claimed lives in all parts of the empire. In Syria half a million Ottomans, or one in seven, starved to death. Their death, in part, was the result of an Anglo-French strategy to starve the empire's Arab population into rebellion against the Ottoman government in Istanbul. As intended, a full-fledged famine eroded the Ottoman state's legitimacy in Syria and beyond. And while today in Lebanon and Syria, World War I is remembered as "the war of hunger," the Ottoman experience has been largely forgotten in the vast scholarship on hunger and protest in the European context during World War I.

[1] Ihsan Turjman, *Year of the Locust: A Soldier's Diary and the Erasure of Palestine's Ottoman Past*, edited and introduced by Salim Tamari (Berkeley, CA: University of California Press, 2011), 141–3.

Over the course of four years of war, feeding a hungry population became a critical and, for some regimes, the most significant avenue to exercising political legitimacy. As war burned on, hungry and starving civilians grew convinced their governments had failed them as their families foraged for food, queued up in lines, or, in the most severe cases, contended with starvation. Empty stomachs and barren pantries often were the primary drivers of political action. Civilians, as this chapter shows, were not passive recipients of state-imposed provisioning policies. Instead, all of the societies that entered the conflict, and even those who had avoided the cauldron of war, faced increasing calls for food in their cities and the countryside. Perhaps it comes as no surprise that as hunger became widespread, protest intensified; hence, the question of how increasingly war-weary and food-deprived societies marshaled their resistance into collective action and fought a war behind the war deserves close attention.

Wartime governments faced fierce resistance from citizens, who held the state responsible for their deprivations or searched for alternative sources of provisioning. Indeed, questioning political leadership became the order of the day. Though not in a linear fashion nor on the same clock, societies at war in Europe and the Ottoman empire made their voices heard through a variety of actions: civilians demanded food through petitions, rioting, political protests, labor strikes, and, finally, through rebellion and revolution. This process varied from country to country and unfolded highly unevenly within each affected state. What was common across European and Ottoman cities, towns, and the countryside, however, was a deep sense of injustice and violation, and, in political terms, of government failure. Patriotism and propaganda, in the end, could do little to counter hunger. After the war, political legitimacy hinged on any government's or party's ability to restore agricultural production and rebuild markets.

Citizens understood and largely accepted that war required sacrifice. Their contributions to the war effort, in turn, afforded new spaces to make demands on the state. The historian Geoff Eley has likened this activism to a "cashing in of the patriotic check": the expectation for social and political reforms in return for war sacrifices.[2] One such sacrifice, no doubt, was privation on the home front in relation to food supplies and related social disciplining, such as rationing. Floods of petitions, complaints in the press, marches, demonstrations, protests in public spaces, secret and public calls for revolution, made up civilians' wartime "repertoires of contention."[3] That hunger was a serious

[2] Geoff Eley, "War and the Twentieth Century," *Daedalus* 124:2 (1995), 165.

[3] Charles Tilly, *Contentious Performances* (Cambridge: Cambridge University Press, 2008), 45.

danger to the state became nowhere more visible than in Russia. Hunger engendered not only the overthrow of the tsar and his regime, but also its replacement by a new state that promised food and equality. At the same time, state authorities acknowledged the need to provision civilians. Feeding subjects and citizens, it became increasingly clear, was crucial to stabilizing home fronts and preserving public order. While states developed systems of rationing, distributing food, and setting prices, states also responded with violence: from Habsburg Moravia to Russian Bogorodsk to Ottoman Baghdad, authorities met civilian protests with armed force.

In short, civilian provisioning and food policies were not, as often assumed, set by governments.[4] Instead, as this chapter reveals, negotiations around food were determined not only by state and local political leaders but also civilian populations, in a complex politics of provisioning. In the following, we introduce the Ottoman home front experience and provide a comparative discussion of the range of popular demands that politicized hunger. We explore how that process varied across and within the warscapes of Ottoman and European societies, and how hunger, as a catalyst, altered existing political structures and gave rise to new forms of political organization by both elite and non-elite groups. Finally, we ask how political parties and organizations used food procurement and provisioning of civilians amidst hunger as an avenue to achieve, expand, or preserve political significance. The addition of the Ottoman context confirms that the delivery of food or the inability to do so played significantly into perceptions of legitimacy, and brings to the fore yet another important dimension of the politics of hunger: hunger redrew the Ottoman map along perceived ethno-religious lines. As the state questioned the political loyalty of many of its communities – Arab Christians and Muslims from Aleppo to Baghdad; Greek Orthodox Christians in Anatolia; Jews in Palestine; and, especially, Armenian Christians in eastern Anatolia – these communities saw in hunger not only a government failure but also a punishment for their allegedly missing patriotism. As a result, they saw hunger as their government's weapon against their respective communities. The inability of Ottoman and European states to secure their citizens' survival resulted in massive discontent that reconfigured the "relationship of the state and an emergent citizenry" for the long-term.[5] Governments lost support, were voted

[4] Antoon Vrints, "Beyond Victimization: Contentious Food Politics in Belgium during World War I," *European History Quarterly* 45:1 (2015), 84.

[5] Maureen Healy, *Vienna and the Fall of the Habsburg Empire: World War and the Everyday Life in World War I* (Cambridge: Cambridge University Press, 2004), 33.

out, or overthrown. In many states, new political forces emerged and rose to the top. In Syria, in the great hunger's aftermath, French colonial authorities strategically employed food in order to stifle resistance to foreign occupation, while in other regions of the empire new independent states took root, acquiring legitimacy through the provisioning of food.

Hunger Arrives: Petitions

The scarcity of food and the widening of hunger led civilians all across the Ottoman empire and Europe to question the competency and morality of the state and its local agents. Both in Europe and in the Ottoman empire, shortages, inflation, and high prices of basic necessities drove the people to demand aid and relief from their state. Civilians deployed a broad array of strategies to demand state intervention into the food supply chain that would guarantee them to be fed. They wrote (or had professional petitioners write for them) individual or communal petitions to government offices; at other times they resorted to stealing food supplies and to mobbing stores and bakeries. When food proved inedible, men and women hurled it at state representatives. Across Europe, civilians organized collective action and protested the lack of food. Demanding bread took many forms: at times it was organized by unions or political parties, at other times by spontaneous groups of rioters, gathered, not infrequently, outside empty storefronts.

The act of petitioning, a tool to seek redress from patrons and those in power, has a long history in both the Ottoman empire and Europe. Sidney Tarrow has remarked on the changes in the process of petitioning in Great Britain from individual claims to that of mass petitioning in the late eighteenth century. Tarrow notes that petitioning was transformed into "a public act seeking justice in the name of a general moral claim."[6] In the 1790s, petitions were often launched in the "context of public meetings, accompanied by boycotts, newspaper advertisements and lobbying in extended movement campaigns."[7] So while petitions as direct appeals persisted, they became part of what Charles Tilly called a new collective repertoire of protest that, on the national level, was directed at the state. In the context of World War I, petitions were an important tool to attract state authorities' attention, whether they were drafted by committees, unions, political parties, or, in some instances, groups of concerned mothers. This is particularly true for the Ottoman empire,

[6] Sidney Tarrow, *Power in Movement: Social Movements and Contentious Politics* (New York, NY: Cambridge University Press, 1998), 38.

[7] Tarrow, *Power in Movement*, 38.

where petitions to state authorities increased during the war and today serve as a key historical source offering a glimpse into the everyday wartime experiences of ordinary Ottomans.

In the nineteenth century, new technologies and changes in institutional and legal processes spurred a revival in the use of petitions by the empire's subjects.[8] Complaints about the misconduct of government officials and local elites, business disputes, and various failures in governance flooded state offices. After the 1908 Revolution, petitions were directed to the Ottoman government, parliament, and the courts, rather than the sultan. During the war years, the subject of complaint more often than not concerned the material deprivations across the empire.[9] For instance, speaking on behalf of his town near Çatalca, west of Istanbul, a man named İbrahim sent a scathing protest addressed to the government in December 1914. Conscription had slashed the population of his village in half. The remaining families, he wrote, "depend on charcoal production from the local forest and some agricultural work." Men in uniforms had assailed and mistreated the villagers "every day." The soldiers stole the timber that his fellow villagers had cut down and transported with great physical effort, commandeered the village's animals, and helped themselves to the villagers' axes, the very tools of their survival. If these conditions prevailed, İbrahim concluded, "our entire existence and livelihood will be destroyed."[10]

Ottoman women wrote petitions and telegrams addressed to the state. Frequently the petitions complained that "their husbands' and sons' military service was at odds with these women's welfare."[11] On 27 September 1916, for instance, over forty women from Edirne province turned to Istanbul. After presenting themselves as the "mothers and families of our dear soldiers," their telegram demanded protection from the state's aggressive wartime tax collectors. "We sent our sons and husbands to the war," they protested. "We farmed by gripping the plow." Despite these contributions, the state behaved unjustly, the women continued. Tax collectors denied food to their children. Nor could they feed whatever beasts of burden were left in the village. The women were desperate:

[8] Yuval Ben-Bassat, "Bedouin Petitions from Late Ottoman Palestine: Evaluating the Effects of Sedentarization," *Journal of the Economic and Social History of the Orient* 58:1 (2015), 140.

[9] Yuval Ben-Bassat, "The Ottoman Institution of Petitioning When the Sultan no Longer Reigned: A View from Post-1908 Ottoman Palestine," *New Perspectives on Turkey* 56 (2017), 87–103.

[10] Osmanlı Arşivi (BOA), DH/SYS 123-9/21-3, Muhtar İbrahim bin Ahmed, 7 Kanun-u evvel 1330 (December 20, 1914). The village is today's Başak Köyü, near Çatalca.

[11] Yiğit Akın, *When the War Came Home: The Ottomans' Great War and the Devastation of an Empire* (Stanford, CA: Stanford University Press, 2018), 158.

"We will go hungry. We beg that you have pity on us." The women, however, received no special consideration, or aid. The Interior Ministry investigated the women's complaint, but the local governor denied any wrongdoing and assured the central government that war taxes were simply being levied in line with all regulations. For the moment, nothing could be done.[12]

There is a great number of cases of women making similar demands. For example, on May 7, 1918, a group of twelve women from near Ankara wrote to the Interior Ministry. They claimed that some eighty people were perishing from hunger in their district every day. Authorities there were distributing about 640 grams of bread for a family of four, or about 160 grams per person. At the same time, these women and their district were ordered to pay war taxes in grain, something they believed to be as impossible as it was unjust: if these taxes were collected, they admonished officials, they would surely die![13] The warning was reiterated by a "large group of women" in Kırkkilise, who did all of the agricultural work previously performed by menfolk: "We sent our sons and husbands to the army. They [governmental officials] don't leave anything [any grain] for our subsistence. They want to seize everything we produce. They don't take into account what we've given so far. We will starve!"[14] Petitions and complaint telegrams became "a major vehicle" for women to urge the central government's intervention in local "politics of subsistence" on their behalf. These petitions depicted the state as surrogate husbands, that is, as the key provisioner of Ottoman families.[15]

Petitions were not a uniquely Ottoman mechanism for challenging government. Citizens of belligerent and neutral states in Europe, too, demanded their leaders' attention to their suffering through petitions. Such complaints came from political parties, labor organizations, community committees, and what might be termed ad hoc communities of suffering. In October and November 1915, for example, the Amsterdam and The Hague chapters of the Social-Democratic Womens' Club sent several petitions to members of the Dutch parliament. In them they argued for increased food subsidies and government controls over agricultural business interests.[16] At times, villagers and townspeople, believing there

[12] Elif Mahir Metinsoy, "Writing the History of Ordinary Ottoman Women during World War I," *Aspasia* 10:1 (2016), 28.

[13] Metinsoy, "Writing the History of Ordinary Ottoman Women," 29.

[14] Akın, *When the War Came Home*, 159.

[15] Akın, *When the War Came Home*, 158.

[16] Ivo Kuypers, *In de Schaduw van de Grote Oorlog. De Nederlandse arbeidersbeweging en de overheid, 1914–1920* (Amsterdam: Aksant, 2002), 93.

would be strength in numbers, collectively addressed the state through such petitions. A letter written by the women of Wallachisch Klobouk/ Valašské Klobouky in Moravia to the Habsburg Office of Provisioning (*Amt für Volksernährung*) denounced the inequities of food distribution by local officials, demanding that authorities in Vienna step in on their behalf:

> So again we make this profound request, we poor women whose husbands are fighting in the war, so that the k. u. k. Ministry hears our request … and so that it will show compassion and take care of us when our leaders no longer do. And so that we do not have to die from hunger.[17]

When the inspector visited Wallachisch Klobouk in March 1918, however, he – not unlike his Ottoman counterpart in the case of the Edirne women – deemed the supply to be relatively good.

In July 1916, a group of German lower civil servants for the first time presented their chancellor "with an urgent petition for aid."[18] In late 1915 demands had increased across Germany for a government-appointed "food dictator," tasked with bringing the food situation under control and ensuring fair distribution of foodstuffs between the different municipalities. These popular demands led to the creation of the Office of Wartime Provisioning (*Kriegsernährungsamt*) and the appointment of a food minister, Adolf Tortilowicz von Batocki-Friebe, in May 1916. While this new government bureaucracy did not produce the desired results, it did provide an agency and a representative to whom complaints could be lodged.[19] Before long, the Office of Wartime Provisioning in Berlin became flooded with requests, especially after the German rationing scheme granted special accommodation for pregnant women and the sick. Family members of ailing Berliners, who had not received their special allotments of milk or butter, wrote to insist on what the government had promised them. The high number of complaints from officials at hospitals, sanatoria, and from the sick themselves suggests that the provisioning of the sick, in particularly, was largely ignored in regions across Germany.[20]

In the same way that civilian populations in the Ottoman empire addressed their petitions directly to the sultan or the parliament, those

[17] Report from the Brünn/Brno food inspector including the original letter (November 28, 1917), ÖStA, AdR, Volksernährungsamt, AR, K129, no. 2858, March 3, 1918.

[18] Belinda Davis, *Home Fires Burning: Food, Politics, and Everyday Life in World War I Berlin* (Chapel Hill, NC: University of North Carolina Press, 2000), 118.

[19] Mary Elisabeth Cox, *Hunger in War & Peace: Women & Children in Germany, 1914–1924* (London and New York, NY: Oxford University Press, 2019), 76–7, 338–9.

[20] Official Circular from the Office of the President of the KEA, February 1, 1917, BLHA Rep. 1A, Staatliche Verteilungstelle Groß-Berlin.

in the Habsburg empire, too, often hoped to circumvent local leaders and sent their petitions directly to the emperor, "the imperial father."[21] Whether penned by a scribe or written by citizens themselves, letters appealed "in some way to the fatherly authority and magnanimity of the Emperor."[22] The practice of writing "*Bittgesuche* (petitions)" to the emperor here, too, was not new, but increased in volume during the war. As Maureen Healy has illustrated, the emperor was "besieged" by requests for concrete material assistance.[23] A petition from Trieste to the Ministry of Agriculture in Vienna signed "One for All," and dated 6 March 1918, made the following plea:

> We can no longer stand so much misery and pain. We are Austrian subjects. Our fathers, sons, brothers have shed their blood for the fatherland, so many of them are invalids, blinded, sick, or ruined forever. Our poor women and children at home are hungry and in the most squalid misery; suffering the greatest privations and pains. We implore your excellency for help. We demand to be awarded only ¼ kg bread and ¼ kg flour or legumes per day and per person. We demand relatively little just to be able to survive.[24]

At the heart of many grievances was not necessarily the government's inability to make available greater quantities of food, but rather its perceived failure to divide up foodstuffs equitably and evenly. Nor were authorities sufficiently policing fellow citizens who broke the law to secure additional sources of food. In these petitions, citizens were calling governments to account – for now, on paper only – for not exercising authority over such internal enemies, "one's neighbors and colleagues" transgressing the rules of provisioning.[25]

A petition from the small town of Nixdorf/Mikulášovice (in Northern Bohemia, near the German border) to the emperor read:

> In the name of the population of Nixdorf, I apologize to our dear lord and ruler that we have to make a request to Your Majesty the Emperor. As the population of Nixdorf has to suffer great misery and as we are all soldiers' wives, we must ask your Majesty to stand by our side. We have one kilogram of bread per person per week and nothing else: no potatoes, no flour, no meat, no butter or lard, no salt and nothing in the soup, now we must get even less bread and continue to work. Our mayor makes it difficult for us to survive. If we come to the war kitchen and we want to get something to eat, we are kicked around and yelled at by police as if we are dogs and not human beings whose husbands must fight. The youth

[21] Healy, *Vienna and the Fall of the Habsburg Empire*, 284–8, quote from 287.

[22] Healy, *Vienna and the Fall of the Habsburg Empire*, 286.

[23] Healy, *Vienna and the Fall of the Habsburg Empire*, 284–8.

[24] Petition from Trieste to the Ministry of Agriculture in Vienna. ÖStA, AdR, Volksernährungsamt, AR, K148, no. 13589, March 6, 1918.

[25] Healy, *Vienna and the Fall of the Habsburg Empire*, 2.

get blows instead of food, and the policemen have already drawn their sabres against the children instead of pouring them soup. We believe, though, that our dear Emperor does not desire such actions and will help us. The food in the war kitchen cannot be eaten and many have already died from hunger.[26]

As scarcities deepened with every year of war, frustration exceeded what a telegram or letter could assuage and civilians staged more visible forms of protest and collective action.

Hunger Becomes Widespread: Riots, Protests, and Strikes

Food riots during the war became a widespread occurrence. The factors bringing about food riots have been the subject of rich and longstanding historical analysis. In the 1970s, E. P. Thompson argued that food riots were not simply reactionary and sparked by a lack of food, but rather animated by a shared moral economy that stood against changes of capitalist market economies and that rebuked elites for not preserving economic order.[27] The war no doubt was a powerful agent of change for upsetting such a moral economy as proposed by Thompson. Reframing civilians' unrest and dissension as political activity was more than an impulsive response and revealed a politics of provisioning defined by the specific social, economic, and political wartime circumstances of each belligerent society. Food politics as expressed in collective action, in the words of Antoon Vrints, is a "negotiation process between various authorities, private structures and social groups on reconciling claims to food."[28] The negotiation process ranged from "traditional" food riots – localized appeals to the "paternalist duties of the elites" – to a new repertoire of collective action that tended to be "national rather than local [in] scope," as described by Charles Tilly.[29] In some cases, food disturbances were, in fact, however carefully orchestrated strikes aimed at central authorities; in other instances they were spontaneous, localized food riots. More importantly, what the war highlights is that one form of collective action did not foreclose others.

In the Ottoman empire, collective action in the form of protests and riots often was aimed at local merchants and officials representing the

26 Petition from Nixdorf/Mikulášovice to the Emperor, ÖStA, AdR, BMfVE, Amt für Volksernährung, K148, no. 54300, April 18, 1918.
27 Vrints, "Beyond Victimization," 85.
28 Vrints, "Beyond Victimization," 84.
29 For a brief discussion of Thompson, Bohnstedt, and Tilly, see Vrints, "Beyond Victimization," 85.

central government. In March 1916, in the city of Izmir, women who described themselves as members of soldiers' families broke into a bakery and took whatever bread and flour they could find. They defended their action by claiming that despite the Ottoman state's promise to take care of the families of men in military service, the women had not received any relief. The provincial governor immediately demanded money from the government to prevent any further such incidents. In this case, the Finance Ministry provided 40,000 liras in aid.[30] When petitions, telegrams, and local complaints went unheeded, groups of civilians at times felt they had no other choice but to confront state authorities directly. For example, signed by an Ottoman woman named Hatice, a telegram from December 1916 to the central government in Istanbul claimed to speak for over 200 women from Bursa. Hatice explained that their earlier appeals for aid addressed to local officials had fallen on deaf ears and that therefore the women were planning to travel to the capital personally to make their demands heard. To prevent this from happening, state officials sent aid immediately,[31] but warnings of pending civil unrest were not always given or requested help forthcoming.

In the streets of the empire's main cities such as Beirut, Istanbul, and Jerusalem, hungry citizens took action by gathering and breaking into stores or municipal warehouses, attacking merchants and government agents as they transported supplies. For example, the American consul at Beirut recalled, "Yesterday, while some wagons loaded with a few bags of flour were being hauled through the streets they were attacked by a number of frantic and famished women who ripped the bags open with knives and wolfishly scooped up the flour as it flowed out into the road."[32] An employee of the Syrian Protestant College, Edward Nickoley, described bands of women and children who, "frantic with hunger overwhelmed the keepers of bread shops and vegetables and meat stands." The police stood by, according to Nickoley, as women and children carried away what they could and returned the next day for more.[33] The same was true for Istanbul, the capital. As Ahmet Yalman recounts, "large quantities of bread or flour if seen in the streets, ran the risk of being seized by the mob."[34] In Jerusalem, "women and children formed long queues

30 Elif Mahir Metinsoy, *Ottoman Women during World War I: Everyday Experiences, Politics, and Conflict* (Cambridge: Cambridge University Press, 2017), 61.
31 Metinsoy, *Ottoman Women during World War I*, 60.
32 Melanie S. Tanielian, *The Charity of War: Famine, Humanitarian Aid, and World War I in the Middle East* (Stanford, CA: Stanford University Press, 2018), 97.
33 Tanielian, *The Charity of War*, 97.
34 Ahmet Emin Yalman, *Turkey in the World War* (New Haven, CT: Yale University Press, 1930), 111.

in front of bakeries and fought for meager amounts of bread."[35] It was not only the large cities that saw food protests. Women of the small Bekaa Valley town of Rayaq, for example, retaliated against the government by throwing the uneatable bread at the military commander Jamal Pasha as he passed through the town.[36] In the Anatolian provinces of the empire, food riots and protests increased toward the end of the war. In April 1918, for instance, a group of villagers, mostly women, had "illegally" opened a warehouse and "parceled out the provisions among themselves."[37] In some places, protests and looting continued after the armistice. In July 1919, the inhabitants of nearly a dozen villages in Bursa province attacked the harvest shipments and plundered warehouses filled with grain designated as government tax payments.[38] Bread riots continued to be reported in the Syrian hinterlands into the fall of 1920.[39]

In Europe, hunger marches, public protests, riots, and strikes became commonplace as trust in political elites and in societal solidarity between classes in both towns and the countryside gradually broke down. In Berlin, food shortages, starting with bread and potatoes, were felt almost immediately. Already in 1914, poor and urban working class Berliners, in response to rising prices of potatoes, protested and accused food administrators of "indifference, incompetence, and subservience to the politically powerful" landowners.[40] By the middle of the war, German civilians questioned the competence of the state, which some citizens characterized as having transformed from a "rational state" to a "lunatic asylum."[41] Queues and crowds outside of stores functioned as novel, quasi-political fora and "loci of micro-mobilization."[42] By 1915 food protests in Berlin were commonplace; within the span of five days from 14–20 October, police records showed "over fifty displays of 'excesses' or riots."[43] Dubbed the "butter riots," these at times involved several thousand women gathering in working class neighborhoods of the capital.[44]

35 Turjman, *Year of the Locust*, 51.
36 Leila Tarazi Fawaz, *A Land of Aching Hearts: The Middle East in the Great War* (Cambridge, MA: Harvard University Press, 2014), 98.
37 Metinsoy, *Ottoman Women during World War I*, 61.
38 Metinsoy, *Ottoman Women during World War I*, 61–2.
39 Fawaz, *In the Land of Aching Hearts*, 105.
40 Davis, *Home Fires Burning*, 65.
41 Ute Daniel, *Arbeiterfrauen in der Kriegsgesellschaft: Beruf, Familie und Politik im Ersten Weltkrieg* (Göttingen: Vandenhoeck & Ruprecht, 1989), 168.
42 Klaus Weinhauer, "Labour Movements and Strikes, Social Conflict and Control, Protest and Repression (Germany)," in *1914–1918-online. International Encyclopedia of the First World War*, edited by Ute Daniel et al. (Berlin: Freie Universität Berlin, 2017), 4.
43 Davis, *Home Fires Burning*, 80.
44 Davis, *Home Fires Burning*, 80ff.

Women and adolescent youth protested the arrogance and – whether perceived or real – the hoarding practices of shop owners. They also bemoaned the inadequate supplies provided by the municipal authorities directly, and the apparent lack of any control over ever-skyrocketing prices of food: "Without a cut in prices, calm will not return."[45] Berliners' demands were unequivocal. A coordinated food policy had to come from above to end the cycles of protests. In mid-1916, the press sounded alarm bells about the increasing instances of "riots in working class Berlin" as women's threats and violence against police officers jumped. A distinct nervousness set in among officials, who began to view such street protests as linked to radical politics and feared revolution. The devastating Turnip Winter of 1916/17 meant further protests. The call now was for strict equality in food distribution, denouncing extra rations for munition workers, for example, but also for the ill and children. At this point, in Germany, street protests became accompanied by workers' strikes "over wages, food supplies, and the general 'food calamity'" and the failure of the government to curb wartime profiteering.[46]

In the Netherlands, organized calls for demanding food initially were mostly limited to political rallies, put on by trade unions. These protests were closely aligned with the major political parties of the day and tightly controlled by their leadership. As a result, street protests remained at first relatively unthreatening to the central government. By 1917, however, as in Germany, protests intensified. Men and women denounced the meagre rations they were allotted and accused the government of short-changing urban workers over the economic interests of big business.[47] In Eastern Europe, street demonstrations, riots, and, toward the end of the war, labor strikes became common occurrences. As the food crisis deepened, in occupied Poland lower-class women played a key role in inciting Warsaw's food riots in 1916. Here over twenty municipal food stores were ransacked and looted.[48] Warsaw's hungry civilians frequently blamed the conditions on German authorities and the German occupation. Charges of German callousness and corruption turned ever louder. In spring 1917, an "explosion of strikes and demonstrations" marked the urban landscape in Poland.[49]

Public discontent also deepened across the Habsburg empire. Life in the Habsburg lands was shaped by a variety of legal and political regimes from Austria to the Kingdom of Hungary to Bosnia-Herzegovina and

45 Davis, *Home Fires Burning*, 86.
46 Davis, *Home Fires Burning*, 195.
47 Kuypers, *In de Schaduw van de Grote Oorlog*, 152–3.
48 Robert Blobaum, *A Minor Apocalypse: Warsaw during the First World War* (Ithaca: Cornell University Press, 2017), 181–2.
49 Blobaum, *A Minor Apocalypse*, 90–1.

Croatia and Galicia.[50] Hence, as Maureen Healy has suggested, we may no longer talk about fronts and home fronts but rather think in terms of "spaces of war."[51] Still food shortages were felt across these spaces of war and in turn generated public demonstrations as a way of pressuring the state and local governments to feed the hungry. Habsburg officials worried out loud about how much more of the food crisis citizens could endure. Asked by the Interior Ministry if the population could stand another winter of war in 1917, the Moravian governor responded unequivocally: "a half-decent possibility of subsistence" was an "imperative prerequisite for the population to be able to bear the continuation of the war in the coming winter."[52]

Continued requisitioning policies caused disobedience among all strata of society and much of this disobedience took the form of public protests. In the Bohemian lands of the Habsburg empire, for example, the number of food riots more than doubled from 31 in 1915 to 70 in 1916, and then more than tripled to 252 in 1917 and 235 in 1918 (by October).[53] In Prague, hungry residents responded to increasing scarcity "with riots, theft and demonstrations."[54] By January 1918, a large wave of strikes and demonstrations rolled across the Habsburg empire's major industrial centres, involving over 700,000 workers from Trieste to Lemberg, including 100,000 workers in Vienna alone.[55] Large demonstrations took place in Cracow, while 50,000 people demonstrated in the streets of Prague.[56] Demonstrators pressed authorities for greater government aid.[57] A report from the district committee in Haida/Bor (in today's Czech Republic) noted in April 1918 that "the population [was] truly starving and gather[ed] every day in front of the municipality to

[50] Tamara Scheer and Nancy M. Wingfield, "Habsburg Home Fronts during the Great War," *European Review of History: Revue européenne d'histoire* 24:2 (2017), 176.

[51] Maureen Healy, "Introductory Remarks: Space, Chronology and the Habsburg Home Fronts," *European Review of History: Revue européenne d'histoire* 24:2 (2017), 178.

[52] Report from the Moravian governor to the Interior Ministry, ÖStA, AVA, MdI, Präs, sig. 22, 1917, K2070, no. 15456, August 4, 1917.

[53] Peter Heumos, "'Kartoffeln her oder es gibt eine Revolution': Hungerkrawalle, Streiks und Massenproteste in den böhmischen Ländern, 1914–1918," in *Der Erste Weltkrieg und die Beziehungen zwischen Tschechen, Slowaken und Deutschen*, edited by Hans Mommsen, Dušan Kováč, Jiří Malíř, and Michaela Marek (Essen: Klartext, 2001), 153.

[54] Maureen Healy, Dana Bronson, and Musa Jemal, "Social Conflict and Control, Protest and Repression (Austria-Hungary)," in *1914–1918-online. International Encyclopedia of the First World War*, edited by Ute Daniel et al. (Berlin: Freie Universität Berlin, 2015), 9.

[55] Borislav Chernev, *Twilight of Empire: The Brest-Litovsk Conference and the Remaking of East-Central Europe, 1917–1918* (Toronto: University of Toronto Press, 2017), 118.

[56] Numbering 50,000 in the police reports, 70,000 according to newspaper *Národní listy*, see Claire Morelon, *Streetscapes of War and Revolution: Prague, 1914–1920* (Cambridge: Cambridge University Press, 2024), 223.

[57] Peter Heumos, "Kartoffeln her oder es gibt eine Revolution."

demonstrate."[58] By 1918, citizens took increasingly extreme measures. On May 10 in Nová Paka/Neupaka, in Bohemia, a crowd broke into the private apartments of the mayor and the district officer rampaging their homes.[59] The published collection of weekly reports on demonstrations in Bohemia reveals a growth in such violent incidents during the war's last year, while the gendarmerie and sometimes even the army increasingly intervened.[60] The number of people involved in these protests varied from several dozens to a thousand or more in some cases.

The Habsburg government's responses were often violent. In 1917 the American Wolf von Schierbrand, in Vienna at the time, described witnessing several "famine riots." Their goal was to force the mayor to distribute food to those without any means to provide for themselves. Schierbrand noted "many of the women" appearing "haggard, desperate and famished. Some," he wrote, "had pallid babies clinging to their wasted bosoms."[61] In one of them, "a score of determined men and women ... numbering several thousand" had charged through lines of police. Seeking to fight their way to Schönbrunn, the imperial residence, this had now transformed into a political act. Before reaching their destination, however, the rioters were "dispersed by force."[62] In Moravia, the most violent repression against civilians took place in Prostějov/Prossnitz in April 1917, when army units sent to control the crowd panicked and opened fire, killing twenty-three. News of the massacre spread quickly and was taken up in parliament.[63] Following another massive demonstration in Prague in late May 1917, authorities issued a ban declaring any such future gatherings illegal.[64] As hunger turned into desperation, in a riot in Frankstadt/Frankštát, in northern Moravia, women asked provocatively whether they ought to strangle their children and go to jail, where they would at least be fed.[65]

[58] Report from the district committee in Haida/Bor, ÖStA, AdR, Volksernährungsamt, AR, K148, no. 57649, April 18.

[59] See the weekly reports from the Bohemian Governor's Office reproduced in Libuše Otáhalova, ed. *Souhrnná hlašení presidia pražkého místodržitelství o protistátní, protirakouské a protivalené činnosti v Čechách 1915–1918*, no. 2702 (Prague: Nakladatelství Československé akademie věd, 1957), 355.

[60] Published weekly reports from the Bohemian Governor's Office, record of all the protests/demonstrations/riots in Bohemia in 1917 and 1918 (location, number of participants) in Otáhalova, ed. *Souhrnná hlašení.*

[61] Wolf von Schierbrand, "The Food Situation in Austria-Hungary," *North American Review* 205:734 (1917), 49.

[62] von Schierbrand, "The Food Situation," 48.

[63] See *Národní Listy*, July 2, 1917, 3.

[64] Morelon, *Streetscapes of War and Revolution*, 214.

[65] Demonstration on March 6, 1917, of circa 300 women. ÖStA, AVA, MdI, Präs, 20, 1884, 1917–1918, no. 4694.

In Russia the situation was tense very early on in the war. For example, in Bogorodsk near Moscow, on October 1, 1915, some thirty women workers protested the lack of sugar and other foods. They castigated shop owners for hiding goods and selling these on the black market. The women then took matters into their own hands. They broke into one of the shops and looted whatever was available. Confronted by the police, the women marched into the town square. There they were joined by others, eventually comprising a rioting crowd of several thousand, mostly women and youths. The riot had continued for three days when special Cossack troops charged the demonstrators with live bullets, killing two and injuring more. The riots spread to neighboring towns, reaching a total number of demonstrators of some 80,000.[66] At what point did riots become revolutions, demanding a complete overthrow of the wartime government?

Hunger Becomes Unbearable: Revolution

Hunger played a central role in the various revolutionary movements in World War I. Both in the Ottoman empire and in Europe, demands for food catalyzed social dissent into movements that now insisted no longer only on the end to hunger but also on radically new, post-war political and social orders.[67]

Revolutionary movements in the Ottoman empire and in Europe did not appear only with World War I, of course. In fact, the Ottoman wartime government itself – the Committee of Union and Progress, also known as the Unionists or the Young Turks – was one of them. The Ottoman government was the product of the 1908 Revolution, which had curbed the sultan's powers and transferred them, first, to the Ottoman parliament, and then, second, when that body turned too independent-minded, to the Unionists themselves. During the war, however, revolutionary movements confronted new social and political conditions of which hunger became a crucial, if not defining, aspect. Hunger, on the one hand, undermined the legitimacy of the Unionist government in Istanbul, and, on the other hand, became a site for political mobilization against it. Already in August 1914, an Anglo-French fleet took up formation off the Syrian coast, stretching from Alexandria in British-occupied Egypt in the south to Izmir/Smyrna on the Aegean in the north. As seen

66 Barbara Alpern Engel, "Not by Bread Alone: Subsistence Riots in Russia during World War I," *The Journal of Modern History*, 69:4 (1997), 696–7.

67 For an excellent overview, see Chad R. Fulwider, "Revolutions," in *1914–1918-online. International Encyclopedia of the First World* War, edited by Ute Daniel et al. (Berlin: Freie Universität Berlin, 2014), 2.

from London, the purpose of this *de facto* blockade – declared formally a blockade only in spring 1915 – aimed at causing a food and hunger crisis that, in due course, would result in an Arab revolution against the Ottoman ruling regime. It was not without success. İhsan Turjman, the Jerusalem conscript with whom this chapter began, heard the news of an Arab revolt proclaimed by Sharif Husayn of Mecca on July 10, 1916. Sharif Husayn, as the custodian of the holy sites at Mecca and Medina, was both a central religious figure and a powerful political and military ruler in southwestern Arabia.[68] "Could this be the beginning?," Turjman asked. Turjman's indignation over the government and its incompetence became an argument for ethno-nationalism: "Every Arab should be pleased about this news."[69]

As we saw above, hunger and the demand for food engendered local protests and dominated petitions addressed to the Ottoman government. By 1916, it was no longer the government's inability to protect agricultural production and preserve markets that came under heavy civilian fire, but the very legitimacy of the government itself. In June 1916, Sharif Husayn of Mecca launched an uprising that precipitated the end of Ottoman rule over the empire's Arab lands. Backed by British materiel and cash, Sharif Husayn was able to offer food and provisioning to an army of some 4,000 fighters whose livelihood had become increasingly threatened by the Istanbul government's wartime conduct.[70]

In 1917, hunger set off the February Revolution in Russia, where "the immediate cause was worker demonstrations over food supply shortages in the capital, Petrograd."[71] A country that was the largest grain exporter before the war, transformed into a space in which hunger became a fountainhead of political mobilization. When soldiers and moderate opposition members joined the strikers, a worker rebellion turned into revolution.[72] In Russia, it was the home front that collapsed first.[73] The scarcity of foodstuffs and the violent expressions of protest that followed were crucial in triggering revolution in Russia and continued to cascade

[68] Hasan Kayalı, *Arabs and Young Turks: Ottomanism, Arabism, and Islamism in the Ottoman Empire, 1908–1918* (Berkeley, CA: University of California Press, 1997), 174–205.

[69] Turjman, *Year of the Locust*, 155, entry for July 10, 1916.

[70] On this process in the Habsburg Empire, see Pieter Judson, *The Habsburg Empire: A New History* (Cambridge, MA: Harvard University Press, 2016), 417–41. Similar to what happened in the Ottoman context, the inability of the Habsburg state to provide for its population increased calls for national revolutions.

[71] Peter Holquist, *Making War, Forging Revolution: Russia's Continuum of Crisis, 1914–1921* (Cambridge, MA: Harvard University Press, 2002), 44.

[72] Holquist, *Making War*, 44.

[73] Dominic Lieven, *The End of Tsarist Russia: The March to World War I and Revolution* (New York, NY: Penguin, 2016), 344.

through Eastern Europe. On February 23, 1917, in Petrograd, large crowds gathered to demand bread. Slogans of "Down with high prices" and "Down with hunger" quickly turned into "Down with the tsar" and "Down with the war."[74] Soldiers' wives in particular mobilized to an unprecedented degree and rioted when their demands went unmet.[75]

In the Netherlands, too, public protests increased in number, often sparked by either continued agricultural exports or over (rumours of) war profiteering by agricultural interests. For example, when in 1917 a respectable potato harvest was sold on the free market with rather poor oversight and no rationing orders from the leadership of the Dutch Minister of Agriculture, Industry, and Trade, it resulted in extreme prices of this important staple. In Amsterdam, civilians responded by ransacking and looting potato barges and stores in the city center. The government, in turn, deployed military units with deadly consequence.[76] The dire food situation, it has been argued, contributed to a call for revolution in 1918, propagated by the Dutch majority socialist leader P. J. Troelstra.[77] Revolution would not be forthcoming, but increasing discontent translated into continued protests, riots, and eventual violent government responses nonetheless and eventually spreading across the Netherlands and persisting until the end of the war.[78]

In Finland, workers turned militant in 1917. The situation for workers' families had deteriorated significantly. Minutes from a gathering of the Finnish carpenters' union record how "workers with large families who have not had butter for months on end … had to go without bread for a number of days, not to mention milk, which for many is already a distant memory from the past."[79] In their meeting on 17 October 1917, members of the carpenters' union excoriated the injustices separating the rich from the poor: "What could be done to prevent our having to eat lichen [a moss-like shrub], which the bourgeoisie are starting to feed us," they demanded to know.[80] Closely following the revolutionary developments unfolding in Russia, union members were determined "that there was no other way but to seize power once and for all." If they had "to eat lichen,

[74] Engel, "Not by Bread Alone," 697.

[75] Engel, "Not by Bread Alone," 710–11.

[76] Maartje M. Abbenhuis, *The Art of Staying Neutral; The Netherlands in the First World War, 1914–1918* (Amsterdam: Amsterdam University Press, 2006), 220–2.

[77] Wim Klinkert, Samuël Kruizinga, and Paul Moeyes, eds. *Nederland Neutraal: De Eerste Wereldoorlog 1914–1918* (Amsterdam: Boom, 2014), 445–9.

[78] Abbenhuis, *The Art of Staying Neutral*, 220–2.

[79] Minutes for October 5, 1917, in David Kirby, *Finland and Russia, 1808–1920: From Autonomy to Independence* (London, 1975), 216.

[80] Minutes for 17 October 1917, in Kirby, *Finland and Russia*, 216.

then the bourgeoisie will have to eat the same helping as the worker," they demanded.[81] In response, workers attacked employers and fellow workers who refused to join the strike. At the Trade Union Congress held in November 1917, delegates maintained that Finnish workers "too will be compelled to seize power sooner or later" if conditions persisted.[82] Workers, another delegate argued, had a decision to make, either to "submit through hunger to bourgeoisie rule or take up a struggle which will either take us to victory or defeat." To be clear, defeat meant "grim death." Workers "feel that we cannot stand this general starvation anymore."[83] The revolution found support in the United States, where a Finnish diaspora pledged its support.[84] The very first issue of its newspaper demanded action to mitigate the hunger back home: "Starvation in Finland" and "The Finnish People Face to Face with Starvation," the headlines declared.[85] As the war grinded on, food shortages and hunger, as revolutions and revolutionary movements highlight, increasingly endangered the state's legitimacy.

Hunger's Continued Claims: New States and the Specter of Colonialism

As regimes requisitioned resources necessary to feed and equip their armies, the war effort endangered civilian loyalties to the state. Government officials knew full well that food security was essential to their legitimacy and that arguments of a "communal sacrifice" became increasingly difficult to justify. The widespread experiences of hunger had eroded the trust in the states' capability to care for their citizens and to improve matters for years to come.

Governments everywhere were less and less able to convince affected populations of the war's necessity and the sacrifices it entailed. It was not only the old empires that collapsed under the food crisis but also new states that struggled to establish their legitimacy; the war's end after all did not conclude the food crisis or its political impact. In the newly

[81] Kirby, *Finland and Russia*, 216.
[82] Kirby, *Finland and Russia*, 216.
[83] Kirby, *Finland and Russia*, 217.
[84] Finns in the United States in July 1918 formed the Finland Constitutional League of America to support the newly-independent state of Finland and to pledge support for the prospering of democracy there, establishing a new publication, *The Finland Sentinel* as its official organ. In its first issue it presented the League's brief nine-article constitution and listed its founding members. These members included heads of large corporations, academics, and several officials of the American Committee for Armenian and Syrian Relief. *The Finland Sentinel: Official Organ of the Finland Constitutional League of America*, 1:1, 4 July 1918, 2–5.
[85] *The Finland Sentinel*, 10–13.

established state of Czechoslovakia, for instance, supply difficulties continued and contributed to social unrest for another several years. There and elsewhere, citizens' movements threatened the legitimacy of the new state. In fact, the number of strikes in the Bohemian lands after the armistice shot up from 184 in 1918 to 242 the next year and to 590 in 1920.[86] During these post-war protests, crowds were plundering shops or threatened merchants into selling them food at lower prices. In some cases, they carried with them and put on display makeshift gallows to frighten "profiteers." This unprecedented practice of presenting the gallows could be observed in various cities of the new state. In Prague the gallows bore a sign: "Last warning for the profiteers." In Kladno, the crowd led several shopkeepers in a public procession to the gallows, forcing them to swear never again to overcharge their customers.[87]

In a booklet that appeared in early 1919, the Hungarian communist leader, Béla Kun – just prior to his Bolshevist revolution in March – blamed the middle classes for the immense costs of the war and demanded that they pay for having caused such massive suffering and slaughter:

> While there is no bread, clothing, shoes, butter, and milk since the war, there is still money. There is so much of it that those who have it deliver more and more of it to the government. They profit more and more from it and they cannot invest into anything but government loans. It is therefore clear that those who profited from the war must pay for our war debt: the wealthy class, the bourgeoisie.[88]

That food played a role in agitating against the rich is clear. For example, a report published by the American Relief Administration in July 1919 detailed the political function of food in Hungary. The report urged to separate the Hungarian citizenry from the new Bolshevist regime. Food became a key component in the strategy articulated by US authorities who argued that only economic support "brought in by British and American flags" could serve this purpose. The "great majority of the people of Hungary are eager to overthrow the present government and to do away with Bolshevism," the report claimed. It cautioned that outside intervention could have the opposite result and foster national unity behind the Bolshevist regime. The people of Hungary were deemed "not willing to go back to the old regime of government, nor to the gravely

86 Heumos, "Kartoffeln her oder es gibt eine Revolution," 163.

87 Alois Kocman ed. *Souhrnná týdenní hlášení presidia zemské správy politické v Praze o situaci v Čechách 1919–1920* (Prague: Nakladatelství Československé akademie věd, 1959), 57–62.

88 Béla Kun, *Ki fizet a Háboruért? [Who pays for the war?]* (Budapest: A Kommunisták Magyarorszagi Partjának Kiadása, 1919), 6.

unjust distribution of wealth and income which formerly existed." All economic incentive, and relief, could turn popular support against the current government.[89]

In the Ottoman empire, too, the Allied powers understood all too well that food relief offered the most direct route to establishing a new foundation for Anglo-French control in the region. Nicola Ziadeh witnessed the British occupation of Palestine first-hand: "The first change we noticed after the war ended was that we could buy flour, wheat flour, in the shops. It was not, however, the flour of Palestine wheat, but was brought from Australia." Rice, too, arrived with the British. Ziadeh writes that it was Indian rather than the customary Egyptian rice. According to Ziadeh, the people of Palestine rejoiced and celebrated their new ability to purchase rice in the market.[90] Like the British, the French, too, employed food strategically in their new mandatory possession of Syria. Indeed, food aid quickly emerged as an "intrinsic part" of French colonial rule there.[91] The French were fast in lifting the Mediterranean blockade and assuring that food supplies arrived at the port of Beirut. The newly established French mandatory government set up an elaborate system of relief in the region and drew on local elites, and particularly the leaders of the Maronite Church, a long-standing ally of the French, to assure that food would win over the goodwill of the people and display French benevolence. In the lands of the Ottoman empire, as in Europe, ending hunger and providing food became the starting point for the construction of the new political order after the war.

Conclusion

Hunger was a catalyst, a mobilizing force, and a political tool during and after the war.

This chapter examined comparatively European wartime societies, including neutral states, integrating the Ottoman empire into the larger food supply story of World War I. It highlights the war's global

[89] Hoover Institution Library and Archives, Pottle and Durand, "Conditions in Hungary," *American Relief Administration Bulletin*, 19 (1919), 30.

[90] Nicola Ziadeh, "A First-Person Account of the First World War in Greater Syria," in *The First World War as Remembered in the Countries of the Eastern Mediterranean*, edited by Olaf Farschid, Manfred Kropp, and Stephan Dähne (Baden-Baden: Nomos Verlagsgesellschaft, 2006), 271.

[91] Simon Jackson, "Transformative Relief: Imperial Humanitarianism and Mandatory Development in Syria-Lebanon, 1915–1925," *Humanity: An International Journal of Human Rights, Humanitarianism, and Development* 8:2 (2017), 248; and Chris Gratien, "The Sick Mandate of Europe: Local and Global Humanitarianism in French Cilicia, 1918–1922," *Journal of the Ottoman and Turkish Studies Association* 3:1 (2016): 165–90.

effects that, although specific to their own political and historical contexts, reveal similar processes and sentiments. As "traditional institutions that govern food consumption and production" proved inadequate and failed, citizens not only sought alternative strategies of survival in famine-struck areas but also demanded their rights from municipal, regional, and national governing bodies.[92] It is clear that wartime governments everywhere faced requests and, at times, fierce resistance from populations who petitioned their leaders, looted stores, broke into warehouses, raised demands for food dictatorship, but also ultimately actively sought alternative leadership or gave their support to foreign powers in return for being fed. The capacity to deliver food, or the inability to do so, would play a crucial role in shaping perceptions of state legitimacy in the post-war years, leading to political revolution, legitimizing colonial occupation, and, for some, facilitating national independence.

92 Wendy Wolford and Ryan Nehring, "Moral Economies of Food Security and Protest in Latin America," in *Food Security and Sociopolitical Stability*, edited by Christopher Barrett (Oxford: Oxford University Press, 2013), 302.

10 Measuring Food Requirements and Deprivation

Joël Floris and Kaspar Staub

Introduction

Securing enough food was a major issue for European countries during the First World War. Governments and relief organizations asked: how much do people need? They needed numbers to implement rationing, increase agricultural production, provide food aid, and to determine income and anthropometric thresholds for relief. Scientists provided these numbers. This chapter discusses four ways in which scientists assessed hunger during and after the war: first, by providing a scientific basis for nutritional recommendations; second, by trying to influence food policy; third, by assessing nutritional status and measuring deprivation; and fourth, by investigating how war affects birthweights.

In the nineteenth century, politicians and scientists were concerned about whether a state's own resources were sufficient to feed its population. One scientist calculated the nutritional balance of a population based on food import and export figures and average consumption.[1] Another used nutritional values and a survey of staple foods.[2] Yet another looked at the living standards of countries and estimated the amount of food that could be produced to feed everyone on the planet.[3]

In addition to self-sufficiency, studies particularly focused on the living conditions of the industrial working class. Throughout the nineteenth century, social reformers used human heights to understand the

[1] Theodor R. Simler, 'Versuch einer Ernährungsbilanz der schweizerischen Bevölkerung', *Zeitschrift für schweizerische Statistik und Volkswirtschaft*, 9–11 (1873–5), 158–69 and 257–70, 15–26, 1–22.

[2] Karl Keleti, *Die Ernährungs-Statistik der Bevölkerung Ungarns auf physiologischer Grundlage* (Budapest: Act. G. Athenaeum, 1887).

[3] Karl Ballod, 'Wieviel Menschen kann die Erde ernähren?', in *Jahrbuch für Gesetzgebung, Verwaltung und Volkswirtschaft im Deutschen Reich*, edited by Gustav Schmoller (Leipzig: Verlag von Duncker & Humblot, 1912), 81–102.

living conditions of factory workers.[4] In 1829, one study concluded that poverty and prosperity shape the human body.[5] From the mid-nineteenth century, scientists collected data on the budget of working-class families to determine living conditions.[6] Others reported minimal nutritional values in the daily diet of an average worker.[7] They wanted to know what diet was appropriate for people's wellbeing, based on scientific evidence (i.e., experiments).[8] In 1894, a German economist published case studies on diet and productivity of workers in different locations in Great Britain, Ireland, and Germany.[9] Besides scientific curiosity, economic considerations played a role in improving living standards. Other studies were concerned with the extent of poverty and calculated absolute poverty thresholds.[10] Poverty lines ranged from minimum physiological needs to social conventions defining a minimum basket of goods.[11] Therefore household budgets not only reflected physiological, medical, or public health concerns, they also set standards of behaviour.[12]

Current studies of population nutrition, household budgets, poverty thresholds, or food baskets measure whether there is enough to eat on average. They measure the 'supply of inputs to health'[13] and the extent of hunger, assessing whether a diet is adequate for an individual or the

[4] Mary Elisabeth Cox, 'Anthropometrics: The Application of Anthropometrics to Identify and Assess War Crimes', in *War Crimes Trials and Investigations: A Multi-disciplinary Introduction*, edited by Jonathan Waterlow and Jacques Schumacher (Cham: Palgrave Macmillan, 2018), 82.

[5] Louis René Villermé, 'Mémoire sur la taille de l'homme en France', *Annales d'hygiène publique et de médicine légale*, 1 (1829), 351–99, 388.

[6] Édouard Ducpétieux, *Budgets économiques des classes ouvrières en Belgique: subsistance, salaires, populations* (Brussels: M. Hayez, 1855).

[7] Carl von Voit, *Untersuchung der Kost in einigen öffentlichen Anstalten: Für Aerzte und Verwaltungsbeamte* (Munich: R. Oldenbourg 1877), 15.

[8] von Voit, *Untersuchung der Kost*, 1.

[9] Lujo Brentano, *Hours and Wages in Relation to Production* (London: Swan Sonnenschein & Co., 1894).

[10] Charles Booth, *Life and Labour of the People*, 2 vols (2nd Volume: *Labour and Life of the People*) (London: Macmillan and Co., 1889–1891); Benjamin Seebohm Rowntree, *Poverty: A Study of Town Life*, 2nd ed. (London: Maxmillan and Co., 1908).

[11] Joël Floris, Marius Kuster, and Ulrich Woitek, 'Armutsgrenzen in der Stadt Zürich während des Ersten Weltkriegs', *Traverse: Zeitschrift für Geschichte*, 3 (2017), 97.

[12] Jakob Tanner, *Fabrikmahlzeit: Ernährungswissenschaft, Industriearbeit und Volksernährung in der Schweiz, 1890–1950* (Zurich: Chronos 1999), 134–5; Jakob Tanner, 'Der Tatsachenblicke auf die „reale Wirklichkeit": zur Entwicklung der Sozial- und Konsumstatistik in der Schweiz', *Schweizerische Zeitschrift für Geschichte*, 45 (1995), 94–108; United States Bureau of Labor Statistics, *The Consumer Price Index: History and Techniques, Bulletin No. 1517* (Washington, DC: US Government Printing Office, 1966).

[13] Richard H. Steckel, 'Stature and the Standard of Living', *Journal of Economic Literature*, 33 (1995), 1903–40, 1903.

consumption of a group of people. The possible intake, or at least the theoretical and statistical amount of food needed, is considered.

In contrast, anthropometric methods as well as morbidity, mortality rates, and death records are all *outputs* that measure the effects of lack of food. They capture the demands for inputs.[14] The distinction is, however, not clear-cut, especially when measures are considered over time. For instance, household budgets show how families respond to the changing economic environment,[15] and the nutritional value approach assesses both the inputs and the demand for those inputs.

To determine levels of hunger, scientists now also look at the characteristics of malnutrition,[16] deficiencies, excesses, or imbalances in an individual dietary intake relative to the energy needed to maintain the body, grow, move, work, and resist disease. This is known as nutritional status.[17] Current research views hunger as a lack of food embedded in a biological, socioeconomic, and epidemiological environment. Nutritional status is difficult to measure because intake and requirements vary with age, sex, working conditions, and other living conditions. Today, anthropometry is a standard method for determining body shape and monitoring health and nutritional status.[18]

The experience of food shortages in Europe during the First World War shaped discourses on evaluations of nutritional status and minimum standards. While studies have documented relief efforts, rationing, and food shortage during war, the focus has rarely been on the measuring itself: the standards used, where the measurements came from, and how they were implemented.[19] Only a few modern studies have

[14] Steckel, 'Stature and the Standard of Living', 1905.

[15] Brian A'Hearn, Nicola Amendola, and Giovanni Vecchi, 'On Historical Household Budgets', *Institute for New Economic Thinking Working Paper*, 45 (2016), 4.

[16] Sara Millman and Robert W. Kates, 'Towards Understanding Hunger', in *Hunger in History: Food Shortage, Poverty, and Deprivation*, edited by Lucile F. Newman (Cambridge, MA: Basil Blackwell, 1990), 3.

[17] Barry Bogin, *Patterns of Human Growth*, 2nd ed. (Cambridge: Cambridge University Press, 1999); Roderick Floud, Robert W. Fogel, Bernard Harris, and Sok Chul Hong, *The Changing Body: Health, Nutrition, and Human Development in the Western World since 1700* (Cambridge: Cambridge University Press, 2011), 11.

[18] Victor R. Preedy, ed., *Handbook of Anthropometry: Physical Measures of Human Form in Health and Disease* (New York, NY: Springer, 2012); World Health Organization, ed., *The Assessment of the Nutritional Status of the Community* (Geneva: World Health Organization, 1966).

[19] A few works dealing with both world wars have looked at these areas: Stephen Wheatcroft and Cormac Ó Gráda, 'The European Famines of World Wars I and II', in *Famine in European History*, edited by Guido Alfani and Cormac Ó Gráda (Cambridge: Cambridge University Press, 2017), 240–68; Hans-Joachim Voth, 'Civilian Health during WWI and the Cause of German Defeat: A Reexamination of the Winter Hypothesis', *Annales de Démographie Historique (Les réseaux de parenté)* (1995), 291–307; Jay Winter, *The Great War and the British People* (Cambridge, MA: Harvard University Press, 1986).

relied on historical anthropometric data to measure hunger during war, when nutritional access was reduced, illness was prevalent, and therefore growth was slowed or interrupted.[20] Yet, anthropometry was popular before and during the war. Richard E. Scammon's 1927 overview on the child growth literature shows that the number of studies increased exponentially between the second half of the nineteenth century and the 1920s (129 studies of general body growth between 1850 and 1875; 518 between 1875 and 1900; and 900 between 1900 and 1925).[21] And in 1914, a comprehensive biological anthropology textbook contributed to the standardization of anthropometric techniques.[22]

This chapter presents four ways in which hunger was measured during the First World War and in its aftermath, drawing on anthropometric studies from the war that examine the process of measuring, as well as our current scientific understanding of anthropometrics as a tool for understanding hunger and deprivation. In the first two sections, we describe the nutritional concepts adopted across Europe since the end of the nineteenth century and look at the measurements, thresholds, and rationing quantities that were established. In the third section, we describe how scientists began to assess malnutrition and child health and the standards they used. In the fourth section, we look at how hunger shapes the human body at birth, a question often asked by scientists during the war.

20 On historical anthropometrics, see Floud, *The Changing Body;* on how deprivation reduces growth, see James M. Tanner, *Growth at Adolescence*, 2nd ed. (Oxford: Blackwell, 1962); on anthropometrics to measure impact of the war, see Mary Elisabeth Cox, 'Hunger Games: Or How the Allied Blockade in the First World War Deprived German Children of Nutrition, and Allied Food Aid Subsequently Saved Them', *The Economic History Review*, 68 (2015), 600–31; Mary Elisabeth Cox, *Hunger in War and Peace: Women and Children in Germany, 1914–1924* (New York, NY: Oxford University Press, 2019); Joël Floris, Kaspar Staub, and Ulrich Woitek, 'The Benefits of Intervention: Birth Weights in Basle 1912–1920', *University of Zurich Department of Economics Working Paper Series*, 236 (2016), 1–36; Kaspar Staub, 'Der vermessene menschliche Körper als Spiegel der Ernährungs- und Gesundheitsverhältnisse am Ende des Ersten Weltkrieges', in *"Woche für Woche neue Preisaufschläge": Nahrungsmittel-, Energie- und Ressourcenkonflikte in der Schweiz des Ersten Weltkriegs*, edited by Dandiel Krämer, Christian Pfister, and Daniel Marc Segesser (Basel: Schwabe, 2016), 285–308; Bernard Harris, 'The Demographic Impact of the First World War: An Anthropometric Perspective', *Social History of Medicine* 6 (1993), 343–66; Robert Millward and Joerg Baten, 'Population and Living Standards, 1914–1945', in *History of Modern Europe*, volume 2 (1870 to the present), edited by Steven Broadberry and Kevin H. O'Rourke (Cambridge: Cambridge University Press, 2012), 232–63.

21 Richard E. Scammon, 'The Literature on the Growth and Physical Development of the Fetus, Infant, and Child: A Quantitative Summary', *The Anatomical Record* 35 (1927), 248.

22 Rudolf Martin, *Lehrbuch der Anthropologie in systematischer Darstellung: Mit besonderer Berücksichtigung der anthropologischen Methoden* (Jena: Gustav Fischer, 1914).

How Much Do We Need?

In December 1914, Paul Eltzbacher, professor of law and acting rector at the *Handelshochschule* in Berlin, edited the book *Die deutsche Volksernährung und der englische Aushungerungsplan* (*Germany's Food Can It Last?*).[23] This book on the food question was written jointly by 15 eminent German scientists. For them, the food question was about food shortage within Germany, a question of national self-sufficiency.[24] Their estimates of the needs of the German people were based on the nutritional value approach. Max Rubner, one of the book's authors, had discovered the caloric equivalents of nutrients in terms of protein, fat, and carbohydrates.[25] He had been assistant to the physiologist Carl von Voit, who in the 1870s had popularized the idea that a diet of an average German male worker should contain 118 grams of protein, 56 grams of fats, and 500 grams of carbohydrates.[26] The authors of *Germany's Food Can It Last?* used Voit's work to emphasise the nutritional needs of the human body. They started with the amounts of food and nutrients needed by individuals under different conditions. These values were then extrapolated to match the need of the entire population. Together with figures on consumption, trade, and domestic production in Germany before the First World War, they estimated possible food shortages in 1914 and discussed measures to overcome them.

An English translation of the book was published in June 1915. The aim was to show the English public the case of German food supply.[27] British physician Augustus Desiré Waller discussed the data presented, which he believed showed that the Germans would be able to meet their physiological needs (Table 10.1). Waller was critical of the stated minimum protein requirement of 80 grams per man per day. He argued that this minimum was adequate in a physiological experiment of short duration, but would hardly be valid over a longer period, assuming a country

[23] Paul Eltzbacher, ed., *Die deutsche Volksernährung und der englische Aushungerungsplan* (Braunschweig: Vieweg, 1914); English translation: Paul Eltzbacher, *Germany's Food Can It Last? The German Case as Presented by German Experts*, Sidney Russel Wells (translator) (London: University of London Press, 1915).

[24] Christian Gerlach, 'Hunger in der Geschichte des 20. Jahrhunderts', *Aus Politik und Zeitgeschichte* 65:49 (2015), 20; Ellen Messer and Laurie F. DeRose, 'Food shortage', in *Who's Hungry? And How Do We Know? Food Shortage, Poverty, and Deprivation*, edited by Laurie DeRose, Ellen Messer, and Sara Millman (Tokyo: United Nations University Press, 1998), 53–91.

[25] Max Rubner, *Die Gesetze des Energieverbrauchs bei der Ernährung* (Leipzig: Franz Deuticke, 1902).

[26] von Voit, *Untersuchung der Kost*, 20.

[27] Wells, *Germany's Food*, ix.

Table 10.1 *Total protein and energy assets of Germany*

	Protein		Energy	
	Grams per head per day	Grams per man per day	Calories per head per day	Calories per man per day
Consumption 1912/13	93	116	3,642	4,779
Physiological minimum	64	80	2,287	3,000
Home production	62.5	78	2,727	3,577
Increased production	81.5	102	3,274	4,295

Source: S. Russel Wells, *Germany's Food Can It Last?*, xvi and xxi.

under siege.[28] For Waller the calorie calculations showed no risk of starvation. However, as he notes, they were based almost entirely on the supply of potatoes and beetroot, the validity of previous official returns, and the estimate of the expansion of production.[29]

Eltzbacher's book was based on the nutritional value approach. Max Rubner advocated 'rational nutrition', a public policy program that used physiology and economics to improve people's nutritional habits.[30] The human body was perceived as a machine that converts nutrients into work, as exemplified in *Germany's Food Can It Last?*: the body is 'a machine into whose furnace or cylinder materials are introduced which are there transformed by processes comparable to the burning of fuel. The chemical energy of the introduced materials is changed into the main activities of the machine man, namely, mechanical energy and heat.'[31] Nutrition, however, is not only a source of energy for human work, it is also required for the maintenance of the body.[32] Studies have argued that this physiological–scientific human–machine metaphor also had an economic rationale: to increase the efficiency and performance of the industrial worker.[33] In this case, however, the focus was on national self-sufficiency and the survival of the population, although this too had an economic dimension.

28 Wells, *Germany's Food*, xix.
29 Wells, *Germany's Food*, xxi–xxii.
30 Corinna Treitel, 'Max Rubner and the Biopolitics of Rational Nutrition', *Central European History*, 41 (2008), 2.
31 Wells, *Germany's Food*, 20.
32 Wells, *Germany's Food*, 20–4.
33 Anson Rabinbach, *The Human Motor: Energy, Fatigue, and the Origins of Modernity* (Berkley, CA: University of California Press, 1990); Jakob Tanner, *Fabrikmahlzeit*, 53–88.

Many scientists followed Voit's physiological model. Alfred Gigon, lecturer at the Medical Clinic of the University of Basel, reported many nutritional value studies (Table 10.2) in his own study on workers' nutrition in Basel.[34] The main focus was on workers, but Armand Gautier, for instance, professor at the medical faculty in Paris, had also included dietary estimates for newborns, young children, adolescents, pregnant women, breastfeeding mothers, and postmenopausal women in his comprehensive book.[35]

Some studies in Gigon's table report actual population diets based on consumption or trade statistics, while others are based on physiological experiments. But during the First World War an economist criticized that the physiological and economics literature often failed to clearly distinguish between the actual and experimental approach.[36]

The experimental approach was considered the only scientific approach for appropriate dietary advice, but physiologists knew that their results depended on living conditions, weight, age, sex, diet, and workload.[37] Note the variation in dietary standards of protein in Table 10.2.

Voit's nutritional recommendations became a standard reference, but they did not remain unchallenged. The adequate amount of (animal) protein (arguments for and against vegetarianism) and the right proportions of nutrients in a healthy diet were debated.[38] Gigon argued that 'the diet of soldiers, workers, prisoners etc. must correspond to this 'normal diet'. The question of nutrition does not only concern physiology and medicine; it is also a major economic issue.'[39] He concludes his section with Brillat-Savarin's aphorism, 'the destiny of nations depends on the manner in which they are fed', which is an apt description of the situation during the First World War; the war influenced the scientific debate on nutrition.

For Mikkel Hindhede, a Danish physician and head of the State Laboratory for Nutrition Research in Copenhagen from 1910 to 1932, 'the Danish food regulation [during war] was [the] most interesting problem' and 'a low protein experiment on a largescale, with about 3,000,000 subjects being available.'[40] He belonged to the *Lebensreform* movement,

[34] Alfred Gigon, *Die Arbeiterkost nach Untersuchungen über die Ernährung Basler Arbeiter bei freigewählter Kost* (Berlin: Springer Verlag, 1914).

[35] Armand Gautier, *L'alimentation et les régimes chez l'homme sain et chez les malades* (Paris: Masson et Cie, 1904), chapter XXXIII.

[36] Salome Schneider, 'Die Erzeugung und der Verbrauch von Nährwerten in der Schweiz', *Zeitschrift für Schweizerische Statistik und Volkswirtschaft* 53 (1917), 275–335.

[37] Wells, *Germany's Food*, 29–38.

[38] Gigon, *Die Arbeiterkost*, 1.

[39] Gigon, *Die Arbeiterkost*, 1.

[40] Mikkel Hindhede, 'The Effect of Food Restriction on Mortality in Copenhagen during War', *Journal of the American Medical Association* 74 (1920), 381–2.

Table 10.2 *Daily diets and dietary standards of workers in different cities and countries*

Author Year	Location and type of work	Proteins (g)	Fat (g)	Carbo-hydrates (g)	Calories	Remarks
Voit, 1877	Worker in Munich, moderate work	118.0	56.0	500.0	3,054.0	Rounded values according to own analyses
Voit, 1881	Worker in Munich, hard work	135.0	80.0	500.0	3,347.5	
Forster, 1873	Worker in Munich	131.9	81.5	457.4	3,174.1	Average values of own analyses
Erismann, 1889	Factory worker in Russia	131.8	79.7	583.8	3,675.2	Average values of own analyses
Hultgren and Landergren, Sweden, 1891	Hard work	188.6	110.1	714.4	4,726.2	Average values of own analyses
	Moderate work	134.4	79.4	522.0	3,436.0	
Atwater, United States, 1896	Worker, moderate work	150.0	150.0	500.0	4,060.0	Rounded values according to own analyses
	Worker, hard work	175.0	250.0	650.0	5,705.0	
Gautier, Paris, 1904	Diet in Paris	102.1	56.5	400.4	2,585.7	Official trade statistics
	Adult, at total rest	80.0	56.5	250–300	1,818–2,083	According to surveys in different countries
	Adult, at relative rest	107.2	64.5	407.5	2,711.0	
	Worker, hard work	152.0	85.0	630.0	3,884.0	
Koenig, Germany, 1904	Rest and light work	100.0	50.0	400.0	2,515.0	Average values from various statistics
	Moderate work	120.0	60.0	500.0	3,100.0	
	Hard work	140.0	100.0	450.0	3,344.0	
Sundström, Finland, 1907	Urban worker, moderate work	124.0	105.0	380.0	3,011.0	Own investigations, without analysis of the meals
	Urban worker, hard work	167.0	153.0	554.0	4,378.0	
Slosse and Waxweiler, Belgium, 1910	Medium hard work	104.6	105.8	392.8	3,023.0	Average values of own analyses
Albertoni and Rossi, Italy, 1907	Abbruzzo Farmer	72.8	53.3	450.0	2,746.4	Average values of own analyses
Inaba, Japan, 1912	Worker, 55–60 kg	90–95	16.0	560–600	2,800–3,000	Own analyses (?)

Table 10.2 (*cont.*)

Author Year	Location and type of work	Proteins (g)	Fat (g)	Carbo-hydrates (g)	Calories	Remarks
Kreis, Basel, 1908	Prison food	137.3	77.3	631.3	3,870.0	Average values of own analyses
Gigon, Basel, 1914	Worker	106.7	94.2	450.0	3,157.6	Average values of own analyses
Schneider, Switzerland, 1917	Swiss actual diet	137.5	108.8	583.8 (601.09)	4,031.0 (4,256.0)	Estimated (incl. alcohol)
Modern, (DACH), 2018	Reference values g/day for adults (25–51, male)	57.0	80.0	225–275	2,300–3,000	If 200 kcal, PAL 1.4–1.8

DACH reference values for nutrient intake published by the German (D), Austrian (A), and Swiss Nutrition Societies (CH).
Source table: Gigon, *Die Arbeiterkost*, 39 and Schneider, 'Die Erzeugung', 331.

which criticized the postulated high protein requirements. The reformers' own nutritional experiments resulted in much lower amounts of protein (23–30 g).[41] This was remarkably low compared to Eltzbacher's 80 g and Voit's 118 g, and even lower than the current modern recommendation of 57 g.[42]

Max Rubner's position, however, was nuanced. In Eltzbacher's book, the authors conceded that 'the physiological protein minimum can be extraordinarily small'.[43] But they argued that it was not a theoretical minimum that was important, but 'the smallest quantity of protein which a man can take without harm to his constitution or his activity.'[44] The authors underlined that Voit felt it crucial to avoid the danger of protein deficiency in the diet, and therefore deliberately included a safety margin in his 118 g recommendation.[45] After considering the literature, they recommended 80 grams.[46]

As the war dragged on and food became increasingly scarce, scientists across Europe studied the effects on people of falling below the supposed minimum food requirement.[47] Diet specialists in the Habsburg Monarchy relied on international literature on calories. In 1915 and 1916, doctors and scientists in Prague conducted experiments to find ways to keep the Austro-Hungarian war effort going on reduced food supplies.[48] Others published on consumption levels before, during, and after the war. For instance, a comparison of the Swiss diet in 1912 and 1917 was published in 1919.[49] The author reported that protein consumption decreased from 137.5 grams to 90.5 grams, and total caloric intake decreased from 4,031 to 2,789 calories.[50] War became a 'mass

41 Uwe Heyll, 'Der „Kampf ums Eiweißminimum“: Zum Konflikt zwischen wissenschaftlicher Ernährungslehre und Ernährungsreform in Deutschland im 19. und 20. Jahrhundert', *Deutsche Medizinische Wochenschrift*, 132 (2007), 2768–73.

42 Dietary reference values in Germany (D), Austria (A), and Switzerland (CH), DACH-Reference Values, German Nutrition Society, 25 April 2023, www.dge.de/wissenschaft/referenzwerte/.

43 Wells, *Germany's Food*, 31.

44 Wells, *Germany's Food*, 32.

45 Wells, *Germany's Food*, 32. Uwe Heyll writes that Max Rubner used the same argument in 1914: Heyll, 'Der "Kampf ums Eiweißminimum"', 2771.

46 Wells, *Germany's Food*, 29–38.

47 For Germany, see Anna Roerkohl, *Hungerblockade und Heimatfront: Die kommunale Lebensmittelversorgung in Westfalen während des Ersten Weltkrieges* (Stuttgart: Franz Steiner Verlag, 1991), 114.

48 Rudolf Kučera, *Rationed life: Science, Everyday Life, and Working-class Politics in the Bohemian Lands, 1914–1918* (New York, NY: Berghahn Books, 2016), 21–7.

49 Salome Schneider, 'Die schweizerische Volksernährung vor und während dem Kriege', *Zeitschrift für Schweizerische Statistik und Volkswirtschaft*, 55 (1919), 7–20.

50 Schneider, 'Die schweizerische Volksernährung', 13.

nutrition experiment' as the Swiss Commission for War Nutrition recurrently underlined during the Second World War.[51]

In 1920, Mikkel Hindhede argued that this 'natural nutrition experiment' did not have a negative outcome in Denmark. The forced change in diet counterintuitively led to lower mortality rates.[52] In his study on the improvement in civilian living standards and health among poor British people during the war, historian Jay Winter made a similar argument but shifted away from measuring protein to measuring adequacy of overall diet.[53] While Mikkel Hindhede argued that the change of diet from meat to a vegetarian diet led to lower mortality rates, Winter argued that these results were a combination of the maintained level of diets, the reduction of socio-economic differences, and wartime welfare policies.[54] Winter's argument has been since criticized with authors emphasizing continuity in mortality patterns.[55] However, neither the British nor the Danish case is representative of other countries. In most countries, especially in the occupied territories and in Central and Eastern Europe, the 'mass experiment' of war caused a significant deterioration in the health status of the civilian population.

For many scientists, the self-sufficiency of the state and its population was at the forefront of their work at the beginning of the war. Later, however, the war also provided an opportunity to re-discuss scientific issues, such as the question of the vegetarian diet and the correct balance of nutrients in an adequate diet. The physiological studies were linked to the economic conditions and the population's standard of living. It was clear to the scientists that the results of their experiments depended on the circumstances. During the war it was not primarily a question of increasing the productivity of the industrial worker, but of ensuring adequate nutrition during a crisis. In combining physiology and economics, the aim was to determine the extent of food shortage and to recommend measures to overcome or completely prevent it. These measures, however, were only partly taken up by politicians.

Advising People and Policy-makers

Many scientists felt that it was their duty to help win the war. Eltzbacher and his co-authors addressed their book to the general public and governmental agencies. For them, Germany could become invincible to

51 Tanner, *Fabrikmahlzeit*, 383–4 and 415–24.
52 Hindhede, 'The Effect of Food Restriction', 381–2.
53 Winter, *The Great War*.
54 Winter, *The Great War*, 244.
55 Harris, 'The Demographic Impact of the First World War', 345–51.

the Allied Blockade through the correct action on nutrition. Their goal was 'to help ensure that the success of our arms is not brought to naught by economic shortcomings.'[56] Thus they emphasized the relationship between military success, nutrition, and the economy. With its national focus, and use of science in service of the fatherland, the book showed the authors' commitment to the war effort. This was consistent with the well-known *Manifesto of the Ninety-Three*, published on 4 October 1914 by prominent German scientists and artists, and the *Declaration of the University Teachers of the German Reich*, released on 16 October 1914 and signed by over 3,000 German teachers.[57] Max Rubner, one of the main authors of *Germany's Food Can It Last?* was also a signatory of the *Manifesto of the Ninety-Three*. Germany was becoming an isolated economy, and the question the authors posed was: how could it survive?[58]

Scientific advice was an integral part of the emerging nutrition sciences.[59] Findings on metabolism and nutritional values were disseminated to experts and the general public. The 'rational nutrition' program aimed to influence the eating habits of citizens and to discipline the lower social strata.[60] Diet had changed dramatically since the mid-nineteenth century. It was now centred on meat, wheat bread, sugar, fruits, vegetables, and milk products, and meals became varied.[61] Although the diet was not balanced by today's standards, and many poor families still lacked adequate nutrition, some were eating better than ever before.[62] The changes in dietary habits concerned many contemporaries. In 1915, physician Josef Kafka promoted an 'economical, self-sufficient, and healthy alimentation', arguing that contemporary diets were too rich. He advocated the replacement of the old motto 'only cook as much as you eat' with 'only cook as much as you need'.[63] He criticized the habit of eating five times a day, recommending only three meals.

A major concern in the debate on the adequate dietary level of (animal) protein was growing meat consumption.[64] Many scientists saw

[56] Wells, *Germany's Food*, xxxi (Eltzbacher, *Die deutsche Volksernährung*, iv: 'mitzuhelfen, dass die Erfolge unserer Waffen nicht durch wirtschaftliche Fehler zu Schanden werden.').

[57] Wolfgang U. Eckart and Rainer Godel, ed., *"Krieg der Gelehrten" und die Welt der Akademien 1914–1924* (Stuttgart: Wissenschaftliche Verlagsgesellschaft, 2016).

[58] Wells, *Germany's Food*, p. 10 (Eltzbacher, *Die deutsche Volksernährung*, pp. 8–9).

[59] Kari Tove Elvbakken, 'Physiology and Hygiene in the History of Nutrition Science: The Norwegian Case 1870–1970', *Social History of Medicine* 33:1 (2018), 1–21.

[60] Tanner, *Fabrikmahlzeit*, 89.

[61] Treitel, 'Max Rubner', 7.

[62] Treitel, 'Max Rubner', 7.

[63] Josef Kafka, *Úsporná výživa* (Prague: F. Šimáčka, 1915), 5.

[64] Treitel, 'Max Rubner', 9.

meat as an essential source of protein and a vital food. The 'superfood' meat was key because it was the only foodstuff that could adequately provide the supposedly required 118 grams of protein.[65] The thesis of undersupply also became widespread; the lack of protein was seen as the main problem of popular nutrition, and the protein gap was a central issue in the 'social question' debates.[66] Others, such as Mikkel Hindehede, who advised the Danish government, and the Swiss physician Maximilian Oskar Bircher-Benner, advocated a vegetarian diet and criticized the increasing meat consumption.[67] During the war, scientists in the Bohemian Lands tried to find alternative sources of protein to mitigate shortages and they too criticized the traditional meat-heavy diet of the working class. Diet expert Julius Stoklasa, for example, recommended introducing mucilage (a plant extract) to food to replace protein from animals.[68]

Max Rubner also complained about the high meat consumption in Germany, thus standing in opposition to the prevailing scientific and public opinion. He criticised the new meat-based sandwich diet of workers in Berlin. To investigate, he bought twenty-eight sandwiches and analysed their nutritional values.[69] For him, urbanization had promoted meat eating and caused undernourishment because sandwiches were low in nutritional value and high in monetary cost.[70] Unsurprisingly, these guidelines also featured in Eltzbacher's book:

> A decrease in our consumption of meat is in no way a misfortune. In the course of the nineteenth century the consumption of meat has risen very much ... Our consumption is greater than that of most other nations, and we could without harm approach the customs of our fathers. We should then live very much more healthily and certainly more cheaply.[71]

Some measures from the book were indeed adopted, the most famous resulting in the destruction of some 9 million swine because they were viewed as 'co-eaters' with humans and an inefficient use of land for caloric production. Consequently, the editor of the English translation, Sidney Russell Wells, was convinced that the book was 'the text-book on which the German Government and people [were] acting.'[72]

[65] Treitel, 'Max Rubner', 9; Tanner, *Fabrikmahlzeit*, 71–3.
[66] Tanner, *Fabrikmahlzeit*, 71–3.
[67] Heyll, 'Der "Kampf ums Eiweißminimum"', 2768–73.
[68] Kučera, *Rationed Life*, 21–7.
[69] Treitel, 'Max Rubner', 5–10.
[70] Treitel, 'Max Rubner', 5–10.
[71] Wells, *Germany's Food*, 188.
[72] Wells, *Germany's Food*, xi.

Before Eltzbacher's book, some of the authors had already published a booklet on nutrition during war.[73] The study published in 1915 by statistician Robert Kuczynski and physiologist Nathan Zuntz (both Eltzbacher's co-authors) aimed to learn from the past and quantify the effectiveness of measures already taken and make demands for the future.[74]

German scientists published advice for authorities and the wider public but were generally not closely involved in policy making.[75] Although they were consulted, they were not directly involved in framing government policy. Moreover, the competitive situation between military authorities and civilian authorities reduced the effectiveness of policy advice. In contrast, the British nutrition experts were closer to the political decision-makers. And some policy-makers in England had been directly involved in dietary research before the war. They knew that the solution to the nutrition issue needed to consider social inequalities.

With the founding of the Royal Society (War) Committee in June 1915, which provided scientific advice to the British government on war issues, a physiological section was established. Under the leadership of Ernest Henry Starling, physiology Professor at University College London, the issues of nutrition in Great Britain and enemy states were brought to the fore. In December 1916, a separate Food (War) Committee was formed to deal exclusively with nutritional issues. British nutrition experts were closer to politics, but this caused problems.[76] The question of bread rationing was controversial: the Minister of Food, Lord Davenport, proposed bread rationing, but scientific experts strongly opposed it, arguing that bread was a staple food and that the amounts were too small. Scientific opinion prevailed. Bread was not rationed, and the food minister was replaced. In February 1917, a scheme of voluntary rationing was introduced to reduce consumption of food in short supply. State-wide rationing was introduced in July 1918.[77]

[73] Paul Eltzbacher, Hedwig Heyl, Carl Oppenheimer, Max Rubner, and Nathan Zuntz, *Ernährung in der Kriegszeit: Ein Ratgeber für Behörden, Geistlicher, Ärzte, Lehrer und Lehrerinnen, Gewerkschaftsbeamte, Hausfrauen und alle die raten und helfen wollen* (Wiesbaden: Springer Fachmedien, 1914).

[74] Robert Kuczynski and Nathan Zuntz, *Unsere bisherige und unsere künftige Ernährung im Kriege* (Braunschweig: Friedrich Vieweg & Sohn, 1915).

[75] Mikuláš Teich, 'Science and Food during the Great War: Britain and Germany', in *The Science and Culture of Nutrition, 1840–1940*, edited by Harmke Kamminga and Andrew Cunningham (Amsterdam: Rodopi, 1995), 229–30; Andrew J. Hull, 'Food for Thought?: The Relations between the Royal Society Food Committees and Government, 1915–19', *Annals of Science*, 59 (2002), 263–98.

[76] Teich, 'Science and Food during the Great War', 227–8.

[77] Richard J. Hammond, *Food Volume I. The Growth of Policy* (London: HMSO, 1984), 3.

Although not directly implemented everywhere, the nutritional value approach remained central. For example, Voit's recommendation became the de facto standard for Dutch scientific thought about nutritional requirements.[78] Physicians and domestic science schoolteachers incorporated them in textbooks and cooking classes for the working poor. A prominent Dutch advocate of the von Voit-Rubner school, Dr F. A. Steensma, collaborated with cookbook author Martine Wittop-Koning; they influenced discussions on rations and broader ideas about wartime nutrition.[79]

Voit/Rubner's ideas formed the basis for the menus in the Wittop-Koning wartime Dutch bestsellers *How Do We Feed Ourselves Well and Cheaply* in 1914 and *Rationed: Suggestions for Housewives* in 1917.[80] Such scientific cookbooks appeared everywhere, even before the War. German Hedwig Heyl, Eltzbacher's co-author, had published in 1885 *Das ABC der Küche* which became a standard German cookbook.[81] She also published *Kleines Kriegskochbuch* in 1914 including a leaflet on the *Volksernährung in der Kriegszeit* by Franz Bumm, Paul Eltzbacher, Max Rubner, Nathan Zuntz, and herself.[82] In addition, authorities invested in scientific endeavours to fabricate unavailable foodstuffs. Replacement foodstuffs (over 10,000 items in October 1917 in Germany alone)[83] or diluting and mixing foodstuffs with additives became necessary. War cooking recipes were also published in France. Some of them had already been published in the Franco-Prussian War of 1870 and were reissued; some were reissued again during the Second World War.[84] The restrictions imposed by the war were sold by the authorities as good for everyone, even beneficial, and in 1917 a scientific society advocating a rational nutrition embraced the lack of meat.[85]

As soon as food rationing was introduced (see Chapter 3), the measurement of adequate rations became an important concern for governments. The official rations in Vienna (Tables 10.3 and 10.4) were in

[78] T. van den Briel-van Ingen, 'Beknopte geschiedenis van de voedingswetenschap in Nederland', *Voeding*, 44 (1983), 160–70.

[79] Anneke H. van Otterloo, 'Voedzaam, smakelijk en gezond: kookleraressen en pogingen tot verbetering van eetgewoonten tussen 1880 en 1940', *Amsterdams Sociologisch Tijdschrift* 12 (1985–86), 495–542.

[80] Martine Wittop Koning, *Hoe voeden wij ons 't goedkoopst en toch goed? Raadgevingen en inlichtingen betreffende de keus, de bereiding en de inmaak van deugdelijk en smakelijk goedkoop voedsel* (Amsterdam: Elsvier, 1914); Martine Wittop Koning, *Op rantsoen. Wenken voor de huisvrouw* (Zaltbommel: Nutsuitgeverij, 1917).

[81] Thirteen editions had been published by 1926. Hedwig Heyl, *Das ABC der Küche*, 13th ed. (Berlin: Carl Habel, 1926). First edition in 1885.

[82] Hedwig Heyl, *Kleines Kriegskochbuch* (Berlin: Carl Habel, 1914); see also Chapter 5.

[83] Roerkohl, *Hungerblockade und Heimatfront*, 224.

[84] Eric Alary, *La Grande Guerre des civils: 1914–1919* (Paris: Perrin, 2013), 386–400.

[85] Alary, *La Grande Guerre des civils*, 386–400.

Table 10.3 *Official rations in Vienna for an adult who was not a self-supporter*

Food type	Daily amount at the beginning of rationing (1915) (g)	Daily amount at the beginning of rationing (cal.)	Daily amount at the end of war (1918) (g)	Daily amount at the end of war (cal.)
Flour	100	300	35.7	107.1
Bread	140	350	180	450
Fat	17.1	153.9	5.7	51.3
Meat	28.5	28.5	17.8	17.8
Milk	1/8 L	82.5		
Potatoes	214	171.2	71.4	57.1
Sugar	41.6	166.4	25	100
Marmalade	23.8	47.6	23.8	47.6
Coffee	8.9			
Total		1,300.1		830.9

Table 10.4 *Official rations in Vienna for an adult doing heavy labour*

Food type	Daily amount at the beginning of rationing (1915) (g)	Daily amount at the beginning of rationing (cal.)	Daily amount at the end of war (1918) (g)	Daily amount at the end of war (cal.)
Flour	150.0	450.0	35.7	107.1
Bread	210.0	525.0	320.0	800.0
Fat	21.4	192.6	5.7	51.3
Meat	28.5	28.5	17.8	17.8
Milk	1/8 L	82.5		
Potatoes	214.0	171.2	71.4	57.1
Sugar	54.1	216.4	50.0	200.0
Marmalade	29.7	59.4	29.7	59.4
Coffee	8.9		8.9	
Total		1,725.6		1,292.7

Source: Loewenfeld-Russ, *Die Regelung der Volksernährung im Kriege*, 335.

force until 1918, but all too often quantities could not be delivered.[86] The total calorific values were below the modern daily recommendation of 2,000 (female) and 2,500 (male) calories per day. The basal metabolic

[86] Hans Loewenfeld-Russ, *Die Regelung der Volksernährung im Kriege* (Vienna: Hölder Pichler Tempsky, 1926), 335.

rate (BMR) is the energy required to keep the body functioning at rest. It ranges between 1,350 and 2,000 kcal per day, depending on height, weight, age, and sex.[87] But this is not enough to survive. Eating, digesting, moving, and essential hygiene activities require more energy: 'a survival diet is 1.27 BMR.'[88] Therefore, the Austrian values of 1,300 to 1,725 calories per day at the start of rationing and between 830 and 1292 at the end literally meant a 'starvation diet'. In Bochum, the average amount was 1,446 (1916), 1,495 (1917), and 1,702 (1918), and in Bielefeld 1,213 (1917) and 1,388 (1918) calories per day.[89] The official rations were clearly insufficient.

The many nuances of rationing systems make it difficult to measure the impact of science on food policy. The ration quotas were set to reach the desired minimum caloric intake spread over three key nutrients: protein, fat, and carbohydrates. The value of any type of foodstuff was considered for its contribution to the recommended daily caloric intake, not *sui generis*, or its contribution in terms of vitamins. The Dutch government, for instance, advocated converting pastures to arable farmland in 1917. They argued that a hectare of pasture produced 150 kg of protein and 150 kg of fat yearly, which corresponded to only 2.5 million calories, whereas a hectare of farmland produced 8 to 12 million calories (about 350 kg of protein and 100 kg of fat), depending on whether they were sown with wheat, legumes, or potatoes.[90] The practice of calculating how many calories a unit of land could produce depending on whether it was used for grain or different livestock was the same method used by Rubner et al. in *Germany's Food Can It Last?*

The nature and function of vitamins were debated, and perceptions of their value differed.[91] In 1918, Paul Lauener, school medical officer in Bern, stated that their essence had not yet been clarified.[92] He underlined the importance of fruits and vegetables for their salt contribution but added that, if the vitamin question was correct, they were rich in vitamins too.[93] Max Rubner, for example, neglected them, while British

[87] Floud, *The Changing Body*, 43.
[88] Floud, *The Changing Body*, 43.
[89] Roerkohl, *Hungerblockade und Heimatfront*, 348.
[90] C. Broekema, 'Landbouw', in *Nederland in den oorlogstijd: de geschiedenis van Nederland en van Nedeerlandsch-Indie tijdens den oorlog van 1914 tot 1919, voor zoover zij met dien oorlog verband houdt*, edited by H. Brugmans (Amsterdam: Elsevier, 1920), 303.
[91] Teich, 'Science and Food during the Great War', 223–7.
[92] Paul Lauener, 'Die Bedeutung der Ernährung für unsere Jugend', *Jahrbuch der Schweizerischen Gesellschaft für Schulgesundheitspflege* 19 (1918), 121.
[93] Lauener, 'Die Bedeutung der Ernährung', 121–2.

experts were much more aware of the need for vitamins in the diet.[94] Yet, because knowledge of vitamins was at an early stage, it had no direct impact on food policies.

Though the *Schweinemord* of 1915 traced back to Rubner's recommendations, direct influence of scientists on politics was limited, and their advice was often ignored.[95] Other core aspects of general policy such as defence, law, economy, and public health were important in decision-making.[96] Moreover, food policy was not always coherent: measures were taken by different authorities, they were not always clear, issued ad hoc, or partially interfered with each other. It is not surprising that Max Rubner criticised the government rationing system in 1916.[97] He thought the bread rations were too low and pointed to substitution effects, with people increasing consumption of other foodstuff too much.[98] He criticized the lack of coordination in the rationing of individual food items, as the total quotas did not provide an adequate diet.[99]

Assessing and Documenting Hunger: Medical Action

Physicians and other health professionals were directly involved in measuring hunger and monitoring nutritional status. As part of the *Carnegie Series on the Economic and Social History of the World War*, Clemens Pirquet, professor at the Vienna University Children's Hospital, published an anthology in 1926 on people's health in Austria and Hungary during the war.[100] Pirquet's chapter focused on the nutritional status of children in Vienna, including those admitted to the Vienna children's hospital in 1918.[101] Of 498 children admitted to the hospital, 440 were

94 Teich, 'Science and Food during the Great War', 223–7; Hull, 'Food for Thought?', 270.

95 Reinhard Güll, 'Der "Schweinemord" oder die "Professorenschlachtung"', *Statistisches Monatsheft Baden-Württemberg*, 6 (2004), 55; Dieter Baudis, 'Vom Schweinemord zum Kohlrübenwinter: Streiflichter zur Entwicklung der Lebensverhältnisse in Berlin im ersten Weltkrieg (August 1914 bis Frühjahr 1917)', *Jahrbuch für Wirtschaftsgeschichte*, (1986), 129–52; For the designation 'Professorenschlachtung' see also August Skalweit, *Die Deutsche Kriegsernährungswirtschaft* (Stuttgart: Deutsche Verlagsanstalt, 1927), 95.

96 Hull, 'Food for Thought?', 297.

97 Max Rubner, *Deutschlands Volksernährung im Kriege* (Leipzig: Verlag "Naturwissenschaften," 1916).

98 Max Rubner, *Deutschlands Volksernährung*, 28.

99 Max Rubner, *Deutschlands* Volksernährung, 37; Roerkohl, *Hungerblockade und Heimatfront*, 287–315.

100 Clemens Pirquet, ed., *Volksgesundheit im Krieg vol. I* (*Wirtschafts- und Sozialgeschichte des Weltkrieges: Österreichische und ungarische Serie*, edited by James T. Shotwell) (New Haven, CT: Yale University Press, 1926).

101 Pirquet, 'Ernährungszustand der Kinder in Österreich während des Krieges und der Nachkriegszeit', in *Volksgesundheit im Krieg I*, 151–79.

classified as undernourished.[102] On children that were not sent to hospitals he reports on examinations by his assistant Edmund Nobel. In May and July 1918, 71,851 children from the larger cities of Austria and the German-Bohemian regions were sent for a period to the rural regions in Hungary to recover.[103] A doctor examined 56,849 of these children, assessing their skin's blood content, fat deposits, and muscle development. Only 4,637 were considered to be adequately nourished. Children suffering from illness were not allowed to leave, so the children who went to Hungary were not even the worst off. Pirquet further reported that in 1918 the Vienna Municipal Youth Welfare Office (*Wiener städtisches Jugendamt*) examined 50,000 of a total 200,000 schoolchildren: 63 per cent of the children (32,403) were classified medium or thin (level 3), thin (4), thin or very thin (5), or very thin (6) on a scale of 1 to 7.

Among a variety of paediatric measures he created as part of a uniform system of assessing children's health, Clemens Pirquet developed the *Pelidisi Index* to measure body shape, in particular to measure child malnutrition.[104] The index is a ratio between weight and sitting height.[105]

$$\left(\text{Pelidisi Index} = \frac{10 * \text{weight}_{(g)}}{\text{sitting height}^3_{(cm)}}\right)$$

The American Relief Administration (ARA) used the Pelidisi Index to select children from Central Europe for relief, but dropped his other measures aimed at measuring strength and blood flow, for example.[106] Children with a Pelidisi score below 94 were considered undernourished, between 95 and 100 well nourished and above 100 over nourished; adolescents were undernourished below a score 98 (boys) and 99 (girls).[107] Between November 1920 and January 1921, 420,000 children

[102] Pirquet, 'Ernährungszustand der Kinder', 155.

[103] Pirquet, 'Ernährungszustand der Kinder', 155–6; For more on child transports, see Chapter 7 in this book. See also Friederike Kind-Kovács, 'The "Other" Child Transports: World War I and the Temporary Displacement of Needy Children from Central Europe', *Revue d'histoire de l'enfance «irrégulière»*, 15 (2013), 1–33.

[104] Mary Elisabeth Cox, 'L'indice Pelidisi (1920–1921): Une réévaluation contemporaine d'un indicateur nutritif oublié', in *Les Fronts intérieurs européens: l'arrière en guerre (1914–1920)*, edited by Laurent Dornel et Stéphane Le Bras (Rennes: Presses universitaires de Rennes, 2018), 179–98.

[105] Pelidisi formula: $10 \times 72{,}900$ g / 90 cm^3 = 1 corresponds to 100 Pelidisi. Pe-li-di-si: Pe for pondus decies, li for linear, di for divisio, si for sedentis altitudine.

[106] Frank M. Surface and Raymond L. Bland, *American Food in the World War and Reconstruction Period. Operations of the Organizations under the Direction of Herbert Hoover 1914 to 1924* (Stanford, CA: Stanford University Press, 1931), 158; Cox, 'L'indice Pelidisi (1920–1921)'.

[107] Cox, 'L'indice Pelidisi (1920–1921)'; Pirquet, 'Ernährungszustand der Kinder', 160.

were examined throughout Austria. In total 75 per cent were considered undernourished and 25 per cent of the 75 per cent were severely undernourished (Pelidisi value below 91).[108]

Growth curves are another way of detecting malnutrition. While the Pelidisi Index is based on the ratio of body measurements, growth curves show change over time. In both cases, reference values are needed to specify that a Pelidisi value below 94 should be considered critical or to judge that a child has a deviant growth curve. At the end of the nineteenth century, the first precursors of modern paediatric growth curves emerged, and many tables with weight and length data for different age groups were published.[109]

However, all anthropometric measurements can be misleading when used alone. In an issue of the *American Relief Administration Bulletin*, a physician reported the examination of 900 Christian and 400 Jewish children in Poland.[110] Out of the 900 Christians, 349 (or 43.8 per cent) had a Pelidisi index of 95 and above and were thus considered sufficiently nourished. However, 55 of those children (13.9 per cent) had signs of anaemia, in 120 cases (30.6 per cent) enlarged glands were present, and 21 children were suffering from rickets (5.3 per cent). The Polish physician noted that only 193 of the 394 children (42.2 per cent) with a Pelidisi index of 95 and above could be registered as normal healthy children after a 'merely superficial examination'.[111] Similar problems arose in Russia, where the Pelidisi was used to measure children suffering from severe famine. The Pelidisi was only useful for children who were undernourished to some degree; it was not helpful for those who were so deprived that they were physically deformed.[112]

Nevertheless, the Pelidisi index was useful in triage for rapid assessment of thousands of children or for monitoring population health. On its own, however, it was inadequate for assessing individual nutritional status, as shown in Poland and Russia.[113] The recurrent criticism of the Body Mass Index, the closest analogue to the Pelidisi along with the Rohrer's Index (or Ponderal Index), as the standard method for assessing weight follows the same pattern.

108 Pirquet, 'Ernährungszustand der Kinder', 161–7.

109 Tim J. Cole, 'The Development of Growth References and Growth Charts', *Annals of Human Biology* 39/5 (2012), 382–94; James Allen Young, 'Height, Weight, and Health: Anthropometric Study of Human Growth in Nineteenth-Century American Medicine', *Bulletin of the History of Medicine* 53:2 (1979), 214–43.

110 Dr. Podhorecki, 'IV Pelidisi Results in Poland', *American Relief Administration Bulletin*, 2:20 (1922), 29–31.

111 Podhorecki, 'IV Pelidisi Results in Poland', 29.

112 Cox, 'L'indice Pelidisi (1920–1921)', 189–91.

113 Cox, 'L'indice Pelidisi (1920–1921)', 189–91.

Measuring nutritional status for use in triage and in monitoring health after the war was the basis for food relief. For Eastern Europe, the ARA decreed that:

> only children who have been carefully examined by a doctor and pronounced to be undernourished (according to the Dr. Pirquet system of weight and measurements) are given cards admitting them to the kitchens. The children partaking of the feeding are weighted at frequent intervals, and any child who has increased in weight so as to approach the normal is excluded, to make place for another undernourished one.[114]

This 'From the body to relief'[115] was not a neutral medical procedure to provide relief. It was embedded in a wider political and social context. It shaped the humanitarian discourse in the interwar period and was linked to political interests.[116] The procedure required a norm for comparison. The more a child deviated from an expected norm, the more the child became an object of humanitarian and medical intervention.[117]

In addition to assessing nutritional status using anthropometric measures, Clemens von Pirquet also analysed other consequences of famine. The relative infant mortality rate increased by 30 per cent in Vienna between 1914 and 1919 (i.e. considering the decrease in birth rates). The mortality of children aged 5–14 increased as well. There were more deaths from tuberculosis between the ages of 5 and 20, as well as more cases of scurvy and rickets caused by a poor diet.[118]

In the same anthology, Johann v. Bókay, president of the *Hungarian Central Committee of the ARA*, and Adolf Juba reported on the nutrition of children in Hungary.[119] In Budapest, the total number of deaths was 16,000 in 1909, in 1918 it had risen to 30,000. The authors cite poorer nutrition, worsening public sanitation, deterioration of housing conditions, and the emergence of epidemic diseases. With regard to poorer nutrition, they refer to a study on insufficient rationing quantities by Leo von Liebermann, Professor of Hygiene at Budapest University. The total calorific value of the official rations was estimated at 1,273 calories per

[114] C. G. Bowden, 'Economic Conditions and Relief in Hungary' (19 January 1921), *American Relief Administration Bulletin* 2:12 (1 May 1921), 13.

[115] Friederike Kind-Kovács, 'The Great War, the Child's Body and the American Red Cross', *European Review of History* 23 (2016), 41.

[116] Kind-Kovács, 'The Great War'; Valérie Gorin, '"Millions of children in deadly peril": utilisation des photographies d'enfants affamés par le *Save the Children Fund* pendant l'entre-deux-guerres', in *Perceptions et mises en scène médiatiques de la famine au XXe siècle*, (Itinera), edited by Angela Müller and Felix Rauh (Basel: Schwabe, 2014): 95–112.

[117] Gorin, '"Millions of children in deadly peril"', 95–112.

[118] Pirquet, 'Ernährungszustand der Kinder', 171–9.

[119] Johann v. Bókay and Adolf Juba, 'Ernährungszustand der Kinder in Ungarn', in *Volksgesundheit im Krieg*, 180–224.

person day, per day.[120] Like many Central European cities, Budapest also saw an increase in infant and child mortality and tuberculosis cases.

In the autumn of 1919, 127,076, Hungarian children aged 6 to 14 years were examined and classified as 'well nourished', 'medium', and 'undernourished' (without specifying how this distinction were made): 73 per cent were considered poorly fed, 24 per cent medium-nourished, and 3 per cent well-fed.[121] Bókay compared the weight and height values with those of Friedrich Camerer, a German physician who had published weight and height tables by age at the end of the nineteenth century, which were frequently used as reference values in German-speaking countries, even though his sample size was small.[122] The weight curves of all children in Budapest were below the Camerer values (on average across all age groups and the two sexes by 6 kg in 1919 and by 2 kg in 1920).[123] These children were examined by Bókay and Juba over the course of the ARA relief mission and came from poor or middle-class families with modest income. Grammar school pupils from better-off families, measured by Adolf Juba, were heavier and taller than children from poorer families in 1919, but on average they too weighed less than they had before the war.

Adolf Juba also measured the heights and weights of pupils at the St. Stephan Gymnasium in the VIIth district of Budapest continuously from 1908 to 1921 (approximately 1,000 pupils per year, aged 10 to 20).[124] He reported that in 1919 nearly all pupils weighed significantly less than before the war (0.40 to 4.17 kg). He also found lower values for height. In addition, Bókay and Juba also reported negative consequences due to a deterioration of physical conditions: increased absenteeism due to illness, and increased incidence of goitre.

A similar survey of 2,147 schoolchildren (six years old) for the year 1917/18 was conducted in Prague (Table 10.5).[125] A total of 60 per cent of the children suffered from undernourishment and 67 per cent had poor teeth; 14 per cent of the children had bone disease, 17 per cent had visual impairments, 11 per cent had scrofula, 9 per cent had speech impairments, and 2 per cent had tuberculosis. The ARA survey completed in May and June 1921 of over 50,000 schoolchildren in

[120] Bókay, 'Ernährungszustand der Kinder in Ungarn', 184.

[121] Bókay, 'Ernährungszustand der Kinder in Ungarn', 192; János Bókay, 'The Result of the 1921 Feeding from a Medical Standpoint', *American Relief Administration Bulletin*, 2:23 (1922), 44–8.

[122] Wilhelm Camerer, *Der Stoffwechsel des Kindes von der Geburt bis zur Beendigung des Wachstums* (Tübingen: Verlag der H. Laupp'schen Buchhandlung, 1894).

[123] Bókay and Juba, 'Ernährungszustand der Kinder in Ungarn', 191–204.

[124] Bókay and Juba, 'Ernährungszustand der Kinder in Ungarn', 204–24.

[125] Philip Skinner Platt, *Přehled veřejného zdravotnictví Velké Prahy* (V Praze: Ministerstvo sociální péče, 1920), 72.

Table 10.5 *Survey of 2,147 schoolchildren in Prague, 1917/18*

	Number	%
Well-fed children	862	40
Sufficiently fed children	1032	48
Poorly fed children	253	12
Children with healthy teeth	705	33
Children with satisfactory teeth	1255	57
Children with bad teeth	217	10
Children with 'handicaps'	557	26
Children with rickets	278	13
Children with distorted spine and other diseases	76	4
Anaemic children	599	28

Source: Philip Skinner Platt, *Přehled veřejného zdravotnictví Velké Prahy*, 72.

Table 10.6 *American Relief Administration schoolchildren survey in Czechoslovakia, May and June 1921*

City population	Number examined	Percentage schoolchildren examined	Seriously undernourished (%)	Subnormal (%)
Over 500,000 (Prague)	4,694	3.5	9	46
100,000 to 300,000 (Brno)	6,176	14	18	48
20,000 to 100,000	21,490	15	15	50
10,000 to 20,000	11,741	18	14	53
Under 10,000	4,298	22	9	36

Source: The American Relief Administration, *The American Relief Administration in Czecho-Slovakia*, 11.

Czechoslovakia also demonstrated the serious health consequences of the war (Table 10.6).[126] Children had a subnormal nutritional status with 36 to 53 per cent, and 9 to 18 per cent were considered seriously undernourished.

The impact of war on children's health depended on the food supplies available in each country. The health of children in combatant states in Central and Eastern Europe declined rapidly. The health of children in

[126] The American Relief Administration, *The American Relief Administration in Czecho-Slovakia: A Sketch of the Child-feeding Operations of the A.R.A. Mission to Czecho-Slovakia, 1919–1921* (New York, NY: The American Relief Administration, 1921), 11.

Belgium and occupied France was also poor.[127] In Belgium, the average weight and height of schoolchildren aged 6 to 14 decreased progressively between 1915 and 1918. The difference in average weight between 1913 and 1918 corresponded to a year's weight gain.[128] In occupied France, children's growth suffered from inadequate food rations (adult rations were rarely over 1,600 calories, often only 1,400 calories).[129] In Lille, it was reported shortly after the war that 14-year-old children looked like 10-year-olds,[130] and an average development lag of 18 to 24 months was measured in the départements Nord and Ardennes.[131]

In the city of Berne in neutral Switzerland the declining trend in rickets (1913–1930) was interrupted by an increase in 1918.[132] The supply of food was difficult for Switzerland even though it was a neutral country because of the Allied blockades. In Bern, the shortage was reflected in the heights of 15-year-old children: the percentage of schoolchildren below the threshold of 148 cm increased in 1918 (boys) and 1919 (girls) compared to the years 1914 to 1917.[133] In contrast, there is little evidence of an effect on growth of first-grade children.[134]

Not only the war situation of the country – whether belligerent, neutral, occupied, near the front – has to be taken into account, but also local conditions. In France, the supply situation was apparently worse in cities than in the countryside.[135] In Germany, too, some argue that the rural population benefited from proximity to farms, although recent studies suggest economic status was more relevant than the urban/rural divide.[136] In Central Europe children were sent from the cities to the countryside to recover from the stresses of war.[137] However, the growth and body weight of the rural children was also

[127] Andrew Donson, 'Children and Youth', in *1914–1918-online. International Encyclopedia of the First World War*, edited by Ute Daniel et al. (Berlin: Freie Universität Berlin, 2014); Jean Houssiau and Christian Vreugde, 'Brussels Schoolchildren during the First World War', *Cahiers Bruxellois* 46 (2014), 39–52.

[128] Jean Demoor and Auguste Slosse, 'L'Alimentation des Belges pendant la guerre et ses conséquences', *Bulletin de l'Académie royale de Médecine de Belgique* 30 (1920), 501.

[129] Albert Calmette, 'Considérations sur l'état sanitaire de la ville de Lille pendant l'occupation allemande', *Bulletin de l'Académie de Medicine* 81 (1919), 120–5.

[130] Calmette, 'Considérations sur l'état sanitaire', 120–5

[131] Joseph Genevrier and Georges Heuyer, 'L'état sanitaire des enfants dans les départements libérés', *Bulletins de la Société de Pédiatrie de Paris* 17 (1919), 59–65.

[132] Staub, 'Der vermessene menschliche Körper', 293.

[133] Staub, 'Der vermessene menschliche Körper', 292–3.

[134] Staub, 'Der vermessene menschliche Körper', 292–3.

[135] Alary, *La Grande Guerre*, 337.

[136] Cox, *Hunger in War and Peace*, 170; Eberhard Demm, 'Deutschlands Kinder im Ersten Weltkrieg: Zwischen Propaganda und Sozialfürsorge', *Militärgeschichtliche Zeitschrift* 60 (2001), 51–98.

[137] Kind-Kovács, 'The "Other" Child Transports', 75–109; Demm, 'Deutschlands Kinder im Ersten Weltkrieg', 65.

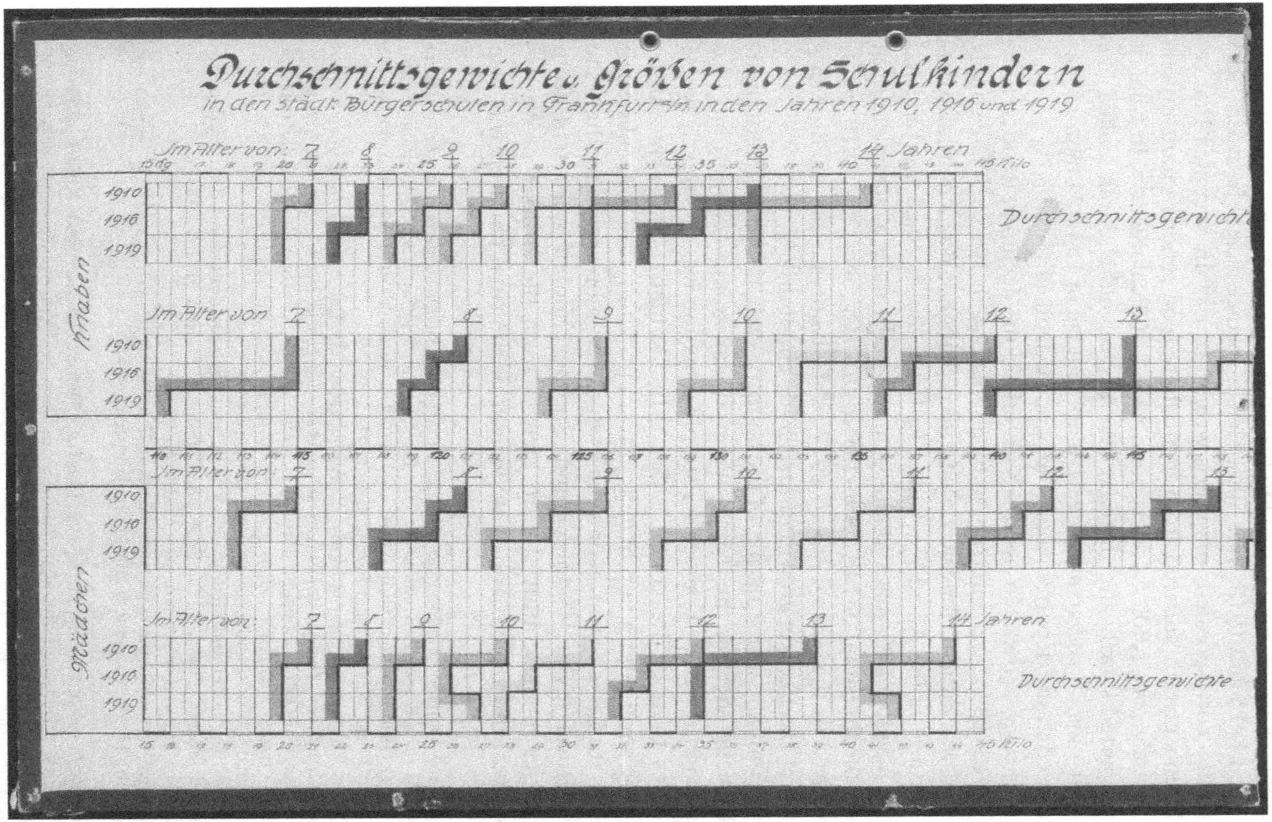

Figure 10.1 Graph showing average height and weight of schoolchildren in Frankfurt, 1910, 1916, and 1919.
Source: AEG, Archives privées 92.10.9 (2)

affected. Although those in rural areas may have benefited from a better nutritional situation, they needed more energy for heavy physical work. For instance, in the Schopfheim school district (in southern Germany), urban boys (aged 6 to 10) were 2.7 kg heavier and girls 2.4 kg heavier.[138] It would have been no different in Poland, where 12- to 15-year-old boys and girls worked in the fields if their older siblings and fathers had been mobilised.[139]

The variety of measures used and the different conditions in the regions make it difficult to make meaningful comparisons of these surveys of children across Europe. Figure 10.1 shows a table of measurements for schoolchildren in Frankfurt. In some of the examples given, authors reported the percentage of children that were 'undernourished' or 'thin' without stating the methods used to obtain these results. Nevertheless, our review suggests that the war impact on children's body shape was greater in Central and Eastern Europe (and the occupied territories) than in non-occupied France or Britain, or in neutral countries. This section has highlighted the efforts of physicians to quantify the impact of war on children's health and the role of measurements in determining food aid. These anthropometric-health studies were part of 'a more general expansion of the welfare state for youth and children in Europe'.[140] Practical applications often went hand in hand with the development of scientific knowledge. The final section of this chapter examines a lesser studied measure of wartime hunger that interested scientists: birthweights.

War Effects on Neonatal Health and Birth Weight

In 1916, the Royal Women's Hospital at the University of Berlin (*Kgl. Universitäts-Frauenklinik*) was asked to report on the effects of bad nutritional conditions on neonates and their mothers during and after pregnancy.[141] The hospital was specifically asked if there was a need for an extra protein allowance for pregnant and breastfeeding women. To answer the question, physician Carl Ruge II compared the average birthweight of all children born at the hospital between July 1915 and July 1916 with the average birthweight in 1913. Finding a difference of

[138] Demm, 'Deutschlands Kinder im Ersten Weltkrieg', 80.

[139] Jan Molenda, 'War, Children and Youth: The Impact of the First World War upon Changes in the Position of Children in the Peasant Family and Community', *Acta Poloniae Historica* 79 (1999), 172–3.

[140] Donson, 'Children and Youth'.

[141] Carl Ruge II, 'Über den Einfluß der Kriegsernährung auf Fruchtentwicklung und Laktation', *Zentralblatt für Gynäkologie* 40 (1916), 680–4.

30 grams, he concluded that the mothers' wartime diets only had little effect on the foetus' development. Nevertheless, he added that an adequate diet was important for women to prepare their bodies for the extra demands of pregnancy and breastfeeding.

Similar studies have been designed to answer specific scientific (medical) questions. Ruge, for instance, was interested in the effect of war on the sex ratio at birth and on the incidence of eclampsia.[142] Others wanted to see if better nutrition could make labour easier.[143] Before caesarean sections became common, this question was debated in cases where the pelvis was too narrow to deliver babies.[144] The influence of the mother's diet on the foetus was also discussed in relation to specific nutrients.[145] Once again the war was seen as an opportunity for research.[146]

In most cases these studies were authored by medical doctors from obstetrical clinics and maternity hospitals. In 1924, Sigmund Peller and Friedrich Bass reviewed forty studies quantifying the effect of war on birthweight in German cities.[147] First, they summarized the studies of birthweights that had been published during the war until 1917 and found no change in wartime birthweights compared with pre-war birthweights. Some might have concluded that war had no effect on the nutritional status of mothers and their newborns.[148] Despite the lack of change, Peller and Bass argued against such a conclusion, pointing

[142] Ruge, 'Über den Einfluß der Kriegsernährung', 680–4.

[143] F. Binz, 'Einiges über den Zusammenhang zwischen Krieg und Geburt', *Münchener medizinische Wochenschrift* (1919), 12–14.

[144] Otto Günther, *Das Gewicht der Neugeborenen in der Kriegs- u. Nachkriegszeit* (Munich: Rudolph Müller & Steinicke, 1927).

[145] Dr. Momm, 'Hat die eiweiß- und fettarme Nahrung einen Einfluß auf die Entwicklung der Frucht?', *Zentralblatt für Gynäkologie* 40 (1916), 545–50; Hans Abels, 'Über die Wichtigkeit der Vitamine für die Entwicklung des menschlichen fötalen und mütterlichen Organismus', *Klinische Wochenschrift* 1 (1922), 1785–7; H. Katz and W. König, 'Über die Abhängigkeit des Geburtsgewichtes des Neugeborenen vom Vitamin-Gehalt der mütterlichen Nahrung', *Klinische Wochenschrift* 2 (1923), 2077–9.

[146] A. Hamm, 'Geburtshilflich-gynäkologische Kriegsfragen', *Zentralblatt für Gynäkologie* 42 (1918), 82–90; Binz, 'Einiges über den Zusammenhang'; Michael Dávid, 'Über Kriegsneugeborene', *Zentralblatt für Gynäkologie* 46 (1922), 795–802; Günther, *Das Gewicht der Neugeborenen*.

[147] Sigismund Peller and Friedrich Bass, 'Die Rolle exogener Faktoren in der intrauterinen Entwicklung des Menschen mit besonderer Berücksichtigung der Kriegs- und Nachkriegsverhältnisse', *Archiv für Gynäkologie* 122 (1924), 208–38.

[148] Binz, 'Einiges über den Zusammenhang'; Hamm, 'Geburtshilflich-gynäkologische Kriegsfragen'; Dr. Mössmer, 'Über "Kriegsneugeborene"', *Zentralblatt für Gynäkologie*, 40 (1916), 684–6; Momm, 'Hat die eiweiß- und fettarme Nahrung einen Einfluß?'; M. Pfaundler, 'Ueber Körpermasse von Münchener Schulkinder während des Krieges', *Münchener Medizinische Wochenschrift* 66 (1919), 859–62; Ruge II, 'Über den Einfluß der Kriegsernährung auf Fruchtentwicklung und Laktation'; A. Tschirch, 'Zur Frage der Kriegsneugeborenen', *Münchener Medizinische Wochenschrift* 63 (1916), 1650–1.

out that only few studies covered the entire war period. The period after 1917 did indeed see a decline in birthweight.[149]

Survey periods and specific nutritional situations explain the differences.[150] The war effect depends on the duration, severity, and timing of malnutrition. Human growth and development is slowed or interrupted when affected by malnutrition or disease.[151] When conditions improve, growth returns to its previous path through accelerated growth or a longer period of growth. However, this occurs only if the negative impact was not too harsh and too long. The timing of the negative effect is also important. Effects can be particularly strong during sensitive periods of human growth. Moreover, malnutrition, infection, and immune defence are interrelated and mutually reinforcing, affecting development and body growth.[152] The shape of the human body and growth are directly affected by the nutritional status.[153] Neonatal size at birth and child height and weight are considered to reflect the immediate nutritional conditions at the time of measurement and are therefore considered to be sensitive indicators of short-term shocks.[154]

The war impact was evident in the height and weight of children, especially when looking at the data produced by the ARA after the war. The scientific evidence on the effect on birthweight, however, was mixed. In 1947, the physician Hosemann summarized the debate by pointing out that it was only with the studies on Russian children born during the famine after 1918 that it had been 'proven' that severe maternal malnutrition led to lower birthweights and an increase in premature births and infant mortality.[155] Similarly, a 1954 textbook stated that both the world

149 Peller and Bass, 'Die Rolle exogener Faktoren', 218.

150 A. O. Gerschenson, 'Zur Frage des Einflusses einiger Faktoren auf das Gewicht der Neugeborenen', *Zeitschrift für Kinderheilkunde* 51 (1931), 20–30.

151 Tanner, *Growth at Adolescence*.

152 Peter G. Lunn, 'Nutrition, immunity and infection', in *The Decline of Mortality in Europe*, edited by Roger Schofield, David S. Reher, and Alain Bideau (Oxford: Clarendon Press, 1991), 131–45.

153 Floud, *The Changing Body*.

154 Floris, 'The benefits of intervention'; Carlos Varea, José Manuel Terán, Cristina Bernis, Barry Bogin, and Antonio González-González, 'Is the economic crisis affecting birth outcome in Spain? Evaluation of temporal trend in underweight at birth (2003–2012)', *Annals of Human Biology* 43 (2016), 169–82; Bastiaan T. Heijmans et al., 'Persistent Epigenetic Differences Associated with Prenatal Exposure to Famine in Humans', *PNAS* 105 (2008), 17046–9; Zena Stein, Mervyn Susser, Gerhart Saenger, and Francis Marolla, *Famine and Human Development: The Dutch Hunger Winter of 1944–1945* (New York, NY: Oxford University Press, 1975).

155 H. Hosemann, 'Ernährung und fötale Entwicklung', *Deutsche Medizinische Wochenschrift* 72 (1947), 507–11.

wars and the subsequent hunger years had shown that severe malnutrition reduced average birthweight.[156]

Hosemann, however, also pointed out that birthweight is a poor indicator because only severe malnutrition has a sizeable effect on average birthweight.[157] He referred to animal experiments to support his argument. The reference to animal experiments was a common argument in studies during the war and its aftermath.[158] Scientific research in the 1920s suggested that birthweight was determined by many factors including gestational age, vital status, infant sex, maternal age, parity, multiple births, parental ethnicity, genetics, maternal health and nutritional status, maternal body size, and parental socio-economic background.[159]

Many contemporary authors knew as well as we do today that average birthweight was not a perfect measure and they knew that birthweight was an anthropometric measure embedded in a biological, socioeconomic, and epidemiological environment. The war affected birth rates, the sex ratio at birth, gestational age, the rate of premature birth, and the number of stillbirths.[160] For many reasons, it remains difficult to compare the birthweights of children born in hospitals over time and space. Complicated births were more common in hospitals.[161] During the war, hospitals registered more births. Due to shortage of money, food, housing, heating materials, and clothing, people chose hospitals where food was available and a heating system kept the building warm.[162] The shortage of physicians also increased the number of births in hospitals, as fewer physicians could attend home births.[163] For the same reasons, it is reported that women in Vienna tended to stay longer in hospital before giving birth.[164] It is therefore not unreasonable to assume that they also stayed longer after the birth, but these data are not available. The socio-economic

[156] Joachim Brock, ed., *Biologische Daten für den Kinderarzt: Gründzüge einer Biologie des Kindesalters*, 2nd ed. (Berlin: Springer Verlag, 1954), 17.

[157] Hosemann, 'Ernährung und fötale Entwicklung'.

[158] Ruge II, 'Über den Einfluß der Kriegsernährung auf Fruchtentwicklung und Laktation'; Hamm, 'Geburtshilflich-gynäkologische Kriegsfragen'; Binz, 'Einiges über den Zusammenhang'; Dávid, 'Über Kriegsneugeborene'.

[159] Bogin, *Patterns of Human Growth*, 58–66.

[160] Binz, 'Einiges über den Zusammenhang'; Dávid, 'Über Kriegsneugeborene; Josef Bondi, 'Das Gewicht der Neugeborenen aus der Kriegs- und Nachkriegszeit', *Wiener klinische Wochenschrift* 37 (1924), 1093–6.

[161] Binz, 'Einiges über den Zusammenhang'.

[162] Binz, 'Einiges über den Zusammenhang'; Dávid, 'Über Kriegsneugeborene'.

[163] Binz, 'Einiges über den Zusammenhang'.

[164] Sigismund Peller, 'Die Maße der Neugeborenen und die Kriegsernährung der Schwangeren', *Deutsche Medizinische Wochenschrift* 43 (1917), 178–80.

composition of those giving birth in hospitals also changed during the war.[165]

Generally, trends in size at birth are not synchronous with trends in height at other ages during the twentieth century. For the United States, mean birthweight values reached their current levels by the late nineteenth century.[166] For Switzerland, Germany, and Norway there was an increase during the first half of the twentieth century.[167] Two studies in 1942 on the question of a 'secular' increasing trend in average birthweight in Prague and Budapest present only a slight increase in average birthweight.[168]

Looking for studies reporting either original or summarized anthropometric data from neonates from various countries from 1910 to 1950, we found 17 studies on birthweight that report weights of neonates for the entire war period and shortly thereafter (Table 10.7). These birthweight data originate mainly from larger maternity hospitals in cities, and thus primarily reflect more urban populations. Moreover, all home births are missed by these data, which is biased against certain socioeconomic groups. There is a lack of modern studies assessing how neonate size at birth in Europe developed during the First World War.[169]

With the seventeen studies at hand, we attempt to summarize the quantitative evidence on birthweights during the war in a comparative way. However, because of the varying inclusion and exclusion of criteria regarding vital status, parity, and maturity, the average birthweight levels are not directly comparable between the studies and cities. Moreover, the

165 Binz, 'Einiges über den Zusammenhang'; Peller, 'Die Maße der Neugeborenen'.

166 Eric Schneider, 'Fetal Health Stagnation: Have Health Conditions in utero Improved in the United States and Western and Northern Europe over the Past 150 Years?', *Social Science & Medicine* 179 (2017), 18–26.

167 Tim J. Cole, 'Secular Trends in Growth', *Proceedings of the Nutrition Society* 59 (2000), 317–24; Tim J. Cole, 'The Secular Trend in Human Physical Growth: A Biological View', *Economics and Human Biology* 1 (2003), 161–8; K. Solth and K. Abt, 'Die Veränderung des Geburtsgewichtes in den letzten fünfzig Jahren: Vergleich deutscher Kliniken mit dem Frauenspital Basel', *Schweizerische Medizinsche Wochenschrift*, 81 (1951), 58–61; W. Peter Ward, *Birthweight and Economic Growth: Women's Living Standards in the Industrializing West* (Chicago, IL: University of Chicago Press, 1993); Emily Oken, 'Secular trends in birthweight', in *Recent Advances in Growth Research: Nutritional, Molecular and Endocrine Perspectives*, edited by Matthew W. Gillman, Peter D. Gluckman, and Ron G. Rosenfeld (Nestlé Nutrition Institute Workshop Series) (Basel: S. Karger, 2013), 103–14.

168 Heinz v. Braitenberg, 'Zur Frage der Entwicklungsbeschleunigung der Neugeborenen', *Archiv für Gynäkologie* 174 (1942), 193–203; Imre Korompai, 'Untersuchungen über die Gewichtsverhältnisse der Neugeborenen auf Grund des 40jährigen Materials der Klinik', *Zeitschrift für Geburtshilfe und Gynäkologie* 124 (1942), 36–43.

169 Schneider, 'Fetal Health Stagnation'; Ward, *Birth Weight and Economic Growth.*

Table 10.7 *Studies included*

Study	City	Data source	N	Author	Inclusion criteria
A	Berlin	Frauenklinik Charité	ca. 13,000	Solth, 1950	Only singletons, weight ≥1,000 g, gestational age ≥250 days, 3 y moving averages
B	Würzburg 1	Universitäts-Frauenklink	ca. 11,000	Solth, 1950	Only singletons, weight ≥1,000 g, gestational age ≥250 days, 3 y moving averages
C	Würzburg 2	Universitäts-Frauenklink	ca. 2,100	Wolf, 1939	Only first parities, mature neonates, gestational age ≥280 days
D	Marburg	Universitäts-Frauenklink	ca. 8,000	Solth, 1950	Only singletons, weight ≥1,000 g, gestational age ≥250 days, 3 y moving averages
E	Frankfurt	Universitätsklinik	ca. 6,600	Kemper, 1940	All neonates, by parents' SEP
F	Munich	Wöchnerinnenheim Rotes Kreut	ca. 1,400	Günther, 1927	Only lower SEP mothers and first parity
G	Basel	Frauenspital Universität	ca. 15,000	Solth/Abt, 1951	All neonates, 3 y moving averages
H	Vienna 1	Universitäts-Frauenklink	ca. 14,000	Katz/König, 1923	Only singletons with weight ≥1,500 g
I	Vienna 2	Wöchnerinnenheim Lucina	ca. 1,700	Bondi, 1924	All neonates
J	Budapest 1	Universitäts-Frauenklink	ca. 13,000	David, 1922	All neonates
K	Budapest 2	Universitäts-Frauenklink	ca. 12,000	Korompai, 1942	Only mature neonates (weight ≥2,500 g)
L	Milano	Clinica L. Mangiagalli	ca. 5,000	Capelli-Vegni, 1932	All neonates
M	Odessa	Two unspecified maternity hospitals	ca. 12,000	Gerschenson, 1931	Only live births, singletons, and mature neonates
N	Petrograd 1	Schreder Hospital	ca. 3,000	Ltschkus/Valtsky, 1921	Only singletons and mature neonates

O	Petrograd 2	State Clinic, Obstetrical Institute	ca. 6,700	Lure/Belugina, 1923	Only mature births
P	Moscow 1	Abrikosova Maternity Hospital	ca. 20,000	Troipkaya, 1922	Only mature births
Q	Moscow 2	University Obstetrical Clinic	ca. 2,500	Troipkaya, 1922	Only mature births

Sources: K. Solth, 'Die Veränderung des Geburtsgewichtes im Laufe der letzten Jahrzehnte', *Archiv für Gynäkologie* 177 (1950), 678–92; Martha Wolf, *Ist die Größe des Neugeborenen von Einflüssen der Umwelt abhängig?* (Dissertation Julius-Maximilian-Universität Würzburg), (Borna-Leipzig: Robert Noske, 1939); Rudolf Kemper, *Stat. Arbeit über Gewicht und Größe der Neugeborenen sowie des Gewichts der Placenta* (Dissertation Johann Wolfgang Goethe-Universität Frankfurt a. M.), (Gelnhausen: F. W. Kalbfleisch, 1940); Otto Günther, *Das Gewicht der Neugeborenen in der Kriegs- u. Nachkriegszeit* (Dissertation Ludwigs Maximilians-Universität München), (München: Rudolph Müller & Steinicke, 1927); K. Solth and K. Abt, 'Die Veränderung des Geburtsgewichtes in den letzten fünfzig Jahren'; Floris, 'The Benefits of Intervention'; H. Katz and W. König, 'Über die Abhängigkeit des Geburtsgewichtes des Neugeborenen vom Vitamin-Gehalt der mütterlichen Nahrung', *Klinische Wochenschrift* 2 (1923), 2077–9; Josef Bondi, 'Das Gewicht der Neugeborenen aus der Kriegs- und Nachkriegszeit', *Wiener klinische Wochenschrift* 37 (1924), 1093–6; Michael Dávid, 'Über Kriegsneugeborene', *Zentralblatt für Gynäkologie* 46 (1922), 795–802; Imre Korompai, 'Untersuchungen über die Gewichtsverhältnisse der Neugeborenen auf Grund des 40jährigen Material der Klinik', *Zeitschrift für Geburtshilfe und Gynäkologie* 124 (1942), 36–43; Adele Capelli-Vegni, 'Contributo di osservazioni intorno allo sviluppo ponderale del neonato in rapporto alla professione della madre e intorno a variazioni di peso di neonati partoriti tra il 1911 e il 1931 nella clinica „L. Mangiagalli" die Milano', *Annali die ostetricia e ginecologia* (1932), 1457–98; A. O. Gerschenson, 'Zur Frage des Einflusses einiger Faktoren auf das Gewicht der Neugeborenen', *Zeitschrift für Kinderheilkunde* 51 (1931), 20–30. English transliterations of the Russian studies: L. G. Ltschkus and L. A. Valtsky, 'K voprosu o vliyanii nedoedaniya na techenie beremennosti i rodov na ves i smertnost' novorozhdennykh i na molokootdelenie', *Vrachebnoe Delo* 1–6 (1921), 31–4; R. G. Lure and I. V. Belugina, 'O vese beremennykh i donoshennykh novorozhdennykh voennogo i golodnogo vremeni', *Russkiĭ Ginekologicheskiĭ Vestnik* 1:3 (1923), 310–35; L. S. Troipkaya, 'Izmeneniya vesa donomennogo ploda za 6 dete 1914 po 1919 god po materialam rodnl'nogo doma imeni A. Abrivosovoj i akusherskoĭ Kliniki 2 Moskovekogo Gos. Universiteta', *Meditsinskiĭ Zhurnal* 1–3 (1922).

geographical variation in the size of neonates complicates direct comparison.[170] Some studies smoothed their data using moving averages, blurring the immediate effects in their series. To ensure temporal comparability within the single studies, we only included data series that use identical measurement standards and inclusion criteria over the observed time period.[171] Overall, we present aggregated and published data on average birthweight from the German Empire (six studies), Austria-Hungary (four studies), Switzerland (one study), Italy (one study), and Russia (five studies). We reproduce the mean values untreated, as reported in the original studies.

The German cities Berlin, Marburg, Würzburg, Frankfurt, and Munich, and Basel in Switzerland, experienced a rather moderate decrease in average birthweight with local minima 1918/1919 and recovery thereafter in 1920–1922 (Figure 10.2). Overall, the loss in average birthweight was 100 grams in these cities. Milano had a similar decrease in average birthweight at the same time, and the percentage of neonates below 3,000 grams doubled from 25 per cent prior to the war to 50 per cent in 1918. Other authors also showed an increase in the number of children weighing less than 3,000 grams and a decrease in the number of children weighing more than 3,500 grams, while the number of children with a birthweight between 3,000 and 3,500 grams remained stable.[172] Vienna and partially Budapest show a more marked and substantial decrease in average birthweight over the war period until 1918. Information on recovery is, however, lacking because most studies do not cover the post-war period.

In Moscow and Petrograd, the decrease in average birthweight was even more pronounced and sustained. In Petrograd, average birthweight did not recover until 1922, and in Odessa average birthweight first increased again in 1923. Overall, the loss in average birthweight in the cities in Austria-Hungary and Russia was 200–300 grams and thus more pronounced than in the cities in the German Empire, Switzerland, and Italy.[173] In Petrograd, malnutrition not only reduced the size of newborn babies, it also reduced the average weight of pregnant women when they arrived at the maternity hospital to give birth. The mean

[170] Leary et al. 'Geographical variation in neonatal phenotype' *Acta Obstetricia et Gynecologica Scandinavica* 85:9 (2006), 1080–9.

[171] The number of studies not included is too large to be reported here. A summary of the literature is provided by Peller and Bass, 'Die Rolle exogener Faktoren'; Additional studies can be found in *Berichte über die gesamte Gynäkologie und Geburtshilfe sowie deren Grenzgebiete* edited by the Deutsche Gesellschaft für Gynäkologie.

[172] Peller and Bass, 'Die Rolle exogener Faktoren'; Bondi, 'Das Gewicht der Neugeborenen'; Gerschenson, 'Zur Frage des Einflusses einiger Faktoren'.

[173] Gerschenson, 'Zur Frage des Einflusses einiger Faktoren'.

weight of these heavily pregnant women was 6–10 kg lighter in 1919 than it was in 1913, although both groups were equally tall (approximately 156 cm by average). This suggests that nutritional status of the expecting mothers suffered first due to reduced nutritional input, and that the birthweight of their neonates reacted to these adverse maternal conditions.

Gerschenson, the author of the Odessa study from 1931, suggested that the larger and more lasting loss in birthweight in Russia compared to the German Empire was the result of the more pronounced famine situations in some Russian areas.[174] For instance, he describes that in Odessa people attained less than half of their protein and fat needs.[175] Gerschenson also mentions that the observation of the following years also revealed that these children born in famine conditions showed poorer physical development, weakened immune defence against infections, and increased mortality compared with children born in non-war years.[176] Thus, Gerschenson and many other authors of these and similar studies made connections between the value of average birthweight for measuring hunger, and of the health consequences and outcomes of the affected children later in life.

This fits well with more recent research on the long-term negative consequences of an unhealthy early life environment on later life outcomes such as morbidity, mortality, and educational achievement; research that builds on David Barker's hypothesis of foetal and infant origins of adult disease.[177] Similar results were also found for the Dutch hunger winter of 1944/1945. Depending on when babies were born during the First World War, they may also have received fewer inputs in the first years after birth, when the fastest increase in stature occurs (0–2 years). Thus, the negative effects on physical and cognitive development of the next generation may have been multiplied under these circumstances.

[174] Gerschenson, 'Zur Frage des Einflusses einiger Faktoren', 23; famines were common in Russia in the first half of the twentieth century, see Chapter 12.

[175] Gerschenson, 'Zur Frage des Einflusses einiger Faktoren', 23.

[176] Gerschenson, 'Zur Frage des Einflusses einiger Faktoren', 24.

[177] David J. P. Barker, 'The Fetal and Infant Origins of Adult Disease: The Womb May Be More Important Than the Home', *BMJ*, 301 (1990), 1111; Stein, *Famine and Human Development*; David J. P. Barker, *Mothers, Babies, and Health in Later Life*, 2nd ed. (Edinburgh: Churchill Livingstone, 1998); Douglas Almond and Janet Currie, 'Killing Me Softly: The Fetal Origins Hypothesis', *Journal of Economic Perspectives* 25 (2011), 153–72; while Barker's name has become synonymous with the foetal origins hypothesis, he was not the first one to explore later health effects of early life conditions. See A. Forsdahl, 'Are Poor Living Conditions in Childhood and Adolescence an Important Risk Factor for Arteriosclerotic Disease?', *British Journal of Preventive and Social Medicine* 31 (1977), 91–5.

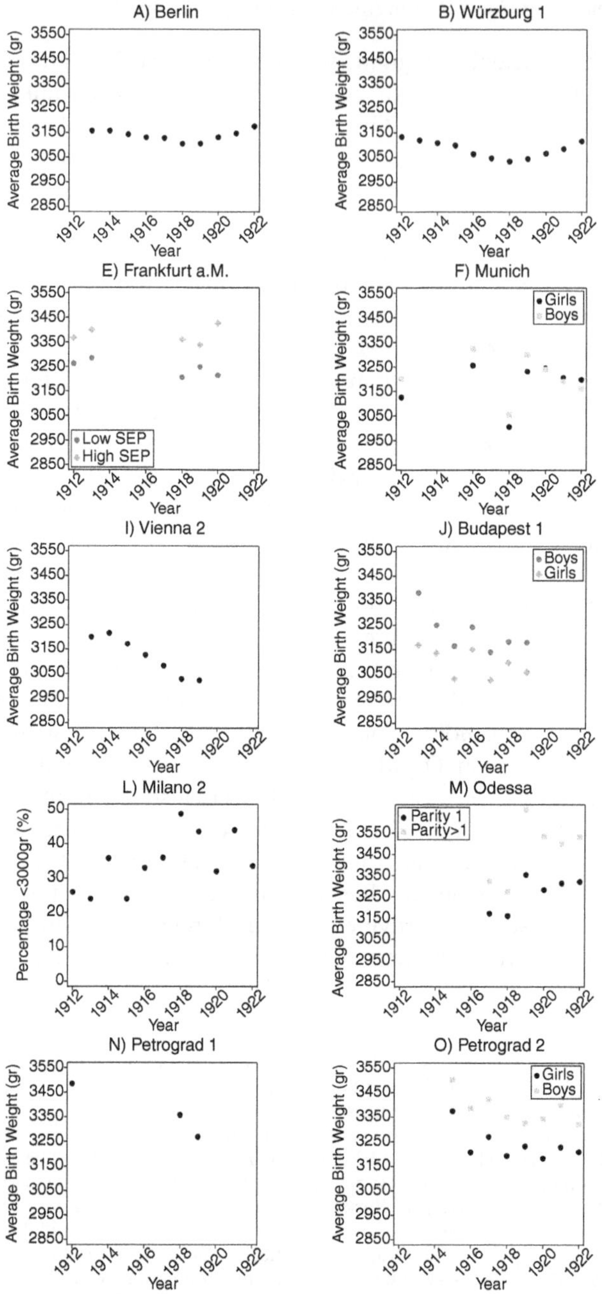

Figure 10.2 Average birthweight of neonates in various cities, 1912–22 (SEP, socio-economic position in graphs E and H, age of mothers in years in graph P).

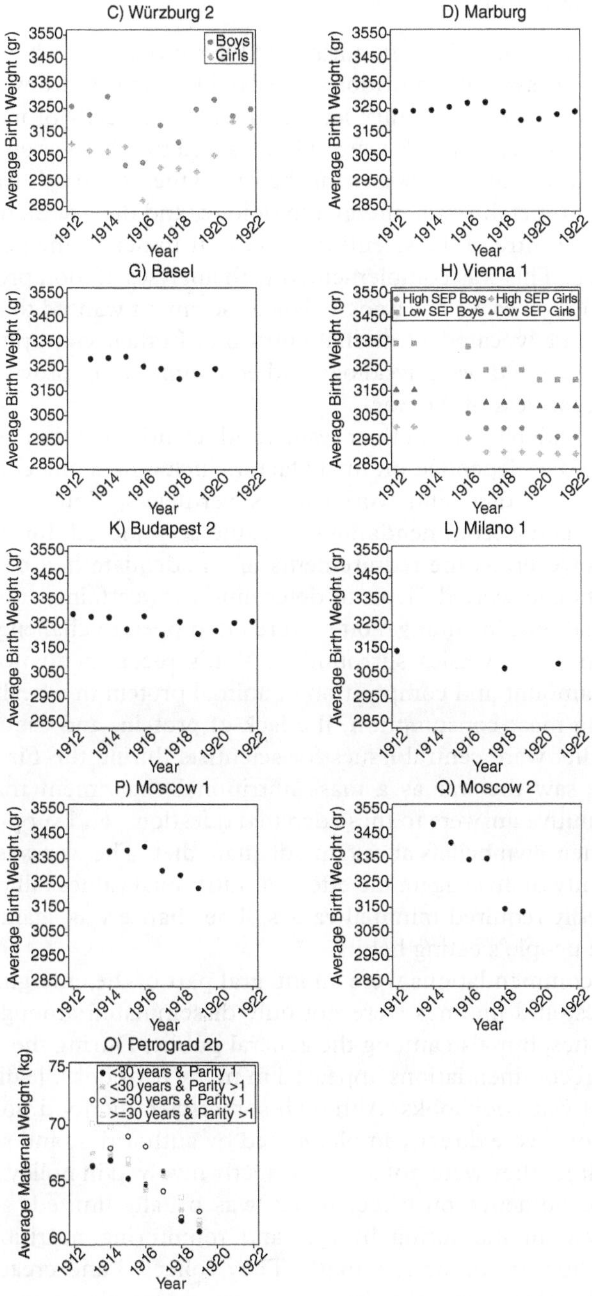

Figure 10.2 (Continued)

Conclusion

Scientists created large datasets during the First World War while measuring hunger and assessing nutritional needs. They analysed how to overcome food shortages at country level and what the needs of individuals and the population as a whole were. They wanted to help their own people survive. Some saw their work as contributing to their country's war effort.

Research in metabolism, energy physiology, and dietary thermogenesis was at the centre of the scientific endeavour to determine population dietary needs. This was complemented with analyses of food production and consumption as well as trade balance. Scientists wanted to help and many of them advocated a 'rational nutrition'. In their view, public policy programs should use physiology and economics to improve people's nutrition, regardless of the war.

Scientists understood that their results and scientific recommendations on adequate diet depended on many factors including living conditions, weight, age, sex, diet, and workload. Nevertheless, Voit's nutritional calculations and recommendations became a standard for scientific thought. However, as the requirements of an adequate diet depend on many factors and were difficult to determine with certainty, nutritional recommendations, including Voit's, were often open to challenge.

The main controversies surrounding Voit's recommendations were the correct amount and composition of animal protein in a healthy diet. The growing meat consumption, the lack of protein, and the role of a vegetarian diet were central issues for scientists during the First World War. Many saw the war as a mass nutritional experiment that could provide definitive answers to these debated questions, and support arguments for their own beliefs about an adequate diet. The war was seen as an opportunity to investigate the effect of nutritional values falling below the supposedly required minimal values. The chance was again opened to influence people's eating habits.

Public recommendations were an integral part of the emerging nutrition sciences, and findings were not only disseminated among experts and authorities, but also among the general public. During the war, scientific diet recommendations appeared in many textbooks, leaflets, and especially in war cookbooks. Although some scientific food policy recommendations were directly implemented by authorities, and scientists were consulted, they were not always directly involved in policy making.

While the influence on direct policy was usually limited, scientists were involved in measuring hunger and monitoring nutritional status during the war and its aftermath. They collected and created huge amounts of anthropometric data to assess malnutrition in children and newborns. In some cases, new indexes were created to measure nutritional deprivation, most notably the *Pelidisi Index* in Austria. Other anthropometric measurements, such as birthweight and height and weight measurements taken at schools, had a longer history but took on greater meaning for scientists during and especially after the war as they used them to try to understand shifting living standards. In measuring nutritional status to do triage and monitor health, scientists were also determining thresholds for food relief and help. It was not a neutral procedure to show how war had affected children and their bodies; it shaped the humanitarian discourse and programmes during the interwar period on who received aid.[178]

The many studies investigating the effects of war on birthweight suggest that the war was seen as an opportunity to resolve an old scientific question. However, the studies provided mixed evidence and the debate remained open during the 1920s and 1930s. It is only the cumulative experience of both world wars and the following hunger years that made it clear that malnutrition of the mother had a negative effect on birthweight.

But the mixed evidence in the 1920s also showed that birthweight was determined by many factors including gestational age, vital status, sex of the child, maternal age, parity, multiple births, parental ethnicity, genetics, maternal health and nutritional status, maternal body size, and socio-economic background of the parents. Scientists were aware that birthweight was embedded in a biological, socioeconomic and epidemiological environment, and thus was notoriously difficult to compare. It became clear that the resulting average birthweights were influenced by the survey period, the composition of the sample, and the duration, severity, and timing of malnutrition. Our analysis of 17 of those contemporary studies on birthweight shows that during the war and its aftermath all groups had lower birthweights than before the War, but these losses were not the same. In cities in Austria-Hungary and Russia, neonates weighed 200–300 grams less than they had before the War; in cities in the German Empire, Switzerland, and Italy, they weighed approximately 100 grams less.

The combination of anthropometric history analysis with modern research on the impact of adverse environmental conditions both before and immediately after birth on health and wellbeing outcomes later in life, together with an historical analysis on how those measurements were created and interpreted, offers a fascinating avenue for further research on the immediate, short, medium, and long-term legacy of the

[178] On humanitarian aid after the First World War, see Chapter 13.

First World War. And, especially as 'there is no area in which custom and biology are more intermixed than in problems of nutrition'[179] the question of how hunger shaped the human body during the First World War is also a question about the impact of war decades later and even on subsequent generations.

[179] S. L. Washburn, 'Review of Josef Brozek, ed., *Body Measurements and Human Nutrition* (Detroit, MI: Wayne State University Press, 1956)', *American Anthropologist* 60 (1958), 207–8.

11 The Science of Hunger and Malnutrition

Mark Harrison

It is often said that war is a catalyst for progress in science and medicine,[1] and in certain respects this is true. But the relationship is usually a complicated one, for conflict tends to accelerate research into subjects vital to the war effort while side-lining others.[2] Gains made during war may also be difficult to consolidate in the very different conditions of peacetime.[3] The scientific understanding of hunger and malnutrition is no exception but far less is known about the impact of the First World War in this regard than the Second. The war of 1939–45 has received more attention because scientific studies conducted during and immediately after the conflict continue to inform recovery regimes for the severely malnourished.[4] In addition to numerous observations on the effects of starvation among prisoners and persons in formerly occupied countries,[5] experiments were also conducted on human volunteers and these subsequently informed the relief of distressed populations.[6] This research

[1] E.g. Guy Hartcup, *The War of Invention: Scientific Developments, 1914–18* (London: Brasseys, 1988); Solly Zuckerman, *Scientists and War: The Impact of Science on Military and Civil Affairs* (New York, NY: Harper and Row, 1967); Zachary Cope, 'The Medical Balance Sheet of War', in his *Some Famous General Practitioners and other Medical Historical Essays* (London: Pitman, 1961).

[2] Roger Cooter, 'Medicine and the Goodness of War', *Canadian Bulletin of Medical History* 12 (1990), 147–59; Linda Bryder, 'The First World War: Healthy or Hungry?' *History Workshop Journal* 24 (1987), 141–57.

[3] Roger Cooter, *Surgery and Society in Peace and War: Orthopaedics and the Organization of Modern Medicine, 1880–1948* (London: Macmillan, 1993).

[4] Hisham Mehanna, Paul C. Nankivell, Jamil Moledina and Jane Travis, 'Refeeding Syndrome – Awareness, Prevention and Management', *Head and Neck Oncology* 1:4 (2009), doi:10.1186/1758-3284-1-4.

[5] E.g. E. P. Trepman, 'Rescue of the Remnants: The British Emergency Medical Relief Operation in Belsen Camp 1945', *Journal of the Royal Army Medical Corps* 145 (2001), 281–93; M. A. Schnitker, P. E. Mattman and T. L. Bliss, 'A Clinical Study of Malnutrition in Japanese Prisoners of War', *Annals of Internal Medicine* 35:1 (1951), 69–96; Douglas Stevenson, 'Famine Oedema among Prisoners of War', *British Medical Journal* 1:4349 (1944), 658–60.

[6] Todd Tucker, *The Great Starvation Experiment: The Heroic Men Who Starved So That Millions Could Live* (New York, NY: Free Press, 2006).

is sometimes regarded as the foundation of the modern science of hunger[7] and has tended to eclipse work that was undertaken during the era of the First World War.[8] As this chapter will argue, this earlier research was in many respects equally significant, bringing substantial progress in the understanding of deficiency disease and the pathology of starvation. However, as with most medical advances in wartime, progress was uneven and some of the lessons learned during the war were soon forgotten or overshadowed.

Nutrition and Medicine before the War

The pathology and physiology of hunger and nutritional deprivation was in its infancy in 1914. There was much confusion, and often acrimonious debate, about the nature and causes of illnesses said to be linked to impoverished diet; not least because hunger was a potent political issue. But the uncertainty shrouding these conditions owed much to the fact that they appeared as changeable clusters of symptoms, frustrating diagnosis and the attribution of causes. The relationship of these diseases to diet was also obscured by alternative hypotheses, ranging from exposure to cold and damp to infection with 'germs'. From the 1870s, a series of discoveries identifying the causal agents of diseases such as cholera and tuberculosis led some to believe that bacteria were responsible for many of the conditions that we know to be caused by malnutrition. Although the acceptance of germ theory did not lead to research into nutrition being shelved, some physicians and scientists pursued what ultimately turned out to be an infertile hypothesis. This can be seen most clearly in the case of beriberi, which we now know is caused by lack of vitamin B1 or thiamin. Prior to the First World War, beriberi was frequently encountered among prisoners and certain isolated populations; it was attributed to a variety of factors including exhaustion, inclement weather and infection. Even though

[7] British Nutrition Foundation, 'How the War Changed Nutrition: From There to Now', https://archive.nutrition.org.uk/nutritioninthenews/wartimefood/warnutrition.html [last accessed March 1, 2022]; Laura C. Schultz, 'The Dutch Hunger Winter and the Developmental Origins of Health and Disease', *Proceedings of the National Academy of Science of the United States of America* 107:39 (2010), 16757–58.

[8] In the case of Britain, for example, scholarship has tended to focus on rationing, rather than detailed investigations of the effects of malnutrition during wartime. See David F. Smith, 'Nutrition Science and the Two World Wars', in *Nutrition in Britain: Science, Scientists and Politics in the Twentieth Century*, edited by David F. Smith (London: Routledge, 1997), 142–65; L. Margaret Barnett, *British Food Policy during the First World War* (London: Routledge, 1985); Jose Harris, 'Bureaucrats and Businessmen in British Food Control, 1916–19', in *War and the State: The Transformation of British Government*, edited by K. Burk (London: George Allen and Unwin, 1982), 135–56.

dietary deficiency figured in most accounts of this disease, population studies and dietary experiments on animals failed to yield conclusive results.[9] However, an important breakthrough came in the 1890s when the scientist Christiaan Eijkman (1858–1930), working in the Dutch East Indies, noticed that beriberi only developed among animals that were fed polished rice, as opposed to grains that were still covered by their husk. This research was followed up by his younger colleague Gerrit Grijns, who proposed that the husks of rice contained a substance that was necessary to preserve health.[10]

A similar conclusion was reached by the English-trained physician (later Admiral and Baron) Takaki Kanehiro (1849–1920), who recommended adding Western dietary items to naval rations and mixing rice with barley. As a result, beriberi (known as *kak'ke* in Japan) was eliminated from the navy by 1895. The army knew of the navy's success but believed that it would be much harder for it to follow the same path, due to the difficulty of supplying troops in the field. Moreover, most army doctors and the Tokyo medical elite were influenced heavily by German laboratory science. They were more inclined to the theory that beriberi was caused by bacteria and suffered over 80,000 cases during the war against Russia in 1904–5 as a result of their refusal to supplement rations. Afterwards, the Minister of War, General Terauchi, forced the army to mix barley with its rice ration but a good deal of resistance to the dietary theory remained.[11]

The Japanese case shows that powerfully entrenched professional interests could affect debates about science and medicine. It also shows that the debate over the aetiology of beriberi was still very much alive. Even among advocates of the nutrition theory, there was little agreement about the identity of the vital element that seemed to be contained in the husks of rice and some other foods. However, in 1912, there were two important developments. The Cambridge University physiologist Frederick Gowland Hopkins (1861–1947) used animal feeding experiments to show that there must be substances other than protein, fats and carbohydrates that were necessary for growth. He referred to these as 'accessory

[9] E.g. Herbert E. Durham, 'Notes on Beriberi in the Malay Peninsula and on Christmas Island (Indian Ocean)', *Epidemiology and Infection* 4:1 (1904), 112–55; C. Barry, 'Notes on Beri-beri in Rangoon', *Indian Medical Gazette* (September 1900), 343–5.

[10] Kenneth J. Carpenter, 'The Discovery of Thiamin', *Annals of Nutrition and Metabolism* 61 (2012), 219–23.

[11] Alexander Bay, *Beriberi in Modern Japan: The Making of a National Disease* (Rochester, NY: University of Rochester Press, 2012); Alan Hawk, 'The Great Disease Enemy, Kak'ke (Beriberi) and the Imperial Japanese Army', *Military Medicine* 171:4 (2006), 333–9.

food factors'.[12] In the same year, the Polish biochemist Casimir Funk (1884–1967) identified four chemicals (amines) which he claimed were linked to vital processes in the human body. He called these substances 'vitamines' (vital amines), one of which was the substance (B1) that prevented beriberi, the others preventing scurvy, rickets and pellagra.[13]

Although the importance of these discoveries is clear in retrospect (Hopkins and Eijkmann received the Nobel Prize in 1929 for their work, though not Funk), they did not lead to an immediate change in the ways in which most doctors viewed diseases linked to nutrition. Many resisted the idea that the lack of vitamins (the 'e' was soon dropped) was sufficient to cause disease. This can be seen clearly in the case of rickets, which was the most common problem related to dietary deficiency in European countries. Rickets was regularly diagnosed among the urban poor and the muscular weakness, stunted growth and skeletal deformity that characterised the disease were potent symbols of deprivation. In Britain, the prevalence of such conditions had long been associated with physical deterioration; a concern that was heightened in the years following the war in South Africa (1899–1902). During that conflict, there had been difficulty in obtaining recruits who could fulfil the physical criteria for enlistment and these revelations spurred a series of initiatives intended to regenerate the urban poor. Most of these – such as the provision of free milk to children, classes in motherhood and school medical inspection – focused on the improvement of nutrition.[14] But while the majority of physicians accepted that rickets was linked to nutrition, many were uncertain whether it was a single disease or whether other factors might be involved. Lack of sunlight entering dense urban conurbations and atmospheric pollution were commonly implicated in the causation of rickets, as were infections such as diarrhoea and syphilis.[15]

There was evidently no consensus about the causes of diseases in which poor nutrition had been implicated, which meant that doctors

[12] Frederick G. Hopkins, 'Feeding Experiments Illustrating the Importance of Accessory Factors in Normal Dietaries', *The Journal of Physiology* 44 (1912), 425–60.

[13] Anna Piro, Giuseppe Tagarelli, Paolo Lagonia, Antonio Tagarelli and Aldo Quattrone, 'Casimir Funk: His Discovery of the Vitamins and Their Deficiency Disorders', *Annals of Nutrition and Metabolism* 57:2 (2010), 85–8.

[14] Bernard Semmel, *Imperialism and Social Reform* (London: Allen & Unwin, 1960); Geoffrey R. Searle, *The Quest for National Efficiency* (Oxford: Oxford University Press, 1971); Anna Davin, 'Imperialism and Motherhood', *History Workshop* 5 (1978), 9–65; Deborah Dwork, *War is Good for Babies and Other Young Children: A History of the Infant and Child Welfare Movement in England 1898–1918* (London: Tavistock, 1987).

[15] J. S. Fowler, 'The Nutritive Diseases of Infancy: A Review', *Edinburgh Medical Journal* 13:6 (1914), 469–77; Anne Hardy, 'Commentary: Bread and Alum, Syphilis and Sunlight: Rickets in the Nineteenth Century', *International Journal of Epidemiology* 32:3 (2003), 337–40.

who encountered such diseases during the war had no clear template for dealing with them. The same was true of conditions arising from starvation. The little that was known about such conditions was derived from work conducted in the European colonies, especially British India, which experienced a number of severe famines in the decades before the First World War.[16] In the 1870s, medical officers such as William Cornish began to calculate diets for those employed temporarily in famine relief works. Some administrators disagreed with his assessments, believing them to be too generous but Cornish's view prevailed.[17] A related controversy arose over the use of opium to stem the effects of hunger. Some critics of the British administration in India claimed that famines were partly due to the fact that too much land was given over to the cultivation of opium. This was dismissed by government medical officers who pointed out that food was often comparatively abundant in opium growing areas. Likening 'anti-opiumists' to anti-vaccinators in their failure to acknowledge facts, they maintained that opium was the 'salvation of thousands' because it enabled them to endure hardship and hunger and exercised a 'prophylactic influence' over the fevers that tended to occur during and after famines.[18] This dispute was part of a wider debate over opium, which saw a widening gulf between opinion – including medical opinion – in India and in Britain.[19]

British India was also the source of most studies of the pathology of hunger, particularly the condition known as 'famine dropsy' or 'epidemic dropsy', which was characterised by swelling, initially in the legs and then in other parts of the body. This disease was observed by Cornish among prisoners in South Indian jails during the mid-1860s and again in his work on the great famine of 1877–8. Other writers made similar observations during the latter famine and the condition was widely discussed in medical journals over the coming years.[20] Kenneth McLeod, a senior officer of the Indian Medical Service and editor of the *Indian Medical Gazette* was one of the most frequent contributors to these discussions. McLeod worked on a range of issues related to famine but

[16] Mike Davis, *Late Victorian Holocausts: El Niño Famines and the Making of the Third World* (London: Verso, 2001).

[17] David Arnold, 'The 'Discovery' of Malnutrition and Diet in Colonial India', *Indian Economic and Social History Review* 31:1 (1994), 1–26.

[18] William Moore, 'Famine: Its Effects and Relief', *Transactions of the Epidemiological Society of London*, n.s., 11 (1891), 27–46.

[19] Paul C. Winther, *Anglo-European Science and the Rhetoric of Empire: Malaria, Opium, and British Rule in India, 1756–1895* (Lanham, MD: Lexington Books, 2003).

[20] Alexander Porter, *The Diseases of the Madras Famine of 1877–78* (Madras: Government Press, 1889); Kenneth McLeod, 'Epidemic Dropsy in Calcutta', *Indian Medical Gazette* 10 (1881), 148.

dropsy became his chief concern and he collected a huge amount of clinical, pathological and epidemiological information related to that condition. McLeod concluded that the disease was communicable, though not directly: some form of medium or media seemed to be involved. Its communicability also appeared to depend on seasonal factors and exposure to the elements.[21]

Contemporaneous with these studies, a number of laboratory investigations were directed to understanding the histological changes resulting from a severely impoverished diet. The most important of these were conducted by Dr D. D. Cunningham, one of the scientific officers attached to the Government of India's Sanitary Department. Cunningham undertook experiments with nutritional deprivation on plants and also on tadpoles, which were selected because their tissues were transparent, allowing microscopic investigations to be easily carried out. Cunningham noted that food deprivation led to fatty degeneration of the epithelium of the intestinal canal and wasting of other organs. Furthermore, he believed that there were similarities between the appearances found in the intestines of the tadpoles and the dysentery suffered by many people subject to famine.[22]

Although Cunningham's work failed to convince many other scientists at the time, some of those working during the First World War were interested in similar questions (see also, Chapter 10). The much larger body of work on epidemic dropsy was also important even though it has recently been dismissed as a 'diversion' from research on 'internationally recognised' diseases such as beriberi.[23] This judgement is misleading in several respects. Firstly, famine-related oedema ('dropsy') was not clearly distinguished from beriberi at this time and although some authors (like McLeod) insisted that it was a disease *sui generis*, others were unsure.[24] Secondly, famine-related dropsy was at least as prevalent among the civilian population of India during the late nineteenth century as beriberi and it is no wonder that it was deemed a subject worthy of research.[25] Finally, the research done in India was subsequently

[21] Kenneth McLeod, 'Epidemic Dropsy', *Indian Medical Gazette* 29:1 (1894), 14–17; Kenneth McLeod, 'Epidemic Dropsy', *Indian Medical Gazette* 28:8 (1893), 257–9; Moore, 'Famine: Its Effects and Relief'.

[22] D. D. Cunningham, *On Certain Effects of Starvation on Vegetable and Animals Tissues* (Calcutta: Superintendent of Government Printing, 1879).

[23] David Arnold, 'British India and the "Beriberi Problem," 1798–1942', *Medical History* 54 (2010), 306.

[24] T. H. Delany, 'Epidemic Dropsy or Beri-Beri in Eastern Bengal', *Indian Medical Gazette* 43 (1908), 167–74.

[25] E.g. E. D. W. Greig, *Epidemic Dropsy in Calcutta, Scientific Memories by Medical Officers of the Medical and Sanitary Departments of the Government of India*, 45 (Calcutta:

recognised as important by those who worked on famine oedema during the First World War.

Prior to 1914, medical officers in India had also begun to examine the relationship between severe nutritional deprivation and diseases generally thought to be infectious. Epidemics of 'fever' were common in times of famine and were often observed among malnourished prisoners in Indian jails. However, there were different opinions on whether these diseases were directly produced by famine or incidental to it.[26] Most reports were wary of attributing the outbreaks to poor diet because it would have reflected badly on the British administration.[27] But some medical officers who worked in areas which suffered regularly from malaria and famine believed them to be causally related.[28] This connection was not thoroughly investigated until 1908, when Punjab and the neighbouring province of United Provinces suffered extremely high mortality from malaria. The government of India dispatched S. R. Christophers of the Indian Medical Service to determine the causes of the epidemic and he concluded that it had been triggered by a period of prolonged drought, in which food had become scarce and prices high. Having reached the point of starvation, the population became vulnerable to malaria.[29] This work became very influential and subsequently formed the basis for anti-malaria intervention in northern India.[30] It also seems to have shaped the outlook of some of those who served in the First World War.

Starvation

The research conducted in India served as a foundation for investigations of severe nutritional deprivation during the First World War. India was one of the few places in which 'hunger' or 'famine' oedema had been described in detail. But while Indian research informed work conducted during the war, it is inaccurate to state that 'colonial' methods (i.e. reliance on large-scale population studies rather than laboratory research)

Superintendent Government Printing, 1911); T. C. Rutherford, 'An Epidemic of Dropsy', *Indian Medical Gazette* 43 (1908), 174–6.

[26] E.g. 'Review of R. T. Lyons, *On Relapsing, or Famine Fever* (London: King and Co., 1872)', *Indian Medical Gazette*, 8 (1873), 106–8.

[27] E.g. W. J. Buchanan, 'A Note on the Nutritive Values of the Dietaries of Bengal Jails', *Indian Medical Gazette* 31 (1896), 153–8.

[28] E.g. *Annual Report of the Sanitary Commissioner for the North West Provinces and Oudh* (Allahabad: Government Press, 1897), 28.

[29] S. R. Christophers, *Malaria in the Punjab, Scientific Memoirs by Officers of the Medical and Sanitary Departments of the Government of India*, 46 (Calcutta: Superintendent Government Printing, 1911).

[30] Sheila Zurbrigg, *Weakened by Want: Epidemic Malaria and Hunger in Colonial Punjab* (Abingdon: Routledge, 2019).

were imported into Europe in order to study such diseases.[31] There are some similarities between wartime and colonial research but not all previous work on famine oedema stemmed from the colonies. Some studies of starved populations in Europe used a similar methodology; for example, the Swiss physician Friedrich Erismann observed swellings and other symptoms similar to those recorded in India in Russia, during the war against Turkey in 1877–8.[32] More importantly, there is no evidence that doctors facing the problem of starvation in Europe consciously imported a model of research from the colonies. Rather, their methods seem to have evolved in response to the problem they faced. Population-level studies were the obvious first step in dealing with a new mass phenomenon. The hypotheses generated by these large-scale clinical studies were also followed up by research in the laboratory. Much of this research was informed by the work of the physiologist Ernest H. Starling (1866–1927) at University College London, who showed (in 1896) that oedema was the result of osmotic imbalance.[33] By 1918, the main hypothesis was that this imbalance was caused by nutritional deprivation.

In Europe, cases of oedema began to appear in large numbers in 1915, when Dr Hermann Strauss described a 'hunger disease' in parts of Poland and Galicia in which the poor had an insufficient and monotonous diet. About the same time, in July 1915, Drs B. Budzynski and J. M. H. Chelchowski described a similar condition among the inhabitants of certain towns in Poland, which appeared to result from deprivation caused by the German occupation. The name 'hunger swelling' was given to this condition because it was characterised by oedema. All the patients who suffered from this disease were in a state of semi-starvation.[34] In Germany, war oedema first made its appearance in prison camps, in July 1915, when it was recorded by Dr Theodor Rumpel. Rumpel initially considered relapsing fever to be responsible for oedema because this louse-borne disease was extremely common in prisoner of war (POW) camps.[35] However, in 1916, when many cases with dysenteric symptoms occurred in prison camps free from relapsing fever, Rumpel

[31] Dana Simmons, 'Starvation Science: From Colonies to Metropole', in *Food and Globalization: Consumption, Markets and Politics in the Modern World*, edited by A. Nützenadel and F. Trentmann (Oxford: Berg, 2008), 173–92.

[32] Peter F. Krug, 'The Debate over the Delivery of Health Care in Rural Russia: The Moscow Zemstvo, 1864–1878', *Bulletin of the History of Medicine* 50:2 (1976), 226–41.

[33] Ernest H. Starling, 'On the Absorption of Fluids from the Connective Tissue Spaces', *Journal of Physiology* 19:4 (1896), 312–26.

[34] B. Budzynski and J. M. H. Chelchowski, 'Hunger Swelling in Poland', *Journal of Tropical Medicine* 19 (1916), 141–2.

[35] Theodor Rumpel, 'Zum Aetiologie der Oedemkrankheiten in russichen Gefangenenlagern', *Deutsche Medizinische Wochenschrift* 41 (1915), 1021–2.

and his colleague A. V. Knack concluded that dysentery was the main cause.[36] At this time, oedema was also reported among Russian soldiers at the front and, in early 1917, there were many cases among civilians in Germany and Austria-Hungary.[37] Their number continued to grow throughout the war.

According to Budzynski and Chelchowski, and the German scientists C. Maase and H. Zondek, oedema was caused by the absence of fats from the diet of the poor and the rotten potatoes consumed in some areas affected by the Allied blockade.[38] The diet in these areas was composed mostly of carbohydrates, which was reflected in the popular name for oedema: *Mehlnahrschaden* or 'flour dystrophy'. It was particularly noticeable among children who had been weaned on a diet comprised predominantly of cereal flour. However, some observers also attributed oedema to the fact that most of the sufferers consumed a watery diet comprised largely of soups and broths. Others speculated that it might be due to a disorder of the heart or circulatory failure but radiography showed no indication of such problems.[39] However, in the last two years of the war, there was accumulating evidence to support Starling's hypothesis that hunger oedema was due mainly to deficiency of protein in the blood, which lowered osmotic pressure. A succession of authors published evidence to support this hypothesis, finding low quantities of protein (albumin) in the blood of patients with oedema. This became the dominant interpretation and was confirmed at the end of the war by feeding experiments using rats.[40] Some investigators of oedema believed that other factors were probably involved, including the low salt content of diets and lack of rest,[41] but some of these hypotheses, such as the salt theory, were later disproved as a result of animal-feeding experiments.[42]

[36] Theodor Rumpel and A. V. Knack, 'Dysenterieartige Darmerkrankungen und Oedeme', *Deutsche Medizinische Wochenschrift* 42:46 (1916), 1412–14.

[37] Ulrike Thoms, 'Hunger – ein Bedürfnis zwischen Politik, Physiologie und persönliche Erfahrung (Deutschland, 19. Und 20. Jahrhundert', *Body Politics* 3:5 (2015), 154–5.

[38] Budzynski, 'Hunger Swelling in Poland'; C. Maase and H. Zondek, 'Ueber eigenartige Oedeme', *Deutsche Medizinische Wochenschrift* 43 (1917), 487–85.

[39] Hermann Strauss, 'Die Hungerkrankheit', *Die Medizinische Klinik* 39 (1915), 854–6.

[40] E. A. Kohman, 'The Experimental Production of Edema as Related to Protein Deficiency', *American Journal of Physiology* 51 (1920), 378–405.

[41] C. Maase and H. Zondek, *Das Hungerödem* (Lepizig: Georg Thieme, 1920); J. A. Nixon, 'Famine-Dropsy as Food-Deficiency Disease', *The Bristol Medico-Chirurgical Journal* 37 (1920), 138–48; J. I. Enright, 'War Oedema in Turkish Prisoners of War', *The Lancet* 195:5032 (1920), 314–16; Michael H. N. Golden, 'Oedematous malnutrition' *British Medical Bulletin* 54:2 (1918), 433–4.

[42] A. Harden and S. S. Zilva, 'Oedema Observed in a Monkey Fed on a Diet Free from the Fat-Soluble "A" Accessory Food Factor and Low in Fat', *The Lancet* 2 (1919), 780–1.

Wartime research was pivotal in the expansion of knowledge concerning famine oedema but it was built on foundations erected by Cornish and others in India in the preceding decades.[43] By the end of the war, most authors believed that the conditions described in India and those observed during the war were essentially the same and very different from what had come to be known as 'deficiency diseases'. Rather than being the result of the lack of vitamins, 'epidemic dropsy', 'famine oedema' and 'war oedema' (now often termed 'nutritional oedema') appeared to result from a diet deficient in protein.[44] Subsequent research, including observations made during the Second World War, confirmed the protein hypothesis.[45] Nutritional oedema was later given the name *kwashiorkor*, which originated from colonial research in the 1930s, or was referred to as 'oedematous malnutrition'. It was found that the disease could be treated successfully in a matter of weeks using milk-based foods or special preparations using peanut oil, supplemented by vitamins and minerals, among other things.[46]

The work conducted on famine oedema during the First World War provided important new insights into its causation. However, the conflict provided other opportunities to study the pathology of starvation, including among combatants. One of the contexts in which chronic starvation was observed was among British and Indian forces besieged at Kut, in Mesopotamia (Iraq). This siege lasted from 4 December 1915 to 29 April 1916, or 148 days. At the beginning of the siege, the strength of the force was 14,586, including followers, over 10,000 of which were Indian. During the siege, the Assistant Director of Medical Services of 6th (Poona) Division, Patrick (later Maj-Gen. Sir Patrick) Hehir of the Indian Medical Service was able to keep a record of the effects of worsening food shortages among the troops under his charge. They had already been weakened by a severe epidemic of malaria in Lower Mesopotamia and by the exceptional strain of the march to the battle of Ctesiphon, which preceded their retreat to Kut. Whereas British troops were able to obtain sufficient amounts of protein during the siege, Indians were not, as nearly 90 per cent of them refused to consume horseflesh. British

[43] E.g. John B. Youmans, Austin Bell and Dorothy Donley, 'Endemic Nutritional Edema: 1. Clinical Findings and Dietary Studies', *Archives of Internal Medicine (Chicago)* 50:6 (1932), 843–54.

[44] Maria Maver, 'Nutritional Edema and "War Dropsy"', *Journal of the American Medical Association* 74:14 (1920), 934–41; Nixon, 'Famine Dropsy as a Food-Deficiency Disease'.

[45] E.g. R. B. Frisch, R. B. Mendel and J. P. Peters, 'The Production of Edema and Serum Protein Deficiency in White Rats by Low Protein Diets', *Journal of Biological Chemistry* 84 (1929), 167–77; Stevenson, 'Famine Oedema in Prisoners of War'.

[46] Golden, 'Oedematous Malnutrition'.

troops suffered at least a 50 per cent reduction in their fat consumption but the reduction was larger for Indians (averaging 66 per cent) as most were reliant for their fat intake on a diminishing supply of ghee (clarified butter). Carbohydrate loss was serious in both sets of men, the intake again being reduced by at least half of normal rations. There was a similar reduction in the intake of salts.

Throughout the nineteen-week siege, Hehir weighed 400 British and 800 Indian troops at regular intervals. The average weight loss among British troops was 12.5 lbs and 17 lbs among Indians, on top of a significant loss of bodyweight as a result of the privations of the earlier marches. Hehir noticed that chronic starvation tended to produce a gradual reduction in body temperature and pulse rate, an inclination to sleep and a general state of debility. However, the most serious effect was the increasing susceptibility to infectious disease, many men succumbing to diarrhoea which caused over 200 deaths among the garrison and even more (649) to dysentery.[47] Perhaps the most valuable finding of Hehir's study concerned the treatment of persons with starvation, particularly the need for caution in returning patients to normal diets. He noted that many of those who gorged themselves after starvation died because their 'atrophied digestive systems' were unable to cope.[48] Hehir did not fully elaborate the physiological processes which led to what is now known as 'refeeding syndrome' but his observations anticipated those made in the Second World War, which are usually thought to be the first to describe this problem.[49]

Hehir's observation that food shortages and other marked changes in diet could lower resistance to infection was echoed by other medical practitioners. In Mesopotamia, this seemed to be most evident in the case of intestinal diseases.[50] But in other theatres associations were noted in respect of other diseases. Lt-Col. E. J. Williams of the Canadian Army Medical Corps, who worked at different places in the Mediterranean theatre, noted this connection in the case of malaria, for example.[51] Looking back on the war in 1937, Hehir also concluded that 'lowered bodily nutrition' was probably one of the reasons why prophylaxis with quinine failed to work among troops during the First World War, in

47 Patrick Hehir, 'Effects of Chronic Starvation during the Siege of Kut', *British Medical Journal* 1:3205 (1922), 865–8.

48 Hehir, 'Effects of Chronic Starvation', 868.

49 'Refeeding Syndrome', editorial, *British Medical Journal* 328 (2004), 908.

50 Carey F. Coombs, 'Medicine and Surgery in Mesopotamia', *Bristol Medico-Chirurgical Journal* 34:131 (1916), 138.

51 E. J. Williams, 'Malaria in the Army', *Canadian Medical Association Journal* 8:6 (1918), 523–9.

contrast to military populations in peacetime.[52] Epidemics of malaria in many parts of Eastern and Southern Europe after the First World War – which admittedly had many causes – were similarly ascribed (by the League of Nations Malaria Commission) to the impoverishment and poor nutrition of the afflicted populations. For example, the Commission made a point of emphasising the relationship between famine in Ukraine and Russia and the serious epidemic of malaria occurring there in the early 1920s.[53] All told, it seems that the First World War accelerated the recognition of diseases such as malaria as 'social diseases' affected by nutrition. It also brought greater realisation of the complexity of mortality crises during and immediately after conflicts.

Vitamin Deficiency

The eastern theatres of the war were also important locations for research into diseases caused by the lack of micronutrients or vitamins as they were becoming known. As mentioned earlier, the notion of vitamins was new in 1914 and their role in maintaining health was presumed rather than proven. By 1918, knowledge of vitamin deficiency had changed substantially due to numerous cases of diseases that appeared to be connected to malnutrition. One of these was scurvy; a disease that had once plagued mariners around the world but which had been largely eradicated due to the extensive use of citrus juices. However, scurvy remained a significant problem on land and occurred periodically among prisoners and in garrisons or expeditionary forces in areas in which it was difficult to obtain fresh produce. While the role of diet in scurvy was generally accepted, there was still some uncertainty over which foods contained the antiscorbutic element or vitamin. The influence of non-dietary factors was also considered to be important in the causation of scurvy and only a few regarded it as a deficiency disease pure and simple. Weather, hygiene, exhaustion and state of mind were all still implicated in its causation.[54]

Before the First World War, the Indian Army often suffered from scurvy in detachments sent to remote outposts on the Northwest Frontier.[55] However, the scale of the outbreak in Mesopotamia was unprecedented.

52 Patrick Hehir, *Malaria in India* (London: Oxford University Press, 1937), 281.

53 Gabriel Gachelin and Annick Opinel, 'Malaria Epidemics in Europe After the First World War: The Early Stages of an International Approach to the Control of the Disease', *Historia Ciencias Saude Manguinhos* 18:2 (2011), 431–69.

54 Myer Coplans, 'On the Etiology of Scurvy', *The Lancet* 163 (1904), 79–116; Kenneth J. Carpenter, *The History of Scurvy & Vitamin C* (Cambridge: Cambridge University Press, 1986), 133–57.

55 Mark Harrison, 'Scurvy on Sea and Land: Political Economy and Natural History, c.1780–c.1850', *Journal for Maritime Research* 15 (2013), 7–26.

In the last six months of 1916, over 11,000 Indian troops succumbed to scurvy, as well as other deficiency diseases. The starvation of the men besieged at Kut and the failure to supply troops in forward areas were the immediate causes. But there was an underlying problem that made Indian troops uniquely vulnerable to this disease. The amount of food supplied in their rations was much lower than for British troops because of the custom of providing sepoys with an allowance to purchase such food as was compatible with their religious requirements. The ration they were given was also high in cereals and low in fresh meat and vegetables. Both were hard to obtain in the areas in which troops were fighting in 1916.[56]

By the end of 1916, an overhaul of logistics had improved supplies to forward areas and this began to stem the flow of casualties. Indian ration scales were also revised and the monetary allowance given to individual sepoys was reduced accordingly, making diets more uniform. Most of these improvements flowed from the advice given to commanders by temporary Lt-Col. (later Sir) William Willcox, a physician at St Mary's Hospital, London and Consulting Physician to the British-led forces in Mesopotamia.[57] Together with other officers of the Royal Army Medical Corps, he worked to perfect treatments for scurvy, which were not only dietary but included rest, physical exercise and antiseptic mouthwashes to remove the ulcers typical of the disease. However, one of his most important findings was that scurvy could be prevented and treated by eating fresh meat. There had been some indication of this before the war, for example during Scott's 1902 Antarctic expedition, but experiences in Mesopotamia showed that this was definitely the case, as meat was the only dietary advantage enjoyed by British troops, none of whom suffered from the disease.[58]

Willcox also conducted research on beriberi, most of which occurred among British troops, with slightly more cases among officers than other ranks. Willcox suspected that this was due to their diet, with officers suffering more because they substituted some items of the ration with food they purchased locally. Based on a clinical study of over fifty cases treated in Mesopotamia and the Mediterranean in 1915, Willcox noted that the disease was principally due to the lack of the 'anti-beriberi vitamin', which

[56] Mark Harrison, 'The Fight against Disease in the Mesopotamia Campaign', in *Facing Armageddon: The First World War Experienced*, edited by H. Cecil and P. H. Liddle (London: Leo Cooper, 1996), 475–89.

[57] P. H. A. Willcox, *The Detective-Physician: The Life and Work of Sir William Willcox 1870–1941* (London: Heinemann, 1970).

[58] W. H. Willcox, 'Discussion on the Treatment and Management of Diseases due to Dietetic Deficiencies', *Proceedings of the Royal Society of Medicine* 13:3 (1920), 7–22.

seemed to be absent from the tinned foods which constituted a large part of the British ration. By contrast, patients responded well to foods rich in yeast, which demonstrated that the vitamin must be abundant in yeast as well as in unpolished rice. Beriberi could therefore be prevented and treated by issuing foods high in yeast, such as Marmite. However, Willcox also found that another factor was at work, which he termed a 'toxic influence' following attacks of dysentery, diarrhoea and jaundice.[59]

Marmite was issued to troops in Mesopotamia as a prophylactic from October 1916, with good results. Willcox's research also provided a major stimulus to what he termed the 'scientific rationing' of troops. He worked tirelessly to ensure that rations comprised a balance of the main food groups but also foods that were thought to contain vitamins. Some of these changes were resisted by officers at Indian Army headquarters because they believed that alterations to Indian rations would provoke unrest among troops. However, this did not occur – at least, not as a result of alterations to rations – and such objections were overruled. Comparisons with other colonial troops, including African soldiers under German command, revealed that they had fared far better than the Indians.[60] Such differentials could not be allowed to continue.

After the war, in a lecture to the Royal Society of Medicine, Willcox declared that, 'The experiences of the War, especially in distant countries such as Mesopotamia, called for special attention to the scientific rationing of troops. The old idea of sufficiency of calories, or of proteins, fat and carbohydrates, is quite inadequate to meet the needs.'[61] He added that the Mesopotamia campaign had 'conclusively established that both scurvy and beriberi are essentially deficiency diseases and are due to a deficiency in the respective vitamins in the dietary associated with their causation'.[62] In retrospect, it might seem that the vitamin theory was already pretty well established but Willcox was correct to insist on the probative value of the research in Mesopotamia. As late as April 1917, the *Indian Medical Gazette* still regarded the theory as unproven, at least in respect of beriberi.[63]

Willcox was not the only person working on beriberi at this time. Important research was also being carried out in London by a group of

[59] W. H. Willcox, 'Beriberi with Special Reference to Prophylaxis and Treatment', *The Lancet* 187:4828 (1916), 553–7.

[60] *Further Report of Brigadier-General Vaughan's Ration Committee Re-assembled for the Purpose of Considering the Criticisms by Certain Branches of Army Headquarters in the Original Report* (Calcutta: Superintendent of Government Printing, 1918).

[61] Willcox, 'Discussion on the Treatment and Management of Diseases', 21.

[62] Willcox, 'Discussion on the Treatment and Management of Diseases', 7.

[63] 'Medical Diseases of the War', *Indian Medical Gazette*, 52 (1917), 151.

scientists that included many women, one of whom was the biochemist Harriette (later Dame Harriette) Chick (1875–1977), who, after the war, would go on to lead a team of scientists investigating the causes of rickets. In 1905, Chick became the first woman to obtain a position at the Lister Institute of Preventive Medicine in London, where she worked as an assistant to Charles Martin, the director. In 1916, Martin was posted to the Mediterranean where he encountered many cases of beriberi and scurvy, which he was convinced were diseases of nutritional deficiency. He asked Chick to conduct animal feeding trials to determine foods that could be used in rectifying these diseases. She recruited a group of women to work with her, using a series of feeding experiments on guinea pigs. Chick concluded that beriberi could be prevented by using whole-grain cereals, pulses, dried eggs and cheese. Her experiments on scurvy confirmed Willcox's observation that fresh meat was useful in preventing scurvy when fresh fruits and vegetables were not available. It also showed that the process of canning destroyed the antiscorbutic qualities of vegetables because of the heating of foods.[64] However, she also found that freshly germinated pulses had antiscorbutic properties and they were used successfully to treat Serbian soldiers suffering from scurvy in 1918.[65]

Important animal-feeding experiments were conducted simultaneously in India by the Indian Medical Service officer Lt-Col. Robert (later Sir Robert) McCarrison (1878–1960). McCarrison's interest in nutrition stemmed from a period as medical officer in the North West Frontier Province, where he recorded the diet and lifestyle of the Hunza people of the Western Himalayas, whose powerful physique and good health were much admired by the British. McCarrison attributed their stature and longevity to a wholefood diet, sparking a lifelong interest in such diets as a factor in human health. After leaving the frontier, McCarrison went to work at the Pasteur Institute of South India in Coonoor, still in the capacity of an Indian Medical Service officer. There, he conducted a series of studies examining the impact of diet on health, using monkeys and pigeons.[66] These diets consisted almost entirely of polished rice, which allowed McCarrison to study the aetiology of beriberi and the

[64] Mabel E. D. Campbell and Harriette Chick, 'The Antiscorbutic and Growth Promoting Value of Canned Vegetables', *The Lancet* 194:5008 (1919), 320–22.

[65] Kenneth J. Carpenter, 'Harriette Chick and the Problem of Rickets', *The Journal of Nutrition* 138:5 (2008), 827–32; H. W. Wiltshire, 'A Note on the Value of Germinated Beans in the Treatment of Scurvy and some Points in Prophylaxis', *The Lancet* 192:4972 (1918), 811–13.

[66] Robert McCarrison, 'The Pathogenesis of Deficiency Disease', *British Medical Journal* 15 (1919), 177–9; Robert McCarrison, 'The Effects of Deficient Dietaries on Monkeys', *British Medical Journal* 1 (1920), 249–53.

more general effects of a diet high in refined starch, such as that eaten by many people in lowland India. McCarrison was convinced that such diets were less healthy than those consisting of wholegrains, like those of the Hunza.[67]

McCarrison's work contributed to the elucidation of the pathology of beriberi but he made other significant observations. One was that vitamin deficiency seemed to reduce immunity to infection. As he put it, such deficiency rendered the body 'very liable to be overrun by the rank growth of bacteria'.[68] Another observation, which recalls the much earlier animal experiments of Cunningham, was on the effects of vitamin deprivation on the intestines (in this case of pigeons). McCarrison observed both atrophy of the bowel and – like Cunningham – erosion of its mucous membrane.[69] The problem of famine dysentery, that Cunningham had also commented on, was taken up tangentially by McCarrison through his work on monkeys, which showed that vitamin C deficiency seemed to predispose to gastro-intestinal disease.[70]

When McCarrison published his monograph on deficiency disease in 1921, it referred to both his observations in India and those that had been made in Europe during the recent war. His work examined the aetiology and pathogenesis of deficiency diseases and medical conditions that were linked to it, such as gastro-intestinal disorders. As well as addressing a range of cultural factors – such as dietary preferences – McCarrison touched almost inevitably on the controversial matter of poverty and its relationship to disease. He concluded that government, particularly local government, should have a role in ensuring the provision of nutritious food.[71] The issue of poverty was never far below the surface of wartime research into another deficiency disease – pellagra. Caused by the lack of vitamin B3 (niacin) and the amino acid tryptophan, pellagra is characterised by diarrhoea, dementia and dermatitis and in extreme cases can be fatal. Prior to 1914, it was recorded in some parts of Asia and Europe (e.g. Italy)[72] but was more prominent in the Americas, among those whose diets were comprised largely of maize. Maize is a poor source of

[67] G. T. Wrench, *The Wheel of Health: A Study of a Very Healthy People* (C.W. Daniel, 1938).

[68] McCarrison, 'The Pathogenesis of Deficiency Disease', 179.

[69] Robert McCarrison, 'The Influence of Deficiency of Accessory Food Factors on the Intestine', *British Medical Journal* 2 (1919), 36.

[70] Robert McCarrison, 'Deficiency Disease with Special Reference to Gastro-Intestinal Disorders', *British Medical Journal* 1 (1920), 822–6.

[71] Robert McCarrison, *Studies in Deficiency Disease* (London: Henry Frowde and Hodder & Stoughton, 1921).

[72] Monica Ginnaio, 'La pellagra en Italie à la fin du XIXe siècle: les effets d'une maladie de carence', *Population* 66 (2011), 671–98.

niacin and tryptophan, which are abundant in foods such as meat, eggs, fish and peanuts. An epidemic of pellagra in the southern United States in the 1900s led to the disease being studied more closely and in 1915 William Goldberg, who had been deputed to examine the disease by the United States Public Health Service, showed that it was linked to diet by studying cases in orphanages and mental hospitals. However, powerful economic interests were at stake. Cotton production had displaced mixed farming in the American South and, having few other means of subsistence, rural labourers had become reliant on cheap maize produced on farms in the Midwest.[73] Goldberg's study revealed the social costs of this new economic order and was heavily criticised by physicians allied with agricultural interests in the South, particularly H.M. Green, Chairman of the Pellagra Commission of the National Medical Association, Knoxville, Tennessee, who referred to the nutritional theory as 'unbalanced food propaganda'.[74]

In light of these disputes, research carried out on populations affected by the war was potentially of political as well as military importance. Much of this work was conducted by Allied doctors, who were compelled to delve more deeply into the problem on account of complaints made to the International Committee of the Red Cross (ICRC) by the Ottoman government, which alleged that Turkish POW were being neglected.[75] POW hospitals such as that in Abbassia (El-Abaseya), Egypt, had many cases of deficiency and infectious disease. It was chiefly for this reason that an investigative delegation of the ICRC was dispatched to the camps in 1917. All of them were found to be in an excellent sanitary condition and the ICRC confirmed that 'the diet of the prisoners in Egypt is nothing less than we would expect'.[76] Nevertheless, the heavy strain placed on POW facilities in the last year of the war meant that it was difficult to cope. In early October 1918, a committee was formed under F. D. Boyd, the Consulting Physician with the Egyptian Expeditionary

[73] Ajay Bollet, 'Politics and Pellagra: The Epidemic of Pellagra in the U.S. in the Early Twentieth Century', *Yale Journal of Biology and Medicine* 65:3 (2006), 211–21.

[74] H. M. Green, 'Some Observations on Pellagra in Reply to the Report of the Public Health Committee', *Journal of the National Medical Association* 2:2 (1916), 73.

[75] See Mark Harrison, 'War, Epidemics and Empire: British Military Government in the Middle East, 1914–18', in A. Cormack (ed.), 'A Long, Long Trail A-Winding: Centenary Perspectives on the Great War' (Dorchester: The Dorset Press, 2018, 33–55) *Journal of Army Historical Research*, Special Publication No. 18.

[76] Committee of the International Red Cross, 'Rapport sur la visite aux camps de prisonniers Ottomans en Egypte en Décembre 1916 et Janvier 1917', Documents publiés a l'occasion de la Guerre Européenne (1914–1917) (Geneva: Librarie George & Co., 1917): Rapports de MM. le Dr F. Blanchod, F. Thormeyer & Em. Schloch sur leur inspection des camps de prisonniers turcs en France, en Corse et an Egypte Décembre 1916 et Janvier 1917 (Geneva: Librarie George & Co., 1917), 67–8.

Force, and Lt-Col. P. S. Lelean, Assistant Professor of Hygiene at the Royal Army Medical College, to investigate an alleged epidemic of pellagra among Turkish POW at containment camps in Kantara, on the eastern side of the Suez Canal. After conducting interviews with fifty prisoners, the committee reported in December 1918 that the disease was in fact pellagra but added that Turkish POW were pellagrous before their capture and that there was no evidence of any increase due to local conditions.[77]

Observations made at the camp reinforced some of the conclusions reached in a related clinical study. One hundred cases of pellagra among newly captured prisoners were transferred to Cairo for close examination, accompanied by two of their own medical officers who acted as interpreters. They were kept at No. 2 POW Hospital in Abbasia, which the Army ran in co-operation with the Egyptian Public Health Department. Civilian experts in deficiency disease were used to conduct the study, as most medical officers had not previously encountered pellagra. The study reported that pellagra patients responded well to diets high in protein and recommended that the protein content of rations be increased.[78]

On the basis of this evidence, the committee absolved the British authorities of blame. It concluded that pellagra occurred only among those prisoners who had been deprived of adequate nutrition prior to their internment and non-Ottoman prisoners appear to have been exempt. However, the committee was less sure about whether the labour performed by prisoners had contributed to the problem. Although it seemed that the rations were sufficient for most, the heaviest men and those suffering from illness or impaired digestion could become pellagrous on a diet adequate for average needs.[79] Two thousand Germans had been imprisoned in the camps alongside the Turks and had been pellagra-free for two years despite having arrived from Arabia in poor physical condition. Many had showed signs of pellagra as well as dysentery and malaria.[80] Their health had steadily improved but all had been able to supplement their rations using money given to them by their consulate.[81] In view of this, the committee could not claim that the ration was sufficient to protect prisoners against pellagra in all cases. It therefore

[77] Wellcome Collection Archives and Manuscripts, RAMC 567, 'Report of a Committee of Enquiry Regarding the Prevalence of Pellagra among Turkish Prisoners of War', 4.

[78] Wellcome Collection, RAMC 567, 'Report of a Committee of Enquiry', 8–9.

[79] Wellcome Collection, RAMC 567, 'Report of a Committee of Enquiry', 4, 19.

[80] The National Archives of the UK. 'The War Diary of No.2 POW Hospital, Abassia, September 21, 1916 and September 20', 1916, WO/95/4750.

[81] Wellcome Collection, RAMC 567, 'Report of a Committee of Enquiry', 14, 18.

recommended not only that the protein content of rations be increased but that it was inadvisable to employ Turkish POW as labourers.[82]

Most of the studies conducted in Egypt confirmed the importance of foodstuffs containing protein but the relationship was complicated – as in the case of hunger oedema – by levels of physical activity. After the war, this research was presented as articles in scientific journals and published lectures, one of which given by F. D. Boyd who had returned to his position of Professor of Clinical Medicine at Edinburgh University. Boyd described the clinical appearance of pellagra in some detail – low blood pressure, skin pigmentation, loss of muscular tone and depression – as well as some of the metabolic effects of the disease. One important observation was that deficient assimilation of protein in the lower bowel made it easier for pathogenic microbes to become established, further compounding the absorption of protein and resulting in diarrhoea. In other words, there was a vicious circle of protein depletion. Moving onto the causes of the disease, Boyd presented data which showed both the total calorific intake of prisoners and the amount of each food type. This demonstrated that there was no relationship between overall calorie intake and the onset of pellagra or with the intake of fats or carbohydrates. Pellagra only began to show itself when the dietary level of protein fell below 40 grams.[83] Researchers who had examined other populations during the war came to similar conclusions. W. H. Wilson, Professor of Physiology at the Egyptian School of Medicine, found in his studies of Armenian refugees in Port Said that the chief causal factor in pellagra was deficiency of protein below 40 grams, a figure of 50 grams being necessary to sustain hard labour. However, Wilson also undertook a major review of other studies of pellagra (probably the most thorough of its kind), in Europe and the Americas, with a view to tracing common factors. Among other things, he examined the controversial issue of maize dependency, concluding that the link was due simply to the fact that it contained a highly variable quantity of protein.[84]

Most American studies published at the end of the war ignored these findings. Green and his colleagues, who had earlier opposed the tendency to focus on diet, continued to do so, stressing other factors such as poor sanitation and hygiene.[85] This disconnection was noted in 1920

82 Wellcome Collection, RAMC 567, 'Report of a Committee of Enquiry', 5, 21.

83 F. D. Boyd, 'Pellagra', *Transactions of the Medico-Chirurgical Society of Edinburgh* 34 (1921), 10–17.

84 William H. Wilson, 'The Diet Factor in Pellagra', *Journal of Hygiene* 20 (1921), 1–59.

85 Charles H. Johnson, 'Some Observations on Pellagra', *Journal of the National Medical Association* 9 (1918), 113–17; H. M. Green, 'Report of the Pellagra Commission', *Journal of the National Medical Association* 9 (1918), 82–6.

by a British physician, Edward J. Wood, who had worked on pellagra in the United States. While praising the 'brilliant investigations' that had been stimulated by the war, Wood observed that the question of the aetiology of pellagra was still disputed in the US, where diets and modes of life were very different from those encountered in Asia and Europe.[86] Although northern US physicians placed the blame for pellagra firmly on southern diets, their studies seldom made reference to wartime research.[87] A conspicuous exception was Goldberger, who not only read but actively engaged with studies of pellagra in other countries. In 1920, he was among several physicians (including W. H. Wilson) who took exception to an article by a British military doctor, Capt. J. I. Enright, who claimed that pellagra among German POW he had treated in the War Hospital at Cairo was unrelated to diet.[88] Enright had earlier stressed non-dietary factors in the production of war oedema and his work on both diseases went against the emerging consensus.[89] In the United States, however, the issue of pellagra remained contentious for many years. Goldberg provided additional proof that protein deficiency was a factor in the disease but he faced a long struggle to gain acceptance for his conclusions.[90] One of the problems was that it was not the absence of protein *per se* but of substances within protein-rich foods that were the cause of pellagra. It was not until 1937 that the American biochemist Conrad Elvehjem (1901–62) showed that vitamin B3 could be used to treat pellagra in dogs; Tom Spies (1902–60) and other researchers demonstrated the same thing among humans the year afterwards.[91]

Conclusion

During the First World War, the science of hunger and malnutrition progressed as a result of the accumulation of evidence from many nations and theatres of war rather than as a result of any specific breakthrough. But the combined effect of these many small advances was transformative. At the beginning of the war, the vitamin theory was unproven and

[86] Edward J. Wood, 'The Etiology of Pellagra from the Standpoint of Deficiency Disease', *Transactions of the Royal Society of Tropical Medicine and Hygiene* 14:1 (1920), 1–7.

[87] E.g. E. A. Robinson, 'Pellagra', *Journal of the National Medical Association* 13 (1921), 91–3.

[88] J. Goldberger, 'The Pellagra Outbreak in Egypt', *The Lancet*, 196:5053 (1920), 41–2; W. H. Wilson, 'The Pellagra Outbreak in Egypt', *The Lancet*, 196:5066 (1920), 719–20.

[89] J. I. Enright, 'The Pellagra Outbreak in Egypt. I: Pellagra amongst German Prisoners of War', *The Lancet* 195:5045 (1920), 998–1004; Enright, 'War Oedema'.

[90] Alan M. Kraut, *Goldberger's War: The Life and Work of a Public Health Crusader* (New York, NY: Hill and Wang, 2003).

[91] C. J. Koehn and C. A. Elvehjem, 'Further Studies on the Concentration of the Antipellagra Factor', *Journal of Biological Chemistry* 118:3 (1937), 693–9.

the causes of most deficiency diseases and famine-related conditions were unclear. By 1918, the causes of hunger oedema had been established and the primary causal relationship of nutrition deficiency had been established to most scientists' satisfaction in the case of scurvy, beriberi and pellagra. The treatment and prevention of these conditions using dietary and other means had also improved and the research done by physicians, physiologists and biochemists was beginning to have some impact upon military and civilian rations.

These were significant achievements but it would be a mistake to claim too much for the war as an agent of medical and scientific change. The promise of an international standard of nutrition took years to realise and other scientific research conducted during the war inevitably focused on problems that were deemed to be of military or strategic importance.[92] Diseases that had less immediate impact on the war effort, such as rickets, were consequently neglected and research into them did not resume until after the war had ended. Indeed, publications on the aetiology of rickets in 1918 differed little from those immediately before the war.[93] Even where progress had been made, as in the case of pellagra, it sometimes failed to make an immediate impression on civilian health and medicine, especially where opinions were firmly entrenched, as in the United States. Despite these caveats, the advances made in the field of nutritional science during the First World War were probably as significant as those in the Second.

[92] Cooter, 'Medicine and the Goodness of War'.

[93] E.g. Eric Pritchard, 'The Causation and Treatment of Rickets', *The British Medical Journal* 2:3072 (1919), 627–9.

12 Famine in Russia and parts of Europe, 1914–22

Stephen G. Wheatcroft

All of Europe experienced hunger in these years, but the extent and locations in which it resulted in famine with sharply elevated mortality for a prolonged period of time remains disputed.[1] Russia experienced hunger with elevated mortality to a much greater extent than the rest of Europe, and in Russia famine continued until 1922. For Russia, there were consequently two stages of food problems. The first covered the Great War itself from 1914–19 and was characterised by mutual international blockades that upset regular international trade and caused general hunger with some elevated mortality. In this stage the signs of food shortage and hunger were clear amongst all European countries although the elevation of mortality to famine levels was only clearly visible in Romania in 1917 and in the major Russian, Polish and Finnish towns in 1918, and in Germany and Austria in the final year of the war and the first months of the armistice. The second stage of Russia's food problems followed the Great War and extended for four years from 1919 to 1922. At this time the rest of Europe saw a resumption of international grain imports and the receipt of US aid which relieved to some extent their hunger. But in Soviet Russia hunger and famine did not disappear and became much more severe. For part of this time, Russia remained subject to blockade and to civil and international war. US relief for Soviet Russia only began in 1921, the final and most terrible year of the famine.

This chapter begins with a definition of famine mortality and then provides a survey of the normal levels of mortality and of patterns of food supply in the different zones of Europe before the war. The second part looks at how these patterns of supply were strained during the First World War, especially in areas where mortality rose to famine levels. It concentrates on the difficult situation in Russia, Poland, Romania, Germany and Austria, the most seriously affected countries during the war. The third section looks at the more serious famine that developed in Soviet Russia in the later period. The conclusions return to consider the

[1] See the next section of this chapter for definitions of famine mortality levels.

political changes resulting from these food problems in both December 1918 and in 1922.

Famine Mortality and Pre-war Levels of Mortality and Food Supply before the First World War

In this chapter famine[2] is taken to be an extreme extent of food shortages and hunger causing mortality to rise above 40 per thousand population or by more than 50 per cent.[3] Famine mortality normally has a short duration and narrow coverage. It does not normally cover entire countries for whole years. The spread and duration of famine mortality need to be considered when assessing the seriousness of famine hunger. The rates most often cited refer to annual figures for whole countries measured in calendar years. Crop years from July to June capture the harvests better. Monthly mortality rates are difficult to compare because of seasonal patterns. Fortunately, the seasonal patterns tend to be regular. Monthly mortality rates have been converted into their annual equivalents to make them comparable with rates per thousand per year, but in comparing monthly mortality we need to ensure that we are comparing rates from similar months.

Mortality levels had been falling sharply throughout Europe in the decades before World War One. The most significant factor driving this was the decline in infant mortality.[4] In Western Europe, levels of infant mortality fell on average by a third from about 160 per thousand in 1900, to about 100 in 1913. In central Europe the decline varied, but from a higher 1900 level. The decline was greater in Germany by 34 per cent (from 229 to 151), but lower in Austria by 22 per cent from 231 to 180 and even more so in Hungary by 10 per cent from 223 per thousand to 201. In Russia the decline was smaller still (6 per cent) from an even higher level of 252 in 1900, to 237 in 1911. A much lower birth rate

2 Different languages have different words to distinguish between different levels of hunger on a spectrum. Most have words to distinguish between hunger and famine as in English, although traditionally the Slavic languages did not. *Golodomor* in Russian and *Holodomor* in Ukrainian are words that have only recently been invented to distinguish famine causing death from hunger: *golod* and *holod*.

3 These are arbitrary numbers, but they generally work. Forty per thousand is close to the maximum birth rate possible, so, mortality rates over 40 per thousand imply a negative population growth rate. A growth of 50 per cent has been chosen because when applied to countries with a crude death rate of 30 per thousand it would bring the level up to 45 per thousand. Countries which had much lower normal death rates, say 20 per thousand, should not need to face a higher level of increase in hunger-related death rates to be included in the famine category.

4 Stephen Wheatcroft and Cormac O'Grada, 'The European Famines of World Wars I and II', in *Famines in European History*, edited by G. Alfani and C. O'Grada (Cambridge University Press, 2017), 249–50 (Figures 11.1–11.2).

in the west resulted in a smaller proportion of the population in high-mortality cohorts, given standard age-specific mortality rates, resulted in great differences in crude death rates per thousand population. This makes using crude death rate indicators (not differentiated by age and sex) problematic when making comparisons of relatively small changes in mortality. This problem can be overcome by using age-specific mortality rates or more simply infantile mortality rates. However, when we are dealing with large increases in mortality, rising to 40 per thousand or more, then even crude indicators can be usefully used.[5]

On the eve of the First World War, grain was by far the most important foodstuff and Europe imported about 12 million tons of grain from New World areas outside Europe. This was probably about 8 per cent of the grain that Europe needed for human consumption, industrial use seed and livestock feed.[6] Within Europe different countries had different degrees of external dependence on grain imports, with some exporting grain. Europe can be divided into predominantly grain-deficit countries in the west and countries with large grain surpluses in the east. Generally, the more industrialised and urbanised the country or region, the greater the grain deficit. Regions that were normally grain surplus and those that were normally grain deficient experienced hunger very differently.

Apart from receiving extra grain from the New World outside Europe, European food-deficit countries received a similar amount: about 12 million tons of grain from the three European countries that had large grain-surplus regions. The largest amount (about 9 to 10 million tons) came from the Russian Empire, and the rest (about 3 million tons) from the Danube Basin (Romania and Hungary). This was probably another 10 per cent of the grain that the European deficit countries needed.

The Russian Empire with a population of 140 million and a low level of industrialization and urbanization (only 20 per cent urban) was at one extreme. It was the largest grain surplus country in the world, let alone in Europe. In the years before the First World War it exported an average of just under 10 million tons of grain a year. This was roughly 12 per cent of its own grain use. Given this large surplus of grain production, Russia was expected to be secure from hunger in the war. At the other extreme was the highly industrialised and urbanised United Kingdom with a population of about 45 million (80 per cent urban) which imported more than 10 million tons of grain per year or about 60 per cent of its basic

[5] On infantile mortality, see Wheatcroft and Grada, 'The European Famines'; on age specific mortality rates, see Jay Winter and Jean-Louis Robert, *Capital Cities at War*, volume 1 (Cambridge University Press, 1997).

[6] Wheatcroft, 'The European Famines', 241–2.

grain requirements. Western Continental Europe (WCE) had an external dependency rate for grain imports of about 15 per cent overall. It was higher in Germany (22 per cent) and Denmark (19 per cent), but lower in France (8 per cent). In the centre of Europe the complex Empire of Austria-Hungary was much less dependent on extra-European grain, importing in these years only half a million tons of grain, just 2 per cent of its needs. But the Empire was itself split with the western, more industrial part of Austria, Bohemia and Moravia importing 10 per cent of their grain use, while Hungary to their east on the Danube plain exported 3 per cent of its grain production. Further to the east on the Danube was Romania, which exported 2.4 million tons of its grain, a massive 36 per cent of its production. Most Romanian grain initially went Southeast through the mouth of the Danube to the Black Sea, the Mediterranean and on to Western Europe. A small amount went northwest, up the Danube to Austria-Hungary.

The Russian Empire was not just a grain surplus producing country. Besides its three main grain surplus regions in the south, the centre and the east, it also contained two grain deficit regions: a large Northern Consumer Region (NCR) and a much smaller Southern Consumer Region (SCR). Our main interest is with the NCR, which on the eve of the First World War contained not only parts of Russia, but also Poland, Finland and the Baltic Provinces, which were grain deficit regions which would gain their independence from Russia after the Revolution. Within Russia itself there were the two large capital cities of St Petersburg and Moscow, and many of Russia's industrial towns. The SCR centred on the oilfields of Baku in the Transcaucasus and the cotton fields of the Ferghana valley in Russian Central Asia, arnd is of less importance for this study.

The Russian Empire's NCR on the eve of the First World War required over 6 million tons of grain imports per year, which was more grain than Germany imported and more than half as much as the largest European importer, the UK. This Russian deficit had traditionally been provided by the old supply region of the centre, the Central Producer Region (CPR) of Central Black Earth and the Volga. In the good years of 1909–13 the CPR provided about 5 million tons of grain, which was most of the grain needed by the NCR. But increasingly, in bad years, other new supply areas were needed, to cover all the northern deficit. In 1909–13 the new supply region in the East EPR (Urals, Siberia and Kazakhstan) supplied half a million tons of grain. This left Russia's New World Region in the south – the Southern Producer Region (SPR) of Ukraine and North Caucasus – to export most of its surplus grain, which in 1913 amounted to about 9 million tons.

Disruptions in Food Supply in the First World War Causing Elevation of Mortality to Famine Levels

Blockades, during and immediately after the war, disturbed the previous flows of Russian and Transatlantic grain into Western and Central Europe. The Allied blockades on food for Germany were not fully lifted until 12 July 1919. For the three months of November, December and January 1919 the blockade even intensified and spread to the Baltic, grounding German fishing vessels and stopping smuggling.[7] The Allies extended their blockade on food to Russia in late 1917 and that blockade lasted much longer, until 1920.

Germany and the Austro-Hungarian Empire, 1914–19

Before the First World War, Germany imported about 7 million tons of grain, of which 2.4 million tons were wheat. Russia supplied about 40 per cent (1 million tons) of the wheat. Another 50 per cent (1.2 million tons) came from across the Atlantic (with Argentina providing 0.5 million tons, the USA 0.4 million tons, Canada 0.2 million tons and Australia 0.1 million tons), most of the rest about 8 per cent (another 0.2 million tons) came from Romania. The second largest import was rye, with most of it coming from Russia. All of this grain was subject to blockade. Russian supplies were blocked at source until 1918, when Russia left the war. Canadian supplies were blocked at source throughout the war. American supplies were controlled by British regulations in the passage across the Atlantic Ocean before being blocked at source when America joined the war in April 1917. Romanian supplies, which were normally shipped out of the mouth of the Danube and through the Black Sea and Mediterranean to Western Europe were initially blocked. Grain was purchased by British and German agents and stored, but neither side could ship it out of Romania. Then in late 1915 Romania agreed to sell 2.5 million tons of grain to the central powers, which was to be shipped up the Danube to Germany and Austria.[8] This arrangement faltered in the third year of the war after the 1916 harvest when in late August 1916 Romania switched sides and, in the hope of annexing Transylvania, joined Russia in attacking Austria-Hungary. This led to Germany invading and occupying Romania when Romanian grain stocks, including those previously bought and stored by the British were captured and transported to Germany. The following year, Germany began requisitioning grain from Romanian producers. As a result

[7] See M. Cox, *Hunger in War and Peace: Women and Children in Germany, 1914–1924* (Oxford University Press, 2019), 207.

[8] D. Hamlin, 'The Fruits of Occupation: Food and Germany's Occupation of Romania in the First World War', *First World War Studies* 4:1 (2013), 82.

of these efforts, 1.9 million tons of grain was extracted from Romania from the 1917 harvest, of this sum 0.8 million tons was sent to Germany and the rest went to Austria. According to Hamlin these forced grain extractions from Romania may have resulted in excess deaths of civilians in Romania as high as 400,000 out of a population of 7.5 million.[9]

On the eve of the war, the Austrian parts of the Austro-Hungarian Empire received most of the grain that they needed from the less industrialised Hungarian parts of the Empire. Consequently, the Empire, as a whole, only had a deficit of 0.5 million tons of grain, which was easily covered by Romanian surpluses. For the first two years of the war a Romanian blockade made it impossible for Austria to access these Romanian surpluses. The Romanian and Russian attacks on Hungarian Transylvania and the excessively droughty weather of 1916 reduced Hungary's ability to provide all the grain needed. The food supply situation in Hungary became desperate in late 1916 and throughout 1917. But in early 1918, with Russia leaving the war, Austria looked as though it would be able to find some temporary relief. However, the increase in nationalism in Hungary and Bohemia resulted in a further final deterioration in the Austrian food supply situation after the 1918 harvest, when these and other parts of the Empire began to faulter in delivering grain to the German parts of the Empire.

The December 1918 Hunger Map marks Germany, Austria and Hungary as unclassified (See Map 14.1), and Romania as "already receiving US aid". Available mortality data show very serious elevations of mortality in the former, and famine levels in Romania (see Table 12.1).

Table 12.1 *Crude death rates and infantile mortality in Germany, Austria and Hungary*

Crude death rates				Infantile mortality				
				Per 1,000 birth			Compared to 1913	
	1913	1918	Percentage	1913	1915	1918	1915 (%)	1918 (%)
Germany	15.0	24.8	165	151	148	158	98	105
Austria	20.2	26.4	131	190	218	193	115	102
Romania	26.1	40.8	154					
Hungary	23.2	25.7	111	201	264	217	131	108

Source: Germany, Austria, Hungary from: Wheatcroft, 'The European Famines', 249–51; Romania from Tudorel Andrei and Vasile Gheţău, *Serii istorice de date: populaţia României 1860–2020* (Bucharest: Institutul Naţional de Statistică, 2021), pp. 28–29.

[9] Hamlin, 'The Fruits of Occupation', p. 91.

Within Germany, Austria and Hungary, there were undoubtedly regions where mortality reached famine proportions, and the situation was worse in the months from October 1918 to February 1919.[10]

Food Disruptions in the Russian Empire

Before the war Poland, Finland and the Baltic States were all part of the Northern Consumer Region of the Russian Empire, but during the war Poland and two of the Baltic provinces were occupied by German forces and fell outside the Russian grain supply area. In times of emergency and food shortage, many of the remaining areas in the NCR would receive less priority than food supplies designated for the army and the two capital cities, which were themselves running short of grain. This naturally contributed to the subsequent disintegration of these parts of the Russian Empire.

On the eve of the First World War, the Imperial Northern Consumer Region, taken together, received about 6 million tons[11] of grain a year by rail alone from the three surplus producing regions and another couple of million tons by waterway. These supply patterns were greatly disturbed during the war. The previous trend of bringing regional grain price differentials between the consumer and producer regions closer was reversed and the price differential greatly rose.

Poland and Baltic Provinces

The German advance into the nine provinces of Tsarist Poland and three of the four Baltic provinces in 1915 and 1916 caused a major upset in these occupied regions. Food supplies from Russia were immediately cut off and the retreating Russian army laid waste the land and took away as much of the available supplies as it could. In 1913 the nine Polish provinces had produced about 3.5 million tons of grain and imported 1.4 million tons of grain, about 29 per cent of their total supply. The four Baltic provinces produced about 1.7 million tons of grain and imported 1.2 million tons of grain from Russia. This was about 41 per cent of their total supplies. These were normally the wealthiest, most industrialised parts of the Empire. These grain supplies would be very seriously affected by the war and the changing frontlines. Poland was occupied

[10] See Winter, *Capital Cities at War*.

[11] A total of 5.5 million tons by rail for all of the Empire excluding Finland calculated from *Statisticheskiye Danniye ob otpravlenii I pribitii prodovolsstvennykh gruzov po Russkim Zheleznym dorogam s raspredeleniam po guberniyam I oblastam za 1912, 1913, 1914gg.* Petrograd 1918; plus 0.5 million tons for Finland.

by German forces in 1915, after the retreating Russian Army had laid waste the country and forced a large part of its population to flee the country. The productivity of the wasted country was greatly reduced. Imports from Russia ceased, and the invading Germans refused to take responsibility for feeding the remaining population. International relief measures like those set up by Hoover in Belgium were not successful, and the occupied population began to starve. Available mortality figures for Russian Poland (Kingdom) show crude mortality in 1918 to have risen by 47 per cent from 19 per thousand in 1913 to 28 per thousand in 1918. This was significantly more than the 17 per cent rise in Austrian Poland (i.e. Galicia) from 23 per thousand in 1913 to 27 per thousand in 1918.[12] Regions within Poland would have certainly reached famine levels of mortality.

The December 1918 Map of Hunger correctly shows Poland as already an independent country outside the Russian Empire and experiencing famine (see Map 14.1 in Chapter 14 of this book). The future Baltic republics are shown as experiencing famine, but not yet independent of Russia.

Finland

Finland normally imported about half a million tons of grain from Russia, about one third of its total needs. It normally produced about 0.75 million tons. After deducting seed and industrial use, about 1.3 million tons would be left for human and livestock consumption. With a population of 3.2 million this left about 0.35 tons per person per year. For the first two years of the war into 1916, grain production and imports remained high. But in 1917 imports fell from over 550,000 tons to less than 60,000 with a serious decline in domestic production. This reduced and halved the amount of grain available for human and livestock consumption from over 350 kg per person per year to 171 kgms. In 1918 imports from Russia fell to only 12,000 tons; although grain production remained at the same level as previously, this reduced the amount for per capita consumption to 162 kgms per year. The years 1917 and 1918 were the two worst of famine for Finland when livestock numbers were drastically cut, and many humans starved. Crude mortality is reported to have risen from 17.1 per thousand in 1913 to 18.8 per thousand in 1917 and then to 30.4 per thousand in 1918. This was 78 per cent above the 1913 level and certainly indicated famine mortality.

[12] *Historia Polski w liczbach: ludność terytorium* (Warsaw: Główny Urząd Statystyczny, 1994) 116–17.

The famished situation in Russia at this time, and their inability to feed other parts of the Empire meant that they would have found it very difficult to have kept hold of Finland whatever the military outcome.

Bessarabia and Ukraine

Bessarabia and Ukraine were two of the major grain surplus regions of the Tsarist Empire. Before the war, the nine gubernia (administrative regional units) of Ukraine supplied over 1 million tons of grain for the Russian Empire, as well as 5 to 6 million tons for export. The Bessarabia gubernia alone provided about 0.6 million tons of grain to the Empire and more for export. All international exports through the Dardanelles were halted once Turkey joined the war on the side of the Central Powers, and it was widely believed that millions of tons of grain were accumulating in the South. Bessarabia had been occupied by Romania when it entered the war on the side of the Central Powers in 1916, but Ukraine was believed to have continued to produce large amounts of grain that could have been available to other parts of the Empire until the collapse of 1917. There has been much dispute about what happened to the Ukrainian surpluses from 1914 to 1916. Most likely they would have been consumed by the peasants and their livestock. Presumptions that they would still be available years later are clearly false.

Russian access to Bessarabian grain surpluses was lost in 1916, along with its access to Ukrainian surpluses from 1917 when Ukraine claimed its independence. This was followed in early 1918 with the German occupation, after the first Brest Litovsk Treaty.

The loss of connections with many of its supply regions was the main reason for the Russian North being plunged into famine in 1918, as we will see below. Despite their efforts, the Central Powers were unable to extract sufficient grain from these regions to save themselves. Nevertheless, the internal supply situation in Ukraine broke down and the Ukrainian capital experienced severe hunger. Available mortality data for Kiev shows that mortality rose from 16.0 per thousand in 1914 to 24.4 in 1917 and then in 1918 under German occupation to 38.5 per thousand. This was an excess of 53 per cent in 1917 and of 140 per cent in 1918, indicating a famine situation in Kiev at this time (note that part of the 1918 elevation could have been caused by Spanish flu, see Table 12.4).

When German forces withdrew from Ukraine in December 1918, Ukraine had declared its independence and was correctly classified as a separate country from Russia in the American Hunger Map. Unlike its neighbours, Ukraine normally had sufficient food supplies, and if grain was not being confiscated or requisitioned by an alien power it would not have had a shortage.

The Northern Food Deficit Regions within Russia (NCR)

The northern deficit region of Russia excluding Finland, Poland and the Baltic Provinces comprises three sub-regions with a combined rail grain deficit of just under 3 million tons in 1913. The three sub-regions were: the Petrograd Industrial and Northern Region that produced 1.8 million tons of grain and received 1 million tons of grain imports per year (that is, imports were 36 per cent of its needs); the Moscow Industrial Region that produced over 5 million tons of grain in 1913 and required another 1.5 million tons of grain to be imported (that is, 23 per cent of its needs); and finally, the Western region that would later incorporate the Byelorussian Soviet Socialist Republic (BSSR). It produced 4.2 million tons of grain in 1913 and probably exported to Poland as much grain as it received from the supply regions of Russia.

The northern cities of Russia were areas that would see the most dramatic developments in these troubled times. Inadequate reserves were held. The rapidly increasing amount of grain collected by the state for the army interfered with the normal transfers required by the civilian population in the Northern Consumer Region. When the state took responsibility for feeding the civilian population in the north, as well as the army, it failed to do both adequately. The table below, based on data provided by the leading pre-revolutionary economist and revolutionary politician Kondratiev,[13] shows a growth in grain collections by the state from 8.2 million tons in 1915/6 to 8.8 million tons in 1916/7 i.e. by 0.6 million (7 per cent), but this was 19 per cent less than the growth that had been planned (see Table 12.2).

Table 12.2 *State grain procurements, grain transported for military and civilian use and grain not transported in million tons*

		Transported for:				
				Of which:		
	All collections	Army	Other	Population	Rail workers	Not transported
1914/5	5.0	3.0	2.0	–	–	–
1915/6	8.2	5.7	2.5	–	–	–
1916/7 plan	10.8	8.1	2.7	2.4	0.3	–
1916/7 actual	8.8	4.7	0.8	0.7	0.07	3.3
1917/8 actual	1.6	–	–	–	–	–

Source: Calculated from data in Kondratiev, *Rynok Khlebov*, 365–7, 413–6.

[13] N. D. Kondratiev, *Rynok Khlebov i ego regulirovaniye vo vremya voiny I revolyutsii* (Moscow: Nauka, 1991) (originally 1922).

But, it also shows that the main problem was that only 5.5 million tons of this 8.8 million tons of grain collected in 1916/7 was transported to the army, consumer populations or railway workers. In 1916/7 the army received 4.7 million tons, which was 1 million tons (or 18 per cent) less than in 1915/16, and 3.4 million tons or 42 per cent less than planned. The designated civilian population including railway workers were much worse off; they received only 0.8 million tons which was 1.7 million tons less than the 2.5 million tons they had received in 1915/6, and 1.9 million tons less than the 2.7 million tons planned. Altogether, 3.3 million tons of grain (about 38 per cent) could not be transported. The reason for the critically low level of food for the army and consumer population in 1916/17 was not peasant resistance to collections, but the government's inability to transport the collected grain.

The situation the following year, 1917/18, was even more catastrophic, when only 1.6 million tons of grain were collected. This was clearly insufficient to sustain the army, let alone the civilian population. The government had no alternative but to disband the army, that it could not feed. This was not a political decision made by the Bolsheviks. The situation required it, and the Bolsheviks were the only party that wanted to do this and could survive doing it.

There were two other important decisions that were made in 1918, and had to be made, because there was no alternative. The Russian government had to let go of those parts of the Empire that needed central allocations of food but could not get them from the new Soviet government. These included Poland, Finland and the Baltic Provinces, as explained above. Also, the feeding of the population of Petrograd, in a food deficit region over 1,000 km away from food surplus regions was not feasible. There was no choice other than to move the capital 700 km South-East, and closer to the food surplus regions to Moscow.

These three major steps to reduce Russia's food problem were important, but not enough. As we will see below, food prices moved sharply upwards in Petrograd in comparison with Moscow, and in the whole NCR in comparison with the producer regions. Table 12.3 below shows the drastic reduction of the net amount of grain shipped by rail into the three remaining subregions of NCR (excluding exports).

The drastic decline in grain going to the Petrograd, Lakes and North regions caused severe hunger, and the food riots and demonstrations that brought about the February Revolution.

Relative price data for grain on the limited markets that remained reflect the dynamic processes of these years and the sharp deterioration from 1916. In 1909/13, rye prices in the Lake District where Petrograd was located were the highest by far in the Russian Empire. They were 8 per cent higher than in the Moscow Industrial Region and 25 per cent

Table 12.3 *Net amount of grain shipped by rail into the three subregions of NCR which would remain in the USSR after 1917 in million tons (excluding exports)*

	1913	1914	1915	1916	1917	Percentage of 1913 in 1917
Petrograd, Lakes and North	1.67	1.64	3.16	1.46	0.65	39
Moscow Industrial	0.92	0.89	1.03	0.78	0.32	35
West	0.32	0.51	0.46	−0.1	0.05	16
All NCR (later in USSR)	2.9	3.08	4.69	2.1	1.0	34

Note: 1) Poland, Baltic Provinces and Finland are not listed; 2) West excludes grain exported to Poland and Baltic provinces.
Source: Trudy Tsentral'nogo statisticheskogo upravleniia, 6:2 (1923), 169–70.

higher than in the CPR or SPR. In 1915 the price differentials began to open with the Petrograd Region 14 per cent higher than Moscow Industrial and 50 per cent higher than the CPR and SPR. This was to be expected given the inability of grain to be exported abroad from the SPR.

In 1916 there were signs of much greater price instability. In the spring of 1916, the Petrograd region prices were 25 per cent cheaper than the Moscow region, but in the autumn of 1916 the relationship was reversed, and Petrograd prices were double Moscow prices. The relative difference between Producer Region and Consumer Region prices increased progressively from spring 1916 for most regions apart from Central Volga. This was a sign of the increasing fracturing of the market.

For Moscow the food crisis hit a little later. The Moscow Index of average retail prices from Kondratiev's Conjuncture Institute indicates that while inflation was driving up all prices, food prices were rising less sharply than non-food prices up to September 1917 when their differential was only 54 per cent of their 1913 relationship, but by January 1918 they were double and by May 1918 quadruple the 1913 relationship.[14] This was the peak level of the split.

There was a reluctance amongst the most talented economists and administrators to accept that the situation was as catastrophic as it was. After citing statistics showing the catastrophic decline in grain production and trade in 1916 and 1917, Kondratiev, who had presided over food supplies for the provisional government in 1917, wrote in 1922 that there

[14] Price data from *Vestnik Statistiki*, 210, no. 1–4 (Moscow, 1921), 210 and A. L. Vainshtein, *Tseny i tsenoobrazovaniye v SSSR v vosstanovitel'nii period, 1921–28* (Moscow: Nauka, 1972), 157–9 analysed and presented in table form in S.G. Wheatcroft, 'Famine and Factors Affecting Mortality in the USSR :The Demographic Crises of 1919–22 and 1927–33' (Birmingham University CREES, SIPS Discussion Papers, Birmingham University, 1982), 26–7 and reproduced with my permission in Lars T. Lih, *Bread and Authority in Russia, 1914–1921* (Berkeley: University of California Press, 1990), 245.

was no real shortage of food in the country at that time, because of the large surpluses that had been accumulated after the good harvests of 1914 and 1915.[15] His argument was that the major scaling back of grain exports after the 1914 and 1915 harvests should have resulted in large grain reserves being accumulated in the countryside, that he thought should have been available for use in the years of poor harvest in 1916 and 1917.

As Amartya Sen has famously pointed out, following his analysis of the Bengal famine of 1946/7 food supply administrators were prone to the error of assuming that food was instantly geographically transferable through time and location, and that if they had calculated that enough grain had been produced in the country then it would be available.[16]

There undoubtedly had been much grain available in the south following the 1914 and 1915 harvests, when little could be exported, but it was wrong to assume that this grain would not be used (fed to humans, or animals, or converted into vodka) and that it would still be available two years later when the harvests were much poorer. Later Soviet politicians were to continue using similar arguments into the 1930s.

Mortality data from the main towns indicate that deaths in Petrograd, Saratov and Kiev were already greatly elevated in 1917 and that by the end of 1918, and 1919, all the main towns of Russia had famine levels of mortality (see Table 12.4).[17]

Table 12.4 *Mortality data in main cities*

	1913	1917	1918	1919	% of 1913 in 1917	% of 1913 in 1918	% of 1913 in 1919
Crude death rate							
Petrograd	20.9	27.9	64.2	79.7	133	307	381
Moscow	24.7	23.7	29.9	45.4	96	121	184
Saratov	29.3	34.1	47.5	69.5	117	162	237
Kiev	16.0	24.4	38.5	61.6	153	241	385
Infantile mortality per thousand births							
Petrograd	231	243	308	434	105	133	188
Moscow	234	268	267	333	115	114	142
Saratov	260	512	372	395	197	143	152
Kiev	–	150	249	304	–	–	–

Source: S. G. Wheatcroft, 'Famine and Factors', 4–12.

[15] Kondratiev, *Rynok Khlebov*, 127.

[16] Amartya Sen, *Poverty and Famines: An Essay on Entitlement and Deprivation* (Oxford University Press, 1981), 80–3.

[17] For monthly mortality indicators showing the sharp onset of famine mortality in Russian cities in early 1918 see S. G. Wheatcroft, 'Eastern Europe (Russian and the USSR)', in

The Second Stage: Further Disruption of Russian and East European Grain Supplies from 1919 to 1922

After the war, most European countries received US relief to help them overcome their food difficulties. The official record of US aid shows that US relief was already flowing into Germany, Austria, Poland, Finland and the Allied occupied regions of Russia in the late Armistice period.[18] The situation was very different in those parts of the former Russian Empire that had already experienced major elevation of mortality in 1918 and which remained under Bolshevik control. The wars of intervention and civil wars which continued until 1920 ensured that famines in the Consumer Regions of Russia remained in place until 1920. But instead of the situation improving with the first peacetime harvest of 1921, there was a further and more terrible famine, now located in the normal producer regions in the Volga and parts of the Urals and Ukraine. This was the terrible result of drought coming at a time when reserves had been depleted by three previous years of famine, assisted by the harsh procurement policies carried out by the starving population of the north or its agents.

Finland

Available food production and transportation data show a great improvement in 1919, with a slight increase in domestic grain production by 20,000 tons, and a massive increase in grain imports by 260,000 tons from outside Europe. US relief data show that Finland also received 2,000 tons of grain and grain produce relief and 3,000 tons of all relief in the Reconstruction period. This additional supply of grain would have lifted Finland out of serious famine in the second half of 1919.

Famine in European History, edited by G. Alfani and C. O. Grada (Cambridge University Press, 2017), 228.

[18] See F. M. Surface and R. L. Bland, *American Food in the World War and Reconstruction Period: Operations of the Organizations under the Direction of Herbert Hoover, 1914 to 1924* (Stanford University Press, 1931). The USA divides the aid period into three stages: during the war, 1914–18; the Armistice period, November 1918 to June 1919; and the Reconstruction period, June 1919 to 1924. During the war period 19 million tons of grain and flour were provided mainly to Italy (6.9 million tons), UK (4.7 million tons), France and Belgium (3.5 million tons each). During the late Armistice period 2 million tons of grain were provided mainly to Germany (0.72 million tons), Czechoslovakia (0.37 million tons), Poland (0.25 million tons), Finland and Romania (0.18 million tons each), Yugoslavia (0.07 million tons) and 15,000 tons were provided to the British occupied areas in the northwest of Russia. During the Reconstruction stage, 1.4 million tons were provided: to Russia (0.64 million tons), Poland (0.30 million tons), Austria (0.24 million tons) and Armenia (0.05 million tons).

Poland and the Baltic Republics

Having received 350,000 tons of US relief, of which most was grain, by 1920 Poland was strong enough to launch an attack on Ukraine, capturing Kiev in May 1920. This is normally interpreted as a nationalist attempt to restore the medieval boundaries of the Polish Lithuanian Empire, but in a still hungry and recently starved Europe, Ukraine with its abundant grain would have had other practical attractions. However, this last Polish attack was met with a serious rebuff from the Russian side and an invasion of Poland by the Red Army reaching Warsaw in August in 1920. This was seen at the time as an early stage in the attempt to extend world communism into Western Europe, rather than an attempt at re-building the Russian Empire. The failure of the Red Army to capture Warsaw led to the Russian retreat and Peace Treaty of Brest Litovsk; redrawing the map to recognise Poland as a separate country from Russia. There were good military reasons for this, but the fact that Russia was still not able to feed itself made the loss of this grain deficit region easier to accept.

The situation in the three newly declared Baltic Republics took on a similar pattern. They were all now importing grain from across the Atlantic. Local grain production was improving and the Baltic states were also receiving food relief from Hoover.[19] Given Russia's famished situation at this time, and their inability to feed these deficit regions, the reconquest of these regions was less attractive than the reconquest of Ukraine and Bessarabia.

Bessarabia and Ukraine

In the final year of the war when the Eastern Front collapsed after the October Revolution, Romania and Germany came to an agreement over the division of Bessarabia and Ukraine. Germany agreed to Romanian annexation of Bessarabia in exchange for Romania allowing Germany the free passage of German troops to invaded Ukraine in March 1918.

In the following years of the civil war and Polish invasion of Ukraine in 1920 the Ukrainian grain fields were intensely fought over. Romania remained in control of most of Bessarabia apart from the small East Dnestrian part, which the Soviets eventually regained naming it the Moldovan ASSR. The Red Army, having failed to retake Poland in

[19] Latvia and Estonia were each receiving twice as much assistance as Finland: for Latvia, 4,000 tons of grain and 7,000 tons of all aid; for Estonia, 3,000 tons of grains and 6,000 tons for all aid; while Lithuania (excluding Vilnius at this time) received 1,000 tons of food aid.

1920 was able to withdraw and redraw part of the map to restore Ukraine and Moldovan ASSR to the entity that would in 1922 become the USSR.

The Soviet Parts of the Former Tsarist Empire

Despite cutting supplies to the army, losing Poland, Finland and the Baltic Provinces, and shifting the capital from Petrograd to Moscow, the Bolshevik government was still unable to command all the grain that it needed to build a smaller army and stop the famine in the north. After a year of chaos, the state took control of the independent food detachments and began constructing them into a food army to carry out centralised grain procurements for both the army and the food deficit regions of the northern cities.

The amount of grain produced in Russia is difficult to assess because of problems over the unreliability of grain production data that was subject to under-reporting from the producers and exaggeration by the desperate procurement officials.[20] Available price, transport and procurement data allow us to construct a picture of the deteriorating food situation in the different food zones of Russia.

The hole in grain procurements caused by the loss of the south is visible in the following table (see Table 12.5) showing the regional sources of centrally state-collected grain.

Table 12.5 *State grain procurement in million tons*

		From producer regions			
	All	South	Centre	East	Total
1916/17	8.9	4.0	2.7	1.5	8.2
1917/18	1.2	0.4	0.2	0.5	1.1
1918/19	1.8	–	1.5	0.3	1.8
1919/20	3.4	–	1.7	1.5	3.2
1920/21	5.9	2.1	1.3	2.0	5.4
1921/22	3.8	1.4	0.7	0.9	3.0
1922/23	5.9	2.3	1.8	1.0	5.1

Source: Calculated from data in *Itogi Desyatiletiya Oktyabrskoi Revolyutsii* (Moscow, 1928), 379.

[20] This was not a uniquely Russian problem. It happened everywhere there were attempts at planning food supplies. Adam Tooze described the same problem in Germany. J. Adam Tooze, *Statistics and the German State, 1900–1945: The Making of Modern Economic Knowledge* (Cambridge University Press, 2001), 69–70.

Table 12.6 *Flows of grain into the northern deficit region*

	1913	1917	1918	1919	1920	1921	1922
Total grain procurements	–	1.2	1.8	3.4	5.9	3.8	5.9
Transport data to:							
Petrograd, Lakes and North	2.20	–	–	–	1.35	0.28	0.25
Moscow Industrial	2.08	–	–	–	0.71	0.41	0.76
West	2.0	–	–	–	1.10	0.68	0.82
All NCR (later in Soviet Union)	6.28	–	–	–	3.16	1.37	1.83

Source: Trudy TsSU, 19:2 (1925), pp. 6–11; Rail only excluding exports *Trudy TsSU*, 6:2 (1923), 169–70.

We lack transport data for the three crucial years of collapse in the north 1917–19, but the figures for 1920–22, in comparison with the 1913 figures show us the regional recovery process from 1920 (see Table 12.6).

In the years following the collapse of the state central grain procurement system in 1917 very little grain was centrally collected in the following year. Bagmen and worker detachments used force to take grain wherever they could, and their collections and transports were not all included in the haulage statistics. Gradually when military action and blockade stopped in 1920, the state was able to strengthen the collection system and collect 5.9 million tons of grain in 1920. The shipping of 3.2 million tons of grain into the different subregions of NCR in 1920 was enough to stop the decline in NCR, but the following years saw a reversal of this recovery, as the drought brought famine to the south.

The state had attempted to reform the system, to give the peasant an incentive to produce more grain and market more by abolishing requisitioning and replacing it with a tax in kind. This would have allowed the peasants to trade their surplus grain. But before this occurred the Volga region, in the South-East, suffered a very severe drought. The intensity of the drought is clear from available meteorological data.

The relationship of food prices to non-food prices in Moscow, which had already moved to be quadruple their 1913 relationship in 1918 would remain high and more than triple the normal level for the next two years and in January 1930 would still be 390 per cent the normal level to 152 per cent in January 1921, 130 per cent in January 1922, before falling to 66 per cent in the famous 'scissors' in January 1923.[21] These clearly show that the 1921/2 food shortages in Moscow were less serious than the 1918/19 ones.

[21] See data cited in footnote 14.

Food consumption surveys, which had just been developed on a national basis, were now used to check on the situation. They showed the appalling situation in the northern towns in March 1919 when these surveys began, and the subsequent improvements. Moscow and Petrograd recorded a slight deterioration in the spring, but a substantial improvement in 1922, when the famine was at its worse in the Volga. The surveys from the city of Saratov in the Volga in 1921–22 showed levels of per capita consumption like those experienced a few years earlier by Petrograd and Moscow in the northern famine. Data from the network of rural peasant food investigations become available from February 1920, when they showed fairly high levels of consumption. But they fell catastrophically to 30 or 40 per cent of normal levels in Orenburg, Samara, Saratov and Ekaterinoslav in the Volga, the Urals, and North Kazakstan regions.[22]

The growing differentials in grain prices noted in 1916 and 1917 increased in 1918–20, indicating increasing food shortages. This led to the inhabitants of the famished Consumer Regions taking drastic action to find food. In 1918 local food requisition detachments were formed spontaneously with the aim of taking the grain, not only from the few local supply regions, which were clearly insufficient, but also from more distant traditional supply regions. Later the central government took control of these groups and organised them into a food army in parts of the traditional supply region that were still under Soviet control. This resulted in the northern disorganised famished state raiding the south and forcibly (with arms) extracting and requisitioning any grain that it could find. This policy, known as War Communism, naturally led to increased hostility with the southern peasantry, but in the complexity of the time when other hostile military groups were also invading these areas and carrying out similar policies, the Bolsheviks may not have appeared the worse option.

The civil war between northern consumers and southern producers became mixed into a civil war between Reds and Whites. The war between Nationalists and integrationists in Ukraine was mixed into a war with Poland, and ultimately the Bolsheviks emerged victorious and redrew the map re-integrating the Southern Producer Region including Ukraine into the USSR.

The consequences of continued food problems and drought was continued elevation of mortality, especially in rural areas (see Saratov uezd [administrative subdivision] in Table 12.7 below). The situation did,

[22] S. G. Wheatcroft, 'Soviet Statistics of Nutrition and Mortality during Times of Famine, 1917–1922 and 1931–33', *Cahiers du Monde russe* 38:4 (1997), 1–34.

Table 12.7 *Mortality data in main cities and Saratov region*

	1913	1919	1920	1921	1922	% of 1913 in 1921	% of 1913 in 1922	% of 1919 in 1921	% of 1919 in 1922
	Crude death rate								
Petrograd city	21.4	71.7	48.5	31.0	29.0	145	136	43	40
Moscow city	24.7	45.4	36.3	25.5	29.0	103	117	56	64
Saratov town	26.1	71.4	59.8	66.6	82.8	255	317	93	116
Saratov uezd	29.5	29.1	35.9	28.1	37.2	95	116	97	128
Kiev	16.0	61.8	68.7	–	–	–	–	–	–
	Infantile mortality per thousand births								
Petrograd	231	434	187	155	244	67	106	36	56
Moscow	234	333	233	206	247	88	106	62	74
Saratov	384	395	298	424	393	110	102	107	100
Kiev	–	304	251	–	–	–	–	–	–

Source: S. G. Wheatcroft, 'Famine and Factors', 4–12.

however, ease a little in Moscow and Petrograd cities in comparison with the terrible year of 1919. But this was still higher than in 1913.

Reconnecting the northern deficit region and the capitals with the three traditional supply regions greatly improved the position in the northern towns and prepared the way for general recovery. In March 1921 the prospects for recovery were further boosted when the government introduced the New Economic Policy, replacing requisitioning with a tax in kind and re-establishing the market. However, before these favourable circumstances were able to have any effect on the countryside, a massive drought devastated the poor economies in the Volga and the south that had experienced five years of harsh procurements. The results were visible in the food consumption surveys that had been introduced and in a reversal in regional grain price differentials, with grain appearing to be cheaper in the Consumer Regions than in the Producer Regions. Despite the country receiving large amounts of international aid (mainly US aid through the American Relief Administration), very large levels of famine mortality were recorded in these Producer Regions. Recovery only came with the 1922 harvest.

Conclusions: Famine and Redrawing the Map of Eastern Europe

The towns in the NCR experienced serious hunger and famine from late 1916 to 1920. The early stages of the hunger contributed to the demonstrations and changes that led to the February Revolution of 1917. The situation in the south and in rural regions at this time was not so serious. Continued food crises in the north led to extraordinary measures to take grain from the countryside in the south. The situation was further complicated by the civil and interventionist wars, culminating in the Polish invasion. Eventually the Bolsheviks were successful in expelling invaders and winning the civil war. This enabled them to redraw their borders and re-incorporate most of the grain surplus regions of the south and east back into the USSR.

For Germany and Austria, the redrawn map emerging from war and famine remained in place until the mid 1930s and Second World War when Germany, the main grain deficit region of continental Europe, under Nazi control, attempted again to redraw the map to incorporate both of the main grain surplus regions of Europe. This attempt failed in the Second World War and for the next 45 years these main grain surplus regions of Europe reverted to Soviet and Soviet Allied control, but by this time, Europe was no longer grain deficient and global food supplies from outside Europe had become far less important.

If the first stage of Europe's food problems (to December 1918) could be characterised as hunger redrawing the map of Europe and destroying its Empires, the second stage in Eastern Europe (up to 1922) was concerned with re-redrawing the map to re-establish vital food supply links to the main food deficit region in Russia's NCR. In many ways this could be seen as the re-establishment of traditional imperial and colonial links, even though it was being carried out by a revolutionary state that was claiming to be anti-imperialist and may well have thought of itself as such in other matters.

13 Healing Hunger
Post-War Humanitarian Action

Ēriks Jēkabsons

Introduction

The First World War changed more than the political map of the world. The deterioration of local and national economies also worsened the humanitarian situation of civilians. Difficult living conditions were especially acute in territories that experienced direct warfare or occupation. The humanitarian crises were particularly prolonged and exasperated across the Ottoman Empire and in Eastern European countries (Finland, the Baltic States, Poland, Hungary, Russia, and others) where fighting did not end in 1918, but continued on for several years in the wake of imperial collapse.[1] The focus of this chapter is on healing from hunger through international intervention. While the forces that brought misery and hunger to millions of people across Europe and the Ottoman Empire were indeed strong, so too were the efforts to feed others and to bring relief.

Many of the international aid organizations that exist today had their genesis in the era of the First World War. Others saw their operations and scope materially expand during the war. Some institutions, even large ones, began during the war and ended soon after. To write a comprehensive history of humanitarian foreign aid, even for a single organization or geographic location, would take much more space than the present chapter allows.[2] This chapter examines some of the main operations of the organizations that sent food aid from the United States, especially the American Relief Administration (ARA), which provided by far the

[1] See Robert Gerwarth, *The Vanquished: Why the First World War Failed to End* (London: Allen Lane, 2016).

[2] Humanitarianism in the wake of the First World War is a growing field of research. See, among others, Branden Little, ed. "Humanitarianism in the Era of the First World War," *First World War Studies* 5:1 (March 2014), 1–16; Bruno Cabanes, *The Great War and the Origins of Humanitarianism, 1918–1924* (Cambridge: Cambridge University Press, 2014); Elisabeth Piller and Neville Wylie, eds. *Humanitarianism and the Greater War, 1914–24* (Manchester: Manchester University Press, 2023).

most amount of food aid.[3] In addition to the efforts of the ARA, there were many other aid givers and organizations involved in post-war relief: The League of Nations Health Organization, the Red Cross, as well as local, international, religious and secular groups.[4] A brief summary of a handful of some of these other major international players involved with food aid is included here.

This chapter is organized first with a discussion of the widespread priority given by nations to the feeding of militaries over civilians in times of need. This is followed by a discussion of local concerns over national health and the role that concerns over children played in conceptions of a future state. The next section introduces several of the other major international aid players before moving to the primary discussion of the ARA, the largest provider of aid on the continent.

Nutritional Needs of Militaries and Concerns over National Health

Governments all over the world were aware of the importance of the food supplies and of its direct link to national health. Indeed, food security was so significant that governments created special ministries with the responsibility of supplying their inhabitants with food.[5] Many of these ministries, including those from Czechoslovakia,[6]

[3] Tammy Proctor, *Saving Europe: First World War Relief and American Identity* (Oxford: Oxford University Press, 2025); Ēriks Jēkabsons, *Latvijas un Amerikas Savienoto Valstu attiecības 1918.-1922.gadā* (Riga: Latvijas vēstures institūta apgāds, 2018); Doina Anca Cretu, "Humanitarian Aid in the 'Bulwark Against Bolshevism': The American Relief Administration and the Quest for Sovereignty in Post-World War I Romania," *Journal of Romanian Studies* 1:2 (2019), 65–88; Franz Adlgasser, *American Individualism Abroad. Herbert Hoover, die American Relief Administration und Österreich, 1919–1923* (Vienna: VWGÖ, 1993); Matthew Adams, "Herbert Hoover and the Organization of the American Relief Effort in Poland (1919–1923)," *European Journal of American Studies* 4 (2009), 2; Suda Bane, ed. *Documents of the American Relief Administration European Operations 1918–1922*. Vol. I-XXII (Stanford: Stanford University Press, 1932); Suda Bane and Ralph Lutz, ed. *The Blockade of Germany After the Armistice 1918–1919*: *Selected Documents of the Supreme Economic Council Superior Blockade Council, American Relief Administration, and Other Wartime Organizations* (Stanford: Stanford University Press, 1942); Frank Surface and Raymond Bland, *American Food in the World War and Reconstruction Period: Operations of the Organizations under Herbert Hoover 1914 to 1924* (Stanford, CA: Stanford University Press, 1931).

[4] Many of these organizations were American, but there were also organizations from other European countries including, for example, the British *Save the Children*, which was soon internationalized with headquarters in Geneva, British Quakers, as well as the Lady Paget mission and many others.

[5] For more on government actions see Chapter 3 in this book.

[6] The Czechoslovak ministry for supply of the population was created in 1918 and dissolved in 1933, *Sbírka zákonů a nařízení*, Zákon č. 142/1933 Sb., kterým se ruší úřad (ministerstvo) pro zásobování lidu, July 19, 1933.

Germany,[7] Austria,[8] and Great Britain,[9] remained in function through the early 1920s, demonstrating the centrality of this issue during and after the war. Similarly, The French ministry of supply was created in 1917 and merged with the ministry of commerce in 1920.[10]

Often there were not enough foodstuffs to feed both the military and civilian populations. In a world of decreased food supplies, governments intervened by choosing to feed soldiers over civilians. In Germany and Austria-Hungary,[11] France,[12] Russia, and the Ottoman Empire,[13] for example, the military would routinely requisition food supplies at the expense of civilian populations. It was worse when civilians met foreign militaries. The German military regularly acquisitioned foodstuffs in Belgium, Poland, Romania, and the Baltics.[14] The English requisitioned men and animals in Palestine and Syria after 1917.[15] Soldiers needed enough energy to engage in the ongoing war, and their immediate needs were often viewed as more pressing than supplying food to civilian populations. Leaders believed that failing to feed an army during war might endanger its survival.

The question of supplying food to the armed forces remained acute in countries where warfare continued after the formal end of the First

[7] Germany's *Kriegsernährungsamt* or War Nutrition Office began on May 16, 1916. It was dissolved during the Armistice when it became the Reichsernährungsamt. The Reichsarnährungsamt later became part of the agricultural department during the Weimar Republic.

[8] The Austrian ministry of Public Nutrition ceased to exist in 1923, "Bundesgesetz vom 20. Juli 1922 über die Auflassung des Bundesministeriums für Volksernährung," *Bundesgesetzblatt* 527 (1922), 999.

[9] The Food Council in Great Britain had a memorandum for the demobilization of food control as early as November 10, 1918, and by the end of 1918 governmental constraints on breads, tea, and pork had been removed. However, deregulation itself was done in stages over time. The Ministry of Food itself was dissolved on March 31, 1921. See William Beveridge, *British Food Control* (London: Oxford University Press, 1928), 267–79, 308.

[10] Erik Langlinay, "Consommation et ravitaillement en France durant la Première Guerre mondiale (1914–1920)," in *Au nom du consommateur: Consommation et politique en Europe et aux États-Unis au XXe siècle*, edited by Alain Chatriot (Paris: La Découverte, 2005), 27–44.

[11] Holger H. Herwig, *The First World War: Germany and Austria-Hungary, 1914–1918* (2nd ed., London: Bloomsbury, 2014), 280–1.

[12] Langlinay, "Consommation et ravitaillement en France."

[13] Yiğit Akın, *When the War Came Home: The Ottomans' Great War and the Devastation of an Empire* (Stanford, CA: Stanford University Press, 2018), 111.

[14] On Poland, see Jesse Kauffman, *Elusive Alliance: The German Occupation of Poland in World War I* (Cambridge, MA: Harvard University Press, 2015), Chapter 1. On Romania, see David Hamlin, "'Dummes Geld': Money, Grain, and the Occupation of Romania in WWI," *Central European History* 42:3 (2009), 451–71.

[15] Michael Crowder, "The First World War and Its Consequences," in *General History of Africa vol. VII: Africa under Colonial Domination, 1880–1935*, edited by A. Adu Boahen (Berkeley, CA: University of California Press, 1985), 295.

World War such as the Baltic States, Poland, Romania, and Hungary and the priority given to soldiers continued.

The variability in the available foodstuffs rather than a uniform ration suggests the precarity and rapidly changing food situation. These 1919 summer rations for Latvian soldiers (see Table 13.1) also allow us to make estimates of the total caloric value. As Table 13.2 shows, rations for Latvian soldiers in the summer of 1919 contained around 2,900 calories.

The number of calories an individual needs depends on their size and health, and on the type of physical activity they are engaged in. Typically, adult females need about 2,200 calories per day to maintain their daily activities, and adult males need about 2,500. Rations for US soldiers in

Table 13.1 *Rations of Latvian soldiers, summer 1919*

Either/or		Add. substitution
750 grams bread	563 grams flour	
200 grams meat (later 250)	400 grams fresh fish (or 300 grams of salted fish)	3 eggs, 50 grams fats
500 grams potatoes		
200 grams root veg. (or 250 sauerkraut)	250 grams sauerkraut	

Source: Data for table in Inta Pētersone (ed.) *Latvijas Brīvības cīņas. Enciklopēdija* (Riga: Preses nams, 1999), 229.

Table 13.2 *Estimated calories from Latvian soldiers' summer ration, 1919*

	Caloric value per 1 gram	100 grams in ration	Total calories
Flour	3.74	563	2,105.62
Fresh fish (pike)	0.905	400	362
Potatoes (russet) flesh and skin	0.77	500	385
Sauerkraut	0.19	250	47.5
Daily total caloric value (estimate)			2,900.12

Source: Caloric values taken from the "Food Calorie Calculator," powered by the USDA National Nutrient Database, caloriecontrol.org.

Note: As pike is the most common fish in Latvia, the average of the two pike species listed in the calculator were taken. The content of the flour is difficult to know for certain (see previous chapter on substitutions) so the lowest and highest flour types by calorie (carob and sesame) were taken and averaged. Calorie per food type was listed in 100 grams. This is listed as gram in the table.

the mid 1990s were set at 3,600 calories per day.[16] Although Latvian soldiers rations were below this, they were also well above starvation rates and 400 calories above what is recommended for normal activity for males. A fuller picture would require estimates of total proteins, carbohydrates, vitamins, and fats.

Food supplies for militaries give an indication of the capacity of countries to provide for their civilian population. When soldiers were fed less than optimal diets, rations for civilians were even smaller. Regular civilians in Latvia would have eaten less than members of the military. Contemporary reports suggest that in many of the Latvian towns that had been recently freed from the Bolsheviks, the majority of inhabitants were hungry and nearing starvation.[17] The changes in the supply rate of the armies during the First World War are indicative on their own, showing a gradual decrease in the capability of states to supply their inhabitants with appropriate amounts of food.[18]

Beyond the immediate need to supply military troops, belligerent countries also had to contend with the dangers posed by hunger to the long-term future health of the nation. In many states, governments observed the negative impact of war on their population's health.[19] They were concerned that these conditions could negatively influence popular perceptions of the state's strength. For example, in 1916, an article in the *Hungarian Journal of Folk Teachers* stated:

> This news [of the high child mortality rate] is … particularly sad, from the perspective of the nation's future, if we compare our own growth of population with the one of competing nations. … Therefore, it is the duty of all educated people in the land of our country to take up the fight in this field, to undertake war service in this direction, which is almost as important from the perspective of the future of our nation as the one the valiant warriors are fulfilling in the plains of Russia and the mountains of the Balkans.[20]

After the turmoil of war, the post-war corresponded to a moment of fear surrounding the health of the nation. Public health experts played an

[16] BM Marriott (ed.), "Military Recommended Dietary Allowances, AR 40–25," table 2–3, in *Food Components to Enhance Performance: An Evaluation of Potential Performance-Enhancing Food Components for Operational Rations* (Washington, DC: National Academies Press, 1994).

[17] See Jānis Šiliņš. *Padomju Latvija 1918–1919* (Riga: Vēstures izpētīšanas un popularizēšanas biedrība, 2013), 142–5.

[18] See more in Chapter 1 of this book.

[19] A notable exception to this is in Britain. See Jay M. Winter, *The Great War and the British People* (London: Macmillan, 1985); Ian Gazeley and Andrew Newell, "The First World War in Working-Class Food Consumption in Britain," *European Review of Economic History* 17 (2013), 71–91; Mary E. Cox, "Food," in *The British Home Front and the First World War*, edited by Hew Strachan (Cambridge: Cambridge University Press, 2023), 469–86.

[20] Juba Adolf, "A gyermek táplálása és a háború," *Néptanitók lapja* 40:4 (1916), 4–6.

important role in the debate on how to best create a healthy and modern nation in this context of reconstruction. Many efforts to improve public health were based on scientific theories for the biological and social improvement of the nation, often influenced by eugenic discourses.[21] The recognition of the importance of a healthy population for building and maintaining a strong future state meant that particular attention was devoted to the health of the younger generation. Children were often the primary target group in the efforts of both local and international relief organizations. Governments and organizations understood that receiving adequate amounts of foodstuffs during childhood had an immediate impact on a child's health as well as on their future as adult citizens. They were therefore prioritizing the proper feeding of children. This manifested itself in different ways, including special rations; for example, children were often allotted special milk rations.[22] In other instances, children were temporarily moved to locations where they would be better fed.[23]

In terms of state survival, institutional priority of limited resources was given first to feeding soldiers if conflict continued, and second to feeding children. If during wartime children were viewed more from the viewpoint of their future military capacity, after the war children were seen as a guaranty for the future of the state, though the two ideas were often related and could be intertwined. Children were also prioritized by non-governmental charitable and religious groups fuelled by conceptions of children as innocent victims.[24] The focus on feeding children first was a universal response by aid givers both foreign and domestic.

International Relief

Governments in countries devastated by the war in 1918 did what they could to care for the health of their people. Local aid organizations and charities were widespread, and not only through official government channels. Many charitable institutions sought to alleviate hunger for the

[21] On Poland, see Katrin Steffen, "Who Belongs to the Healthy Body of the Nation? Health and National Integration in Poland and the Polish Army after the First World War," in *From the Midwife's Bag to the Patient's File: Public Health in Eastern Europe*, edited by Heike Karge, Friederike Kind-Kovács, and Sara Bernasconi (Budapest: CEU Press, 2017), 119–44; on Hungary: Marius Turda, *Eugenics and Nation in Early 20th Century Hungary* (Basingstoke: Palgrave, 2014); see also Barbara Klich-Kluczewska, Joachim von Puttkamer and Immo Rebitschek, eds., *Biopolitics in Central and Eastern Europe in the 20th Century: Fearing for the Nation* (London: Routledge, 2023).

[22] For example in Freiburg, Germany: Roger Chickering, *The Great War and Urban Life in Germany: Freiburg, 1914–1918* (New York, NY: Cambridge University Press, 2007), 254.

[23] See Chapter 7 for more information on children moving between urban and rural areas.

[24] On the concept of children as quintessential victims of war see Tara Zahra, *The Lost Children: Reconstructing Europe's Families after World War II* (Cambridge, MA: Harvard University Press, 2011), chapter 1.

most needy. In Bohemia, for example, the Agrarian political party set up *Česke srdce* or Czech Heart, to provide food for hungry children.[25] The governor of Beirut, Jamal Pasha, set up centers for refugees and poor women that were supported by the elite women.[26] Although technically voluntary, both Pasha's refugee centers in Beirut and the *Česke srdce* in Bohemia were at least in part initiated, organized, and administered with political backing. In war-torn Europe and the Ottoman Empire, people often sought to help those with whom they held a kinship, typically based on a shared locality, religion, or language. Still, the possibilities for local people and governments to rapidly solve a situation that had developed over the course of four years of war were often limited. Internal aid efforts were often insufficient. An immediate reduction of hunger in the war-torn countries was practically impossible without the aid of foreign countries because there was simply not enough food.

The main source of food relief in Europe and the Ottoman Empire came from the United States. The Americans were also outsized in terms of the amount of food that they were able to sell or donate. Food production in the United States actually increased during the war,[27] unlike in Europe or the Ottoman Empire,[28] where, in addition to blockades and other losses associated with the war, there were significant reductions in agricultural output.[29] The large agricultural surpluses in the United States gave it a unique capacity to provide relief.[30] With its vast bread basket across the plains, there was more than enough food for domestic consumption with much more left over.

Indeed, the United States-led organizations fed millions of people across the Ottoman Empire and Europe during and especially after the First World War. This chapter will mostly focus on the American Relief

[25] Claire Morelon, *Streetscapes of War and Revolution* (Cambridge: Cambridge University Press, 2024), 199–200.

[26] Melanie S. Tanielian, *The Charity of War: Famine, Humanitarian Aid, and World War I in the Middle East* (Stanford, CA: Stanford University Press, 2018), 174.

[27] Herbert Hoover, "Introduction," in *History of the United States Food Administration 1917–1919*, edited by William Clinton Mullendore (Stanford, CA, Stanford University Press, 1941), 9–12.

[28] Tanielian, *The Charity of War*, 69–79; see also Fritz Grobba, *Die Getreidewirtschaft Syriens und Palästinas seit Beginn des Weltkrieges* (Hannover: Orient-Buchhandlung Heinz Lafaire, 1923); see also Graham Pitts, "Organization of War Economies (Ottoman Empire/Middle East)," in *1914–1918-online. International Encyclopedia of the First World War*, edited by U. Daniel, Peter Gatrell, Oliver Janz, et al. (Berlin: Freie Universität Berlin, 2015).

[29] See Chapter 14 in this book and https://hungerdrawsthemap.history.ox.ac.uk/hunger-during-and-after-first-world-war [last accessed March 1, 2022] to view maps of annual agricultural production in European countries.

[30] US Department of Agriculture, *Yearbook of the United States Department of Agriculture 1919* (Washington, DC: Government Printing Office, 1920), 23–4.

Administration but they worked within a network of several other major aid players, which must be briefly introduced. The largest international aid organization operating in the Ottoman Empire in 1918 came from the United States: Near East Relief. It was founded in 1915 as "The American Committee for Armenian and Syrian Relief" as a direct response to massacres of Armenians, Syrians, and Greeks, and provided material relief for orphans and widows.[31] While the name of the organization changed several times, it grew in scope and supplies. By the time the war ended, it had helped people of many different backgrounds from across the region. A report dated from September 30, 1918, gave the total receipts for relief at US$12,604,127.70.[32] Relief increased into the 1920s, and enjoyed US congressional support.

While Near East Relief was the largest foreign aid organization operating in the Ottoman Empire, it was not alone. The American Jewish Joint Distribution Committee also did substantial work in the area, although as an institution the Joint's focus was on relieving suffering Jews rather than on geographic location. Subsequently it had operations in Europe as well. Similar to Near East Relief, the Joint began during the war itself in direct response to need.[33] During the war the Joint distributed some US$13.75 million in funds to Jews in need in the Ottoman Empire and parts of Eastern Europe.[34] Relief efforts only increased once fighting slowed and aid became easier to deliver. Many other international aid groups operated in the Ottoman Empire besides Near East Relief and the American Joint Distribution Committee, but these two numbers can give the reader a minimal idea on how much aid was being donated and received.[35]

While the Joint and Near East were started in the United States during the war, other aid organizations that had a longer history, such as the American Red Cross, actively increased their operations during and following the war. The American Red Cross (ARC) was active in Western and Central European countries throughout the First World

[31] American Committee for Relief in the Near East, *The American Committee for Relief in the Near East, Its History, Its Work and the Need for Support as Outlined by President Wilson and Others* (Publisher unknown, 1918), 1.

[32] American Committee for Relief in the Near East, *The American Committee for Relief in the Near East*, 14.

[33] Jaclyn Granick, "Waging Relief: the Politics and Logistics of American Jewish War Relief in Europe and the Near East (1914–1918)," *First World War Studies* 5:1 (2014), 55–68.

[34] Granick, "Waging Relief," 57.

[35] Relief in the region came from a variety of sources. See Tanielian, *The Charity of War*; on French efforts, see Simon Jackson, "Transformative Relief: Imperial Humanitarianism and Mandatory Development in Syria-Lebanon, 1915–1925," *Humanity, An International Journal of Human Rights, Humanitarianism and Development* 8:2 (2017), 247–68.

War, and worked with all sides in the conflict to help wounded soldiers. It also began to help civilians, especially after the war, eventually providing free medical care and clothes to civilians and soldiers alike. In Eastern and Central European countries after the war, the ARC concentrated its humanitarian aid on the poor, and in these efforts, it cooperated with local organizations (for example with the Women's Aid Corps in Latvia or similar women's organizations in other countries, local Red Cross organizations and others). It also provided assistance in the form of medications and sanitary supplies. Special clinics for children were set up in various countries.

The ARC grew immensely during the First World War. In 1914 it had 107 sections with 17,000 members, but by 1918 there were 3,864 sections with some 20 million members. In 1917, the Junior Red Cross was established and both organizations together numbered more than 30 million members. The ARC operated in around twenty-five countries outside the United States and these activities were supervised by the ARC Europe Commission, situated in Paris. In November 1918, ARC commissions were in operation in Great Britain, France, Belgium, Italy, Palestine, North Russia, Siberia, Serbia, and Greece (activities in Romania were ended shortly before). In the beginning of 1920, activities were ceased in Great Britain, France, Belgium, and Italy, but at the same time became more intense in Balkan countries, Poland and the Baltic States (still called "Western Russia" at the time).[36]

American Relief Actions

Commission for the Relief in Belgium

American involvement in helping hungry European civilians started early in the war. Under Herbert Hoover's management as the first president of the Commission for the Relief in Belgium (CRB), the US government and its citizens were generously involved, though it remained an international agency. The CRB was formed in 1914 as Belgium, occupied by German forces and subject to the British-Allied blockade, faced a severe food shortage. This organization gathered donations and then exported

[36] See: Henry Davison, *The American Red Cross in the Great War* (New York, NY: Macmillan, 1919); Herbert Hoover, *An American Epic: Famine in Forty-five Nations. Organization Behind the Front, 1914–1923. Vol. II* (Chicago, IL: Henry Regnery Company, 1960), 189–200; Lavinia Dock et al. *History of American Red Cross Nursing* (New York, NY: Macmillan, 1922), 387–1133; Foster Dulles, *The American Red Cross: A History* (New York, NY: Harper, 1950), 1–212; Julia Irwin, *Making the World Safe: The American Red Cross and Nation's Humanitarian Awakening* (Oxford: Oxford University Press, 2013).

them through the blockade (with the permission of the governments of Britain, Germany and France), and delivered the imported food to the people of Belgium and Northern France.[37] In both countries, the CRB partnered with local committees which managed the food distribution, primarily the *Comité National de Secours et d'Alimentation* in Belgium and the *Comité d'Alimentation du Nord de la France* in Northern France. Municipal committees were then in charge of food repartition to inhabitants through a system of rationing tickets.[38] The amount of supplies necessary to feed the hungry was huge and averaged 100,000 tons of food per month for almost five years. The coordination of such a high number of food imports to occupied territories was a massive endeavour.[39] In total, the CRB received 5,174,431 tons of food between 1914 and 1918.[40] The CRB operated until 1919, but official American involvement ceased with the declaration of war on Germany in April 1917, as Americans could not operate as a neutral force anymore. The operation of the organization was transferred into the hands of the Spanish and Dutch officials. All in all, the CRB was one of the most visible international relief organizations during the war itself, and certainly the largest. The successful actions of the CRB earned Herbert Hoover extensive experience in relief work and an excellent reputation, both of which he later used to his advantage in the management of armistice and post-war relief efforts by the American Relief Administration. Crucially, they also gave him experience in feeding large groups of children, and an understanding of some of the practical and political challenges in food provisioning.

United States Food Administration

After the United States entered the world war, Hoover stepped down from his role of president of the CRB. He became the head of the newly

[37] Clotilde Druelle, *Feeding Occupied France during World War I: Herbert Hoover and the Blockade* (Cham: Palgrave Macmillan, 2019).

[38] For Belgium, see Sophie de Schaepdrijver, "A Civilian War Effort: the Comité National de Secours et d'Alimentation in Occupied Belgium, 1914–1918," in *Remembering Herbert Hoover and the Commission for Relief in Belgium* (Brussels: Fondation Universitaire, 2007), 24–37; for Northern France see Alex Dowdall, "Entre improvisation et intervention: le rôle des autorités locales dans le ravitaillement en nourriture des villes du front français," in *Les mises en guerre de l'État: 1914–1918 en perspective*, edited by Sylvain Berstchy and Philippe Salson (Lyon: ENS Editions, 2018), 226–89.

[39] Branden Little, "The Commission for Relief in Belgium," in *1914–1918-online. International Encyclopedia of the First World War*, edited by Ute Daniel et al. (Berlin: Freie Universität Berlin, 2014).

[40] George I. Gay and H. H. Fisher, *Public Relations of the Commission for Relief in Belgium. Documents* (Stanford, CA: Stanford University Press, 1929), vol. 2, 474.

Table 13.3 *US food exports to Europe, pre-war – 1919*

Commodity	3-year pre-war avg.	1917–1918	1918–1919
	In tons		
Wheat and rye	3,720,398	4,590,928	10,382,094
Other cereals	1,607,296	4,584,633	3,221,624
Pork	498,115	868,551	1,472,154
Beef	93,187	350,983	551,133
Vegetable oils	165,116	75,732	148,910
Dairy products	13,019	306,940	439,294
Sugar*	511,884	1,279,351	1,893,914
Fruit and vegetables	350,040	269,796	558,255
Totals	6,959,055	12,326,914	18,667,378

Source: M. E. Cox, *Hunger in War and Peace*, 237.
*Sugar includes exports from Cuba.

created United States Food Administration (USFA), created in May 1917. Its aims were to increase food supplies that could be shipped to US Allies through increasing domestic agricultural production, organizing food storage, distribution, exports and imports, and regulating food prices. "Food will win the war" became a slogan (USFA).[41] Table 13.3 shows the increase of US food exports to Europe.

The organization was successful in increasing food production. Supplies of wheat, pork, and other products exported to Europe had increased significantly in the United States during the war itself. Much of these exports were financed to the Allies through US loans.

Thanks to this activity, when fighting slowed in 1918, there was a food surplus in the United States. This extra supply of food needed to be used.[42] In the immediate post-war period, many European governments integrated food and appeals for aid into their diplomatic relations with the United States. The new leaders of Czechoslovakia, for example, despite having spent the war away from their country, were very aware of the urgency of the food situation in their homeland and of its potential political impact. In a letter to Edvard Beneš in November 1918, Tomáš Masaryk, then in Washington, considered that the first question to be discussed was: "Will our [people] at home have enough bread?" He then suggested that the United States should be asked

[41] Hoover Herbert, *An American Epic: Famine in Forty-five Nations. Organization Behind the Front, 1914–1923. Vol. II* (Chicago, IL: Henry Regnery Company, 1960), 2.
[42] Cox, *Hunger in War and Peace*, 226–40.

for help.[43] Even the Netherlands, during the spring of 1919, tried to dispel the perception of having been a war profiteer as a way to justify their requests for international aid relief.[44]

The USFA ended during the armistice period.[45] However, Hoover realised as early as the autumn of 1918 that the need to sell and distribute food from the United States after the war would continue. He wanted to create a new structure to assist in the renewal of Europe. On 12 November 1918, he travelled to Europe to assess how the United States, in cooperation with other powers, could help the inhabitants of Central and Eastern Europe affected by the war.[46]

Hoover was by then already aware of the severity of the food crisis in this region of Europe, as demonstrated by his efforts to organize relief for the Polish people in 1915.[47] Another attempt to provide aid in Eastern Europe during the war was the project to send shipments to newly independent Finland in late 1917. The members of the USFA and War Trade Board, seeing the hunger threat for the inhabitants of newly founded Finland, began preparations to send food there. There too, unfortunately, efforts failed, although for a different reason. Civil war in Finland worsened the situation and the country did not receive aid until 1919.[48]

The American Relief Administration

Near the end of the war, President Woodrow Wilson and Herbert Hoover created an aid plan for those countries in Central and Eastern Europe that were most devastated by the war. This assistance was offered for humanitarian, religious, political, and economic reasons.[49] The United States needed a market for the surplus production of agricultural goods

[43] Letter from November 3, 1918 in Dagmar Hájková, Ivan Šedivý, eds., *Korespondence T.G. Masaryk – Edvard Beneš 1914–1918* (Prague: Masarykův Ústav, 2004), 297.

[44] Dutch National Archives, 2.05.23/842, folder A250 N.P. "Economic losses suffered by Holland as a consequence of the War," [brochure, 1919], sent by foreign minister H.A. van Karnebeek to all Dutch envoys in Allied countries, not dated [circa April 1919]; on German appeals to the United States, see Elisabeth Piller, "German Child Distress. US Humanitarian Aid and Revisionist Politics, 1918–24," *Journal of Contemporary History* 51:3 (2016), 453–86.

[45] Herbert Hoover, *Preface to a Report of the United States Food Administration* (Publisher unknown, April 1920), 3.

[46] Hoover Institution Library & Archives, ARA, Box 542, Folder 21 (Statistical Report on the work of Director General of Relief in Europe During the Post Armistice Period, November 11, 1918, to September 1919. Prepared by F. Surface, 7).

[47] Adams, "American Relief Effort in Poland."

[48] United States Committee on Public Information, "Ten Shiploads of U.S. Grain Diverted to Starving Finns," *American Food Journal* 13:1 (1918), 56.

[49] Cox, *Hunger in War and Peace*, 224–40.

that were a direct result of the USFA's aims to increase food that could be used to supply the Allies. It was argued that food supplies could blunt the spread of Bolshevism and would ensure US interests in Europe.

Hoover was aware of the severity of the food crisis in Europe. Yet to orchestrate the division of millions of tons of foodstuffs required knowledge on the local level. He requested estimates of food needs from local governments in addition to sending men to assess needs on the ground. The process of estimating nutritional needs of an entire population also set a precedent for estimating the nutritional needs of nations.[50]

Hoover ordered the first food shipments to Europe before he left the United States, which left port on November 16, 1918.[51] Those first ships arrived via Rotterdam on January 4, 1919.[52] Working closely with Herbert Hoover, US President Woodrow Wilson sent a letter to the major Allied governments on December 15, 1918, outlining US food supplies and a plan to lift the Allied blockade. With the backing of the president, Hoover then met with the Inter-Allied Blockade Council on December 22, 1918 to work on this plan. While the blockade was not lifted until much later, efforts to distribute food supplies continued. The ARA was officially founded with the US Congress decision on February 24, 1919 to make US$100 million available for helping European countries.[53] The day after the bill passed, the ARA office in Paris was established by President Wilson to coordinate this action and put under the general direction of Herbert Hoover. A total of around 4,000 paid employees, mainly demobilized army officers, participated in the work of the ARA in European countries and were assisted by many more volunteers.

Decision-making on the distribution of millions of tons of food to a hungry world after the war, and the control of financial markets this implied, was a powerful tool.[54] Herbert Hoover wanted to keep the distribution of US foods in US hands. With the founding of the ARA, Hoover hoped to create an instrument for economic cooperation, comparable to what Woodrow Wilson envisioned the League of Nations to be for political cooperation, and that would include a leading role for the United States in it.[55]

[50] Mullendore, *History of US Food Administration*, 324–5.

[51] Sidney Brooks, *America and Germany, 1918–1925* (2nd ed., New York, NY: Macmillan, 1927), 75.

[52] Brooks, *America and Germany*, 76.

[53] Surface, *American Food*, 39.

[54] Cox, *Hunger in War and Peace*, 256–57.

[55] Kendrick Clements, *The Life of Herbert Hoover: Imperfect Visionary 1918–1928* (New York, NY: Palgrave Macmillan, 2010), 2–3.

The ARA office in Paris operated in close cooperation with the Grain Corporation of the US Food Administration.[56] It used its trade connections as a business agent in both the United States and Europe. The ARA gave their orders to the New York office, which organized purchases and shipments that were further supervised by the London office of the Grain Corporation (which supervised ARA accounting as well).[57]

The ARA operated closely with other aid organizations as well, large and small. In February 1919, for example, Herbert Hoover approached the American Red Cross leadership to explain the plans of the ARA and confirm that they in no way wished to interfere with the sphere of work of the ARC. He extended an invitation to the ARC to cooperate with the ARA.[58] This cooperation helped the ARA to adapt to difficult domestic conditions across the globe and cope with problems of destroyed infrastructure, particularly in transportation. Furthermore, many countries in Eastern Europe were the site of post-war conflicts between different national groups to dispute the new borders. Due to the importance of the mission work for local inhabitants, local governments tended to respect the opinions and wishes of both the ARA and the ARC, especially in cases when both organizations presented a coordinated viewpoint.[59]

To give just a few examples of the ARA's rapid movement of foodstuffs, in the winter and spring of 1919 the ARA delivered more than 300,000 tons of food supplies on credit to Poland. This helped stabilize the internal situation while the fight over the borders continued.[60] The Baltics and Poland were engaged in direct warfare against Bolshevik

[56] Suda Bane and Ralph Haswell Lutz (eds.), *Organization of American Relief in Europe 1918–1919* (Stanford, CA: Stanford University Press, 1943), 335.

[57] Hoover Institution Library and Archives, American Relief Administration, European operation records, Box 542, Folder 21 (Statistical Report on the work of Director General of Relief in Europe, 11); Frank Surface, *The Grain Trade during the World War Being a History of the Food Administration and the United States Grain Corporation* (New York: Macmillan Co., 1928), 398–412.

[58] National Archives of the United States, Herbert Hoover Presidential Library, Herbert Hoover to Henry P. Davison, February 22, 1919; R. Olds to H. Hoover, February 25, 1919, *American Relief Administration Bulletin*, April 8, 1919.

[59] See Gerwarth, *The Vanquished*; Jochen Böhler, *Civil War in Central Europe: the Reconstruction of Poland, 1918–1921* (Oxford: Oxford University Press, 2018).

[60] American Relief Administration European Children's Fund Mission to Poland, *Polsko-Amerykański Komitet Pomocy Dzieciom. 1919–1922* (Warsaw, 1922), 7; see also: *Amerykańska przyjaźń. Herbert Hoover a Polska. Wystawa w Zamku Królewskim w Warszawie 12 listopada 2004–16 stycznia 2005. American Friendship. Herbert Hoover and Poland. Exhibition in the Royal Castle in Warsaw November 12, 2004–Jaunuary 16, 2005* (Warsaw: "Agraf," 2004), 9–119.

troops and were also the site of violence by paramilitary groups.[61] By the end of 1918 Hoover and the organizations he led were involved with supplying food to the Baltics. There was immense devastation in this region, and Americans wished to contain Bolshevism. If local governments were more concerned with the physical health of the nation being affected by hunger, the ARA also addressed hunger in Europe as a way to combat Bolshevism.[62] In the ARA's conception, Bolshevism was a "disease" that needed to be fought and prevented: "the psychological effect of seeing persons from Allied countries going about in the different towns plus the hard fact of getting food will do more to combat Bolshevism than any army can – for Bolshevism, they find there, is like a disease or a germ rather than an armed enemy."[63] This political disease could not be stopped by force, but it might be "by food."[64]

In the summer of 1919, Herbert Hoover detailed more of the structure of the recently founded ARA. It was to be based on a national committee and sub-committees in individual countries, which would be composed of people with a high position in society. This structure would give a chance for local people to organize relief work on their own, leaving for Americans the functions of initiative and oversight, but not total leadership over the actual work, as this would prevent local initiative from building up, something viewed as essential to ensure continuation of the relief work later on, after the Americans had left. The explicit aim of the American Relief Administration was to provide short-term emergency relief, not substitute or replace existing welfare structures in the various societies in which it operated.[65] By June 1919, the ARA was intervening in the following countries: Armenia, Austria, Bulgaria, Czechoslovakia, Denmark, Estonia, Finland, Germany, Hungary, Latvia, Lithuania, Greater Serbia, Northern France, Poland, Romania, and parts of Russia.[66] Keeping with Hoover's plan to appoint local individuals in high positions of society, national representatives were often chosen for

[61] On Poland, see Böhler, *Civil War in Central Europe*; on Lithuania: Tomas Balkelis, *War, Revolution, and Nation-Making in Lithuania, 1914–1923* (Oxford: Oxford University Press, 2018).

[62] See: Neal Pease, *Poland, the United States and the Stabilization of Europe, 1919–1933* (New York, NY: Oxford University Press, 1986), 4.

[63] Hoover Institution Library and Archives, American Relief Administration, European operation records, Box 344, Folder 10 (undated report).

[64] Pease, *Poland, the United States and the Stabilization of Europe*, 4.

[65] "Organization of the American Relief Administration European Children's Fund," *American Relief Administration Bulletin*, July 25, 1919.

[66] National Archives of the United States, Herbert Hoover Presidential Library. American Relief Administration Bulletins Series I Box I, No. 16–19. "A Report on Relief Operations from the Minutes of the Supreme Economic Council for June 23, 1919 (Minute No. 234)," 1–3.

their expertise and esteem. For example, Clemens von Pirquet, a famous medical doctor and professor in Vienna, was appointed as the head of Austrian section.[67] Under Pirquet's direction, the methods he developed in Vienna during the war on assessing nutritional deprivation of children were applied across Austria.[68]

The unitary principles of how food aid was distributed were similar for different countries; this was particularly true when helping children. The main operational principles included a classification of children in categories, depending on their health condition, with children grouped as the most deprived receiving food aid first. Special cards could be shown or exchanged for food; and food was cooked in specific, designated kitchens overseen by local committees. Children could only eat at designated feeding centers, and had to show their feeding card to be allowed in. This prevented food being shared or given to others instead of the children it was intended for.[69] One aim of the ARA was to assist countries with food supplies while simultaneously developing the capability of these countries to care for their children themselves. This was part of the rationale behind requesting a small amount of financial assistance or other form of participation by local governmental or municipal structures.[70] Sharing leadership gave local communities and domestic governments ownership of the child feeding, and benefited children. In Germany, this took of the form of free train transportation for food for German children, reducing transportation costs once food reached the country, thus allowing more money to be spent on food.

On May 20, 1919, Herbert Hoover reminded ARA employees in Europe that the work needed to be completed with absolute impartiality; the single aim was to avert hunger, anarchy, and economic collapse. He wrote that participation in any local political affairs was

[67] American Relief Administration. European Children's Fund, *Three Years Work of the American Relief Administration in Austria* (Vienna, 1921), 3; Nils Hansson and Daniela Angetter-Pfeiffer, "Remembering Innovative Paediatrician Clemens von Pirquet on the 150th Anniversary of His Birth," *Acta Paediatrica* 113 (2024), 1778–80.

[68] Mary E. Cox, "L'indice Pelidisi (1920–1921). Une réévaluation contemporaine d'un indicateur nutritif oublié," in *Les Fronts intérieurs européens: l'arrière en guerre (1914–1920)*, edited by Laurent Dornel and Stéphane Le Bras (Rennes: Presses universitaires de Rennes, 2018), 179–96.

[69] For examples of this practice in Latvia see Jēkabsons, *Latvijas un Amerikas Savienoto Valstu attiecības*, 529–43; for Germany see Cox, *Hunger in War and Peace*, 307–13.

[70] See: Adams, "American Relief Effort in Poland," 4–5; Mary E. Cox, "Hunger Games: Or How the Allied Blockade in the First World War Deprived German Children of Nutrition, and Allied Food Aid Subsequently Saved Them," *Economic History Review* 68, 2 (2015), 621–4; American Relief Administration European Children's Fund, *Final Report of the Work in Hungary* (Budapest: American Relief Administration, 1920), 6–7.

forbidden, as was criticism of any local leaders or government officials.[71] This was a needed reminder in places such as Latvia. Because assistance rendered by the ARA was so essential, local governments yielded to the Americans' demand that certain civil servants of Baltic German extraction be retained in their posts. Americans aspired to implement principles of fairness and equity, which was considerably influenced by the poor relationship prevailing between Latvians and the former elite: Baltic Germans. As elsewhere, the ARA mission in Latvia tried to remain neutral with regard to Latvia's internal affairs. Yet, during this complicated phase of transition, they sometimes came into conflict with the retreating German troops and other political and military actors. The situation was similar in nearby Lithuania, where the ARA's headquarters in Kaunas were attacked by German armed soldiers a day after the Americans' arrival in the city.[72] Any perceived political support for one of the conflicting groups could have caused tensions with other parties and so reduced the effectiveness of the ARA's activities.

Still, despite its goal to remain impartial, members of the ARA often influenced national institutions. This was true in Poland, where they participated in Polish decision making.[73] In Latvia, ARA worker Thomas Orbison openly expressed his sympathies towards the Latvians in their fight against Bermondt's forces and the Bolsheviks. This, along with Orbison's extraordinary activity and initiative, earned him great popularity, which caused complications for the ARA leadership in London and later within Latvia itself. Orbison eventually assumed that he could regulate certain administrative matters related to agencies for children. This brought him into direct conflict with social democrat Latvians in municipalities who wished to influence the destination of American aid. As a result, a drawn-out public feud ensued. In London, Orbison was eventually chastised for getting involved in Latvia's domestic affairs as an ARA member, which was strictly forbidden.[74]

One of the difficulties ARA officers faced in Eastern Europe was to carry out their work in the middle of a war. In Poland, for example,

[71] Hoover Institution Library and Archives, American Relief Administration, European operation records, Box Box 692, Folder 14 (Hoover to all Representatives of the Relief Administration and the Grain Corporation in Europe, May 20, 1919).

[72] Balkelis, *War, Revolution, and Nation-Making*, 1.

[73] Davide Rodogno, Francesca Piana, and Shaloma Gauthier, "Shaping Poland: Relief and Rehabilitation Programmes by Foreign Organizations, 1918–1923," in *Shaping the Transnational Sphere: Experts, Networks, and Issues from the 1840s to the 1930s*, edited by Davide Rodogno, Bernhardt Struck, and Jakob Vogel (New York, NY: Berghahn Books, 2015), 259–78.

[74] Jēkabsons, *Latvijas un Amerikas Savienoto Valstu attiecības*, 478–517.

the ARA followed the advance of troops eastwards. Revolutions also disturbed the course of their operations, as in Hungary after Béla Kun came to power in spring 1919.[75] Furthermore, relationships with local committees were not always smooth as they relied on previous institutions and local volunteers. In Lithuania, the rules the ARA introduced to regulate food distribution led some volunteers to quit, which slowed distribution.[76] The Austrian head of the ARA in Austria, Clemens von Pirquet, was so upset by his American counterpart in Vienna, Herman Raymond Geist, that he threatened to resign.[77] Geist was removed and sent back to the United States.[78] The customary separation of welfare committees in many locations according to nationality irritated American welfare workers. An American journalist visiting Czechoslovakia after the war noted that national tensions could have an influence on local food distribution:

> If the child is hungry they [the Americans] aim to feed it. The people among whom they work, however, don't always feel that way about it. In many towns which have Czech majorities the Czechs frequently try to fix things so that German children won't be fed. In towns with German majorities the Germans often take steps to deprive the Czech children of food. The American Relief Administration has been forced to recognize this condition, and they have to be very careful that the feeding committees are carefully mixed.[79]

All these aspects had to be taken into account by ARA officers, while maintaining political neutrality and so ensuring equal respect by all parties.

It should be stressed that the ARA sought to supply relief to many countries that were in need of it, including former enemies of the United States and other Allied countries. In March 1919 in reference to Germany, Austria, Hungary, Bulgaria, and Turkey, it was stressed:

75 On the Hungarian revolution and the ARA see: John Oskison, "An Adventure in Food Relief," *American Relief Administration Bulletin* 4 (1919), 27–9.

76 Andrea Griffante, "Fighting over Children. Relief, Rehabilitation and Childhood in Lithuania, 1914–1923," *Journal of the University of Latvia History / Latvijas Universitates Zurnals. Vesture* 3:98 (2017), 124–37.

77 National Archives of the United States, Herbert Hoover Presidential Library, BAEF: ARA Personnel Box 115, American Relief Administration Personnel Files, Geist Herman, 1919–1945. "Memorandum Concerning Dr. Geist" by Clemens von Pirquet (December 30, 1919.)

78 National Archives of the United States, Herbert Hoover Presidential Library, BAEF: ARA Personnel Box 115, American Relief Administration Personnel Files, Geist Herman, 1919–1945. Letter from G. B. Stockton to Mr. Brown (January 20, 1919).

79 Kenneth Lewis Roberts, *Europe's Morning After* (New York, NY: Harper & Bros, 1921), 157.

> These areas are as much in need of relief as the rest of Europe, although obviously not subject to such sympathetic attention. But as the primary object of relief is to prevent anarchy and its spread and to encourage the establishment of good government, relief must be furnished to the enemy as well as friends.[80]

Still, despite these efforts, lifting the British and Allied blockade was slow work. And because of the limit that no food from the US$100,000,00 emergency relief fund passed by US Congress could be used to help former enemies, this meant that countries such as Germany needed to pay for their food in gold and foreign currencies.[81] After the armistice was signed in June 1919, there were technically no more 'enemy' countries.

During the first stage of its operations in the spring and summer 1919, the ARA carried out a "Program of General Relief" by distributing food to all groups of inhabitants that were in need of it (see Figure 13.1). During this stage, governments of the relief-receiving countries partly paid or promised to pay for the food. From the summer of 1919 until the summer 1920 and again from 1921 to 1922, the Children's Relief Program was carried out as part of the General Relief Programme, during which the food was financed from private donations raised in the United States and was distributed completely without payment. Although, as mentioned, local governments and volunteers participated in the process of feeding the children. Relationships between the ARA and the governments they worked with were regulated by treaties. One early treaty was between the ARA and the government of Czechoslovakia, signed on 24 February 1919. This treaty not only set out the obligations of both parties, but also explicitly stressed that the treaty was in force because the government of Czechoslovakia had appealed to the United States, Great Britain, France, and Italy "for foodstuffs in order to prevent starvation among the people of Czecho-Slovakia and to assist the Czecho-Slovak National Republic in the maintenance of order and to stop the spread of anarchy from other countries."[82] Similar contracts were made between the ARA and governments of Poland, Yugoslavia, and Romania. In April 1919, Hoover proposed relief for Soviet Russia, but their government did not agree to the conditions attached to the help including a neutral commission, total equality in food distribution among classes, and the halt to

[80] National Archives of the United States, Herbert Hoover Presidential Library, "Relief of Enemy States," *American Relief Administration Bulletin* 1 (March 17, 1919), 3.

[81] National Archives of the United States, Herbert Hoover Presidential Library, "ARA Bulletins Series I Box I, Folder ARA Bulletin Series 1 No. 1–4," *American Relief Administration Bulletin* 1 (March 17, 1919), 3; Herbert Hoover, *The Memoirs of Herbert Hoover: The Years of Adventure, 1874–1920* (New York, NY: Macmillan, 1951), 347.

[82] Hoover Institution Library and Archives. "Contract between the American Relief Administration and the Czecho-Slovak National Republic," *American Relief Administration Bulletin* 2 (1919), 12.

Figure 13.1 ARA warehouse in Vienna.
Source: HILA, ARA, EOR, Box 851, Folder D

invasion.[83] The ARA would subsequently organize a separate programme of food relief to Soviet Russia during the famines of 1921–1923.[84]

In Czechoslovakia, ARA missions started operating just in time, but still they experienced complications from the first days of their work. The deficiencies of the transportation infrastructure after the war meant that supplies could not easily reach the land-locked country and food intended for Czechoslovakia was stuck in the port of Trieste.[85] The ARA mission during the following months helped not only through the import of American foodstuffs, but also in facilitating transportation through Germany, repairing communications to allow gold remittances from Czech-Americans into the country and supervising a child relief program.[86] These difficulties were not limited to Czechoslovakia but were present in much of Central and Eastern European countries where the infrastructure had either been destroyed or coal shortages reduced train traffic. In Latvia, for example, transportation problems were particularly acute. The first American shipment of flour only arrived at the beginning of April 1919. The Americans assessed that humanitarian conditions were dire, the provisional government weak, and the military and political situation complicated. At the end of May the mission began distributing flour to the municipalities of Liepāja and other cities, which improved the local inhabitants' circumstances, but found itself in conflict with British missions that accepted the status quo of German dominance and saw such help as politically unwise.[87]

As in Czechoslovakia and Germany, Americans encountered difficulties in areas "far from civilization," especially because of poor infrastructure and transportation.[88] The situation was further complicated

[83] Cabanes, *The Great War and the Origins of Humanitarianism*, 213.

[84] The ARA's operations in Russia constitute a separate and more well-known chapter in the history of the organization, for which we do not have sufficient space. For more details see Harold Fisher, *The Famine in Soviet Russia 1919–1923: The Operations of the American Relief Administration* (New York: Macmillan Co., 1927); Benjamin Weisssman, *Herbert Hoover and Famine Relief to Soviet Russia: 1921–1923* (Stanford, CA: Hoover Institution Press, 1974); Bertrand Patenaude, *The Big Show in Bololand: The American Relief Expedition to Soviet Russia in the Famine of 1921* (Stanford, CA: Stanford University Press, 2002). See also Chapter 12 in this book.

[85] Hoover Institution Library and Archives, American Relief Administration, European operation records, Box 342, Folder 5, 9, "History of the American Relief Administration Mission at Prague."

[86] Hoover Institution Library & Archives, American Relief Administration, European operation records, Box 342, Folder 5, 11 (August 15, 1919).

[87] The National Archives of the United Kingdom, "Wolter Cowan to Admirality, Report, May 11, 1919," Foreign Office, 608/185, 139, 290; Jēkabsons, *Latvijas un Amerikas Savienoto Valstu attiecības*, 166–70.

[88] Hoover Institution Library and Archives, American Relief Administration, European operation records, Box 423, Folder 3 (Letter from J. Smith in Liepāja to W. Atwood, May 29, 1919).

in Latvia by the unregulated financial system and logistical difficulties. Despite these obstacles, shipments of American flour reached more remote, less populated areas, thus saving many inhabitants who suffered from a lack of provisions.[89]

The intensive relief work could not be kept up indefinitely. It was intended, after all, as a temporary emergency measure to help countries affected by war overcome the crisis period. Initially, the ARA authorities believed it would be feasible to end the general relief program by the end of the summer 1919. In his announcement from 9 June 1919 about the termination of relief work in Europe, Hoover stated that help had already been given to people in Finland, Estonia, Latvia, Lithuania, Poland, Belgium, Czechoslovakia, Austria, Hungary, Serbia, Romania, Bulgaria, Turkey, Armenia, Germany, and parts of Russia, in addition to help that had been given to all inhabitants and 3,500,000 underfed children in the liberated countries. Hoover enumerated reasons why relief was necessary and stated that an administrative basis had been created for the supply and distribution of foodstuffs. He expected that with the signing of peace and the new harvest, a priority could be given to food shipments, and that the overall situation would continue to improve.[90]

Focus on Child Feeding

The first food shipments used specifically to feed children in Europe from the ARA began during the Armistice period, from an initial gift of US$7,500,000 from the US people. "The total supplies distributed under the Relief Administration from December 1st (1918) to May 30th (1919) was 2,486,230 tons comprising 512 shiploads and of a value of approximately $636,175,000."[91] These foodstuffs fed children in Finland, Estonia, Lithuania, Latvia, Czechoslovakia, Austrian Republic, Serb-Croat-Slovene State, Poland, and Romania.[92] Indeed, while still engaging in general relief work, the ARA began to provide assistance focused on children early on after its founding. In March 1919, Hoover underlined:

[89] Jēkabsons, *Latvijas un Amerikas Savienoto Valstu attiecības*, 149–70.

[90] Bane and Lutz, *The Blockade of Germany*, 513–14; see also: Hoover, *The Memoirs*, 353–431.

[91] National Archives of the United States, Herbert Hoover Presidential Library ARA Bulletins Series I Box I, No. 16–19. "A Report on Relief Operations from the Minutes of the Supreme Economic Council for June 23, 1919 (Minute No. 234)," 1–3.

[92] "A Memorandum on Children's Relief Work," June 4, 1919, in Bane and Lutz, *Organization of American Relief in Europe*, 532.

It is necessary to at once provide a special ration for these children and to systematically organize such agencies as we conducted in Belgium for some years by way of creation of systematic handling of the debilitated children and the provision of supplementary rations through the schools, which shall be independent of the general rationing of populations.[93]

Thus, the best practices developed in the child feeding program of the Committee for the Relief for Belgium were passed on to the child feeding programs of Europe as a whole. Upon its arrival, the mission began preparations for the feeding of children, but also organized additional activities through the local committees, such as providing children with medical check-ups. Americans everywhere worked side by side with local doctors.

As had been the case in the "General Relief" program, during the execution of the "Children's Relief Program," the Americans were careful to see to it that their actions would promote cooperation among local political and ethnic groups, erasing the contradictions and conflicts between them in their combined efforts to feed children. In Czechoslovakia, the Children's Relief action, active from April 1919, brought together associations which had previously worked separately, including the Czech Heart. According to Joseph Shaw, who was in charge of the Children's Relief: "This organization is working down separatism, both political and racial. As an instance of the spirit of cooperation, three of the most powerful organizations of the country, which have hitherto been functioning independently, have now formally come together to work under this National Organization."[94] In Poland, a child welfare commission was created following the American model of the Child Welfare Bureau.[95]

The numbers of children fed in Central and Eastern European countries increased rapidly from April 1919 and reached a total of 1,146,511 children by July 1919 (see Table 13.4).

As the United States prepared to move out of Europe with the signing of the Treaty of Versailles, Herbert Hoover remained concerned about children in Europe. On July 7, 1919, just a month after his June 9, 1919

93 "Necessity for a Special Ration for European Children and the Policy of the American Red cross Regarding the Inauguration of a Child Feeding Scheme." Letter by Herbert Hoover to Henry Davison (ARC), Paris, February 22, 1919, Reprinted in Bane and Lutz, *Organization of American Relief in Europe*, 287–8.

94 Hoover Institution Library and Archives, American Relief Administration, European Operation Records, Box 344, Folder 10, Letter from Joseph Shaw to Robert Taft, April 30, 1919.

95 Rodogno, "Shaping Poland," 267. On the tensions with established child protection associations in Poland, see Morgane Labbé, "Les débuts de la protection sociale infantile à Łodz: Associations locales et réseaux transnationaux (1900–1919)," *Revue d'histoire de la protection sociale* 11 (2018/1), 46–71.

announcement that the work would be finished by the end of the summer, he sent a telegram requesting that an organization be set up to focus solely on children. This became the European Children's Fund, or ECF. While the ECF was an outgrowth of the ARA, it was technically a private organization and was organized under charter as a private charity in New York. However, it can also be considered quasi-governmental because it received and distributed funds provided by the US President's National Security and Defence Fund as well as US Congressional appropriation. In practice, the ECF continued operations begun by the ARA food missions that were implementing the "general program" as had the Children's Relief Program.[96]

This new period of work in Europe by the American Relief Administration with the European Children's Fund began in August 1919 and its first phase lasted until August 1920. In contrast to the previous period, it was formally an American non-governmental organization. The assistance to European countries was possible because of funds collected during the ARA's donation drive. A wide network of children's soup kitchens was created by ARA committees throughout each country. The local public was involved, with the Americans administering oversight through "central relief committees" or other organizations with supervisory functions, and the ARA firmly controlled respect of norms and regulations (such as the size of rations, guidelines for food distribution, equality of nationalities, etc.). Aid to children also included medical assistance, clothing, and shoes. Help with sanitation was extended to prisons. Local authorities were usually exceptionally welcoming to the ARA.[97] Additionally, until the spring of 1920, the number of recipients of daily meals in Europe overall was constantly growing, reaching over 3 million in March–May (April: 3,303,907).[98]

Germany was a special case because during the Armistice ARA funds were not allowed to be used on "enemies." The majority of American food into Germany came therefore not directly from the ARA, but from the American Friends Service Committee (AFSC). Their action is nonetheless worth mentioning in this context given how closely these organizations worked together, and the huge number of German children fed. In the summer of 1919, Hoover asked the AFSC to extend their feeding operations to Germany, as this was something that US public opinion was not ready to engage in.[99] The widespread feeding of children in

[96] Surface, *American Food*, 73–4; Hoover, *An American Epic*, 378; Adams, "American Relief Effort in Poland."
[97] Jēkabsons, *Latvijas un Amerikas Savienoto Valstu attiecības*, 477–528.
[98] Table 13.4: Number of children fed by the ARA April 1919 – December 1922.
[99] Surface, *American Food*, 117.

Table 13.4 *Number of children fed by the ARA, April 1919–December 1922*

	Finland	Esthonia	Latvia	Lithuania	Poland	ČSR	Austria	Hungary	Rumania	Jugo-Slavia	Germany	Danzig	Calc. Totals	Totals given
Apr-19	0	0	0	0	0	4,000	0	0	0	0	0	0	4,000	4,000
May-19	1,9291	0	0	13,200	125,000	63,000	15,000	0	11,100	100,000	0	0	346,591	347,091
Jun-19	50,945	81,374	8,000	18,275	300,000	97,000	63,534	0	74,000	200,000	0	0	893,128	893,128
Jul-19	52,010	54,821	19,000	12,945	400,000	166,000	116,735	0	125,000	200,000	0	0	1,146,511	1,146,511
Aug-19	79,394	59,950	21,000	22,905	52,5000	365,660	141,855	35,900	150,000	200,000	0	0	1,601,664	1,601,664
Sep-19	98,260	54,950	22,840	17,875	600,000	412,775	180,217	36,000	42,100	150,000	0	0	1,615,017	1,643,317
Oct-19	94,535	54,950	59,000	16,945	700,000	547,786	186,915	36,000	8,600	150,000	0	0	1,854,731	1,888,231
Nov-19	96,015	66,050	59,400	18,870	900,000	547,786	213,616	44,710	0	150,000	0	0	2,096,447	2,105,047
Dec-19	97,315	66,050	80,000	15,990	975,000	547,786	211,654	73,992	0	150,000	0	0	2,217,787	2,217,787
Jan-20	127,770	73,050	81,000	16,000	1,080,722	547,786	216,267	89,392		150,000			2,381,987	2,381,897
Feb-20	127,525	77,550	81,000	17,500	1,128,818	547,786	227,521	106,328		150,000			2,464,028	2,464,028
Mar-20	126,220	84,000	81,000	17,500	1,222,680	547,786	249,884	107,706		150,000	708,589		3,295,365	3,295,365
Apr-20	66,524	84,000	81,000	17,500	1,268,313	547,786	269,887	110,357		150,000	708,589		3,303,956	3,303,907
May-20	66,420	84,000		17,500	1,315,490	394,140	294,887	65,300		150,000	708,589		3,096,326	3,177,335
Jun-20	50,000			1,000	969,296	394,140	296,376	31,670		50,000	708,589		2,501,071	2,501,080
Jul-20				1,000	545,325	394,140	265,619	31,499		5,0000	708,589		1,996,172	1,996,181
Aug-20					350,869	394,140	226,655	34,657		30,000	708,589		1,744,910	1,744,919
Sep-20					327,058	106,010	199,777	7,651		20,000	346,933		1,007,429	1,007,429
Oct-20					407,194	106,010	219,845	7,651			390,629		1,131,329	1,181,327
Nov-20					529,018	106,010	245,568	7,651			465,893		1,354,140	1,354,140
Dec-20					675,058	106,010	274,829	7,651			569,165		1,632,713	1,630,713
Jan-21					863,544	106,010	284,678	10,447			653,316		1,917,995	1,917,996
Feb-21		43,000	240,246		1,100,000	82,050	288,588	21,107			672,000		2,446,991	2,230,771
Mar-21		43,000	24,428	5,000	1,221,721	89,650	307,619	31,084			736,001		2,458,503	2,458,503
Apr-21		43,000	44,349	5,000	1,236,200	135,840	360,287	34,751			736,000	4,501	2,599,928	2,596,098

May-21		30,695	41,153	5,000	1,187,319	158,310	357,615	35,264	20,000	820,000	6,542	2,661,898	2,661,898
Jun-21	5,000	22,879	31,980	5,000	113,309	131,385	362,309	33,637	20,000	997,000	7,250	1,729,749	2,749,749
Jul-21	5,000	27,435	46,548	5,000	922,962	57,698	276,476	15,472	20,000	800,000	7,274	2,183,865	2,183,865
Aug-21	5,000	20,000	21,700	5,000	701,000	55,000	214,000	8,000	20,000	177,000	1,900	1,228,600	1,248,600
Sep-21	5,000	12,000	42,700		488,200		169,900	10,900	20,000	130,000	2,200	880,900	871,900
Oct-21	5,000	20,000	41,800		495,200		16,4000	16,900	20,000	360,500	3,300	1,126,700	1,126,700
Nov-21	5,000	10,000	39,600		512,213		180,500	13,000		500,000	3,300	1,263,613	1,263,613
Dec-21	5,000	10,000	41,200		466,000		190,600	19,200		500,000	3,200	1,235,200	1,230,200
Jan-22		10,000	40,278		440,500		173,700	11,875			4,351	680,704	680,804
Feb-22		10,000	41,519		428,138		168,999	17,871			4,250	670,777	670,777
Mar-22		10,000	39,600		430,840		165,190	17,500			4,330	667,460	667,460
Apr-22		10,000	46,900		440,600		157,700	17,200			4,130	676,530	676,528
May-22		10,000	41,503		421,469		142,461	18,100				633,533	633,533
Jun-22		10,000	40,490		176,647		72,405					299,542	299,542
Jul-22		10,000	21,830		197,155		45,474					274,459	274,459
Aug-22		10,000	19,574				20,476					50,050	50,050
Sep-22							16,604				4,000	20,604	20,604
Oct-22											4,000	4,000	4,000
Nov-22											4,000	4,000	4,000
Dec-22											4,000	4,000	4,000

Note: This does not include other feeding groups or agencies; the statistics can only be taken as rough estimates and cannot form the basis of accurate comparison, as the dates and numbers are incomplete for some countries. Hoover Institution Library and Archives, American Relief Administration, European Operation Records, Box 544, Folder 32. (Numbers of persons fed daily from April 1919 to June 30, 1923). Another version was published in the ARA bulletin with this caveat: "The figures in this table are close approximations only. In most cases they represent a monthly average of the numbers of children fed, although in some cases the number for the month is the number fed on the first or last day of the month." *American Relief Administration Bulletin* 2:22 (March 1922), 45.

Germany began February 26, 1920.[100] By June 1, 1920, the Quakers had served 44.6 million hot meals to German children, pregnant women, and nursing mothers. In 1922, the largest number of children being fed in any one day was up to 1,010,000. At this point, the Quakers decided to remove their missionaries and to deliver aid directly to German charities. Still, they continued to provide food daily for 500,000 children, but in January 1923, when the Ruhr was invaded, the AFSC decided to return to Germany and continued their work for some time, feeding approximately 1 million German children every day.[101]

Child feeding in Germany lasted beyond 1924, but in most other countries it ended earlier. For example, in Latvia, the ARA operated until 1922 through two overlapping stages: an initial programme of general relief to all groups of society active until the summer of 1919, and a relief programme targeted expressly to children called the American Relief Administration European Children's Fund. Indeed, by August 1920, the ARA child feeding program in many countries was terminated. On August 18, 1920, the main office in New York officially announced the closure of Children's Relief work in Finland and the Baltic States. Conditions had improved in these countries and local governments themselves, with help from Americans, had created an effective system to care for their children. It was also announced that the ARA program would also be reduced in Yugoslavia, Czechoslovakia, and Hungary. The relief work continued only in Austria, Germany, and in the part of Poland not in the hands of Bolsheviks, where a considerably diminished number of children were fed.[102] In Poland the numbers of children fed daily was reduced from 1.3 million in May and June 1920 to 350,000 in August, in Czechoslovakia from 547,000 in April to 106,000 in September, in Hungary from 110,000 in April to 7,600, and only remained around previous levels in Austria.[103] As mentioned, these numbers should be taken as indications only and provide a partial picture of the amount of relief delivered. The blurry line between ARA child feeding programs and local programs that continued in later years make precise assessment of when "American" programs ended difficult.[104]

Unfortunately, after the American food distribution was discontinued, the situation in many Central and Eastern European countries continued to be dire, and local governments could not cope with the social

[100] Surface, *American Food*, 118.
[101] Cox, *Hunger in War and Peace*, 241–73; See also Cox, "Hunger Games."
[102] "End Relief Work in Latvia: American Aid to be Withdrawn in Other Countries Also," *The New York Times* 22,853 (August 19, 1920), 8.
[103] Table 13.4: Number of children fed by the ARA April 1919 – December 1922.
[104] On Romania, see Cretu, "Nationalizing International Relief."

situation. The new states could not provide adequate amounts of food for its poorest inhabitants and local public organizations could not take over all that had been previously done by the ARA. For example, in Latvia in August 1920, the Food Board of the Riga City Council was forced to recognize that the ceasing of ARA activities on 23 July had meant, that "at least 10,000 poor children are now in a desperate situation." An attempt was proposed to organize local public organizations and try to continue the feeding of the children. Estimates of the necessary food amount were made, but lack of finances prevented further action.[105] The seriousness of the situation attracted the attention of the ARA leadership. A telegram from the American Red Cross mission in the Baltic States from December 17, 1920 detailed that at least 200,000 children in the Baltics were in need of the additional food that had been provided by the ARA before, otherwise child mortality would increase considerably during the winter. Eventually new treaties were signed with the governments of Latvia and Estonia that guaranteed the participation of governments in the feeding of children by the ARA. Feeding was then resumed based on the same organizational principles as before.[106]

At the beginning of 1921, the number of children fed continued to grow. Feeding operations were resumed in the Baltic states and Yugoslavia. The highest number of children fed by the ARA during this period as recorded in Table 13.4 was reached in June 1921, when a total of 2,749,749 children received daily meals in all the countries combined (Finland, Estonia, Latvia, Lithuania, Poland, Czechoslovakia, Austria, Hungary Germany, Romania, Yugoslavia, Germany, free city of Danzig). Figure 13.2 shows children in a kitchen in Mostar (Kingdom of Serbs, Croats and Slovenes). The ARA then started to gradually lower the number of supplied children, ending their actions in Danzig in April 1922, in Hungary in May 1922, and during the summer – in Latvia, Estonia, Poland, and Austria.[107]

The ARA concentrated much of its relief work on the millions of children in hunger-devastated Russia up until the summer of 1923, with the exception of Germany, where children continued to be fed. Relief in Central Europe ended, but by 1921–1923 many organizations together

[105] Jānis Riekstiņš, "Izdziedētā brūce. Bāreņu un trūcīgo bērnu aprūpe Latvijas brīvvalsts pirmajos gados," *Latvijas Arhīvi* 3–4 (1996), 113–14.

[106] Hoover Institution Library and Archives, American Relief Administration, European operation records, Box Box 692, Folder16, Box 335, Folder18 ("Special Agreement between the American Relief Administration European Children's Fund and the Latvian Government," December 31, 1920, and "Special Agreement … [with] the Estonian Government," January 4, 1921).

[107] Table 13.4: Number of children fed by the ARA April 1919–December 1922.

Figure 13.2 Kitchen in Mostar, European Children's Fund.
Source: HILA, Charles Nelson Leach papers, Box 3, ARA albums

with the American Relief Administration were involved in humanitarian relief in Soviet Russia, which was a huge undertaking and a separate story in itself. Foreign relief helped millions of people in Russia to avoid death. The total number of persons fed every day reached 9.5 million people.[108]

Although ARA leaders everywhere tried to ensure that national organizations would gradually take over their activities by the time they left, this strategy only partially succeeded, as often governments simply did not have enough resources to finance it.[109] However, some activities, like the summer camps on the seashore in Latvia and elsewhere, grew into a tradition.[110] A park in Liepaja retained the name of ARA Food missionary Thomas Orbison until 1940. Similar cases may be found in several other countries as well. For example, as a way of thanking Herbert Hoover for the relief given to Poland, he received the title of honorary citizen of Poland. A city square in Warsaw was named after him and a monument of gratitude was erected at the square.[111] A symbolic representation of the value and importance of the relief work undertaken by the ARA is the huge amount of gifts, cards, and drawings sent to the locally operating ARA officers both by high government representatives and politicians and by the European children who ARA missions helped to feed and supply with necessary items.[112]

Conclusion

Feeding civilians in the aftermath of the First World War was one way that organizations and people from across the world, especially the United States, responded to the hunger that faced some millions of people in Europe and in the Ottoman Empire. Some of this help was politically based; Americans made no attempt to hide their contempt for Bolshevism and their belief that hunger and starvation could result

[108] For more details about healing hunger in Soviet Russia see Fisher, *The Famine in Soviet Russia;* Weisssman, *Herbert Hoover and Famine Relief to Soviet Russia*; Patenaude, *The Big Show in Bololand.*

[109] See for an example of the assertion in the Latvian press about the lack of money for the continuing of children's feeding, see "Amerikāņu palīdzība," *Jaunākās Ziņas* 162 (July 25, 1922), 4.

[110] Elza Klaustiņa, "Amerikāņu palīdzības darbs 1921. gadā," *Latvju Sieviete* 6 (1952), 19.

[111] Nick Siekierski, "Herbert Hoover and Poland," https://researchteacher.com/wp-content/uploads/2015/10/Herbert-Hoover-and-Poland-Nicholas-Siekierski.pdf [last accessed March 1, 2022].

[112] See, for example, numerous gifts and thank you messages sent to T. Orbison, ARA officer in Latvia. Hoover Institution Library and Archives, T. Orbison's collection, Box 1–3. On children's gratitude, see also Cox, *Hunger in War and Peace*, chapter 9.

in it. Occasionally local American leaders got tangled up in local politics despite careful instructions not to. For an operation that, from the American side, fed some 83 million people, such inevitable conflicts should not be seen as a surprise. What is more surprising is how well the ARA, European Children's Fund, and other groups achieved their aims of feeding millions of people. Given the context of lost infrastructure, new borders, and the continuance of fighting, it was by no means a foregone conclusion. These acts themselves, if not capable of healing the deep emotional wounds that came from battles and bereavement, were at least able to reduce the physical suffering of millions.

14 "Hunger Draws the Map"

Mary Elisabeth Cox and Claire Morelon

> We hope that in the future no one on hearing the name "Attigny" will automatically adjust his bifocals for long distance. It is one thing to feel off the map, and quite another to be it ...We ask you, oh Map-owner, to take your Rand McNally or your Taride – or whatever you have comme map. Unroll it far to the west. Make a dot in the margin, in the upper left-hand corner. Make it in ink, and remember: it's us.[1]

Esther Sayles Root penned these words from the French Ardennes for the short-lived American Friends Service Committee (AFSC) magazine *Reconstruction*, in September 1919. She was a reconstructionist and humanitarian who originally moved to France in the autumn of 1916 to assist with the war effort.[2] Her enthusiastic embrace of maps reflected a widespread popular use of them in the early twentieth century, the "age of cartophilia."[3] The use of maps was often incorrect or incomplete, as were the maps themselves, yet they were nonetheless omnipresent. Indeed, using and making maps was part of the *zeitgeist* of the First World War era. They were a vital tool for militaries as they planned, attacked, and defended territory. Maps were no less important to established states, imperial powers, and the new would-be states in the aftermath of the conflict. The Paris Peace Conference famously saw a proliferation of maps. As American geographer Charles Seymour recalled: "Each side, whether stressing justice or political interest, appealed to the geographer for assistance ... Maps were everywhere. They were not all good. ... But the appeal to the map in every discussion was constant."[4]

1 Esther Sayles Root, "Do You Own A Map"? *Reconstruction* II:6 (September 1919), 86–7, American Friends Service Committee Archives (AFSCA).

2 Esther Sayles Root and Marjorie Crocker, *Over Periscope Pond: Letters from Two American Girls In Paris. October 1916 – January 1918* (Boston, MA: Houghton Mifflin Company and Cambridge: The Riverside Press, 1918).

3 Catherine Tatiana Dunlop, *Cartophilia: Maps and the Search for Identity in the French-German Borderland* (Chicago, IL: The University of Chicago Press, 2015), 4.

4 Charles Seymour, *Geography, Justice, and Politics at the Paris Conference of 1919* (New York: American Geographical Society, 1951), 9–10.

In the wake of the First World War, geography was conceived of as an objective and scientific tool to help produce a new world. Maps showing language skills, ethnicity, and plebiscites, helped form and break national boundaries. The conference powers relied on the expertise of the 'map men' to redraw the borders of East Central Europe and the Middle East.[5] The goal of these men was not just to draw boundaries based on ethnicity, but also to balance idealistic demands for historical justice with economic realities.[6] Maps were not only a tool to produce supposed ethno-historical certainties and justify territorial claims, but also a way to understand economic realities in the wake of imperial collapse in order to aid reconstruction. Maps at the time played a central role in the depiction of global trade flows, transportation links, and economic processes.[7] Despite this, the use of maps for ethnographic purposes in the era of the First World War has received far more attention than their role in economic and humanitarian projects.

Humanitarians like Esther Sayles Root relied on maps as they responded to the human suffering described in this book. Fixing roads and delivering food, clothing, and medical supplies to people in need was something – with organization, effort, and verve – that many believed could be accomplished. Roads could be repaired. Food could be grown, purchased, measured, divided, shipped, and distributed. New clothes and shoes could be sewn. Hospitals could be built or repaired and stocked with medical equipment and supplies.[8] Even the bodies of aid recipients could be measured before and after they had participated in feeding programs, showing who needed food most, and the extent to which any improvement had been made. Maps were part of all these processes, both big and small. On a basic level, maps helped aid workers and their supplies reach their destinations. They were a way to make sense of the locations where they intervened. Maps brought order. Yet, maps also presented interpretations of how the world was, and possibilities for how it could be changed. However benign many of these maps might have appeared, they also implied where food supplies and volunteers *should* go, and *who* should receive assistance.

[5] Steven Seegel, *Map Men: Transnational Lives and Deaths of Geographers in the Making of East Central Europe* (Chicago, IL: The University of Chicago Press, 2018); Maciej Górny, *Drawing Fatherlands: Geographers and Borders in Inter-war Europe* (Leiden: Brill, 2022).

[6] Leonard V. Smith, *Sovereignty at the Paris Peace Conference of 1919* (Oxford: Oxford University Press, 2018), 115–16.

[7] Slobodian, Quinn, "How to See the World Economy: Statistics, Maps, and Schumpeter's Camera in the First Age of Globalization," *Journal of Global History*, 10 (2015), 307–32.

[8] Bertrand M. Patenaude and Joan Nabseth Stevenson, *Bread + Medicine: American Famine Relief in Soviet Russia, 1921–1923* (Stanford: Hoover Institution Press, 2023.)

Figure 14.1 American Relief Administration Mapping Department, Paris.
Source: HILA, ARA, EOR, Box 851, Folder B

Many aid organizations, including the American Friends Service Committee where Esther Sayles Root worked, not only used widely published maps from companies like Rand McNally or Taride, they also produced their own. At least one aid organization, the American Relief Administration (ARA), even had their own mapping department in Paris (see Figure 14.1).

The fact that the ARA had their own mapping department underscores the centrality of maps and mapmaking in their humanitarian projects. The organization's ethos centered around providing aid through efficient and scientific techniques. Statistics and maps played an important role in these efforts, and in their assessments of need.[9] Maps helped rationalize the difficult question of logistics and how to transport a large quantity of food in regions with damaged transportation systems from the war. They were also a tool to ameliorate and to understand the

[9] Cabanes, *Great War and Origins of Humanitarianism*, 229.

economic strengths of regions to help stabilize new countries.[10] The ARA did not only want to provide food as a charity would, they also wanted to kickstart the economic reconstruction of the continent. As the ARA director for Central Europe, Thomas T. C. Gregory recalled: "The real work, and the one which conferred the greatest benefit to all of these stunned people, was a galvanizing again into activity the economic processes of the countries, which were at dead center."[11] The production of maps by the ARA on topics as varied as industrial capacity, coal production, agricultural output, and transportation links contributed to this larger mission of rebuilding the continent.

Professional photographic portraits of ARA personnel most often contained blank backgrounds. When photos were taken inside with something other than a blank background, it is noticeable how many of the portraits include maps in the image.[12] This portrait of ARA personnel member in Paris, J. S. McKnight, depicts him sitting in uniform in front of a map of Europe, showing many connecting lines through water ways and landmasses (see Figure 14.2). Perched in McKnight's right hand is a telephone, with his left hand pressing the receiver up to his ear. This photograph offers clues to the image of the efficient humanitarian embodied by the ARA, flanked with modern modes of communication and a map as symbols of the rational aid delivered.

A photograph of the office of Herbert Hoover, the head of the American Relief Administration, in the Hôtel de Crillon in Paris, also demonstrates the centrality of maps in the self-presentation of American humanitarians (Figure 14.3). Amid the splendor of a marble desk, upholstered chairs with upturned legs, white plastered walls, and landscaped etchings, Hoover's office had maps and graphs pinned to the walls. Centered behind his desk, and partially covering the centered mirror, was a large map of pre-war Europe. In the old-world elegance of the room, the maps, along with the telephone, conveyed the serious, rationalized work undertaken by the 'food czar' and his role in redrawing Europe. Maps were a demonstration of power. In a world where new boundaries and countries were not only argued and created with

[10] On humanitarians' goals to reform the social system in the Middle East, see Watenpaugh, *Bread from Stones*; on Romania, see Doina Anca Cretu, *Foreign Aid and State-Building in Interwar Romania* (Stanford, CA: Stanford University Press, 2024).

[11] Thomas T. C. Gregory, "A Sketch of the Activities of Herbert Hoover and his Band of Americans in Central Europe following the Great War," 1919, HILA, Thomas T. C. Gregory papers, Box 1, p. 3.

[12] See American Relief Administration Mapping Department, Paris. American Relief Administration European Operational Records Box 851, Folder B "ARA PERSONELL" for more examples.

Figure 14.2 ARA Personnel Paris Office, J. S. McKnight.
Source: HILA, ARA, EOR, Box 851, Folder B

lines on a paper, but entire groups of people were fed based on their location, maps – as objects – were powerful.

Maps take data linked to geographical locations and visually portray them to explain or to persuade. Data going into maps may be disputed, incomplete, inconstant, or wrong. And yet, by freezing the temporal into an intemporal form, maps provide a snapshot of not only the data they contain, but also of the map maker's interpretations and preferences. As Jill Desimini writes, "the map describes the near past or even the far past intentionally in the case of historic maps – while often contributing to a reading, and even constructing, of a future."[13] In distilling the complex into visual form, maps bring order to a subject that might otherwise not be easily understood. This singular strength of simplification is also the inherent weakness of maps. Multifaceted problems can be understood, to a degree, with a single glance, but the inherent or explicit biases of the mapmakers often go unstated.

[13] Jill Desimini, "Cartographic Grounds: The Temporal Cases," in *Mapping Landscapes in Transformation: Multidisciplinary Methods for Historical Analysis*, edited by Thomas Coomans, Bieke Cattoor, and Krista De Jong (Leuven: Leuven University Press, 2019), 17.

Figure 14.3 Herbert Hoover's office in Paris.
Source: HILA, ARA, EOR, Box 851, Folder B, Herbert Hoover's Office, Paris, Hotel de Crillon, June 1919

Hunger Maps

Hunger, though perhaps mapped less frequently than other kinds of data, fluctuates. Food supplies are constantly consumed, but may not as consistently be replenished. While analyzing these life-changing fluctuations at the scale of families, communities, societies, and even nations, the complexity of creating a single snapshot of hunger for disparate regions of the world as a printed one-dimensional map is obvious. Superimpose upon this something as complex as a war, with people on the move and political and national boundaries contested, and the difficulty of drawing straight lines and symbols to represent actual hunger levels and food supplies of diverse populations would have been daunting. Despite this difficulty, many hunger maps were produced in the era of the First World War, especially after 1918.

Perhaps the most reproduced hunger map was one entitled *Hunger Draws the Map* (Map 14.1). First published as early as November

Map 14.1 Hunger Draws the Map.
Source: HILA

25, 1918,[14] though dated December 1, 1918, *Hunger Draws the Map* came out just weeks after the initial armistice between Germany and the Western Allies on November 11, 1918. Created by the US Food Administration, it portrayed hunger in Europe as they understood it in the fall of 1918. Its geographical boundaries were set by Portugal in the west, the Persian Gulf and Siberia in the east, Scandinavian countries in the north, and the Mediterranean and top of Africa in the south. The map drew comparisons between hunger levels in different countries through one of six categorizations: "famine conditions," "food shortage

[14] Though dated December 1, the map was published as early as November 25, 1918. See for example "Hunger Draws the Map," *Petaluma Daily Morning Courier*, November 25, 1918, 5.

approaching famine point," "serious food shortage," "sufficient present food supply but future serious," "peoples already receiving American aid," and "unclassified." Exactly how current the data were that created this snapshot of hunger, and what types of data were used is unknown. Furthermore, no absolute numbers of hunger or food supplies were delineated on the map.

Hunger Draws the Map was published at least 1,233 times in newspapers in the United States between 1918 and 1919,[15] and at least once in 1922.[16] During this period political borders changed, especially borders in the former Austrian-Hungarian, German, Russian, and Ottoman Empires as smaller new states were created and fought over in the aftermath of the demise of Empires. Yet the borders portrayed in this version of *Hunger Draws the Map* never changed. Hunger levels on the map stayed the same. So too did the supposed equalities within countries, and the inequalities between countries.

For its superficial appearance of neutrality and empiricism, *Hunger Draws the Map* was political. Food was power in the wake of WWI, and the decision to distribute or withhold food aid had huge physiological and psychological impacts on the intended recipients. For example, in Map 14.1, both Germany and Austria-Hungary were marked as "unclassified." At the time the original map was created, reports were still coming in about conditions on the ground in those areas. The Germans did not finish their official report on food conditions in their country for the US government until December 27, 1918, weeks after the map was printed.[17] The United States had a more accurate idea of the needs of allies and neutrals because they had been involved in selling foodstuffs to them during the War itself. Still, one way to consider the countries in *Hunger Draws the Map* marked as "unclassified" is to note that when the map was first published in late November 1918, Germany and Austria-Hungary were still official enemies of the Entente, and the borders of the new states created in the wake of Austria-Hungary were still uncertain. Coding their levels of hunger as "unclassified" allowed both responsibility and culpability for hunger on the ground to be avoided.[18] As they

[15] At time of writing, we used "newspapers.com" to view and count the newspapers that published this map. While this commercial company has scanned and published the majority of newspapers across the United States for this time period, it has not published all newspapers. Therefore, the total number of times "Hunger Draws the Map" was published was likely higher.

[16] "Hunger Draws the Map," *The Severance News* [Kansas], January 27, 1922.

[17] *Hauptbericht der freien wissenschaftlichen Kommission zum Studium der jetzigen Ernährungsverhältnisse in Deutschland* (publisher and place unknown, 1919).

[18] Mary Cox, *Hunger in War and Peace: Women & Children in Germany 1914–1924* (Oxford: Oxford University Press, 2019), 252.

Map 14.2 Hunger Draws the Map, Hunger Map of Europe.
Source: 'Hunger Draws The Map', American war posters from the First World War, BANC PIC 2005.001:123 – AX (Berkeley, CA: The Bancroft Library, University of California)

stand on the map, the borders do not correspond to any historic reality. "Austria-Hungary" stands next to the new Central European states. The lands of the Ottoman Empire were replaced with "Turkey" and "Armenia" only. What is even more telling are the countries not included in the map at all. At the edges of the map, "Siberia" and "Africa," both with hungry populations in 1918, are listed, but no information on them was provided.

This is not to suggest that the people who made *Hunger Draws the Map* did not make changes. They did. In one iteration, the words "Hunger Map of Europe" either replaced the title "Hunger Draws the Map" or were added as a subtitle (see Map 14.2). Other than these additional words, the rest of the map remained unchanged. As a replacement or an addition, "Hunger Map of Europe" was used at least 111 times in US newspapers between 1918–1919 for maps that, other than this text, were exactly the same as *Hunger Draws the Map* (Map 14.1).[19] Through specifying *Hunger Draws the Map* as a "Hunger Map of Europe," the map became more inclusive. Without the additional words "Hunger Map of Europe," the first map could be read that Europe was where all the hunger was in the world, or where hunger was worth considering. Still, in both iterations, the focus of the map on Europe revealed Western biases and concern with hunger in that part of the world over other regions of the world.

Despite being repeatedly printed in the press, the American Relief Administration (the successor organization of the US Food Administration) did produce and use more current hunger maps after the original *Hunger Draws the Map* and *Hunger Draws the Map, Hunger Map of Europe* (Maps 14.1 and 14.2). This included the *Hunger Map of Europe, August 1921* (Map 14.3) and *Hunger Map of Europe, October 1, 1921* (Map 14.4).

These maps included important updates. First, both maps covered a different geographic area, zooming in more on Central and Eastern Europe, slopping off Portugal, Spain, and the British Isles in the West (regions categorized as "Sufficient food at Present but future Serious" in previous hunger maps). Second, these two iterations of *Hunger Map of Europe* (Maps 14.3 and 14.4) contain more updated borders of the new states that had emerged from the disintegration of the Austro-Hungarian Empire and the Russian Empire. Third, the map legend changed in substantive ways. Instead of six levels of famine in the legend, the August 1921 *Hunger Map of Europe* (Map 14.3) halved that into just three: "Areas from which the ARA has withdrawn," "Areas in which the ARA is now operating," and "Russian Famine Area." In *Hunger Map of Europe, October 1, 1921* (Map 14.4), the legend changed from having three levels of famine and aid to four: "Areas from which the ARA has withdrawn," "Areas in which the ARA is now operating," "Milk ration only: 50,000 being distributed," and "Russian Famine Area." This legend, similar to the previous hunger maps, mixed measuring levels of famine with aid being received in the same map, showing how the ARA equated its withdrawal with improved conditions. In the case of Czechoslovakia, the transition from full ARA operations in August to only milk distribution in October appeared as progress.

[19] At time of writing, we used "newspapers.com" to view and count newspapers that published "Hunger Map of Europe" as part of *Hunger Draws the Map*.

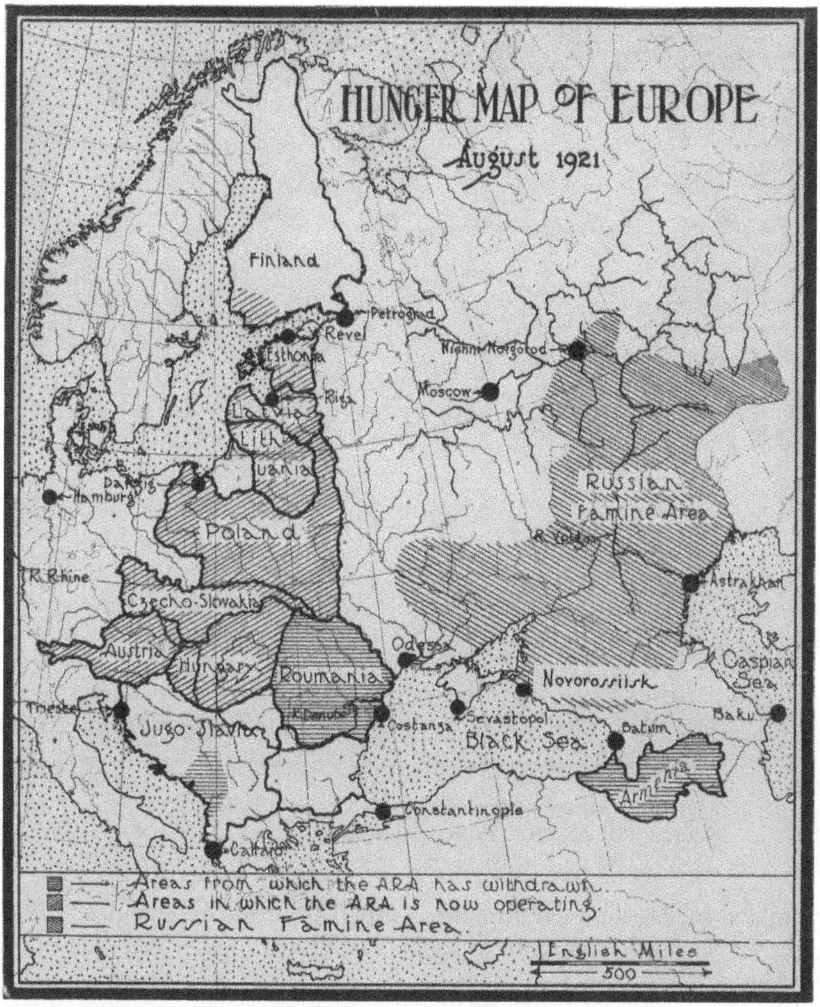

Map 14.3 Hunger Map of Europe, August 1921.
Source: HILA, ARA, EOR, Box 531, Folder 9

Why were hunger maps such as these made, and how were they used? The explicit aim of the hunger maps was to show where hunger was greatest so that aid could be directed to those areas. Each of these hunger maps matched famine levels to national borders, and other than maps showing some variation within Russia, denoted a single hunger level within country-level borders, suggesting uniformity of hunger levels within each state. This hid any geographic hunger differences within a single state,

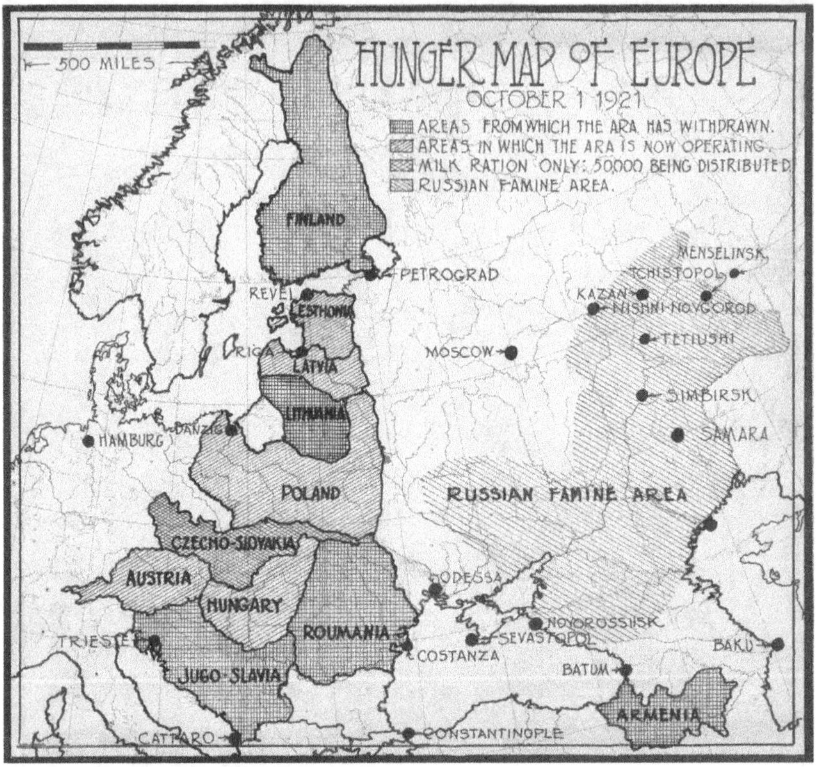

Map 14.4 Hunger Map of Europe, October 1, 1921.
Source: HILA, ARA, EOR, Oversize Folder 6

masking socio-economic disparities, urban and rural inequalities, different hunger levels according to sex or age, and any other inequality that might have been present. Yet as this book confirms, hunger across a single state is never uniform. Simplifications made in the hunger maps made them easier to understand at a glance. In creating a snapshot of hunger, hunger maps, in their various forms, faced the same problem of ephemerality that other maps did and masked their subjective and emotional origins. We argue that hunger maps were used as instruments of persuasion, tools for efficient distribution, and to document conditions.

For the public, *Hunger Draws the Map* was an attempt both to explain and to persuade, to contribute "to a reading, and even a constructing, of a future." The repeated image of *Hunger Draws the Map* in national and local newspapers in the United States, hundreds and hundreds of times, was often accompanied with text related to the acute needs of hungry people in Europe, and to urge the American people to help. This example from the *Deseret Evening News* in Salt Lake City, Utah, was typical:

> If we fail to lighten the black spots on the hunger map or if we allow any portions to become darker the very peace for which we fought and bled will be threatened ... That Utahns will respond heartily to this cry of need is believed assured. It is a cry of humanity that will not go unheeded. Ever to the fore in answering the calls made upon it, the Beehive state will not fail in this.[20]

This article and a copy of *Hunger Draws the Map* (Map 14.1) was published on December 28, 1918, eight weeks before the Sixty-fifth Congress of the United States passed "An Act providing for the relief of such populations in Europe, and countries contiguous thereto, outside of Germany, German-Austria, Hungary, Bulgaria, and Turkey, as may be determined upon by the President as Necessary" on February 25, 1919.[21] This Act provided 100 million US dollars to be sent to "Europe, and countries contiguous thereto" outside of enemy countries to the United States. The geographic focus on Europe corresponds exactly to what the early hunger maps (Maps 14.1–14.4) kept their focus on. The act also stated "that Armenians, Syrians, Greeks, and other Christian and Jewish populations of Asia Minor, now or formerly subjects of Turkey may be included within the populations to receive relief under this act."[22] Herbert Hoover, head of the US Food Administration that printed the map, asked US President Woodrow Wilson for 200 million US dollars on November 9, 1918,[23] weeks before the official publication date of *Hunger Draws the Map* on December 1, 2018. By showering small and large newspapers with *Hunger Draws the Map*, particularly over the holiday period when many congressmen would have been home among their constituents, Herbert Hoover and the US Food Administration wanted to persuade politicians, and Americans at large, to support feeding Europe (see Figure 14.4). While the map was titled *Hunger Draws the Map*, it was, in reality, re-drawing the map. "Lighten[ing] the black spots" and not "allow[ing] any portions to become darker."

[20] "Hunger Draws the Map," *Deseret Evening News*, December 28, 1918.

[21] Richardson, *A Compilation of the Messages and Papers of the Presidents*, p. 8690; *United States Statutes at Large*, 40 Stat. 1161 (1919).

[22] *Combined Annual Reports of the World War Foreign Debt Commission: With Additional Information Regarding Foreign Debts Due to the United States. Fiscal Years 1922, 1923, 1924, 1925, and 1926* (Washington, DC: United States Government Printing Office, 1927), 313.

[23] Letter from Herbert Hoover to Woodrow Wilson, November 9, 1918, Herbert Hoover Subject Collection, Box no. 8, Folder: "Correspondence, Wilson Woodrow, November 1918," Hoover Institution Library & Archives as cited in Cox, *Hunger in War and Peace*, 212.

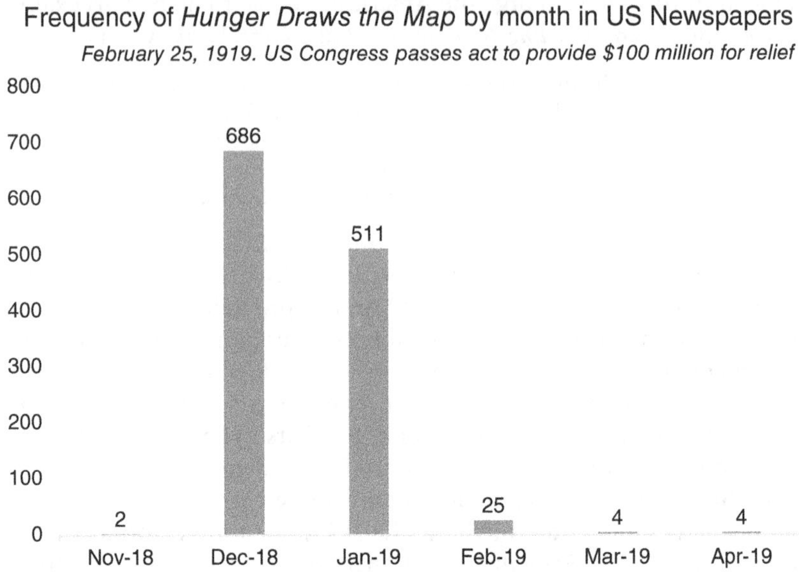

Figure 14.4 Frequency of *Hunger Draws the Map* by month.

As part of their efforts to obtain donations, aid organizations often employed images of women and children to trigger empathy.[24] Overlooked in the literature of the visualization of aid, however, is the use and power of maps to do the same thing. Like images of desperate women and waifish children, maps could inform and create empathy. While *Hunger Draws the Map* by the US Food Administration may have been the most ubiquitous, other aid organizations used maps that were no less compelling. Some, such as *Where the Victims Are* (1918 or 1919) (Map 14.5), used by The American Committee For Relief in the Near East, includes statistics overlaid on the map and a plea to "SAVE THE SURVIVORS." This map is more of an appeal for assistance than an explanation of the situation. Yet, like most hunger maps, it is both. While the text, in order from largest to smallest, includes "SAVE THE SURVIVORS," followed by "WHERE THE

[24] See Heide Fehrenbach and Davide Rodogno, eds. *Humanitarian Photography: A History* (Cambridge: Cambridge University Press, 2015); Michelle Tusan, "Genocide, Famine and Refugees on Film: Humanitarianism and the First World War," *Past & Present* 237:1 (2017), 197–235; Lina Sturfelt "Visualizing War Victims, Rädda Barnen's Humanitarian Reporting in the Interwar Years," in *War Remains: Mediations of Suffering and Death in the Era of the World Wars*, edited by Marie Cronqvist and Lina Sturfelt (Lund: Nordic Academic Press, 2018).

Map 14.5 Where the Victims Are, American Committee for Relief in the Near East.
Source: HILA, Poster collection, US 3437 [Exact date unknown. 1918 or 1919]

VICTIMS ARE" followed by "3,950,000 STARVING PEOPLE" and "CAMPAIGN FOR $30,000,000," (about the same size) are quite large, the map also contains smaller text. The smaller text consists of statistics on how large the area was, how many had "died of massacre and starvation," and how many "Non-Moslems, (Christians, chiefly)" had lived in the area in 1914 (see Map 14.5).[25] These details, while sharing information, were also, clearly, meant to trigger empathy and solicit donations.

Yet hunger maps were more than an additional form of education or art of persuasion. They were also tools outright, used by aid workers like Esther Sayles Root and others. Map 14.6 shows a copy of the same *Hunger Map of Europe* that was produced in August 1921, but with hand-written annotations and statistics of how much was being shipped to each country. Even the month, August, is crossed out with "March" penned in instead. Notes indicate the amount of "relief furnished" in metric tons that different countries on the map had received. This example shows how the maps were repurposed internally to communicate different information.

As tools of explanation, the original *Hunger Draws the Map* (Map 14.1), like many that came after it, mixed the level of famine in various locations with aid – whether a place was receiving aid, or had been receiving aid. In some examples, like *Hunger Map of Europe*, October 1, 1921 (Map 14.4), how much aid had been received was also mixed with famine areas. An area under famine, and an area receiving aid, are linked, but they are not the same. As ARA activities grew, maps increasingly focused on where they were operating, and/or how much and what kind of aid was being delivered. This occurred on an international level, a regional level, a national level, and even for specific cities. For example, at the national level, a detailed map of Poland indicated the intensity of the ARA feeding action in a proportion of the population.[26] At the city level, a detailed map of Budapest shows the location of ARA-funded kitchens and feeding centers.[27]

25 Special sympathy for Christians in this part of the world was not new. See Davide Rodogno, *Against Massacre: Humanitarian Interventions in the Ottoman Empire, 1815–1914* (Princeton University Press, 2011).

26 The American Relief Administration, "Poland: Intensity of the feeding action according to the administrative districts in May 1921," in *American Relief Administration European Children's Fund Mission to Poland* (Warsaw: The American Relief Administration, 1922), 77.

27 The American Relief Administration, "Map of Budapest, Hungary indicating location ARA ECF child feeding stations," in *American Relief Administration European Children's Fund: Final Report of the Work in Hungary* (Budpapest: The American Relief Administration, 1920), 14–15.

Map 14.6 Hunger Map of Europe, August 1921, with handwritten annotations.
Source: HILA, ARA, EOR, Box 531, Folder 9

At the international level, the ARA maps show the evolution of their areas of operation. One of the earliest, "Map Showing Territory Reached by American Relief Administration" (Map 14.7) was produced on March 24, 1919. Its key includes four levels: "Port visited by A.R.A. vessels," "Relief supplies (routes)," "Relief supplies projected," and "Approximate

Map 14.7 Map Showing Territory Reached by American Relief Administration, March 24, 1919.
Source: HILA, Frank M. Surface Papers, Box 6

boundaries of actual occupation." While "Russia" is included (taking up perhaps a fourth of the entire space on the map), it is bare.

By 1921 and 1922, Russia, Ukraine, and Belarus had more ARA routes than the rest of the map combined, as both "Relief Operations of the ARA, July 1, 1921–March 31, 1922" (Map 14.8) and "Movement of Supplies, A.R.A. 1921–1922" (Map 14.9), show. The map not only showed areas where the ARA was still no longer active, but also how supplies reached underfed areas. Both maps indicate feeding stations, food remittance warehouses, as well as ports and railroads. By the time "Movement of Supplies, A.R.A. 1921–1922" (Map 14.9) was published in October 1922, seven months later, the representation of warehouses increased in Russia, at least on the map. Map 14.9 also highlights the clear relationship between the placement of these warehouses and railroads. All of the Central Child Feeding Stations and all but one of the Food Remittance Warehouses are either directly on or next to railroad lines.

Placing warehouses along train routes was a practical solution for food distribution. A clear example of how ARA workers used maps as tools to re-draw the map can also be seen in maps of Serbia. In these maps, "Serbian Railways" (Map 14.10) and "Children's Relief in Serbia Proper" (Map 14.11), it appears that the ARA copied the railroad map of Serbia and then used it to place their feeding centers for children. Both might also have been produced from some other map of Serbia that contained railroad lines. Lines showing where children were being fed (Map 14.11) predominantly follow the railroad lines in Maps 14.10 and 14.11.

Finally, hunger maps were also used to create records of the work of aid organizations for future generations. Organizations wanted to preserve a record of their efforts, and the maps themselves were part of this evidence. Some of the hunger maps used in this chapter include references to the ARA mapping department on the front or back of the map or the back of a photograph. One even references "the ARA Historical Department" in the bottom right corner (Map 14.8). Thus, maps produced by the ARA were to have both immediate as well as long-term functions as aid workers attempted to provide scientific knowledge of conditions on the ground. Visualizing statistics through maps was an important part of their scientific humanitarianism. This ARA map of the "Net Crop of Food Grains in Russia," for example, published in May 1922 (see Map 14.12), roughly matches what we know today were the worst places of the Russian famine. Like many other ARA maps, it relied on statistics from the national statistical office. Unlike other hunger maps examined so far, this map denotes hunger by examining the "Net Crop

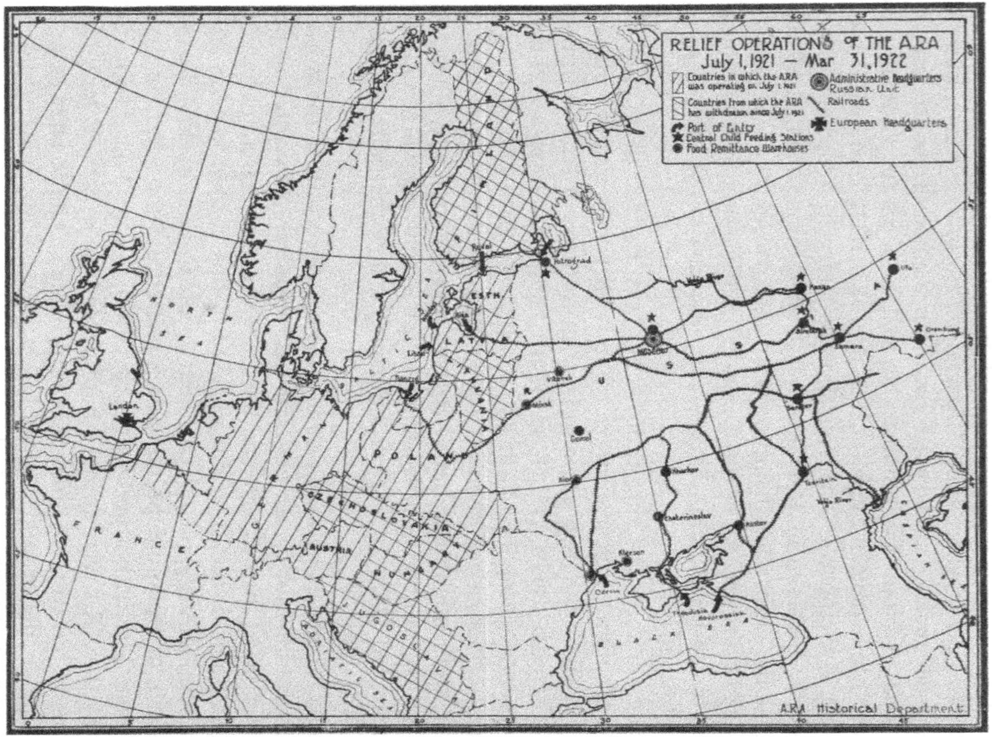

Map 14.8 Relief Operations of the ARA, July 1, 1921–March 31, 1922.
Source: HILA, ARA, EOR, Box 531, Folder 5

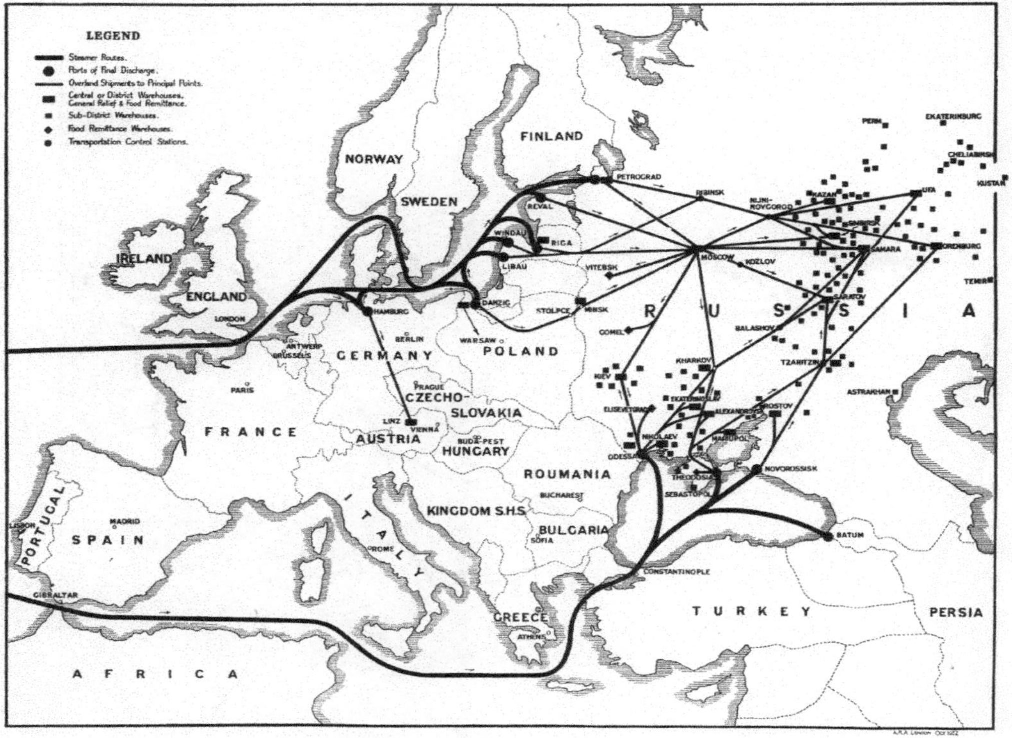

Map 14.9 Movement of Supplies, ARA 1921–1922.
Source: U.S. National Archives, Herbert Hoover Presidential Library and Museum

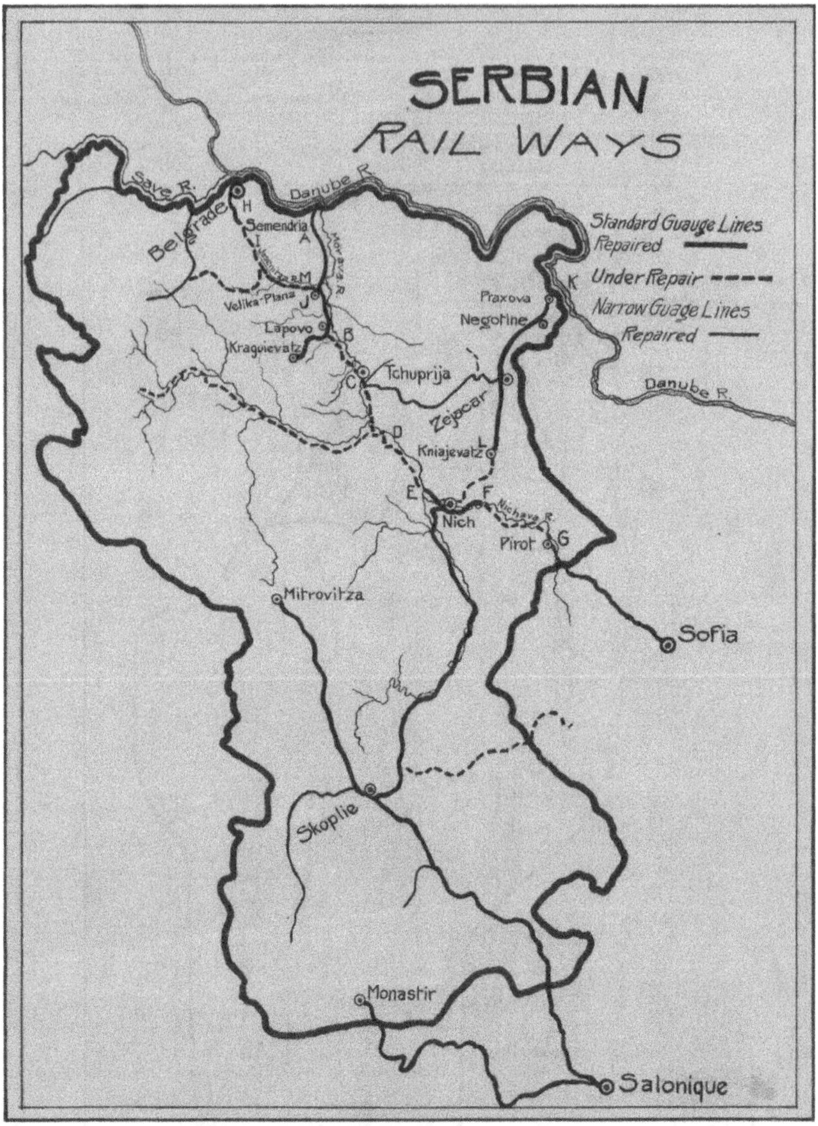

Map 14.10 Serbian Railways.
Source: HILA, ARA, EOR, Oversize Folder 7

of Food Grains per Capita of the Rural Population." The darkest "black spots" in the map are places with "crop less than seed needs" meaning that there were not enough grains to plant for the next harvest.

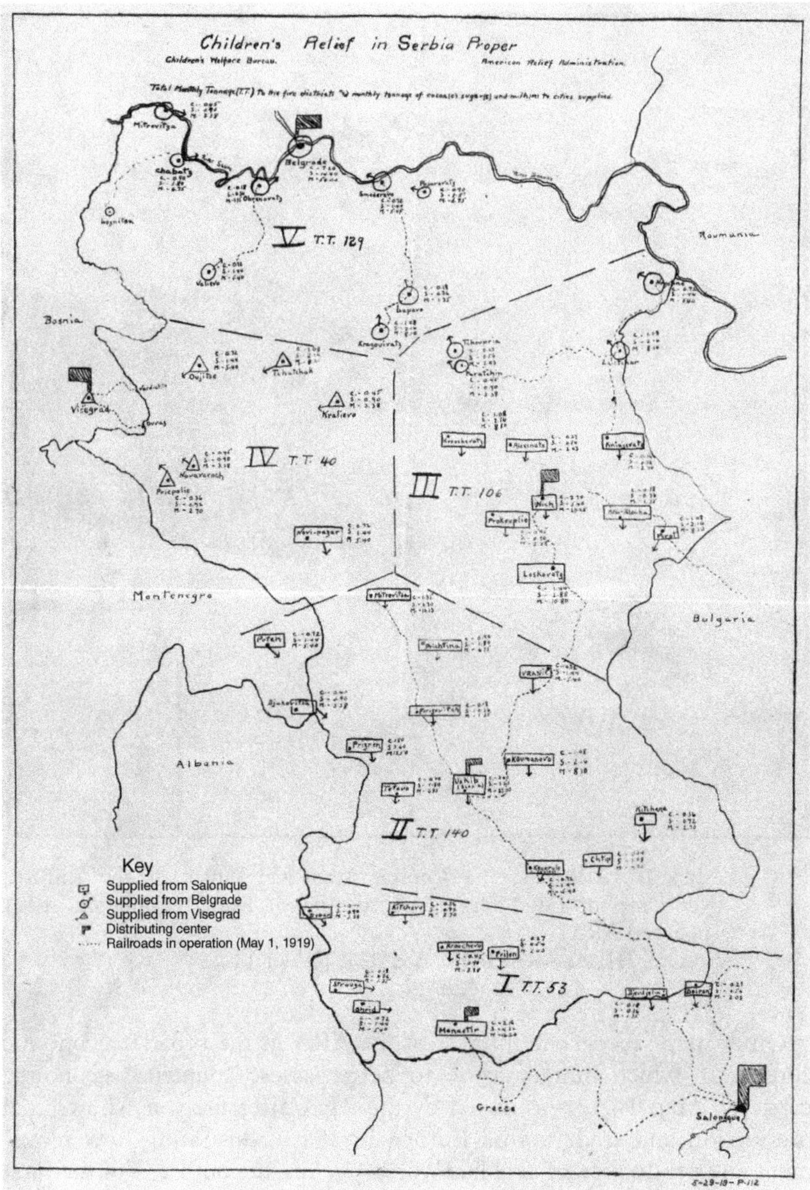

Map 14.11 Children's Relief in Serbia Proper, May 29, 1919.
Source: HILA, ARA, EOR, Oversize Folder 7

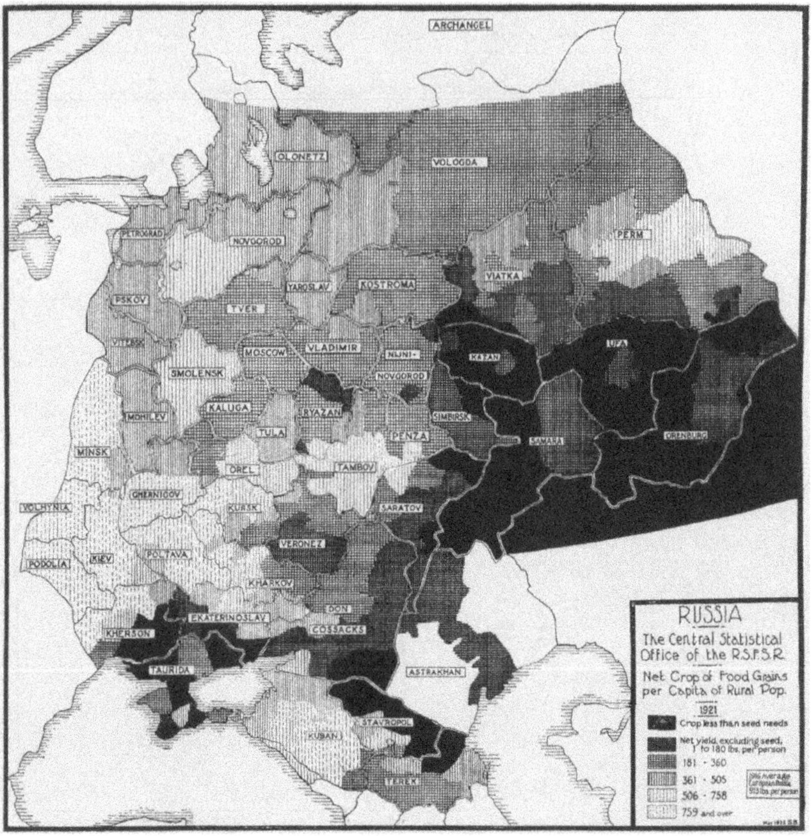

Map 14.12 Russia, the Central Statistical Office of the RSFSR: Net Crop of Food Grains per Capita of Rural Population, 1921 (believed ARA).
Source: HILA, ARA, EOR, Box 531, Folder 11

Other maps reveal the interest of the ARA in the broader economic context in which hunger arose to better assess countries' economic capacity. Map 14.13, produced by the ARA after the war, shows coal production and trade across Europe in 1913, illustrating how movement and production of coal had worked before the outbreak of the First World War. Maps like this illustrate how the ARA deemed it important to understand coal production and the pre-war economy as part of their aid efforts. Shortages of coal were deeply intertwined with hunger: coal, which had often been coopted by belligerent countries for war-making, was essential for the transportation of foodstuff from

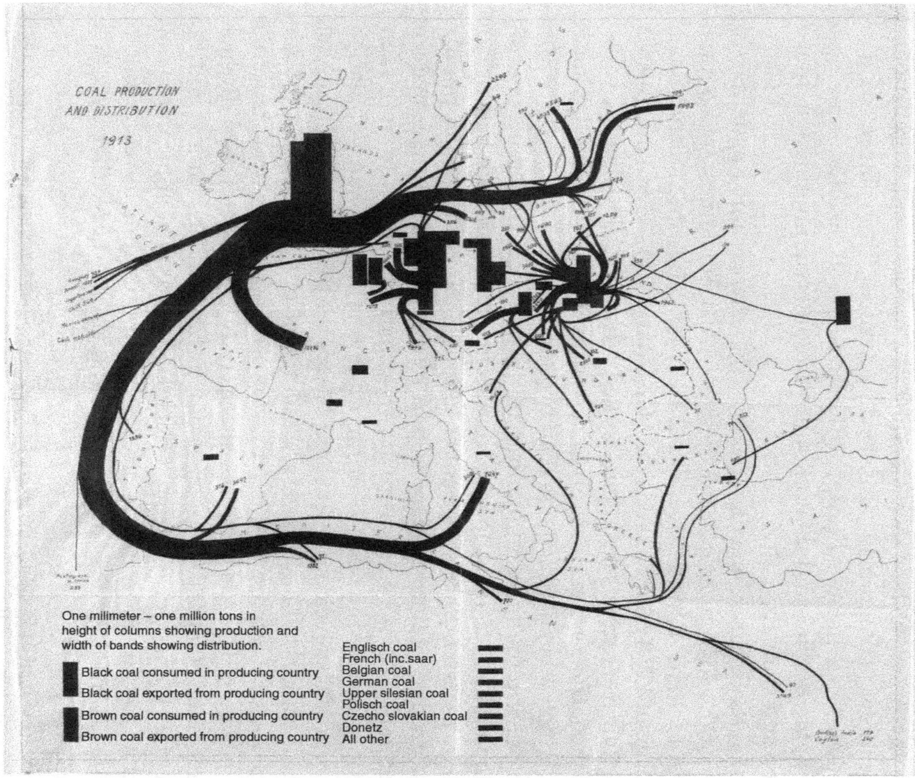

Map 14.13 Coal production and distribution map, 1913.
Source: HILA, ARA, EOR, Oversize Folder 6

producer to consumer. A map of industrial production in Poland meanwhile showed attempts to assess the means of comprehensive economic recovery of countries in the wake of war.[28]

The ARA was not the only aid organization to use and create hunger maps as instruments of persuasion or as tools in their work. This "Famine Zone" map (Map 14.14) created by the American Jewish Joint Distribution Committee (JDC) was used in an internal draft report with other maps such as the "Location of Pre-war Jewish Populations," "Migrations," "Pogroms," "Bolshevik Advances," that illustrated dangers to Jews in Eastern Europe.[29] These maps all take the same basic geographic outline, and then fill it in with different information, movements, and symbols.

The JDC Famine Zone map (Map 14.14) shares similar patterns with many of the ARA hunger maps. Besides visual similarities, it also mixes levels of famine with the level of aid received. The same locations as in the original 1918 *Hunger Draws the Map* (Map 14.1) – Germany, Austria, and Hungary – are marked "unclassified." It is plausible that the widely published *Hunger Draws the Map* served as a guide for this US-made map, which was published less than two months later.

Before international humanitarian agencies began publishing and producing hunger maps, local governments during the war had already tried to ascertain levels of hunger among their own civilian populations, producing hunger maps as part of this process. Hunger maps of Cisleithania (Map 14.15) were drawn as part of a report from the censorship office in June 1917 on the morale of the civilian population. The report was based on censored letters sent from the Austrian half of the Empire.[30] They provide a picture of hunger levels in the different regions: Alpine Lands (roughly present-day Austria, Slovenia, and parts of Croatia and Northern Italy), Dalmatia and Bosnia-Herzegovina, Galicia (in present-day Poland and Ukraine), and the Bohemian Lands (present-day Czech Republic). The four maps show red dots for famine areas (*Hungersnot*) and blue dots for emergencies (*Notstand*). Most cities and larger towns are marked either by a blue

[28] "Industrial map of Poland," in *American Relief Administration European Children's Fund Mission to Poland*, 73.

[29] Famine Zone map collected from the National Library of Israel, special collections. Permission to use image obtained from the American Jewish Joint Distribution Committee.

[30] OeStA/KA FA AOK Evb/NA Akten 3578, Evidenzbüroakt Nr. 11609 ex. 1917. On censored letters, see Péter Hanák, "Vox Populi: Intercepted Letters in the First World War," in *The Garden and the Workshop: Essays on the Cultural History of Vienna and Budapest* (Princeton, NJ: Princeton University Press, 1998), 179–212.

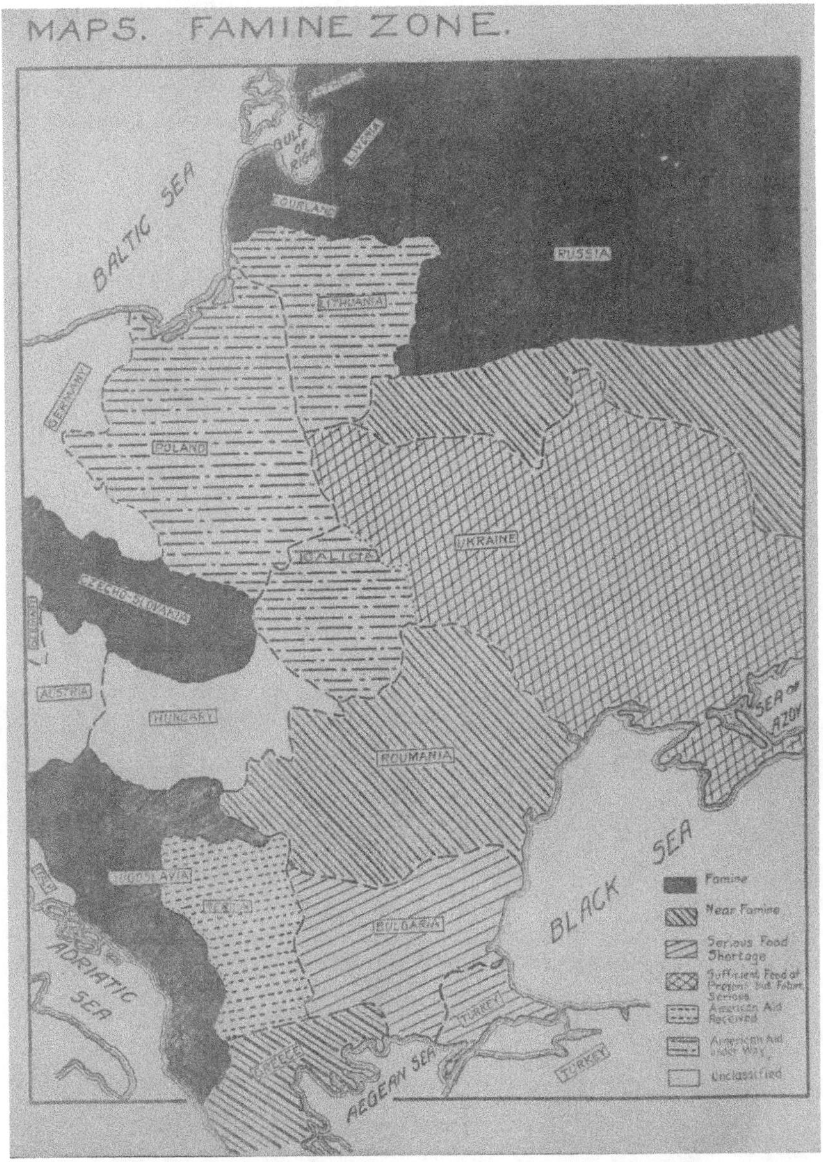

Map 14.14 JDC Famine Zone.
Source: "Map 5. Famine Zone." Draft of memorandum on constructive relief in the eastern war zones. Submitted to the committee on constructive relief of the joint distribution committee. January 23, 1919. 2=35 B 888, C.1. Archives. National Library of Israel

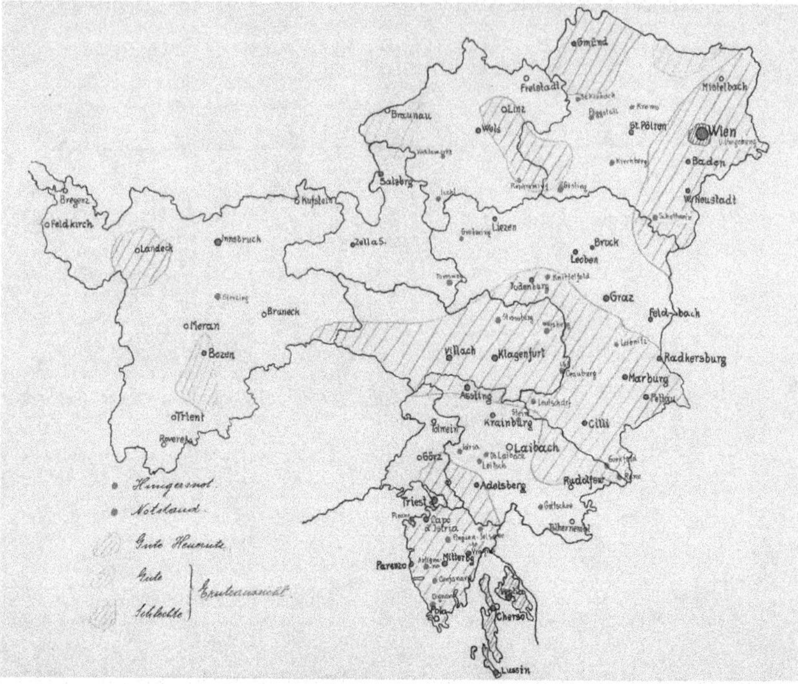

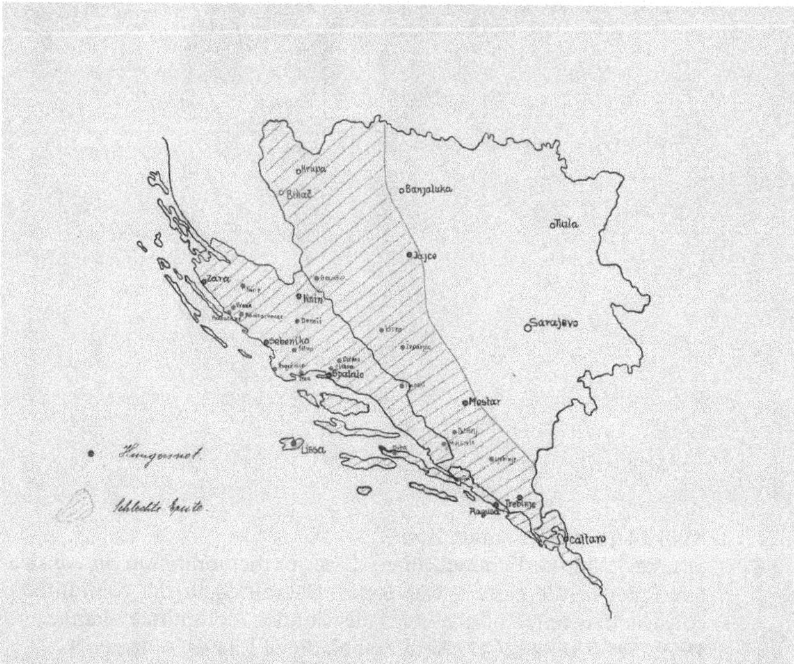

Map 14.15 Hunger maps of Cisleithania.
Source: OeStA/KA FA AOK Evb/NA Akten 3578, Evidenzbüroakt Nr. 11609 ex. 1917

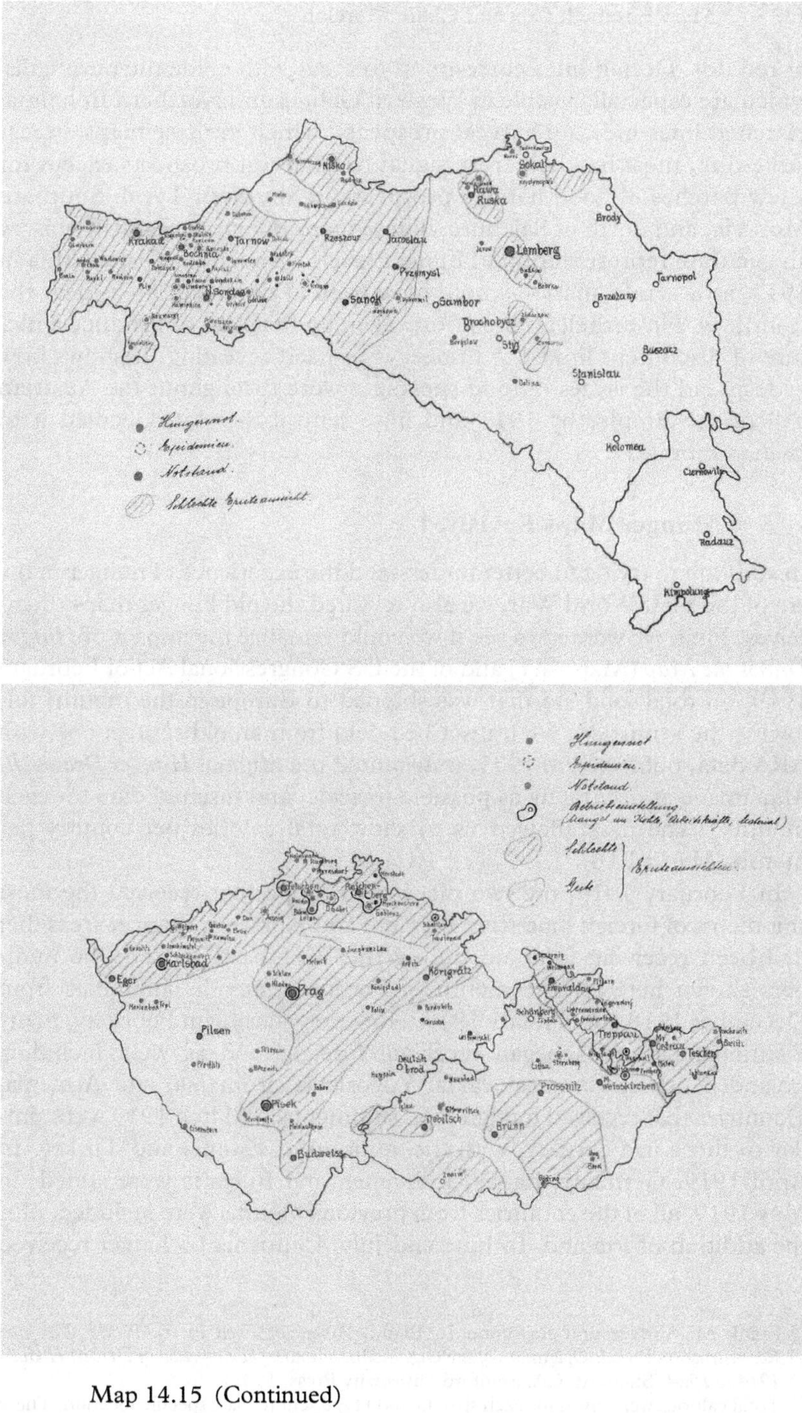

Map 14.15 (Continued)

or red dot. Dotted lines correspond to areas with epidemic outbreaks, which are especially visible in Western Galicia and Northern Bohemia. Hatched lines indicate harvest prospects, which in these maps appear quite dire; most hatched areas signal bad harvest prospects except for a few patches of good harvest prospects in Southern Tyrol, Southern Moravia, and north of Salzburg. These maps do not necessarily convey an accurate representation of hunger levels throughout Cisleithania in 1917, as less information would have been available for areas near the frontlines. Nevertheless, the effort taken by the state to produce a picture of discontent linked to hunger is in itself revealing. It shows how widespread the issues of food shortages were throughout the Austrian half of the Empire by 1917 and how central the state deemed it to civilian morale.

Hunger Maps Revisited

In addition to trying to better understand the experience of hunger in the era of the First World War, we also revisited the old hunger maps themselves. First, we wanted to see if we could visualize the impact of *Hunger Draws the Map* (Map 14.1) and of the US Congressional Act of February 1919, on total food aid that was shipped to Europe in the months following the armistice. We transcribed data from an old sourcebook with ARA data, published in 1931, transmuted the original *Hunger Draws the Map* image as accurately as possible to scale, and inserted data for each month.[31] The data allowed us to show total calories per country per month (Map 14.16).[32]

In February 1919, the two places in Europe that received the most shipments of foreign food were Belgium and Northern France, areas that had been receiving food aid during the War itself. Indeed, the numbers shown here for the month of February include shipments from December 1918 and January 1919. However, starting in February, many additional countries began receiving foreign food as well, including Poland, Austria, Czechoslovakia, Yugoslavia, Romania, and Armenia. Countries that received foreign food shipments in March 1919 were similar to those in February, with the addition of Estonia and Turkey. In April 1919, Germany, Latvia, Lithuania, and Bulgaria were added. In May 1919, all of the countries from previous months were included, plus the addition of Finland. In June and July, Lithuania no longer received

[31] Frank M. Surface and Raymond L. Bland, *American Food in the World War and Reconstruction Period: Operations of the Organizations under the Direction of Herbert Hoover, 1914 to 1924* (Stanford, CA: Stanford University Press, 1931).

[32] Total calories were given for each specific food type sent to each specific location. These calories per food type per location were totalled for each country.

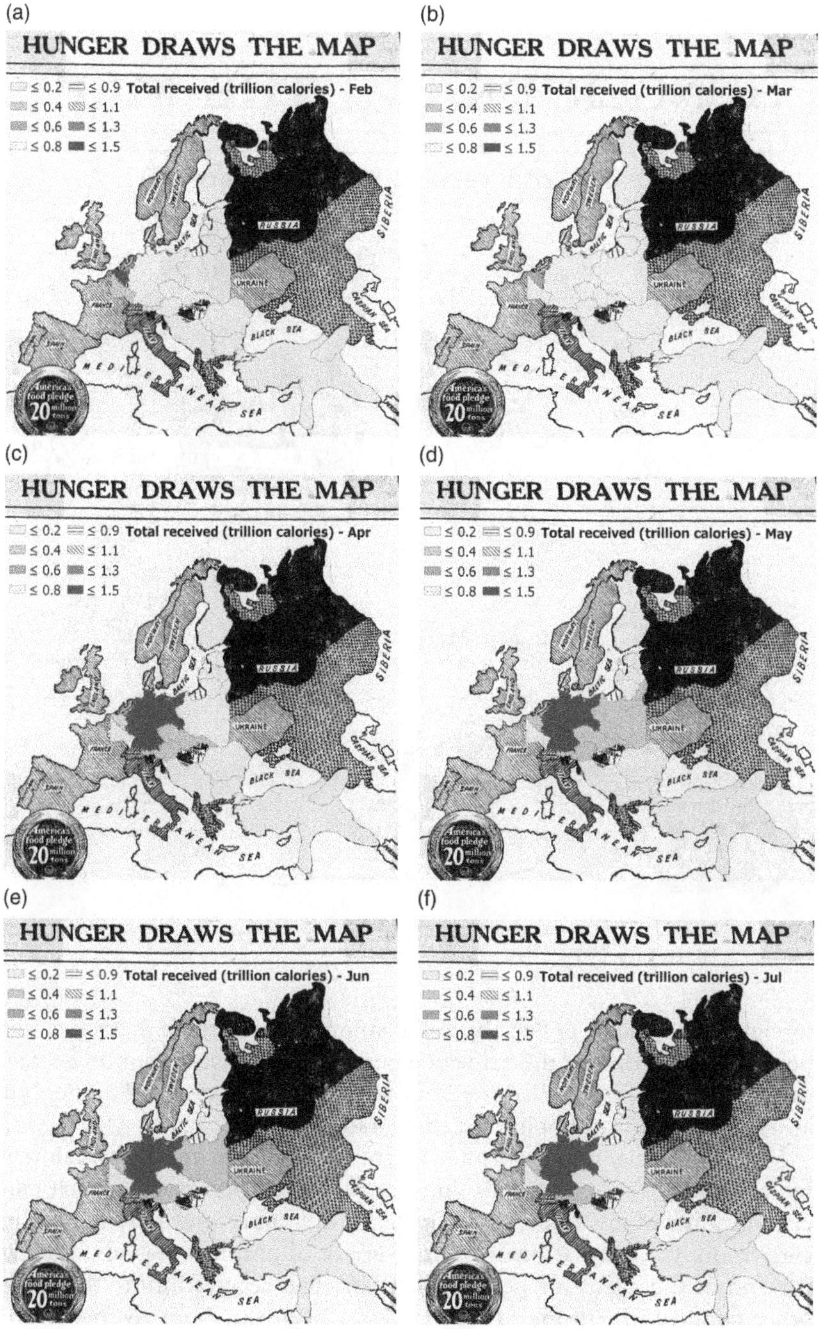

Map 14.16 Total monthly calories sent to different European countries by US and allies, February–July 1919.[33]

[33] Special thanks to Thomas Caton Harrison for his help creating these maps.

Map 14.17 Total calories shipped by America and allies, December 1918–July 1919.

foreign food, at least not a substantial amount. From these maps it could be argued that during the armistice period the changing monthly totals and countries that received food aid were not based on need alone, but also on feasibility and political considerations.

Map 14.17 clearly shows that Germany obtained the most calories by far. Again, these are totals and not portrayed per capita, which can explain some of the differences. Germany did not receive food aid in the early months of the armistice for a variety of political reasons, but by the end of the armistice period, Germany had received more than any other country in Europe. This may have been due both to the severe famine conditions experienced there, as well as to the fear of the spread of unrest fueled in part by hunger, as the Allies tried to negotiate peace.

To make comparisons more immediately visible, we have produced other maps to visualize European reduced food supplies in wartime, showing both the reduction in agricultural output and changes in trade. For example, we collected and transcribed country-level data to create new maps that show historical levels of agricultural production. To accomplish this, historical maps were sketched into ArcGIS using old borders. We share many of the same limitations as the creators of the original *Hunger Draws the Map* in creating spatial images to represent complex, temporal processes. Yet these new maps, like the original hunger maps of a hundred years ago, show a great deal of information with a single glance. It should be emphasized that the production and import data for the belligerent countries during the war years is less reliable, but we have tried to go back to national statistics to include as much data as possible. Over 300 maps were created, and all are available on the following website: https://hungerdrawsthemap.history.ox.ac.uk/hunger-during-and-after-first-world-war.[34] These maps can be displayed and compared in a variety of ways by using the dropdown menus.

The maps on crop yields show a marked decline in agricultural production across the continent, both in absolute totals and in averages per surface grown.[35] The decrease in total yields was particularly visible in countries directly affected by the conflict, while neutral countries and Great Britain fared much better (see Map 14.19). Map 14.18 compares wheat production in 1918 with pre-war averages. Production had significantly fallen in Germany, France, the Austrian half of Austria-Hungary, Belgium, and, to a lesser extent, Italy. Many of these countries had arable land that became unusable because it was located near the frontlines, reducing the harvested surface. However, the total loss of production is not explained by loss of arable land alone. A comparison of yields per surface harvested as done in Map 14.20 for wheat also shows a decline in yields. The reasons for lower crop yields are not shown in these maps but are explained throughout the book: reduced manpower with men

[34] We thank Thomas Caton Harrison for his work in creating these maps. We followed the same order of precedence for grains as the League of Nations.

[35] Statistics on crop yields found in: *Annuaire International de Statistique Agricole 1909 à 1921* (Rome: Institut international d'agriculture, 1922); *200 jaar statistiek in tijdreeksen, 1800–1999* (The Hague: Centraal Bureau voor de Statistiek, 2001) and various statistical yearbooks: *Österreichisches statistisches Handbuch, etc.* (Vienna: Gerold & Sohn, 1913–1917); *Statistisches Handbuch fur die Republik Oesterreich* (Vienna: Österreichische Staatsdruckerei, 1920); *Annuaire statistique de la Belgique et du Congo belge* (Brussels: impr. A. Lesigne, 1922–1924); *Statistisches Jahrbuch für das Deutsche Reich* (Berlin: Puttkammer & Mühlbrecht, 1920–1924); *Annuario Statistico Italiano, Seconda Serie*, Vol. III-IX (Rome: Istituto Nazionale di Statistica, 1913–1925); *Zasiewy I zbiory w roku 1918* (Warsaw: Nakł. Głównego Urzędu Statystycznego, 1920); *Magyar Statisztikai Évkönyv* (Budapest: Központi Statisztikai Hivatal, 1914–1925).

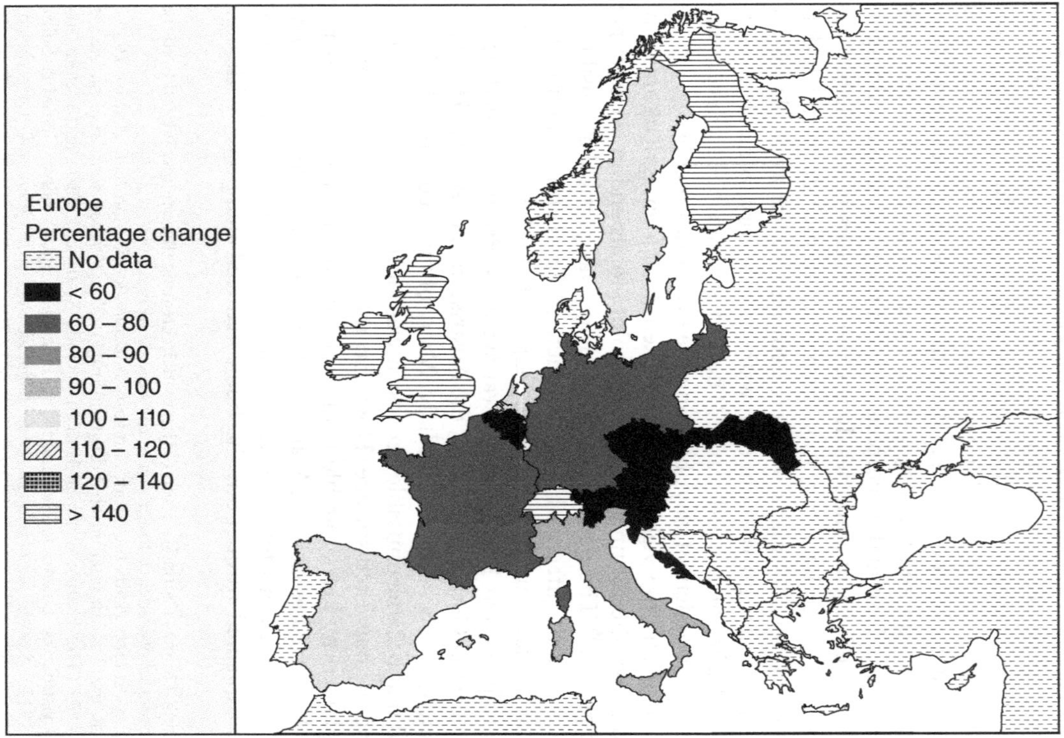

Map 14.18 Wheat production change in 1918 compared to pre-war (1909–1913) average.
Credit: Geodienst

being away fighting, requisitioned horses, reduced availability of fertilizers, and poor weather. While agricultural workers may have been incentivized to report smaller crop yields in order to sell goods clandestinely for larger profits, poor weather and other environmental calamities, as well as shifts in the labor force away from young men in their prime, suggests that at least some of the reported reductions in agricultural output were real. Furthermore, there was a loss of both international and local infrastructure as roads and routes were destroyed throughout the war. Even when infrastructure was not physically destroyed, the shipments of food and fertilizer were often blockaded.

Yields per hectare are a relatively comparable measure that confirms the significant negative impact of the war on the agriculture of the whole continent. Yields per surface varied enormously across Europe before the war because of different environmental factors and levels of agricultural modernization, but they were reduced in all countries directly affected by war. The loss of total production may have been greater in countries such as France, Belgium, or Austria with a large amount of land destroyed, but yields per surface show significant decline in other countries such as Germany, Hungary, and Italy. The decline was slightly more pronounced in countries such as Belgium and Sweden which had higher yield levels before the war, but the fall was still significant in places like Italy or Hungary, for example. Overall, production only gradually returned to pre-war levels after 1921 (as is visible in Map 14.20). The maps clearly show that the recovery of agricultural production was a very slow process after 1918. Production was impeded by destruction, continued warfare, manpower issues, and lack of fertilizers.

Maps 14.19 and 14.20 only show the decline for wheat, but our other maps to be found online show similar decline for all the major crops (wheat, barley, rye, oat, and corn). For most European countries, wheat was the most important crop, but wheat numbers are, for example, relatively insignificant for Finland, where mostly rye and oat were cultivated. A full picture of the different grains shows how other crops, such as potatoes, were often substituted, which explains some of the variation.

Reduced trade made it more difficult for countries to counterbalance these losses. The reduction in imports and exports shows how individual countries could not rely on foreign markets to compensate for their insufficient domestic production as they had before the onslaught of hostilities. Map 14.21 shows a series of seven maps of grain and starch imports for 1913. Map 14.22 shows maps of grain exports for 1913 for the same products. These maps are missing data for the Russian Empire, which we know produced and exported a huge amount of grain to the rest of the continent.

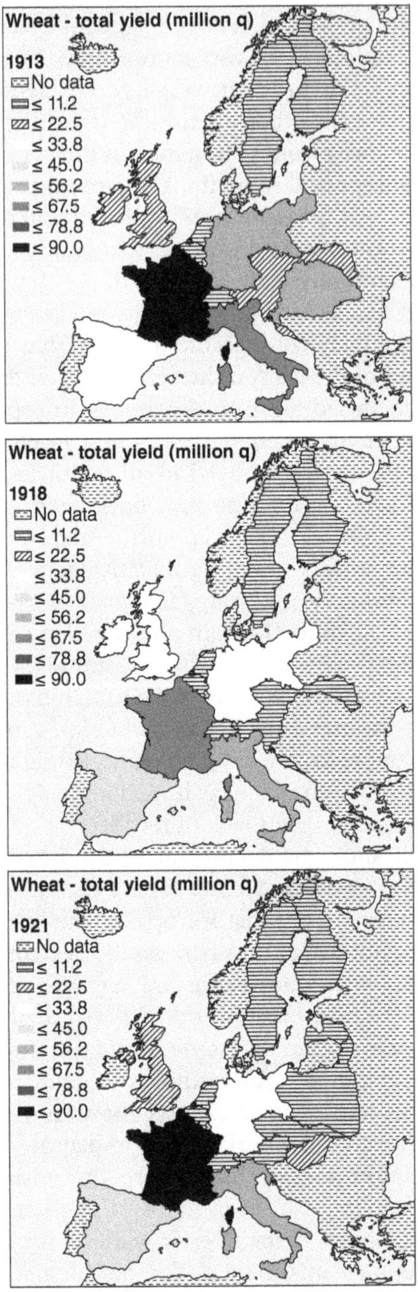

Map 14.19 Total yields for wheat, 1913, 1918, and 1921.

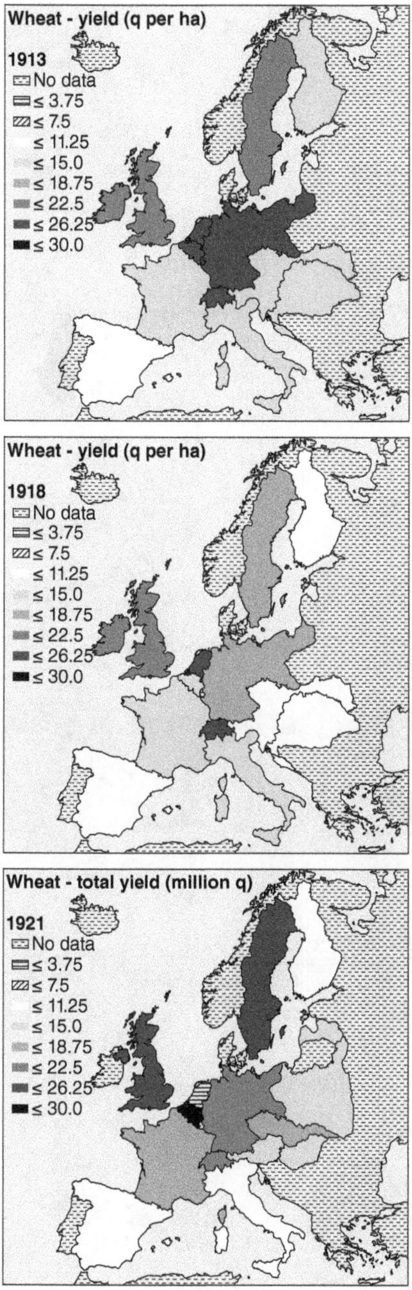

Map 14.20 Yields per surface area for wheat, 1913, 1918, and 1921.

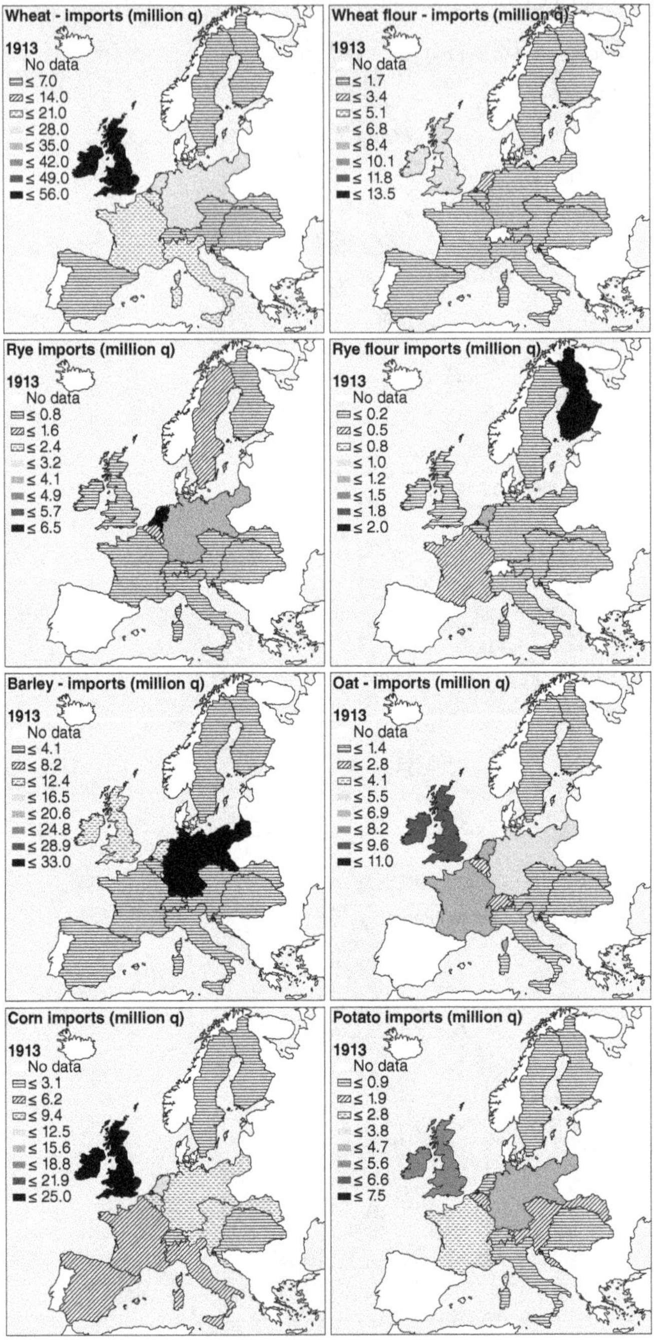

Map 14.21 Grain imports in Europe, 1913.

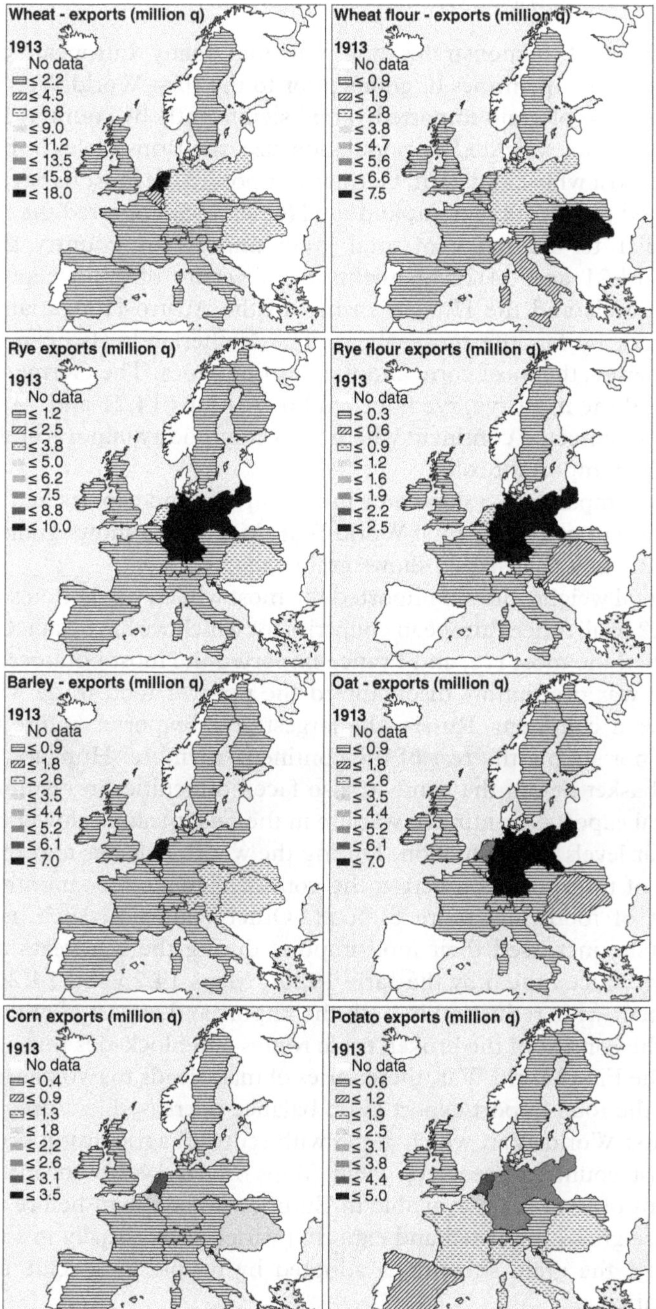

Map 14.22 Grain exports in Europe, 1913.

Map 14.21 demonstrates not only that many European countries imported vast quantities of grains prior to the First World War, but also that the type of grain imported varied significantly by country. In aggregate terms not weighted by population size, the British Isles imported by far the most wheat and corn, Germany imported the most barley, Finland imported the most rye flour, and the Netherlands imported the most rye.

Similar to the range of total grain imports by country shown in Maps 14.21 and 14.22 highlights the diversity of grain exports. The Netherlands and the Hungarian half of the Austro-Hungarian Empire exported, by far, the most wheat. The Netherlands also exported the most barley, the most corn, and the most potatoes. The German Empire exported the most rye, rye flour, and oats. Maps 14.21 and 14.22 show an interconnected continent where food commodity imports and exports played an important role.

As a comparison to show how much imports and exports had changed in the aftermath of the First World War, Map 14.23 shows grain imports for 1922, and Map 14.24 shows grain exports.

In total weight, Britain imported the most wheat, wheat flour, and oats in 1922 of all other European countries for which we have data. Germany imported the most rye, and France imported the most potatoes.

The war profoundly disorganized the pre-war food trade within the European continent. Russia, the largest grain exporter before the war, could not supply the rest of the continent anymore. Hungary, another breadbasket before the conflict, also faced difficulties in resuming agricultural exports. Continued warfare in the East meant a slower return to pre-war levels of production. During the war, blockades and the breakdown of transportation across the continent made the smooth import/export of foodstuffs more difficult. Other countries, such as France and Italy, increased their food imports during the war years and only slowly reduced them by the early 1920s. Maps 14.23 and 14.24 show a continent-wide reduction in both the import and export of grains.

In the context of the broken trade routes and blockades that accompanied the First World War, these series of maps leads to two observations. First, the total import/export grain balance decreased in Europe during the First World War, which along with reduced agricultural production in most countries (see crop yield Maps 14.18–14.20) meant that the amount of total grain available in Europe was less than before. Second, because grains imported and exported varied substantially in Europe by country, the grain substitutes adopted by people in specific countries also varied.

The maps show the changes in the European food supply through the war at the macro level, highlighting the devastated agricultural

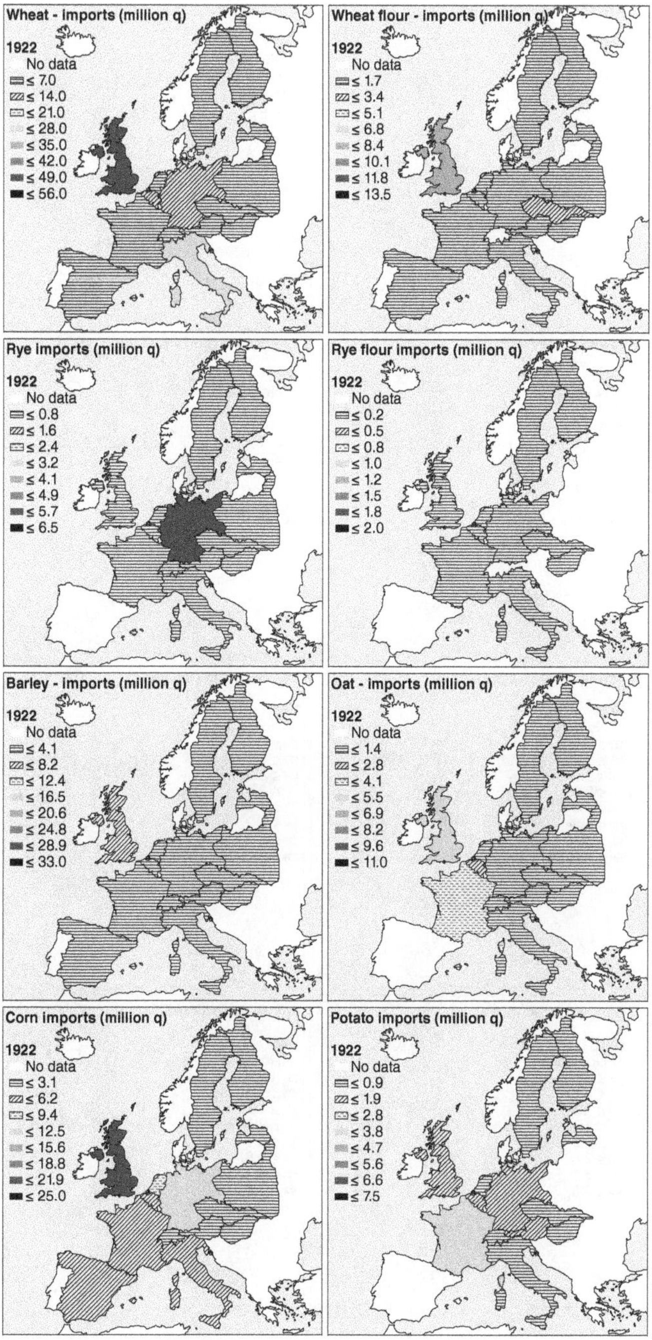

Map 14.23 Grain imports in Europe, 1922.

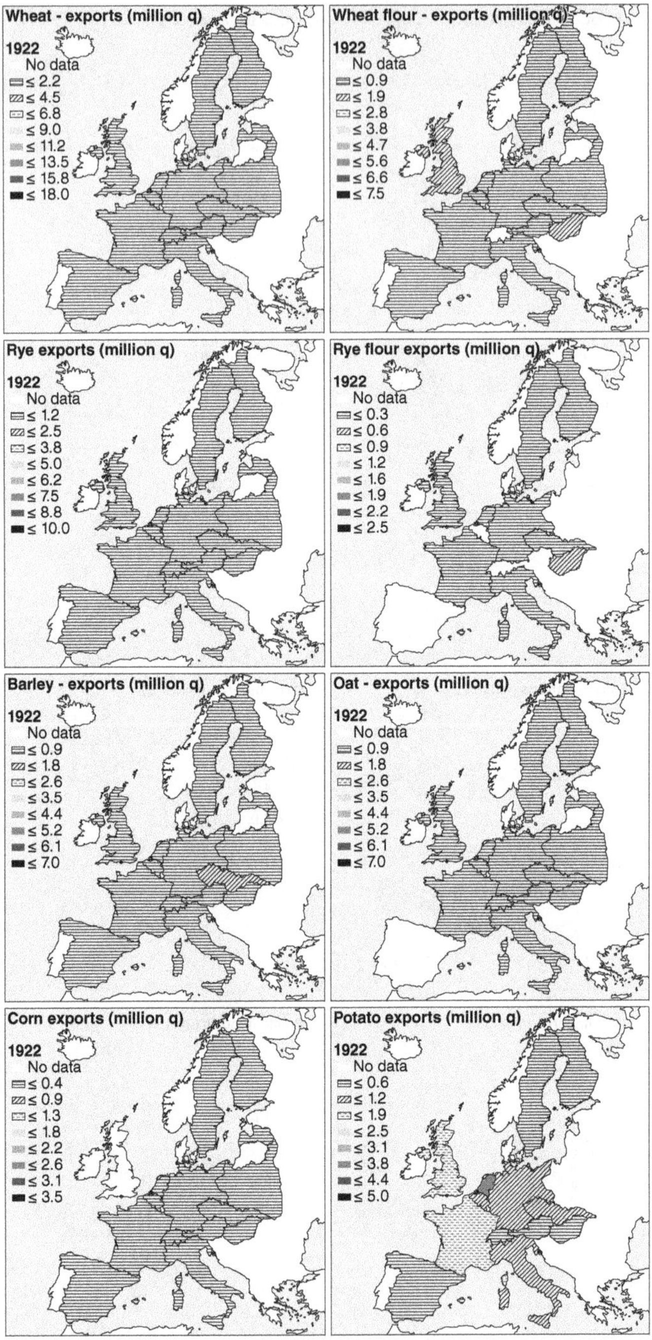

Map 14.24 Grain exports in Europe, 1922.

production throughout the continent and the reduced ability to import in the Central Powers, while increased reliance on imports dominated in the West during the war (France and Italy). Taken together, they suggest a clear decline in consumption across the continent as both production and imports went down from pre-war levels. Europe had less food after the war than before. The internal and external sources of cereals ceased to be available and many countries who might have made up for the shortfall of production with increased imports were unable to do so (especially with weak currencies in an inflationary context). The disappearance of the complex organization of pre-war food supply maintained by imports and efficient transportation spelled hunger. Maps 14.19 to 14.24 make vivid the disruptions to the food system in Europe in a single glance. They show the profound damage to agriculture and interruptions in the trade of grains. Because the maps span several years, they also illustrate that neither yields nor trade had returned to pre-War standards by 1918. All of this explains how reliance on imports could become such a salient issue in the post-war period.

Our book has explored the various consequences of this reduced food consumption across the continent. The authors of this volume reassess hunger and food shortages during and following the First World War, offering new perspectives on how hunger impacted societies. As a graphic construct, *Hunger Draws the Map* helped to incentivize the approval of millions of dollars for food aid, trigger assistance for the recipients of that food aid, and determine where food was distributed. It was not created simply to reflect the status quo. Playing on the title of this old map, this book has argued that hunger truly did re-draw the map, and in a much broader sense than where and how Americans appropriated aid. Hunger was a central experience at the personal and familial level for millions of people and was fundamental in the disintegration and creation of different societies and countries. When scholars assess the era of the First World War in the future, we hope they will consider the primacy of hunger and recognize its sweeping influence.

Bibliography

Archival Sources

Austria

Österreichisches Staatsarchiv (National Archives of Austria) (ÖStA)

Archiv der Republik (Archives of the Republic, AdR)

Arbeit und Soziales, Volksernährungsamt, Allgemeine Reihe (Office for the Alimentation of the Population, AuS, BMfVE, AR)

Arbeit und Soziales, Bundesministerium für soziale Verwaltung, Volksgesundheit, Akten

Bundeskanzleramt-Inneres, Sonderlegungen, Kriegsflüchtingsfürsorge

Allgemeines Verwaltungsarchiv (General Administrative Archives, AVA)

Ministerium des Innern, Präsidium (Ministry of the Interior, Presidium, MdI, Präs)

Kriegsarchiv, Feldakten, Armeeoberkommando, KA, FA, AOK

Gemeinsames Zentralnachweisbüro (GZNB)

Evidenzbüro des Generalstabs (Evb/NA)

Belgium

Archives of the City of Brussels (Archief van de Stad Brussel/Archives de la Ville de Bruxelles)

'Museum Betreffende de Bederving en de Vervalsching der Eetwaren.' [Poster], 1917.

Belgian State Archives

Archiepiscopal Archive, First World War Reports

Brussels, Archives et Musée de la Littérature

Georges Eekhoud

Czech Republic

Národní archiv (Czech National Archives) [CNA]

Ministerstvo pro zdraví lidu/Rakousko (Ministry for the Population's Health/ Austria, MZd/R)

Prezidium policejního ředitelství (Presidium of the Prague Police Headquarters, PP), 1916–1920; Hauptstelle 1915–1918

Prezidium českého místodržitelství (Presidium of the Bohemian Governor's Office, PM), 1911–1920

Cirkuláře a vyhlášky (Memoranda and announcements)

Státní Okresní Archiv Plzeň Sever (State District Archives Plzeň North)

Farní Archiv, Vysoká Libyně, Kronika fary (Parish archives, Vysoká Libyně, parish chronicle)

Germany

Brandenburgisches Landeshauptarchiv (Brandenburg Main State Archive) (BLHA)

Staatliche Verteilungstelle Groß-Berlin

Bundesarchiv Berlin

R3601, Reichsministerium für Ernährung und Landwirtschaft

R3101, Reichswirtschaftsministerium

Israel

National Library of Israel, Special Collections.

V 770 / 1 Joint Distribution Committee Vienna Collection

Italy

Fondazione Museo storico del Trentino

Archivio della Scrittura Popolare

Museo Storico Italiano della Guerra (MSIG)

Archivio fotografico (AF)

Netherlands

Nationaal Archief (Dutch National Archives)

2.05.23/842, Ministry of Foreign Affairs, A-dossiers

2.21.026.07/9, Dr Folkert Evert Posthuma (1874-1943)

Switzerland

Archives d'Etat de Genève (State Archives of Geneva)

Archives privées 92, Archives de l'Union internationale de secours aux enfants (Archive of the Save the Children International Union)

United Kingdom

National Archives of the United Kingdom (TNA)
Foreign Office 608/185
War Office 95/4750

Wellcome Collection Archives and Manuscripts
Royal Army Medical Corps Muniments Collection (RAMC)

United States

American Friends Service Committee Archives

'New Worlds to Old' Films
Reconstruction

Archives Center, National Museum of American History, Smithsonian Institution

American Relief Administration, European Children's Fund Collection

Hoover Institution Library and Archives (HILA)

American Relief Administration Bulletin
American Relief Administration, European Operation Records (ARA, EOR)
American Relief Administration, European unit
Graham Lusk Papers
Poster Collection
T. Orbison's collection
U.S. Food Administration Records, Office of Foreign Information (USFAR)

Bancroft Library, University of California, Berkeley

American war posters from the First World War

National Archives of the United States, Herbert Hoover Presidential Library

American Relief Administration Personnel Files
Movement of Supplies, A.R.A. 1921–1922 [Map].

Turkey

Ottoman Archives of the Prime Minister's Office (BOA)
Osmanlı Arşivi, DH/SYS 123-9/21-3

Other Non-Published Sources

Private Collection of Mary Elisabeth Cox [MEC]

Postcards

Recorded Interviews

Interview by Mary Elisabeth Cox with Ruth Steiner (daughter of Hans Steiner) completed in Vienna on September 21, 2021.

Digital Sources

Czech Academy of Sciences

Digital Archive of Journals [online]. Prague: Institute for Czech Literature of the CAS, accessible from: http://archiv.ucl.cas.cz/

Periodicals

Historical Press

8 Órai Ujság
American Food Journal
Belgian Bulletin
Berliner Zeitung am Mittag
Budapesti Hírlap
Darba Dzīve
Deutsche Zeitung Bohemia
Die Frau
Die Muskete
Egyenlőség
Fővárosi Közlöny
Friss Ujság
Helsingin Sanomat
Humoristické listy
Jaunākās Ziņas
Kirekiki
Kiskun-Halas Helyi Értesítője
La Croix
La Libre Belgique
Lāčplēsis
Latvijas Sargs
Latvju Sieviete
Līdums
Národní Listy
Národní Politika
Nebelspalter: das Humor-und Satire-Magazin
Néptanitók lapja
Neues Wiener Journal

Neues Wiener Tagblatt
North American Review
Nyírvidék
Öffentliche Sicherheit: Polizei-Rundschau
Österreichische Volks-Zeitung
Pesti Napló
Policijas Vēstnesis
Prager Tagblatt
Satirische Zeitung
Segodnia
Suomen Kuvalehti
Tagesbote aus Mähren und Schlesien
The New York Times
Tolnai Világlapja
Tygodnik Ilustrowany
Uz Priekšu
Vragen des Tijds
Wiener Neueste Nachrichten
Zeltene

Medical Journals

American Journal of Physiology
Annals of Internal Medicine
Annales d'hygiène publique et de médicine légale
Archiv für Gynäkologie
Archives of Internal Medicine (Chicago)
British Medical Bulletin
British Medical Journal
Bulletin de l'Académie de Medicine
Bulletin de l'Académie royale de Médecine de Belgique
Bulletins de la Société de Pédiatrie de Paris
Canadian Medical Association Journal
Deutsche Medizinische Wochenschrift
Die Medizinische Klinik
Edinburgh Medical Journal
Epidemiology and Infection
Indian Medical Gazette
Jahrbuch der Schweizerischen Gesellschaft für Schulgesundheitspflege
Journal of Biological Chemistry
Journal of Hygiene
Journal of Physiology
Journal of the American Medical Association
Journal of the National Medical Association
Journal of Tropical Medicine
Klinische Wochenschrift
Meditsinskiĭ Zhurnal
Münchener medizinische Wochenschrift
Proceedings of the Royal Society of Medicine

Russkiĭ Ginekologicheskiĭ Vestnik
Schweizerische Medizinsche Wochenschrift
The Anatomical Record
The Annals of the American Academy of Political and Social Science
The Bristol Medico-Chirurgical Journal
The Journal of Physiology
The Lancet
Transactions of the Epidemiological Society of London
Transactions of the Medico-Chirurgical Society of Edinburgh
Transactions of the Royal Society of Tropical Medicine and Hygiene
Vrachebnoe Delo
Wiener klinische Wochenschrift
Zentralblatt für Gynäkologie
Zeitschrift für Geburtshilfe und Gynäkologie
Zeitschrift für Kinderheilkunde

Governmental and Institutional Periodicals

Bundesgesetzblatt
Capital Bulletin
Deutsches Reichsgesetzblatt
Ekonomicheskii byulleten Kon'yunturnogo Instituta
International Labour Review
Jahrbuch für Gesetzgebung, Verwaltung und Volkswirtschaft im Deutschen Reich
Sbírka zákonů a nařízení
Trudy TSU
Verhandlungen des Reichstages
Vestnik Statistiki
Zeitschrift für Schweizerische Statistik und Volkswirtschaft

Published Primary Sources

Aereboe, Friedrich, *Der Einfluss des Krieges auf die landwirtschaftliche Produktion in Deutschland* (Stuttgart: Deutsche Verlags-Anstalt, 1927).

Akten der Reichskanzlei, Weimarer Republik (Boppard am Rhein: H. Boldt, 1971).

American Committee for Relief in the Near East, *The American Committee for Relief in the Near East, Its History, Its Work and the Need for Support as Outlined by President Wilson and Others* (s.n.: s.l., 1918).

American Relief Administration, *A Review of the Work of the American Relief Administration in Austria* (Vienna: The American Relief Administration, 1921).

American Relief Administration, *The American Relief Administration in Czecho-Slovakia: A Sketch of the Child-Feeding Operations of the A.R.A. Mission to Czecho-Slovakia, 1919–1921* (New York: The American Relief Administration, 1921).

American Relief Administration, *Three Years Work of the American Relief Administration in Austria* (Vienna: The American Relief Administration, 1922).

American Relief Administration European Children's Fund, *Final Report of the Work in Hungary* (Budapest: The American Relief Administration, 1920).

American Relief Administration European Children's Fund Mission to Poland, *Polsko-Amerykański Komitet Pomocy Dzieciom. 1919–1922* (Warsaw: The American Relief Administration, 1922).

Annuaire International de Statistique Agricole 1909 à 1921 (Rome: Institut international d'agriculture, 1922).

Annual Report of the Sanitary Commissioner for the North West Provinces and Oudh (Allahabad: Government Press, 1897).

Aprovisace obce pražské za války a po válce 1914–1922 (Prague: Aprovisační ústav hlavního města Prahy, 1923).

Augé-Laribé, Michel, *L'agriculture pendant la guerre* (Paris: Les Presses Universitaires de France, 1925).

Bachi, Riccardo and Gaetano Zingali, *L'alimentazione e la politica annonaria in Italia: con una appendice su 'Il rifornimento dei viveri dell'esercito italiano' di Gaetano Zingali* (Rome: G. Laterza, 1926).

Bane, Suda, ed., *Documents of the American Relief Administration European Operations 1918–1922* (Stanford: Stanford University Press, 1932), vol. I–XXII.

Bane, Suda and Ralph Lutz, eds, *The Blockade of Germany after the Armistice 1918–1919, Selected Documents of the Supreme Economic Council, Superior Blockade Council, American Relief Administration, and Other Wartime Organizations* (Stanford: Stanford University Press, 1932).

Bane, Suda and Ralph Lutz, eds, *Organization of American Relief in Europe 1918–1919 Including Negotiations Leading up to the establishment of the Office of Director General of Relief at Paris by the Allied and Associated Powers. Documents* (Stanford: Stanford University Press, 1943).

Barber, Oswald, *Einrichtung Und Aufgaben Der Zentral-Einkaufsgesellschaft* (Berlin: Stellvertretendes Generalkommando VI. Armeekorps, 1917).

Baumann, Wilhelm, 'Das Sinken Der Grundrente Landwirtschaftliche Grossbetriebe Durch Den Weltkrieg' (unpublished PhD thesis, Universität Frankfurt a/Main, 1921).

Bell, A. C., *A History of the Blockade of Germany and of the Countries Associated with Her in the Great War, Austria-Hungary, Bulgaria, and Turkey 1914–1918* (London: His Majesty's Stationery Office, 1937; not publicly available until 1961).

Bettauer, Hugo, *Die Freudlose Gassse: ein Wiener Roman aus unseren Tagen* (Vienna: R. Löwit, 1925).

Beveridge, William H., *Peace in Austria: A Study of Social and Industrial Conditions with a Programme for Reconstruction Based on a Personal Visit to Austria* (London: Fight the Famine Council, 1920).

Beveridge, William H., *British Food Control* (London: Oxford University Press, 1928).

Bloch, I. S., *Modern Weapons and Modern War, Being an Abridgement of "The War of the Future in its Technical, Economic and Political Relations,"* with a prefatory conversation with the author by W. T. Stead (London: Grant Richards, 1900).

Bloch, Jean de, *La guerre, traduction de l'ouvrage russe La Guerre Future aux points de vue technique, économique et politique,* 6 vols (Paris: Guillaumin, 1898–1900).

Blunt, Katherine and Florence Powdermaker, *Food and the War: A Textbook for College Classes* (Boston: Houghton Mifflin Company, 1918).
Booth, Charles, *Life and Labour of the People*, 2 vols. (*2nd Volume: Labour and Life of the People*) (London: Macmillan and Co., 1889–1891).
Bosshardt, Oscar, *Die Schweizer Hilfsaktion für die hungernde Stadt Wien* (Bern: Francke, 1921).
Brentano, Lujo, *Hours and Wages in Relation to Production* (London: Swan Sonnenschein & Co., 1894).
Brooks, Sidney, *America and Germany, 1918–1925*, 2nd ed. (New York: Macmillan and Co., 1927).
Brugmans, Hajo, ed., *Nederland in den oorlogstijd: de geschiedenis van Nederland en van Nedeerlandsch-Indie tijdens den oorlog van 1914 tot 1919, voor zoover zij met dien oorlog verband houdt* (Amsterdam: Elsevier, 1920).
Callwell, Charles E., *Small Wars: Their Principles and Practice*, 3rd ed. (London: His Majesty's Stationery Office, 1909).
Camerer, Wilhelm, *Der Stoffwechsel des Kindes von der Geburt bis zur Beendigung des Wachstums* (Tübingen: Verlag der H. Laupp'schen Buchhandlung, 1894).
Cangardel, Henri, *La marine marchande française et la guerre* (Paris: Les Presses Universitaires de France, 1927).
Carnegie Endowment for International Peace: Division of Intercourse and Education, *Report of the International Commission to Inquire into the Causes and Conduct of the Balkan Wars*: publication no. 4 (Washington, DC: Carnegie Endowment, 1914).
Christophers, S. R., *Malaria in the Punjab, Scientific Memoirs by Officers of the Medical and Sanitary Departments of the Government of India*, 46 (Calcutta: Superintendent Government Printing, 1911).
Clémentel, Etienne, *La France et la politique économique interalliée* (Paris: Les Presses Universitaires de France, 1928).
Cochin, Denys, *Les organisations de blocus en France pendant la guerre (1914–1918)* (Paris: Plon, 1926).
Combined Annual Reports of the World War Foreign Debt Commission: With Additional Information Regarding Foreign Debts Due to the United States – Fiscal Years 1922, 1923, 1924, 1925, and 1926 (Washington, DC: United States Government Printing Office, 1927).
Committee of the International Red Cross, *Rapport sur la visite aux camps de prisonniers Ottomans en Egypte en Décembre 1916 et Janvier 1917, Documents publiés a l'occasion de la Guerre Européenne (1914–1917)* (Geneva: Librarie George & Co., 1917).
Committee of the International Red Cross, *Rapports de MM. le Dr F. Blanchod, F. Thormeyer & Em. Schloch sur leur inspection des camps de prisonniers turcs en France, en Corse et an Egypte Décembre 1916 et Janvier 1917* (Geneva: Librarie George & Co., 1917).
Corbett, Julian, *Some Principles of Maritime Strategy* (London: Longmans, Green, 1911; the 1988 edition published by the Naval Institute Press and ed. by Eric Grove).
Cunningham, D. D., *On Certain Effects of Starvation on Vegetable and Animals Tissues* (Calcutta: Superintendent of Government Printing, 1879).

Dähne, S., O. Farschid, and M. Kropp, eds, *The First World War as Remembered in the Countries of the Eastern Mediterranean* (Baden-Baden: Nomos Verlagsgesellschaft, 2006).

De Bas, W. G., *25 jaar geschiedenis van Nederland 1898–1923: gedenkboek, uitgegeven ter gelegenheid van het zilveren regeeringsfeest van Hare Majesteit Koningin Wilhelmina der Nederlanden* (Amsterdam: Fongers & Co, 1923).

Deppe, Ludwig, *Mit Lettow-Vorbeck durch Afrika* (Berlin: August Scherl, 1919).

Die Amerikanische Kinderhilfsaktion in Wien (Vienna: Generalkomiss. d. A. K. H. A., 1921).

Die amtlichen Befehle, Verordnungen u. Bekanntmachungen für Libau, erlassen in d. Zeit vom 7. Mai 1915 bis 3. März 1918 (Libau: Gottl. D. Meyer, 1918).

Duch české ženy za války [The spirit of the Czech woman during the war] (Praha: Ženský obzor, 1928).

Ducpétieux, Édouard, *Budgets économiques des classes ouvrières en Belgique: subsistance, salaires, populations* (Brussels: M. Hayez, 1855).

Edmonds, James E., ed., *History of the Great War Based on Official Documents: Military Operations: France and Belgium, 1917*, 3 vols (London: Macmillan and Co., 1940–1948).

Edmonds, James E. and L. Oppenheim, *Land Warfare: An Exposition of the Laws and Usages of War on Land for the Guidance of Officers of His Majesty's Army* (London: His Majesty's Stationery Office, [1912]).

Eltzbacher, Paul, ed., *Die deutsche Volksernährung und der englische Aushungerungsplan* (Braunschweig: Vieweg, 1914).

Eltzbacher, Paul, ed., *Germany's Food Can It Last? The German Case as Presented by German Experts*, trans. by Sidney Russel Wells (London: University of London Press, 1915).

Eltzbacher, Paul, *Ernährung in der Kriegszeit: Ein Ratgeber für Behörden, Geistlicher, Ärzte, Lehrer und Lehrerinnen, Gewerkschaftsbeamte, Hausfrauen und alle die raten und helfen wollen* (Wiesbaden: Springer Fachmedien, 1914).

Endres, Karl, *Die völkerrechtlichen Grundfäßte der Kriegführung zu Lande und zur See* (Berlin: Decker, 1909).

Ernst, Margit, *Wiener Kinder in der Schweiz* (Vienna: Seram Velag, 1925).

Fayle, Charles Ernest, *History of the Great War Based on Official Documents: Seaborne Trade*, 3 vols (London: John Murray, 1920–1924).

Fayle, Charles Ernest, *The War and the Shipping Industry* (London: Humphrey Milford, 1927).

Fisher, Harold, *The Famine in Soviet Russia 1919–1923: The Operations of the American Relief Administration* (New York: Macmillan and Co., 1927).

Foley, Robert T., ed., *Alfred von Schlieffen's Military Writings* (London: Frank Cass, 2003).

Fry, A. Ruth, *A Quaker Adventure: The Story of Nine Years' Relief and Reconstruction* (London: Nisbet, 1926).

Further Report of Brigadier-General Vaughan's Ration Committee Re-assembled for the Purpose of Considering the Criticisms by Certain Branches of Army Headquarters in the Original Report (Calcutta: Superintendent of Government Printing, 1918).

Gautier, Armand, *L'alimentation et les régimes chez l'homme sain et chez les malades* (Paris: Masson et Cie, 1904).

Gay, George I. and H. H. Fisher, *Public Relations of the Commission for Relief in Belgium: Documents* (Stanford: Stanford University Press, 1929).

Gigon, Alfred, *Die Arbeiterkost nach Untersuchungen über die Ernährung Basler Arbeiter bei freigewählter Kost* (Berlin, Heidelberg: Springer Verlag, 1914).

Gille, Louis, *Cinquante mois d'occupation allemande*, ed. by Paul Delandsheere and Alphonse Ooms (Brussels: Dewit, 1919).

Giuffrida, Vincenzo, and Gaetano Pietra, *Provital: approvvigionamenti alimentari d'Italia durante la grande guerra 1914–1918* (Padua: Cedam, 1936).

Gollin, Kamil, *Ket'asová zpověd': autentické líčení života, zákulisí a tajů řetězového obchodu po dobu pěti měsíců ve válce od 1. srpna 1917 až do ledna 1918* (Prague: A. Svěcený, 1918).

Gratz, Gustav and Richard Schüller, *Der wirtschaftliche Zusammenbruch Österreich-Ungarns die Tragödie der Erschöpfung* (Vienna: Hölder-Pichler-Tempsky, 1930).

Greig, E. D. W., *Epidemic Dropsy in Calcutta, Scientific Memories by Medical Officers of the Medical and Sanitary Departments of the Government of India*, 45 (Calcutta: Superintendent Government Printing, 1911).

Greven, H. B., ed., *The Netherlands and the World War: Studies in the War History of a Neutral* (New Haven: Yale University Press, 1928).

Grobba, Fritz, *Die Getreidewirtschaft Syriens und Palästinas seit Beginn des Weltkrieges* (Hanover: Orient-Buchhandlung Heinz Lafaire, 1923).

Großen Generalstabe, Kriegsgeschichtliche Abteilung I, *Studien zur Kriegsgeschichte und Taktik: VI: Heeresverpflegung* (Berlin: Mittler, 1913).

Guichard, Louis, *The Naval Blockade 1914–1918*, trans. and ed. by Christopher Turner (London: Philip Allan, 1930).

Günther, Otto, *Das Gewicht der Neugeborenen in der Kriegs- u. Nachkriegszeit* (Munich: Rudolph Müller & Steinicke, 1927).

Hájková, Dagmar and Eva Kalivodová, eds, *Deníky Edvarda a Hany Benešových z období první světové války (1915–1918)* (Prague: Masarykův archiv, 2013).

Hájková, Dagmar and Ivan Šedivý, eds, *Korespondence T.G. Masaryk – Edvard Beneš 1914–1918* (Prague: Masarykův Ústav, 2004).

Hartmann, Fritz, *Die Heeresverpflegung in Volkswirtschaftliche Abteilung des Kriegsernährungsamts: Beiträge zür Kriegswirtschaft* (Berlin: Verlag der Beiträge zur Kriegswirtschaft, 1917).

Hauptbericht der freien wissenschaftlichen Kommission zum Studium der jetzigen Ernährungsverhältnisse in Deutschland (s.l.: s.n., 1919).

Heckscher, Ely F. and Wilhelm Keilhau, *Sweden, Norway, Denmark and Iceland in the World War* (New Haven: Yale University Press, 1930).

Hehir, Patrick, *Malaria in India* (London: Oxford University Press, 1937).

Heller, Victor, 'Government Price Fixing and Rationing in Austria during the War of 1914–18', *Report for the National Bureau of Economic Research*, January 1941.

Henry, Albert, *Le ravitaillement de la Belgique pendant l'occupation allemande* (Paris: Presses Universitaires de France, 1924).

Heyl, Hedwig, *Das ABC der Küche*, 13th ed. (Berlin: Carl Habel, 1926).

Heyl, Hedwig, *Kleines Kriegskochbuch* (Berlin: Carl Habel, 1914).

Holland, Thomas Erskine, *The Laws of War on Land (Written and Unwritten)* (Oxford: Clarendon Press, 1908).

Hoover, Herbert, *Preface to a Report of the United States Food Administration* (Publisher unknown, April 1920).

Hoover, Herbert, *The Memoirs of Herbert Hoover: The Years of Adventure, 1874–1920* (New York: Macmillan and Co., 1951).

Hoover, Herbert, *An American Epic: Famine in Forty-five Nations: Organization Behind the Front, 1914–1923*, Vol. II (Chicago: Henry Regnery Company, 1960).

Hudson Middleton, Thomas, *Food Production in War* (Oxford: Clarendon Press, 1923).

Ibáñez, Vicente Blasco, *Los cuatro jinetes del Apocalipsis*, 1916.

International Institute of Agriculture, *Annuaire international de statistique agricole 1909 à 1921* (Rome: Institut international d'agriculture, 1922).

Ionesco-Sisesti, G., *L'Agriculture de la Roumanie pendant la guerre* (Paris: Les Presses Universitaires de France, 1929).

Jablońska z Seifertów, Helena, *Dziennik z Oblężonego Przemyśla (1914–1915)*, ed. by Stanisław Stępień (Przemyśl: Południowo-Wschodni Instytut Naukowy w Przemyślu, 2017).

Kafka, Josef, *Úsporná výživa* (Prague: F. Šimáčka, 1915).

Käppeli, Josef and Max Riesen, *Die Lebensmittelversorgung der Schweiz unter dem Einfluss des Weltkrieges von 1914 bis 1922*, Separatdruck aus dem Landwirtschaftlichen Jahrbuch der Schweiz 1925 (Bern: Verbandsdruckerei A. & G., 1925).

Keleti, Karl, *Die Ernährungs-Statistik der Bevölkerung Ungarns auf physiologischer Grundlage* (Budapest: Act. G. Athenaeum, 1887).

Kellogg, Vernon and Alonzo Taylor, *The Food Problem* (New York: Macmillan and Co., 1917).

Kemper, Rudolf, *Stat. Arbeit über Gewicht und Größe der Neugeborenen sowie des Gewichts der Placenta* (dissertation, Johann Wolfgang Goethe-Universität Frankfurt a. M.) (Gelnhausen: F. W. Kalbfleisch, 1940).

Kiendl, Gerold, ed., *Nessis Tagebuch aus dem Ersten Weltkrieg*, www.zenker.se/History/nessi_tagebuch.shtml

Klemperer, Victor, *Curriculum Vitae: Erinnerungen 1881–1918*, ed. by Walter Nowojski (Berlin: Aufbau-Verlag, 1996).

Klopfer, Volkmar, *Die Verbesserung des Brotes durch Aufschliessung der Kleie und Vervollkommung des Backverfahrens* (Dresden: Globus, 1918).

Kocman, Alois, ed., *Souhrnná týdenní hlášení presidia zemské správy politické v Praze o situaci v Čechách 1919–1920* (Prague: Nakladatelství Československé akademie věd, 1959).

Kruijt, Jakob P., *België: boeren en arbeiders sedert den Wereldoorlog* (Groningen-Batavia: Noordhoff, 1932).

Kuczynski, Robert and Nathan Zuntz, *Unsere bisherige und unsere künftige Ernährung im Kriege* (Braunschweig: Friedrich Vieweg & Sohn, 1915).

Kun, Béla, *Ki fizet a Háboruért? [Who pays for the war?]* (Budapest: A Kommunisták Magyarorszagi Partjának Kiadása, 1919).

Landwehr, [Ottokar], *Hunger: Die Erschöpfungsjahre der Mittelmächte 1917–18* (Vienna: Amalthea, 1931).

Larisch, Anna, *150 Kochrezepte für die Kriegszeit* (Brünn: k. k. Hofbuchhandlung Carl Miniker, 1915).

League of the Nations, *Agricultural Production in Continental Europe during the 1914–18 War and the Reconstruction Period* (Geneva: League of the Nations, 1943).

Leoni, Diego and Camillo Zadra, eds, *La città di legno: Profughi trentini in Austria (1915–1918)* (Trento: TEMI, 1981).

Lilar, Suzanne, *Une enfance gantoise* (Paris: Grasset, 1976).

Loewenfeld-Russ, Hans, *Ernährungswirtschaftliche Gegenwartsprobleme in Österreich: Vortrag geh. In d. Vollversammlung d. N.-ö Gewerbevereines am 28. Nov. 1919* (Vienna: Mainz, 1919).

Loewenfeld-Russ, Hans, *Die Regelung der Volksernährung im Kriege* (Vienna: Hölder Pichler Tempsky, 1926).

Loewenfeld-Russ, Hans, *Im Kampf gegen den Hunger: aus den Erinnerungen des Staatssekretärs für Volksernährung, 1918–1920* (Munich: Oldenbourg, 1986).

Loveling, Virginie, *In oorlogsnood. Oorlogsdagboek 1914–1918*, ed. by Bert Van Raemdonck (Ghent: KANTL/UGent, 2005).

Maase, C. and H. Zondek, *Das Hungerödem* (Leipzig: Georg Thieme, 1920).

Mackenzie, Compton, *Greek Memories* (London: Chatto and Windus, 1939).

Majérus, Benoît, and Sven Soupart, Sven, eds, *Journal de guerre de Paul Max. Notes d'un Bruxellois pendant l'occupation (1914–1918)* (Brussels: Archives de la Ville de Bruxelles, 2006).

Martin, Rudolf, *Lehrbuch der Anthropologie in systematischer Darstellung: Mit besonderer Berücksichtigung der anthropologischen Methoden* (Jena: Gustav Fischer, 1914).

Mayow Hastings Lloyd, Edward, *Experiments in State Control at the War Office and the Ministry of Food* (Oxford: Clarendon Press, 1924).

McCarrison, Robert, *Studies in Deficiency Disease* (London: Henry Frowde and Hodder & Stoughton, 1921).

Methods of Compiling Cost of Living Index Numbers: Report Prepared for the Second International Conference of Labour Statisticians (Geneva: International Labour Office, 1925).

Minutes Second Chamber Dutch Estate General, Session 1916–1917 (Den Haag: Departement van landbouw, nijverheid en handel, 1918).

Moulinasse, Julienne, *Enghien: histoire, monuments, souvenirs* (Brussels: Van Buggenhoudt, 1931).

Nédelf, Lieutenant-Colonel, *Les operations en Macédoine. L'épopée de Doïran 1915–1918*, trans. by Commandant Goetzmann (Sofia: Imprimerie Armeyski Voeno-Isdatelski Fond, 1927).

Neumann, Rudolf Otto, *Die im Kriege 1914–1918 verwendeten und zur Verwendung empfohlenen Brote, Brotersatz- und Brotstrechmittel unter Zugrundelegung eigener experimenteller Untersuchungen* (Berlin: Springer, 1920).

Nussbaum, Anna and Else Feldmann, eds, *Das Reisebuch des Wiener Kindes: Eine Sammlung von Briefen, Aufsätzen und Zeichnungen der Wiener Schulkinder im Ausland* (Vienna: Gloriette-Verlag, 1921).

Oberkommando des Heeres, *Der Weltkrieg, Die Kriegführung im Frühjahr 1917, Band 12* (Berlin: Mittler, 1939).

Orga, Irfan, *Portrait of a Turkish Family* (first published 1950; London: Eland, 2011).

Otáhalova, Libuše, ed., *Souhrnná hlašení presidia pražkého místodržitelství o protistátní, protirakouské a protivalené činnosti v Čechách 1915–1918* (Prague: Nakladatelství Československé akademie věd, 1957).

Pánek, Rudolf, *Od černého orla k bílému lvu: 1918–1928* [*From the Black Eagle to the White Lion*] (Praha: Alois Lapáček, 1928).

Pearl, Raymond, *The Nation's Food: A Statistical Study of a Physiological and Social Problem* (Philadelphia & London: W.B. Saunders Company, 1920).

Pinot, Pierre, *Le Contrôle du ravitaillement de la population civile* (Paris: Presses Universitaires de France, 1925).

Pirenne, Henri, *La Belgique et la Guerre Mondiale* (Paris: Presses Universitaires de France, 1928).

Pirenne, Jacques and Maurice Eugène Auguste Vauthier, *La Législation et l'administration allemandes en Belgique* (Paris: Les Presses Universitaires de France, 1925).

Pirquet, Clemens, *Volksgesundheit im Krieg* (New Haven: Yale University Press, 1926).

Pitkin, Walter, ed., *Columbia War Papers* (New York: Division of Intelligence and Publicity of Columbia University, 1917).

Porter, Alexander, *The Diseases of the Madras Famine of 1877–78* (Madras: Government Press, 1889).

Ranieri, Liane, *Emile Francqui ou l'intelligence créatrice: 1863–1935* (Paris: Duculot, 1985).

Reichsarchiv, *Der Weltkrieg. Die Operationen des Jahres 1915*, Band 8 (Berlin: Mittler, 1932).

Reischl, Friedrich ed., *Mitteilungen der American Relief Administration B and I* (Vienna: Unknown Publisher, 1921).

Rem, Georges [pseud. of Georges Rémy], *Le roman de ma maison* (Ans: Printex, 1975).

Ricci, Umberto, *La politica annonaria dell'Italia durante la Guerra* (Bari: Laterza, 1939).

Ritter, P. H. Jr., *De donkere poort. Een boek, behelzende tal van Persoonlijke Herinneringen van vooraanstaande Mannen, Stemmingsbeelden, Indrukken, Beschouwingen, Belangrijke en Onbelangrijke Gebeurtenissen, Verhalen en Anecdoten over Nederland in de jaren 1914–1918* ('s-Gravenhage: Daamen, 1931).

Roberts, Adam and Richard Guelff, *Documents on the Laws of War*, 3rd ed. (Oxford: Oxford University Press, 2000).

Roberts, Kenneth Lewis, *Europe's Morning After* (New York & London: Harper & Bros, 1921).

Roland, J., *Unsere Lebensmittel: Ihr Wesen, Ihre Veränderung und ihre Konservierung* (Dresden and Leipzig: Verlag von Theodor Steinkopf, 1917).

Rowntree, Seebohm Benjamin, *Poverty: A Study of Town Life*, 2nd ed. (London: Macmillan and Co., 1908).

Royal Society, *The Food Supply of the United Kingdom: A Report Drawn up by a Committee of the Royal Society at the Request of the President of the Board of Trade* (London: His Majesty's Stationery Office, 1917).

Rubin, Harry R., *Armistice 1918* (New Haven: Yale University Press, 1944).

Rubmann, Max, *Hunger! Wirkungen moderner Kriegsmethoden* (Berlin: Verlag von Georg Reimer, 1919).

Rubner, Max, *Die Gesetze des Energieverbrauchs bei der Ernährung* (Leipzig and Vienna: Franz Deuticke, 1902).

Rubner, Max, *Deutschlands Volksernährung im Kriege* (Leipzig: Verlag Naturwissenschaften, 1916).

Salter, Arthur, *Allied Shipping Control: An Experiment in International Administration* (Oxford: Clarendon Press, 1921).

Schaeffer, Werner, *Krieg Gegen Frauen und Kinder: Englands Hungerblockade gegen Deutschland 1914–1920* (Stuttgart: Berlin Deutsche Verlag, 1940).

Schneider, Paul, *Die Verpflegung des Feldheeres* (Berlin: Mittler, 1912).

Seymour, Charles, *Geography, Justice, and Politics at the Paris Conference of 1919* (New York: American Geographical Society, 1951).

Skalweit, August, *Die deutsche Kriegsernährungswirtschaft* (Stuttgart: Deutsche Verlagsanstalt, 1927).

Sierakowska, Katarzyna, ed., *Śmierć Wygnanie Głód w dokumentach osobistych: Ziemie polskie w latach Wielkiej Wojny 1914–1918 [Death Exile Hunger in Personal Documents: Polish Lands in the Years of the Great War 1914–1918]* (Warsaw: Institute of History, Polish Academy of Sciences, 2015).

Skinner Platt, Philip, *Přehled veřejného zdravotnictví Velké Prahy* (V Praze: Ministerstvo sociální péče, 1920).

Statisicheskiye Danniye ob otpravlenii I pribitii prodovolsstvennykh gruzov po Russkim Zheleznym dorogam s raspredeleniam po guberniyam I oblastam za 1912, 1913, 1914gg (Petrograd: s.n., 1918).

Statistics of the Military Effort of the British Empire during the Great War 1914–1920 (London: His Majesty's Stationery Office, 1922).

Statististche Amt der Stadt Zürich, *Die Aufwendungen der Stadt Zürich für Armenfürsorge und Sozialpolitik, 1893 bis 1951* (Zurich: s.n., 1953).

Statistischen Reichsamt, *Deutschlands Wirtschaftslage Unter Den Nachwirkungen Des Weltkrieges. Unter Verwendung von Amtlichen Material Zusammengestellt Im Statistischen Reichsamt* (Berlin: Zentralverlag, 1923).

Stavěl, Josef, *Zum Aufbau der Psychodiagnostik* (Prague: n.p., 1936).

Struce, P. B., *Food Supply in Russia during the World War* (New Haven: Yale University Press, 1930).

Surface, Frank M., *The Grain Trade during the World War: Being a History of the Food Administration Grain Corporation and the United States Grain Corporation* (New York: The MacMillan Company, 1928).

Surface Frank M. and Raymond Bland, *American Food in the World War and Reconstruction Period: Operations of the Organizations under Herbert Hoover 1914 to 1924* (Stanford: Stanford University Press, 1931).

Tīmoshenko, Vladīmir Prokopovīch, *Agricultural Russia and the Wheat Problem* (Stanford: Pub. jointly by the Food Research Institute and the Committee on Russian Research of the Hoover War Library, 1932).

Townshend, Charles V. F., *My Campaign in Mesopotamia* (London: Thornton Butterworth, 1920).

Treub, M. W. F., *Herinneringen en Overpeinzingen* (Haarlem: H.D. Tjeenk Willink & Zoon, 1931).

Tytgat, Charles, *Bruxelles sous la botte allemande* (Brussels: Charles Bulens, 1919).
US Department of Agriculture, *Yearbook of the United States Department of Agriculture 1919* (Washington, DC: Government Printing Office, 1920).
Urban, Gisela, *Österreichisches Kriegs-Kochbuch vom k.k. Ministerium des Innern überprüft und genehmigt* (Vienna: Stefan, 1915).
Van Nuffel, Petrus, *De Duitschers in Aalst* (Aalst: Vooruitgang, 1921).
Vanhemelryck, F., J.-P. Peeters, and G. Janssens, eds., *Mensen in Oorlogstijd* (Brussel: UFSAL, 1988).
Vieulzoeuf, Josef, *Memoáry pražského knihaře* [Memoirs of a Prague bookbinder] (Prague: Svaz pomocnictva knihařského, 1929).
Voit, Carl von, *Untersuchung der Kost in einigen öffentlichen Anstalten: Für Aerzte und Verwaltungsbeamte* (Munich: R. Oldenbourg, 1877).
Volkswirtschaftlichen Abteilung des Kriegsernaehrungsamts, ed. *Beiträge Zur Kriegswirtschaft 5* (Berlin: Volkswirtschaftlichen Abteilung des Kriegsernaehrungsamts, 1917).
Vondráček, Vladimír, *Lékař vzpomíná 1895–1920* [*A Physician Remembers*] (Prague: Avicenum, 1978).
Vožický, F. P., *Kronika světové války 1914–1919* (Na Král Vinohradech: F.P. Vožický, 1919–1921).
Whitlock, Brand, *Belgium: A Personal Narrative* (New York: D. Appleton and Company, 1919).
Wiener Kinder in Norwegen 1. Was die norwegischen Pflegeeltern schreiben: eine Sammlung von Briefen mit zahlreichen Illustrationen (Oslo: Norwegischen Hilfsaktion in Kristiania, 1925).
Wittop Koning, Martine, *Hoe voeden wij ons 't goedkoopst en toch goed? Raadgevingen en inlichtingen betreffende de keus, de bereiding en de inmaak van deugdelijk en smakelijk goedkoop voedsel* (Amsterdam: Elsvier, 1914).
Wittop Koning, Martine, *Op rantsoen. Wenken voor de huisvrouw* (Zaltbommel: Nutsuitgeverij, 1917).
Wolterek, Richard, *Hilfsaktion für kranke deutsche Kinder in der Schweiz* (Bern: A. Francke, 1919).
Wullus-Rudiger, J., *Flamenpolitik: suprême Espoir allemande de domination en Belgique* (Brussels: Rossel, 1922).
Yalman, A. E., *Turkey in the World War* (New Haven: Yale University Press, 1930).
Žipek, Alois, ed., *Domov za války: svědectví účastníků* (Praha: Pokrok, 1929).
Zombory, László, *Gyermekvédelem a Háború Alatt* (Budapest: Stephaneum, 1916).

Secondary Sources

A'Hearn, Brian, Niccola Amendola, and Giovanni Vecchi, 'On Historical Household Budgets', *Institute for New Economic Thinking Working Paper*, 45 (2016), 1–43.
Abbenhuis, Maartje M., *The Art of Staying Neutral: The Netherlands in the First World War, 1914–1918* (Amsterdam: Amsterdam University Press, 2006).

Abbenhuis, Maartje M. and Ismee Tames, *Global War, Global Catastrophe: Neutrals, Belligerents and the Transformations of the First World War* (London & New York: Bloomsbury Academic, 2022).

Adams, Matthew, 'Herbert Hoover and the Organization of the American Relief Effort in Poland (1919–1923)', *European Journal of American Studies*, 2 (2009). http://journals.openedition.org/ejas/7627.

Addington, Larry H., *The Blitzkrieg Era and the German General Staff* (New Brunswick: Rutgers University Press, 1971).

Adlgasser, Franz, *American Individualism Abroad: Herbert Hoover, Die American Relief Administration und Österreich, 1919–1923* (Vienna: VWGÖ, 1993).

Aizsilnieks, Arnolds, *Latvijas saimnieciskā vēsture 1914–1945* (Stockholm: Daugava, 1968).

Akarca, Halit Dundar, 'The Imperial Transformation of a Russian-Occupied Ottoman City during the First World War', *War & Society*, 41.1 (2022), 21–35.

Akın, Yiğit, 'War, Women, and the State: The Politics of Sacrifice in the Ottoman Empire during the First World War', *Journal of Women's History*, 26.3 (2014), 12–35.

Akın, Yiğit, *When the War Came Home: The Ottomans' Great War and the Devastation of an Empire* (Stanford, CA: Stanford University Press, 2018).

Alary, Eric, *La Grande Guerre des civils: 1914–1919* (Paris: Perrin, 2013).

Albert, Anaïs, *La Vie à crédit. La consommation des classes populaires à Paris (années 1880–1920)* (Paris: Éditions de la Sorbonne, 2021).

Alfani, Guido and Mario Rizzo, 'Politiche annonarie, provvedimenti demografici e capitale umano nelle città assediate dell'Europa moderna', in *Nella morsa della guerra. Assedi, occupazioni militari e saccheggi in età preindustriale*, ed. by G. Alfani and M. Rizzo (Milan: Franco Angeli, 2013), pp. 15–46.

Alfani, Guido, and Cormac Ó Gráda, ed., *Famine in European History* (Cambridge: Cambridge University Press, 2017).

Alvi, Maddalena, 'The Land of Cockaigne: The German Art Market and the First World War', *German History*, 38.4 (2020), 594–615.

Allen, Keith, 'Sharing Scarcity: Bread Rationing and the First World War in Berlin, 1914–1923', *Journal of Social History*, 32.2 (Winter 1998), 371–93.

Allen, W. E. D., and Paul Muratoff, *Caucasian Battlefields: A History of the Wars on the Turco-Caucasian Border 1828–1921* (Cambridge: Cambridge University Press, 1953).

Almond, Douglas, and Janet Currie, 'Killing Me Softly: The Fetal Origins Hypothesis', *Journal of Economic Perspectives*, 25 (2011), 153–72.

al-Qattan, Najwa, 'When Mothers Ate Their Children: Wartime Memory and the Language of Food in Syria and Lebanon', *International Journal of Middle East Studies*, 46 (2014), 719–36.

Amara, Michaël, and Hubert Roland, eds, *Gouverner en Belgique occupée: Oskar von der Lancken-Wakenitz – rapports d'activité 1915–1918* (Brussels: Peter Lang, 2004).

Amerykańska Przyjaźń. *Herbert Hoover a Polska. Wystawa w Zamku Królewskim w Warszawie 12 listopada 2004–16 stycznia 2005. American Friendship. Herbert Hoover and Poland. Exhibition in the Royal Castle in Warsaw November 12, 2004–Jaunuary 16, 2005* (Warsaw: "Agraf," 2004).

Anderson, Kyle J., *The Egyptian Labor Corps: Race, Space, and Place in the First World War – The Egyptian Labor Corps* (Austin: University of Texas Press, 2022).

Arnold, David, 'The "Discovery" of Malnutrition and Diet in Colonial India', *Indian Economic and Social History Review*, 31.1 (1994), 1–26.

Arnold, David, 'British India and the "Beriberi Problem," 1798–1942', *Medical History*, 54 (2010), 295–312.

Balderston, Theo, 'Industrial Mobilization and War Economies', in *A Companion to World War I*, ed. by John Horne (London: Wiley-Blackwell, 2010), pp. 217–33.

Balkelis, Tomas, *War, Revolution, and Nation-Making in Lithuania, 1914–1923* (Oxford: Oxford University Press, 2018).

Banerji, Arup, *Merchants and Markets in Revolutionary Russia, 1917–30* (London: Palgrave Macmillan, 1997).

Barker, David J. P., *Mothers, Babies, and Health in Later Life*, 2nd ed. (Edinburgh: Churchill Livingstone, 1998).

Barnett, L. Margaret, *British Food Policy during the First World War* (Boston: Allen & Unwin, 1985).

Barthel, Stephan, 'Resilience', in *A Companion to Urban Anthropology*, ed. by Donald M. Nonini (Oxford: Wiley Blackwell, 2014), pp. 428–46.

Bas, Mehmet Fatih, 'War Losses (Ottoman Empire/Middle East) 1914–1918', in *1914–1918-online. International Encyclopedia of the First World War*, ed. by U. Daniel, Peter Gatrell, Oliver Janz, et al. (Berlin: Freie Universität Berlin, 2015).

Baudis, Dieter, 'Vom Schweinemord zum Kohlrübenwinter: Streiflichter zur Entwicklung der Lebensverhältnisse in Berlin im ersten Weltkrieg (August 1914 bis Frühjahr 1917)', *Jahrbuch für Wirtschaftsgeschichte*, (1986), 129–52.

Bauerkämper, Arnd, and Elise Julien, eds, *Durchhalten!: Krieg und Gesellschaft im Vergleich 1914–1918* (Göttingen: Vandenhoeck & Ruprecht, 2010).

Baughan, Emily, *Saving the Children: Humanitarianism, Internationalism, and Empire* (Berkeley: University of California Press, 2021).

Bay, Alexander, *Beriberi in Modern Japan: The Making of a National Disease* (Rochester: University of Rochester Press, 2012).

Becker, G., *A Treatise on the Family* (Cambridge, MA: Harvard University Press, 1991).

Becker, Jean-Jacques, *1914, comment les Francais sont entrés dans la guerre. Contribution à l'étude de l'opinion publique printemps-été 1914* (Paris: Presses de la Fondation nationale des sciences politiques, 1977).

Becker, Jean-Jacques, 'Union Sacrée et idéologie bourgeoise', *Revue Historique*, 264.1 (1980), 65–74.

Becker, Peter, and Natasha Wheatley, eds, *Remaking Central Europe: The League of Nations and the Former Habsburg Lands* (Oxford: Oxford University Press, 2021).

Bellwald-Roten, Andreas, and Marco Jorio, 'Wirtschaftliche Landesversorgung', *Historisches Lexikon Schweiz*, online ed., 2015 www.hls-dhs-dss.ch/textes/d/D42887.php [accessed 26 April 2023].

Belzer, Allison Scardino, *Women and the Great War: Feminity under Fire in Italy* (New York: Palgrave Macmillan, 2010).

Ben-Bassat, Y., 'Bedouin Petitions from Late Ottoman Palestine: Evaluating the Effects of Sedentarization', *Journal of the Economic and Social History of the Orient*, 58.1 (2015), 135–62.

Ben-Bassat, Y., 'The Ottoman Institution of Petitioning When the Sultan no Longer Reigned: A View from Post-1908 Ottoman Palestine', *New Perspectives on Turkey*, 56 (2017), 87–103.

Bendtsen, Bjarne Søndergar, 'Neutral Merchant Seamen at War: The Experience of Scandinavian Seamen during the First World War', in *Scandinavia in the First World War: Studies in the War Experience in the Northern Neutrals*, ed. by Claes Ahlund (Lund: Nordic University Press, 2012), 327–54.

Benschop, Bob, *Kanongebulder in de verte: Hellevoetsluis en omgeving tijdens de mobilisatie 1914–1918* (Zaltbommel: Aprilis, 2008).

Berend, Ivan T., *An Economic History of Twentieth-Century Europe: Economic Regimes from Laissez-Faire to Globalization* (Cambridge: Cambridge University Press, 2016).

Berglund, R. Bruce, '"We Stand on the Threshold of a New Age": Alice Masarykova, the Czechoslovak Red Cross, and the Building of a New Europe', in *Aftermaths of War: Women's Movements and Female Activists, 1918–1923*, ed. by Matthew Stibbe and Ingrid Sharp (Leiden: Brill, 2011), pp. 355–74.

Bernardo y Garcia, Luis Angel, *Le Ventre des Belges: Une histoire alimentaire des temps d'occupation et de sortie de guerre* (Bruxelles: Algemeen Rijksarchief, 2017).

Bertrand, François, *La presse francophone de tranchée au front belge 1914–1918* (Brussels: Musée royal de l'armée, 1971).

Bianchi, Bruna, '"That Massacre of the Innocents Has Haunted Us for Years": Women Witnesses of Hunger in Central Europe', in *Living War, Thinking Peace (1914–1924): Women's Experiences, Feminist Thought, and International Relations*, ed. by Bruna Bianchi and Geraldine Ludbrook (Newcastle: Cambridge Scholars, 2016), pp. 64–92.

Bignon, Vincent, *Black Markets and Grey Networks for Illegal Exchanges in post WW2 Germany* (Geneva: Graduate Institute for International and Development Studies, 2007).

Blobaum, Robert, *A Minor Apocalypse: Warsaw During the First World War* (Ithaca: Cornell University Press, 2017).

Boch, Rudolf, *Staat und Wirtschaft im 19: Jahrhundert* (Munich: Oldenbourg, 2004).

Bogin, Barry, *Patterns of Human Growth*, 2nd ed. (Cambridge: Cambridge University Press, 1999).

Böhler, Jochen, *Civil War in Central Europe: The Reconstruction of Poland, 1918–1921* (Oxford: Oxford University Press, 2018).

Bollet, Ajay, 'Politics and Pellagra: The Epidemic of Pellagra in the U.S. in the Early Twentieth Century', *Yale Journal of Biology and Medicine*, 65.3 (2006), 211–21.

Borrero, Mauricio, *Hungry Moscow: Scarcity and Urban Society in the Russian Civil War, 1917–1921* (New York: Peter Lang, 2006).

Bouloc, François, *Les profiteurs de guerre, 1914–1918* (Bruxelles: Complexe, 2008).

Brand, Tylor, *Famine Worlds: Life at the Edge of Suffering in Lebanon's Great War* (Stanford: Stanford University Press, 2023).

Breen, Rodney, 'Saving Enemy Children: Save the Children's Russian Relief Operation, 1921–23', *Disasters: The Journal of Disaster Studies and Management*, 18.3 (September 1994), 221–37.

Briel-van Ingen, T. van den, 'Beknopte geschiedenis van de voedingswetenschap in Nederland', *Voeding*, 44 (1983), 160–70.

Broadberry, Stephan and Mark Harrison, eds., *The Economics of World War I* (Cambridge: Cambridge University Press, 2005).

Brock, Joachim, ed., *Biologische Daten für den Kinderarzt: Gründzüge einer Biologie des Kindesalters*, 2nd ed. (Berlin: Springer Verlag, 1954).

Bronson, D., M. Healy, and M. Jemal, 'Social Conflict and Control, Protest and Repression (Austria-Hungary)', in *1914–1918-online. International Encyclopedia of the First World War*, ed. by U. Daniel, Peter Gatrell, Oliver Janz, et al. (Berlin: Freie Universität Berlin, 2015).

Brudek, Paweł, Jan Molenda, and Jerzy Z. Pająk, 'The Great War in Polish Correspondence Intercepted by Austro-Hungarian Censorship: Materials of Polish Censorship Groups from 1914–1918', in *Metamorfozy Społeczne 21: The First World War on Polish Lands; Expectations, Experiences, Consequences*, ed. by Włodzimierz Mędrzecki (Warsaw: Tadeusz Manteuffel Institute of History, Polish Academy of Sciences, 2018), pp. 199–224.

Bründel, Steffen, *Volksgemeinschaft oder Volksstaat. Die 'Ideen von 1914' und die Neuordnung Deutschlands im Ersten Weltkrieg* (Berlin: Akademie Verlag, 2003).

Bryder, Linda, 'The First World War: Healthy or Hungry?', *History Workshop Journal*, 24 (1987), 141–57.

Burk, Kathleen, ed., *War and the State: The Transformation of British Government, 1914–1919* (London and New York: Routledge, 2014).

Burnett, John, and Derek Oddy, eds, *The Origins and Development of Food Policies in Europe* (London: Leicester University Press, 1994).

Cabanes, Bruno, *The Great War and the Origins of Humanitarianism, 1918–1924* (Cambridge: Cambridge University Press, 2014).

Capelli-Vegni, Adele, 'Contributo di osservazioni intorno allo sviluppo ponderale del neonato in rapporto alla professione della madre e intorno a variazioni di peso di neonati partoriti tra il 1911 e il 1931 nella clinica "L. Mangiagalli" die Milano', *Annali di ostetricia e ginecologia*, (1932), 1457–98.

Carpenter, Kenneth J., *The History of Scurvy & Vitamin C* (Cambridge: Cambridge University Press, 1986).

Carpenter, Kenneth J., 'Harriet Chick and the Problem of Rickets', *Journal of Nutrition*, 138.5 (2008), 827–32.

Carpenter, Kenneth J., 'The Discovery of Thiamin', *Annals of Nutrition and Metabolism*, 61 (2012), 219–23.

Chambers, Frank Pentland, *The War behind the War 1914–1918: A History of the Political and Civilian Fronts* (London: Faber & Faber, 1939).

Charle, Christophe, *La Crise des sociétés impériales: Allemagne, France, Grande-Bretagne (1900–1940). Essai d'histoire sociale comparée* (Paris: Seuil, 2001).

Chickering, Roger, *Imperial Germany and the Great War, 1914–1918*, 2nd ed. (Cambridge: Cambridge University Press, 2004).

Chickering, Roger, *The Great War and Urban Life in Germany: Freiburg, 1914–1918* (New York: Cambridge University Press, 2007).

Chickering, Roger, 'Imperial Germany's Peculiar War, 1914–1918', *Journal of Modern History*, 88.8 (2016), 856–94.

Clavin, Patricia, 'The Austrian Hunger Crisis and the Genesis of International Organization after the First World War', *International Affairs*, 90.2 (2014), 265–78.

Clements, Kendrick, *The Life of Herbert Hoover: Imperfect Visionary 1918–1928* (New York: Palgrave Macmillan, 2010).

Clingan, Edmunc C., 'More Construction, More Crisis: The Housing Problem of Weimar Germany', *Journal of Urban History*, 26.5 (2000), 630–44.

Cobb, Stephen, *Preparing for Blockade 1885–1914: Naval Contingency for Economic Warfare* (London: Routledge, 2013).

Cole, Tim J., 'Secular Trends in Growth', *Proceedings of the Nutrition Society*, 59 (2000), 317–24.

Cole, Tim J., 'The Secular Trend in Human Physical Growth: A Biological View', *Economics and Human Biology*, 1 (2003), 161–68.

Cole, Tim J., 'The Development of Growth References and Growth Charts', *Annals of Human Biology*, 39 (2012), 382–94.

Collingham, Lizzie, *The Taste of War: World War Two and the Battle for Food* (New York: Penguin Books, 2011).

Compagnon, Olivier, and Pierre Purseigle, 'Geographies of Mobilization and Territories of Belligerence during the First World War', *Annales: Histoire, Sciences Sociales*, 71.1 (2016), 37–60.

Connolly, James, *The Experience of Occupation in the Nord 1914–1918: Living with the Enemy in First World War France* (Manchester: Manchester University Press, 2018).

Cooter, Roger, 'Medicine and the Goodness of War', *Canadian Bulletin of Medical History*, 12 (1990), 147–59.

Cooter, Roger, *Surgery and Society in Peace and War: Orthopaedics and the Organization of Modern Medicine, 1880–1948* (London: Macmillan and Co., 1993).

Cope, Zachary, 'The Medical Balance Sheet of War', in *Some Famous General Practitioners and Other Medical Historical Essays* (London: Pitman, 1961), pp. 169–83.

Corni, Gustavo, 'Occupation during the War', in *1914–1918-online. International Encyclopedia of the First World War*, ed. by U. Daniel, Peter Gatrell, Oliver Janz, et al. (Berlin: Freie Universität Berlin, 2015).

Corni, Gustavo and Francesco Frizzera, 'Die Diskussion um die "Zwangswirtschaft" während des Ersten Weltkrieges und in der Nachkriegszeit', *Journal for Agricultural History and Sociology – Zeitschrift für Agrargeschichte und Agrarsoziologie*, 66.1 (2018), 23–25.

Corni, Gustavo and Francesco Frizzera, 'Erster Teil: Vom Ersten Weltkrieg bis zum Ende der Weimarer Republik', in *Agrarpolitik im 20. Jahrhundert: Das Bundesministerium für Ernährung und Landwirtschaft und seine Vorgänger*, ed. by H. Möller and others, (Berlin and Boston: De Gruyter Oldenbourg, 2020), pp. 13–19.

Cottier, Maurice, *Liberalismus oder Staatsintervention: die Geschichte der Versorgungspolitik im Schweizer Bundesstaat* (Zürich: Verlag Neue Zürcher Zeitung, 2014).

Cox, Mary Elisabeth, 'Hunger Games: Or How the Allied Blockade in the First World War Deprived German Children of Nutrition, and Allied Food Aid Subsequently Saved Them', *Economic History Review*, 68.2 (2015), 600–31.

Cox, Mary Elisabeth, 'Anthropometrics: The Application of Anthropometrics to Identify and Assess War Crimes', in *War Crimes Trials and Investigations: A Multi-disciplinary Introduction*, ed. by Jonathan Waterlow and Jacques Schumacher (Cham, Switzerland: Palgrave Macmillan, 2018), pp. 81–109.

Cox, Mary Elisabeth, 'L'indice Pelidisi (1920–1921): Une réévaluation contemporaine d'un indicateur nutritif oublié', in *Les Fronts intérieurs européens: l'arrière en guerre (1914–1920)*, ed. by Laurent Dornel and Stéphane Le Bras (Rennes: Presses universitaires de Rennes, 2018), pp. 179–98.

Cox, Mary Elisabeth, *Hunger in War and Peace: Women & Children in Germany, 1914–1924* (London and New York: Oxford University Press, 2019).

Cox, Mary Elisabeth, 'The Blockade in the First World War' in *From Harfleur to Hamburg. Five Centuries of British and English Violence in Europe*, Brendan Simms and David Trim, eds (London: Hurst Publishers, 2024).

Crampton, R. J., 'The Balkans 1914–1918', in *The Oxford Illustrated History of the First World War*, ed. by Hew Strachan (Oxford: Oxford University Press, 1998), 66–79.

Cretu, Doina Anca, 'Humanitarian Aid in the "Bulwark Against Bolshevism": The American Relief Administration and the Quest for Sovereignty in Post-World War I Romania', *Journal of Romanian Studies*, 1.2 (2019), 65–88.

Cretu, Doina Anca, 'Child Assistance and the Making of Modern Refugee Camps in Austria-Hungary during the First World War', *Central European History*, 55 (2022), 510–27.

Cretu, Doina Anca, *Foreign Aid and State Building in Interwar Romania: In Quest of an Ideal* (Stanford: Stanford University Press, 2024).

Creveld, Martin van, *Supplying War: Logistics from Wallenstein to Patton* (Cambridge: Cambridge University Press, 1977).

Cronier, Emmanuelle, 'Food and Nutrition', in *1914–1918-online. International Encyclopedia of the First World War*, ed. by Ute Daniel, Peter Gatrell, Oliver Janz, et al. (Berlin: Freie Universität Berlin, 2021).

Crowder, Michael, 'The First World War and its Consequences', in *General History of Africa vol. VII: Africa under Colonial Domination, 1880–1935*, ed. by A. Adu Boahen (Berkeley: University of California Press, 1985), pp. 132–142.

Curran, Declan, Lubomy Luciuk, and Andrew G. Newby, eds., *Famines in European Economic History: The Last Great European Famines Reconsidered* (London and New York: Routledge, 2015).

Daly, Selena, Martina Salvante, and Vanda Wilcox, eds., *Landscapes of the First World War* (Cham: Palgrave Macmillan, 2018).

Daniel, Ute, *Arbeiterfrauen in der Kriegsgesellschaft: Beruf, Familie und Politik im Ersten Weltkrieg* (Göttingen: Vandenhoeck & Ruprecht, 1989).

Daniel, Ute, *The War from Within: German Women in the First World War* (Oxford: Berg, 1997).

Davin, Anna, 'Imperialism and Motherhood', *History Workshop*, 5 (1978), 9–65.

Davis, Belinda J., *Home Fires Burning: Food, Politics, and Everyday Life in World War I Berlin* (Chapel Hill: University of North Carolina Press, 2000).

Davis, Lance E., and Stanley E. Engerman, *Naval Blockades in Peace and War: An Economic History since 1750* (Cambridge: Cambridge University Press, 2006).

Davis, Mike, *Late Victorian Holocausts: El Niño Famines and the Making of the Third World* (London: Verso, 2001).

Davis, Thomas and Elizabeth Spilman, 'Proto-Economic Nationalism in the Early Nineteenth Century', in *History and Culture of Economic Nationalism in East-Central Europe*, ed. by Helga Schulz and Eduard Kubo (Berlin: Berliner Wissenschafts-Verlag, 2006), pp. 89–108.

De Zwarte, Ingrid, *The Hunger Winter: Fighting Famine in the Occupied Netherlands, 1944–1945* (Cambridge: Cambridge University Press, 2020).

Deák, István, 'The Habsburg Empire', in *After Empire: Multiethnic Societies and Nation-Building – The Soviet Union and the Russian, Ottoman, and Habsburg Empires*, ed. by Karen Barkey and Mark von Hagen (Boulder: West View Press, 1997), pp. 129–41.

Degen, Bernard, 'Rationierung', *Historisches Lexicon der Schweiz*, online ed., 2010, www.hls-dhs-dss.ch/textes/d/D13782.php.

Demm, Eberhard, 'Deutschlands Kinder im Ersten Weltkrieg: Zwischen Propaganda und Sozialfürsorge', *Militärgeschichtliche Zeitschrift*, 60 (2001), 51–98.

Dentoni, Maria Concetta, *Annona e consenso in Italia, 1914–1919* (Milan: Franco Angeli, 1995).

Desimini, Jill, 'Cartographic Grounds: The Temporal Cases', in *Mapping Landscapes in Transformation: Multidisciplinary Methods for Historical Analysis*, ed. by Thomas Coomans, Bieke Cattoor and Krista De Jong (Leuven: Leuven University Press, 2019), pp. 17–26.

Dewey, P. E., *British Agriculture in the First World War* (London: Routledge, 1989).

Dix, P. E., *Wirtschaftskrieg und Kriegswirtschaft. Zur Geschichte des deutschen Zusammenbruchs* (Berlin: Mittler, 1920).

Dogelis, Povilas, *Mano gyvenimo prisiminimai* (Kaunas: "Šešupės" spaustuvė Marijampolėje, 1936).

Donson, Andrew, 'Children and Youth', in *1914–1918-online. International Encyclopedia of the First World War*, ed. by U. Daniel, Peter Gatrell, Oliver Janz, et al. (Berlin: Freie Universität Berlin, 2014).

Dornik, Wolfram, 'Verwaltung des Mangels: die österreichisch-(ungarisch) en Kriegszentralen 1914–1918', in *Wirtschaft. Macht. Geschichte: Brüche und Kontinuitäten im 20. Jahrhundert*, ed. by Gerald Schöpfer and Barbara Stelzl-Marx (Graz: Leykam, 2012), pp. 261–74.

Dornik, Wolfram, and Peter Lieb, 'Die Wirtschaftliche Ausnutzung', in *Die Ukraine Zwischen Selbstbestimmung Und Fremdherrschaft 1917–1922*, ed. by Wolfram Dornik (Graz: Leykam, 2011), pp. 281–323.

Dowdall, Alex, 'Entre improvisation et intervention: le rôle des autorités locales dans le ravitaillement en nourriture des villes du front français', in *Les mises en guerre de l'État: 1914–1918 en perspective*, ed. by Sylvain Berstchy and Philippe Salson (Lyon: ENS Editions, 2018), pp. 226–89.

Dowdall, Alex, *Communities under Fire: Urban Life at the Western Front, 1914–1918* (Oxford: Oxford University Press, 2020).

Downes, Alexander B., *Targeting Civilians in War* (Ithaca: Cornell University Press, 2008).

Drozdowska, Agnieszka, *Kobiety w czasie Pierwszej wojny światowej* (Białystok: Książnica Podlaska im. Łukasza Górnickiego, 2018).

Druelle, Clotilde, *Feeding Occupied France during World War I: Herbert Hoover and the Blockade* (London: Palgrave Macmillan, 2019).

Duffett, Rachel, *The Stomach for Fighting: Food and the Soldiers of the Great War* (Manchester: Manchester University Press, 2012).

Dunlop, Catherine Tatiana, *Cartophilia: Maps and the Search for Identity in the French-German Borderland* (Chicago: The University of Chicago Press, 2015).

Duroselle, Jean-Baptiste, *La France et les Français 1914–1920* (Paris: Perrin, 1972).

Dwork, Deborah, *War Is Good for Babies and Other Young Children: A History of the Infant and Child Welfare Movement in England 1898–1918* (London and New York: Tavistock, 1987).

Eckart, Wolfgang U. and Rainer Godel, eds, *'Krieg der Gelehrten' und die Welt der Akademien 1914–1924* (Stuttgart: Wissenschaftliche Verlagsgesellschaft, 2016).

Eggens, Albert, *Van daad tot vonnis: Door Drenten gepleegde criminaliteit voor en tijdens de Eerste Wereldoorlog* (Assen: Van Gorcum, 2005).

Eldem, Vedat, *Harp ve Mütareke Yıllarında Osmanlı İmparatorluğu'nun Ekonomisi* (Ankara: Türk Tarih Kurumu Basımevi, 1994).

Eley, G., 'War and the Twentieth Century', *Daedalus*, 124.2 (1995), 155–75.

Elvbakken, Kari Tove, 'Physiology and Hygiene in the History of Nutrition Science: The Norwegian Case 1870–1970', *Social History of Medicine*, 33.1 (2020), 1–21.

Engel, B. A., 'Not by Bread Alone: Subsistence Riots in Russia during World War I', *Journal of Modern History*, 69.4 (1997), 696–721.

Ermacora, Matteo, 'Rural Society', in *1914–1918-online. International Encyclopedia of the First World War*, ed. by U. Daniel, Peter Gatrell, Oliver Janz, et al. (Berlin: Freie Universität Berlin, 2015).

Es, Bart van, *The Cut Out Girl: A Story of War and Family, Lost and Found* (London: Penguin Books, 2018).

Farrar, Marjorie Millbank, *Conflict and Compromise: The Strategy, Politics and Diplomacy of the French Blockade, 1914–1918* (The Hague: Martinus Nijhoff, 1974).

Fawaz, Leila Tarazi, *A Land of Aching Hearts: The Middle East in the Great War* (Cambridge, MA: Harvard University Press, 2014).

Federico, Giovanni, 'The Growth of World Agricultural Production 1800–1938', *Research in Economic History*, 22 (2004), 125–81.

Federico, Giovanni, *Feeding the World: An Economic History of Agriculture 1800–2000* (Princeton and Oxford: Princeton University Press, 2009).

Federico, Giovanni and Antonio Tena-Junguito, 'World Trade, 1800–1938: A New Data-Set', European Historical Economics Society Working Papers 0093 (2016). https://doi.org/10.13140/RG.2.1.4013.1602.

Fehrenbach, Heide and Davide Rodogno, eds., *Humanitarian Photography: A History* (Cambridge: Cambridge University Press, 2015).

Feinstein, Charles Hilliard, Peter Temin, and Gianni Toniolo, *The World Economy between the World Wars* (Oxford: Oxford University Press, 2008).

Feldman, Gerald D., *Army, Industry and Labor in Germany 1914–1918* (Princeton: Princeton University Press, 1966).
Feldman, Gerald D., *The Great Disorder: Politics, Economics, and Society in the German Inflation, 1914–1924* (New York: Oxford University Press, 1993).
Figes, Orlando, *A People's Tragedy: The Russian Revolution* (London: Bodley Head, 2017).
Findlay, Ronald and Kevin H. O'Rourke. *Power and Plenty: Trade, War, and the World Economy in the Second Millennium* (Princeton and Oxford: Princeton University Press, 2007).
Fischer-Kattner, Anke, and Jamel Ostwald, eds, *The World of the Siege: Representations of Early-Modern Positional Warfare* (Leiden: Brill, 2019).
Fleissig, Adrian R., and Gerald A. Whitney, 'Belgium Relief Fund, Post War food Shortages and the "True" Cost of Living', *Explorations in Economic History*, 58 (2015), 93–106. https://doi.org/10.1016/j.eeh.2015.05.001.
Flemming, Jans, *Landwirtschaftliche Interessen Und Demokratie. Ländliche Gesellschaft, Agrarverbände Und Staat 1890–1925* (Bonn: Verlag Neue Gesellschaft, 1978).
Floris, Joël, Kaspar Staub, and Ulrich Woitek, 'The Benefits of Intervention: Birth Weights in Basle 1912–1920', *University of Zurich Department of Economics Working Paper Series*, 236 (2016), 1–36.
Floris, Joël, Marius Kuster, and Ulrich Woitek, 'Armutsgrenzen in der Stadt Zürich während des Ersten Weltkriegs', *traverse: Zeitschrift für Geschichte*, 3 (2017), 97–112.
Floud, Roderick, Robert W. Fogel, Bernard Harris et al., *The Changing Body: Health, Nutrition, and Human Development in the Western World since 1700* (Cambridge: Cambridge University Press, 2012).
Forsdahl, A., 'Are Poor Living Conditions in Childhood and Adolescence an Important Risk Factor for Arteriosclerotic Disease?', *British Journal of Preventive and Social Medicine*, 31 (1977), 91–95.
Förster, Stig, 'Der deutsche Generalstab und die Illusion des kurzen Krieges, 1871–1914. Metakritik eines Mythos', *Militärgeschichtliche Mitteilungen*, 54 (1995), 61–95.
Foster, Zachary J., 'The 1915 Locust Attack in Syria and Palestine and Its Role in the Famine during the First World War', *Middle Eastern Studies*, 51.3 (2015), 370–94.
Francisco, Jason, 'War Photography in the Twentieth Century: A Short Critical History', JasonFrancisco.net, 2005, http://jasonfrancisco.net/war-photography.
François, Marie-Thérèse, 'La production et la consommation du sucre dans le monde', *Revue de botanique appliquée et d'agriculture coloniale*, 17.191 (1937), 496–513.
Frémeaux, Jacques, *Les Colonies dans la Grande Guerre. Combats et Épreuves des Peuples d'Outre-Mer* (Saint-Cloud: 14–18 éd., 2006).
Frey, Marc, 'Deutsche Finanzinteressen an den Vereinigten Staaten und den Niederlanden im Ersten Weltkrieg', *Militärgeschichtliche Mitteilungen*, 53.2 (1994), 327–53.
Frey, Marc, 'Trade, Ships, and the Neutrality of the Netherlands in the First World War', *International History Review*, 19 (1997), 542–46.

Frey, Marc, *Der Erste Weltkrieg und die Niederlande: Ein neutrales Land im politischen und wirtschaftlichen Kalkül der Kriegsgegner* (Berlin: Akademie, 1998).

Frey, Marc, 'Bullying the Neutrals: The Case of the Netherlands', in *Great War, Total War: Combat and Mobilisation on the Western Front, 1914–1918*, ed. by Stig Förster and Roger Chickering (Cambridge and New York: Cambridge University Press, 2000), pp. 227–46.

Friedrichs, Jörg, 'Escapology, or How to Escape Malthusian Traps', in *Scarcity in the Modern World: History, Politics, Society and Sustainability, 1800–2075*, ed. by Fredrik Albritton Jonsso, John Brewer, Neil Fromer et al. (London: Bloomsbury Academic, 2019), pp. 115–31.

Fritz, Judith, 'Vom Strecken, Wässern und Dünnen', https://ww1.habsburger.net/de/kapitel/vom-strecken-waessern-und-duennen.

Fulwider, C. R., 'Revolutions', in *1914–1918-online. International Encyclopedia of the First World War*, ed. by U. Daniel, Peter Gatrell, Oliver Janz, et al. (Berlin: Freie Universität Berlin, 2014).

Gachelin, Gabriel, and Annick Opinel, 'Malaria Epidemics in Europe after the First World War: The Early Stages of an International Approach to the Control of the Disease', *Historia Ciencias Saude Manguinhos*, 18.2 (2011), 431–69.

Gardner, Nikolas, 'Sepoys and the Siege of Kut-al-Amara, December 1915–April 1916', *War in History*, 14 (2004), 307–26.

Gatrell, Peter, *Government, Industry and Rearmament in Russia, 1900–1914: The Last Argument of Tsarism* (Cambridge: Cambridge University Press, 1994).

Gatrell, Peter, *A Whole Empire Walking: Refugees in Russia during World War I* (Bloomington: Indiana University Press, 1999).

Gatrell, Peter, *Russia's First World War: A Social and Economic History* (London: Pearson, 2005).

Gatrell, Peter, 'World Wars and Population Displacement in Europe in the Twentieth Century', *Contemporary European History*, 16.4 (2007), 415–26.

Gatrell, Peter, 'Organization of War Economies (Russian Empire)' in *1914–1918-online. International Encyclopedia of the First World War*, ed. by U. Daniel, Peter Gatrell, Oliver Janz, et al. (Berlin: Freie Universität Berlin, 2014).

Gatrell, Peter and Lyubov Zhvanko, eds., *Europe on the Move: The Great War and Its Refugees* (Manchester: Manchester University Press, 2017).

Gazeley, Ian, and Andrew Newell, 'The First World War and Working-Class Food Consumption in Britain', *European Review of Economic History*, 17 (2013), 71–94.

Gerhard, Gesine, *Nazi Hunger Politics: A History of Food in the Third Reich – Rowman & Littlefield Studies in Food and Gastronomy* (London: Rowman & Littlefield Publishers, 2015).

Gerlach, Christian, 'Hunger in der Geschichte des 20. Jahrhunderts', *Aus Politik und Zeitgeschichte*, 65.49 (2015), 20–26.

German Nutrition Society, 'Dietary reference values in Germany (D), Austria (A) and Switzerland (CH), DACH-Reference Values', 25 April 2023, www.dge.de/wissenschaft/referenzwerte/.

Gerwarth, Robert, *The Vanquished: Why the First World War Failed to End, 1917–1923* (London: Allen Lane, 2016).

Gerwarth, Robert and Erez Manela, eds., *Empires at War: 1911–1923* (Oxford: Oxford University Press, 2014).

Gerwarth, Robert and John Horne, eds, *War in Peace: Paramilitary Violence in Europe after the Great War* (Oxford: Oxford University Press, 2012).

Geyer, Martin and Verkehrte Welt, *Revolution, Inflation und Moderne, München 1914–1924* (Göttingen: Vandenhoeck & Ruprecht, 1998).

Ginnaio, Monica, 'La pellagra en Italie à la fin du XIXe siècle: les effets d'une maladie de carence', *Population*, 66 (2011), 671–98.

Główny Urząd Statystyczny, *Historia Polski w Liczbach: Ludność terytorium* (Warsaw: Zakl. Wyd. Statyst., 1994).

Goeschel, Christian, *Suicide in Nazi Germany* (Oxford: Oxford University Press, 2009).

Goldman, Wendy Z. and Donald Filtzer, eds, *Hunger and War: Food Provisioning in the Soviet Union during World War II* (Bloomington: Indiana University Press, 2015).

Golubinov, Iaroslav, 'Food and Nutrition (Russian Empire)', in *1914–1918-online. International Encyclopedia of the First World War*, ed. by U. Daniel, Peter Gatrell, Oliver Janz, et al. (Berlin: Freie Universität Berlin, 2015).

Gorin, Valérie, '"Millions of children in deadly peril": l'utilisation des photographies d'enfants affamés par le Save the Children Fund pendant l'entre-deux-guerres', in *Perceptions et mises en scène médiatiques de la famine au XXe siècle, (Itinera)*, ed. by Angela Müller and Felix Rauh (Basel: Schwabe, 2014), pp. 95–112.

Graff, Michael, A. G. Kenwood, and A. L. Lougheed, *Growth of the International Economy, 1820–2015* (London: Routledge, 2014).

Granick, Jaclyn, 'Waging Relief: The Politics and Logistics of American Jewish War Relief in Europe and the Near East (1914–1918)', *First World War Studies*, 5.1 (2014), 55–68.

Granick, Jaclyn, *International Jewish Humanitarianism in the Age of the Great War* (Cambridge: Cambridge University Press, 2021).

Gratien, C., 'The Sick Mandate of Europe: Local and Global Humanitarianism in French Cilicia, 1918–1922', *Journal of the Ottoman and Turkish Studies Association*, 3.1 (2016), 165–90.

Grayzel, Susan R., and Tammy M. Proctor, eds, *Gender and the Great War* (Oxford: Oxford University Press, 2017).

Gregory, Adrian, *The Last Great War: British Society and the First World War* (Cambridge: Cambridge University Press, 2008).

Griffante, Andrea, 'Food and Nutrition (East Central Europe)', in *1914–1918-online. International Encyclopedia of the First World War*, ed. by U. Daniel, Peter Gatrell, Oliver Janz, et al. (Berlin: Freie Universität Berlin, 2015).

Griffante, Andrea, 'Fighting over Children. Relief, Rehabilitation and Childhood in Lithuania, 1914–1923', *Journal of the University of Latvia History/Latvijas Universitates Zurnals. Vesture*, 3.98 (2017), 124–37.

Grillini, Anna, *La guerra in testa: Esperienze e traumi di civili, profughi e soldati nel manicomio di Pergine Valsugana (1909–1924)* (Bologna: Il Mulino, 2018).

Grünfeld, Ernst, *Die deutsche Aussenhandelskontrolle (Die Politik der Sperren) vom Kriegsausbruch bis zum Inkrafttreten des Friedensvertrages* (Bonn and Leipzig: Schroeder, 1922).

Güll, Reinhard, 'Der "Schweinemord" oder die "Professorenschlachtung"', *Statistisches Monatsheft Baden-Württemberg*, 6 (2004), 55.

Günther, Otto, *Das Gewicht der Neugeborenen in der Kriegs- u. Nachkriegszeit* (Munich: Rudolph Müller & Steinicke, 1927).

Hadry, Susan, 'Ernährungskrise, Revolution Und Der Bauernbund – Zur Geschichte Des Ersten Bayerischen Staatsministeriums Für Landwirtschaft (1919–1932)', *Archivalische Zeitschrift*, 92.1 (2011), 209–75.

Hagen, Antje. 'Anglo-German Economic Relations before, during and after the War', in *Change and Inertia, Britain under the Impact of the Great War*, ed. by Hartmut Berghoff and Robert von Friedeburg (Bodenheim: Philo, n.d.), pp. 67–89.

Haider, Edgar, *Wien 1918: Agonie der Kaiserstadt* (Vienna: Böhlau, 2018).

Hajtó, Vera, 'The "wanted" Children: Experiences of Hungarian Children Living with Belgian Host Families during the Interwar Period', *History of the Family*, 14 (2009), 203–16.

Hajtó, Vera, *Milk Sauce and Paprika: Migration, Childhood and Memories of the Interwar Belgian-Hungarian Child Relief Project* (Leuven: Leuven University Press, 2016), pp. 33–35.

Hallwirth, Lena, *Die Versorgung der Zivilbevölkerung mit Lebensmitteln und Ersatzlebensmitteln während des Ersten Weltkriegs*, Social Ecology Working Paper 171, Alpen-Adria Universität, Klagenfurt, 2016, www.aau.at/wp-content/uploads/2017/04/WP171_Web.pdf.

Halpern, Paul, *The Naval War in the Mediterranean 1914–1918* (London: Allen and Unwin, 1987).

Halpern, Paul, ed., *The Royal Navy in the Mediterranean 1915–1918* (Aldershot: Navy Records Society, 1987).

Halpern, Paul, *A Naval History of World War I* (London: UCL Press, 1994).

Hamlin, David, '"Dummes Geld": Money, Grain, and the Occupation of Romania in WWI', *Central European History*, 42.3 (September 2009), 451–71.

Hamlin, David, 'The Fruits of Occupation: Food and Germany's Occupation of Romania in the First World War', *First World War Studies*, 4.1 (2013), 81–95.

Hamlin, David, *Germany's Empire in the East: Germans and Romania in an Era of Globalization and Total War* (Cambridge: Cambridge University Press, 2017).

Hammond, Richard J., *Food, Volume 1: The Growth of Policy* (London: HMSO, 1984).

Hanák, Péter, '*The Garden and the Workshop: Essays on the Cultural History of Vienna and Budapest* (Princeton: Princeton University Press, 1998).

Hanebrink, Paul, *In Defense of Christian Hungary: Religion, Nationalism, and Antisemitism, 1890–1944* (Ithaca: Cornell University Press, 2006).

Hardach, Gerd, *The First World War, 1914–1918* (Berkeley and Los Angeles: University of California Press, 1981).

Hardy, Anne, 'Commentary: Bread and Alum, Syphilis and Sunlight: Rickets in the Nineteenth Century', *International Journal of Epidemiology*, 32.3 (2003), 337–40.

Harris, Bernard, 'The Demographic Impact of the First World War: An Anthropometric Perspective', *Social History of Medicine*, 6 (1993), 343–66.

Harris, Jose, 'Bureaucrats and Businessmen in British Food Control, 1916–19', *War and the State: The Transformation of British Government*, ed. by K. Burk (London: George Allen and Unwin, 1982), pp. 135–56.

Harrison, Mark, 'The Fight against Disease in the Mesopotamia Campaign', in *Facing Armageddon: The First World War Experienced*, ed. by H. Cecil and P. H. Liddle (London: Leo Cooper, 1996), pp. 475–89.

Harrison, Mark, 'Scurvy on Sea and Land: Political Economy and Natural History, *c.*1780–*c.*1850', *Journal for Maritime Research*, 15 (2013), 7–26.

Harrison, Mark, 'War, Epidemics and Empire: British Military Government in the Middle East, 1914–18', in *A Long, Long Trail A-Winding: Centenary Perspectives on the Great War*, ed. by A. Cormack (Dorchester: The Dorset Press, 2018), pp. 33–55.

Hart, Basil Liddell, *A History of the World War, 1914–1918* (London: Faber, 1934).

Hartcup, Guy, *The War of Invention: Scientific Developments, 1914–18* (London: Brasseys, 1988).

Hawk, Alan, 'The Great Disease Enemy, Kak'ke (Beriberi) and the Imperial Japanese Army', *Military Medicine*, 171.4 (2006), 333–39.

Healy, Maureen, *Vienna and the Fall of the Habsburg Empire: Total War and Everyday Life in World War I* (Cambridge: Cambridge University Press, 2004).

Healy, Maureen, 'Introductory Remarks: Space, Chronology and the Habsburg Home Fronts', *European Review of History: Revue européenne d'histoire*, 24.2 (2017), 176–84.

Heijmans, Bastiaan T., Elmar W. Tobi, Aryeh D. Stein et al., 'Persistent Epigenetic Differences Associated with Prenatal Exposure to Famine in Humans', *PNAS*, 105 (2008), 17046–49.

Herwig, Holger H., *The First World War: Germany and Austria-Hungary, 1914–1918* (London and New York: Arnold, 1997).

Heumos, Peter, '"Kartoffeln her oder es gibt eine Revolution": Hungerkrawalle, Streiks und Massenproteste in den böhmischen Ländern, 1914–1918', in *Der Erste Weltkrieg und die Beziehungen zwischen Tschechen, Slowaken und Deutschen*, ed. by Hans Mommsen, Dušan Kováč, Jiří Malíř et al. (Essen: Klartext, 2001), pp. 255–86.

Heyll, Uwe, 'Der "Kampf ums Eiweißminimum": Zum Konflikt zwischen wissenschaftlicher Ernährungslehre und Ernährungsreform in Deutschland im 19. und 20. Jahrhundert', *Deutsche Medizinische Wochenschrift*, 132 (2007), 2768–73.

Heywood, Antony, 'Post-War Economies (Russian Empire)', in *1914–1918-online. International Encyclopedia of the First World War*, ed. by U. Daniel, Peter Gatrell, Oliver Janz, et al. (Berlin: Freie Universität Berlin, 2015).

Hionidou, Violetta, *Famine and Death in Occupied Greece, 1941–1944* (Cambridge: Cambridge University Press, 2006).

Hirschfeld, Gerhard, Gerd Krumeich, and Irina Renz, *1918: Die Deutschen zwischen Weltkrieg und Revolution* (Berlin: Ch. Links Verlag, 2018).

Hirschfeld, Magnus, *Sittengeschichte des Ersten Weltkriegs*, 2nd ed. (Hanau: Müller & Kiepenhauder, n.d.) [original edition: *Sittengeschichte des Weltkrieges*, 1929, 2 vols].

Högselius, Per, Arne Kaijser, and Erik van der Vleuten, *Europe's Infrastructure Transition: Economy, War, Nature* (Houndsmills: Palgrave Macmillan, 2016).

Holquist, P., *Making War, Forging Revolution: Russia's Continuum of Crisis, 1914–1921* (Cambridge, MA: Harvard University Press, 2002).

Holtfrerich, Carl-Ludwig, *The German Inflation 1914–1923: Causes and Effects in International Perspective* (New York: Walter de Gruyter, 2013).

Hong, Young-Sun, *Welfare, Modernity, and the Weimar state, 1919–1933* (Princeton, NJ: Princeton University Press, 1998).

Horel, Catherine, 'Il Compromesso austro-ungherese alla prova della Grande guerra', in *La Grande guerra e la dissoluzione di un Impero multinazionale*, ed. by Paolo Pombeni (Trento: FBK Press, 2017), pp. 201–17.

Horrell, S. and D. Oxley, 'Crust or Crumb?: Intrahousehold Resource Allocation and Male Breadwinning in Late Victorian Britain', *Economic History Review* 52.3 (1999), 494–522.

Houssiau, Jean and Christian Vreugde, 'Brussels Schoolchildren during the First World War', *Cahiers Bruxellois*, 46 (2014), 39–52.

Howard, Michael, *The Franco-Prussian War: The German Invasion of France, 1870–1871* (London and New York: Routledge, 1990), pp. 220–24.

Howard, N. P., 'The Social and Political Consequences of the Allied Food Blockade of Germany, 1918–19', *German History*, 11.2 (1993), 182–84.

Howe, Paul and Stephen Devereux, 'Famine Intensity and Magnitude Scales: A Proposal for an Instrumental Definition of Famine', *Disasters*, 28.4 (December 2004), 353–72.

Hubertus, Jahn, *Patriotic Culture in Russia During World War I* (Ithaca: Cornell University Press, 1995).

Hull, Andrew J., 'Food for Thought?: The Relations between the Royal Society Food Committees and Government, 1915–19', *Annals of Science*, 59 (2002), 263–98.

Hull, Isabel V., *A Scrap of Paper: Breaking and Making International Law during the Great War* (Ithaca: Cornell University Press, 2014).

Innerhofer, Ian, 'Post-War Economies (South East Europe)' in *1914–1918-online. International Encyclopedia of the First World War*, ed. by U. Daniel, Peter Gatrell, Oliver Janz, et al. (Berlin: Freie Universität Berlin, 2015).

IPC, 'What is Famine?' www.ipcinfo.org/famine-facts/.

Irish, Tomás, *Feeding the Mind: Humanitarianism and the Reconstruction of European Intellectual Life, 1919–1933* (Cambridge: Cambridge University Press, 2024).

Irwin, Julia, *Making the World Safe: The American Red Cross and a Nation's Humanitarian Awakening* (Oxford: Oxford University Press, 2013).

Jackson, Simon, 'Transformative Relief: Imperial Humanitarianism and Mandatory Development in Syria-Lebanon, 1915–1925', *Humanity: An International Journal of Human Rights, Humanitarianism and Development*, 8.2 (2017), 247–68.

Jacob, Frank, *East Asia and the First World War* (Oldenbourg: De Gruyter, 2022).

Jacques, Catherine, and Valérie Piette, 'Une grande bataille: sauver l'enfance', in *Une guerre totale ? La Belgique dans la Première Guerre mondiale*, ed. by Serge Jaumain, Michaël Amara, Benoît Majerus et al. (Brussels: Rijksarchief, 2005), pp. 171–82.

Jēkabsons, Ē., 'Latvijos ginkluotųjų pajėgų partizanų daliniai 1919 metais', in *Paramilitarism in the Eastern Baltics, 1918–1940: Cases Studies and comparisons*, ed. by Vytautas Jokubauskas, Vasilijus Safronovas, and Vygantas Vareikis (Klaipėda: Klaipėdos universiteto leidykla, 2014), pp. 57–71.

Jēkabsons, Ē., *Latvijas un Amerikas Savienoto Valstu attiecības 1918.-1922.gadā* (Rīga: Latvijas vēstures institūta apgāds, 2018).

Jones, Heather, 'A Forgotten Front? The Mediterranean Blockade in the First World War', *The International History Review*, 46.4 (2024), 426–43.

Judson, Pieter M., *The Habsburg Empire: A New History* (Cambridge, MA: Belknap Press: An Imprint of Harvard University Press, 2016).

Kammelar, Rob, Jacques Sicking, and Menno Wielinga, eds, *Het monster van de oorlog. Nederlandse liedjes en gedichten over de Eerste Wereldoorlog* (Amsterdam: Nijgh & Van Ditmar, 2004).

Kaplan, Steven L., *Pour le pain* (Paris: Fayard, 2020).

Kauffman, Jesse, *Elusive Alliance: The German Occupation of Poland in World War I* (Cambridge, MA: Harvard University Press, 2015).

Kayalı, H., *Arabs and Young Turks: Ottomanism, Arabism, and Islamism in the Ottoman Empire, 1908–1918* (Berkeley: University of California Press, 1997).

Keller, Tait, 'Destruction of the Ecosystem', in *1914–1918-online. International Encyclopedia of the First World War*, ed. by U. Daniel, Peter Gatrell, Oliver Janz, et al. (Berlin: Freie Universität Berlin, 2015).

Kenez, Peter, *A History of the Soviet Union from the Beginning to the End* (Cambridge: Cambridge University Press, 2006).

Kennedy, Greg, 'Intelligence and the Blockade 1914–1917: A Study in Administration, Friction and Command', *Intelligence and National Security*, 22 (2007), 699–721.

Kennedy, Greg, 'Strategy and Power: The Royal Navy, the Foreign Office and the Blockade, 1914–1917', *Journal of Defence Studies*, 8 (2008), 190–206.

Kennedy, Paul, *The Rise and Fall of British Naval Mastery* (London: Macmillan and Co., 1983).

Keren, Célia, Fabio Giomi, and Morgane Labbé, eds., *Public and Private Welfare in Modern Europe: Productive Entanglements* (London: Routledge, 2022).

Keys, Ancel, *The Biology of Human Starvation* (Minneapolis: University of Minnesota Press, 1950), vol. II.

Kind-Kovács, Friederike, 'The "Other" Child Transports: World War I and the Temporary Displacement of Needy Children from Central Europe', *Revue d'histoire de l'enfance «irrégulière»*, 15 (2013), 76–109.

Kind-Kovács, Friederike, 'The Great War, the Child's Body and the American Red Cross', *European Review of History*, 23 (2016), 33–62.

Kind-Kovács, Friederike, *Budapest's Children: Humanitarian Relief in the Aftermath of the Great War* (Bloomington: Indiana University Press, 2022).

Kirby, D., *Finland and Russia, 1808–1920: From Autonomy to Independence* (London: Macmillan and Co., 1975).

Klemann, Hein, 'Ontwikkeling door isolement. De Nederlandse economie 1914–1918', in *Wankel evenwicht. Neutraal Nederland en de Eerste Wereldoorlog*, ed. by Martin Kraaijestein and Paul Schulten (Soesterberg: Aspekt, 2007), pp. 271–309.

Klinkert, Wim, Samuël Kruizinga, and Paul Moeyes, *Nederland neutraal: de Eerste Wereldoorlog 1914–1918* (Amsterdam: Boom, 2014).

Klovland, Jan Tore, 'Navigating through Torpedo Attacks and Enemy Raiders: Merchant Shipping and Freight Rates during World War I', Norwegian School of Economics Discussion Paper 04, no. 17 (2017).

Kluge, Ulrich, *Die deutsche Revolution: 1918/1919; Staat, Politik und Gesellschaft zwischen Weltkrieg und Kapp-Putsch* (Berlin and Frankfurt am Main: Suhrkamp, 1997).

Kluge, Ulrich, *Agrarwirtschaft und ländliche Gesellschaft im 20. Jahrhundert* (Munich: Oldenbourg, 2005).

Knoepfli, Adrian, 'Mit Kaninchenzucht gegen den Hunger. Winterthur im Ersten Weltkrieg', in *Kriegs- und Krisenzeit. Zürich während des Ersten Weltkriegs*, ed. by Erika Hebeisen, Peter Niederhäuser, and Regula Schmid (Zürich: Chronos, 2014), pp. 37–48.

Koblik, Steven, *Sweden. The Neutral Victor. Sweden and the Western Powers 1917–1918. A Study of Anglo-American-Swedish Relations* (Stockholm: Läromedelsförlagen, 1972), pp. 15–64.

Koblik, Steven, *'Sweden 1917: Between Reform and Revolution', Neutral Europe between war and revolution, 1917–23*, ed. by Hans A. Schmitt (Charlottesville: University Press of Virginia, 1988), pp. 111–32.

Kofman, Jan, *Economic Nationalism and Development: Central and Eastern Europe between the Two World Wars* (Boulder: Westview Press, 1997).

Kondratiev, N. D., *Rynok Khlebov i ego regulirovaniye vo vremya voiny I revolyutsii* (Moscow: Nauka, 1991 [originally 1922]).

Korompai, Imre, 'Untersuchungen über die Gewichtsverhältnisse der Neugeborenen auf Grund des 40jährigen Materials der Klinik', *Zeitschrift für Geburtshilfe und Gynäkologie*, 124 (1942), 36–43.

Kosi, Jernej, '"Yugoslavia Has Nothing. Yugoslavia Has No Bread. But Hungary Gives Us Bread": Access to Food and (Dis)Loyalty in a "Redeemed" Yugoslav Borderland', *Austrian History Yearbook*, 55 (2024), 283–97.

Kovačević, Ognjen, 'Putujuća škola: Izveštaj profesora Miloša S. Moskovljevića o srpskim đacima u Rusiji za vreme Prvog svetskog rata', *Istorijske sveske*, 11 (2014), 25–28.

Kraaijestein, Martin, 'Lokale noden en lokaal beleid', in *Leven naast de catastrophe. Nederland tijdens de Eerste Wereldoorlog*, ed. by Hans Binnenveld (Hilversum: Uitgeverij Verloren, 2001), pp. 63–77.

Krämer, Daniel, Chrisian Pfister, and Daniel Marc Segesser, eds., *'Woche für Woche neue Preisaufschläge': Nahrungsmittel-, Energie-, und Ressourcenkonflikte in der Schweiz des Ersten Weltkrieges* (Basel: Schwabe, 2016).

Krauss, Karl-Peter, ed., *Agrarreformen und Ethnodemographische Veränderungen. Südosteuropa Vom Ausgehenden 18. Jahrhundert Bis in Die Gegenwart* (Stuttgart: Franz Steiner Verlag, 2009).

Kraut, Alan M., *Goldberger's War: The Life and Work of a Public Health Crusader* (New York: Hill and Wang, 2003).

Krejčí, J., and P. Machonin, *Czechoslovakia, 1918–92: A Laboratory for Social Change* (Basingstoke, UK: Macmillan and Co., 1998).

Krug, Peter F., 'The Debate over the Delivery of Health Care in Rural Russia: The Moscow Zemstvo, 1864–1878', *Bulletin of the History of Medicine*, 50.2 (1976), 226–41.

Kruizinga, Samuël, 'NOT Neutrality. The Dutch Government, the Netherlands Oversea Trust Company, and the Entente blockade of Germany, 1914–1918', in *Caught in the Middle: Neutrals, Neutrality, and the First World War*, ed. by Johan den Hertog and Samuël Kruizinga (Amsterdam: Amsterdam University Press, 2011), pp. 85–104.

Kruizinga, Samuël, *Overlegeconomie in oorlogstijd. De Nederlandsche Overzee Trustmaatschappij en de Eerste Wereldoorlog* (Zutphen: Walburg Pers, 2012).
Kruizinga, Samuël, 'Sailing in Uncharted Waters. Dutch Steamship Companies and the First World War', *International Journal of Maritime History*, 27.2 (2015), 227–49.
Kučera, Rudolf, 'Entbehrungen Und Nationalismus. Die Erfahrung Tschechischer Soldaten Der Österreichisch-Ungarischen Armee 1914–1918', in *Jenseit Des Schützengrabens. Der Erste Weltkrieg Im Osten: Erfahrung-Wahrnemung-Kontext*, ed. by Bernhard Bachinger and Wolfram Dornik (Innsbruck: Studien Verlag, 2013), pp. 121–38.
Kučera, Rudolf, *Rationed Life: Science, Everyday life, and Working-Class Politics in the Bohemian Lands, 1914–1918* (New York and Oxford: Berghahn, 2016).
Kurasawa, Fuyuki, 'The Making of Humanitarian Visual Icons: On the 1921–1924 Russian Famine as Foundational Event', in *Iconic Power: Materiality and Meaning in Social Life*, ed. by Jeffrey Alexander, Dominik Bartmański, and Bernhard Giesen (New York: Palgrave Macmillan, 2012), pp. 67–84.
Kuypers, I., *In de Schaduw van de Grote Oorlog. De Nederlandse arbeidersbeweging en de overheid, 1914–1920* (Amsterdam: Aksant, 2002).
Labbé, Morgane, 'Les débuts de la protection sociale infantile à Łodz: Associations locales et réseaux transnationaux (1900–1919)', *Revue d'histoire de la protection sociale*, 1.11 (2018), 46–71.
Lambert, Andrew D., 'The Crimean War Blockade, 1854–56', in *Naval Blockades and Seapower: Strategies and Counter-strategies, 1805–2005*, ed. by Bruce Elleman and S. C. M. Paine (London: Routledge, 2006), pp. 46–60.
Lambert, Nicholas A., *Planning Armageddon: British Economic Warfare and the First World War* (Cambridge, MA: Harvard University Press, 2012).
Lampe, John R., and Marvin R. Jackson, *Balkan Economic History, 1550–1950: From Imperial Borderlands to Developing Nations* (Bloomington: Indiana University Press, 1982).
Langlinay, Erik, 'Consommation et ravitaillement en France durant la Première Guerre mondiale (1914–1920)', in *Au nom du consommateur: Consommation et politique en Europe et aux États-Unis au XXe siècle*, ed. by Alain Chatriot (Paris: La Découverte, 2005), pp. 27–44.
Langthaler, Ernst, 'Food and Nutrition (Austria-Hungary)', in *1914–1918-online. International Encyclopedia of the First World War*, ed. by Ute Daniel, Peter Gatrell, Oliver Janz, et al. (Berlin: Universität Berlin, 2016), https://encyclopedia.1914-1918-online.net/article/food_and_nutrition_austria-hungary. https://doi.org/10.15463/ie1418.10796.
Leary, Sam, C. Fall, C. Osmond, et al., 'Geographical Variation in Neonatal Phenotype', *Acta Obstetricia et Gynecologica Scandinavica*, 85.9 (September 2006), 1080–89.
Lembré, Stéphane, *La guerre des bouches: Ravitaillement et alimentation à Lille, 1914–1919* (Villeneuve-d'Ascq, France: Presses universitaires du Septentrion, 2016).
Leonhard, Jörn, *Die Büchse der Pandora: Geschichte des Ersten Weltkrieges* (Munich: C.H. Beck, 2014).
Lieven, Dominic, *The End of Tsarist Russia: The March to World War I and Revolution* (New York: Penguin, 2016).

Lih, Lars T., 'Bolshevik Razverstka and War Communism', *Slavic Review*, 45.4 (1986), 673–88.

Lih, Lars T., *Bread and Authority in Russia, 1914–1921* (Berkeley and Los Angeles: University of California Press, 1990).

Little, Branden, 'An Explosion of New Endeavours. Global Humanitarian Responses to Industrialized Warfare in the First World War era', *First World War Studies*, 5.1 (2014), 1–16.

Little, Branden, 'The Commission for Relief in Belgium', in *1914–1918-online. International Encyclopedia of the First World War*, ed. by U. Daniel, Peter Gatrell, Oliver Janz, et al. (Berlin: Freie Universität Berlin, 2015).

Liulevicius, Vejas Gabriel, *War Land on the Eastern Front: Culture, National Identity and German Occupation in the World War I* (Cambridge: Cambridge University Press, 2000).

Livezeanu, Irina, Thomas Ort, and Alex Drace-Francis, 'The Cultures of East Central Europe: Imperial, National, Revolutionary', in *The Routledge History of East Central Europe since 1700*, ed. by Irina Livezeanu and Arpad von Klimo (Abingdon and New York: Routledge, 2017), pp. 325–426.

London, Barbara, *Photography*, 8th ed. (Upper Saddle River: Prentice Hall, 2005).

Loriaux, Florence, *Le chômeur suspect: histoire d'une stigmatisation* (Brussels: Centre d'Animation et de Recherche en Histoire Ouvrière et Populaire (CARHOP)/ Centre de Recherche et d'Information Socio-Politiques (CRISP), 2015).

Luiten van Zanden, Jan, 'The First Green Revolution: The Growth of Production and Productivity in European Agriculture, 1870–1914', *Economic History Review*, 44.2 (n.d.), 215–39.

Lunn, Peter G., 'Nutrition, Immunity and Infection', in *The Decline of Mortality in Europe*, ed. by Roger Schofield, David S. Reher, and Alain Bideau (Oxford: Clarendon Press, 1991), pp. 131–45.

Magri, Susanne, 'Les propriétaires, les locataires, la loi. Jalons pour une analyse sociologique des rapports de location, Paris 1850–1920', *Revue française de sociologie*, 37.3 (1996), 397–418.

Maguire, Anna. '"A Pageant of Empire?" Untangling Colonial Encounters in Military Camps', in *Colonial Encounters in a Time of Global Conflict, 1914–1918*, ed. by Santanu Das, Anna Maguire, and Daniel Steinbach (London: Routledge, 2021), pp. 37–56.

Majérus, Benoît, 'War Losses (Belgium)', in *1914–1918-online. International Encyclopedia of the First World War*, ed. by U. Daniel, Peter Gatrell, Oliver Janz, et al. (Berlin: Freie Universität Berlin, 2016).

Majérus, Benoît, and Anne Roekens, 'Deadly Vulnerabilities. The Provisioning of Psychiatric Asylums in Occupied Belgium (1914–1918)', *Journal of Belgian History*, 47.4 (2017), 18–48.

Malle, Silvana, *The Economic Organization of War Communism 1918–1921* (Cambridge: Cambridge University Press, 2002).

Marcus, Nathan, *Austrian Reconstruction and the Collapse of Global Finance, 1921–1931* (Cambridge, MA: Harvard University Press, 2018).

Markevich, Andrei, Natalya Naumenko, and Nancy Qian, 'The Causes of Ukrainian Famine Mortality, 1932–33', National Bureau of Economic Research, Working Paper 29089, July 2021, revised May 2023.

Marriott, B. M., ed., *Food Components to Enhance Performance: An Evaluation of Potential Performance-Enhancing Food Components for Operational Rations* (Washington, DC: National Academies Press, 1994).

Martin, Jamie, 'Globalizing the History of the First World War: Economic Approaches', *Historical Journal*, 65 (2022), 838–55.

Masuy-Stroobant, Godelieve, 'Les enfants et la guerre', in *Une guerre totale? La Belgique dans la Première Guerre mondiale*, ed. by Serge Jaumain and others (Brussels: Rijksarchief, 2005), pp. 157–70.

May, Arthur J., 'The Novibazar Railway Project', *Journal of Modern History*, 10.4 (1938), 496–527.

Mayerhofer, Lisa, 'Making Friends and Foes: Occupiers and Occupied in First World War Romania, 1916–1918', in *Untold War: New Perspectives in First World War Studies*, ed. by Heather Jones, Jennifer O'Brien and Christoph Schmidt-Supprian (Leiden: Brill, 2008), pp. 119–50.

McGuire, Michael, 'At (Red) Cross Purposes: American Red Cross Humanitarian "arrogance" and France's Great War Relief and Reconstruction, 1917–20', *European Review of History: Revue Européenne d'histoire*, 30.5 (2023), 705–26.

McNeill, William H., *The Pursuit of Power: Technology, Armed Force, and Society since A.D. 1000* (Oxford: Basil Blackwell, 1983).

Mehanna, Hisham, Paul C. Nankivell, Jamil Moledina, and Jane Travis, 'Refeeding Syndrome – Awareness, Prevention and Management', *Head and Neck Oncology*, 1.4 (2009).

Menning, Bruce W., *Bayonets before Bullets: The Imperial Russian Army 1861–1914* (Bloomington: Indiana University Press, 1992).

Messer, Ellen, and Laurie F. DeRose, 'Food Shortage', in *Who's Hungry? And How Do We Know? Food Shortage, Poverty, and Deprivation*, ed. by Laurie DeRose, Ellen Messer, and Sara Millman (Tokyo: United Nations University Press, 1998), pp. 53–91.

Metinsoy, E. M., 'Writing the History of Ordinary Ottoman Women during World War I', *Aspasia*, 10.1 (2016), 18–39.

Metinsoy, E. M., *Ottoman Women during World War I: Everyday Experiences, Politics, and Conflict* (Cambridge: Cambridge University Press, 2017).

Mick, Christoph, *Kriegserfahrungen in einer multiethnischen Stadt: Lemberg 1914–1947* (Wiesbaden: Harrassowitz, 2010).

Millman, Sara and Robert W. Kates, 'Towards Understanding Hunger', in *Hunger in History: Food Shortage, Poverty, and Deprivation*, ed. by Lucile F. Newman (Cambridge, MA: Basil Blackwell, 1990), pp. 32–34.

Millward, Robert and Joerg Baten, 'Population and Living Standards, 1914–1945', in *History of modern Europe, Volume 2 (1870 to the Present)*, ed. by Steven Broadberry and Kevin H. O'Rourke (Cambridge: Cambridge University Press, 2012), pp. 232–63.

Mitrović, Andrej, *Serbia's Great War, 1914–1918* (West Lafayette: Purdue University Press, 2007).

Moeller, Robert G., 'Winners as Losers in the German Inflation: Peasant Protest over Controlled Economy, 1920–1923', in *Die Deutsche Inflation: Eine Zwischenbilanz*, ed. by Gerald D. Feldman and Gerald Merkin (Berlin and New York: De Gruyter, 1982), pp. 257–88.

Moeller, Robert G., *Peasants and Lords in Modern Germany: Recent Studies in Agricultural History* (Winchester: Allen & Unwin, 1986).

Mokyr, Joel and Cormac Ó. Gráda, 'What Do People Die of During Famines: The Great Irish Famine in Comparative Perspective', *European Review of Economic History*, 6.3 (December 2002), 339–63.

Molenda, Jan, 'War, Children and Youth: The Impact of the First World War upon Changes in the Position of Children in the Peasant Family and Community', *Acta Poloniae Historica*, 79 (1999), 162–84.

More, Alexander F., Christopher Loveluck, Heather Clifford, et al., 'The Impact of a Six-Year Climate Anomaly on the "Spanish Flu" Pandemic and WWI', *GeoHealth*, 4.9 (2020). https://doi.org/10.1029/2020GH000277.

Morelon, Claire, 'A Threat to National Unity?: The Urban-Rural Antagonism in Prague During the First World War in a Comparative Perspective', in *Frontwechsel. Österreich-Ungarns "Grosser Krieg" im Vergleich*, ed. by Wolfram Dornik, Julia Walleczek-Fritz, and Stefan Wedrac (Vienna: Böhlau, 2014), pp. 325–42.

Morelon, Claire, *Streetscapes of War and Revolution: Prague 1914–1920* (Cambridge: Cambridge University Press, 2024).

Mûelenaere, Nel de, 'International Development Contested: The American Child Health Section in Belgium (1922–1924)', *European Review of History: Revue Européenne d'histoire*, 30.5 (2023), 747–69.

Mullendore, William Clinton, *History of the United States Food Administration 1917–1919* (Stanford: Stanford University Press, 1941).

Müller, Klaus-Peter, *Politik und Gesellschaft im Krieg: Der Legitimitaetsverlust des badischen Staates 1914–1918* (Stuttgart: Kohlhammer, 1988).

Naert, Jan, 'Ventre Affamé n'a Pas d'oreilles: Une Histoire Sociale de l'approvisionnement par les Autorités Locales dans les Territoires Occupés en Belgique et en France (1914–1918)', *Guerres mondiales et conflits contemporains*, 272.4 (2018), 35–50.

Nath, Giselle, *Voedselschaarste en voedselbedeling,tactieken en strategieën. Twee episodes uit de Belgische bezetting tijdens de Eerste Wereldoorlog* (Master's thesis, University of Ghent, 2011).

Nehring, R., and W. Wolford, 'Moral Economies of Food Security and Protest in Latin America', in *Food Security and Sociopolitical Stability*, ed. by C. Barrett (Oxford: Oxford University Press, 2013).

Nekrasov, George, *North of Gallipoli: The Black Sea Fleet at War, 1914–1917* (Boulder: East European Monographs, 1992).

Nivet, Philippe, *La France occupée 1914–1918*, 2nd ed. (Paris: Armand Colin, 2014).

Nouailhat, Yves-Henri, *France et Etats-Unis août 1914–avril 1917* (Paris: Publications de la Sorbonne, 1979).

Offer, Avner, 'The Working Classes, British Naval Plans and the Coming of the Great War', *Past and Present*, 107 (May 1985), 204–26.

Offer, Avner, *The First World War: An Agrarian Interpretation* (Oxford: Oxford University Press, 1989).

Oğuz, Çiğdem, *Moral Crisis in the Ottoman Empire: Society, Politics, and Gender during WWI* (London: I.B. Tauris, 2021).

Oken, Emily, 'Secular Trends in Birthweight', in *Recent Advances in Growth Research: Nutritional, Molecular and Endocrine Perspectives*, ed. by Matthew W. Gillman, Peter D. Gluckman, and Ron G. Rosenfeld (Nestlé Nutrition Institute Workshop Series) (Basel: S. Karger, 2013), pp. 103–14.

Oliver, G. J., *War, Food, and Politics in Early Hellenistic Athens* (Oxford: Oxford University Press, 2007).

Olson, Mancur, *The Economics of the Wartime Shortage: A History of British Food Supplies in the Napoleonic War and in World Wars I and II* (Durham: Duke University Press, 1963).

Osborne, Eric W., *Britain's Economic Blockade of Germany 1914–1919* (London: Frank Cass, 2004).

Otter, Chris, *Diet for a Large Planet: Industrial Britain, Food Systems, and World Ecology* (Chicago: University of Chicago Press, 2020).

Palmer, Svetlana and Sarah Wallis, *A War in Words* (London: Simon and Schuster, 2003).

Paret, Peter, Beth Irwin Lewis, and Paul Paret, *Persuasive Images: Posters of War and Revolution from the Hoover Institution Archives* (Princeton: Princeton University Press, 1992).

Parker, Geoffrey, *Global Crisis: War, Climate Change and Catastrophe in the Seventeenth Century* (New Haven and London: Yale University Press, 2013).

Patenaude, Bertrand M., 'Peasants into Russian: The Utopian Essence of War Communism', *Russian Review*, 54.4 (1995), 552–70.

Patenaude, Bertrand M., *The Big Show in Bololand: The American Relief Expedition to Soviet Russia in the Famine of 1921* (Stanford: Stanford University Press, 2002).

Patenaude, Bertrand M., and Joan Nabseth Stevenson, *Bread + Medicine: American Famine Relief in Soviet Russia, 1921–1923* (Canada: Hoover Institution Press, 2023).

Pati, Budheswar, *India and the First World War* (New Delhi: Atlantic Publishers and Distributors, 1996).

Patin, Nicolas, 'Histoire d'un chiffre. Réflexions autour des victimes allemandes du blocus de 1914–1918', *Les Cahiers Sirice*, 26 (2021), 95–107.

Payk, Marcus M., and Roberta Pergher, eds. *Beyond Versailles: Sovereignty, Legitimacy, and the Formation of New Polities After the Great War* (Bloomington: Indiana University Press, 2019).

Pease, Neal, *Poland, the United States and the Stabilization of Europe, 1919–1933* (New York: Oxford University Press, 1986).

Pedersen, Susan, *Family, Dependence, and the Origins of the Welfare State: Britain and France, 1914–1945* (Cambridge: Cambridge University Press, 1993).

Peeling, Siobhan, 'War Communism', in *1914–1918-online. International Encyclopedia of the First World War*, ed. by U. Daniel, Peter Gatrell, Oliver Janz, et al. (Berlin: Freie Universität Berlin, 2015).

Peri, Alexis, *The War Within: Diaries from the Siege of Leningrad* (Cambridge, MA: Harvard University Press, 2020).

Perren, Richard. 'Farmers and Consumers under Strain: Allied Meat Supplies in the First World War', *Agricultural History Review*, 52.2 (2005), 212–28.

Perry, Heather R., 'Onward Kitchen Soldiers' Gender, Food and Health in Germany's Long Great War', in *Food, Culture and Identity in Germany's Century of War*, ed. by Heather Merle Benbow and Heather R. Perry (Cham: Palgrave Macmillan, 2019), pp. 17–44.

Pētersone, Inta, ed., *Latvijas Brīvības cīņas. Enciklopēdija* (Rīga: Preses nams, 1999).

Petersson, Niels P., 'Das Kaiserreich in Prozessen ökonomischer Globalisierung', in *Das Kaiserreich transnational: Deutschland in der Welt 1871–1914*, ed. by Sebastian Conrad and Jürgen Osterhammel (Göttingen: Vandenhoeck & Ruprecht, 2004), pp. 49–67.

Petrungaro, Stefano, 'Soup Kitchens and Yugoslav Poor Relief between the Two World Wars', *European Review of History: Revue Européenne d'histoire*, 26.1 (2019), 141–162.

Piller, Elisabeth, 'German Child Distress, American Humanitarian Aid and Revisionist Politics, 1918–1924', *Journal of Contemporary History*, 51.3 (2016), 453–86.

Piller, Elisabeth and Neville Wylie, eds., *Humanitarianism and the Greater War, 1914–24* (Manchester: Manchester University Press, 2023).

Piro, Anna, Giuseppe Tagarelli, Paolo Lagonia, et al., 'Casimir Funk: His Discovery of the Vitamins and Their Deficiency Disorders', *Annals of Nutrition and Metabolism*, 57.2 (2010), 85–88.

Pitts, Graham, 'The Ecology of Migration: Remittances in World War I Mount Lebanon', *The Arab Studies Journal*, 26.2 (Fall 2018), 102–29.

Pitts, Graham, 'Organization of War Economies (Ottoman Empire/Middle East)', in *1914–1918-online. International Encyclopedia of the First World War*, ed. by Ute Daniel, Peter Gatrell, Oliver Janz, et al. (Berlin: Freie Universität Berlin, 2018).

Pitts, Graham, 'Was Capitalism the Crisis? Mount Lebanon's World War I Famine', *Arcadia*, no. 3 (2021), Arcadia Collection: Terms of Disaster.

Plumpe, Werner, 'Die Logik des Modernen Krieges und die Unternehmen: Überlegungen Zum Ersten Weltkrieg', *Jahrbuch für Wirtschaftsgeschichte*, 56.2 (2015), 325–57.

Poulain, Caroline, ed., *Manger et boire entre 1914 et 1918* (Dijon: Bibliothèque municipale de Dijon, 2015).

Preedy, Victor R., ed., *Handbook of Anthropometry: Physical Measures of Human Form in Health and Disease* (New York: Springer, 2012).

Proctor, Tammy M., *Civilians in a World at War: 1914–1918* (New York and London: New York University Press, 2010).

Prost, Antoine, 'War Losses', in *1914–1918-online. International Encyclopedia of the First World War*, ed. by U. Daniel, Peter Gatrell, Oliver Janz, et al. (Berlin: Freie Universität Berlin, 2014).

Purseigle, Pierre, 'Mirroring Societies at War: Pictorial Humour in the British and French Popular Press during the First World War', *Journal of European Studies*, 31 (2001), 289–328.

Qvarnström, Sofi, 'Sweden', in *1914–1918-online. International Encyclopedia of the First World War*, ed. by U. Daniel, Peter Gatrell, Oliver Janz, et al. (Berlin: Freie Universität Berlin, 2015).

Quine, Maria Sophia, *Italy's Social Revolution: Charity and Welfare from Liberalism to Fascism* (Basingstoke: Palgrave, 2002).

Rabinbach, Anson, *The Human Motor: Energy, Fatigue, and the Origins of Modernity* (Berkeley: University of California Press, 1990).

Rauchensteiner, Manfred, *Der Erste Weltkrieg und das Ende der Habsburgermonarchie 1914–1918* (Wien: Böhlau, 2013).

Rechter, David, 'Galicia in Vienna: Jewish Refugees in the First World War', *Austrian History Yearbook*, 28 (1997), 113–30.

Rechter, David, *The Jews of Vienna and the First World War* (London: The Littman Library of Jewish Civilization, 2008).

Régis, Nina, '1917, année de rupture: le rôle du pain de guerre (Kriegsbrot) en Allemagne', *Revue d'Allemagne et des pays de langue allemande*, 49.2 (2017), 407–22.

Régis, Nina, *Le pain de guerre allemand : une histoire culturelle de l'arrière (1914–1919)* (unpublished doctoral thesis, Université de Toulouse-Jean Jaurès, November 2022).

Reill, Dominique Kirchner, *The Fiume Crisis: Life in the Wake of the Habsburg Empire* (Cambridge, MA: Harvard University Press, 2020).

Reill, Dominique Kirchner, Ivan Jeličić, and Francesca Rolandi, 'Redefining Citizenship after Empire: The Rights to Welfare, to Work, and to Remain in a Post-Habsburg World', *The Journal of Modern History*, 94.2 (2022), 326–62.

Renouvin, Pierre, 'Les buts de guerre du gouvernement français 1914–1918', *Revue historique*, 235 (1966), 1–38.

Révész, Tamás, 'A National Army under the Red Banner? The Mobilisation of the Hungarian Red Army in 1919', *Contemporary European History*, 31 (2022), 71–84.

Richardson, Matthew, *The Hunger War: Food, Rations & Rationing 1914–1918* (Barnsley: Pen and Sword, 2015).

Richter, Klaus, 'The Catastrophe of the Present and That of the Future: Expectations for European States from the Great War to the Great Depression', *Contemporary European History*, 33.3 (2024), 1002–20.

Riekstiņš, Jānis, 'Izdziedētā brūce. Bāreņu un trūcīgo bērnu aprūpe Latvijas brīvvalsts pirmajos gados', *Latvijas Arhīvi*, 3–4 (1996), 111–19.

Rigó, Máté, *Capitalism in Chaos: How the Business Elites of Europe Prospered in the era of the Great War* (Ithaca: Cornell University Press, 2022).

Ritter, Gerhard, *The Schlieffen Plan: Critique of a Myth* (London: Oswald Wolff, 1958).

Rodogno, Davide, *Against Massacre: Humanitarian Interventions in the Ottoman Empire, 1815–1914* (Princeton: Princeton University Press, 2011).

Rodogno, Davide, Piana Francesca, and Gauthier Shaloma, 'Shaping Poland: Relief and Rehabilitation Programmes by Foreign Organizations, 1918–1923', in *Shaping the Transnational Sphere: Experts, Networks, and Issues from the 1840s to the 1930s*, ed. by Davide Rodogno, Bernhardt Struck, and Jakob Vogel (New York: Berghahn Books, 2015), pp. 259–78.

Roerkohl, Anna, *Hungerblockade und Heimatfront: Die kommunale Lebensmittelversorgung in Westfalen während des Ersten Weltkrieges* (Stuttgart: Franz Steiner Verlag, 1991).

Rogan, Eugene, *The Fall of the Ottomans: The Great War in the Middle East* (New York: Basic Books, 2015).

Romsics, Ignác, 'The Peasantry and the Age of Revolutions: Hungary, 1918–1919', *Acta Historica Academiae Scientiarum Hungaricae*, 35.1/4 (1989), 113–33.

Rosenberg, William G., *States of Anxiety: Scarcity and Loss in Revolutionary Russia* (Oxford: Oxford University Press, 2023).

Roskill, Stephen, *Hankey: Man of Secrets*, 3 vols (London: Collins, 1970–1974).

Rothwell, V. H., *British War Aims and Peace Diplomacy 1914–1918* (Oxford: Oxford University Press, 1971).

Rubel, William, *Bread: A Global History* (London: Reaktion, 2011).

Ruchti, Jacob, *Geschichte der Schweiz während des Weltkrieges 1914–1919: politisch, wirtschaftlich und kulturell*, 2 vols. (Bern: Haupt, 1930).

Samson, Andrea and James Gross, 'Humour as Emotion Regulation: The Differential Consequences of Negative versus Positive Humour', *Cognition & Emotion*, 26 (2012), 375–84.

Saraiva, Tiago, *Fascist Pigs: Technoscientific Organisms and the History of Fascism* (Cambridge: MIT Press, 2016).

Savouret, Edwige, Jean-Paul Amat, Olivier Cantat et al. 'Au Temps Météorologique de la Grande Guerre. Approche Séquentielle des Périodes Contraignantes dans les Tranchées sur le Front de la Marne et de La Meuse, 1914–1918', *Climatologie*, 8 (2011), 59–77.

Schaepdrijver, Sophie De, *La Belgique et la Première Guerre mondiale* (Brussels: Peter Lang, 2004).

Schaepdrijver, Sophie De, 'A Civilian War Effort: The Comité National de Secours et d'Alimentation in Occupied Belgium, 1914–1918', in *Remembering Herbert Hoover and the Commission for Relief in Belgium*, ed. by Patrick Hilgers and Robert Fergloute (Brussels: Fondation Universitaire, 2007), pp. 24–37.

Schaepdrijver, Sophie De, 'Military Occupation, Political Imaginations, and the First World War', *First World War Studies*, 4.1 (2013), 1–5.

Schaepdrijver, Sophie De, *Gabrielle Petit: The Death and Life of a Female Spy in the First World War* (London: Bloomsbury Academic, 2015).

Scheer, T. and N. M. Wingfield, 'Habsburg Home Fronts during the Great War', *European Review of History: Revue européenne d'histoire*, 24.2 (2017), 985–1002.

Schindler, John R., *Fall of the Double Eagle: The Battle for Galicia and the Demise of Austria-Hungary* (Nebraska: Potomac Books, 2015).

Schmidt, Stefan, *Frankreichs Außenpolitik in der Julikrise 1914. Ein Beitrag zur Geschichte des Ausbruchs des Ersten Weltkrieges* (Munich: De Gruyter, 2009).

Schneider, Eric, 'Fetal Health Stagnation: Have Health Conditions in Utero Improved in the United States and Western and Northern Europe over the Past 150 Pears?', *Social Science & Medicine*, 179 (2017), 18–26.

Scholliers, Peter, 'La faim à Bruxelles en '14-'18. Soupe populaire et restaurants économiques', in *Bruxelles en '14-'18: la guerre au quotidien*, ed. by Serge Jaumain and Valérie Piette (Brussels: La Fonderie, 2005), pp. 34–40.

Schoups, Martin, 'Prosecuting Food Profiteers after the Armistice: A Transitional-justice Perspective, 1919–1923', in *Doing Justice in Wartime: Multiple Interplays between Justice and Populations during the Two World Wars*, ed. by Melanie Bost and Anton Vrints (Cham: Springer, 2021), pp. 45–68.

Schultz, Laura C., 'The Dutch Hunger Winter and the Developmental Origins of Health and Disease', *Proceedings of the National Academy of Science of the United States of America*, 107.39 (2010), 16757–58.

Schumacher, Martin, *Land und Politik. Eine Untersuchung über Politische Parteien und Agrarische Interessen, 1914–1923* (Düsseldorf: Droste Verlag, 1978).

Schwarz, Peter, '"Die Opfer sagen, es war die Hölle": Vom Tremolieren, Faradisieren, Hungern und Sterben: Krieg und Psychiatrie in Wien', in *Im Epizentrum des Zusammenbruchs: Wien im Ersten Weltrieg*, ed. by Alfred Pfoser and Andreas Weigl (Wien: Metroverlag, 2013), pp. 330–34.

Scott-Smith, Tom, *On an Empty Stomach: Two Hundred Years of Hunger Relief* (Ithaca: Cornell University Press, 2020).

Scriba, Arnulf, 'Ersatzprodukte', Deutsches Historisches Museum, Berlin, 2014, www.dhm.de/lemo/kapitel/erster-weltkrieg/alltagsleben/ersatzprodukte.html

Searle, Geoffrey R., *The Quest for National Efficiency* (Oxford: Oxford University Press, 1971).

Seegel, Steven, *Map Men: Transnational Lives and Deaths of Geographers in the Making of East Central Europe* (Chicago: The University of Chicago Press, 2018).

Seidl, Alois, *Deutsche Agrargeschichte* (Frankfurt am Main: DLG-Verlag, 2013).

Semmel, Bernard, *Imperialism and Social Reform* (London: Allen & Unwin, 1960).

Sen, Amartya, *Poverty and Famines: An Essay on Entitlement and Deprivation* (Oxford: Clarendon Press, 1981).

Siekierski, Nick, 'Herbert Hoover and Poland', https://researchteacher.com/wp-content/uploads/2015/10/Herbert-Hoover-and-Poland-Nicholas-Siekierski.pdf

Šiliņš, Jānis, *Padomju Latvija 1918–1919* (Rīga: Vēstures izpētīšanas un popularizēšanas biedrība, 2013).

Simmons, Dana, 'Starvation Science: From Colonies to Metropole', in *Food and Globalization: Consumption, Markets and Politics in the Modern World*, ed. by A. Nützenadel and F. Trentmann (Oxford and New York: Berg, 2008), pp. 173–92.

Siney, Marion, *The Allied Blockade of Germany, 1914–1916* (Ann Arbor: University of Michigan Press, 1957).

Slobodian, Quinn, 'How to See the World Economy: Statistics, Maps, and Schumpeter's Camera in the First Age of Globalization', *Journal of Global History*, 10 (2015), 307–32.

Slobodkin, Yan, *The Starving Empire: A History of Famine in France's Colonies* (Ithaca: Cornell University Press, 2023).

Smith, David F., 'Nutrition Science and the Two World Wars', in *Nutrition in Britain: Science, Scientists and Politics in the Twentieth Century*, ed. by David F. Smith (London: Routledge, 1997), pp. 142–65.

Smith, Leonard, *Sovereignty at the Paris Peace Conference of 1919* (Oxford: Oxford University Press, 2018).

Smith, Leonard, Stéphane Audoin-Rouzeau, and Annette Becker, *France and the Great War, 1914–1918* (Cambridge: Cambridge University Press, 2003).

Sorgeloos, C. and G. Veirman, 'La guerre du silence ou le journal de la Comtesse d'Oultremont', *Revue belge d'Histoire militaire*, 29 (1991), 123–44 and 209–28.

Southerton, Dale, *Encyclopedia of Consumer Culture* (London: Sage, 2011).

Soutou, Georges-Henri, *L'Or et le sang: les buts de guerre économiques de la première guerre mondiale* (Paris: Fayard, 1989).

Sprenger-Seyffarth, Jenny, *Kriegsküchen in Wien und Berlin: Öffentliche Massenverpflegung und private Familienmahlzeit im und nach dem Ersten Weltkrieg* (Berlin: Transcript, 2023).

Stabile, D. R. and A. F. Kozak, *Markets, Planning and the Moral Economy: Business Cycles in the Progressive Era and New Deal* (Cheltenham: Edward Elgar Publishing, 2012).

Steckel, Richard H., 'Stature and the Standard of Living', *Journal of Economic Literature*, 33 (1995), 1903–40.

Steeg, Heinrich, 'De Extensivierung Der Rheinischen Landbaus Unter Der Wirkung Der Hoechstpreise Und Der Zwangswirtschaft' (unpublished PhD thesis, Universität Koeln, 1923).

Steffen, Katrin, 'Who Belongs to the Healthy Body of the Nation? Health and National Integration in Poland and the Polish Army after the First World War', in *From the Midwife's Bag to the Patient's File: Public Health in Eastern Europe*, ed. by Heike Karge, Friederike Kind-Kovács, and Sara Bernasconi (Budapest: CEU Press, 2017), pp. 119–44.

Stein, Zena, Mervyn Susser, Gerhart Saenger, and Francis Marolla, *Famine and Human Development: The Dutch Hunger Winter of 1944–1945* (New York: Oxford University Press, 1975).

Stergar, Rok, 'L'expérience des soldats austro-hongrois sur le front austro-italien: le problème du ravitaillement en vivres', in *Soldati e quotidianità della guerra*, ed. by Giovanni L. Fontana and Marco Mondini (Ospedaletto: Pacini editore, 2019), pp. 13–30.

Stibbe, Matthew, *Civilian Internment during the First World War: A European and Global History, 1914–1920* (Cham: Palgrave Macmillan, 2019).

Stovall, Tyler, *Paris and the Spirit of 1919: Consumer Struggles, Transnationalism, and Revolution* (Cambridge: Cambridge University Press, 2012).

Strachan, Hew, *The First World War, I: To Arms* (Oxford: Oxford University Press, 2001).

Strachan, Hew, *Financing the First World War* (Oxford: Oxford University Press, 2004).

Strachan, Hew, 'The First World War as a Global War', *First World War Studies*, 1.1 (2010), 3–14.

Strachan, Hew, ed., *The British Home Front and the First World War* (Cambridge: Cambridge University Press, 2023).

Strotmann, Christine, 'Nitrogenous Fertilisers in Germany – Paths of Distribution from Chile Saltpetre to Haber-Bosch-Ammonia and Cyanamide (ca 1914–1930)', *Jahrbuch Für Wirtschaftsgeschichte*, 62.1 (2021), 159–89.

Sumida, Jon T., 'Forging the Trident. British Naval Industrial Logistics, 1914–1918', in *Feeding Mars: Logistics in Western Warfare from the Middle Ages to the Present*, ed. by John A. Lynn (Boulder: Westview Press, n.d.), pp. 217–50.

Sumpf, Alexandre, *La grande guerre oubliée: Russie, 1914–1918* (Paris: Perrin, 2014).
Sypher, Wylie ed., *Comedy: An Essay on Comedy* (New York: Doubleday, 1956).
Taithe, Bertrand, *Defeated Flesh: Medicine, Welfare, and Warfare in the Making of Modern France* (Lanham: Rowman and Littlefield, 1999).
Tamari, S., and I. Turjman, eds, *Year of the Locust: A Soldier's Diary and the Erasure of Palestine's Ottoman Past* (Berkeley: University of California Press, 2011).
Tanielian, Melanie S., 'Feeding the City: The Beirut Municipality and the Politics of Food during World War I', *International Journal of Middle East Studies*, 46.4 (November 2014), 737–58.
Tanielian, Melanie S., 'Politics of Wartime Relief in Ottoman Beirut (1914–1918)', *First World War Studies*, 5.1 (2014), 69–82.
Tanielian, Melanie S., 'Food and Nutrition (Ottoman Empire/Middle East)', in *1914–1918-online. International Encyclopedia of the First World War*, ed. by U. Daniel, Peter Gatrell, Oliver Janz, et al. (Berlin: Freie Universität Berlin, 2015).
Tanielian, Melanie S., *The Charity of War: Famine, Humanitarian Aid, and World War I in the Middle East* (Stanford: Stanford University Press, 2017).
Tanner, Jakob, 'Der Tatsachenblicke auf die "reale Wirklichkeit": zur Entwicklung der Sozial- und Konsumstatistik in der Schweiz', *Schweizerische Zeitschrift für Geschichte*, 45 (1995), 94–108.
Tanner, Jakob, *Fabrikmahlzeit: Ernährungswissenschaft, Industriearbeit und Volksernährung in der Schweiz, 1890–1950* (Zurich: Chronos, 1999).
Tanner, James M., *Growth at Adolescence*, 2nd ed. (Oxford: Blackwell, 1962).
Tarrow, S., *Power in Movement: Social Movements and Contentious Politics* (New York: Cambridge University Press, 1998).
Teich, Mikuláš, 'Science and Food during the Great War: Britain and Germany', in *The Science and Culture of Nutrition, 1840–1940*, ed. by Harmke Kamminga and Andrew Cunningham (Amsterdam: Rodopi, 1995), pp. 213–34.
Teuteberg, Hans-Jürgen, 'Die Rolle von Brot und Kartoffeln in der historischen Entwicklung der Nahrungsgewohnheiten', *Ernährungs-Umschau*, 26.5 (1979), 146–54.
Thoms, Ulrike, 'Hunger – ein Bedürfnis zwischen Politik, Physiologie und persönliche Erfahrung (Deutschland, 19. und 20. Jahrhundert', *Body Politics*, 3.5 (2015), 154–55.
Tilly, C., *Contentious Performances* (Cambridge: Cambridge University Press, 2008).
Todd, Selina, 'Class, Experience and Britain's Twentieth Century', *Social History*, 39.4 (2014), 489–508.
Tönsmeyer, Tatjana, Peter Haslinger, and Agnes Laba, eds, *Coping with Hunger and Shortage under German Occupation in World War II* (London: Palgrave, 2018).
Tooze, Adam, *Statistics and the German State, 1900–1945: The Making of Modern Economic Knowledge* (Cambridge: Cambridge University Press, 2001).
Tooze, Adam, *The Deluge: The Great War and the Remaking of the Global Order, 1916–1931* (London: Allan Lane, 2014).
Torp, Cornelius, *Die Herausforderung der Globalisierung: Wirtschaft und Politik in Deutschland 1860–1914* (Göttingen: Vandenhoeck & Ruprecht, 2005).

Tracy, Michael, *Government and Agriculture in Western Europe 1888–1988*, 3rd ed. (New York: New York University Press, 1989).

Treitel, Corinna, 'Max Rubner and the Biopolitics of Rational Nutrition', *Central European History*, 41 (2008), 1–25.

Treitel, Corinna, *Eating Nature in Modern Germany: Food, Agriculture, and Environment, c. 1870 to 2000* (Cambridge: Cambridge University Press, 2017).

Trentmann, Frank, and Flemming Just, eds., *Food and Conflict in Europe in the Age of the Two World Wars* (New York: Palgrave Macmillan, 2006).

Trepman, E. P., 'Rescue of the Remnants: The British Emergency Medical Relief Operation in Belsen Camp 1945', *Journal of the Royal Army Medical Corps*, 145 (2001), 281–93.

Tucker, Richard P. ed., *Environmental Histories of the First World War* (Cambridge: Cambridge University Press, 2018).

Tucker, Todd, *The Great Starvation Experiment: The Heroic Men Who Starved So That Millions Could Live* (New York: Free Press, 2006).

Tunstall, Graydon A., *Written in Blood: The Battles for Fortress PrzemyšlPrzemyśl in WW1* (Bloomington: Indiana University Press, 2016).

Turda, Marius, *Eugenics and Nation in Early 20th Century Hungary* (Basingstoke, UK: Palgrave, 2014).

Tusan, Michelle, 'Genocide, Famine and Refugees on Film: Humanitarianism and the First World War', *Past & Present*, 237.1 (2017), 197–235.

United States Army, Center of Military History, *The U.S. Army in World War I: Complete History of the U.S. Army in the Great War, Including the Mobilization, The Main Battles & All Official Documents of the U.S. Government during the War*, ed. by Eric B. Setzekorn (Washington, DC: Madison & Adams Press, 2018).

United States Bureau of Labor Statistics, *The Consumer Price Index: History and Iechniques*, Bulletin No. 1517 (Washington, DC: U.S. Government Printing Office, 1966).

United States Department of Agriculture, 'Food Calorie Calculator', *National Nutrient Database*, http://caloriecontrol.org.

Valk, J. P. de and M. van Faassen, *Dagboeken en aantekeningen van Willem Hendrik de Beaufort 1874–1918* (The Hague: Huygens Instituut voor Nederlandse Geschiedenis, 1993).

Van der Velden, Annie, 'Gemeentevis en regeringsvarkens: Voedselvoorziening in Utrecht 1914–1918', *Oud-Utrecht*, 81.6 (2008), 162–66.

Van Genabeek, Joost, and Louise Rietbergen, *De S.D.A.P. en de volkshuisvesting. Inhoud en resultaten van het sociaaldemocratische volkshuisvestingsbeleid in Nederland (1894–1940)* (Utrecht: n.p., 1991).

Van Kamp, Robert, *De kolenvoorziening van Nederland gedurende de Eerste Wereldoorlog* (Amsterdam: Het Parool, 1968).

Van Otterloo, Anneke H., 'Voedzaam, smakelijk en gezond: kookleraressen en pogingen tot verbetering van eetgewoonten tussen 1880 en 1940', *Amsterdams Sociologisch Tijdschrift*, 12 (1985–1986), 495–542.

Varea, Carlos, José Manuel Terán, Cristina Bernis et al., 'Is the Economic Crisis Affecting Birth Outcome in Spain? Evaluation of Temporal Trend in Underweight at Birth (2003–2012)', *Annals of Human Biology*, 43 (2016), 169–82.

Veit, Helen Zoe, *Modern Food, Moral Food: Self-Control, Science, and the Rise of Modern American Eating in the Early Twentieth Century* (Chapel Hill: University of North Carolina Press, 2013).

Verduyn, Marijke, and Sietske van Weerden, eds, *Getuigen van een Generatie. Waarden, idealen en het leven van alledag in de jaren na de Eerste Wereldoorlog in Nederland* (Zoetermeer, Netherlands: Meinema, 1992).

Verhey, Jeffrey, *The Spirit of 1914: Militarism, Myth and Mobilization in Germany* (Cambridge and New York: Cambridge University Press, 2006).

Vernon, James, *Hunger: A Modern History* (Cambridge, MA: Harvard University Press, 2007).

Verseput, Jan, 'Gevolgen van de gesloten wapenstilstands- en vredesverdragen, welke een einde aan de eerste wereldoorlog maakten, voor Rotterdam', *Rotterdams Jaarboekje*, 8 (1960), 228–44.

Vincent, Paul, *The Politics of Hunger: The Allied Blockade of Germany 1915–1919* (Athens: Ohio Press University, 1985).

Voth, Hans-Joachim, 'Civilian Health During WWI and the Cause of German Defeat: A Reexamination of the Winter Hypothesis', *Annales de Démographie Historique (Les réseaux de parenté)* (1995), 291–307.

Vrints, Antoon, 'Beyond Victimization: Contentious Food Politics in Belgium during World War I', *European History Quarterly*, 45.1 (2015), 83–107.

Vrints, Antoon, 'Food and Nutrition (Belgium)', in *1914–1918-online. International Encyclopedia of the First World War*, ed. by U. Daniel, Peter Gatrell, Oliver Janz, et al. (Berlin: Freie Universität Berlin, 2015).

Wall, Robert and Jay Winter, *The Upheaval of War: Family, Work and Welfare in Europe, 1914–1918*, ed. by (Cambridge: Cambridge University Press, 1988).

Ward, W. Peter, *Birth Weight and Economic Growth: Women's Living Standards in the Industrializing West* (Chicago: University of Chicago Press, 1993).

Wargelin, Clifford F., 'A High Price for Bread: The First Treaty of Brest-Litovsk and the Break-up of Austria-Hungary, 1917–1918', *The International History Review*, 19.4 (1997), 757–88.

Washburn, S. L., 'Review of Josef Brozek (ed.), Body Measurements and Human Nutrition (Detroit: Wayne State University Press, 1956)', *American Anthropologist*, 60 (1958), 207–8.

Watson, Alexander, *Ring of Steel: Germany and Austria-Hungary at War 1914–1918* (London: Allen Lane, 2014).

Wegs, Robert J., 'Transportation: The Achilles Heel of the Habsburg War Effort', in *The Habsburg Empire in World War I*, ed. by Robert A. Kann, Béla Király, and Paula S. Fichtner (New York: Columbia University Press, 1977), pp. 121–34.

Weindling, Paul, *International Health Organisations and Movements, 1918–1939* (Cambridge: Cambridge University Press, 1997).

Weinhauer, K., 'Labour Movements and Strikes, Social Conflict and Control, Protest and Repression (Germany), in *1914–1918-online. International Encyclopedia of the First World War*, ed. by U. Daniel, Peter Gatrell, Oliver Janz, et al. (Berlin: Freie Universität Berlin, 2015).

Weinreb, Alice, *Modern Hungers: Food and Power in Twentieth Century Germany* (Oxford: Oxford University Press, 2016).

Weissman, Benjamin, *Herbert Hoover and Famine Relief to Soviet Russia: 1921–1923* (Stanford: Hoover Institution Press, 1974).

Weitensfelder, Hubert, 'Die Ersatzmittel-Ausstellung im Prater 1918', https://ww1.habsburger.net/de/kapitel/die-ersatzmittel-ausstellung-im-prater-1918.

Wentholt, C. J. F. M., ed., *Den Haag '14-'18: fragmenten uit een dagboek* (The Hague: Haags Gemeentemuseum, 1986).

Wheatcroft, S. G., 'Soviet Statistics of Nutrition and Mortality during Times of Famine, 1917–1922 and 1931–33', *Cahiers du Monde Russe*, 38.4 (1997), 525–57.

Wheatley, Natasha, 'Central Europe as Ground Zero of the New International Order', *Slavic Review*, 78 (2019), 900–11.

Wilk, Richard, 'Rethinking the Relationships between Scarcity, Poverty and Hunger: An Anthropological Perspective', in *Scarcity in the Modern World: History, Politics, Society and Sustainability, 1800–2075*, ed. by Fredrik Albritton Jonsso, John Brewer, Neil Fromer et al. (London: Bloomsbury Academic, 2019), pp. 47–62.

Willcox, P. H. A., *The Detective-Physician: The Life and Work of Sir William Willcox 1870–1941* (London: Heinemann, 1970).

Wilson, Keith, 'Hankey's Appendix: Some Admiralty Manoeuvres during and after the Agadir Crisis', *War in History*, 1 (1994), 81–97.

Wingfield, Nancy, *The World of Prostitution in Late Imperial Austria* (Oxford: Oxford University Press, 2017).

Winkler, Heinrich August, *La Repubblica di Weimar: 1918–1933: storia della prima democrazia tedesca* (Roma: Donzelli Editore, 1998).

Winter, Jay, *The Great War and the British People* (Cambridge, MA: Harvard University Press, 1986).

Winter, Jay, ed., *The Cambridge History of the First World War* (Cambridge: Cambridge University Press, 2014), 3 vols.

Winter, Jay, *The Day the Great War Ended, 24 July 1923: The Civilianization of War* (Oxford: Oxford University Press, 2022).

Winter, Jay, and Jean-Louis Robert, eds., *Capital Cities at War: Paris, London, Berlin 1914–1919* (Cambridge: Cambridge University Press, 1997).

Winter, Jay, and Jean-Louis Robert, eds., *Capital Cities at War: Paris, London, Berlin 1914–1919: A Cultural History* (Cambridge: Cambridge University Press, 2007).

Winther, Paul C., *Anglo-European Science and the Rhetoric of Empire: Malaria, Opium, and British Rule in India, 1756–1895* (Lanham: Lexington Books, 2003).

Witzig, Heidi, 'Alltagsleben und Alltagserleben während des Ersten Weltkriegs. Frauen und Männer der Mittel- und Oberschicht im Zürcher Oberland', in *Kriegs- und Krisenzeit. Zürich während des Ersten Weltkriegs*, ed. by Erika Hebeisen, Peter Niederhäuser, and Regula Schmid (Zürich: Chronos Verlag, 2014), pp. 75–86.

Wolf, George, 'Emil Abderhalden: His Contribution to the Nutritional Biochemistry of Protein', *Journal of Nutrition*, 126.4 (April 1996), 794–8.

Wolf, Martha, 'Ist die Größe des Neugeborenen von Einflüssen der Umwelt abhängig?' (dissertation Julius-Maximilian-Universität Würzburg) (Borna-Leipzig: Robert Noske, 1939).

Wood, David, 'American Indian Farmland and the Great War', *Agricultural History*, 55.3 (1981), 249–65.

World Health Organization (ed.), *The Assessment of the Nutritional Status of the Community* (Geneva: World Health Organization, 1966).

Wrench, G. T., *The Wheel of Health: A Study of a Very Health People* (London: C.W. Daniel, 1938).

Wright, Gavin, and Howard Kunreuther, 'Cotton, Corn and Risk in the Nineteenth Century', *Journal of Economic History*, 35.3 (1975), 526–51.

Wrigley, Chris, 'The War and the International Economy', in *The First World War and the International Economy*, ed. by Chris Wrigley (Cheltenham, UK: Edward Elgar, 2000), pp. 1–33.

Xu, Guoqi, *Strangers on the Western Front: Chinese Workers in the Great War* (Cambridge, MA: Harvard University Press, 2011).

Young, James Allen, 'Height, Weight, and Health: Anthropometric Study of Human Growth in Nineteenth-Century American Medicine', *Bulletin of the History of Medicine*, 53.2 (1979), 214–43.

Zaccaria, Massimo, '"Not a Hectare of Land Shall Remain Uncultivated This Year!" Food Provisions for Italy and the Role of the Colonies, 1917–1918', *Afriche e Orienti*, 21.3 (2019), 25–41.

Zahra, Tara, *Kidnapped Souls: National Indifference and the Battle for Children in the Bohemian Lands, 1900–1948* (Ithaca: Cornell University Press, 2011).

Zahra, Tara, *The Lost Children: Reconstructing Europe's Families after World War II* (Cambridge, MA: Harvard University Press, 2011).

Zahra, Tara, *The Great Departure: Mass Migration from Eastern Europe and the Making of the Free World* (New York: W. W. Norton & Company, 2016).

Zahra, Tara, *Against the World: Anti-Globalism and Mass Politics between the World Wars* (New York: W.W. Norton & Company, 2023).

Zahra, Tara, Peter Becker, Kate Brown, et al., 'A World of Contradictions: Globalization and Deglobalization in Interwar Europe', *The American Historical Review*, 128.2 (2023), 703–881.

Zariņš, Klāvs, *Policies of the German Military Administration in the occupied Courland Governorate (May 1915–March 1918)* (dissertation, University of Latvia, January 2023).

Ziegler, Dieter, 'Die Kriegswirtschaft Im Ersten Weltkrieg – Trends Der Forschung', *Jahrbuch Für Wirtschaftsgeschichte*, 56.2 (2015), 313–23.

Ziemann, Benjamin, *War Experiences in Rural Germany: 1914–1923* (Oxford and New York: Berg, 2011).

Zuckerman, Solly, *Scientists and War: The Impact of Science on Military and Civil Affairs* (New York: Harper and Row, 1967).

Zurbrigg, Sheila, *Weakened by Want: Epidemic Malaria and Hunger in Colonial Punjab* (Abingdon: Routledge, 2019).

Zweiniger-Bargielowska, Ina, Rachel Duffett, and Alain Drouard, eds, *Food and War in Twentieth Century Europe* (London: Routledge, 2011).

Index

Page numbers in *italic* referes to figures, tables and maps.

Printed by Integrated Books International,
United States of America